# GRADUATE TEXTS IN COMPUTER SCIENCE

*Editors*
David Gries
Fred B. Schneider

Springer

*New York*
*Berlin*
*Heidelberg*
*Barcelona*
*Budapest*
*Hong Kong*
*London*
*Milan*
*Paris*
*Santa Clara*
*Singapore*
*Tokyo*

# GRADUATE TEXTS IN COMPUTER SCIENCE

*Apt and Olderog*, Verification of Sequential and Concurrent Programs, Second Edition

*Fitting*, First-Order Logic and Automated Theorem Proving, Second Edition

*Li and Vitányi*, An Introduction to Kolmogorov Complexity and Its Applications, Second Edition

*Nerode and Shore*, Logic for Applications, Second Edition

*Schneider*, On Concurrent Programming

*Smith*, A Recursive Introduction to the Theory of Computation

*Socher-Ambrosius and Johann*, Deduction Systems

Fred B. Schneider

# ON CONCURRENT
# PROGRAMMING

 Springer

Fred B. Schneider
Department of Computer Science
Cornell University
Ithaca, NY 14853-7501, USA

*Series Editors*

David Gries
Fred B. Schneider

Department of Computer Science
Cornell University
Upson Hall
Ithaca, NY 14853-7501, USA

Library of Congress Cataloging-in-Publication Data
Schneider, Fred B.
     On concurrent programming / Fred B. Schneider.
        p.   cm. — (Graduate texts in computer science)
     Includes bibliographical references and index.
     ISBN 0-387-94942-9 (hardcover: alk. paper)
     1. Parallel programming (Computer science)     I. Title
     II. Series
     QA76.642.S36     1997
     005.2'75—dc21                                    97-1017

Printed on acid-free paper.   5/17/44

Production managed by Steven Pisano; manufacturing supervised by Joe Quatela.
Photocomposed copy prepared from the author's TROFF files.
Printed and bound by R.R Donnelley and Sons, Harrisonburg, VA.
Printed in the United States of America.

9 8 7 6 5 4 3 2 1

ISBN 0-387-94942-9 Springer-Verlag New York Berlin Heidelberg   SPIN 10556809

*To my father, Sidney,*
*and*
*the memory of my mother, Rose*

**About the Cover.** A concurrent program is just a collection of atomic actions. Each atomic action may transform only a small part of the system state, but when executed together, rich and complex behaviors emerge. There is an obvious parallel with pointillism, the nineteenth-century style of painting, where only small dots of pure color are placed on the canvas and the dots merge into regions of color and light at normal viewing distance. A well-known example of pointillist painting is reproduced on the cover:

> Georges Seurat, *A Sunday on La Grande Jatte–1884*, 1884–86, oil on canvas, 207.5 × 308 cm, Helen Birch Bartlett Memorial Collection, photograph copyright 1996, The Art Institute of Chicago. All Rights Reserved.

Many know this painting by another title, "Sunday Afternoon on the Island of La Grande Jatte." Investigations by a curator at The Art Institute of Chicago, however, found that *A Sunday on La Grande Jatte–1884* (in French) was the title used by Seurat when he first publicly exhibited the painting in 1886. Seurat put the date in the title to claim credit for pioneering pointillism, because other artists had adopted the style in the two years it took Seurat to put the finishing touches on his painting.

# Preface

> *It is a profoundly erroneous truism, repeated by all the copybooks, and by eminent people when they are making speeches, that we should cultivate the habit of thinking of what we are doing. The precise opposite is the case. Civilization advances by extending the number of operations which we can perform without thinking about them. Operations of thought are like cavalry charges in a battle—they are strictly limited in number, they require fresh horses, and must only be made at decisive moments.*
>
> Alfred North Whitehead, *An Introduction to Mathematics*

So much of today's software depends on concurrent programming. One must marvel at our past successes, given the primitive tools that programmers had available for the task. But contemplate a future built using those same tools! We are building concurrent programs that put lives at stake, yet our development methods are dependent on fresh horses and cavalry charges.

It happens that a few simple techniques suffice for reasoning about concurrent programs. They replace cavalry charges with straightforward (even dull) symbol manipulation. This book is about these techniques—assertional methods for developing concurrent and distributed programs. As I wrote the text, I had in mind first-year computer science graduate students, but senior-level undergraduates in computer science should have the necessary mathematical maturity as well. And to ensure a broad readership, previous experience with neither logic nor concurrency is assumed.

The defining characteristic of assertional methods is the use of logical formulas to characterize sets of states and sets of program behaviors. A program is analyzed by manipulating these logical formulas, rather than by mentally simulating execution. Assertional methods also provide a compelling way to motivate and to understand the operational topics associated with concurrent programming:

- synchronization and communication mechanisms
- protocols that solve key concurrent-programming problems

So, these topics are covered in addition to the programming logics. Details of concurrent programming notations—once a dominant theme of this field—are deliberately not covered. Better programming notations have not made writing concurrent programs appreciably easier (although bad notations indeed exacerbate the problems).

## Treatment of Logic

The text discusses logics at some length, but from a user's point of view. Soundness proofs, completeness proofs, and other topics of interest primarily to logicians are left to the references. The book is for programmers and computer scientists—not logicians. I consciously chose rich collections of axioms and inference rules over spare ones so proofs could be constructed more easily and presented more compactly. Short axiomatizations are appealing when proving things *about* a logic but not when proving things *in* the logic.

The methods presented are based on first-order predicate logic, linear-time temporal logic, and Hoare-style asserted programs (herein called proof outlines). To anyone familiar with these logics, the formulas in the text will not only look familiar but will have their expected meanings. This, however, required that the logics be changed in nontrivial ways. Unifying temporal logic and proof outlines meant revising the semantics of these logics. Frequent use of logical puns was necessary.

An alternative would have been to introduce a new notation and logic. But I wanted to equip readers with the background needed to access other literature in formal methods and programming logics. I hoped that this book would not be their last exposure to formal methods. Inventing a new logic would not have served that purpose well, whereas employing familiar notations with their familiar meanings does.

## Expository Dilemmas

Concurrent programs are not discussed until Chapter 5. This is the price for a self-contained treatment, something I regard as critical in an introductory textbook. Temporal logic and proof outlines both extend first-order predicate logic, which, in turn, extends propositional logic; concurrent programs are built from sequential ones. Those preliminaries add up to over one-hundred pages of material.

One benefit of writing a self-contained book was that it kept me honest by allowing me to work out proofs in full. However, to simplify the exposition and provide focus, the proofs actually appearing in any given chapter often omit details concerning logics introduced in previous chapters. All the logics are here—even if all the proofs are not—and the reader is given all the tools needed for the complete picture.

I tried to strike a balance between writing a readable book and a reference book. For example, I put a historical-notes section at the end of each chapter rather than including citations in the body of the chapter. This, I felt, would make the text more readable, because it enabled related literature to be discussed and put into context. Each historical-notes section contains pointers to papers that introduce key ideas, to papers that explain those ideas particularly well, and to papers from which I took ideas for the chapter. I enjoyed my forays as an armchair historian, and I tried as best I could to give credit where credit was due. Additions or corrections are most welcome.

Some readability of the text has been sacrificed because axioms, inference rules, and key techniques are always identified by a number as well as a descriptive label. The number makes it possible to find the place in the book where the item was first introduced; the descriptive label is intended to make finding that place unnecessary. In addition, I employ the following conventions:

- The defining occurrence of each technical term is what gets typeset in italics. I often exploit this convention to omit phrases like "is defined to be" when giving the definition of a term.

- The abbreviation "iff" is used in place of "if and only if."

- The new word "truthify" is used in place of the phrase "to make true." For example, I might write "execution of the program truthifies $P$ or falsifies $Q$."

Finally, none of the proofs in the text have been checked mechanically. They were checked manually—by careful readers—but errors doubtless remain. For these, I apologize. I will be maintaining a list of corrections, and the list will be available to anyone who requests a copy.

## Some Technical Details

I started with mature programming logics, or so I thought. Too often, however, what I found in the literature did not work in the setting I required, and I was forced to make extensions. Some extensions were motivated by one or another aspect of how real concurrent programs execute; other extensions were necessary in order to integrate temporal logic with a logic of proof outlines. Let me briefly mention a few of the issues.

The programming notation I employ is designed specifically to avoid unrealistic simplifications about atomicity. For example, its alternative and iterative statements involve identifiable and separate guard evaluation actions—something rarely addressed by programming logics but invariably present in real programs. Another example is the assignment statement I chose, which can read and modify several variables in a single atomic action. Unrealistically coarse-grain atomic actions are easily programmed using this multiple assignment statement. However, its expressive power provides impetus for discussions (in Chapter 9) regarding realistic assumptions about granularity and decomposition of coarse-grain atomic actions into fine-grain ones. Moreover, some processors do have instructions that are specific instances of the multiple assignment, and I wanted to provide the tools for reasoning about these instructions.

"Vanilla" proof outlines were not usable for direct reasoning about safety properties, much to my dismay. Hoare-style programming logics generally avoid axiomatizing the control state and instead employ auxiliary variables. Control predicates may be ugly, but auxiliary variable deletion can be unsound (as discussed in Chapter 7), so I avoided using auxiliary variables. But adding control predicates to proof outlines is subtle—for example, the usual axiom for **skip**, $\{P\}$ **skip** $\{P\}$, is not sound unless restrictions are placed on $P$. And the $wp$ predicate transformer is not defined for control predicates.

My desire to use proof outlines for reasoning about all safety properties led to the "past" extensions of Chapter 7. I could instead have simply required that safety properties involving the past be proved directly in temporal logic, as I require for liveness properties. But I knew that escalation to temporal logic was theoretically unnecessary for reasoning about safety properties (whereas for liveness properties it is), and proof outlines were too useful a program development tool to abandon. Support for the past extensions, however, reverberated through the book. For example, the derived terms of predicate logic are not only convenient, but they become necessary for expressiveness; anchored sequences are the only clean way to give a temporal logic semantics to proof outlines with past terms; and so on.

## A One-Semester Course

The book contains more than enough material for a one-semester course. At Cornell, the course I teach has 39 one-hour lectures.

The heart of the book is Chapter 3 (on temporal logic), Chapters 4 and 5 (on proof outlines), and Chapters 6 and 8 (on proving properties using temporal logic). When lecturing on Chapter 3, I concentrate on the meanings of temporal logic formulas, rather than going over all the axioms and inference rules. Recently, I have been skipping §3.5 (on modal logics) for lack of time. In Chapter 4, I omit §4.4 (assignment to composite variables) and devote only a few minutes to §4.5 (weakest preconditions and program derivation)—material that I bring up as it is needed. I cover Chapter 5 (concurrency) and Chapter 6 (invariance properties) thoroughly in class, for these show the methodology in action by illustrating the derivation of concurrent programs. Chapter 8 (verifying temporal logic properties) can be covered in two or three lectures if small examples are selected, leaving students to read the larger case studies in the chapter on their own.

Chapter 1 (an introduction) is quite brief and can be covered as part of the first lecture or assigned as reading. How Chapter 2 is covered should depend on the background of the students. Students who are not comfortable with first-order predicate logic will have problems with all that follows, so spend whatever time is needed. The key parts of Chapter 7 (past extensions) can be covered in two lectures. Note that no later part of the book depends on this material, so it can be skipped without harm.

Chapters 9 through 11 deal with various synchronization mechanisms. These chapters are largely independent of each other, and any of them can be omitted. Make time to cover at least one, though, to show how the logics of the preceding chapters become a powerful program development tool.

## Acknowledgments

This book started over a decade ago as a joint effort with Greg Andrews, and the final product is certainly better for that collaboration. The material matured and the presentation profited from successive offerings of Cornell's CS613 as well as from short courses I had the privilege to teach at the University of Helsinki (Finland), Noordwijkerhout (the Netherlands), IBM Corporation (Endicott and Kingston, NY), and Marktoberdorf (Germany). I am grateful to all those who listened and provided feedback on my lectures and the early drafts of this material.

I have received research funding from a variety of sources over the years. Early in my career, support from NSF was instrumental in helping me to establish a research program. Funding from ONR and an IBM Faculty Development Award gave a needed boost to the initial phases of writing this book. I am currently funded by ARPA and AFOSR, and I couldn't hope for more supportive or engaging program managers.

Collaborations with Bard Bloom, Limor Fix, and Scott Stoller contributed to the development of proof outline logic. Each of them found time to understand the details of the logic and help me tackle technical difficulties—assistance that went far beyond the call of duty.

I am grateful to Julie Zeftel and The Art Institute of Chicago for granting permission to reproduce Georges Seurat's *A Sunday on La Grande Jatte − 1884*. Thanks to them, putting a masterpiece on the cover of this book was like a walk in the park.

Amir Pnueli, although writing a competing text, nevertheless welcomed my email questions about temporal logics. He answered questions both about his work and about the ramifications of alternatives, being as willing to talk about my axiomatizations as about his. I have learned a lot from Amir—not only about temporal logic but about being a first-rate scholar.

Many of the ideas on which this book is based can be traced to Leslie Lamport. I am privileged to include him among my friends and collaborators. He has been willing to chat about technical problems whenever I needed help. And he is always happy to share his newest ideas with me, providing inspiration as well as a rare view of how research ought to be done.

I don't know how to express my gratitude to David Gries. He, more than anyone, is responsible for my skills as a writer; he introduced me to and has guided me through the world of programming methodology; and he provided extremely useful line-by-line comments on the final draft of this text. One often hears of how valuable a mentor can be. It's true—and thanks to David, I can speak from personal experience.

Finally, I owe an enormous debt to my wife, Mimi Bussan, who has been supportive and patient while I finished this book, a process that took far longer than either of us ever imagined. It is a debt I shall repay, with interest (and pleasure)!

Fred B. Schneider
Ithaca, New York

# Contents

# List of Figures

# Chapter 1

# Introduction

## 1.1 Concurrent Programs

A *concurrent program* consists of processes and shared objects. A *process* is a sequential program executing on some processor; the shared objects are built using shared memory or a computer-communication network.

Concurrent programs are often found in *reactive systems*—systems whose outputs may affect their environment and, therefore, may influence subsequent inputs. Thus, a reactive system can control ongoing activities. Contrast this with a *transformational system*, whose output is, by definition, unaffected by its input. A transformational system implements a function from input to output, and its correctness is defined in terms of its initial state (which includes its inputs) and its final state (which includes its outputs). Correctness for a reactive system concerns initial, final, as well as intermediate states.

Operating systems are probably the oldest examples of concurrent programs. An operating system manages execution of user tasks and controls processors and input/output devices that run in parallel. It has a natural specification as a concurrent program, with a separate process controlling each user task and each hardware resource. Concurrent programs are not the sole province of those who design operating systems, however. Concurrent programs are useful whenever an application involves real or apparent parallelism—in database systems, networks, industrial automation, and so on.

Even when there is no real or apparent parallelism, structuring a system as a collection of processes and shared objects has proved effective for organizing large, complex systems. We master complexity by decomposing a system into processes and shared objects whose interfaces are of concern and whose internals are not.

## 1.2  Communication and Synchronization

In order to cooperate, processes must communicate. *Communication* allows one process to influence execution of another; it is accomplished by writing and reading shared variables or by sending and receiving messages. Either can involve delays. Time might elapse between when a shared variable is written and when it is read, and time can elapse between when a message is sent and its receipt. This potential for delay means that information obtained by a process might reflect a past state of the sender. Orchestrating cooperation among processes when the exact state of the system is unavailable to any of them is one of the things that makes designing concurrent programs difficult.

Communication using a shared object is possible only if the shared object is read after it is written—reading the object before it is written can return a meaningful, but erroneous, value. Thus, communication between asynchronous processes cannot occur without some kind of *synchronization*. Two forms of synchronization are prevalent in concurrent programs. The first, *mutual exclusion*, involves grouping actions into *critical sections* and blocking execution of a critical section in one process whenever a critical section from another has started but not completed. Mutual exclusion ensures that a state resulting from execution of only part of a critical section is never visible to another process. The second form, *condition synchronization*, blocks a process until the system state satisfies some specified condition. This is useful for ordering events that occur at different processes.

The following example illustrates these two types of synchronization in a system with shared memory. Communication between a producer process and consumer process is often implemented using a shared buffer. The producer writes values into the buffer; the consumer reads them. Mutual exclusion is used to ensure that a partially written value is not read—access to the buffer by the producer and consumer is made mutually exclusive. Condition synchronization is used to ensure that a value is not overwritten or read twice—the producer is prevented from overwriting a value that has not yet been read, and the consumer is prevented from reading the buffer until a new value has been written.

## 1.3  Understanding Concurrent Programs

A program *state* associates a value with each variable. Variables include those explicitly declared by the programmer as well as *implicit variables*, which cannot be read or written in assignment statements. The *program counter* for a process is an example of an implicit variable. It denotes the next action to be executed by that process, and its value is changed as a result of executing that action (but it cannot appear in assignment statements). A shared communications channel is another example of an implicit variable. Sending or receiving a message is usually the only way to change the value of this implicit variable.

Execution of a concurrent program is defined in terms of *atomic actions*, each of which transforms the system from one state to another without appearing to pass through any intermediate states. We can formalize program execution using a potentially infinite *history*

$$s_0 \xrightarrow{\alpha_1} s_1 \xrightarrow{\alpha_2} \cdots \xrightarrow{\alpha_i} s_i \xrightarrow{\alpha_{i+1}} s_{i+1} \xrightarrow{\alpha_{i+2}} \cdots$$

where the $s_i$ denote program states, the $\alpha_i$ denote atomic actions, and execution of each $\alpha_{i+1}$ in state $s_i$ can terminate in state $s_{i+1}$. State $s_0$ need not be an initial state of the program. For a concurrent program, sequence $\alpha_1 \alpha_2 \ldots$ is the result of interleaving atomic actions from each of the component processes in the order these actions were executed. Finite histories correspond to terminating executions; the final state of a finite history must be one in which no atomic action can be executed.

Note that even parallel execution can be modeled using interleavings of atomic actions. Consider, for example, two atomic actions that execute in parallel, so neither finishes before the other has started. Since atomic actions are indivisible, we conclude that the two necessarily access disjoint objects. If the two actions do not share objects, then the effects of neither action can depend on the other. Execution of these two atomic actions serially, then, produces the same state as is produced by their parallel execution.

We might try basing a formal representation of histories either on (i) the sequence of states or (ii) state $s_0$ and the sequence of atomic actions. Both representations allow us to recover the history, but under different restrictions.

- From a sequence of states, we reconstruct the missing atomic actions by looking at program-counter values in adjacent states to see which atomic action was scheduled between them. This works only if every atomic action alters the program counter.

- From a sequence of atomic actions, we reconstruct the missing states by simulating execution starting from $s_0$. This works only if atomic actions are deterministic, because with nondeterministic atomic actions it would be impossible to simulate execution and recover the unique next state of a history.

A requirement that each atomic action alters the program counter is not a significant limitation, but a requirement prohibiting nondeterministic atomic actions would be. So, there is a compelling reason to prefer sequences of states, and we base our formalisms on that representation.

A program $S$ defines a set of histories. A *property* of a program also is a set of histories. Program $S$ *satisfies* a property $\mathcal{P}$ iff[1] the histories of $S$ are a subset of $\mathcal{P}$, because then every execution of $S$ is an execution allowed by $\mathcal{P}$. For example, the property "$x$ is never 0" contains all histories whose states satisfy $x \neq 0$, and a program $S$ satisfies "$x$ is never 0" if, in every history of $S$, $x \neq 0$ holds in all states.

---

[1]Here and throughout, we write "iff" to abbreviate "if and only if."

For all but trivial concurrent programs and properties, the corresponding sets of histories are apt to be quite large—too large to enumerate. Therefore, the approach we take for proving that one set of histories is a subset of another is based on a *programming logic*. Theorems of the logic define properties satisfied by the program at hand, and these theorems are derived directly from that program's text.

Our definition of property will restrict what we can reason about. We define a property $\mathcal{P}$ in terms of a method to determine whether or not a history is an element of $\mathcal{P}$. The membership test must depend only on the history; it may not depend on other histories. This definition rules out formalizing as properties requirements described in terms of "sometimes," like "the program sometimes terminates," which constrains the entire set of histories but not the individual histories in the set. Similarly, our definition of property rules out formalization of requirements involving probabilities, such as "with probability 0.95 the program computes the correct answer." Rarely should one be interested in a program that is correct only sometimes, so the restriction on properties is not significant.

By defining properties as we have, every property is equivalent to some combination of safety properties and liveness properties:[2]

(1.1)   **Safety.**   A *safety property* asserts that no "bad thing" happens during execution.                                                                                       □

(1.2)   **Liveness.**   A *liveness property* asserts that some "good thing" eventually happens.                                                                                     · □

The key attribute of a safety property is that once the proscribed "bad thing" happens, no subsequent execution can cause the safety property to hold. The key attribute of a liveness property is that no partial execution is irremediable: it always remains possible for the prescribed "good thing" to occur during subsequent execution.

For example, *total correctness* is a property asserting that a program inevitably produces the correct answer. This property can be formulated using one safety property and one liveness property. Safety property *partial correctness* asserts that the program never terminates with the wrong answer. Partial correctness is a safety property because terminating with the wrong answer is the "bad thing," and once this "bad thing" has occurred, no subsequent execution can correct it. Liveness property *termination* asserts that the program eventually does terminate. Termination is a liveness property because terminating is the "good thing," and even though a program has not yet terminated, it might do so in the future.

---

[2]The proof of this statement appears in §2.4, where formal definitions of property, safety, and liveness are given.

We might also desire that a program satisfy real-time constraints in producing answers. Real-time constraints are safety properties. The "bad thing" is that the clock (an implicit variable) reaches a certain value before the program counter (also an implicit variable) denotes the statement following the one that generates the result.

As a final example, *mutual exclusion* is a safety property asserting that at most one process is executing in its critical section at any given time. The "bad thing" is a state in which the program counters for two or more processes denote atomic actions inside critical sections. One usually expects that a process attempting entry to a critical section will eventually succeed provided that no process remains forever in a critical section. This is a liveness property, the "good thing" being entry into a critical section.

## 1.4  A Preview

Programming is the activity of constructing a program that satisfies some given specification. We will make a distinction between concurrent programming and parallel programming based on the nature of that specification. In *concurrent programming*, a decomposition into processes is given; in *parallel programming*, such a decomposition is not given and must be devised.

Concurrent programming problems naturally arise in operating systems and distributed computing, where processes are imposed by the problem, are imposed by geography, or are used as a structuring tool. Parallel programming problems arise in scientific computing and other applications where parallelism is being used to decrease response time. Clearly, both concurrent programming and parallel programming are important. Moreover, both require mastery of concurrent programming, since whether a decomposition into processes is given or must be devised, the next step is the design of a concurrent program.

This textbook is about concurrent programming. It presents mental tools to help develop and understand concurrent programs, notations and programming constructs for describing concurrent computations, and some problems that crop up frequently in writing concurrent programs. The mental tools we present are based on an integrated set of programming logics for proving that a program satisfies safety and liveness properties. The programming constructs include various synchronization mechanisms that have been studied by researchers and employed by systems programmers. The programming problems we tackle are standards from the literature.

### Historical Notes

Here, we mention some textbooks devoted to concurrent programming and reasoning methods similar to the ones used in this text.

Brinch Hansen wrote the first textbook devoted exclusively to concurrent programming [Brinch Hansen 77]. It describes the design of three operating systems and contains Concurrent Pascal programs for them. [Holt et al. 78] and its successor [Holt 83] cover those aspects of concurrent programming most closely related to operating systems.

Another undergraduate text, [Ben-Ari 82], discusses some important synchronization mechanisms and shows how to construct informal correctness proofs for concurrent programs. In [Fillman & Friedman 84], models, languages, and heuristics for concurrent programming are treated.

Several advanced texts discuss programming logics for concurrent programs. An early survey of different verification methods for safety properties appears in [Barringer 85]. See [de Bakker et al. 86] for an overview of various formal methods for use with concurrent programs. An assertional methodology for designing parallel programs well suited for various architectures is the subject of [Chandy & Misra 88b]. In [Andrews 91], the emphasis is on programming languages and paradigms for concurrent systems, but a logic like that in Chapters 4 and 5 is presented and used informally. A similar logic appears in [Bernstein & Lewis 93], along with a discussion of topics that arise in connection with database systems and fault-tolerant distributed systems. The treatment in [Apt & Olderog 91] is more oriented toward semantic and formal logical issues, again using a logic like that of Chapters 4 and 5. The logics of [Andrews 91], [Bernstein & Lewis 93], and [Apt & Olderog 91] handle only a subset of the properties that ours does, allowing those logics to be simpler than ours. Temporal logics, like the logic in Chapters 4 and 8, are discussed in [Hailpern 82], [Kroger 87], [Manna & Pnueli 92], and [Manna & Pnueli 95].

## Exercises

**1.1.** Consider the intersection of two busy streets. Due to a high incidence of accidents, a traffic light with left-turn arrows for each direction has been installed. A *safe* configuration of lighted signals is one in which two cars cannot collide at the intersection if neither has gone through a red light.

   (a)   Assume that drivers always obey the lit traffic light signals and that left turns are made only when the corresponding left-turn arrow is lit. Without listing each of them, characterize all safe configurations of green, red, and left-arrow-green lit signals for each of the directions.

   (b)   Give a scheme for generating a sequence of configurations that guarantees that all drivers will have an opportunity to make progress through the intersection.

**1.2.** Suppose a concurrent program contains $N$ deterministic, straight-line processes, and each process executes $M$ distinct atomic actions. Prove that

$$\frac{(N\,M)!}{(M!)^N}$$

different histories are possible.

**1.3.** A maximum of $2^N$ distinct values can be represented using $N$ bits $b_1, ..., b_N$. Execution of a concurrent program with $N$ processes, where each process $p_i$ alternately sets and resets $b_i$, produces some subset of these $2^N$ values. The number of values that actually arise during a single execution depends on the exact interleaving of the processes. Assuming that no process executes only a finite number of instructions, what is the *minimum* number of distinct values that can arise during a single execution of this $N$ process concurrent program?

**1.4.** In the early days of railroads, the section of track between any two stations could accommodate at most one train at a time. However, each station had a siding on which a train could be parked in order to clear the main track. A primitive signaling scheme was provided to allow an engineer at either end of a track segment to set or unset a semaphore that was visible at both ends of that track segment. Devise a protocol involving a single such semaphore to prevent collisions on a given track segment. Your protocol should avoid unnecessary waiting on sidings.

**1.5.** Consider a group of $N$ gnomes, where one is the leader. The leader wishes to notify the other gnomes of a pending catastrophe using the only available communication facility: a telegraph service. Unfortunately, some gnomes will die of despair upon receiving the bad news.

(a) Devise a protocol to ensure that the message is disseminated to all gnomes, even if the leader dies during its execution. You may assume that a live gnome can send a telegram to another live gnome and that any gnome can write telegrams while other telegrams written by that gnome are being delivered.

(b) Suppose it takes $E$ seconds to write a telegram and $D$ seconds to deliver a telegram. What strategy will ensure that the message is disseminated to all in a minimum length of time.

**1.6.** A collection of ships in the middle of an ocean communicate using radio. Due to differing antenna heights and atmospheric conditions, the fact that ship $A$ can receive broadcasts from ship $B$ does not imply that $B$ can receive broadcasts from $A$. Devise a protocol that allows the ships to construct a graph giving the interconnection topology of the network, assu.ning that (i) there is always a path (involving one or more ships) between every pair of ships and that (ii) the interconnection topology does not change while the protocol is executing.

**1.7.** One way to view an execution of a distributed system is in terms of a partial order. Define $\ll$ to be a relation on pairs of system states. Assume that no system state ever repeats and that for states $s$ and $t$, $s \ll t$ holds if the fact that the system is in state $t$ could have been influenced—directly or indirectly—by the system previously being in state $s$. Are there any properties of all executions of a system that can be described using this semantics, but not the history semantics of §1.3? Are the two semantics equally expressive? Explain.

**1.8.** For each of the following, state whether it is a safety or liveness property and identify the "bad thing" or "good thing" of interest.

(a) At most five people are in the elevator at a time.

(b) Patrons are serviced first-come, first-served.

(c) The cost of living never decreases.

(d) Two things are certain in this world: death and taxes.

(e) All good things (must) come to an end.

(f) The book improves with each rewriting.

(g) A hungry philosopher eventually eats.

(h) At most one person should be speaking at a time; any number of people can be listening.

(i) No errors by commission.

(j) No errors by omission.

# Chapter 2

# Formal Logic

The methods in this textbook for reasoning about programs are based on using formal logic to characterize program execution. Here, we review some rudiments of logic and show how logic can be used to formalize safety and liveness. Our study of logic is done from the programmer's viewpoint, not the logician's. For us, logic is simply a tool. However, as with most tools, it must be understood to be used effectively.

## 2.1 Formal Logical Systems

A *formal logical system* consists of

- a set of symbols,
- a set of *formulas* constructed from the symbols,
- a set of distinguished formulas, called *axioms*, and
- a set of inference rules.

The set of formulas is called the *language* of the logic; it is defined by a giving a syntax for constructing formulas from the symbols.

The *inference rules* of the logic allow formulas to be derived from other formulas. We specify inference rules using the notation

$$\frac{P_1, P_2, ..., P_n}{C}$$

where *premises* $P_1, P_2, ..., P_n$ and *conclusion* $C$ are either formulas or schematic representations of formulas. An inference rule can be used to derive a formula $F$ from formulas $F_1, ..., F_n$ if $F$ is an instantiation of the conclusion of the rule and $F_1, ..., F_n$ are instantiations of its premises. We give an example shortly.

A *proof* in a formal logical system is a sequence of formulas in which each formula is an axiom or can be derived by using an inference rule whose premises are axioms or previous formulas in the sequence. Any formula in a proof is called a *theorem*. Thus, theorems are special only in that they are axioms or the result of applying inference rules to axioms and other theorems. We use the notation $\vdash_L F$ to assert that $F$ is a theorem of logic $L$ and the notation $A_1, A_2, ..., A_n \vdash_L F$ to assert that $F$ is a theorem of the logical system resulting when $A_1$ through $A_n$ are added to $L$ as axioms.

To illustrate these ideas, we investigate a simple formal logical system, PQ–L:

**Symbols:**  P, Q, –

**Formulas:**  Formulas have the form $a\,P\,b\,Q\,c$, where $a$, $b$, and $c$ each represents a finite sequence of zero or more dashes ("–").

**Axioms:**
(2.1)   $- P - Q - -$
(2.2)   $- - P - Q - - -$

**Inference Rule:**

(2.3)   $$\frac{a\,P\,b\,Q\,c, \quad d\,P\,e\,Q\,f}{a\,d\,P\,b\,e\,Q\,c\,f}$$

Examples of PQ–L formulas are:

$- - - P - Q - -$
$P\,Q -$
$- P - Q - -$

We now give an example of a PQ–L proof. Strictly speaking, the justification delimited by « and » that precedes each formula is not part of the proof. However, such justifications simplify reading the proof, so they are usually included.

«Axiom (2.1)»
  1.  $- P - Q - -$
«Axiom (2.2)»
  2.  $- - P - Q - - -$
«Rule (2.3) with 1 and 2»
  3.  $- - - P - - Q - - - - -$
«Rule (2.3) with 1 and 3»
  4.  $- - - - P - - - Q - - - - - - -$

Formulas 1 and 2 are axioms of PQ–L; formula 3 is the result of using inference rule (2.3) with formulas 1 and 2 as premises; and formula 4 results from using inference rule (2.3) with formulas 1 and 3 as premises. Note that this proof contains four theorems—one theorem on each line.

## *Models and Interpretations*

A digital computer could be instructed in the rules of some formal logic and would thereafter be able to prove theorems of the logic. Such theorems would probably not be very useful, though. A formal logical system stops being an exercise in symbol pushing and becomes a powerful tool when its theorems are true statements of some domain of discourse that concerns us. An *interpretation* for a logic $L$ gives a meaning to formulas of $L$ in terms of a domain of discourse by mapping each formula to *true* or *false*. For example, we might be interested in statements about the domain "integers and addition," and we would expect an interpretation to map formula $1+3=4$ to *true* and $1+4=6$ to *false*.

Interpretations usually deal with some class of mathematical objects, such as sets, relations, mappings, or sequences. For example, when program states are the domain of discourse, the class of possible interpretations is the set of mappings from program variables to values; when program executions are the domain of discourse, the class might be sequences of such mappings.

An interpretation $\iota$ is a *model for a formula P*, denoted by $\iota \models P$, if $P$ is mapped to *true* by $\iota$. Thus, an interpretation that maps the symbols "0" to zero, "1" to one, "+" to the function we know as integer addition, and "=" to equality is a model for the formula $1+0=1$, but so is an interpretation that instead maps "0" to *false*, "1" to *true*, and "+" to logical-or. Not only can a formula have more than one model, but a given interpretation can be a model for more than one formula. For example, both of the interpretations just described are models for $0+1=1, 0+0=0, 1+0=1$, and many other formulas.

An interpretation $\iota$ is a *model for a logic L* if it is a model for every theorem of $L$. For example, PQ–L has the following model:

(2.4) **Addition-Equality Interpretation.** A formula $a\,P\,b\,Q\,c$ is mapped to *true* iff $|a|+|b|=|c|$, where $|x|$ is the number of dashes in sequence $x$. $\qquad\square$

To see that Addition-Equality Interpretation (2.4) is a model for PQ–L, first note that it is a model for each PQ–L axiom. (Under the interpretation, axiom (2.1) asserts $1+1=2$ and (2.2) asserts $2+1=3$.) Next, observe that formulas obtained using inference rule (2.3) have Addition-Equality Interpretation (2.4) as a model, because if $a+b=c$ and $d+e=f$ hold, then so does $(a+d)+(b+e)=(c+f)$. Thus, all theorems of PQ–L have Addition-Equality Interpretation (2.4) as a model.

The following interpretation is also a model for PQ–L.

(2.5) **Addition-Inequality Interpretation.** A formula $a\,P\,b\,Q\,c$ is mapped to *true* iff $|a|+|b|\leq|c|$, where $|x|$ is the number of dashes in sequence $x$. $\qquad\square$

This interpretation is not the same as Addition-Equality Interpretation (2.4). Some formulas have Addition-Inequality Interpretation (2.5) as a model but not Addition-Equality Interpretation (2.4). An example of such a formula is:

(2.6)   $-P--Q----$

If every element in some set $R$ of interpretations is a model for $P$, then $P$ is said to be *R-valid*. This is denoted by $R \vDash P$. When $R$ is clear from the context, it may be omitted. A formula $P$ is *R-satisfiable* if at least one interpretation in $R$ is a model for $P$. Observe that $R$-satisfiable formulas need not be $R$-valid and that $R$-valid formulas need not be theorems. For example, consider any set of interpretations containing Addition-Equality Interpretation (2.4) and Addition-Inequality Interpretation (2.5). PQ–L formula (2.6) is then satisfiable but not valid because Addition-Inequality Interpretation (2.5) is a model but Addition-Equality Interpretation (2.4) is not.

An important attribute of a logic is soundness relative to a set of interpretations $R$. An axiom is *R-sound* iff it is $R$-valid. An inference rule is *R-sound* iff any formula derived using that rule is $R$-valid whenever all its premises are $R$-valid. And a logic is *R-sound* iff all of its axioms and inference rules are. If a logic is $R$-sound, then facts about a domain of discourse characterized by $R$ can be deduced in a purely mechanical fashion—theorems of the logic are derived mechanically by applying inference rules, and soundness means that theorems are true statements about the domain of discourse.

Soundness of a logic is rarely an accident. A logic is usually intended to facilitate reasoning about a given domain of discourse, so the logic is defined with a particular set $R$ of interpretations in mind. Each axiom is defined so that all interpretations in $R$ are models; each inference rule is formulated so that any formula derived using it will be $R$-valid whenever its premises are $R$-valid.

A logic $L$ is *complete* iff every $R$-valid formula is a theorem. If we let *FACTS* be the set of $R$-valid formulas of $L$ and *THMS* be the set of theorems, then soundness means that *THMS⊆FACTS* and completeness means that *FACTS⊆THMS*. For example, Addition-Inequality Interpretation (2.5) is a model for formula (2.6), but (2.6) is not provable in PQ–L, so PQ–L is not complete with respect to formulas that are valid according to Addition-Inequality Interpretation (2.5). A logic that is both sound and complete allows exactly the $R$-valid formulas to be proved. Our failure to prove that an $R$-valid formula is a theorem in such a logic cannot be attributed to weakness of the logic.

Unfortunately, the domains of discourse of concern to us—arithmetic truths, program behavior, and so on—do not have sound and complete axiomatizations. This is a consequence of Gödel's incompleteness theorem, which states that no formal logical system that axiomatizes arithmetic can be both sound and complete.[1] Fortunately, this incompleteness is not a problem in practice. The theorems we will have to prove when reasoning about most programs are ones for which proofs can be constructed with ease.

---

[1]More precisely, no logical system in which the set of axioms is recursive can provide a sound and complete axiomatization of arithmetic.

In order to isolate sources of incompleteness in a logic, the logic can be defined in a hierarchical fashion. Logic $L$ is an *extension* of logic $L'$ if the symbols, formulas, axioms, and inference rules of $L'$ are included in $L$. We say that $L$ is *complete relative to $L'$* if adding as axioms to $L$ every $R$-valid formula of $L'$ results in a complete formal logical system. If a logic $L$ is complete relative to $L'$, then $L$ introduces no source of incompleteness beyond that already in $L'$. The logics we will define for reasoning about programs are extensions of logics for reasoning about integers under the arithmetic operations, sequences under the usual sequence operations, and so on. In light of Gödel's incompleteness theorem, the best we can then hope for is relative completeness.

A final important property for a logic is *expressiveness*. A logic is *expressive* with respect to a domain of discourse insofar as it allows statements about that domain of discourse to be expressed as formulas. For example, the syntax of PQ–L does not allow statements like $3+1=1+3$ to be made. PQ–L is not very expressive.

### Formal and Informal Proofs

The point of a proof is to provide convincing evidence of the correctness of some statement that is expressed as a formula. What is convincing evidence? Imagine a logical system for which the soundness of each axiom and inference rule can be accepted without question. A formal proof using such a logic will constitute convincing evidence, because each step in the proof is, by supposition, truth-preserving. Moreover, although such a proof might be tedious, it can be checked mechanically.

Consider an informal proof written as English text. Although perhaps easier to read, such a proof might leave steps out or contain subtle errors, since English is rich but ambiguous. Thus, one might argue that such a text cannot be construed as convincing evidence.

On the other hand, a good informal proof can be viewed as an outline, or set of instructions, for constructing a formal proof in some specified formal logical system. In that case, such an informal proof might well be considered convincing evidence. Informal proofs are legitimate reasoning tools when they are constructed to serve as descriptions of formal proofs.

## 2.2 Propositional Logic

*Propositional Logic*, the first nontrivial formal logical system we study, is the basis for all the other logical systems discussed in this text. It is a formalization of the type of reasoning most would call common sense. A *proposition* is a statement that is either *true* or *false*. In Propositional Logic, *propositional variables* are used to denote propositions, and *propositional connectives* are used to form formulas from propositional variables and propositional constants.

Various sound and complete axiomatizations of Propositional Logic have been proposed. The one described below has the virtue of brevity; it is impressive how powerful such a small logical system can be.

**Symbols:**  Propositional connective:  $\Rightarrow$
Propositional constant: *false*
Propositional variables:  $p,\ q,\ r,\ ...$
Grouping symbols:  $(\,,)$

**Formulas:**  *false* is a formula.

Each propositional variable is a formula.

For $P$ and $Q$ formulas: $(P \Rightarrow Q)$ is a formula; $P$ is called the *antecedent* and $Q$ the *consequent*. Parentheses may be omitted when no ambiguity results.

**Axioms:**

(2.7)   *Affirmation of the Consequent*:  $p \Rightarrow (q \Rightarrow p)$

(2.8)   *Self-Distributive Law of Implication*:
$$(r \Rightarrow (p \Rightarrow q)) \Rightarrow ((r \Rightarrow p) \Rightarrow (r \Rightarrow q))$$

(2.9)   *Double Negation*:  $(((p \Rightarrow false) \Rightarrow false) \Rightarrow p)$

**Inference Rules:**

(2.10) *Modus Ponens*:  $\dfrac{P,\ (P \Rightarrow Q)}{Q}$

(2.11) *Substitution*: Let $P_Q^q$ denote the formula obtained by substituting formula $Q$ for every occurrence of propositional variable $q$ in formula $P$.  Then:
$$\frac{P}{P_Q^q}$$

The following proof in Propositional Logic establishes that $p \Rightarrow p$ is a theorem:

«Self-Distributive Law of Implication (2.8)»
  1.  $(r \Rightarrow (p \Rightarrow q)) \Rightarrow ((r \Rightarrow p) \Rightarrow (r \Rightarrow q))$
«Substitution (2.11) into 1 using $s$ for $p$»
  2.  $(r \Rightarrow (s \Rightarrow q)) \Rightarrow ((r \Rightarrow s) \Rightarrow (r \Rightarrow q))$
«Substitution (2.11) into 2 using $p$ for $q$»
  3.  $(r \Rightarrow (s \Rightarrow p)) \Rightarrow ((r \Rightarrow s) \Rightarrow (r \Rightarrow p))$
«Substitution (2.11) into 3 using $p$ for $r$»
  4.  $(p \Rightarrow (s \Rightarrow p)) \Rightarrow ((p \Rightarrow s) \Rightarrow (p \Rightarrow p))$
«Substitution (2.11) into 4 using $q$ for $s$»
  5.  $(p \Rightarrow (q \Rightarrow p)) \Rightarrow ((p \Rightarrow q) \Rightarrow (p \Rightarrow p))$
«Affirmation of the Consequent (2.7)»
  6.  $p \Rightarrow (q \Rightarrow p)$

«Modus Ponens (2.10) using 6, 5»
   7. $(p \Rightarrow q) \Rightarrow (p \Rightarrow p)$
«Substitution (2.11) into 7 using $q \Rightarrow p$ for $q$»
   8. $(p \Rightarrow (q \Rightarrow p)) \Rightarrow (p \Rightarrow p)$
«Modus Ponens (2.10) using 6, 8»
   9. $p \Rightarrow p$

In addition to the propositional constant and connective defined above, another propositional constant, *true*, and other connectives, "¬" (read "not") for logical negation, "∨" (read "or") for disjunction, "∧" (read "and") for conjunction, and "=" (read "equals") to denote equivalence, can be viewed as abbreviations, according to:

| | |
|---|---|
| *true*: | $false \Rightarrow false$ |
| $\neg P$: | $P \Rightarrow false$ |
| $P \vee Q$: | $(P \Rightarrow Q) \Rightarrow Q$ |
| $P \wedge Q$: | $\neg(\neg P \vee \neg Q)$ |
| $P = Q$: | $(P \Rightarrow Q) \wedge (Q \Rightarrow P)$ |

When parentheses are omitted, the connectives are assumed to have precedence given by these binding strengths:

$$\neg \qquad = \qquad \wedge \qquad \vee \qquad \Rightarrow$$

Tightest                                              Weakest

In addition, all except the equals connective are assumed to be left associative. For example:

| | | |
|---|---|---|
| $P \wedge Q \wedge R$ | is an abbreviation for | $(P \wedge Q) \wedge R$ |
| $\neg P \Rightarrow Q$ | is an abbreviation for | $(\neg P) \Rightarrow Q$ |
| $P \vee Q \wedge R$ | is an abbreviation for | $P \vee (Q \wedge R)$ |

The equals connective is assumed to be *conjunctional*, which means that $P = Q = R$ is an abbreviation for $(P = Q) \wedge (Q = R)$.

Formulas of Propositional Logic are interpreted by functions, called *states*, that map each propositional variable to *true* or *false*. The value of a propositional variable $p$ in a state $s$ is denoted by $s[\![p]\!]$.

(2.12) **Interpretation for Propositional Logic.** For a propositional variable $p$ and state $s$:

$$s \vDash p \quad \text{iff} \quad s[\![p]\!] \text{ equals } true$$

For Propositional Logic formulas $P$ and $Q$ and state $s$:

$s \models (\neg P)$   iff   $s \not\models P$

$s \models (P \vee Q)$   iff   $s \models P$   or   $s \models Q$

$s \models (P \wedge Q)$   iff   $s \models P$   and   $s \models Q$

$s \models (P \Rightarrow Q)$   iff   $s \not\models P$   or   $s \models Q$

$s \models (P = Q)$   iff   $s \models P$   equals   $s \models Q$                                                    □

The value of a formula $P$ in a state $s$ need not be computed recursively using Interpretation for Propositional Logic (2.12); instead, it can be computed as follows. First, each propositional variable $p$ in $P$ is replaced by its value $s[\![p]\!]$ in $s$. The resulting formula is then simplified by repeatedly selecting a subexpression that involves a single propositional connective and replacing it with a propositional constant, according to the table below. This process is repeated until it can no longer be carried out; it yields a single propositional constant. That propositional constant is taken to be the value of the original formula $P$.

The following table gives the values for subexpressions that contain a single propositional connective. Each row of the table corresponds to possible values for the constant(s) in the subexpression; each column corresponds to a subexpression containing a single propositional connective. The value of a subexpression is the value that appears in the row and column corresponding to the propositional constant(s) and the subexpression being simplified.

(2.13)  **Meaning of Propositional Connectives:**

| $p$ | $q$ | $\neg p$ | $p \wedge q$ | $p \vee q$ | $p \Rightarrow q$ | $p = q$ |
|-----|-----|----------|--------------|------------|-------------------|---------|
| false | false | true | false | false | true | true |
| false | true | true | false | true | true | false |
| true | false | false | false | true | false | false |
| true | true | false | true | true | true | true |

For example, the value of $\neg p \Rightarrow (p \vee q)$ in a state where $p$ is *false* and $q$ is *true* is computed as follows.

$\neg false \Rightarrow (false \vee true)$    replacing variables by their values.

$true \Rightarrow (false \vee true)$    replacing $\neg false$.

$true \Rightarrow true$    replacing $false \vee true$.

$true$    replacing $true \Rightarrow true$.

## Some Convenient Enhancements

   Although the axiomatization given above for Propositional Logic is complete, using it can be awkward. Completeness of an axiomatization is a far cry from convenience. Therefore, we augment the axiomatization to allow simpler proofs of theorems that tend to arise in practice—theorems of the form $P = Q$ and $P \Rightarrow Q$, where $P$ and $Q$ are formulas of Propositional Logic.

   The laws[2] below are formulated in terms of propositional variables $p$, $q$, and $r$. Substitution (2.11) can be used to replace these variables by arbitrary propositional formulas.

(2.14) *Commutative Laws*: (a) $(p \wedge q) = (q \wedge p)$
                                (b) $(p \vee q) = (q \vee p)$
                                (c) $(p = q) = (q = p)$

(2.15) *Associative Laws*: (a) $(p \wedge (q \wedge r)) = ((p \wedge q) \wedge r)$
                          (b) $(p \vee (q \vee r)) = ((p \vee q) \vee r)$

(2.16) *Distributive Laws*: (a) $(p \wedge (q \wedge r)) = ((p \wedge q) \wedge (p \wedge r))$
                        (b) $(p \wedge (q \vee r)) = ((p \wedge q) \vee (p \wedge r))$
                        (c) $(p \vee (q \wedge r)) = ((p \vee q) \wedge (p \vee r))$
                        (d) $(p \vee (q \vee r)) = ((p \vee q) \vee (p \vee r))$
                        (e) $(p \vee (q = r)) = ((p \vee q) = (p \vee r))$
                        (f) $(p \vee (q \Rightarrow r)) = ((p \vee q) \Rightarrow (p \vee r))$
                        (g) $(p \Rightarrow (q \wedge r)) = ((p \Rightarrow q) \wedge (p \Rightarrow r))$
                        (h) $(p \Rightarrow (q \vee r)) = ((p \Rightarrow q) \vee (p \Rightarrow r))$
                        (i) $(p \Rightarrow (q = r)) = ((p \Rightarrow q) = (p \Rightarrow r))$
                        (j) $(p \Rightarrow (q \Rightarrow r)) = ((p \Rightarrow q) \Rightarrow (p \Rightarrow r))$

(2.17) *De Morgan's Laws*: (a) $\neg (p \wedge q) = (\neg p \vee \neg q)$
                         (b) $\neg (p \vee q) = (\neg p \wedge \neg q)$

(2.18) *Identity Law*: $p = p$

(2.19) *Negation Law*: $p = \neg \neg p$

(2.20) *Excluded Middle Law*: $(p \vee \neg p) = \text{true}$

(2.21) *Contradiction Law*: $(p \wedge \neg p) = \text{false}$

---

[2]Here and throughout, we label as "laws" useful theorems that are not axioms.

(2.22) *Implication Laws*:  (a) $(p \Rightarrow q) = (\neg p \lor q)$
                            (b) $(p \Rightarrow q) = ((p \land q) = p)$

(2.23) *Equality Law*:  $(p = q) = ((p \Rightarrow q) \land (q \Rightarrow p))$

(2.24) *Equality-Simplification Law*:  $p = (p = true)$

(2.25) *Or-Simplification Laws*:  (a) $(p \lor p) = p$
                                  (b) $(p \lor true) = true$
                                  (c) $(p \lor false) = p$
                                  (d) $(p \lor (p \land q)) = p$

(2.26) *And-Simplification Laws*:  (a) $(p \land p) = p$
                                   (b) $(p \land true) = p$
                                   (c) $(p \land false) = false$
                                   (d) $(p \land (p \lor q)) = p$

(2.27) *Implication-Simplification Laws*:  (a) $(p \Rightarrow true) = true$
                                           (b) $(true \Rightarrow p) = p$

(2.28) *Importation/Exportation Law*:  $(p \Rightarrow (q \Rightarrow r)) = ((p \land q) \Rightarrow r)$

(2.29) *Antecedent-Strengthening Law*:  $(p \land q) \Rightarrow p$

(2.30) *Consequent-Weakening Law*:  $p \Rightarrow (p \lor q)$

(2.31) *Implication-Deduction Laws*:  (a) $p \land (p \Rightarrow q) \Rightarrow q$
                                      (b) $\neg q \land (p \Rightarrow q) \Rightarrow \neg p$

(2.32) *Contrapositive Law*:  $(p \Rightarrow q) = (\neg q \Rightarrow \neg p)$

(2.33) *Constructive Dilemma Laws*:
                    (a) $(p \Rightarrow q) \land (r \Rightarrow s) \Rightarrow ((p \land r) \Rightarrow (q \land s))$
                    (b) $(p \Rightarrow q) \land (r \Rightarrow s) \Rightarrow ((p \lor r) \Rightarrow (q \lor s))$

Some additional inference rules will also be convenient. These rules do not allow new theorems to be proved, but they do simplify the construction and presentation of proofs.

The first rules assert that equals can be substituted for equals. As we shall see, this supports an equational style of reasoning that is similar to the familiar one used for manipulating algebraic formulas.

(2.34) *Substitution of Equals*: For any propositional variable $p$:

$$\text{(a)} \quad \frac{Q=R}{P_Q^p = P_R^p} \qquad\qquad \text{(b)} \quad \frac{Q=R}{P_R^p = P_Q^p}$$

Generalizing from Substitution of Equals (2.34), one might try to infer $P_Q^p \Rightarrow P_R^p$ from a theorem $Q \Rightarrow R$. However, such an inference could be unsound. As an example, consider the case where $P$ is $p \Rightarrow q$ and premise $Q \Rightarrow R$ is the theorem $a \Rightarrow (a \vee b)$. $P_Q^p \Rightarrow P_R^p$ would be $(p \Rightarrow q)_a^p \Rightarrow (p \Rightarrow q)_{a \vee b}^p$, which is $(a \Rightarrow q) \Rightarrow ((a \vee b) \Rightarrow q)$ and is not valid. But notice that it is sound to conclude $(p \Rightarrow q)_a^q \Rightarrow (p \Rightarrow q)_{a \vee b}^q$ (i.e., $(p \Rightarrow a) \Rightarrow (p \Rightarrow (a \vee b)))$ from theorem $a \Rightarrow (a \vee b)$.

We seek a sound inference rule that, given a theorem $Q \Rightarrow R$, yields a formula involving two instances of $P$—one instance with some propositional variable $p$ replaced by $Q$ and the other with $p$ replaced by $R$. Towards this end, we define the *parity* of a propositional variable in a formula.

(2.35) **Parity of a Variable.** For $P$ a Propositional Logic formula and $p$ a propositional variable not appearing in an operand of an equivalence[3] in $P$:

- $p$ has *even* parity in $P$ iff each occurrence of $p$ is within an even number of negations and antecedents of implications.

- $p$ has *odd* parity in $P$ iff each occurrence of $p$ is within an odd number of negations and antecedents of implications. ☐

For example, in $p \Rightarrow q$, $p$ has odd parity and $q$ has even parity; in $\neg(p \Rightarrow q)$, $p$ has even parity and $q$ has odd parity.

If $Q \Rightarrow R$ is a theorem, then $P_Q^p \Rightarrow P_R^p$ is valid if $p$ has even parity in $P$, and $P_R^p \Rightarrow P_Q^p$ is valid if $p$ has odd parity in $P$. This can be shown by structural induction on $P$ and is the basis for the following inference rules.

(2.36) *Monotonicity Rule*: For a propositional variable $p$ that has even parity in Propositional Logic formula $P$:

$$\frac{Q \Rightarrow R}{P_Q^p \Rightarrow P_R^p}$$

(2.37) *Antimonotonicity Rule*: For a propositional variable $p$ that has odd parity in Propositional Logic formula $P$:

$$\frac{Q \Rightarrow R}{P_R^p \Rightarrow P_Q^p}$$

---

[3]Recall, any equivalence $A=B$ is equal to $(A \Rightarrow B) \wedge (B \Rightarrow A)$, so precluding equivalences does not really constitute a restriction.

Monotonicity Rule (2.36) allows us to conclude from premise $a \Rightarrow (a \lor b)$ that $(p \Rightarrow a) \Rightarrow (p \Rightarrow (a \lor b))$ and $(\neg a \Rightarrow q) \Rightarrow (\neg (a \lor b) \Rightarrow q)$ are theorems, and Antimonotonicity Rule (2.37) allows us to conclude that $((a \lor b) \Rightarrow q) \Rightarrow (a \Rightarrow q)$ is a theorem.

The next inference rules assert that equality and implication are transitive. They are useful for combining formulas whose principal connective is equals and/or implies.

(2.38)  *Transitivity of Equality*:  $\dfrac{P = Q,\ Q = R}{P = R}$

(2.39)  *Transitivity of Implication*:

$$\text{(a)}\ \frac{P \Rightarrow Q,\ Q \Rightarrow R}{P \Rightarrow R} \qquad \text{(b)}\ \frac{P = Q,\ Q \Rightarrow R}{P \Rightarrow R} \qquad \text{(c)}\ \frac{P \Rightarrow Q,\ Q = R}{P \Rightarrow R}$$

It now becomes possible to write proofs and proof steps in an equational format. This *equational format* consists of a sequence of formulas, each on a separate line, with adjacent lines being separated by equals or implies, along with a justification (delimited by « and »). An example is the following:

(2.40)      $A$
$\quad =$      «Why $A = B$ is a theorem»
$\qquad B$
$\quad \Rightarrow$      «Why $B \Rightarrow C$ is a theorem»
$\qquad C$
$\quad =$      «Why $C = D$ is a theorem»
$\qquad D$

In our equational proofs, a justification "Why $X$ is a theorem" gives only the premise that enables $X$ to be proved whenever the inference rule being used to make that deduction is obvious—and it usually is obvious.

(2.41)  **Equational Proof Justifications.** A justification "Why $X$ is a theorem" in an equational proof must be:

   (i)   The theorem that enables $X$ to be deduced by repeated uses of Substitution (2.11). Details of the substitutions may be omitted when they are obvious.

   (ii)  The theorem that enables $X$ to be deduced according to one of the Substitution of Equals (2.34) rules.

   (iii) The theorem that enables $X$ to be deduced according to Monotonicity Rule (2.36).

   (iv)  The theorem that enables $X$ to be deduced according to Antimonotonicity Rule (2.37).

Without mention, conjuncts or disjuncts in formulas may be reordered, thereby omitting steps that involve Commutative Laws (2.14). □

Equational proof (2.40) establishes $A \Rightarrow D$. Formally, that conclusion follows from repeated use of Transitivity of Equality (2.38) and Transitivity of Implication (2.39) on justifications $A=B$, $B \Rightarrow C$, and $C=D$. But that is not all that can be deduced from (2.40).

(2.42) **Equational Proof Conclusions.**

    (i)  Given a proof of $A \Rightarrow D$ with $A$ a theorem, $D$ is also a theorem.

    (ii)  Given a proof of $A=D$ with $A$ a theorem, $D$ is also a theorem.

    (iii)  Given a proof of $A=D$ with $D$ a theorem, $A$ is also a theorem.   □

The formal justification for part (i) of Equational Proof Conclusions (2.42) is a single Modus Ponens (2.40) step. To justify part (ii), three steps suffice—an equational proof and two steps involving Modus Ponens (2.40).

$$
\begin{aligned}
1.\quad & A=D \\
= \quad & \text{«Equality Law (2.23)»} \\
& (A \Rightarrow D) \wedge (D \Rightarrow A) \\
\Rightarrow \quad & \text{«Antecedent-Strengthening Law (2.29)»} \\
& (A \Rightarrow D)
\end{aligned}
$$

«Modus Ponens (2.40) with $A=D$ (assumed previously proved) and 1»
  2. $A \Rightarrow D$

«Modus Ponens (2.40) with $A$ (assumed previously proved) and 2»
  3. $D$

The justification of part (iii) is similar to that just given for part (ii).

In order to illustrate the virtues of the equational proof format, consider proving:

(2.43)  $(InA \Rightarrow \neg InB) = \neg(InA \wedge InB)$

If $InA$ and $InB$ denote propositions

    $InA$:  "process $A$ is executing in its critical section"

    $InB$:  "process $B$ is executing in its critical section"

then a proof of (2.43) would establish that processes $A$ and $B$ are not both executing at the same time in their critical sections provided that whenever $A$ executes in its critical section, $B$ does not. Here is an equational proof:

$$
\begin{aligned}
& InA \Rightarrow \neg InB \\
= \quad & \text{«Implication Law (2.22a)»}
\end{aligned}
$$

$\neg InA \lor \neg InB$
$=$       «De Morgan's Law (2.17a)»
$\neg (InA \land InB)$

For comparison, here is a nonequational proof of (2.43).

«Implication Law (2.22a)»
   1. $(p \Rightarrow q) = (\neg p \lor q)$
«Substitution (2.11) into 1 using $InA$ for $p$ and $\neg InB$ for $q$»
   2. $(InA \Rightarrow \neg InB) = (\neg InA \lor \neg InB)$
«De Morgan's Law (2.17a)»
   3. $\neg (p \land q) = (\neg p \lor \neg q)$
«Substitution of Equals (2.34b) using $p$ for $P$ and 3 for $Q=R$»
   4. $(\neg p \lor \neg q) = \neg (p \land q)$
«Substitution (2.11) into 4 using $InA$ for $p$ and $InB$ for $q$»
   5. $(\neg InA \lor \neg InB) = \neg (InA \land InB)$
«Transitivity of Equality (2.38) with 2, 5»
   6. $(InA \Rightarrow \neg InB) = \neg (InA \land InB)$

## Decision Procedure for Propositional Logic

In any sound and complete axiomatization of a logic, a formula is valid iff it is a theorem. This fact can be used to determine whether a formula of Propositional Logic is a theorem: simply determine whether the formula is valid.[4]

(2.44) **Decision Procedure for Propositional Logic.** If the value of formula $P$ is *true* in every possible state, then $P$ is a theorem.     □

In order to determine validity of a propositional formula that involves $N$ distinct variables, $2^N$ states must be checked. For example, we show that

$$\neg (p \land q) = (\neg p \lor \neg q)$$

is valid by checking $2^2$ cases:

| $p$ | $q$ | $\neg(p \land q)$ | $\neg p \lor \neg q$ | $\neg(p \land q) = (\neg p \lor \neg q)$ |
|------|------|------|------|------|
| *false* | *false* | *true* | *true* | *true* |
| *false* | *true* | *true* | *true* | *true* |
| *true* | *false* | *true* | *true* | *true* |
| *true* | *true* | *false* | *false* | *true* |

---

[4]The valid formulas in Propositional Logic are sometimes called *tautologies*.

## 2.3   A Predicate Logic

We now turn attention to *Predicate Logic*, a logic that is considerably more expressive than Propositional Logic. Predicate Logic augments Propositional Logic in three ways:

- A new class of variables is introduced to denote values other than *true* and *false*.

- Predicates and functions allow properties of values to be expressed.

- Quantification allows properties about sets of values to be expressed.

This makes the logic well suited for characterizing relationships among program variables.

Various formulations of Predicate Logic have been proposed. The one given below is an extension of Propositional Logic. Thus, it contains all the formulas, axioms, and inference rules given in §2.2. Although not as terse as some axiomatizations of Predicate Logic, it is convenient for reasoning about program states.

### *Formulas*

In our Predicate Logic, *individual variables*, henceforth simply called variables (in contrast to propositional variables), denote values from a fixed domain that includes booleans (i.e., the constants *true* and *false*), integers, reals, sequences, and other values commonly found in programming. *Terms* are defined to be constants, variables, derived terms (discussed below), and function applications (often denoted by infix operators) that involve zero or more terms. The set of functions and operators is presumed to include all those permitted in expressions of the programming language at hand. The value of a term $T$ in a state $s$, denoted by $s[\![T]\!]$, is the value that results from replacing all variables in $T$ by their values in $s$ and applying the designated function(s).

Relationships among terms are characterized in Predicate Logic by using predicates. A *predicate* is a function application that always yields a boolean and is specified by giving a *predicate symbol* and a parenthesized[5] list of zero or more terms: for $p$ a predicate symbol and $T_1$, ..., $T_n$ terms, $p(T_1, T_2, ..., T_n)$ denotes a predicate. To improve readability, predicates are sometimes written using an infix notation, as in $x < y$, where "$<$" is the predicate symbol. Another predicate—different, because it involves different terms—is $x+1 < y+1$. The value of a predicate $p(T_1, T_2, ..., T_n)$ in a state $s$ is either *true* or *false*, based on the meaning of $p$ after $T_1$, $T_2$, ..., $T_n$ is each replaced by its value in $s$.

Predicate symbols in our Predicate Logic include equality[6] ($=$) along with

---

[5]The parentheses may be omitted when the list contains zero terms.

[6]In fact, "$=$" in Propositional Logic was defined to bind tightest of all the binary propositional connectives just so it would have the same precedence as a predicate symbol, and therefore, a single symbol could be employed for both.

all the other standard ones from logic, mathematics, and programming.[7]   Rather than fix this set here, we leave it unspecified and introduce predicate symbols as needed. We rely on the reader's familiarity with the usual meaning associated with a predicate symbol instead of giving axioms for predicates constructed using it.

Predicates and terms are defined for all values of their arguments.[8] Predicates always evaluate to *true* or *false*. Terms, on the other hand, are guaranteed to produce a value but are not guaranteed to produce a value in any given set. Thus, we assume that the term $x/y$, which denotes the result of dividing $x$ by $y$, has a value even when $y=0$ or when $x$ and/or $y$ denote non-numeric values. For example, when $y$ is 0, $x/y$ might equal "abc."

We avoid problems associated with having predicates and terms be defined for all values of their arguments by postulating the existence of other predicates to characterize when a predicate or term is meaningful. For this purpose, it is often convenient to be able to assert that the value of a given variable or term is an element of some set. Figure 2.1 gives a useful collection of such sets. In addition, for each term or predicate $\mathcal{E}$, we postulate a predicate $def_{\mathcal{E}}$ that is *true* in exactly those states where $\mathcal{E}$ is meaningful. As an example, $def_{x/y}$ might be equivalent to

$$x \in \text{Int} \;\; \wedge \;\; y \in \text{Int} \;\; \wedge \;\; y \neq 0$$

---

| | |
|---|---|
| Bool | booleans: *false*, *true* |
| Nat | natural numbers:  0, 1, 2, 3, 4, ... |
| Int | integers:  ..., −3, −2, −1, 0, 1, 2, ... |
| Rat | rationals:  any value $x/y$, where $x \in$ Int, $y \in$ Int, and $y \neq 0$ |
| Real | reals |
| Char | characters |
| $V^*$ | the set of finite-length sequences of values from set $V$ |
| $V^+$ | the set of nonempty finite-length sequences of values from set $V$ |
| $V^\infty$ | the set of finite-length sequences and infinite-length sequences of values from set $V$ |

**Figure 2.1.** Sets of values

---

[7]Due to Gödel's incompleteness theorem, this means that our Predicate Logic is incomplete, since it axiomatizes arithmetic. The logic, however, is complete relative to arithmetic.

[8]This approach is not satisfactory for reasoning about whether terms and predicates are undefined. But we have no need for such reasoning, so we will not be handicapped. Logics that allow reasoning about whether terms and predicates are undefined usually involve three truth-values—*true, false,* and *undefined*—and/or have more complicated axiomatizations than the one given in this chapter.

which is *false* unless $x$ and $y$ are integers and $x/y$ is defined. This means that

(2.45) $def_{x/y} \;\wedge\; z \in \text{Rat} \;\wedge\; (x/y)=z$

is *false* unless $x$ and $y$ are integers, $x/y$ is defined, $z$ is a rational, and $x/y=z$. Therefore, (2.45) is *false* if $y$ is zero, no matter what the (unspecified) value $x/y$ is.

## *Quantification*

It is often useful to be able to assert that values in a given set satisfy some property of interest. We might wish to specify that all values in array $a[1..n]$ are 0. Conjunction would seem suitable for this purpose:

(2.46) $a[1]=0 \;\wedge\; a[2]=0 \;\wedge\; \cdots \;\wedge\; a[n]=0$

Disjunction could be used to assert that some value in a set satisfies a property of interest. Thus,

(2.47) $b[1]=16 \;\vee\; b[2]=16 \;\vee\; \cdots \;\vee\; b[m]=16$

would assert that some element in array $b[1..m]$ equals 16. Unfortunately, this approach is flawed because the ellipses in (2.46) and (2.47) are ambiguous. Formula (2.46) might assert that $a[p]=0$ for all even values of $p$ between 1 and $n$, or for all values of $p$ that are powers of 2 and at most $n$, or for all values of $p$ that are prime numbers and at most $n$, or any number of other things.

Predicate Logic provides *quantified expressions* for unambiguously specifying properties of sets of values. To give a meaning to quantified expressions, it is helpful to have a notation for redefining the value of a variable in a state. For a state $s$, variable $v$, and term $e$, define *augmented state* $(s; v{:}e)$ to be the state that is identical to $s$, except that the value of $v$ equals the value of $e$ in $s$:

(2.48) $(s; v{:}e)[\![x]\!]:\ \begin{cases} s[\![e]\!] & \text{for } \text{``}v\text{''}=\text{``}x\text{''} \\ s[\![x]\!] & \text{for } \text{``}v\text{''}\neq\text{``}x\text{''} \end{cases}$

For example, $(s; w{:}22)[\![w+3]\!]$ equals 25, and $(s; w{:}22)[\![v+3]\!]$ equals $s[\![v+3]\!]$.

Since $(s; v{:}e)$ is itself a state, nested augmented states can be constructed. Thus, state $((s; v{:}9); w{:}88)$ associates 88 with variable $w$, associates 9 with variable $v$, and otherwise associates values according to $s$. Composition of augmented states is defined to be left associative, so:

(2.49) $(s; v{:}e; v'{:}e') \;=\; ((s; v{:}e); v'{:}e')$

For example, $(s; v{:}2; v{:}3)[\![v]\!]$ equals 3 and $(s; v{:}2; w{:}v+2)[\![w]\!]$ equals 4.

Predicate Logic has two types of quantified expressions: one for conjunction and one for disjunction. For Predicate Logic formulas $R$ and $P$ and variable

$x$, the *universally quantified expression* with *range R* and *body P*

(2.50)  $(\forall x\colon R\colon P)$

is *true* in a state $s$ iff for *every* value V, $R \Rightarrow P$ is satisfied in state $(s; x{:}V)$. For this reason, (2.50) is read "For all $x$ satisfying $R$, $P$ holds." An example of a universally quantified expression is

$(\forall i\colon 1{\leq}i{\leq}n \wedge i{\in}\text{Int}\colon a[i]{=}0)$

which is *true* in a state $s$ iff $a[1]$, $a[2]$, ..., $a[n]$ each equals 0 in state $s$, just as was intended by (2.46).

An existentially quantified expression specifies that some value in a set satisfies a property of interest. For Predicate Logic formulas $R$ and $P$, the value of *existentially quantified expression* with *range R* and *body P*

(2.51)  $(\exists x\colon R\colon P)$

in a state $s$ is *true* iff for *some* value V, $R \wedge P$ is satisfied in state $(s; x{:}V)$. Not surprisingly, (2.51) is read "There exists an $x$ satisfying $R$ for which $P$ holds." For example, $(\exists i\colon 1{\leq}i{\leq}m \wedge i \in \text{Int}\colon b[i]{=}16)$ is *true* in a state $s$ iff at least one of $b[1]$, $b[2]$, ..., $b[m]$ equals 16 in state $s$ (as was intended by (2.47)).

In a quantified expression, the variable that follows *quantifier* $\forall$ or $\exists$ is called a *bound variable*, and it is associated with that quantifier. The *scope* of a bound variable is defined by the parentheses that delimit the quantified expression in which it is introduced. This is similar to the way scope of identifiers is defined in a block-structured programming language.

An occurrence of a variable $v$ in a formula of Predicate Logic is considered *free* if $v$ is different from every bound variable whose scope contains that occurrence. An occurrence is considered *bound* if $v$ is the same as some bound variable whose scope contains that occurrence. Here are some examples:

(2.52)  $i < n$

(2.53)  $(\forall i\colon 1{\leq}i < 10\colon i < n)$

(2.54)  $(\forall i\colon 1{\leq}i < 10\colon i < n) \wedge i < n$

In (2.52), the occurrences of $i$ and $n$ are free; in (2.53), the three occurrences of $i$ are bound, and the occurrence of $n$ is free; in (2.54), all but the last occurrence of $i$ are bound, the last occurrence is free, and both occurrences of $n$ are free.

Finally, where convenient, we shorten quantified expressions by employing some abbreviations. ($Q$ represents a quantifier "$\forall$" or "$\exists$.")

$(Q\,i\colon P)$ denotes $(Q\,i\colon \textit{true}\colon P)$

$(Q\,i{\in}V\colon P)$ denotes $(Q\,i\colon i{\in}V\colon P)$

$(Q\,i \in V\colon\ R\colon\ P)$ denotes $(Q\,i\colon\ i \in V \wedge R\colon\ P)$

## Derived Terms

A facility to associate names with terms gives us the power to extend our Predicate Logic with abstractions tailored for a task at hand. To specify such a *derived term*, we give its name, the set of states in which it is defined, and a method for computing its (unique) value in those states.[9] The syntax we employ for defining a derived term $Z$ is:

$$(2.55)\quad Z\colon\ \begin{cases} e_1 & \text{if } B_1 \\ \cdots \\ e_n & \text{if } B_n \end{cases}$$

Each expression and its corresponding guard define a *clause*.

The value of $Z$ in a state $s$ is the value of the unique *expression* $e_i$ for which a corresponding *guard* $B_i$ holds. If no guard holds or more than one guard holds in $s$, then the value of $Z$ is unspecified.

Notice that the notation we have been using for definitions,

$$Z\colon\ e$$

can be regarded as an abbreviation for the following definition of a derived term:

$$Z\colon\ \{\, e \ \ \text{if } true$$

As an illustration of a derived term, here is one named $M$, which equals the maximum of $a$ and $b$.

$$(2.56)\quad M\colon\ \begin{cases} a & \text{if } b < a \\ b & \text{if } a \le b \end{cases}$$

Notice that appearances of $M$ in a formula give no hint to the reader that its value depends on $a$ and $b$. This ability to hide details is important when defining abstractions. But it does create free occurrences of variables in formulas even though those variables do not explicitly appear in the formula. For example, any formula that mentions $M$ may contain free occurrences of $a$ and $b$.[10] A derived

---

[9]By convention, derived terms will be named by identifiers starting with an uppercase letter.

[10]The occurrences of $a$ and $b$ are not necessarily free. For example, $(\forall x\colon\ M \le x)$ contains free occurrences of both $a$ and of $b$, but $(\forall a\colon\ M \le a)$ contains bound occurrences of $a$ and free occurrences of $b$.

term $Z$ contains a *free occurrence* of a variable $v$ whenever an expression or guard containing a free occurrence of $v$ appears in the definition of $Z$.

By imposing restrictions on the definition of a derived term $Z$, we ensure that the value of $Z$ is specified when it ought to be. For a term, derived term, or predicate $\mathcal{E}$, let FDT($\mathcal{E}$) ("free derived terms") be the set of derived terms on which $\mathcal{E}$ depends. FDT($\mathcal{E}$) is defined formally in terms of $fdt(\mathcal{E}, ES)$, the union of a set $ES$ of derived terms and the set of derived terms that are free in term $\mathcal{E}$:

FDT($\mathcal{E}$):   $fdt(\mathcal{E}, \varnothing)$

The definition of $fdt(\mathcal{E}, ES)$ is by induction on the structure of $\mathcal{E}$. It is given in Figure 2.2.

The restrictions on definitions of derived terms are:

(2.57) **Derived Term Restrictions.** A derived term $Z$ defined by (2.55) is *well-defined* provided:

   (i)  $Z \notin \bigcup_{1 \le i \le n} (\text{FDT}(e_i) \cup \text{FDT}(B_i))$

   (ii)  $B_1, ..., B_n$ are pairwise-disjoint predicates.

   (iii) $(B_1 \Rightarrow def_{e_1}) \wedge \cdots \wedge (B_n \Rightarrow def_{e_n})$ is valid.   □

Restriction (i) guarantees termination of the procedure given above for computing the value of $Z$. The alternative, allowing the value of $Z$ to depend on $Z$, could lead to infinite recursion. If restriction (ii) is not satisfied, then a state could satisfy both $B_i$ and $B_j$ (for $i \ne j$), and the value of $Z$ might not be uniquely

---

| $\mathcal{E}$ | $fdt(\mathcal{E}, ES)$ |
|---|---|
| a constant or variable | $ES$ |
| a derived term, where $\mathcal{E} \in ES$ | $ES$ |
| a derived term, where $\mathcal{E} \notin ES$ and defined by: $\mathcal{E}: \begin{cases} e_1 & \text{if } B_1 \\ \cdots \\ e_n & \text{if } B_n \end{cases}$ | $\bigcup_{1 \le i \le n} (fdt(e_i, ES \cup \{\mathcal{E}\}) \cup fdt(B_i, ES \cup \{\mathcal{E}\}))$ |
| a function application or predicate $\mathcal{E}(\mathcal{T}_1, ..., \mathcal{T}_n)$ | $\bigcup_{1 \le i \le n} fdt(\mathcal{T}_i, ES)$ |

**Figure 2.2.** *fdt* definition

determined in that state. Restriction (iii) ensures that $e_i$ is defined whenever $e_i$ is used to compute the value of $Z$.

In light of Derived Term Restrictions (2.57), the value of derived term $Z$ (2.55) is uniquely determined in states that satisfy:

$$def_Z: \quad \underset{1 \leq i \leq n}{\vee} B_i$$

## Syntax and Interpretation for Predicate Logic

With these preliminaries out of the way, we can now give a syntax and semantics for Predicate Logic. The language of Predicate Logic consists of Propositional Logic formulas and Propositional Logic formulas in which all propositional variables have been replaced by predicates and quantified expressions.

Predicate Logic formulas are interpreted with respect to states. The value of a Predicate Logic formula $P$ in state $s$ is the value of the propositional formula that results from replacing every propositional variable, predicate, and quantified expression in $P$ by its value in $s$. This is formalized by:

(2.58) **Interpretation for Predicate Logic.** For a predicate $p(\mathcal{T}_1, ..., \mathcal{T}_n)$ where $p$ is a predicate symbol, $\mathcal{T}_1, ..., \mathcal{T}_n$ are terms, and $s$ is a state:

$$s \vDash p(\mathcal{T}_1, ..., \mathcal{T}_n) \quad \text{iff} \quad p(s[\![\mathcal{T}_1]\!], ..., s[\![\mathcal{T}_n]\!]) \text{ is } true$$

For Predicate Logic formulas $P$ and $Q$ and state $s$:

$$s \vDash (\neg P) \quad \text{iff} \quad s \nvDash P$$
$$s \vDash (P \vee Q) \quad \text{iff} \quad s \vDash P \quad \text{or} \quad s \vDash Q$$
$$s \vDash (P \wedge Q) \quad \text{iff} \quad s \vDash P \quad \text{and} \quad s \vDash Q$$
$$s \vDash (P \Rightarrow Q) \quad \text{iff} \quad s \nvDash P \quad \text{or} \quad s \vDash Q$$
$$s \vDash (P = Q) \quad \text{iff} \quad s \vDash P \quad \text{equals} \quad s \vDash Q$$
$$s \vDash (\forall x: P: Q) \quad \text{iff} \quad \text{For all V:} \quad (s; x{:}V) \vDash (P \Rightarrow Q)$$
$$s \vDash (\exists x: P: Q) \quad \text{iff} \quad \text{Exists V:} \quad (s; x{:}V) \vDash (P \wedge Q) \qquad \square$$

Note (from the final two cases of Interpretation for Predicate Logic (2.58)) that free occurrences of variables obtain their values directly from the state but bound occurrences do not.

## Textual Substitution in Predicate Logic

Propositional Logic uses the notation $P_e^x$ to denote the formula that results from substituting $e$ for each occurrence of variable $x$ in $P$. Thus, the value of $P_e^x$

in a state $s$ is the same as the value of $P$ in state $(s; x{:}e)$. By taking this to be the defining characteristic of textual substitution, we get:

(2.59) **Semantics for Textual Substitution.** For $x$ a variable, $e$ and $\mathcal{T}$ terms, and $P$ a Predicate Logic formula:

(a)  $s[\![\,T^x_e\,]\!] = (s; x{:}e)[\![\,T\,]\!]$

(b)  $s \vDash P^x_e$  iff  $(s; x{:}e) \vDash P$ ☐

Textual substitution of $e$ for $x$ when $\mathcal{T}$ is a constant, variable, or function application is simply a matter of replacing appearances of $x$ with $e$:

(2.60) *Textual Substitution [Constant]*:   For a constant C:  $C^x_e = C$

(2.61) *Textual Substitution [Variable]*:   For a variable $v$:

$$v^x_e = \begin{cases} v & \text{for "}x\text{"}\neq\text{"}v\text{"} \\ e & \text{for "}x\text{"}=\text{"}v\text{"} \end{cases}$$

(2.62) *Textual Substitution [Term]*:   For a function $f$ and terms $\mathcal{T}_1, \mathcal{T}_2, ..., \mathcal{T}_n$:
$$f(\mathcal{T}_1, \mathcal{T}_2, ..., \mathcal{T}_n)^x_e = f((\mathcal{T}_1)^x_e, (\mathcal{T}_2)^x_e, ..., (\mathcal{T}_n)^x_e)$$

It is not difficult to demonstrate that each of these axioms satisfies Semantics for Textual Substitution (2.59) and is, therefore, sound. As an illustration, here is the soundness proof for part of Textual Substitution [Variable] (2.61).

$$s[\![\,v^v_e\,]\!]$$
$$= \quad «\text{Textual Substitution [Variable] (2.61)}»$$
$$s[\![\,e\,]\!]$$
$$= \quad «(2.48)»$$
$$(s; v{:}e)[\![\,v\,]\!]$$

For a derived term $Z$, textual substitution of $e$ for $x$ produces another derived term $Z^x_e$ whose definition is like that of $Z$ but with all its clauses modified to reflect the textual substitution:

(2.63) *Textual Substitution [Derived Term]*:

$$Z^x_e: \begin{cases} (e_1)^x_e & \text{if } (B_1)^x_e \\ \cdots \\ (e_n)^x_e & \text{if } (B_n)^x_e \end{cases}$$

For example, the definition for $M^a_b$, where $M$ is defined by (2.56), is:

$$M_b^a: \quad \begin{cases} b & \text{if } b < b \\ b & \text{if } b \leq b \end{cases}$$

Since $b < b$ is satisfied by no state and $b \leq b$ is satisfied by all states, $M_b^a$ is equivalent to $b$.

Observe that if $Z$ has no free occurrences of $x$, then for all $i$, $(e_i)_e^x = e_i$ and $(B_i)_e^x = B_i$. We conclude:

(2.64) *Derived Term Simplification*: For $Z$ with no free occurrences of $x$:
$$Z_e^x = Z.$$

Thus, according to Derived Term Simplification (2.64), for $M$ defined by (2.56), $M_e^v$ equals $M$ because there are no free occurrences of $v$ in $M$.

We now turn to axioms concerning textual substitution into formulas of Predicate Logic. For predicates and for formulas constructed using propositional connectives, textual substitution behaves as might be expected.

(2.65) *Textual Substitution [Predicate]*: For a predicate symbol $p$ and terms $T_1$, ..., $T_n$:
$$p(T_1, ..., T_n)_e^x \ = \ p((T_1)_e^x, ..., (T_n)_e^x)$$

(2.66) *Textual Substitution [Propositional Connectives]*: For Predicate Logic formulas $P$ and $Q$:

      (a) $(\neg P)_e^x \ = \ \neg(P_e^x)$
      (b) $(P \wedge Q)_e^x \ = \ (P_e^x \wedge Q_e^x)$
      (c) $(P \vee Q)_e^x \ = \ (P_e^x \vee Q_e^x)$
      (d) $(P \Rightarrow Q)_e^x \ = \ (P_e^x \Rightarrow Q_e^x)$
      (e) $(P = Q)_e^x \ = \ (P_e^x = Q_e^x)$

Textual substitution into quantified expressions is tricky because of interactions with bound variables. The naive definition for $(\forall i: R: P)_e^x$ is to perform the designated textual substitutions in $R$ and $P$, obtaining $(\forall i: R_e^x: P_e^x)$. However, without restricting $i$, $x$, and $e$, it is possible for $(\forall i: R: P)_e^x$ and $(\forall i: R_e^x: P_e^x)$ to have different meanings.

To understand the problem, consider the meanings of:

(2.67) $s \vDash (\forall i: R: P)_e^x$

(2.68) $s \vDash (\forall i: R_e^x: P_e^x)$

First, here is the meaning of (2.67).

$$s \vDash (\forall i: R: P)_e^x$$
$$= \quad \text{«Semantics for Textual Substitution (2.59a)»}$$

$(s; x{:}e) \vDash (\forall i{:} R{:} P)$
iff  «Interpretation for Predicate Logic (2.58)»
   For all V:  $(s; x{:}e; i{:}V) \vDash (R \Rightarrow P)$

Here is the meaning of (2.68).

$s \vDash (\forall i{:} R_e^x{:} P_e^x)$
iff  «Interpretation for Predicate Logic (2.58)»
   For all V:  $(s; i{:}V) \vDash (R_e^x \Rightarrow P_e^x)$
iff  «Textual Substitution [Propositional Connectives] (2.66d)»
   For all V:  $(s; i{:}V) \vDash (R \Rightarrow P)_e^x$
iff  «Semantics for Textual Substitution (2.59b)»
   For all V:  $(s; i{:}V; x{:}e) \vDash (R \Rightarrow P)$

Thus, (2.67) and (2.68) are equivalent in a state $s$ iff the value that augmented state $(s; x{:}e; i{:}V)$ assigns to each variable's occurrence in $R \Rightarrow P$ is the same as the value that $(s; i{:}V; x{:}e)$ assigns to that occurrence. In light of (2.48), variables $x$ and $i$ are the only ones whose values might differ; the values assigned to them are summarized in the following table.

| $x$ and $i$ distinct? | variable | value of variable in state | |
|---|---|---|---|
| | | $(s; x{:}e; i{:}V)$ | $(s; i{:}V; x{:}e)$ |
| no | $i$ | V | $(s; i{:}V)[\![e]\!]$ |
| no | $x$ | V | $(s; i{:}V)[\![e]\!]$ |
| yes | $i$ | V | V |
| yes | $x$ | $s[\![e]\!]$ | $(s; i{:}V)[\![e]\!]$ |

From the first pair of rows, we see that if $x$ and $i$ are the same variable, then for (2.67) and (2.68) to be equivalent, V and $(s; i{:}V)[\![e]\!]$ must be the same value. Since V is a constant and $e$ is not, there exist states $s$ in which they are not the same. Therefore, one condition for ensuring the equivalence of (2.67) and (2.68) is to rule out textual substitutions where $x$, the variable being replaced, is not distinct from $i$, a bound variable in the original formula.

From the second pair of rows, we see that even when $x$ and $i$ are distinct, the value assigned to $x$ by one augmented state is not necessarily the same as the value assigned by the other. In particular, the value assigned to $x$ is either $s[\![e]\!]$ or $(s; i{:}V)[\![e]\!]$. These values differ when $i$ appears in $e$. Therefore, a second condition for ensuring equivalence of (2.67) and (2.68) is to rule out textual substitution where $e$, the replacement term, has a free occurrence of $i$, a bound variable in the original formula.

We combine these two restrictions to obtain:

(2.69) *Textual Substitution [Quantification]*: For $i$ distinct from $x$ and distinct from all variables occurring free in $e$:

$$(\forall i{:} R{:} P)_e^x \ = \ (\forall i{:} R_e^x{:} P_e^x)$$

We can circumvent the restrictions on $i$, $x$, and $e$ in Textual Substitution [Quantification] (2.69) by renaming the bound variable to make it distinct from $x$ and every variable occurring free in $e$. For example, bound variable $i$ in $(\forall i: 0 \leq i: i < x)^x_{i+1}$ might first be renamed to $j$, producing $(\forall j: 0 \leq j: j < x)^x_{i+1}$, which does satisfy the restrictions of (2.69) and therefore equals $(\forall j: 0 \leq j: j < i+1)$.

Care must be exercised in choosing a new name for a bound variable. Otherwise, the quantified expression that results from the renaming will have a different meaning than the original. The association of bound variable occurrences with quantifiers must be unchanged, and free occurrences of variables must remain unaltered.

We say that a variable $v$ is *captured* when a free occurrence of $v$ becomes a bound occurrence or when the quantifier with which $v$ has been associated changes. For example, renaming $i$ to $j$ in $(\exists i: i < j)$ results in $(\exists j: j < j)$, a quantified expression in which a free occurrence of $j$ has become captured because it became bound. Bound variables can also be captured by a renaming. Renaming $i$ to $n$ in $(\forall i: (\exists n: i \neq n))$ leads to the capture of $i$ by the universal quantifier: $(\forall n: (\exists n: n \neq n))$.

The examples of the preceding paragraph suggest that bound variable renaming be permitted only when the new name does not cause capture:

(2.70)  *Bound Variable Renaming Rule*:   Provided that

   (i)   $j$ is different from every free variable that occurs in $R$ and $P$,

   (ii)   $j$ is different from every bound variable that occurs in $R$ and $P$,

   then:

$$(Q\,i: R: P) \;=\; (Q\,j: R^i_j: P^i_j)$$

Restriction (i) prevents renaming $i$ to $j$ in $(\exists i: i < j)$. Restriction (ii) prevents renaming $i$ to $n$ in $(\forall i: (\exists n: i \neq n))$ or renaming $i$ to $a$ in $(\exists i: i > M)$ for $M$ defined by (2.56).

The need for restrictions (i) and (ii) in Bound Variable Renaming Rule (2.70) is best seen through the rule's soundness proof. We consider the case where "$Q$" is "$\forall$."

$\qquad\qquad s \vDash (\forall j: R^i_j: P^i_j)$
   iff      «Interpretation for Predicate Logic (2.58)»
$\qquad\qquad$ For all V: $(s; j{:}V) \vDash (R^i_j \Rightarrow P^i_j)$
   iff      «Textual Substitution [Propositional Connectives] (2.66d)»
$\qquad\qquad$ For all V: $(s; j{:}V) \vDash (R \Rightarrow P)^i_j$
   iff      «Semantics for Textual Substitution (2.59b)»
$\qquad\qquad$ For all V: $(s; j{:}V; i{:}j) \vDash (R \Rightarrow P)$
   ·iff      «$(s; j{:}V; i{:}j)=(s; j{:}V; i{:}V)$ due to (2.49) and (2.48)»
$\qquad\qquad$ For all V: $(s; j{:}V; i{:}V) \vDash (R \Rightarrow P)$
   iff      «due to (i) and (ii) $R \Rightarrow P$ does not depend on $j$»

For all V:  $(s; i{:}\text{V})\vDash(R \Rightarrow P)$
iff      «Interpretation for Predicate Logic (2.58)»
$s\vDash(\forall i{:}\ R{:}\ P)$

By combining the above laws for textual substitution, we obtain a reasonably straightforward procedure for performing textual substitutions.

(2.71)  **Textual Substitution.** For a Predicate Logic formula $P$, compute $P_e^x$ as follows.

> (i) First, use Bound Variable Renaming Rule (2.70) to rename bound variables in $P$ so that they are distinct from each other, from $x$, and from every variable that occurs free in $e$.

> (ii) Then, use Textual Substitution [Derived Term] (2.63) to replace every derived term $Z$ in $P$ by $Z_e^x$.

> (iii) Finally, use Textual Substitution [Variable] (2.61) to replace every occurrence of variable $x$ in $P$ by $e$.                    ☐

Textual substitution can be generalized to handle simultaneous replacement of more than one variable. This generalization is particularly useful for reasoning about assignment statements. Let $\bar{x}$ denote a list of (not necessarily distinct) variables $x_1, x_2, ..., x_n$ and let $\bar{e}$ denote a list of terms $e_1, e_2, ..., e_n$, possibly involving the $x$'s. Then for lists $\bar{x}$ and $\bar{e}$, $P_{\bar{e}}^{\bar{x}}$ or $P_{e_1, e_2, ..., e_n}^{x_1, x_2, ..., x_n}$ denotes the *simultaneous substitution* of $\bar{e}$ for $\bar{x}$ in $P$.

Simultaneous substitution specifies that variables are replaced only once by terms; unlike nested textual substitutions, substitutions are not repeatedly made into terms that replace the variables. For example, $(x=y)_{y+1,13}^{x,y}$ is $y+1=13$ and not $13+1=13$. In addition, unlike nested textual substitutions, it is convenient if we define simultaneous substitution to be such that when a variable appears more than once in $\bar{x}$, the rightmost replacement is used. Thus, $(x=y)_{1,2}^{x,x}$ is $2=y$ and not $1=y$.

The following definition of simultaneous substitution formalizes these ideas using nested textual substitutions. In it, the apparent reversal in the order of variables is an artifact of our requirement that the rightmost replacement be used for a variable that appears more than once in $\bar{x}$.

(2.72)  **Simultaneous Substitution.** Let $y1, y2, ..., yn$ be distinct identifiers that do not occur in $\bar{x}$, $\bar{e}$, and $P$:

$$P_{\bar{e}}^{\bar{x}} = ((\ \cdots\ ((((\ \cdots\ (P_{yn}^{xn})\ \cdots\ )_{y2}^{x2})_{y1}^{x1})_{en}^{yn})\ \cdots\ )_{e2}^{y2})_{e1}^{y1}$$    ☐

It is not difficult to prove laws for simultaneous substitution that are analogous to Textual Substitution Laws (2.60) through (2.69). We leave this to the reader.

## Inferences with Textual Substitution

Any theorem of Propositional Logic in which propositional variables are replaced by Predicate Logic formulas is a valid formula of Predicate Logic. This is so because theorems of Propositional Logic are *true* for any values of their propositional variables; Predicate Logic formulas substituted for these variables provide one such set of values. We allow Predicate Logic formulas derived in this manner to become theorems of Predicate Logic by having the following inference rules:

(2.73) *Predicate Logic Substitution*: Let $P_{Q1,Q2,...,Qn}^{q1,q2,...,qn}$ denote the formula obtained by substituting into Propositional Logic formula $P$ Predicate Logic formulas $Q1, Q2, ..., Qn$ for corresponding propositional variables $q1, q2, ..., qn$. Then:

$$\frac{P}{P_{Q1,Q2,...,Qn}^{q1,q2,...,qn}}$$

(2.74) *Predicate Logic Modus Ponens*: Let $P$ and $Q$ be Predicate Logic formulas. Then:

$$\frac{P, P \Rightarrow Q}{Q}$$

We next generalize Substitution of Equals (2.34) to enable individual variables to be replaced.

(2.75) *Substitution of Equals*: For any individual variable $x$:

$$\text{(a)} \quad \frac{Q=R}{P_Q^x = P_R^x} \qquad\qquad \text{(b)} \quad \frac{Q=R}{P_R^x = P_Q^x}$$

A related formulation, which is sometimes more convenient, is:

(2.76) *Substitution Equivalence Law*: $(e_1 = e_2) \Rightarrow (P_{e_1}^x = P_{e_2}^x)$

Substitution Equivalence Law (2.76) asserts that $P_{e_1}^x$ and $P_{e_2}^x$ are equal in states where $e_1$ equals $e_2$; in contrast, Substitution of Equals (2.75) only concerns the case where $e_1$ and $e_2$ are equal in all states.

The next inference rule allows substitution for a derived term $Z$, thereby expanding $Z$ according to its definition.

(2.77) *Derived Term Expansion Rule*: For $Z$ a derived term that is well-defined according to Derived Term Restrictions (2.57)

$$Z: \begin{cases} e_1 & \text{if } B_1 \\ \cdots \\ e_n & \text{if } B_n \end{cases}$$

and $P$ a Predicate Logic formula:

$$\frac{\bigwedge_{1 \le k \le n} (B_k = \neg(\bigvee_{j \ne k} B_j))}{P_Z^x = ((B_1 \wedge P_{e_1}^x) \vee \cdots \vee (B_n \wedge P_{e_n}^x))}$$

We might use this rule to prove that derived term $M$, defined in (2.56), satisfies $(a < M) = (a < b)$.

$a < M$
$=$        «Textual Substitution (2.71)»
          $(a < x)_M^x$
$=$        «Derived Term Expansion Rule (2.77), since $b < a = \neg(a \le b)$»
          $(b < a \wedge (a < x)_a^x) \vee (a \le b \wedge (a < x)_b^x)$
$=$        «Textual Substitution (2.71)»
          $(b < a \wedge a < a) \vee (a \le b \wedge a < b)$
$=$        «Arithmetic»
          $((b < a \wedge false) \vee (a < b))$
$=$        «And-Simplification Law (2.26c)»
          $false \vee a < b$
$=$        «Or-Simplification Law (2.25c)»
          $a < b$

## Laws for Quantification

Textual substitution allows the value of $(\forall x: R: P)$ in a state $s$ to be reformulated as the value in $s$ of an infinite conjunction

(2.78)   $(\forall x: R: P)$ $=$ $((R \Rightarrow P)_{V_1}^x \wedge (R \Rightarrow P)_{V_2}^x \wedge \cdots)$

where $V_1, V_2, \ldots$ are the constants that any variable (e.g. $x$) can assume. Similarly, the value of $(\exists x: R: P)$ in a state $s$ can be reformulated in terms of an infinite disjunction:

(2.79)   $(\exists x: R: P)$ $=$ $((R \wedge P)_{V_1}^x \vee (R \wedge P)_{V_2}^x \vee \cdots)$

These equations, then, enable reasoning informally about quantified expressions by using Propositional Logic.[11] For example, we have the following proof of $(\exists x: R: P) = \neg(\forall x: R: \neg P)$.

$(\exists x: R: P)$
$=$        «Predicate Logic Substitution (2.73) using $(\exists x: R: P)$
              for $p$ in Negation Law (2.19)»
          $\neg(\neg(\exists x: R: P))$
$=$        «(2.79)»

---

[11]Only informal reasoning is possible because (2.78) and (2.79) have ellipses.

$$\neg(\neg((R \wedge P)^x_{\mathrm{V}_1} \vee (R \wedge P)^x_{\mathrm{V}_2} \vee \cdots ))$$

$=\quad$ «repeated application of De Morgan's Law (2.17b)»

$$\neg(\neg(R \wedge P)^x_{\mathrm{V}_1} \wedge \neg(R \wedge P)^x_{\mathrm{V}_2} \wedge \cdots )$$

$=\quad$ «Textual Substitution [Propositional Connectives] (2.66b)»

$$\neg(\neg(R^x_{\mathrm{V}_1} \wedge P^x_{\mathrm{V}_1}) \wedge \neg(R^x_{\mathrm{V}_2} \wedge P^x_{\mathrm{V}_2}) \wedge \cdots )$$

$=\quad$ «repeated application of De Morgan's Law (2.17a)»

$$\neg((\neg R^x_{\mathrm{V}_1} \vee \neg P^x_{\mathrm{V}_1}) \wedge (\neg R^x_{\mathrm{V}_2} \vee \neg P^x_{\mathrm{V}_2}) \wedge \cdots )$$

$=\quad$ «repeated application of Textual Substitution [Propositional Connectives] (2.66a) and (2.66c)»

$$\neg((\neg R \vee \neg P)^x_{\mathrm{V}_1} \wedge (\neg R \vee \neg P)^x_{\mathrm{V}_2} \wedge \cdots )$$

$=\quad$ «repeated application of Implication Law (2.22a)»

$$\neg((R \Rightarrow \neg P)^x_{\mathrm{V}_1} \wedge (R \Rightarrow \neg P)^x_{\mathrm{V}_2} \wedge \cdots )$$

$=\quad$ «(2.78)»

$$\neg(\forall x: R: \neg P)$$

A number of other laws can be discovered in this fashion or by further manipulations. Let $P$, $Q$, and $R$ be formulas of Predicate Logic. The laws are:

(2.80) *De Morgan's Laws*:  (a) $(\exists x: R: P) = \neg(\forall x: R: \neg P)$
$\qquad\qquad\qquad\qquad$ (b) $(\forall x: R: P) = \neg(\exists x: R: \neg P)$

(2.81) *Conjunction Law*:  $(\forall x: R: P \wedge Q) = ((\forall x: R: P) \wedge (\forall x: R: Q))$

(2.82) *Disjunction Law*:  $(\exists x: R: P \vee Q) = ((\exists x: R: P) \vee (\exists x: R: Q))$

(2.83) *Empty-Range Laws*:  (a) $(\forall x: false: P) = true$
$\qquad\qquad\qquad\qquad$ (b) $(\exists x: false: P) = false$

(2.84) *Range Laws*:  (a) $(\forall x: R \wedge P: Q) = (\forall x: R: P \Rightarrow Q)$
$\qquad\qquad\qquad$ (b) $(\exists x: R \wedge P: Q) = (\exists x: R: P \wedge Q)$

(2.85) *Range Partitioning Laws*:
$\qquad\qquad$ (a) $(\forall x: P \vee R: Q) = ((\forall x: P: Q) \wedge (\forall x: R: Q))$
$\qquad\qquad$ (b) $(\exists x: P \vee R: Q) = ((\exists x: P: Q) \vee (\exists x: R: Q))$

(2.86) *Range Narrowing Law*:  $(\forall x: R: P) \Rightarrow (\forall x: R \wedge Q: P)$

(2.87) *Range Widening Law*:  $(\exists x: R: P) \Rightarrow (\exists x: R \vee Q: P)$

(2.88) *Quantification Weakening Laws*:  (a) $(\forall x: R: P) \Rightarrow (\forall x: R: P \vee Q)$
$\qquad\qquad\qquad\qquad\qquad\qquad\quad$ (b) $(\exists x: R: P) \Rightarrow (\exists x: R: P \vee Q)$

(2.89) *Quantification Implication Laws*:
$\qquad\qquad$ (a) $(\forall x: R: P \Rightarrow Q) \Rightarrow ((\forall x: R: P) \Rightarrow (\forall x: R: Q))$
$\qquad\qquad$ (b) $(\forall x: R: P \Rightarrow Q) \Rightarrow ((\exists x: R: P) \Rightarrow (\exists x: R: Q))$

(2.90) *Distributive Laws*:   Provided that $x$ does not occur free in $Q$:

$\quad\quad$ (a) $(Q \wedge (\exists x\colon R\colon P)) = (\exists x\colon R\colon Q \wedge P)$

$\quad\quad$ (b) $(Q \vee (\forall x\colon R\colon P)) = (\forall x\colon R\colon Q \vee P)$

$\quad\quad$ (c) $(Q \Rightarrow (\forall x\colon R\colon P)) = (\forall x\colon R\colon Q \Rightarrow P)$

(2.91) *Distributive Rules*:   Provided that $x$ does not occur free in $Q$:

$\quad$ (a) $\dfrac{(\exists x\colon R)}{(Q \vee (\exists x\colon R\colon P)) = (\exists x\colon R\colon Q \vee P)}$

$\quad$ (b) $\dfrac{(\exists x\colon R)}{(Q \wedge (\forall x\colon R\colon P)) = (\forall x\colon R\colon Q \wedge P)}$

$\quad$ (c) $\dfrac{(\exists x\colon R)}{(Q \Rightarrow (\exists x\colon R\colon P)) = (\exists x\colon R\colon Q \Rightarrow P)}$

The need for premise $(\exists x\colon R)$ in Distributive Rules (2.91) can be seen by choosing *false* for $R$ and observing that the conclusion of the laws need not be valid.

$\quad$ Here are some laws for introducing or removing quantifiers.

(2.92) *Quantification Simplification Laws*:   Provided that $x$ does not occur free in $Q$:

$\quad\quad$ (a) $(\forall x\colon Q) = Q$

$\quad\quad$ (b) $(\exists x\colon Q) = Q$

$\quad\quad$ (c) $(\forall x\colon R\colon \textit{true}) = \textit{true}$

$\quad\quad$ (d) $(\exists x\colon R\colon \textit{false}) = \textit{false}$

(2.93) *One-Point Laws*:   Provided that $x$ does not occur free in $e$:

$\quad\quad$ (a) $P_e^x = (\forall x\colon x=e\colon P)$

$\quad\quad$ (b) $P_e^x = (\exists x\colon x=e\colon P)$

The conditions on $x$ in Quantification Simplification Laws (2.92a) and (2.92b) and in One-Point Laws (2.93a) and (2.93b) prevent capture of $x$.

$\quad$ Next are inference rules that allow introduction and removal of a universal quantifier. If a formula $R \Rightarrow Q$ is valid, then it holds in all states. Thus, $R \Rightarrow Q$ holds for all possible values of any variable, and we have:

(2.94) *Quantification Introduction Rule*:   $\dfrac{R \Rightarrow Q}{(\forall x\colon R\colon Q)}$

$\quad$ If, on the other hand, $(\forall x\colon R\colon Q)$ is valid, then $Q$ holds for every value of $x$ that satisfies $R$. When $R_e^x$ is *false* in a state, $(R \Rightarrow Q)_e^x$ is trivially valid; and when $R_e^x$ is *true* in a state, we conclude from $(\forall x\colon R\colon Q)$ that $Q_e^x$ holds, so $(R \Rightarrow Q)_e^x$ must also be *true* in that state. Thus, whether or not $R_e^x$ holds in a state, we conclude that $(R \Rightarrow Q)_e^x$ holds. This gives:

(2.95) *Quantification Elimination Rule*:  $\dfrac{(\forall x\colon R\colon Q)}{(R \Rightarrow Q)^x_e}$

Finally, here are some rules for manipulating formulas involving nested quantifiers. Such nesting can arise when $R$ and $P$ in $(Q x\colon R\colon P)$ contain quantified expressions.

(2.96) *Quantifier Interchange Laws*: Provided that $x$ does not occur free in $Q$, and $y$ does not occur free in $R$:

$$(a)\ (\forall x\colon R\colon (\forall y\colon Q\colon P)) = (\forall y\colon Q\colon (\forall x\colon R\colon P))$$
$$(b)\ (\exists x\colon R\colon (\exists y\colon Q\colon P)) = (\exists y\colon Q\colon (\exists x\colon R\colon P))$$
$$(c)\ (\exists x\colon R\colon (\forall y\colon Q\colon P)) \Rightarrow (\forall y\colon Q\colon (\exists x\colon R\colon P))$$

Note that the converse of Quantifier Interchange Law (2.96c) is not, in general, valid. For example, $(\forall y\colon (\exists x\colon y \in \text{Int} \wedge x \in \text{Rat} \Rightarrow x{*}y = 1)$ is valid and $(\exists x\colon (\forall y\colon y \in \text{Int} \wedge x \in \text{Rat} \Rightarrow x{*}y = 1)$ is *false*.

## Equational Proofs for Predicate Logic

Equational proofs for Predicate Logic theorems are easier to construct if we can substitute equals for $R$ and $P$ in a quantified expression $(Q x\colon R\colon P)$. However, Substitution of Equals (2.75) cannot be used for this task when $R$ or $P$ have free occurrences of $x$, because Textual Substitution (2.71) would rename bound variable $x$ to be distinct from any variables occurring in $R$ and $P$. For example, using Substitution of Equals (2.75) we would conclude $(\forall x\colon\colon v > 0)^y_{2*x} = (\forall x\colon\colon v > 0)^y_{x+x}$ from premise $2{*}x = x+x$, but this conclusion is not equivalent to $(\forall x\colon\colon 2{*}x > 0) = (\forall x\colon\colon x+x > 0)$.

Rules that do allow equals to be substituted for $R$ and $P$ without bound variables being renamed are:

(2.97) *Equals in Quantified Expressions*: (a) $\dfrac{R = Q}{(\forall x\colon R\colon P) = (\forall x\colon Q\colon P)}$

(b) $\dfrac{R = Q}{(\exists x\colon R\colon P) = (\exists x\colon Q\colon P)}$

(c) $\dfrac{R \Rightarrow (P = Q)}{(\forall x\colon R\colon P) = (\forall x\colon R\colon Q)}$

(d) $\dfrac{R \Rightarrow (P = Q)}{(\exists x\colon R\colon P) = (\exists x\colon R\colon Q)}$

We shall also find it helpful to replace $R$ and $P$ in $(Q x\colon R\colon P)$ by stronger or weaker formulas. Inference rules for these manipulations subsume Range Narrowing Laws (2.86), Range Widening Law (2.87), Quantification Weakening Laws (2.88), and Quantification Implication Laws (2.89).

(2.98) *Monotonicity in Quantified Expressions*:

(a) $$\frac{R \Rightarrow (P \Rightarrow Q)}{(\exists x\colon R\colon P) \Rightarrow (\exists x\colon R\colon Q)}$$

(b) $$\frac{R \Rightarrow (P \Rightarrow Q)}{(\forall x\colon R\colon P) \Rightarrow (\forall x\colon R\colon Q)}$$

(c) $$\frac{R \Rightarrow (P \Rightarrow Q)}{(\exists x\colon P\colon R) \Rightarrow (\exists x\colon Q\colon R)}$$

(d) $$\frac{\neg R \Rightarrow (P \Rightarrow Q)}{(\forall x\colon Q\colon R) \Rightarrow (\forall x\colon P\colon R)}$$

Notice from Monotonicity in Quantified Expressions (2.98d) that the range of a universally quantified expression behaves as if it has odd parity. The other three inference rules suggest that the body of a universally quantified expression, the range of an existentially quantified expression, and the body of an existentially quantified expression, behave as if they each have even parity.

Given these rules, it often is convenient to give as a justification for a step in an equational proof only the premise for the first in a chain of inferences. For example, we might write

$$(\forall x\colon (\forall y\colon (\exists z\colon P)))$$
$$\Rightarrow \quad \text{«}P \Rightarrow Q\text{»}$$
$$(\forall x\colon (\forall y\colon (\exists z\colon Q)))$$

because from premise $P \Rightarrow Q$, Monotonicity in Quantified Expressions (2.98a) derives $(\exists z\colon P) \Rightarrow (\exists z\colon Q)$, and that formula then can be used as a premise for Quantified Expressions (2.98b) to conclude $(\forall y\colon (\exists z\colon P)) \Rightarrow (\forall y\colon (\exists z\colon Q))$, which, in turn, can be used as a premise for Quantified Expressions (2.98b) in order to deduce the desired conclusion:

$$(\forall x\colon (\forall y\colon (\exists z\colon P))) \Rightarrow (\forall x\colon (\forall y\colon (\exists z\colon Q)))$$

For constructing equational proofs, Predicate Logic also has analogues of Propositional Logic inference rules Substitution of Equals (2.34), Monotonicity Rule (2.36), and Antimonotonicity Rule (2.37).

To justify an equational-proof step that asserts $A = B$, we use:

(2.99) *Predicate Logic Substitution of Equals*:   For Predicate Logic formulas $P_Q^p$ and $P_R^p$:

(a) $$\frac{Q = R}{P_Q^p = P_R^p}$$        (b) $$\frac{Q = R}{P_R^p = P_Q^p}$$

In order to formulate Predicate Logic analogues of Monotonicity Rule (2.36) and Antimonotonicity Rule (2.37), we define:

(2.100) **Parity of a Subformula.** For $P_Q^p$ a formula in which subformula $Q$ does not appear in an operand of an equivalence in $P$:

- subformula $Q$ has *even* parity in $P_Q^p$ iff each occurrence of $Q$ is within an even number of negations, antecedents of implications, and ranges of universal quantifications.

- subformula $Q$ has *odd* parity in $P_Q^p$ iff each occurrence of $Q$ is within an odd number of negations, antecedents of implications, and ranges of universal quantifications. $\qquad\Box$

Then we have:

(2.101) *Predicate Logic Monotonicity Rule*: For Predicate Logic formulas $P_Q^p$ and $R$, where subformula $Q$ has even parity in $P_Q^p$:

$$\frac{Q \Rightarrow R}{P_Q^p \Rightarrow P_R^p}$$

(2.102) *Predicate Logic Antimonotonicity Rule*: For Temporal Logic formulas $P_Q^p$ and $R$, where subformula $Q$ has odd parity in $P_Q^p$:

$$\frac{Q \Rightarrow R}{P_R^p \Rightarrow P_Q^p}$$

The conventions concerning justifications for equational proofs in Predicate Logic are summarized by:

(2.103) **Predicate Logic Equational Proof Justifications.** A justification "Why $X$ is a theorem" in an equational proof of a Predicate Logic theorem must be one of the following:

(i)   A law or previously proved theorem $X$ of Predicate Logic.

(ii)  The theorem of Propositional Logic that enables $X$ to be deduced by Predicate Logic Substitution (2.73). Details of the substitutions may be omitted when they are obvious.

(iii) The theorem of Predicate Logic that enables $X$ to be deduced by Substitution of Equals (2.75), Predicate Logic Substitution of Equals (2.99), Predicate Logic Monotonicity Rule (2.101), or Predicate Logic Antimonotonicity Rule (2.102).

(iv)  The theorem that enables $X$ to be deduced by a sequence of one or more other Predicate Logic inference rules. $\qquad\Box$

## 2.4  Safety and Liveness Revisited

We can use Predicate Logic and set theory to formalize the notions of property, safety property, and liveness property. These formalizations then allow us to prove that every property is the conjunction of a safety property and a liveness property. Thus, knowledge of how to prove that a program satisfies safety properties and liveness properties suffices for reasoning about any property.

The formalizations require introducing some notation. Let $\sigma$ be a finite or infinite sequence $s_0 s_1 \dots$ of states; the empty sequence is denoted by $\varepsilon$. Define $|\sigma|$ to be the number of states in $\sigma$ ($|\sigma|=\infty$ if $\sigma$ is an infinite sequence of states), and also define:

$$\sigma[i]: \quad \begin{cases} s_i & \text{for } i\in\text{Int} \wedge 0\leq i<|\sigma| \\ \varepsilon & \text{otherwise} \end{cases}$$

$$\sigma[..i]: \quad \begin{cases} s_0 s_1 \dots s_{\min(i,\,|\sigma|-1)} & \text{for } i\in\text{Int} \wedge 0\leq i \\ \varepsilon & \text{otherwise} \end{cases}$$

$$\sigma[i..]: \quad \begin{cases} s_i s_{i+1} \dots & \text{for } i\in\text{Int} \wedge 0\leq i<|\sigma| \\ \varepsilon & \text{otherwise} \end{cases}$$

An *anchored sequence* is a pair $(\sigma, j)$, where $\sigma$ is a finite or infinite sequence of states and $j$ is a natural number that satisfies $j<|\sigma|$. If $\sigma$ is finite, then $(\sigma, j)$ is called a *finite anchored sequence*. State sequence $\sigma$ in anchored sequence $(\sigma, j)$ is partitioned by $j$ into a sequence $\sigma[0..j-1]$ of *past states*, a *current state* $\sigma[j]$, and a sequence $\sigma[j+1..]$ of *future states*. Thus, not only do anchored sequences describe histories, but they also are expressive enough to describe snapshots of partial executions.

Some sets and operations involving anchored sequences will prove convenient. Let $S^+$ be the set of nonempty finite-length sequences of program states, and let $S^\infty$ be the set of all finite and infinite sequences of program states (including the empty sequence $\varepsilon$). Define sets of anchored sequences:

$$\Sigma_S^+: \{(\sigma,i)\,|\,\sigma\in S^+ \wedge i\in\text{Int} \wedge 0\leq i<|\sigma|\}$$

$$\Sigma_S^\infty: \{(\sigma,i)\,|\,\sigma\in S^\infty \wedge i\in\text{Int} \wedge 0\leq i<|\sigma|\}$$

That $(\sigma, i)$ is a *prefix* of $(\tau, j)$ will be denoted by the infix predicate symbol $\leq$; it is defined as follows:

$$(\sigma,i)\leq(\tau,j): \quad i\leq j \wedge \sigma[..i]=\tau[..i]$$

For describing certain prefixes of anchored sequences, it is useful to have a notation like the one introduced above for describing prefixes of (ordinary) state sequences:

$$(\sigma, i)[..j]: \quad (\sigma[..j], \min(i, |\sigma[..j]|-1))$$

Observe that if $(\sigma, i)$ is an anchored sequence, then by construction, $(\sigma, i)[..j]$ is also one—no matter what value $j$ has.

The length of an anchored sequence is just the length of its sequence of states:

$$|(\sigma, i)|: \quad |\sigma|$$

Finally, we define the *catenation* $(\sigma, i)(\tau, j)$ for anchored sequences $(\sigma, i)$ and $(\tau, j)$ as follows, where $\sigma\tau$ is the sequence obtained by appending $\tau$ to $\sigma$.

$$(\sigma, i)(\tau, j): \quad (\sigma\tau, i)$$

## Formalizing Properties

We model a *property* by a set of anchored sequences. The property Mutual Exclusion, for example, is modeled by a set containing anchored sequences $(\sigma, j)$ such that all states of $\sigma$ are ones in which the program counter for at most one process points to an atomic action inside any critical section. The property Termination might be modeled by the set of anchored sequences $(\sigma, j)$ such that $\sigma$ is finite and $\sigma[|\sigma|-1]$ is a state in which the program counter points to the end of the program. Note that $\sigma$ of an anchored sequence $(\sigma, j)$ in a property need not correspond to a possible execution of a particular—indeed, any—program.

One way to define a set is by giving a *characteristic predicate*—a predicate that is *true* for members of the set and *false* for other values. Use of a characteristic predicate is attractive because it succinctly describes the shared attributes of a set's elements. In addition, Predicate Logic can be used in reasoning about sets defined with characteristic predicates:

(2.104) *Set Membership*: (a) $\gamma \in \{\sigma|P\} = P^\sigma_\gamma$
(b) $\gamma \notin \{\sigma|P\} = \neg P^\sigma_\gamma$

We use characteristic predicates for defining properties. The set

$$\mathcal{P}: \quad \{(\sigma, j)|Q\}$$

where

- $Q$ is a predicate whose only free variables are $\sigma$ and $j$,
- $Q$ implies that $\sigma$ is a sequence of states, and
- $Q$ implies that $j$ is an integer satisfying $0 \leq j < |\sigma|$

defines $\mathcal{P}$ to be the property consisting of all anchored sequences $(\gamma, k)$ such that $Q_{\gamma,k}^{\sigma,j}$ holds. For example, below we formalize the property that stipulates that the state remains constant.

$$\{(\sigma, j) \mid \sigma \in S^{\infty} \ \wedge \ j \in \text{Int} \ \wedge \ 0 \leq j < |\sigma| \\ \wedge \ (\forall i \in \text{Int}: \ 0 \leq i < |\sigma|: \ \sigma[0] = \sigma[i])\}$$

## *Formalizing Safety and Liveness*

Safety (1.1) and Liveness (1.2) of §1.3 are informal definitions. We now formalize them.

Safety (1.1) stipulates that some "bad thing" does not happen. Thus for $\mathcal{P}$ to be a safety property, if an anchored sequence $\alpha$ is not in $\mathcal{P}$, then a "bad thing" must occur in some prefix of $\alpha$. Such a "bad thing" must be irremediable, because a safety property stipulates that the "bad thing" never happens. This suggests that whenever $\alpha \notin \mathcal{P}$ holds, there is a finite prefix $\beta$ that is a "bad thing" for which no $\gamma$ is a mitigating extension.

(2.105) **Safety Property.** A property $\mathcal{P}$ is a safety property iff:
$$(\forall \alpha \in \Sigma_S^{\infty}: \ \alpha \notin \mathcal{P} \ \Rightarrow \ (\exists \beta \in \Sigma_S^+: \ \beta \leq \alpha: \ (\forall \gamma \in \Sigma_S^{\infty}: \ \beta\gamma \notin \mathcal{P}))) \qquad \square$$

Note that the only restriction imposed by this definition on the notion of a "bad thing" is that if the "bad thing" happens in $\alpha$, then there is an identifiable point (i.e., $\beta$) at which it occurs.

Mutual Exclusion satisfies (informal definition) Safety (1.1), the "bad thing" being a state in which more than one process is executing in a critical section. To see that Mutual Exclusion also satisfies our formal definition, observe that there is no way to extend a finite anchored sequence that contains such a state to an anchored sequence in which there are no such states.

Liveness (1.2) stipulates that some "good thing" eventually happens. The thing to observe about a liveness property is that no finite anchored sequence is irremediable. This is because if some finite anchored sequence were irremediable, then this would constitute a "bad thing," and a liveness property cannot proscribe a "bad thing" (a safety property does this) but can only prescribe a "good thing." Thus, if $\mathcal{P}$ is a liveness property, then for any finite anchored sequence $\alpha$, there is a $\beta$, containing the "good thing," such that $\alpha\beta \in \mathcal{P}$ holds.

(2.106) **Liveness Property.** A property $\mathcal{P}$ is a liveness property iff:
$$(\forall \alpha \in \Sigma_S^+: \ (\exists \beta \in \Sigma_S^{\infty}: \ \alpha\beta \in \mathcal{P})) \qquad \square$$

This definition does not restrict what a "good thing" can be. Unlike a "bad thing," a "good thing" can involve an infinite number of states, and it need not occur at an identifiable point.

Recall that Termination satisfies (informal definition) Liveness (1.2), the "good thing" being a state in which the program counter value in the final state of the sequence designates the end of the program. To see that Termination also satisfies our formal definition, for a finite anchored sequence $\alpha$, choose $\beta$ to be any finite anchored sequence whose last state is one in which the program counter value is at the end of the program.

Although the "good thing" for Termination occurs at a single identifiable point—the last state—this is not the case for all liveness properties. Consider the (liveness) property that asserts that each process is executed infinitely often. This property contains anchored sequences $(\sigma, j)$ such that for each process, there is an infinite number of states in $\sigma$ in which the program counter for that process has changed. Here, a "good thing" is not a finite anchored sequence, and this "good thing" cannot be associated with a single identifiable point in the sequence.

## Decomposing Properties into Safety and Liveness

In order to show that every property $\mathcal{P}$ can be expressed in terms of safety and liveness properties, we show how to construct a safety property $Safe(\mathcal{P})$ and a liveness property $Live(\mathcal{P})$ such that $\mathcal{P} = Safe(\mathcal{P}) \cap Live(\mathcal{P})$

$Safe(\mathcal{P})$ contains all anchored sequences in property $\mathcal{P}$ as well as those whose prefixes could be extended in a way that would make them part of $\mathcal{P}$.

(2.107) $Safe(\mathcal{P})$: $\mathcal{P} \cup \{\delta \mid \delta \in \Sigma_S^\infty \wedge (\forall \kappa \in \Sigma_S^+: \kappa \leq \delta: (\exists \iota \in \Sigma_S^\infty: \kappa \iota \in \mathcal{P}))\}$

To see informally that $Safe(\mathcal{P})$ is a safety property, observe the following. For $\alpha$ an anchored sequence, if $\alpha \notin Safe(\mathcal{P})$ holds, then $\alpha \notin \mathcal{P}$ and, by Set Membership (2.104b), $\neg(\forall \kappa \in \Sigma_S^+: \kappa \leq \delta: (\exists \iota \in \Sigma_S^\infty: \kappa \iota \in \mathcal{P}))_\alpha^\delta$ hold. This means that there exists a finite prefix $\kappa$ of $\alpha$ that satisfies $(\forall \iota \in \Sigma_S^\infty: \kappa \iota \notin \mathcal{P})$, so we could consider $\kappa$ to be a "bad thing." An anchored sequence that does not satisfy $\mathcal{P}$ only because it violates a liveness property will satisfy $Safe(\mathcal{P})$.

To show formally that $Safe(\mathcal{P})$ is a safety property, we show that it satisfies Safety Property (2.105).

1.     $\beta \in \Sigma_S^+ \wedge (\forall \iota \in \Sigma_S^\infty: \beta \iota \notin \mathcal{P})$
   $\Rightarrow$    «Range Narrowing Law (2.86)»
       $\beta \in \Sigma_S^+ \wedge (\forall \iota \in \Sigma_S^\infty: \iota = \gamma: \beta \iota \notin \mathcal{P}) \wedge (\forall \iota \in \Sigma_S^\infty: \beta \iota \notin \mathcal{P})$
   $=$    «One-Point Law (2.93a»
       $\beta \in \Sigma_S^+ \wedge \beta \gamma \notin \mathcal{P} \wedge (\forall \iota \in \Sigma_S^\infty: \beta \iota \notin \mathcal{P})$
   $\Rightarrow$    «Consequent-Weakening Law (2.30)»
       $\beta \in \Sigma_S^+ \wedge \beta \gamma \notin \mathcal{P} \wedge (\beta \gamma \notin \Sigma_S^\infty \vee (\forall \iota \in \Sigma_S^\infty: \beta \iota \notin \mathcal{P}))$
   $=$    «One-Point Law (2.93b)»
       $\beta \in \Sigma_S^+ \wedge \beta \gamma \notin \mathcal{P} \wedge (\beta \gamma \notin \Sigma_S^\infty \vee (\exists \kappa: \kappa = \beta: (\forall \iota \in \Sigma_S^\infty: \kappa \iota \notin \mathcal{P})))$
   $\Rightarrow$    «$(\beta \in \Sigma_S^+ \wedge \kappa = \beta) \Rightarrow (\kappa \in \Sigma_S^+ \wedge \kappa \leq \beta \gamma)$»
       $\beta \gamma \notin \mathcal{P} \wedge (\beta \gamma \notin \Sigma_S^\infty \vee (\exists \kappa \in \Sigma_S^+: \kappa \leq \beta \gamma: (\forall \iota \in \Sigma_S^\infty: \kappa \iota \notin \mathcal{P})))$
   $=$    «De Morgan's Laws (2.17) and (2.80)»
       $\beta \gamma \notin \mathcal{P} \wedge \neg(\beta \gamma \in \Sigma_S^\infty \wedge (\forall \kappa \in \Sigma_S^+: \kappa \leq \beta \gamma: (\exists \iota \in \Sigma_S^\infty: \kappa \iota \in \mathcal{P})))$

$\quad$ = $\quad\quad$ «Textual Substitution (2.71)»

$\beta\gamma \notin \mathcal{P} \ \wedge \ \neg(\delta \in \Sigma_S^\infty \ \wedge \ (\forall \kappa \in \Sigma_S^+: \ \kappa \leq \delta: \ (\exists \iota \in \Sigma_S^\infty: \ \kappa\iota \in \mathcal{P})))_{\beta\gamma}^\delta$

$\quad$ = $\quad\quad$ «Set Membership (2.104b)»

$\beta\gamma \notin \mathcal{P} \ \wedge \ \beta\gamma \notin \{\delta \,|\, \delta \in \Sigma_S^\infty \ \wedge \ (\forall \kappa \in \Sigma_S^+: \ \kappa \leq \delta: \ (\exists \iota \in \Sigma_S^\infty: \ \kappa\iota \in \mathcal{P}))\}$

$\quad$ = $\quad\quad$ «definition (2.107) of $\mathit{Safe}(\mathcal{P})$»

$\beta\gamma \notin \mathit{Safe}(\mathcal{P})$

2. $\quad \alpha \in \Sigma_S^\infty \ \wedge \ \alpha \notin \mathit{Safe}(\mathcal{P})$

$\quad$ = $\quad\quad$ «definition (2.107) of $\mathit{Safe}(\mathcal{P})$»

$\alpha \in \Sigma_S^\infty \ \wedge \ \alpha \notin (\mathcal{P} \cup \{\delta \,|\, \delta \in \Sigma_S^\infty \ \wedge \ (\forall \kappa \in \Sigma_S^+: \ \kappa \leq \delta: \ (\exists \iota \in \Sigma_S^\infty: \ \kappa\iota \in \mathcal{P}))\})$

$\quad$ ⇒ $\quad\quad$ «$\alpha \notin (A \cup B) \ \Rightarrow \ \alpha \notin B$»

$\alpha \in \Sigma_S^\infty \ \wedge \ \alpha \notin \{\delta \,|\, \delta \in \Sigma_S^\infty \ \wedge \ (\forall \kappa \in \Sigma_S^+: \ \kappa \leq \delta: \ (\exists \iota \in \Sigma_S^\infty: \ \kappa\iota \in \mathcal{P}))\}$

$\quad$ = $\quad\quad$ «Set Membership (2.104b)»

$\alpha \in \Sigma_S^\infty \ \wedge \ \neg(\delta \in \Sigma_S^\infty \ \wedge \ (\forall \kappa \in \Sigma_S^+: \ \kappa \leq \delta: \ (\exists \iota \in \Sigma_S^\infty: \ \kappa\iota \in \mathcal{P})))_\alpha^\delta$

$\quad$ = $\quad\quad$ «Textual Substitution (2.71)»

$\alpha \in \Sigma_S^\infty \ \wedge \ \neg(\alpha \in \Sigma_S^\infty \ \wedge \ (\forall \kappa \in \Sigma_S^+: \ \kappa \leq \alpha: \ (\exists \iota \in \Sigma_S^\infty: \ \kappa\iota \in \mathcal{P})))$

$\quad$ = $\quad\quad$ «De Morgan's Laws (2.17) and (2.80)»

$\alpha \in \Sigma_S^\infty \ \wedge \ (\alpha \notin \Sigma_S^\infty \ \vee \ (\exists \kappa \in \Sigma_S^+: \ \kappa \leq \alpha: \ (\forall \iota \in \Sigma_S^\infty: \ \kappa\iota \notin \mathcal{P})))$

$\quad$ = $\quad\quad$ «Implication Law (2.22a)»

$\alpha \in \Sigma_S^\infty \ \wedge \ (\alpha \in \Sigma_S^\infty \ \Rightarrow \ (\exists \kappa \in \Sigma_S^+: \ \kappa \leq \alpha: \ (\forall \iota \in \Sigma_S^\infty: \ \kappa\iota \notin \mathcal{P})))$

$\quad$ ⇒ $\quad\quad$ «Implication-Deduction Law (2.31a)»

$(\exists \kappa \in \Sigma_S^+: \ \kappa \leq \alpha: \ (\forall \iota \in \Sigma_S^\infty: \ \kappa\iota \notin \mathcal{P}))$

$\quad$ = $\quad\quad$ «Bound Variable Renaming Rule (2.70)»

$(\exists \beta \in \Sigma_S^+: \ \beta \leq \alpha: \ (\forall \iota \in \Sigma_S^\infty: \ \beta\iota \notin \mathcal{P}))$

$\quad$ = $\quad\quad$ «Quantification Simplification Law (2.92a)»

$(\exists \beta \in \Sigma_S^+: \ \beta \leq \alpha: \ (\forall \gamma \in \Sigma_S^\infty: \ (\forall \iota \in \Sigma_S^\infty: \ \beta\iota \notin \mathcal{P})))$

$\quad$ ⇒ $\quad\quad$ «line 1»

$(\exists \beta \in \Sigma_S^+: \ \beta \leq \alpha: \ (\forall \gamma \in \Sigma_S^\infty: \ \beta\gamma \notin \mathit{Safe}(\mathcal{P})))$

«Quantification Introduction Rule (2.94) with 2»

$\quad$ 3. $\ (\forall \alpha \in \Sigma_S^\infty: \ \alpha \notin \mathit{Safe}(\mathcal{P}): \ (\exists \beta \in \Sigma_S^+: \ \beta \leq \alpha: \ (\forall \gamma \in \Sigma_S^\infty: \ \beta\gamma \notin \mathit{Safe}(\mathcal{P}))))$

$\quad$ 4. $\ (\forall \alpha \in \Sigma_S^\infty: \ \alpha \notin \mathit{Safe}(\mathcal{P}): \ (\exists \beta \in \Sigma_S^+: \ \beta \leq \alpha: \ (\forall \gamma \in \Sigma_S^\infty: \ \beta\gamma \notin \mathit{Safe}(\mathcal{P}))))$

$\quad$ = $\quad\quad$ «Range Law (2.84a)»

$\quad (\forall \alpha \in \Sigma_S^\infty: \ \alpha \notin \mathit{Safe}(\mathcal{P}) \ \Rightarrow \ (\exists \beta \in \Sigma_S^+: \ \beta \leq \alpha: \ (\forall \gamma \in \Sigma_S^\infty: \ \beta\gamma \notin \mathit{Safe}(\mathcal{P}))))$

Since the first line of step 4 is step 3, a theorem, from Equational Proof Conclusions (2.42) we conclude that the final line of step 4 is a theorem. This final line is Safety Property (2.105) instantiated for property $\mathit{Safe}(\mathcal{P})$—we have formally proved that $\mathit{Safe}(\mathcal{P})$ is a safety property.

$\quad Live(\mathcal{P})$ contains all anchored sequences in $\mathcal{P}$ as well as those that violate some safety property in $\mathcal{P}$.

(2.108) $\quad Live(\mathcal{P})$: $\ \mathcal{P} \cup \{\delta \,|\, \delta \in \Sigma_S^\infty \ \wedge \ (\exists \kappa \in \Sigma_S^+: \ \kappa \leq \delta: \ (\forall \iota \in \Sigma_S^\infty: \ \kappa\iota \notin \mathcal{P}))\}$

An informal justification that $Live(\mathcal{P})$ is a liveness property is the following. All anchored sequences $\gamma$ that violate a safety property in $\mathcal{P}$ are in $Live(\mathcal{P})$ because by construction, $\gamma$ will be in $\{\delta \mid \delta \in \Sigma_S^\infty \land (\exists \kappa \in \Sigma_S^+: \kappa \leq \delta: (\forall \iota \in \Sigma_S^\infty: \kappa \iota \notin \mathcal{P}))\}$. Therefore every prefix of an anchored sequence in $Live(\mathcal{P})$ can be extended to produce an anchored sequence in $Live(\mathcal{P})$, and according to Liveness Property (2.106), this is the defining characteristic of a liveness property.

To show formally that $Live(\mathcal{P})$ is a liveness property, we prove below:

$$\alpha \in \Sigma_S^+ \;\Rightarrow\; (\exists \beta \in \Sigma_S^\infty: \alpha\beta \in Live(\mathcal{P}))$$

From this, Quantification Introduction Rule (2.94) yields the desired conclusion, $(\forall \alpha \in \Sigma_S^+: (\exists \beta \in \Sigma_S^\infty: \alpha\beta \in Live(\mathcal{P})))$.

$\qquad\alpha \in \Sigma_S^+$
$=\qquad$ «And-Simplification Law (2.26b)»
$\qquad\alpha \in \Sigma_S^+ \land true$
$=\qquad$ «Excluded Middle Law (2.20)»
$\qquad\alpha \in \Sigma_S^+ \land ((\exists \beta \in \Sigma_S^\infty: \alpha\beta \in \mathcal{P}) \lor \neg(\exists \beta \in \Sigma_S^\infty: \alpha\beta \in \mathcal{P}))$
$=\qquad$ «Bound Variable Renaming Rule (2.70)»
$\qquad\alpha \in \Sigma_S^+ \land ((\exists \beta \in \Sigma_S^\infty: \alpha\beta \in \mathcal{P}) \lor \neg(\exists \iota \in \Sigma_S^\infty: \alpha\iota \in \mathcal{P}))$
$=\qquad$ «De Morgan's Laws (2.80b)»
$\qquad\alpha \in \Sigma_S^+ \land ((\exists \beta \in \Sigma_S^\infty: \alpha\beta \in \mathcal{P}) \lor (\forall \iota \in \Sigma_S^\infty: \alpha\iota \notin \mathcal{P}))$
$=\qquad$ «Distributive Rule (2.91a), since $(\exists \beta: \beta \in \Sigma_S^\infty)$»
$\qquad\alpha \in \Sigma_S^+ \land (\exists \beta \in \Sigma_S^\infty: \alpha\beta \in \mathcal{P} \lor (\forall \iota \in \Sigma_S^\infty: \alpha\iota \notin \mathcal{P}))$
$=\qquad$ «Distributive Law (2.90a)»
$\qquad(\exists \beta \in \Sigma_S^\infty: \alpha \in \Sigma_S^+ \land (\alpha\beta \in \mathcal{P} \lor (\forall \iota \in \Sigma_S^\infty: \alpha\iota \notin \mathcal{P})))$
$\Rightarrow\qquad$ «$A \land (B \lor C) \;\Rightarrow\; B \lor (A \land C)$»
$\qquad(\exists \beta \in \Sigma_S^\infty: \alpha\beta \in \mathcal{P} \lor (\alpha \in \Sigma_S^+ \land (\forall \iota \in \Sigma_S^\infty: \alpha\iota \notin \mathcal{P})))$
$\Rightarrow\qquad$ «$\alpha \in \Sigma_S^+ \land \beta \in \Sigma_S^\infty \;\Rightarrow\; \alpha\beta \in \Sigma_S^\infty$»
$\qquad(\exists \beta \in \Sigma_S^\infty: \alpha\beta \in \mathcal{P} \lor (\alpha \in \Sigma_S^+ \land \alpha\beta \in \Sigma_S^\infty \land (\forall \iota \in \Sigma_S^\infty: \alpha\iota \notin \mathcal{P})))$
$=\qquad$ «One-Point Law (2.93b)»
$\qquad(\exists \beta \in \Sigma_S^\infty: \alpha\beta \in \mathcal{P} \lor (\alpha \in \Sigma_S^+ \land \alpha\beta \in \Sigma_S^\infty \land (\exists \kappa: \kappa = \alpha: (\forall \iota \in \Sigma_S^\infty: \kappa\iota \notin \mathcal{P}))))$
$\Rightarrow\qquad$ «$(\alpha \in \Sigma_S^+ \land \kappa = \alpha) \;\Rightarrow\; (\kappa \in \Sigma_S^+ \land \kappa \leq \alpha\beta)$»
$\qquad(\exists \beta \in \Sigma_S^\infty: \alpha\beta \in \mathcal{P} \lor (\alpha\beta \in \Sigma_S^\infty \land (\exists \kappa \in \Sigma_S^+: \kappa \leq \alpha\beta: (\forall \iota \in \Sigma_S^\infty: \kappa\iota \notin \mathcal{P}))))$
$=\qquad$ «Textual Substitution (2.71)»
$\qquad(\exists \beta \in \Sigma_S^\infty: \alpha\beta \in \mathcal{P} \lor (\delta \in \Sigma_S^\infty \land (\exists \kappa \in \Sigma_S^+: \kappa \leq \delta: (\forall \iota \in \Sigma_S^\infty: \kappa\iota \notin \mathcal{P})))_{\alpha\beta}^\delta)$
$=\qquad$ «Set Membership (2.104a)»
$\qquad(\exists \beta \in \Sigma_S^\infty: \alpha\beta \in \mathcal{P} \lor \alpha\beta \in \{\delta \mid \delta \in \Sigma_S^\infty \land (\exists \kappa \in \Sigma_S^+: \kappa \leq \delta: (\forall \iota \in \Sigma_S^\infty: \kappa\iota \notin \mathcal{P}))\})$
$=\qquad$ «$(a \in \mathcal{P} \lor a \in \mathcal{Q}) = a \in (\mathcal{P} \cup \mathcal{Q})$»
$\qquad(\exists \beta \in \Sigma_S^\infty: \alpha\beta \in (\mathcal{P} \cup \{\delta \mid \delta \in \Sigma_S^\infty \land (\exists \kappa \in \Sigma_S^+: \kappa \leq \delta: (\forall \iota \in \Sigma_S^\infty: \kappa\iota \notin \mathcal{P}))\}))$
$=\qquad$ «definition (2.108) of $Live(\mathcal{P})$»
$\qquad(\exists \beta \in \Sigma_S^\infty: \alpha\beta \in Live(\mathcal{P}))$

Finally, we prove that every property can be specified in terms of a safety property and a liveness property.[12]

$$Safe(\mathcal{P}) \cap Live(\mathcal{P})$$
$=$ «definition (2.107) of $Safe(\mathcal{P})$;  definition (2.108) of $Live(\mathcal{P})$;
$\quad TL$: $\{\delta \,|\, (\forall \kappa \in \Sigma_S^+ \colon \kappa \leq \delta \colon (\exists \iota \in \Sigma_S^\infty \colon \kappa \iota \in \mathcal{P}))\}$»
$\quad (\mathcal{P} \cup (\Sigma_S^\infty \cap TL)) \ \cap \ (\mathcal{P} \cup (\Sigma_S^\infty \cap \sim TL))$
$=$ «distribution of $\cap$ over $\cup$»
$\quad (\mathcal{P} \cap \mathcal{P}) \ \cup \ (\mathcal{P} \cap \Sigma_S^\infty \cap \sim TL) \ \cup \ (\Sigma_S^\infty \cap TL \cap \mathcal{P})$
$\quad \cup \ (\Sigma_S^\infty \cap TL \cap \sim TL)$
$=$ «$A \cap A = A$;  $A \cap \sim A = \varnothing$;  $A \cap \varnothing = \varnothing$;  $A \cup \varnothing = A$»
$\quad \mathcal{P} \ \cup \ (\mathcal{P} \cap \Sigma_S^\infty \cap \sim TL) \ \cup \ (\Sigma_S^\infty \cap TL \cap \mathcal{P})$
$=$ «$(A \cap B) \subseteq A$;  $A \subseteq B \Rightarrow (B \cup A = A)$»
$\quad \mathcal{P} \ \cup \ \mathcal{P} \ \cup \ \mathcal{P}$
$=$ «$A \cup A = A$»
$\quad \mathcal{P}$

Hence, every property $\mathcal{P}$ can be partitioned into a safety component $Safe(\mathcal{P})$ and a liveness component $Live(\mathcal{P})$ whose intersection is $\mathcal{P}$.

### Historical Notes

An introduction to logic, with particular attention to how it relates to computability and artificial intelligence, can be found in [Hofstadter 79]. The book is well written—it won a Pulitzer Prize—and easy to read.

Two popular texts for a first course in logic are [Church 56] and [Enderton 72]. Church's book takes a proof-theoretic point of view, while Enderton's takes a model-theoretic one. A more advanced text, intended for a first-year graduate course, is [Bell & Machover 77]. The text [Gries & Schneider 93], which was written concurrently with this book, treats at an elementary level all the logics in this chapter. See [DeLong 70] for a comprehensive annotated bibliography for formal logic.

The approach to proofs defined in §2.1 is due to Hilbert, although our equational format was inspired by work of Feijen and first reported in [Dijkstra 85]. An alternative style for presenting proofs is based on the way many people devise proofs, where a theorem is proved by identifying goals that imply the desired result and then proving each goal, perhaps by identifying subgoals, and so on. Logical systems that embody this style of reasoning are called *natural deduction systems*. Gerhard Gentzen developed the first such system in 1935. Textbooks [Quine 61] and [Smullyan 68] describe this approach.

Our presentation in §2.1 of formal logical systems was motivated by [Hofstadter 79], and the PQ–L logic is from there. Our axiomatization of Propositional Logic is from [Church 56], where it is called $P_1$. The extensions are based on [Gries & Schneider 93]. Many of our rules for quantified expressions are taken from [Hehner 84] and [Dijkstra & Feijen 84].

---

[12] $\sim A$ denotes the complement of set $A$.

Informal definitions of safety and liveness were first proposed in [Lamport 77a]. The names are borrowed from Petri net theory. The first formal definition of safety did not appear until seven years later [Lamport 85b]. Lamport's definition (Safety Property (2.109) in exercise 2.26) is adequate only for properties that are invariant under stuttering. A formal definition of safety that works for all properties and the first formal definition of liveness are given in [Alpern & Schneider 85]. The first proof that every property is the conjunction of a safety property and a liveness property appeared there as well, although the proof given in §2.4 is based on [Schneider 87]. The relationship between Safety Property (2.109) and Safety Property (2.105) is discussed in [Alpern et al. 86].

Attempts to characterize safety properties and liveness properties in terms of the syntax of the formulas used to express those properties are described in [Sistla 85], [Sistla 86], and [Lichtenstein et al. 85]; automata-theoretic characterizations and an automata-based proof that every property can be decomposed into safety and liveness properties is the subject of [Alpern & Schneider 87]. In [Manna & Pnueli 90], the notions of safety and liveness are further refined into classes based on how that property can be proved. See [Kindler 94] for a survey of research concerned with defining safety and liveness properties.

## Exercises

**2.1.** (a)  Give a finite set of axioms that can be added to PQ–L to make it sound and complete under Addition-Equality Interpretation (2.4).

(b)  Prove that the new logical system is sound and complete. (Hint: To show that a logic is complete, use induction, where the induction hypothesis is that every valid formula with fewer than $i$ symbols is provable.)

**2.2.** Consider the formal logical system defined by

**Symbols:** $M, I, o$.

**Formulas:** Formulas have the form $a \, M \, b \, I \, c$ where each of $a$, $b$, and $c$ is a sequence of zero or more $o$'s.

**Axiom:** $A1. \; o \, o \, M \, o \, o \, I \, o \, o \, o \, o$

**Inference Rules:** For $a$, $b$, and $c$ each a sequence of zero or more $o$'s:

$$R1: \quad \frac{a \, M \, b \, I \, c}{a \, a \, M \, b \, I \, c \, c}$$

$$R2: \quad \frac{a \, M \, b \, b \, I \, c \, c}{a \, a \, M \, b \, I \, c \, c}$$

(a)  Give five formulas in the logic.

(b)  State and prove five theorems of the logic.

(c)  Give an interpretation of the logic that makes multiplication of integers a model.

(d)  Give a formula that is *true* according to your interpretation but is not a theorem. Give additional axioms and/or inference rules to make the logic complete.

**2.3.** Two possible definitions for soundness of an inference rule are:

**Theorem Soundness.** An inference rule is *sound* if a formula derived using that rule is valid whenever the premises used are theorems.

**Model Soundness.** An inference rule is *sound* if a formula derived using that rule is valid whenever the premises used in that inference are valid.

What are the advantages/disadvantages of axiomatizations in which all inference rules satisfy Theorem Soundness versus Model Soundness?

**2.4.** Translate the following English statements into Propositional Logic, assuming:

*Prime_n*:  "*n* is prime"

*Odd_n*:  "*n* is odd"

*Even_n*:  "*n* is even"

(a)    If *n* is not even then it is odd.

(b)    If *n* is prime then it is odd, in which case it is not even.

(c)    If *n* is even and prime then it is also odd.

**2.5.** Define appropriate propositions and then formulate the following statements as formulas of Propositional Logic.

(a)    If I am here then I am not there.

(b)    I cannot be here and there at the same time.

(c)    I cannot be here unless I am not there.

(d)    Whenever the program terminates, it produces the correct answer.

(e)    The program produces the correct answer only if it terminates.

(f)    The program produces the correct answer or it does not terminate.

**2.6.** The formula $P_1 \oplus P_2 \oplus ... \oplus P_n$ is intended to be *true* when exactly one of $P_1, P_2,$ $..., P_n$ is. Show how to translate $P_1 \oplus P_2 \oplus ... \oplus P_n$ into Propositional Logic.

**2.7.** Give proofs using Propositional Logic for the following theorems.

(a)    $((p \wedge q) \Rightarrow r) \Rightarrow (p \Rightarrow (q \Rightarrow r))$

(b)    $(((p \Rightarrow q) \wedge (q \Rightarrow false)) \Rightarrow (p \Rightarrow false))$

(c)    $((p \Rightarrow q) \wedge (p \Rightarrow r)) \Rightarrow (p \Rightarrow (q \wedge r))$

(d)    $(p \Rightarrow (p \Rightarrow false)) \Rightarrow (p \Rightarrow false)$

(e)    $(p \Rightarrow (q \Rightarrow false)) \Rightarrow (q \Rightarrow (p \Rightarrow false))$

(f)    $(p \Rightarrow q) \Rightarrow ((q \Rightarrow false) \Rightarrow (p \Rightarrow false))$

**2.8.** Compute the value of each of the following Propositional Logic formulas in every possible state.

(a)    $p \vee q \vee \neg p$

(b)    $p \vee (p \Rightarrow q)$

(c)    $\neg (p \Rightarrow q) \Rightarrow (p \wedge (q \Rightarrow false))$

(d)    $(p \vee q) \wedge (\neg p \vee q)$

(e)    $(p \wedge q) \vee (\neg p \wedge q)$

(f)    $\neg (\neg p \wedge (q \Rightarrow p)) \vee \neg q$

**2.9.** Replace axioms (2.7)–(2.9) in the axiomatization of Propositional Logic with the following four axioms:

$A1.$  $(p \Rightarrow q) \Rightarrow ((q \Rightarrow r) \Rightarrow (p \Rightarrow r))$

$A2.$  $(((p \Rightarrow q) \Rightarrow p) \Rightarrow p)$

$A3.$  $p \Rightarrow (q \Rightarrow p)$

$A4.$  $false \Rightarrow p$

Show that every theorem of this new axiomatization is also a theorem of the original and vice versa.

**2.10.** A *contradiction* in Propositional Logic is a formula that is *false* in every state.

(a)  Prove, using Propositional Logic, that if $P$ is a theorem then $P \Rightarrow false$ is a contradiction.

(b)  Prove, using Propositional Logic, that if $P$ is a theorem then $\neg P$ is a contradiction.

**2.11.** Suppose we add $p \Rightarrow false$ as an axiom to our axiomatization of Propositional Logic. Show that whenever $P$ is a theorem of the resulting logic, so is $P \Rightarrow false$. What is the consequence of this with respect to the utility of the new logic?

**2.12.** A formula of Propositional Logic is in *conjunctive normal form* if it is a conjunction of formulas, each of which is the disjunction of propositional variables and/or their negations. Show, using Extended Propositional Logic, that it is always possible to translate a formula into conjunctive normal form.

**2.13.** A formula of Propositional Logic is in *disjunctive normal form* if it is a disjunction of formulas, each of which is the conjunction of propositional variables and/or their negations. Show, using Extended Propositional Logic, that it is always possible to translate a formula into disjunctive normal form.

**2.14.** Use the equational proof format and simplify the following formulas.

(a)  $p \vee (q \vee p) \vee \neg q$

(b)  $p \wedge (q \Rightarrow p) \wedge (p \vee \neg q)$

(c)  $\neg p \Rightarrow (\neg p \wedge q)$

(d)  $(p \wedge (q \Rightarrow false)) \ = \ \neg (p \Rightarrow \neg p)$

(e)  $p \Rightarrow (q \Rightarrow (p \wedge q))$

(f)  $(p \wedge q \wedge r) \vee (\neg p) \vee (\neg q) \vee (\neg r)$

(g)  $p \wedge q \Rightarrow (\neg p \wedge \neg q)$

(h)  $p \wedge q \wedge (p \Rightarrow r) \Rightarrow (r \vee (q \Rightarrow r))$

(i)  $p \Rightarrow ((r \vee s) \Rightarrow p)$

(j)  $q \Rightarrow (r \Rightarrow (q \wedge r))$

(k)  $((p \Rightarrow q) \Rightarrow p) \Rightarrow ((p \Rightarrow false) \Rightarrow p)$

**2.15.** Show how the effects of inference rules Substitution of Equals (2.34), Transitivity of Equality (2.38), and Transitivity of Implication (2.39) could be achieved using only axioms (2.7), (2.8), and (2.9) and inference rules Modus Ponens (2.10) and Substitution (2.11) of Propositional Logic.

**2.16.** Show how it is always possible to prove $P$ a theorem of Propositional Logic whenever $(P \Rightarrow true) \wedge (true \Rightarrow P)$ is a theorem by giving a method to extend a proof for $(P \Rightarrow true) \wedge (true \Rightarrow P)$ into one for $P$.

**2.17.** Formulate the following as formulas of Predicate Logic, assuming that $Obj$ is the set of things, $Plc$ is the set of places, and:

   $yech(t)$:  "thing $t$ is rotten"

   $loc(t, p)$:  "thing $t$ is located at place $p$"

   (a)   Everything is rotten.
   (b)   Something is rotten.
   (c)   Nothing is rotten.
   (d)   Something is rotten in Denmark.
   (e)   Nothing in Denmark is rotten, but something someplace else is.
   (f)   Something is rotten someplace and nothing is rotten everywhere.

**2.18.** Write Predicate Logic formulas for the following statements. Assume that $a[1 .. n]$ and $b[1 .. m]$ are arrays of integers.

   (a)   All elements in $a$ are nonzero.
   (b)   Some element in $a$ is zero.
   (c)   Array $a$ is sorted in ascending order.
   (d)   Every element in $a$ is also in $b$.
   (e)   No value in $a$ appears two or more times in $b$.
   (f)   The sequence of elements $a[1], a[2], ..., a[n]$ forms a palindrome. (A *palindrome* is a sequence of characters that reads the same both forwards and backwards, e.g., 1234321.)

**2.19.** Where possible, perform the indicated substitutions into:

   $$E:\ x<y \ \wedge \ (\forall i:\ 0 \le i < n:\ b[i] < y)$$

   (a) $E_z^x$    (b) $E_{x+y}^x$    (c) $E_j^i$    (d) $(E_{w*z}^y)_{a+u}^y$
   (e) $E_{w*z,a+u}^{y,y}$    (f) $(E_{w*z}^y)_{a+u}^z$    (g) $E_{w*z,a+u}^{y,z}$

**2.20.** Use Propositional Logic, informal meaning (2.78) of a universally quantified expression, and informal meaning (2.79) of an existentially quantified expression to justify the following equivalences.

   (a)   Conjunction Law (2.81)
   (b)   Disjunction Law (2.82)
   (c)   Empty-Range Law (2.83a)
   (d)   Empty-Range Law (2.83b)
   (e)   Range Law (2.84a)
   (f)   Range Law (2.84b)
   (g)   Range Partitioning Law (2.85a)

(h)     Range Partitioning Law (2.85b)

(i)     Range Narrowing Law (2.86)

(j)     Range Widening Law (2.87)

(k)     Quantification Weakening Law (2.88a)

(l)     Quantification Weakening Law (2.88b)

**2.21.** Simplify the following formulas.

(a)     $(\forall i: 1 \le i < n: r < A[i]) \;\wedge\; r < A[n]$

(b)     $(\forall i: 1 \le i \le 100: 1 \le i \le 100 \Rightarrow A[i] > 7)$

(c)     $(\forall k: false: k \ne k) \Rightarrow k = k$

(d)     $(\exists k: false: k \ne k) \Rightarrow k = k$

(e)     $(\forall x: R: P) \Rightarrow (\exists x: R: P)$

(f)     $(\forall x: R: P) \Rightarrow (\exists i: P: R)$

**2.22.** Prove the following theorems of Predicate Logic.

(a)     $x = e \;\Rightarrow\; P = P_e^x$

(b)     $(\forall x: R: Q) \Rightarrow (R \wedge Q)_e^x$

(c)     $(\exists x: R: P) \vee (\exists x: R: \neg P)$

(d)     $\neg((\forall x: R: P) \wedge (\forall x: R: P))$

(e)     $(\forall x: P) \Rightarrow (\exists x: x = 22: P)$

(f)     $(\forall x: R: Q) \Rightarrow (\forall x: R: P \Rightarrow Q)$

**2.23.** Show that Equals in Quantified Expressions (2.97a)−(2.97d) can be replaced by a single rule:

$$\frac{P = Q}{(\forall x: P) = (\forall x: Q)}$$

**2.24.** Under what conditions does $(E_{\bar{u}}^{\bar{x}})_{\bar{x}}^{\bar{u}} = E$ hold?

**2.25.** Give either a proof or a counterexample for each of the following claims.

(a)     The intersection of two safety properties is always a safety property.

(b)     The union of two safety properties is always a safety property.

(c)     The complement of a safety property is always a safety property.

(d)     The intersection of two liveness properties is always a liveness property.

(e)     The union of two liveness properties is always a liveness property.

(f)     The complement of a liveness property is always a liveness property.

(g)     The union of any nonempty property and a liveness property is a liveness property.

(h)     Every nontrivial property is the intersection of two nontrivial liveness properties.

**2.26.** Consider the following formal definition for a safety property $\mathcal{P}$

(2.109) **Safety Property:** $(\forall \alpha \in \Sigma_S^\infty:$
$$\alpha \in P = (\forall (\beta, j) \in \Sigma_S^+: (\beta, j) \leq \alpha: (\beta, j)(\beta[|\beta|-1]^\omega, k)) \in P))$$

where $\beta[|\beta|-1]^\omega$ denotes an infinite sequence of $\beta[|\beta|-1]$'s.

(a)     Give an example of a property that satisfies Safety Property (2.105) but not Safety Property (2.109).

(b)     A property $P$ is *invariant under stuttering* iff $\gamma \in P$ then $\delta \in P$ and vice versa, where $\delta$ is $\gamma$ with every state repeated zero or more times. Prove that Safety Property (2.109) is the same as Safety Property (2.105) for properties that are invariant under stuttering.

**2.27.** Prove the following:

(a)     $P$ is a safety property iff $P = Safe(P)$ holds.

(b)     $P$ is a liveness property iff $P = Live(P)$ holds.

**2.28.** Suppose that properties are sets of finite and infinite sequences of states (rather than sets of anchored sequences).

(a)     What would the formal definition be for safety properties?

(b)     What would the formal definition be for liveness properties?

(c)     Give definitions for $Safe(P)$ and $Live(P)$ and prove that for a property $P$:

$Safe(P)$ is a safety property.

$Live(P)$ is a liveness property.

$P = Safe(P) \cap Live(P)$.

# Chapter 3

# Temporal Logic

Predicate Logic allows sets of states to be specified; Temporal Logic allows sets of anchored sequences to be specified. Because properties are modeled by sets of anchored sequences, Temporal Logic is well suited for specifying properties and reasoning about programs. In this chapter, we give an axiomatization for Temporal Logic and explore how the logic relates to other modal logics.

## 3.1  Informal Preview

Formulas of our Temporal Logic are interpreted with respect to anchored sequences (see §2.4). Temporal Logic is an extension of Predicate Logic, so we start by defining when an anchored sequence $(\sigma, j)$ is a model for a *state predicate*—a formula of the Predicate Logic defined in §2.3. Later, in Chapter 7, *past extensions* are given to enhance the expressiveness of that Predicate Logic so that it can specify arbitrary sets of past state sequences.

Anchored sequence $(\sigma, j)$ is a model for a Predicate Logic formula $P$ exactly when $\sigma[..j]$ is, and $\sigma[..j]$ is defined to be a model for a state predicate $P$ iff state $\sigma[j]$ is a model for $P$. Thus, when regarded as a Temporal Logic formula, a Predicate Logic formula $P$ defines a set of models $(\sigma, j)$ by characterizing the past states $\sigma[..j-1]$ and/or current state $\sigma[j]$ of its members. For example, Temporal Logic formula $x=3$ has $(\sigma, j)$ as a model iff the value of $x$ in state $\sigma[j]$ is 3. This is because

(i)  $(\sigma, j)$ is a model for Predicate Logic formula $x=3$ iff $\sigma[..j]$ is, and

(ii)  since $x=3$ is a state predicate, $\sigma[..j]$ is a model for $x=3$ iff $\sigma[j]$ is.

The use of *temporal operators* permits construction of formulas that depend on the current and future states of an anchored sequence. Specifically, the temporal operators characterize allowable suffixes of anchored sequences, where an anchored sequence $(\tau, k)$ is defined to be a *suffix* of $(\sigma, j)$ iff $\sigma = \tau$ and $j \leq k$ hold.

One temporal operator is $\square$. A formula $\square P$ (read "henceforth $P$") is satisfied by $(\sigma, j)$ iff $P$ is satisfied by all suffixes of $(\sigma, j)$. For example, $\square(x=3)$ is satisfied by $(\sigma, j)$ iff $x$ has value 3 in the current state and in every future state, because $\square(x=3)$ is satisfied by $(\sigma, j)$ iff $x=3$ holds on suffixes $(\sigma, j)$, $(\sigma, j+1)$, $(\sigma, j+2)$, ..., and $x=3$ holds in $(\sigma, k)$ iff $x=3$ holds in state $\sigma[k]$.

As another example, the formula

$$(3.1) \quad \square(x=3 \Rightarrow \square(x=3))$$

is satisfied in $(\sigma, j)$ iff starting with the current state, no state that satisfies $x=3$ is followed by a state that satisfies $x \neq 3$. We deduce this as follows. Anchored sequence $(\sigma, j)$ is a model for (3.1) iff every suffix $(\sigma, k)$ is a model for $x=3 \Rightarrow \square(x=3)$. Each $(\sigma, k)$ is a model for $(x=3 \Rightarrow \square(x=3))$ iff it is a model for $x \neq 3$ or for $\square(x=3)$. Suffix $(\sigma, k)$ is a model for $x \neq 3$ iff the value of $x$ in $\sigma[k]$ is not 3; $(\sigma, k)$ is a model for $\square(x=3)$ iff all its suffixes are models for $x=3$, which by the reasoning of the previous paragraph is equivalent to asserting that $x=3$ holds in every state $\sigma[i]$ for $k \leq i < |\sigma|$. Thus, (3.1) asserts that a current or future state that satisfies $x=3$ cannot be followed by a state that satisfies $x \neq 3$.

The other temporal operators are also defined in terms of suffixes. (In these definitions, a finite anchored sequence is being regarded as having its final state thereafter be the current state.)

- $\diamondsuit P$ (read "eventually $P$") iff $P$ holds on some suffix of $(\sigma, j)$.
- $\bigcirc P$ (read "next $P$") iff $P$ holds on suffix $(\sigma, k)$, where $k = \min(j+1, |\sigma|-1)$.
- $P \,\mathcal{U}\, Q$ (read "$P$ unless $Q$") iff $P$ holds on every suffix up until the first (if any) suffix that satisfies $Q$ is found.

For example, $\diamondsuit y=15$ is satisfied in $(\sigma, j)$ iff for some $k$, $j \leq k$, state $\sigma[k]$ satisfies $y=3$; $\bigcirc x=12$ is satisfied in $(\sigma, j)$ iff (i) $\sigma[j+1]$ satisfies $x=12$ or (ii) $\sigma[j]$ is the final state of $\sigma$ and it satisfies $x=12$; and $(0 \leq x) \,\mathcal{U}\, (\diamondsuit y=15)$ is satisfied in $(\sigma, j)$ iff (i) for every $k$, $j \leq k$, $\sigma[k]$ satisfies $0 \leq x$ or (ii) the first suffice of $(\sigma, j)$ that does not satisfy $0 \leq x$ does satisfy $\diamondsuit(y=15)$ (so the first state of some suffix satisfies $y=15$).

Temporal Logic differs from Predicate Logic by having two classes of (individual) variables: *flexible* and *rigid*.[1] Flexible variables, which we typeset in italics, are like the individual variables of Predicate Logic. Rigid variables, which we typeset using uppercase roman letters, have the same values from one state to the next in an anchored sequence; they are like named constants.

---

[1] In the literature, flexible variables are sometimes called *local* or *dynamic* variables; rigid variables are called *global* or *static* variables.

Rigid variables are typically used to relate the values of flexible variables from one state to another. This is illustrated by the formula

(3.2)   $(\forall X: x=X: \Box(x=X))$,

where $x$ is a flexible variable and X is a rigid variable. An anchored sequence $(\sigma, j)$ is a model for (3.2) iff the value of $x$ remains fixed throughout the current and future states. This is because $(\sigma, j)$ is a model for (3.2) iff for every X, $(\sigma, j)$ is a model for $x=X \Rightarrow \Box(x=X)$. There must exist some value X for which $x=X$ holds in $\sigma[j]$, so we infer from $(\sigma, j)$ satisfying $x=X \Rightarrow \Box(x=X)$ that there is some value X for which $(\sigma, j)$ satisfies $\Box(x=X)$. Since $(\sigma, j)$ satisfies $\Box(x=X)$ iff every future state satisfies $x=X$, we conclude that the value of $x$ is the same in every future state as it is in the current state.

We shorten our Temporal Logic formulas somewhat by allowing rigid variables to appear free and then employing the convention that free rigid variables are implicitly universally quantified. This convention is consistent with Predicate Logic (see Quantification Introduction Rule (2.94)). It means that

$x=X \Rightarrow \Box(x=X)$

denotes the same formula as (3.2).

## 3.2  Syntax and Meaning of Formulas

The formulas of Temporal Logic include Propositional and Predicate Logic formulas as well as *temporal formulas* constructed using the unary temporal operators $\Box, \Diamond$, and $\bigcirc$; the binary temporal operator $\mathcal{U}$; the rigid-variable quantifiers $\forall$ and $\exists$; and the propositional connectives $\neg$, $\wedge$, $\vee$, $\Rightarrow$, and $=$. Hereafter, we use the term Predicate Logic formula for those formulas of Predicate Logic that are not also Propositional Logic formulas. The syntax of temporal formulas is given by:

(3.3)   **Syntax of Temporal Formulas.** Every Predicate Logic formula is a temporal formula. For $Q$ and $R$ temporal formulas and X a rigid variable, the following are also temporal formulas: $\Box(Q), \Diamond(Q), \bigcirc(Q), (Q\mathcal{U}R)$, $(\forall X: R: Q), (\exists X: R: Q), (\neg Q), (Q \vee R), (Q \wedge R), (Q \Rightarrow R)$, and $(Q=R)$.                                                                                     □

When parentheses have been omitted, the operators are assigned the precedences given in Figure 3.1, and all operators are assumed to be left-associative except equals, which is conjunctional. For example:

$P\mathcal{U}Q\mathcal{U}R$  denotes  $((P\mathcal{U}Q)\mathcal{U}R)$

$\neg\Box P \vee Q$  denotes  $(\neg(\Box P)) \vee Q$

$\Box P \Rightarrow Q\mathcal{U}\Diamond R \wedge \bigcirc P$  denotes  $(\Box P) \Rightarrow ((Q\mathcal{U}(\Diamond R)) \wedge (\bigcirc P))$

$$
\begin{array}{c}
\neg \\
\square \\
\diamondsuit \\
\bigcirc
\end{array}
\qquad \mathcal{U} \qquad = \qquad \wedge \qquad \vee \qquad \Rightarrow
$$

Tightest                                            Weakest

**Figure 3.1.** Precedence of operators in Temporal Logic formulas

---

We also employ the abbreviations introduced in §2.3 for omitting ranges in a quantified expression with quantifier $Q$:

$(QX\colon P)$ denotes $(QX\colon \textit{true}\colon P)$

$(QX \in V\colon P)$ denotes $(QX\colon X \in V\colon P)$

$(QX \in V\colon R\colon P)$ denotes $(QX\colon X \in V \wedge R\colon P)$

In an anchored sequence $(\sigma, j)$, the states of $\sigma$ assign values to flexible and rigid variables. For rigid variables, it will be convenient to generalize our notation for augmented states, writing $(\sigma; X{:}V)$ to denote a sequence of states that is like $\sigma$ but where the value of X in every state of $\sigma$ is the constant V: $(\sigma[0]; X{:}V)(\sigma[1]; X{:}V)\ldots$ .

With these preliminaries out of the way, we now use structural induction to formalize when an anchored sequence $(\sigma, j)$ is a model for a Temporal Logic formula $P$; that is, we define when $(\sigma, j) \vDash P$ holds.

(3.4) **Interpreting Temporal Logic Formulas.** For anchored sequence $(\sigma, j)$ and Temporal Logic formulas $P$ and $Q$ containing no free occurrences of rigid variables:

$(\sigma, j) \vDash \square P$ iff For all $k \in \mathrm{Int}$, $j \le k < |\sigma|$: $(\sigma, k) \vDash P$

$(\sigma, j) \vDash \diamondsuit P$ iff Exists $k \in \mathrm{Int}$, $j \le k < |\sigma|$: $(\sigma, k) \vDash P$

$(\sigma, j) \vDash \bigcirc P$ iff $(\sigma, \min(j{+}1, |\sigma|{-}1)) \vDash P$

$(\sigma, j) \vDash (P\,\mathcal{U}\,Q)$ iff For all $k \in \mathrm{Int}$, $j \le k < |\sigma|$: $(\sigma, k) \vDash P$   or
               Exists $i \in \mathrm{Int}$, $j \le i < |\sigma|$:
                  $(\sigma, i) \vDash Q$  and
                  For all $k \in \mathrm{Int}$, $j \le k < i$: $(\sigma, k) \vDash P$

$(\sigma, j) \vDash (\forall X\colon P\colon Q)$ iff For all V: $((\sigma; X{:}V), j) \vDash (P \Rightarrow Q)$

$(\sigma, j) \vDash (\exists X\colon P\colon Q)$ iff Exists V: $((\sigma; X{:}V), j) \vDash (P \wedge Q)$

$(\sigma, j) \vDash (\neg P)$ iff $(\sigma, j) \nvDash P$

$$(\sigma, j) \models (P \lor Q) \quad \text{iff} \quad (\sigma, j) \models P \quad \text{or} \quad (\sigma, j) \models Q$$
$$(\sigma, j) \models (P \land Q) \quad \text{iff} \quad (\sigma, j) \models P \quad \text{and} \quad (\sigma, j) \models Q$$
$$(\sigma, j) \models (P \Rightarrow Q) \quad \text{iff} \quad (\sigma, j) \not\models P \quad \text{or} \quad (\sigma, j) \models Q$$
$$(\sigma, j) \models (P = Q) \quad \text{iff} \quad (\sigma, j) \models P \quad \text{equals} \quad (\sigma, j) \models Q$$

For $P$ a formula of Propositional or Predicate Logic:

$$(\sigma, j) \models P \quad \text{iff} \quad \sigma[..j] \models P \qquad\qquad \Box$$

As an example, we characterize models for $\Diamond \Box (x = 0)$.

$(\sigma, j) \models \Diamond \Box (x = 0)$

iff   «Interpreting Temporal Logic Formulas (3.4), $(\sigma, j) \models \Diamond P$»
     Exists $k \in \text{Int}, j \leq k < |\sigma|$: $(\sigma, k) \models \Box (x = 0)$

iff   «Interpreting Temporal Logic Formulas (3.4), $(\sigma, k) \models \Box P$»
     Exists $k \in \text{Int}, j \leq k < |\sigma|$: For all $i \in \text{Int}, k \leq i < |\sigma|$: $(\sigma, i) \models x = 0$

iff   «Interpreting Temporal Logic Formulas (3.4), $(\sigma, i) \models x = 0$»
     Exists $k \in \text{Int}, j \leq k < |\sigma|$: For all $i \in \text{Int}, k \leq i < |\sigma|$: $\sigma[..i] \models x = 0$

iff   «$\sigma[..i] \models x = 0$ iff $\sigma[i] \models x = 0$, since $x = 0$ is a state predicate»
     Exists $k \in \text{Int}, j \leq k < |\sigma|$: For all $i \in \text{Int}, k \leq i < |\sigma|$: $\sigma[i] \models x = 0$

Thus, we conclude that $(\sigma, j)$ is a model for $\Diamond \Box (x = 0)$ iff every state in some suffix of $(\sigma, j)$ satisfies $x = 0$.

If $(\sigma, j)$ is a model for $P$, we say that $P$ holds at position $j$ in $\sigma$. We then may refer to $j$ as the *current position* and call any position $k$ where $j < k < |\sigma|$ a *future position*. Here are some common Temporal Logic formulas, along with a brief description of what each means.

$P \Rightarrow \Box P$       $P$ is an *invariant*—if $P$ holds in the current position, then it holds in all future positions.

$\Box (P \Rightarrow \Diamond Q)$       *P leads to Q*—for every current and future position that satisfies $P$, it or some future position satisfies $Q$.

$\Box \Diamond P$       Among the current and future positions, $P$ holds *infinitely often*.[2]

---

[2]Recall that the last state of a finite sequence $\sigma$ remains the current state forever. Thus, "infinitely often" is a sensible name even with finite anchored sequences.

## Textual Substitution in Temporal Logic

Textual substitution in Temporal Logic formulas is similar to textual substitution in Predicate Logic formulas. In both, it has the same effect as changing the value of a state component—only for an anchored sequence $(\sigma, j)$ the change must be made to every state in $\sigma$.

(3.5)   **Anchored Sequences with Textual Substitution.** For $x$ a variable, $e$ a term, and $P$ a Temporal Logic formula:

$$(\sigma, j) \models P_e^x \quad \text{iff} \quad (\sigma_e^x, j) \models P$$

where

$$\sigma_e^x: \quad (\sigma[0]; x{:}e)(\sigma[1]; x{:}e)(\sigma[2]; x{:}e)\ldots \qquad\qquad \square$$

This leads to axioms that enable manipulation of Temporal Logic formulas involving textual substitutions.

(3.6)   *Textual Substitution [Temporal Formulas]:*   For Temporal Logic formulas $P$ and $Q$:

(a)  $(\square P)_e^x \;=\; \square(P_e^x)$

(b)  $(\Diamond P)_e^x \;=\; \Diamond(P_e^x)$

(c)  $(\bigcirc P)_e^x \;=\; \bigcirc(P_e^x)$

(d)  $(P\,\mathcal{U}\,Q)_e^x \;=\; (P_e^x)\,\mathcal{U}\,(Q_e^x)$

(e)  For X distinct from $x$ and distinct from all variables occurring free in $e$:
$$(\forall \mathrm{X}\colon\ P\colon\ Q)_e^x \;=\; (\forall \mathrm{X}\colon\ P_e^x\colon\ Q_e^x)$$

(f)  For X distinct from $x$ and distinct from all variables occurring free in $e$:
$$(\exists \mathrm{X}\colon\ P\colon\ Q)_e^x \;=\; (\exists \mathrm{X}\colon\ P_e^x\colon\ Q_e^x)$$

(g)  $(\neg P)_e^x \;=\; \neg(P_e^x)$

(h)  $(P \vee Q)_e^x \;=\; (P_e^x) \vee (Q_e^x)$

(i)  $(P \wedge Q)_e^x \;=\; (P_e^x) \wedge (Q_e^x)$

(j)  $(P \Rightarrow Q)_e^x \;=\; (P_e^x) \Rightarrow (Q_e^x)$

(k)  $(P = Q)_e^x \;=\; (P_e^x) = (Q_e^x)$

## 3.3   Axioms and Inference Rules

Temporal Logic, being an extension of Propositional and Predicate Logic, contains their axioms and inference rules. In addition, because theorems of Propositional Logic are *true* for any values of their propositional variables, a theorem of Propositional Logic in which propositional variables have been replaced by temporal formulas is a valid formula of Temporal Logic:

(3.7)  *TL Substitution*: Let $P$ be a Propositional Logic formula whose propositional variables are among $q1, q2, ..., qn$, and let $Q1, Q2, ..., Qn$ be temporal formulas. Then:

$$\frac{P}{P^{q1, q2, ..., qn}_{Q1, Q2, ..., Qn}}$$

(3.8)  *TL Modus Ponens*: Let $P$ and $Q$ be Temporal Logic formulas Then:

$$\frac{P, P \Rightarrow Q}{Q}$$

Temporal Logic has additional axioms and inference rules to permit introduction and manipulation of temporal operators and rigid-variable quantifiers. These and some particularly useful theorems are given below, grouped according to temporal operator. Axioms are identified as such; other theorems are labeled "laws." Throughout, $P, P', Q, Q', R$, and $R'$ denote arbitrary Temporal Logic formulas.

## Henceforth and Eventually

The $\Box$ operator is characterized by two axioms and an inference rule. The axioms are:

(3.10)  $\Box$ *Axioms*:  (a) $\Box P \Rightarrow P$
      (b) $\Box(P \Rightarrow Q) \Rightarrow (\Box P \Rightarrow \Box Q)$

The first axiom is sound because every anchored sequence is, by definition, a suffix of itself. The second axiom asserts that temporal operator $\Box$ is monotonic.

An inference rule allows $\Box$ to be prepended to any theorem.

(3.11)  *Temporal Generalization Rule*:  $\dfrac{P}{\Box P}$

To see that this rule is sound, observe that all suffixes of an anchored sequence are themselves anchored sequences. Thus, if $P$ is valid, and therefore is satisfied by all anchored sequences, then $P$ is also satisfied by all suffixes of any anchored sequence.

We now give an example of a Temporal Logic proof. In it, "propositional reasoning" appears as the justification for any step abbreviating a series of inferences only involving Propositional Logic, TL Substitution (3.7), and TL Modus Ponens (3.8).

«TL Substitution (3.7) with Consequent-Weakening Law (2.30)»
    1. $P \Rightarrow (P \vee Q)$
«Temporal Generalization Rule (3.11) using 1»
    2. $\Box(P \Rightarrow (P \vee Q))$

«□ Axiom (3.10b)»
  3. $\Box(P \Rightarrow (P \vee Q)) \Rightarrow (\Box P \Rightarrow \Box(P \vee Q))$

«TL Modus Ponens (3.8) using 2, 3»
  4. $\Box P \Rightarrow \Box(P \vee Q)$

«TL Substitution (3.7) with Consequent-Weakening Law (2.30)»
  5. $Q \Rightarrow (Q \vee P)$

«Temporal Generalization Rule (3.11) using 5»
  6. $\Box(Q \Rightarrow (Q \vee P))$

«□ Axiom (3.10b)»
  7. $\Box(Q \Rightarrow (Q \vee P)) \Rightarrow (\Box Q \Rightarrow \Box(Q \vee P))$

«TL Modus Ponens (3.8) using 6, 7»
  8. $\Box Q \Rightarrow \Box(Q \vee P)$

«TL Substitution (3.7) with Constructive Dilemma Law (2.33b)»
  9. $(\Box P \Rightarrow \Box(P \vee Q)) \wedge (\Box Q \Rightarrow \Box(Q \vee P))$
    $\Rightarrow ((\Box P \vee \Box Q) \Rightarrow (\Box(P \vee Q) \vee \Box(Q \vee P)))$

«Propositional reasoning using 4, 6, and 9»
  10. $(\Box P \vee \Box Q) \Rightarrow \Box(P \vee Q)$

The theorem just proved and another useful Temporal Logic theorem involving the □ operator are:

(3.12) □ *Distributive Laws:*  (a) $\Box(P \wedge Q) = (\Box P \wedge \Box Q)$
          (b) $(\Box P \vee \Box Q) \Rightarrow \Box(P \vee Q)$

Note that the converse of (3.12b), $\Box(P \vee Q) \Rightarrow (\Box P \vee \Box Q)$, is not valid. This is because $\Box(P \vee Q)$ holds when, for example, $P$ and $Q$ are satisfied on alternate suffixes of $(\sigma, j)$ but neither $\Box P$ nor $\Box Q$ need be satisfied by such a $(\sigma, j)$.

A *derived inference rule* is an inference rule for which there exists a mechanical procedure to transform any proof that uses the rule into a proof that does not use the rule. Two derived inference rules will allow us to prove new theorems of the form $P \Rightarrow \Box Q$ conveniently.

(3.13) □ *Consequence Rule:*   $\dfrac{P \Rightarrow P', \ P' \Rightarrow \Box Q', \ Q' \Rightarrow Q}{P \Rightarrow \Box Q}$

(3.14) □ *Catenation Rule:*   $\dfrac{P \Rightarrow \Box R, \ R \Rightarrow \Box Q}{P \Rightarrow \Box Q}$

The $\Diamond$ operator is defined in terms of the □ operator.

(3.15) $\Diamond$ *Axiom:*   $\Diamond P = \neg\Box\neg P$

Thus, adding $\Diamond$ does not enhance the expressiveness of the logic. However, it is convenient to have a concise notation for expressing eventuality, which is exactly what $\neg\Box\neg P$ means.

The following theorems are helpful for reasoning about formulas containing $\Diamond$.

(3.16) $\Diamond$ *Laws*: (a) $\neg\Diamond P = \Box\neg P$

(b) $\Diamond\neg P = \neg\Box P$

(c) $P \Rightarrow \Diamond P$

(d) $\Box P \Rightarrow \Diamond P$

(e) $\Diamond\Box P \Rightarrow \Box\Diamond P$

(f) $\Box(P \Rightarrow Q) \Rightarrow (\Diamond P \Rightarrow \Diamond Q)$

(g) $\Diamond(P \Rightarrow Q) = (\Box P \Rightarrow \Diamond Q)$

(h) $\Box P \wedge \Diamond Q \Rightarrow \Diamond(P \wedge Q)$

The first two laws reformulate $\Diamond$ Axiom (3.15). The next two, laws (3.16c) and (3.16d), allow $\Diamond P$ to be derived when $P$ holds in the current position. Law (3.16e) asserts that if $P$ holds continuously from some point onward, then $P$ holds infinitely often. Monotonicity of temporal operator $\Diamond$ is stated by law (3.16f). The final two laws are useful for deducing eventualities in various circumstances.

There are also counterparts for $\Diamond$ to $\Box$ Distributive Laws (3.12), as well as laws that characterize how combinations of $\Box$ and $\Diamond$ distribute through conjunction and disjunction.

(3.17) $\Diamond$ *Distributive Laws*: (a) $\Diamond(P \wedge Q) \Rightarrow (\Diamond P \wedge \Diamond Q)$

(b) $\Diamond(P \vee Q) = (\Diamond P \vee \Diamond Q)$

(c) $\Box\Diamond(P \wedge Q) \Rightarrow (\Box\Diamond P \wedge \Box\Diamond Q)$

(d) $\Box\Diamond(P \vee Q) = (\Box\Diamond P \vee \Box\Diamond Q)$

(e) $\Diamond\Box(P \wedge Q) = (\Diamond\Box P \wedge \Diamond\Box Q)$

(f) $(\Diamond\Box P \vee \Diamond\Box Q) \Rightarrow \Diamond\Box(P \vee Q)$

The syntax of Temporal Logic permits arbitrary sequences of $\Box$ and $\Diamond$ operators to precede a formula. However, the next four laws imply that any such sequence is equivalent to a sequence of at most two of these temporal operators.

(3.18) *Absorption Laws*: (a) $\Box\Box P = \Box P$

(b) $\Diamond\Diamond P = \Diamond P$

(c) $\Box\Diamond\Box P = \Diamond\Box P$

(d) $\Diamond\Box\Diamond P = \Box\Diamond P$

Analogous to $\Box$ Consequence Rule (3.13) and $\Box$ Catenation Rule (3.14), the following derived inference rules provide a convenient way to manipulate theorems of the form $P \Rightarrow \Diamond Q$.

(3.19) $\Diamond$ *Consequence Rule*: $\dfrac{P \Rightarrow P', \ P' \Rightarrow \Diamond Q', \ Q' \Rightarrow Q}{P \Rightarrow \Diamond Q}$

(3.20) $\diamond$ *Catenation Rule*:  $\dfrac{P \Rightarrow \diamond Q,\ \ Q \Rightarrow \diamond R}{P \Rightarrow \diamond R}$

## Next and Unless

Operators $\bigcirc$ and $\mathcal{U}$ increase the expressiveness of the logic—formulas written in terms of $\bigcirc$ and $\mathcal{U}$ can describe sets of anchored sequences that cannot be described using only operators $\square$ and $\diamond$. This increased expressiveness is a mixed blessing. In specifications, some things are best left unsaid. For example, in writing a program specification, it is usually best not to constrain the number of atomic actions executed by an implementation. Operator $\bigcirc$, however, can impose such constraints. To illustrate, the following Temporal Logic specification asserts that the value of $x$ in the current state is incremented by 1 and thereafter remains unchanged.

$$(x=X) \Rightarrow \bigcirc\square(x=X+1)$$

The specification constrains implementations to performing the increment using a single atomic action, something that might not have been intended and would not be true for the assignment statements in most programming languages.

Not all uses of operator $\bigcirc$ are evil. It is not possible to obtain a complete axiomatization for the operator $\mathcal{U}$ without a temporal operator having the expressive power of $\bigcirc$. Since the added expressiveness of $\mathcal{U}$ is useful in writing specifications, omitting $\mathcal{U}$ from our logic would be a mistake. Thus, we choose the evils of $\bigcirc$ over having valid but unprovable formulas. A second reason for including $\bigcirc$ in our Temporal Logic is that it allows the semantics of program execution to be formalized using the logic. The semantics of a program should specify which of its actions are atomic, and this is made possible by $\bigcirc$.

Here are the axioms for $\bigcirc$:

(3.21) $\bigcirc$ *Axioms*:   (a) $\bigcirc\neg P = \neg\bigcirc P$
(b) $\bigcirc(P \Rightarrow Q) \Rightarrow (\bigcirc P \Rightarrow \bigcirc Q)$
(c) $\square P \Rightarrow \bigcirc P$
(d) $\square P \Rightarrow \bigcirc\square P$
(e) $\square(P \Rightarrow \bigcirc P) \Rightarrow (P \Rightarrow \square P)$

The first, (3.21a), gives a basis for interchanging $\bigcirc$ and negation. The second, (3.21b), is analogous to $\square$ Axiom (3.10b). However, unlike $\square$ Axiom (3.10b), the converse of (3.21b) is a theorem. The next two axioms state that if $P$ holds on all suffixes of $(\sigma, j)$, then $P$ necessarily holds on some subset of those suffixes—(3.21c) is concerned with the single suffix $(\sigma, \min(j+1, |\sigma|-1))$ and (3.21d) with all suffixes of $(\sigma, \min(j+1, |\sigma|-1))$. The final axiom, (3.21e), asserts that if $(\sigma, \min(j+1, |\sigma|-1))$ is a model for $P$ whenever $(\sigma, j)$ is, then if $(\sigma, j)$ is a model for $P$, all of its suffixes will be too.

From these axioms, it is possible to prove laws that state how $\bigcirc$ distributes over conjunction and disjunction, that $\bigcirc$ can be interchanged with $\square$ and $\diamond$, that a transition from $P$ to $\neg P$ occurs only if there is some point at which $P$ changes from *true* to *false*, and that $\bigcirc$ is monotonic.

(3.22)  $\bigcirc$ *Laws*:   (a) $\bigcirc(P \wedge Q) = (\bigcirc P \wedge \bigcirc Q)$
                (b) $\bigcirc(P \vee Q) = (\bigcirc P \vee \bigcirc Q)$
                (c) $\bigcirc\Box P = \Box\bigcirc P$
                (d) $\bigcirc\Diamond P = \Diamond\bigcirc P$
                (e) $(P \wedge \Diamond\neg P) \Rightarrow \Diamond(P \wedge \bigcirc\neg P)$
                (f) $\Box(P \Rightarrow Q) \Rightarrow (\bigcirc P \Rightarrow \bigcirc Q)$

Just as for $\Box$ and $\Diamond$, a derived inference rule provides a convenient way to strengthen the antecedent and/or weaken the consequent of an implication $P' \Rightarrow \bigcirc Q'$.

(3.23)  $\bigcirc$ *Consequence Rule*:   $\dfrac{P \Rightarrow P', \ P' \Rightarrow \bigcirc Q', \ Q' \Rightarrow Q}{P \Rightarrow \bigcirc Q}$

Axiom (3.21e) forms the basis for two derived inference rules that underlie the methods we will use to establish that a formula $P$ is an invariant, and therefore is not invalidated, by program execution.

(3.24)  *Computational Induction Rules*:   (a) $\dfrac{P \Rightarrow \bigcirc P}{P \Rightarrow \Box P}$

            (b) $\dfrac{P \Rightarrow (Q \wedge \bigcirc P)}{P \Rightarrow \Box Q}$

When a program's history is represented by an anchored sequence, premise $P \Rightarrow \bigcirc P$ of (3.24a) holds iff executing any atomic action in a current state satisfying $P$ leads to its termination in a state satisfying $P$. Therefore, Computational Induction Rule (3.24a) implies that checking the effect of each atomic action in isolation is sufficient to infer that $P$ is not invalidated by execution. Rule (3.24b) extends this reasoning to any $Q$ implied by $P$.

Finally, operator $\bigcirc$ allows characterization of $\Box$ and $\Diamond$ as solutions to recursive equations:

(3.25)  $\Box$ *Fixed-Point Law*:   $\Box P = (P \wedge \bigcirc\Box P)$

(3.26)  $\Diamond$ *Fixed-Point Law*:   $\Diamond P = (P \vee \bigcirc\Diamond P)$

The $\mathcal{U}$ operator is characterized by two axioms. Soundness of the first axiom follows directly from the meaning of $\mathcal{U}$. The second axiom gives a recursive characterization of $\mathcal{U}$.

(3.27)  $\mathcal{U}$ *Axioms*:   (a) $\Box P \Rightarrow P \mathcal{U} Q$
                (b) $P \mathcal{U} Q = (Q \vee (P \wedge \bigcirc(P \mathcal{U} Q)))$

With these axioms, the following theorems can be proved:

(3.28) $\mathcal{U}$ *Insertion Law:*  $Q \Rightarrow P\,\mathcal{U}\,Q$

(3.29) $\Box$ *to* $\mathcal{U}$ *Law:*  $\Box P = P\,\mathcal{U}\,false$

(3.30) $\Diamond$ *to* $\mathcal{U}$ *Law:*  $\Diamond P = \neg((\neg P)\,\mathcal{U}\,false)$

(3.31) $\mathcal{U}$ *Entailment Laws:*  (a) $P\,\mathcal{U}\,Q \Rightarrow \Box P \vee \Diamond Q$
                                           (b) $(P\,\mathcal{U}\,Q \wedge \Box\neg Q) \Rightarrow \Box P$
                                           (c) $(P\,\mathcal{U}\,Q \wedge \neg\Box P) \Rightarrow \Diamond Q$

(3.32) $\mathcal{U}$ *Absorption Laws:*  (a) $(P\,\mathcal{U}\,Q)\,\mathcal{U}\,Q = P\,\mathcal{U}\,Q$
                                           (b) $P\,\mathcal{U}\,Q = P\,\mathcal{U}\,(P\,\mathcal{U}\,Q)$
                                           (c) $(P\,\mathcal{U}\,Q)\,\mathcal{U}\,R \Rightarrow (P \vee Q)\,\mathcal{U}\,R$
                                           (d) $P\,\mathcal{U}\,(Q\,\mathcal{U}\,R) \Rightarrow (P \vee Q)\,\mathcal{U}\,R$

(3.33) $\mathcal{U}$ *Distributive Laws:*  (a) $\Box P \wedge (Q\,\mathcal{U}\,R) \Rightarrow (P \wedge Q)\,\mathcal{U}\,(P \wedge R)$
                                           (b) $(\bigcirc P)\,\mathcal{U}\,(\bigcirc Q) = \bigcirc(P\,\mathcal{U}\,Q)$
                                           (c) $(P \wedge Q)\,\mathcal{U}\,R = (P\,\mathcal{U}\,R \wedge Q\,\mathcal{U}\,R)$
                                           (d) $P\,\mathcal{U}\,(Q \vee R) = (P\,\mathcal{U}\,Q \vee P\,\mathcal{U}\,R)$
                                           (e) $P\,\mathcal{U}\,(Q \wedge R) \Rightarrow (P\,\mathcal{U}\,Q) \wedge (P\,\mathcal{U}\,R)$
                                           (f) $(P\,\mathcal{U}\,R) \vee (Q\,\mathcal{U}\,R) \Rightarrow (P \vee Q)\,\mathcal{U}\,R$
                                           (g) $(P \Rightarrow Q)\,\mathcal{U}\,R \Rightarrow ((P\,\mathcal{U}\,R) \Rightarrow (Q\,\mathcal{U}\,R))$

(3.34) $\mathcal{U}$ *Ordering Laws:*  (a) $(\neg P\,\mathcal{U}\,Q) \vee (\neg Q\,\mathcal{U}\,P)$
                                          (b) $P\,\mathcal{U}\,Q \wedge \neg Q\,\mathcal{U}\,R \Rightarrow P\,\mathcal{U}\,R$
                                           (c) $P\,\mathcal{U}\,(Q \wedge R) \Rightarrow (P\,\mathcal{U}\,Q)\,\mathcal{U}\,R$

(3.35) $\mathcal{U}$ *Monotonicity Laws:*  (a) $\Box(P \Rightarrow Q) \Rightarrow (P\,\mathcal{U}\,R \Rightarrow Q\,\mathcal{U}\,R)$
                                           (b) $\Box(P \Rightarrow Q) \Rightarrow (R\,\mathcal{U}\,P \Rightarrow R\,\mathcal{U}\,Q)$

     Some derived inference rules that are helpful in reasoning about formulas containing $\mathcal{U}$ are:

(3.36) $\mathcal{U}$ *Induction Rule:*  $\dfrac{P \Rightarrow \bigcirc(P \vee Q)}{P \Rightarrow (P\,\mathcal{U}\,Q)}$

(3.37) $\mathcal{U}$ *Introduction-R Rule:*  $\dfrac{R \Rightarrow Q \vee (P \wedge \bigcirc R)}{R \Rightarrow (P\,\mathcal{U}\,Q)}$

(3.38) $\mathcal{U}$ *Introduction-L Rule:*  $\dfrac{Q \vee (P \wedge \bigcirc R) \Rightarrow R}{(P\,\mathcal{U}\,Q) \Rightarrow R}$

(3.39) $\mathcal{U}$ *Strengthening Rule:*  $\dfrac{P \Rightarrow R,\ \ Q \Rightarrow S}{(P\,\mathcal{U}\,Q) \Rightarrow (R\,\mathcal{U}\,S)}$

(3.40) $\mathcal{U}$ *Catenation Rule*:  $\dfrac{P \Rightarrow Q\,\mathcal{U}R,\ \ R \Rightarrow Q\,\mathcal{U}\,S}{P \Rightarrow Q\,\mathcal{U}\,S}$

## *Rigid-Variable Quantified Expressions*

The four axioms and single inference rule that suffice for reasoning about rigid variables and rigid-variable quantified expressions are given in exercise 3.10. The (larger) collection of laws and derived inference rules presented below is easier to use. Many of the laws will be familiar, since they have analogues in Predicate Logic.

(3.41) *Rigid Variable Renaming Rules*: Provided that no occurrence of Y is free or bound in $R$ or $P$:

(a) $\dfrac{(\forall X \colon R \colon P)}{(\forall Y \colon R_Y^X \colon P_Y^X)}$  (b) $\dfrac{(\exists X \colon R \colon P)}{(\exists Y \colon R_Y^X \colon P_Y^X)}$

(3.42) *TL De Morgan's Laws*:  (a) $(\exists X \colon R \colon P) = \neg(\forall X \colon R \colon \neg P)$
(b) $(\forall X \colon R \colon P) = \neg(\exists X \colon R \colon \neg P)$

(3.43) *TL Conjunction Law*:
$(\forall X \colon R \colon P \wedge Q) = ((\forall X \colon R \colon P) \wedge (\forall X \colon R \colon Q))$

(3.44) *TL Disjunction Law*:  $(\exists X \colon R \colon P \vee Q) = ((\exists X \colon R \colon P) \vee (\exists X \colon R \colon Q))$

(3.45) *TL Empty-Range Laws*:  (a) $(\forall X \colon false \colon P) = true$
(b) $(\exists X \colon false \colon P) = false$

(3.46) *TL Range Laws*:  (a) $(\forall X \colon R \wedge P \colon Q) = (\forall X \colon R \colon P \Rightarrow Q)$
(b) $(\exists X \colon R \wedge P \colon Q) = (\exists X \colon R \colon P \wedge Q)$

(3.47) *TL Range Partitioning Laws*:
(a) $(\forall X \colon P \vee R \colon Q) = ((\forall X \colon P \colon Q) \wedge (\forall X \colon R \colon Q))$
(b) $(\exists X \colon P \vee R \colon Q) = ((\exists X \colon P \colon Q) \vee (\exists X \colon R \colon Q))$

(3.48) *TL Range Narrowing Law*:  $(\forall X \colon R \colon P) \Rightarrow (\forall X \colon R \wedge Q \colon P)$

(3.49) *TL Range Widening Law*:  $(\exists X \colon R \colon P) \Rightarrow (\exists X \colon R \vee Q \colon P)$

(3.50) *TL Quantification Weakening Laws*:
(a) $(\forall X \colon R \colon P) \Rightarrow (\forall X \colon R \colon P \vee Q)$
(b) $(\exists X \colon R \colon P) \Rightarrow (\exists X \colon R \colon P \vee Q)$

(3.51) *TL Quantification Implication Laws*:
(a) $(\forall X \colon R \colon P \Rightarrow Q) \Rightarrow ((\forall X \colon R \colon P) \Rightarrow (\forall X \colon R \colon Q))$
(b) $(\forall X \colon R \colon P \Rightarrow Q) \Rightarrow ((\exists X \colon R \colon P) \Rightarrow (\exists X \colon R \colon Q))$

(3.52) *TL Distributive Laws*:   Provided that X does not occur free in $Q$:

(a) $(Q \wedge (\exists X\colon R\colon P)) = (\exists X\colon R\colon Q \wedge P)$

(b) $(Q \vee (\forall X\colon R\colon P)) = (\forall X\colon R\colon Q \vee P)$

(c) $(Q \Rightarrow (\forall X\colon R\colon P)) = (\forall X\colon R\colon Q \Rightarrow P)$

(3.53) *TL Distributive Rules*:   Provided that X does not occur free in $Q$:

(a) $$\frac{(\exists X\colon R)}{(Q \vee (\exists X\colon R\colon P)) = (\exists X\colon R\colon Q \vee P)}$$

(b) $$\frac{(\exists X\colon R)}{(Q \wedge (\forall X\colon R\colon P)) = (\forall X\colon R\colon Q \wedge P)}$$

(c) $$\frac{(\exists X\colon R)}{(Q \Rightarrow (\exists X\colon R\colon P)) = (\exists X\colon R\colon Q \Rightarrow P)}$$

(3.54) *TL Quantification Simplification Laws*:   Provided that X does not occur free in $Q$:

(a) $(\forall X\colon Q) = Q$

(b) $(\exists X\colon Q) = Q$

(c) $(\forall X\colon R\colon true) = true$

(c) $(\exists X\colon R\colon false) = false$

(3.55) *TL Quantification Introduction Rule*:   $$\frac{R \Rightarrow Q}{(\forall X\colon R\colon Q)}$$

(3.56) *TL Equals in Quantified Expressions*:

(a) $$\frac{R = R'}{(\forall X\colon R\colon Q) = (\forall X\colon R'\colon Q)}$$

(b) $$\frac{R = R'}{(\exists X\colon R\colon Q) = (\exists X\colon R'\colon Q)}$$

(c) $$\frac{R \Rightarrow (Q = Q')}{(\forall X\colon R\colon Q) = (\forall X\colon R\colon Q')}$$

(d) $$\frac{R \Rightarrow (Q = Q')}{(\exists X\colon R\colon Q) = (\exists X\colon R\colon Q')}$$

(3.57) *TL Quantifier Interchange Laws*:   Provided that X does not occur free in $R'$, and Y does not occur free in $R$:

(a) $(\forall X\colon R\colon (\forall Y\colon R'\colon Q)) = (\forall Y\colon R'\colon (\forall X\colon R\colon Q))$

(b) $(\exists X\colon R\colon (\exists Y\colon R'\colon Q)) = (\exists Y\colon R'\colon (\exists X\colon R\colon Q))$

(c) $(\exists X\colon R\colon (\forall Y\colon R'\colon Q)) \Rightarrow (\forall Y\colon R'\colon (\exists X\colon R\colon Q))$

(3.58) *TL Monotonicity in Quantified Expressions*:

(a) $$\dfrac{R \Rightarrow (P \Rightarrow Q)}{(\exists X\colon\ R\colon\ P) \Rightarrow (\exists X\colon\ R\colon\ Q)}$$

(b) $$\dfrac{R \Rightarrow (P \Rightarrow Q)}{(\forall X\colon\ R\colon\ P) \Rightarrow (\forall X\colon\ R\colon\ Q)}$$

(c) $$\dfrac{R \Rightarrow (P \Rightarrow Q)}{(\exists X\colon\ P\colon\ R) \Rightarrow (\exists X\colon\ Q\colon\ R)}$$

(d) $$\dfrac{\neg R \Rightarrow (P \Rightarrow Q)}{(\forall X\colon\ Q\colon\ R) \Rightarrow (\forall X\colon\ P\colon\ R)}$$

Not all Predicate Logic laws concerning quantified expressions are sound for reasoning about rigid-variable quantified expressions. One-Point Laws (2.93a) and (2.93b) and Quantification Elimination Rule (2.95) of Predicate Logic, for example, are absent from the above list of Temporal Logic laws for good reason—they would not be sound. This is because replacing a rigid variable by a term involving flexible variables can transform a term that denotes the same value in all states of an anchored sequence to one that denotes a different value in each state.

As an illustration of why One-Point Law (2.93a) is not sound,

(3.59) $(\forall X\colon\ X=y\colon\ \Box(x=X))$

is not equivalent to $(\Box(x=X))_y^X$: the former asserts that $x$ does not change value and equals $y$ in the current state, but the latter asserts that $x$ and $y$ are equal in every state (although their values may differ from state to state).

We say that a term $e$ is *rigidly free for* X *in* P if (i) no free occurrence of X appears in P in the scope of a temporal operator or (ii) no occurrence of any flexible variable is free in $e$. For example, $y$ is not rigidly free for X in $\Box(x=X)$ because X appears in the scope of $\Box$, so condition (i) is violated; and $y$ is a flexible variable, so condition (ii) does not hold either. However, $y$ is rigidly free for X in $x=X$ because condition (i) is satisfied; and Y is rigidly free for X in $x=X$ because condition (ii) is satisfied.

If a term $e$ is rigidly free for X in P, then replacing X in P by $e$ cannot cause a term to change from being constant to having a value that varies from state to state. This allows us to formulate a Temporal Logic version of the Predicate Logic Quantification Elimination Rule (2.95):

(3.60) *TL Quantification Elimination Rule*: Provided that $e$ is rigidly free for X in $R$ and $Q$:

$$\dfrac{(\forall X\colon\ R\colon\ Q)}{(R \Rightarrow Q)_e^X}$$

We can similarly formulate Temporal Logic versions of One-Point Laws (2.93) of Predicate Logic:

(3.61) *TL One-Point Laws*:   Provided that (i) occurrences of X are not free in *e* and (ii) *e* is rigidly free for X in *P*:

$$\text{(a) } P_e^X \;=\; (\forall X\colon X{=}e\colon P)$$
$$\text{(b) } P_e^X \;=\; (\exists X\colon X{=}e\colon P)$$

Observe that because free rigid variables are implicitly universally quantified, TL One-Point Law (3.61a) can be used to instantiate a rigid variable by a constant. For example, (3.61a) allows both $x{=}3 \Rightarrow \Box(x{=}3)$ and $x{=}Y{+}Z \Rightarrow \Box(x{=}Y{+}Z)$ to be inferred from $x{=}X \Rightarrow \Box(x{=}X)$.

Temporal Logic has the following laws for moving temporal operators into and out of rigid-variable quantified expressions. In light of Interpreting Temporal Logic Formulas (3.4), the laws listed below should not be surprising: $\Box$ has a universal nature, $\Diamond$ has an existential nature, the first argument of $P\,\mathcal{U}\,Q$ has a universal nature, and the second argument of $P\,\mathcal{U}\,Q$ has an existential one.

(3.62) $\bigcirc$ *Quantifier Laws*:   (a) $(\forall X\colon \bigcirc P) \;=\; \bigcirc(\forall X\colon P)$
                                    (b) $(\exists X\colon \bigcirc P) \;=\; \bigcirc(\exists X\colon P)$

(3.63) $\Box$ *Quantifier Laws*:   (a) $(\forall X\colon \Box P) \;=\; \Box(\forall X\colon P)$
                                    (b) $(\exists X\colon \Box P) \;\Rightarrow\; \Box(\exists X\colon P)$

(3.64) $\Diamond$ *Quantifier Laws*:   (a) $(\exists X\colon \Diamond P) \;=\; \Diamond(\exists X\colon P)$
                                    (b) $\Diamond(\forall X\colon P) \;\Rightarrow\; (\forall X\colon \Diamond P)$

(3.65) $\mathcal{U}$ *Quantifier Laws*:   Provided that X does not occur free in $Q$:
                                    (a) $(\forall X\colon P\,\mathcal{U}\,Q) \;=\; (\forall X\colon P)\,\mathcal{U}\,Q$
                                    (b) $(\exists X\colon Q\,\mathcal{U}\,P) \;=\; Q\,\mathcal{U}\,(\exists X\colon P)$
                                    (c) $Q\,\mathcal{U}\,(\forall X\colon P) \;\Rightarrow\; (\forall X\colon Q\,\mathcal{U}\,P)$
                                    (d) $(\exists X\colon P\,\mathcal{U}\,Q) \;\Rightarrow\; (\exists X\colon P)\,\mathcal{U}\,Q$
                                    (e) $(\exists X\colon P\,\mathcal{U}\,R) \;\Rightarrow\; (\exists X\colon P)\,\mathcal{U}\,(\exists X\colon R)$
                                    (f) $(\forall X\colon P)\,\mathcal{U}\,(\forall X\colon R) \;\Rightarrow\; (\forall X\colon P\,\mathcal{U}\,R)$

Finally, Temporal Logic has some laws for making inferences based on the constancy of the value of a rigid variable in the current and future states of an anchored sequence. Given a formula $P$ that does not depend on flexible variables, the truth value of $P$ is the same in all suffixes of an anchored sequence. Thus, we have:

(3.66) *Frame Laws*:   For a formula $P$ that has no free occurrences of flexible variables:
                    (a) $P \Rightarrow \bigcirc P$
                    (b) $P = \Box P$

(c) $\Box(P \lor Q) = (P \lor \Box Q)$
(d) $\Diamond(P \land Q) = (P \land \Diamond Q)$

## Well-Founded Induction Rules

For state spaces constructed with values from infinite sets—like integers, lists, and trees—proofs of some theorems require induction. Informally, an inductive proof that a statement $P$ holds for all elements of some (possibly infinite) set $\mathcal{W}$ involves:

(i)   identifying a binary relation $\prec$ on $\mathcal{W}$ such that every nonempty subset of $\mathcal{W}$ contains a $\prec$-minimal element,[3]

(ii)  establishing that $P$ holds for every $\prec$-minimal element of $\mathcal{W}$, and

(iii) establishing that $P$ holds for an arbitrary element $v$ of $\mathcal{W}$ if it holds for every element that is smaller than $v$ (according to $\prec$).

Condition (i) rules out the existence of *infinite descending chains*, infinite sequences $v_1 v_2 \dots$ where for $0 \le i$, $v_i \in \mathcal{W}$ and $v_{i+1} \prec v_i$ hold. Conditions (ii) and (iii) allow us to deduce that $P$ holds on an arbitrary element $v$ of $\mathcal{W}$, as follows.

Because all descending chains in $\mathcal{W}$ have finite length, every element $\mathcal{W}$ is an element of some set $C_n$ for $0 \le n$, where:

$$C_0: \quad \{u \mid \neg(\exists w \in \mathcal{W}: w \prec u)\}$$

$$C_{i+1}: \quad \{u \mid u \in \mathcal{W} \land (\exists w \in C_i: w \prec u)\}$$

Therefore, in order to prove that $P$ holds for every element of $\mathcal{W}$, it suffices to prove that $P$ holds for every element in $C_n$, for any natural number $n$. From (iii), we conclude that $P$ holds for every element in $C_{i+1}$ if $P$ holds for every element in $C_i$. Thus, by repeated application of (iii) and transitivity, we have that $P$ holds for every element in $C_n$ if it holds for every element in $C_0$. Since (ii) establishes that $P$ does hold for every element in $C_0$, we conclude that $P$ holds for every element in $C_n$.

A pair $(\mathcal{W}, \prec)$ is called a *well-founded set* if $\mathcal{W}$ is a set and $\prec$ is a binary relation satisfying (i) above. The set of natural numbers with integer less-than (i.e., $<$) as binary relation $\prec$ is an example of a well-founded set. The set of integers with $<$ is not a well-founded set—it is rife with infinite descending chains.

Some sets are well-founded by virtue of how they are constructed. The *Cartesian product* $\mathcal{W}_1 \times \mathcal{W}_2 \times \cdots \times \mathcal{W}_n$ of sets $\mathcal{W}_1$, $\mathcal{W}_2$, ..., $\mathcal{W}_n$ is a set of $n$-tuples,

---

[3]Element $v$ is a $\prec$-*minimal element* of set $S$ iff $v \in S$ and, for no element $u$ in $S$, $u \prec v$ holds.

$$\{(u_1, u_2, ..., u_n) \mid u_1 \in \mathcal{W}_1 \wedge u_2 \in \mathcal{W}_2 \wedge \cdots \wedge u_n \in \mathcal{W}_n\}.$$

It forms a well-founded set with binary relation

$$(u_1, u_2, ..., u_n) \prec (v_1, v_2, ..., v_n): \begin{array}{l} (u_1 \prec_1 v_1) \ \vee \\ (u_1 = v_1 \ \wedge \ u_2 \prec_2 v_2) \ \vee \\ \vdots \\ (u_1 = v_1 \ \wedge \ u_2 = v_2 \ \wedge \ \cdots \ \wedge \ u_n \prec_n v_n) \end{array}$$

if each $(\mathcal{W}_i, \prec_i)$ is a well-founded set. Thus, the set of $n$-tuples of natural numbers under the usual lexicographic ordering is a well-founded set. The set of $n$-tuples of integers is not well-founded—for any value $(u_1, u_2, ..., u_n)$ there is an infinite decreasing chain:

$$(u_1, u_2, ..., u_n)(u_1, u_2, ..., u_n-1) \ ... \ (u_1, u_2, ..., u_n-k) \ ...$$

Induction is formalized in Temporal Logic by an inference rule whose premise combines (ii) and (iii) as a single Temporal Logic theorem.

(3.67) *Well-Founded Induction Rule*:  For $(\mathcal{W}, \prec)$ a well-founded set and any rigid variable V not occurring free in $P$:

$$\frac{(\forall R \in \mathcal{W}: \ (\forall V \in \mathcal{W}: \ V \prec R: \ P_V^R) \Rightarrow P)}{(\forall R \in \mathcal{W}: \ P)}$$

To understand why this rule is sound, observe that its conclusion is equivalent to $(\forall V \in \mathcal{W}: \ P_V^R)$, due to Rigid Variable Renaming Rule (3.41a). We can then use induction to prove $(\forall V \in \mathcal{W}: \ P_V^R)$. In particular, we use a well-founded set $\mathcal{W}$ for the values over which V ranges (i.e., requirement (i) above) and demonstrate (ii) and (iii), as follows.

The premise of Well-Founded Induction Rule (3.67) formalizes requirement (iii) because it asserts that $P$ holds for a value R if $P$ holds for every V that is ordered smaller by $\prec$. It also formalizes requirement (ii) because when R is $\prec$-minimal, antecedent $(\forall V \in \mathcal{W}: \ V \prec R: \ P_V^R)$ is a universal quantification with empty range. Consequently, by TL Empty-Range Law (3.45a), when R is $\prec$-minimal the premise becomes *true* $\Rightarrow P$. To discharge the premise, therefore, requires showing that $P$ holds when R is $\prec$-minimal.

From Well-Founded Induction Rule (3.67), we can derive an inference rule for proving an eventuality.

(3.68) *Well-Founded $\Diamond$ Induction Rule*:  For $(\mathcal{W}, \prec)$ a well-founded set, rigid variable R not occurring free in $Q$, and rigid variable V not occurring free in $P$ or $Q$:

$$\frac{(\forall R \in \mathcal{W}: \ P \Rightarrow \Diamond(Q \vee (\exists V \in \mathcal{W}: \ V \prec R: \ P_V^R)))}{(\forall R \in \mathcal{W}: \ P \Rightarrow \Diamond Q)}$$

3.3 Axioms and Inference Rules

Informally, the premise of this rule asserts that for any anchored sequence, if $P$ holds for a value R, then for some suffix of that anchored sequence, $Q$ holds or $P$ holds for a value V where V‹R. Due to the absence of infinite-descending chains in $\mathcal{W}$, this means that eventually either $Q$ holds or, for some value V that is ‹-minimal, $P$ holds. And in this latter case, the rule's premise implies $P \Rightarrow \Diamond Q$, because disjunct $(\exists V \in \mathcal{W}: V\langle R: P_V^R)$ is *false* due to TL Empty-Range Law (3.45b).

Specialization of Well-Founded $\Diamond$ Induction Rule (3.68) for the case where the well-founded set is the natural numbers leads to another derived rule for proving eventualities.

(3.69) *Natural Number $\Diamond$ Induction Rule*:  For rigid variable R not occurring free in $Q$ and rigid variable V not occurring free in $P$ or $Q$:

$$\frac{\begin{array}{c} P_0^R \Rightarrow \Diamond Q, \\ (\forall V \in \text{Nat}: \; P_{V+1}^R \Rightarrow \Diamond (Q \vee P_V^R)) \end{array}}{(\forall R \in \text{Nat}: \; P \Rightarrow \Diamond Q)}$$

## Equational Proofs for Temporal Logic

As with the logics in Chapter 2, proofs in Temporal Logic are often easier to read and to construct when an equational format is available. We support this proof style, as follows.

For justifying an equational-proof step that asserts $A=B$, we have the following Temporal Logic inference rule; it is analogous to Predicate Logic Substitution of Equals (2.99):

(3.70) *TL Substitution of Equals*:   For Temporal Logic formulas $P_Q^p$ and $P_R^p$:

$$\frac{Q = R}{P_Q^p = P_R^p}$$

For justifying an equational-proof step that asserts $A \Rightarrow B$, Predicate Logic Monotonicity Rule (2.101) and Predicate Logic Antimonotonicity Rule (2.102) also have Temporal Logic analogues. Parity of a Subformula (2.100) remains unchanged, except that quantified expressions now encompass those involving rigid variables.

(3.71) *TL Monotonicity Rule*:  For Temporal Logic formulas $P_Q^p$ and $R$, where subformula $Q$ has even parity in $P_Q^p$:

$$\frac{Q \Rightarrow R}{P_Q^p \Rightarrow P_R^p}$$

(3.72) *TL Antimonotonicity Rule*:  For Temporal Logic formulas $P_Q^p$ and $R$, where subformula $Q$ has odd parity in $P_Q^p$:

$$\frac{Q \Rightarrow R}{P_R^p \Rightarrow P_Q^p}$$

Finally, we have:

(3.73) **Temporal Logic Equational Proof Justifications.** A justification "Why $X$ is a theorem" in an equational proof of a Temporal Logic theorem must be one of the following:

  (i) A law or previously proved theorem $X$ of Temporal Logic.

  (ii) The theorem of Propositional Logic that enables $X$ to be deduced by TL Substitution (3.7). Details of the substitutions may be omitted when they are obvious. The phrase "Propositional reasoning" is used when the Propositional Logic theorem is obvious and giving it would clutter the proof.

  (iii) The theorem of Temporal Logic that enables $X$ to be deduced by TL Substitution of Equals (3.70), TL Monotonicity Rule (3.71), or TL Antimonotonicity Rule (3.72).

  (iv) The theorem that enables $X$ to be deduced by a sequence of one or more other Temporal Logic inference rules.                                    □

To illustrate, here is an equational proof of Distributive Law (3.12b), $(\Box P \vee \Box Q) \Rightarrow \Box(P \vee Q)$. Because the final line of the equational proof is a theorem, being an instance of Propositional Logic theorem $p=p$, this makes the first line a theorem—thereby proving what we set out to prove. Compare this proof of Distributive Law (3.12b) with the one given just before that law was first introduced.

$$
\begin{aligned}
&\Box P \vee \Box Q \;\Rightarrow\; \Box(P \vee Q) \\
=\quad &\text{«Implication Law (2.22b)»} \\
&((\Box P \vee \Box Q) \wedge \Box(P \vee Q)) \;=\; (\Box P \vee \Box Q) \\
=\quad &\text{«Distributive Law (2.16b)»} \\
&((\Box P \wedge \Box(P \vee Q)) \vee (\Box Q \wedge \Box(P \vee Q))) \;=\; (\Box P \vee \Box Q) \\
=\quad &\text{«Distributive Law (3.12a)»} \\
&((\Box(P \wedge (P \vee Q)) \vee (\Box(Q \wedge (P \vee Q)))) \;=\; (\Box P \vee \Box Q) \\
=\quad &\text{«And-Simplification Law (2.26d) »} \\
&((\Box P \vee (\Box(Q \wedge (P \vee Q)))) \;=\; (\Box P \vee \Box Q) \\
=\quad &\text{«And-Simplification Law (2.26d) »} \\
&(\Box P \vee \Box Q) \;=\; (\Box P \vee \Box Q)
\end{aligned}
$$

## 3.4  Temporal Logic Applications

Temporal Logic formulas can be used to specify and reason about properties and programs. To do this, we identify each program variable with a distinct flexible variable of the logic. Predicate Logic formulas now have program states as models, and Temporal Logic formulas have as models anchored sequences $(\sigma, j)$, where $\sigma$ is a sequence of program states.

## Specifying Properties

Recall from §2.4 that properties are sets of anchored sequences. For each Temporal Logic formula $P$, we write $\{P\}$ to denote the set of anchored sequences that are models for $P$. The phrase "the property specified by $P$," or just "property $P$," then refers to $\{P\}$.

There is a natural correspondence between the propositional connectives of Temporal Logic and set operations on the properties they specify:

(3.74) *Property-Formula Correspondence:* Provided that $P$ and $Q$ have no free occurrences of rigid variables:[4]

      (a) $\{\neg P\} = \sim\{P\}$
      (b) $\{P \wedge Q\} = \{P\} \cap \{Q\}$
      (c) $\{P \vee Q\} = \{P\} \cup \{Q\}$

This correspondence allows complex properties to be specified compositionally. For example, we can specify $\{P\} \cap \{Q\}$ by conjoining Temporal Logic specification $P$ with Temporal Logic specification $Q$.

By defining $\{P\}$ as we have, Temporal Logic can be used for reasoning about properties. This is because establishing

•    that a program satisfies a property or

•    that satisfying one property implies some other property is satisfied

is, by definition, the same as establishing that one property is a subset of another. The following calculation shows how to conclude that a property $\{P\}$ is a subset of a property $\{Q\}$ from the validity of a Temporal Logic formula, $P \Rightarrow Q$. Assume that $P$ and $Q$ have no free occurrences of rigid variables.

      $\vDash (P \Rightarrow Q)$
iff     «definition of $\vDash$»
      For all $(\sigma, j)$: $(\sigma, j) \vDash (P \Rightarrow Q)$
iff     «Interpreting Temporal Logic Formulas (3.4), since $P$ and $Q$
      have no free occurrences of rigid variables»
      For all $(\sigma, j)$: $(\sigma, j) \not\vDash P$ or $(\sigma, j) \vDash Q$
iff     «Implication Law (2.22a)»

---

[4]The requirement that $P$ and $Q$ have no free occurrences of rigid variables is easily satisfied by explicitly quantifying over the rigid variables. The requirement is necessary for Property-Formula Correspondence (3.74c). If $P$ has free occurrences of rigid variable X, and $Q$ has free occurrences of rigid variable Y, then $P \vee Q$ is, by convention, equivalent to $(\forall \text{X, Y}: P \vee Q)$. Formula $(\forall \text{X, Y}: P \vee Q)$ is not equivalent to $(\forall \text{X}: P) \vee (\forall \text{Y}: Q)$. Yet it is $(\forall \text{X}: P) \vee (\forall \text{Y}: Q)$ that must be satisfied by any anchored sequence in property $\{P\} \cup \{Q\}$.

For all $(\sigma, j)$: $(\sigma, j) \vDash P$ implies $(\sigma, j) \vDash Q$
iff        «definition of $\{P\}$ and $\{Q\}$»
           For all $(\sigma, j)$: $(\sigma, j) \in \{P\}$ implies $(\sigma, j) \in \{Q\}$
iff        «definition of $\subseteq$»
           $\{P\} \subseteq \{Q\}$

Given a sound and complete axiomatization of Temporal Logic,[5] $P \Rightarrow Q$ is a theorem iff $\vDash (P \Rightarrow Q)$, so we have:

(3.75) *Subset-Implication Correspondence*:   Provided that $P$ and $Q$ have no free occurrences of rigid variables: $P \Rightarrow Q$ is a Temporal Logic theorem iff $\{P\} \subseteq \{Q\}$ is valid.

As an example of how Subset-Implication Correspondence (3.75) is used in reasoning about properties, recall the mutual exclusion problem formalized by (2.43). There, propositions *InA* and *InB* are defined by:

   *InA*:  "process $A$ is executing in its critical section"

   *InB*:  "process $B$ is executing in its critical section"

Desired is a protocol to prevent processes $A$ and $B$ from executing in critical sections at the same time. Thus, this protocol must satisfy $\Box \neg (InA \wedge InB)$.

   Given a protocol that satisfies $\Box (InA \Rightarrow \neg InB \, \mathcal{U} \neg InA)$, an obvious question is whether mutual exclusion is ensured. One might conjecture that mutual exclusion is guaranteed only if $\Box (InB \Rightarrow \neg InA \, \mathcal{U} \neg InB)$ is also satisfied by the protocol. However,

(3.76)  $\Box (InA \Rightarrow \neg InB \, \mathcal{U} \neg InA) \;\Rightarrow\; \Box \neg (InA \wedge InB)$

is a Temporal Logic theorem, so from Subset-Implication Correspondence (3.75), we conclude that mutual exclusion is implemented by any protocol that satisfies $\Box (InA \Rightarrow \neg InB \, \mathcal{U} \neg InA)$.

   Subset-Implication Correspondence (3.75) can also be used to show that two properties are equal. For Temporal Logic formulas $P$ and $Q$ with no free occurrences of rigid variables, $P = Q$ implies that $\{P\}$ and $\{Q\}$ are equal.

(3.77) *Property Equivalence*:   Provided that $P$ and $Q$ have no free occurrences of rigid variables: $P = Q$ is a Temporal Logic theorem iff $\{P\} = \{Q\}$ holds.

---

[5]In this and subsequent discussions about logics that extend Predicate Logic, "complete" means "complete relative to Predicate Logic."

## Programs That Satisfy Properties

Given a program $S$, we define a set $\mathcal{H}_S$ of anchored sequences to model the histories of $S$:

(3.78) **Program Histories.** For any program $S$, property $\mathcal{H}_S$ contains all anchored sequences $(\sigma, j)$ such that:

  (i)   $\sigma[j]$ is an initial state of $S$.

  (ii)  For all $i$, $j \le i < |\sigma| - 1$: $\sigma[i+1]$ is produced by executing an atomic action from $S$ that is executable in $\sigma[i]$.

  (iii) If $\sigma$ is finite, then no atomic action of $S$ is able to execute in the final state of $\sigma$.                                                                  □

Program Histories (3.78) imposes no constraints on $\sigma[..j-1]$ for an anchored sequence $(\sigma, j)$ in $\mathcal{H}_S$. Another choice would have been to exclude from $\mathcal{H}_S$ anchored sequences $(\sigma, j)$ where $j > 0$ holds. Our choice to include these in $\mathcal{H}_S$ was dictated by an inexpressiveness of the Temporal Logic thus far presented: no formula of that logic has as its models only anchored sequences of the form $(\sigma, 0)$. Were all elements of $\mathcal{H}_S$ required to be of the form $(\sigma, 0)$, we could not characterize $\mathcal{H}_S$ using a Temporal Logic formula, so we could not use the logic for reasoning about program execution.

A program $S$ satisfies a property $\{P\}$ iff $\mathcal{H}_S \subseteq \{P\}$ is valid. Therefore, we can use Subset-Implication Correspondence (3.75) to prove $\mathcal{H}_S \subseteq \{P\}$: Exhibit a Temporal Logic formula $TL(S)$ that has no free occurrences of rigid variables and satisfies $\mathcal{H}_S \subseteq \{TL(S)\}$. Then use Subset-Implication Correspondence (3.75) to infer that $\{TL(S)\} \subseteq \{P\}$ is valid by proving $TL(S) \Rightarrow P$ to be a theorem of Temporal Logic. Transitivity of $\subseteq$ yields $\mathcal{H}_S \subseteq \{P\}$.

As an illustration, consider a simple program that first indivisibly increments $x$ by 2 and then indivisibly increments $y$ by 1:

$S$: **program**
$\quad$ α: increment $x$ by 2;
$\quad$ β: increment $y$ by 1
$\quad$ γ: **end**

The state space for this program includes $x$, $y$, and a program counter $pc$ that ranges over the set $\{\alpha, \beta, \gamma\}$ of labels. The histories of this program are the finite sequences of states in which, for any values X and Y:

  (i)   the first state satisfies $pc = \alpha$, $x = X$, and $y = Y$;

  (ii)  the second state satisfies $pc = \beta$, $x = X+2$, and $y = Y$;

  (iii) the third (and final) state satisfies $pc = \gamma$, $x = X+2$, and $y = Y+1$.

This set of histories is modeled by set $\{TL(S)\}$ of anchored sequences, where:

(3.79) $TL(S)$:    $(\forall X,\ Y:\ x=X \wedge y=Y:$
$$pc=\alpha \wedge$$
$$\bigcirc(pc=\beta \wedge x=X+2 \wedge y=Y \wedge$$
$$\bigcirc\square(pc=\gamma \wedge x=X+2 \wedge y=Y+1))).$$

Note that $\{TL(S)\}$ includes anchored sequences in which the state satisfying $pc=\gamma \wedge x=X+2 \wedge y=Y+1$ is repeated a finite or infinite number of times. A more expressive Temporal Logic (which is given in Chapter 7) could rule out such anchored sequences. The presence of these anchored sequences causes no difficulty, however, since $\mathcal{H}_S \subseteq \{TL(S)\}$ holds, as required.

The property that $S$ does not falsify $x \geq y$ is specified in Temporal Logic by $x \geq y \Rightarrow \square(x \geq y)$. Therefore, to prove that $S$ satisfies $x \geq y \Rightarrow \square(x \geq y)$, it suffices to prove that $TL(S) \Rightarrow (x \geq y \Rightarrow \square(x \geq y))$ is a theorem of Temporal Logic. We leave the proof to the exercises.

Pragmatic considerations limit the utility of an approach that requires proving formulas like $TL(S) \Rightarrow P$ to be theorems of Temporal Logic. For $S$ a nontrivial program, $TL(S)$ is apt to be a long and complex formula—a manipulative nightmare. Also, proving $TL(S) \Rightarrow P$ forces us to reason about program execution from an encoding, $TL(S)$, when it is the program text itself that we seek to understand.

Both of these difficulties are consequences of our definition of validity, which involves a set of interpretations—all anchored sequences—that is larger than necessary. We care only about anchored sequences $(\sigma, j)$ in $\mathcal{H}_S$, because they are the only ones in $\{TL(S)\}$. In fact, antecedent $TL(S)$ is needed in $TL(S) \Rightarrow P$ exactly so that $TL(S) \Rightarrow P$ will be (trivially) satisfied by all other anchored sequences.

We avoid the need to construct and manipulate $TL(S)$ by defining another type of validity for our Temporal Logic. Any set $\mathcal{H}_S^+$ of anchored sequences that satisfies

(3.80)    $\mathcal{H}_S \subseteq \mathcal{H}_S^+$

is one for which the $\mathcal{H}_S^+$-validity of $P$ implies $\mathcal{H}_S \subseteq \{P\}$.

Equation (3.80) does not completely characterize $\mathcal{H}_S^+$. It turns out that by including in $\mathcal{H}_S^+$ certain anchored sequences that are not in $\mathcal{H}_S$, we actually facilitate reasoning about concurrent programs.

(3.81) **Program-Execution Interpretations.** Let $S^\infty$ be the set of all finite and infinite sequences of program states for $S$. Then:

$$\mathcal{H}_S^+:\quad \{(\sigma, j) \mid \sigma \in S^\infty \wedge \sigma[j..] \in sfx(\mathcal{H}_S)\}$$

where

$$sfx(\mathcal{H}_S) = \{\tau[k+i..] \mid (\tau, k) \in \mathcal{H}_S \wedge 0 \leq k+i < |\tau| \}. \qquad \square$$

$\mathcal{H}_S^+$ includes anchored sequences $(\sigma, j)$ for which $\sigma[..j-1]$ is an arbitrary sequence of states and $\sigma[j..]$ satisfies conditions (ii) and (iii) of Program Histories (3.78) but not necessarily condition (i). Such anchored sequences model executions that start in the middle of $S$ (rather than with an initial state), something that occurs in a concurrent program when a process is resumed in the middle of $S$ after (arbitrary) execution by other processes. Thus, $\mathcal{H}_S^+$-validity is ideal for reasoning about a statement $S$ that is part of a concurrent program.

To prove that a program $S$ satisfies a property $\mathcal{P}$, we can now proceed as follows.

(1)   Write a Temporal Logic formula $P$ such that $\mathcal{P} \subseteq \{P\}$.

(2)   Truthify[6] $\mathcal{H}_S^+ \models P$ by proving $P$ a theorem of a sound and complete temporal logic for $\mathcal{H}_S^+$-validity.

Step (1) may require Subset-Implication Correspondence (3.75) to find a Temporal Logic formula $P$ that is easy to prove. Step (2) requires having a temporal logic that is sound and complete for $\mathcal{H}_S^+$-validity.

The Temporal Logic axiomatization of §3.3 is sound with respect to $\mathcal{H}_S^+$-validity. This is because $\mathcal{H}_S^+$ is suffix closed and is a subset of all possible anchored sequences. Soundness of Temporal Generalization Rule (3.11) requires that $\mathcal{H}_S^+$ be suffix closed; soundness of the axioms and other inference rules requires only that $\mathcal{H}_S^+$ be a set of anchored sequences. In fact, by this same argument, we could conclude that the Temporal Logic axiomatization of §3.3 is sound with respect to any suffix-closed set of anchored sequences.

Unfortunately, the Temporal Logic axiomatization of §3.3 is not complete with respect to $\mathcal{H}_S^+$-validity. Completeness would require that every $\mathcal{H}_S^+$-valid formula be provable. A formula satisfied by every anchored sequence in $\mathcal{H}_S^+$ but not satisfied by all anchored sequences is, by definition, not valid. Such a formula would not be provable (nor should it be) using the axiomatization of §3.3; however, it must be provable in a complete axiomatization for $\mathcal{H}_S^+$-validity.

A complete logic for $\mathcal{H}_S^+$-valid formulas can be obtained by extending the axiomatization of §3.3 with axioms and rules that characterize program states and how individual statements and programs execute. We call this logic *S-Temporal Logic*; Chapters 6, 7, and 8 give its axiomatization.

## 3.5   About Modal Logics

Our Temporal Logic is an example of a *modal logic*. By understanding something about modal logics, we enhance our understanding of temporal logics.

---

[6]truth·i·fy: to make true.

[7]In this and subsequent discussions about logics that extend Predicate Logic, "complete" should be taken to mean "complete relative to Predicate Logic."

Formulas of a modal logic are interpreted with respect to a set of *worlds* called a *universe*. Worlds, like states, assign values to flexible variables and assign meanings to predicate and function symbols. However, unlike states, worlds are related by the *accessibility relation* of the modal logic. Two modal operators, $\square$ (read "necessarily") and $\diamond$ (read "possibly")—not to be confused with the temporal operators—allow construction of formulas concerning the necessity or possibility of something holding in accessible worlds. $\square P$ is satisfied by a world $w$ iff $P$ is satisfied in every world accessible from $w$; $\diamond P$ is satisfied by a world $w$ iff $P$ is satisfied in some world accessible from $w$.

Given a modal logic $M$, the meaning of $\square P$ and $\diamond P$ in a world $w$ can be formalized as follows. Let $u\,\mathcal{R}_M v$ denote that world $v$ is accessible from world $u$ according to accessibility relation $\mathcal{R}_M$ for $M$. Define $w \vDash P$ to hold iff $P$ is satisfied in world $w$. By formalizing the informal definitions above for $\square P$ and $\diamond P$, we get:

(3.82) **Interpreting Modal Operators.**

$$w \vDash \square P \quad \text{iff} \quad \text{For all } u,\, w\,\mathcal{R}_M u\text{:}\ u \vDash P$$
$$w \vDash \diamond P \quad \text{iff} \quad \text{Exists } u,\, w\,\mathcal{R}_M u\text{:}\ u \vDash P \qquad\qquad \square$$

We can informally employ Predicate Logic and these definitions to show that the following formulas are valid.[8]

(3.83) *Modal Duality Law*: $\diamond P = \neg\square\neg P$

(3.84) *Modal $\square$ Distribution Law*: $\square(P \Rightarrow Q) \Rightarrow (\square P \Rightarrow \square Q)$

The first follows from informally applying De Morgan's Law (2.80a), the second from Quantification Implication Law (2.89a).

The validity of (3.83) and (3.84) do not depend on any assumptions about the accessibility relation. Therefore, these formulas can be axioms of any modal logic in which the $\square$ and $\diamond$ operators are defined as in Interpreting Modal Operators (3.82). By making assumptions about the accessibility relation, other modal formulas become valid as well. If the accessibility relation is reflexive, then every world is accessible from itself. Thus, if $\square P$ holds in a world $w$, then $P$ holds in every world accessible from $w$, so $P$ will hold in $w$ itself. We have deduced that $\square P \Rightarrow P$ can be an axiom of any modal logic with a reflexive accessibility relation. Modal Duality Law (3.83) then allows $P \Rightarrow \diamond P$ to be inferred by propositional reasoning.

(3.85) *Modal Reflexive Laws*:  (a) $\square P \Rightarrow P$
                                 (b) $P \Rightarrow \diamond P$

---

[8]Formal reasoning in Predicate Logic would require that $u \vDash P$ be a predicate.

If the accessibility relation is both reflexive and transitive, then the set of worlds accessible from a world $w$ and the set of worlds accessible from elements of that set are equal. Thus, when the accessibility relation is reflexive and transitive, the following are valid.

(3.86)  *Modal Transitive Laws*:   (a) $\Box\Box P = \Box P$
$\qquad\qquad\qquad\qquad\qquad\quad$ (b) $\Diamond\Diamond P = \Diamond P$

## Accessibility Relations for Program Execution

Whether two worlds from a universe are related by the accessibility relation of a modal logic depends on the domain of discourse being axiomatized. Two accessibility relations are particularly useful for reasoning about execution of concurrent programs:

(3.87) **Branching-Time Accessibility.** Worlds are program states. Define accessibility relation $\mathcal{R}_{BT}$ such that for worlds $u$ and $v$, $u\mathcal{R}_{BT}v$ holds iff starting from state $u$ and executing zero or more atomic actions can produce state $v$. $\qquad\qquad\qquad\qquad\qquad\qquad\qquad\qquad\qquad\qquad\qquad$ □

(3.88) **Linear-Time Accessibility.** Worlds are anchored sequences $(\sigma, j)$. Define accessibility relation $\mathcal{R}_{LT}$ such that $u\mathcal{R}_{LT}v$ holds iff world $v$ is a suffix of world $u$. $\qquad\qquad\qquad\qquad\qquad\qquad\qquad\qquad\qquad\qquad\qquad$ □

Both accessibility relations are reflexive and transitive, so laws (3.83) through (3.86) are valid in any modal logic based on either.

Branching-Time Accessibility (3.87) and Linear-Time Accessibility (3.88) define modal logics with incomparable expressive powers. To see why, consider the meaning of $\Diamond P$ in each. Under Branching-Time Accessibility (3.87), the fact that $\Diamond P$ holds in a program state implies that it is possible for execution to reach a state satisfying $P$. Thus, $\Diamond P$ does not guarantee that $P$ will eventually hold— only that it might hold. Under Linear-Time Accessibility (3.88), $\Diamond P$ holds on $(\sigma, j)$ if some suffix satisfies $P$. Thus, whenever $\Diamond P$ holds, $P$ is guaranteed to hold eventually. A logic based on (3.88) cannot express properties that involve possibility, and without additional modal operators, a logic based on (3.87) cannot express properties involving eventuality.

It is no accident that modal logic laws (3.83) through (3.86) are identical to axioms of our Temporal Logic. Our Temporal Logic is a modal logic based on Linear-Time Accessibility (3.88). For this reason, it is sometimes called a *linear-time temporal logic*, in contrast to a *branching-time temporal logic*, which would be based on Branching-Time Accessibility (3.87).

An obvious question is why one of these logics should be preferred over the other. The answer depends on how the logic will be used. Our concern is with programs and properties. In light of this, consider what it can mean for the modal logic formula $\Diamond P$ to be valid, for some state predicate $P$.

In a linear-time temporal logic, $\Diamond P$ specifies something that must hold for each execution. In a branching-time temporal logic, $\Diamond P$ can be valid even if some executions do not lead to a state satisfying $P$, because it suffices that it be possible to reach a state satisfying $P$. Thus, formula $\Diamond P$ under Branching-Time Accessibility (3.87) asserts something about some but not all histories, so it does not define (what we are calling) a property. We choose a linear-time temporal logic because of our definition of property. Formulas of a branching-time temporal logic can specify things that are not properties; formulas of a linear-time temporal logic always specify properties.

## Historical Notes

Modal logic (also called *tense logic* or *change logic*) has long been of interest to logicians and philosophers. The use of different modalities (e.g., necessity and possibility) can be traced back to the Megarains and Stoics of ancient Greece. However, A.N. Prior was the first to suggest the temporal interpretation for the $\Box$ and $\Diamond$ modal operators [Prior 57].

A modal logic was used in [Burstall 74] to explain various approaches to sequential program verification. Burstall credits [McCarthy & Hayes 69] with the idea of using a modal logic to avoid having the program state be explicit.

Pnueli was the first to use a temporal logic for reasoning about concurrent programs [Pnueli 77]. This work was motivated by an earlier attempt to reason about nonterminating programs using a logic with an explicit time variable [Francez & Pnueli 76]. The logic in [Pnueli 77] extends Propositional Logic with the (future) temporal operators $\Box$ and $\Diamond$. The need for a logic with greater expressiveness led to an extension, called DX, with the $\bigcirc$ operator [Pnueli 79] and later to DUX, which added an "until" operator [Gabbay et al. 80]. Subsequent work by Manna and Pnueli produced still more expressive temporal logics. In [Manna & Pnueli 81a], a temporal logic is described having universal and existential quantification over rigid variables as well as (future) temporal operators $\Box$, $\Diamond$, $\bigcirc$, and until. In [Lichtenstein et al. 85], a propositional temporal logic with past in addition to future operators is described. A temporal logic that extends Predicate Logic with both past and future operators is given in [Manna & Pnueli 92] and [Manna & Pnueli 95].

Branching time and linear time are distinguished in [Rescher & Urquhart 71]. The ramifications of this distinction for reasoning about concurrent and nondeterministic programs were first explored by Lamport [Lamport 80a]. This initiated a long and heated debate (e.g., [Ben-Ari et al. 81], [Emerson & Halpern 83], and others) about the virtues of branching-time and linear-time temporal logics. Among the most popular branching-time logics is CTL [Emerson & Clarke 81], which is an extension of UB defined in [Ben-Ari et al. 81].

With linear-time Temporal Logics, two kinds of interpretations are popular. The first is for interpretations to be sequences of states. This is called the *floating interpretation* and, until 1989, it was favored. A second popular interpretation is the anchored sequences used in this chapter; anchored sequences were introduced in [Manna & Pnueli 89] and later used in [Manna & Pnueli 92] and [Manna & Pnueli 95]. The floating interpretation is appealing because it allows an intuitive definition of property—as a set of sequences of program states—to be equated with sets of models for Temporal Logic formulas. Anchored sequences, however, lead to a simpler and more uniform handling of formulas with the past extensions of Chapter 7. The same Temporal Logic axiomatization works for both the floating interpretation and anchored sequences.

Another issue that has been debated concerns what temporal operators to include when defining a temporal logic. In [Lamport 80a] and later in [Lamport 83a], the virtues of limiting the expressiveness of the logic are argued. Lamport contends that the ○ operator should be avoided, claiming that a temporal logic being used for specification should be able to express only properties that are invariant under stuttering. In [Lamport 83a], Lamport also explains why specifications should be written using a logic that has existential quantification over functions. However, temporal logic based specification methods without such second-order quantification are described in [Schwartz & Melliar-Smith 81] and [Hailpern 82].

Three general methods for proving that a program $S$ satisfies a temporal logic property $P$ have been investigated over the years. The first, discussed in [Pnueli 79], is to construct a temporal logic formula $TL(S)$ that describes histories of $S$ and then to prove $TL(S) \Rightarrow P$. As mentioned in §3.4, this method is impractical for nontrivial programs because it can result in formulas that are unwieldy to manipulate. A second method, described in [Manna & Pnueli 81b], avoids these difficulties. In this method, in order to prove that $S$ satisfies $P$, $P$ is proved $R$-valid, where $R$ consists of histories of $S$. The third method, similar to the one based on $\mathcal{H}_S^+$-validity, is discussed in [Lamport 80a]. In [Owicki & Lamport 82], axioms and inference rules for such a logic are given, and the logic is used to formalize the concurrent-program verification principles introduced in [Lamport 77a].

Our Temporal Logic is based on an axiomatization that appears in the appendix of [Gabbay et al. 80]. However, the style of presentation and material in §3.2 and §3.3 are derived from [Manna & Pnueli 81c]. The discussion in §3.5 about modal logics is based on [Lamport 80a], [Manna & Pnueli 81a], and [Hughes & Cresswell 68]. Exercises 3.7, 3.8, and 3.10 were inspired by various temporal logic axiomatizations of Manna and Pnueli; exercises 3.18 and 3.20 are based on [Sistla 85].

The reader interested in learning about issues of concern to logicians and philosophers that are raised and resolved by different temporal logics is urged to consult [Gabbay et al. 94], [Prior 67], and [Rescher & Urquhart 71]. See [Hughes & Cresswell 68] for an introduction to modal logic, including axiomatizations of some temporal logics. Textbooks and monographs covering use of temporal logic for specifying and reasoning about concurrent programs include [Goldblatt 87], [Kroger 87], [Manna & Pnueli 92], and [Manna & Pnueli 95]. Kroger's book reformulates Manna and Pnueli's early work ([Manna & Pnueli 81a], [Manna & Pnueli 81b], and [Manna & Pnueli 81c]), but using temporal operator *atnext* [Kroger 84] rather than the until operator. The volumes by Manna and Pnueli give a temporal logic with past and future operators.

## Exercises

**3.1.** Give Temporal Logic formalizations for each of the following properties.

(a) As long as $x$ is 3, $y$ is non-negative.

(b) Every state in which $x$ is 3 is followed immediately by a state in which $y$ is 4.

(c) Every state in which $x$ is 3 is preceded by a state in which $y$ is 4.

(d) The value of $x$ remains 3 until $y$ becomes 4.

(e) Just before $x$ equals 3 for the first time, $y$ equals 4.

(f) At some point, $x$ will be 3, $y$ will be 4, or there will be five successive states in which $z$ will be 5.

(g)     At some point, $x$ will be 3, $y$ will be 4, or there will be five not necessarily successive states in which $z$ will be 5.

(h)     The value of $x$ never exceeds its initial value.

**3.2.** Define suitable predicate symbols and then give Temporal Logic formalizations for each of the following properties.

(a)     Once the dragon was slain, the princess lived happily ever after.

(b)     The dragon was struck repeatedly until it died.

(c)     If she returned before midnight, then all would be well.

(d)     Some enchanted evening, you will meet a stranger.

(e)     It might happen again, but not after that.

(f)     It will not happen again.

(g)     It will not ever happen.

(h)     It ain't necessarily so.

(i)     Après moi, le déluge.

(j)     If at first you don't succeed, try, try again.

(k)     Remain seated until the plane comes to a complete halt.

**3.3.** For each of the following Temporal Logic formulas, either prove the formula a theorem or describe an anchored sequence that does not satisfy the formula.

(a)     $P \Rightarrow \Box P$

(b)     $(\Box P \Rightarrow \Box Q) \Rightarrow \Box(P \Rightarrow Q)$

(c)     $\Box P = (P \wedge \bigcirc \Box P)$

(d)     $\Box P = (P \vee \bigcirc \Diamond P)$

(e)     $\Diamond P \Rightarrow P$

(f)     $\Diamond P \Rightarrow \Box P$

(g)     $\Box \Diamond P \Rightarrow \Diamond \Box P$

(h)     $(\Diamond P \Rightarrow \Diamond Q) \Rightarrow \Box(P \Rightarrow Q)$

(i)     $\Diamond(P \wedge Q) \Rightarrow \Box P \wedge \Diamond Q$

(j)     $\Diamond P \wedge \Diamond Q \Rightarrow \Diamond(P \wedge Q)$

(k)     $(\bigcirc P \Rightarrow \bigcirc Q) \Rightarrow \bigcirc(P \Rightarrow Q)$

(l)     $\bigcirc P \Rightarrow \Box P$

(m)     $(P \Rightarrow \Box P) \Rightarrow \Box(P \Rightarrow \bigcirc P)$

(n)     $P \,\mathcal{U}\, Q \Rightarrow \Box P$

(o)     $P \,\mathcal{U}\, Q \Rightarrow \Diamond Q$

(p)     $\Box P \vee \Diamond Q \Rightarrow P \,\mathcal{U}\, Q$

(q)     $\Box P \Rightarrow (P \,\mathcal{U}\, Q \wedge \Box \neg Q)$

(r)     $\Diamond Q \Rightarrow (P \,\mathcal{U}\, Q \wedge \neg \Box P)$

(r)     $(P \vee Q)\,\mathcal{U}\,R \Rightarrow (P \,\mathcal{U}\, Q)\,\mathcal{U}\,R$

(s)   $(P \lor Q)\mathcal{U}R \Rightarrow P\mathcal{U}(Q\mathcal{U}R)$

(t)   $(P \land Q)\mathcal{U}(P \land R) \Rightarrow \Box P \land (Q\mathcal{U}R)$

(u)   $(P\mathcal{U}Q) \land (P\mathcal{U}R) \Rightarrow P\mathcal{U}(Q \land R)$

(v)   $(P \lor Q)\mathcal{U}R \Rightarrow (P\mathcal{U}R) \lor (Q\mathcal{U}R)$

(w)   $((P\mathcal{U}R) \Rightarrow (Q\mathcal{U}R)) \Rightarrow (P \Rightarrow Q)\mathcal{U}R$

(x)   $(\neg P\mathcal{U}Q) \lor (\neg Q\mathcal{U}P) \Rightarrow (\Diamond P \lor \Diamond Q)$

(y)   $P\mathcal{U}R \Rightarrow (P\mathcal{U}Q \land \neg Q\mathcal{U}R)$

(z)   $(P\mathcal{U}Q)\mathcal{U}R \Rightarrow P\mathcal{U}(Q \land R)$

**3.4.** For each of the following Temporal Logic formulas, either prove the formula a theorem or describe an anchored sequence that does not satisfy the formula.

(a)   $\bigcirc P \Rightarrow \Diamond P$

(b)   $\Box \bigcirc P = \bigcirc \Box P$

(c)   $\Diamond \bigcirc P = \bigcirc \Diamond P$

(d)   $\bigcirc(P \land Q) = (\bigcirc P \land \bigcirc Q)$

(e)   $\bigcirc(P \lor Q) = (\bigcirc P \lor \bigcirc Q)$

(f)   $\bigcirc(P \Rightarrow Q) = (\bigcirc P \Rightarrow \bigcirc Q)$

(g)   $\Box(P \Rightarrow Q) \Rightarrow (\bigcirc P \Rightarrow \bigcirc Q)$

(h)   $(\Box P \land \bigcirc Q) \Rightarrow \bigcirc(P \land Q)$

(i)   $(P \land \Diamond \neg P) \Rightarrow \Diamond(P \land \bigcirc \neg P)$

(j)   $(P \Rightarrow Q) \Rightarrow (\bigcirc P \Rightarrow \bigcirc Q)$

(k)   $(P \land \bigcirc Q) \Rightarrow (P\mathcal{U}Q)$

(l)   $\Diamond P \lor \Box \neg P$

**3.5.** Prove the following Temporal Logic theorems, using only axioms and inference rules of Temporal Logic (but using none of the laws or derived inference rules).

(a)   $\Box$ Distributive Laws (3.12a) and (3.12b)

(b)   $\Diamond$ Laws (3.16a) through (3.16h)

(c)   $\Diamond$ Distributive Laws (3.17a) and (3.17f)

(d)   Absorption Laws (3.18a) through (3.18d)

(e)   $\bigcirc$ Laws (3.22a) through (3.22e)

(f)   $\mathcal{U}$ Insertion Law (3.28)

(g)   $\Box$ to $\mathcal{U}$ Law (3.29)

(h)   $\Diamond$ to $\mathcal{U}$ Law (3.30)

(i)   $\mathcal{U}$ Entailment Laws (3.31a) through (3.31c)

(j)   $\mathcal{U}$ Absorption Laws (3.32a) through (3.32d)

(k)   $\mathcal{U}$ Distributive Laws (3.33a) through (3.33g)

(l)   $\mathcal{U}$ Ordering Laws (3.34a) through (3.34c)

**3.6.** Justify the following derived inference rules of Temporal Logic by regarding the premises as axioms and giving a proof of the conclusion.

(a)    □ Consequence Rule (3.14)

(b)    □ Catenation Rule (3.14)

(c)    ◇ Consequence Rule (3.19)

(d)    ◇ Catenation Rule (3.20)

(e)    TL Substitution of Equals (3.70)

(f)    ○ Consequence Rule (3.23)

(g)    Computational Induction Rule (3.24a)

(h)    Computational Induction Rule (3.24b)

(i)    $\dfrac{P}{\bigcirc P}$

(j)    $\dfrac{P}{\diamondsuit P}$

(k)    $\dfrac{P \Rightarrow Q}{\Box P \Rightarrow \Box Q}$

(l)    Well-Founded ◇ Induction Rule (3.68)

(m)    Natural Number ◇ Induction Rule (3.69)

**3.7.** Suppose we replace □ Axioms (3.10a) and (3.10b), ◇ Axiom (3.15), ○ Axioms (3.21a) through (3.21e), and $\mathcal{U}$ Axioms (3.27a) and (3.27b), by the following.

$$A1: \quad \Box P = P\,\mathcal{U}\,false$$
$$A2: \quad \diamondsuit P = \neg\Box\neg P$$
$$A3: \quad \Box(P \Rightarrow Q) \Rightarrow (\Box P \Rightarrow \Box Q)$$
$$A4: \quad \bigcirc\neg P = \neg\bigcirc P$$
$$A5: \quad \bigcirc(P \Rightarrow Q) \Rightarrow (\bigcirc P \Rightarrow \bigcirc Q)$$
$$A6: \quad \Box P \Rightarrow \bigcirc P$$
$$A7: \quad \Box(P \Rightarrow \bigcirc P) \Rightarrow (P \Rightarrow \Box P)$$
$$A8: \quad P\,\mathcal{U}\,Q = (Q \vee (P \wedge \bigcirc(P\,\mathcal{U}\,Q)))$$
$$A9: \quad \Box P \Rightarrow (P\,\mathcal{U}\,Q)$$

(a)    Show that each of the old axioms is a theorem of this alternative axiomatization.

(b)    Show that each of $A1$ through $A9$ is a theorem of the axiomatization given in §3.3.

**3.8.** The U temporal operator (read "until") can be defined by:

$$(PUQ) = ((P\,\mathcal{U}\,Q) \wedge \diamondsuit Q)$$

Consider a temporal logic that includes this operator, along with the other temporal operators defined in §3.2.

(a)    Explain how to augment Interpreting Temporal Logic Formulas (3.4) to handle formulas including U.

(b)   Show how to translate $\Diamond P$ into a formula involving $\mathbf{U}$ and $P$.

(c)   Show how to translate $\Box P$ into a formula involving $\mathbf{U}$ and $P$.

(d)   What additional axioms or inference rules must be added to §3.3 in order to obtain a sound and complete axiomatization for the extended logic?

**3.9.** The claim was made in connection with Absorption Laws (3.18) that any sequence of $\Box$ and $\Diamond$ operators is equivalent to a sequence consisting of at most two of these operators.

(a)   Justify this claim by giving a procedure to transform any Temporal Logic formula into an equivalent one that contains only minimal-length sequences of $\Box$ and $\Diamond$ operators.

(b)   Explain how to modify this procedure to produce a proof that its input formula is equivalent to its output.

**3.10.** Give Temporal Logic proofs for the laws in §3.3 concerning rigid variables and rigid-variable quantified expressions. Your proofs should use only the axioms and inference rules given in §3.3 and the following axioms and inference rule for reasoning about rigid variables.

> $A1$: $\neg(\exists X\colon R\colon Q) = (\forall X\colon R\colon \neg Q)$
>
> $A2$: If $X$ does not occur free in $e$ and $e$ is rigidly free for $X$ in $R \Rightarrow Q$, then:
> $$(\forall X\colon R\colon Q) \Rightarrow (R \Rightarrow Q)_e^X$$
>
> $A3$: $(\forall X\colon \bigcirc P) = \bigcirc(\forall X\colon P)$
>
> $A4$: If $P$ has no free flexible variables. then:
> $$P \Rightarrow \bigcirc P$$
>
> $R$:   Provided that $X$ does not occur free in $P$:
> $$\frac{P \Rightarrow Q}{P \Rightarrow (\forall X\colon Q)}$$

**3.11.** For each of the following, indicate whether the result is a well-founded set. If it is not well-founded, then describe an infinite descending chain.

(a)   The set of integer finite subsets, where the binary ordering relation is $\subset$.

(b)   The set of sequences of unsigned integers, where the binary ordering relation is $<$.

(c)   The set of sequences of Greek letters, where the binary ordering relation is alphabetic ordering.

(d)   The set of finite binary trees, where the binary ordering relation is "subtree of."

(e)   The set of finite and infinite binary trees, where the binary ordering relation is "subtree of."

**3.12.** Show that if R does not occur free in $P$, then proving the premise of Well-Founded Induction Rule (3.67) requires proving $P$.

**3.13.** The deduction metatheorem for Temporal Logic asserts:
$$\vdash(\Box P \Rightarrow Q) \text{ if } P \vdash Q$$

Give a procedure to transform any proof of $Q$ from an assumption $P$ into a proof of $\Box P \Rightarrow Q$ using no assumptions. (Hint: Transform the original proof one line at a time, starting from the first line.)

**3.14.** Substitution Equivalence Law (2.76) of Predicate Logic, $(e_1 = e_2) \Rightarrow (P^x_{e_1} = P^x_{e_2})$, is not sound for $P$ a Temporal Logic formula.

(a)   Give an example that illustrates that the law can be unsound.

(b)   Give a Temporal Logic formula $Q(A, B)$ involving terms $A$ and $B$ that makes the following law valid in a nontrivial way:
$$Q(A, B) \Rightarrow (P^x_A = P^x_B)$$

**3.15.** Prove Property-Formula Correspondence (3.74a) through (3.74c) when the formal definition of $\{P\}$ is:
$$\{P\}: \ \{(\sigma, j) | P\}$$

**3.16.** Assume that you are given $TL(S)$ and $TL(T)$ for statements $S$ and $T$ of some programming notation. Give $TL(U)$ for each of the following; the statements are executed as in Pascal.

(a)   $U$:  $S; T$

(b)   $U$:  **if** $x > 0$ **then** $S$ **else** $T$ **fi**

(c)   $U$:  **while** $x > 0$ **do** $S$ **od**

(d)   $U$:  **repeat** $S$ **until** $x > 0$

**3.17.** Give a proof of $TL(S) \Rightarrow P$, where $TL(S)$ is defined by (3.79) and $P$ is:

(a)   $x \geq y \Rightarrow \Box(x \geq y)$

(b)   $x = y \Rightarrow \bigcirc(x > y)$

(c)   $even(x) \Rightarrow \Box even(x)$

**3.18.** For Temporal Logic formulas $P$ and $Q$ that define safety properties according to Safety Property (2.105), determine whether

(a)   $\{\Box P\}$ necessarily also satisfies Safety Property (2.105).

(b)   $\{\Diamond P\}$ necessarily also satisfies Safety Property (2.105).

(c)   $\{\bigcirc P\}$ necessarily also satisfies Safety Property (2.105).

(d)   $\{P \mathcal{U} Q\}$ necessarily also satisfies Safety Property (2.105).

**3.19.** For Temporal Logic formulas $P$ and $Q$ that define liveness properties according to Liveness Property (2.106), determine whether

(a)   $\{\Box P\}$ necessarily also satisfies Liveness Property (2.106).

(b)   $\{\Diamond P\}$ necessarily also satisfies Liveness Property (2.106).

(c)   $\{\bigcirc P\}$ necessarily also satisfies Liveness Property (2.106).

(d)   $\{P \mathcal{U} Q\}$ necessarily also satisfies Liveness Property (2.106).

**3.20.** Prove that for a Temporal Logic formula $P$, if $P = \Diamond P$ is valid then $\{P\}$ satisfies Liveness Property (2.106).

**3.21.** (a)   Can a Temporal Logic formula that does not contain a ○ operator define a property that is not invariant under stuttering? (See exercise 2.26 for the definition of invariant under stuttering.)

(b)   Can a Temporal Logic formula that defines a property that is not invariant under stuttering contain a ○ operator?

**3.22.** Determine whether each of the following is valid in a modal logic having an accessibility relation that is reflexive, symmetric, and transitive.

(a)   $\Box\Diamond P = \Diamond P$

(b)   $\Diamond\Box P = \Box P$

**3.23.** Give a modal logic axiom for each proposed property of accessibility relation $\mathcal{R}$:

(a)   For all $u, w$: $(u\mathcal{R}w \Rightarrow w\mathcal{R}u)$

(b)   For all $u$:  Exists $w$:  $u\mathcal{R}w$

(c)   For all $u, w, v$: $((u\mathcal{R}w \wedge u\mathcal{R}v) \Rightarrow w\mathcal{R}v)$

(d)   For all $u, w, v$: $((u\mathcal{R}w \wedge u\mathcal{R}v) \Rightarrow w=v)$

**3.24.** State what property each of the following modal logic axioms implies about accessibility relation $\mathcal{R}$.

(a)   $P \Rightarrow \Box\Diamond P$

(b)   $\Diamond P \Rightarrow \Box\Diamond P$

(c)   $\Box(P \wedge \Box Q \Rightarrow Q) \vee \Box(Q \wedge \Box Q \Rightarrow P)$

(d)   $\Diamond\Box P \Rightarrow \Box\Diamond P$

# Chapter 4

# Notation and Logic
# for Sequential Programming

In order to reason about concurrent programs, one must first be able to reason about their component sequential programs. In this chapter, we describe a sequential programming notation and a logic for reasoning about programs written in the notation. The logic is obtained by extending Predicate Logic with a new type of formula, the proof outline. We also present a calculus to aid in deriving a proof outline along with a program.

## 4.1  Notation for Sequential Programs

In our programming notation, a *program* consists of declarations followed by statements. The *declarations* introduce program variables and associate a type with each. The *statements* define sets of atomic actions. Consequently, a program defines a set of program states and a set of atomic actions. Each *program state* assigns a value of the correct type to the program variables and contains control information to indicate which atomic actions might next execute.

Associated with every program $S$ is also a set of *initial* program states, characterized by a Predicate Logic formula $Init_S$. Initial program states assign unspecified but type-correct values to the program variables. In addition, the control information in these states ensures that execution will begin with the first statement of the program.

### Declarations and Variables

The syntax of a declaration is:

$$\textbf{var } \overline{id}_1 : type_1; \quad \overline{id}_2 : type_2; \quad \cdots \quad \overline{id}_n : type_n$$

Each $\overline{id}_i$ is a list of distinct identifiers, separated by commas. Each $type_i$ is a type

| Type | Example Declaration |
|---|---|
| **enum**( $C_1, C_2, ..., C_n$ ) | *day* : **enum**( *Su, M, T, W, Th, F, Sa* ) |
| **set of** *type* | *primes* : **set of** Nat |
| **seq of** *type* | *name* : **seq of** Char |
| **array** $[a_1 .. b_1,$ <br> $\quad a_2 .. b_2,$ <br> $\quad \cdots$ <br> $\quad a_n .. b_n]$ **of** *type* | $v$ : **array** $[1 .. N]$ **of** Real |
| **record**( $id_1 : type_1;$ <br> $\quad id_2 : type_2;$ <br> $\quad \cdots$ <br> $\quad id_n : type_n$ ) | $q$ : **record**( *strt* : Int; <br> $\quad$ *len* : Int; <br> $\quad$ *elmts* : **array** $[0 .. n]$ **of** Int ) |

**Figure 4.1.** Type constructors

for the variables in $\overline{id_i}$. This type can be Bool, Nat, Int, Rat, Real, or Char (see Figure 2.1), or it can be an enumeration, set, sequence, array, or record, defined using the type constructors in Figure 4.1.

A variable whose type involves the **array** or **record** type constructors is called a *composite variable*, because it has individual components that can be referenced and updated. We use the traditional notation for referencing these components:

- For $a$ an array, $a[i]$ denotes the component of $a$ that is associated with *subscript i*.

- For $r$ a record, $r.id$ denotes the component of $r$ that is associated with *field id*.

## Statements

The execution of a statement consists of executing a sequence of atomic actions, each of which indivisibly transforms the program state. Therefore, we define the semantics of a statement $S$ by giving its atomic actions $\mathcal{A}(S)$ and the effect of each. Statements are constructed using expressions of various kinds. The boolean-valued expressions are a subset of the predicates in our Predicate Logic, and the other expressions are a subset of that logic's terms.

The **skip** statement is a single atomic action whose execution has no effect on any program variable. Its syntax is:

**skip**

The assignment statement is also a single atomic action.[1] Execution of

(4.1)   $x_1, x_2, ..., x_n := e_1, e_2, ..., e_n$

where $x_1, x_2, ..., x_n$ are called *targets*, first computes values for all expressions appearing in the statement (including those in the targets, as in $x[e]$). If (i) any of the $x_i$ is undefined (e.g., $x_i$ is an array reference $x[e]$ and the value of $e$ is outside the range of permissible subscripts) or (ii) the value computed for some expression $e_i$ is not consistent with the type of corresponding target $x_i$, then execution of (4.1) is blocked.[2] Otherwise, execution proceeds by setting $x_1$ to the value computed for $e_1$, then setting $x_2$ to the value computed for $e_2$, and so on.

Statement (4.1) is sometimes called a *multiple assignment statement* because it allows the value of more than one variable to be changed at the same time. For example, $x,y := y,x$ interchanges the values of $x$ and $y$ as a single atomic action. Without a multiple assignment statement, three assignment statements and an additional variable would be required to accomplish this task.

Statement juxtaposition combines two statements $S_1$ and $S_2$ into a new one:

(4.2)   $S_1 \ S_2$

The atomic actions of (4.2) are just the atomic actions of $S_1$ and $S_2$. Execution is performed by executing $S_1$ and, when (and if) it terminates, executing $S_2$.

The syntax of the **if** statement is:

(4.3)   $S$:  **if** $B_1 \to S_1$ [] $B_2 \to S_2$ [] $\cdots$ [] $B_n \to S_n$ **fi**

Each $B_i \to S_i$ is called a *guarded command*. The *guard* $B_i$ is a boolean-valued expression, and $S_i$ is a statement. The atomic actions of $S$ consist of the atomic actions of $S_1$ through $S_n$ and an additional *guard evaluation action*, $GEval_{if}(S)$, which selects one of $S_1$ through $S_n$ for execution. Execution of (4.3) proceeds as follows. First, $GEval_{if}(S)$ is executed. This blocks until at least one of guards $B_1$ through $B_n$ is satisfied. Then some guarded command $B_i \to S_i$ for which guard $B_i$ holds is selected and the corresponding statement $S_i$ is executed.

---

[1]Chapter 9 discusses assignment statements that involve multiple atomic actions.

[2]For example, when $z=0$ holds and $x := y/z$ is executed, some value will be assigned to $x$ if the (unspecified) value of $y/z$ happens to be consistent with the type of $x$; but execution blocks if the value of $y/z$ is not consistent with the type of $x$.

For example, the following program blocks when started in a state where $x = y$ but sets $m$ to $\max(x, y)$ when started in any other state.

**if** $x < y \rightarrow m := y \;\; [] \;\; x > y \rightarrow m := x$ **fi**

The fact that **if** blocks when no guard is *true* might seem troubling. As we will see in Chapter 5, this behavior is useful for expressing synchronization in concurrent programs.

An **if** statement can be *nondeterministic*, meaning that its execution is not completely determined by the state in which it is started, because any guarded command with a *true* guard can be selected for execution. For example,

**if** *true* $\rightarrow x := 1 \;\; [] \;\;$ *true* $\rightarrow x := 2$ **fi**

is nondeterministic and may set $x$ to either 1 or 2.

The **do** statement

(4.4)    $S$:  **do** $B_1 \rightarrow S_1 \;\; [] \;\; B_2 \rightarrow S_2 \;\; [] \;\; \cdots \;\; [] \;\; B_n \rightarrow S_n$ **od**

is used to specify iteration. Its atomic actions are the atomic actions of $S_1$ through $S_n$ plus a guard evaluation action $GEval_{do}(S)$. Execution of (4.4) consists of repeating the following until no *true* guard is found: use $GEval_{do}(S)$ to select a guarded command $B_i \rightarrow S_i$ where $B_i$ is *true*; then, $S_i$ is executed. Note that a different statement might be selected for execution in each repetition.

Occasionally, it is convenient to abbreviate a set of guarded commands in an **if** or **do**. To specify such a set, we write

$\underset{i=1,n}{[]} B \rightarrow S$

where $i$ may occur free in $B$ and $S$, as an abbreviation for the set of guarded commands that result when 1 through $n$ is textually substituted for $i$ in $B \rightarrow S$:

$B_1^i \rightarrow S_1^i \;\; [] \;\; B_2^i \rightarrow S_2^i \;\; [] \;\; \cdots \;\; [] \;\; B_n^i \rightarrow S_n^i$

Note that $i$ is not a program variable and, because of the textual substitution, does not appear in any of the guarded commands in the expansion. For example,

**do** $\underset{i=1,3}{[]} x = i \rightarrow x := x+i$ **od**

is an abbreviation for:

**do** $x=1 \rightarrow x := x+1 \;\; [] \;\; x=2 \rightarrow x := x+2 \;\; [] \;\; x=3 \rightarrow x := x+3$ **od**

## Statement Labels

A label $L$ is associated with a statement by prefixing the statement with $L$ followed by a colon. We use indentation and sometimes a bracket to indicate that a label is associated with the statement resulting from a juxtaposition of two or more statements. For example, in the program of Figure 4.2, indentation is used to indicate that $S_3$ labels the statement juxtaposition formed from the **if** labeled $S_4$ and the assignment statement labeled $S_7$. In the program of Figure 4.6, a bracket is used to associate label $T$ with a juxtaposition of three statements.

We assume that every statement in a program has a unique label. This said, Figure 4.2 illustrates how the inclusion of such labels can result in program texts that are cluttered. Therefore, we often omit statement labels, and when no ambiguity results, we use the text of a statement as a label for that statement.

## 4.2 Reasoning About Program States

The Predicate Logic axiomatization in Chapter 2 must be extended for use in reasoning about program states. Additional axioms, given below, are necessary because the set of program states is a proper subset of the set of all states. The axioms allow us to make inferences based on the types of variables and the correspondence between statement labels and control flow. All of our programming logics are built on this extended Predicate Logic.

### Axioms for Program Variables

The declarations in a program $S$ give rise to a set $VarAx(S)$ of Predicate Logic axioms called *program variable axioms*. These axioms rule out states in which variables have values that are not type-correct. For example, the declarations in the program of Figure 4.2 imply that the following holds for all program states:

(4.5)   $i \in \text{Int} \;\wedge\; m \in \text{Real} \;\wedge\; (\forall e \in \text{Int}: 0 \le e \le n: a[e] \in \text{Real})$

---

**var** $i$ : Int;   $m$ : Real;   $a$ : **array** $[0..n]$ **of** Real

$S_1$: $i, m := 0, a[0]$
$S_2$: **do** $i \ne n \to$   $S_3$: $S_4$: **if** $a[i+1] \le m \to$   $S_5$: **skip**
$\qquad\qquad\qquad\qquad\qquad$ [] $a[i+1] > m \to$   $S_6$: $m := a[i+1]$
$\qquad\qquad\qquad\qquad$ **fi**
$\qquad\qquad\qquad$ $S_7$: $i := i+1$
$\quad$ **od**

**Figure 4.2.** Maximum element of an array

Given an arbitrary program $S$ written in the notation of §4.1, we construct set $VarAx(S)$ as follows.

(4.6)  **Program Variable Axioms.** $VarAx(S)$ is the union of $ValAx(v, t)$ for every program variable $v$ declared in $S$, where $t$ is its type. $ValAx(v, t)$, which is based on type $t$, is defined in Figure 4.3.                            □

The source of (4.5) should now be clear—each conjunct is a program variable axiom. We obtain $i \in$ Int from the declaration of $i$, $m \in$ Real from the declaration of $m$, and $(\forall e \in \text{Int}: 0 \le e \le n: a[e] \in \text{Real})$ from the declaration of $a$.

## Control Predicate Axioms

We now turn to the portion of the state that encodes control information. The *control points* of a program are defined by its atomic actions. Each atomic action has distinct *entry control points* and *exit control points*. For example, the atomic action that implements **skip** has a single entry control point and a single exit control point; a guard evaluation action $GEval_{if}(S)$ is an atomic action having one entry control point and multiple exit control points—one exit control point for each guarded command in $S$.

| type | $ValAx(v, type)$ |
|------|------------------|
| Bool, Nat, Int, Rat, Real, Char | $v \in type$ |
| **enum**$( C_1, C_2, ..., C_n )$ | $v \in \{C_1, C_2, ..., C_n\}$ |
| **set of** *type* | $v \subseteq type$ |
| **seq of** *type* | $(\forall i \in \text{Int}: 0 \le i < |v|: ValAx(v[i], type))$ |
| **array** $[a_1 .. b_1,$ $a_2 .. b_2,$ $\cdots$ $a_n .. b_n]$ **of** *type* | $(\forall e_1 \in \text{Int}, e_2 \in \text{Int}, \cdots, e_n \in \text{Int}:$ $a_1 \le e_1 \le b_1 \wedge a_2 \le e_2 \le b_2 \wedge \cdots \wedge a_n \le e_n \le b_n:$ $ValAx(v[e_1, e_2, ..., e_n], type))$ |
| **record**$( id_1 : type_1;$ $id_2 : type_2;$ $\cdots$ $id_n : type_n )$ | $ValAx(v.id_1, type_1)$ $\wedge ValAx(v.id_2, type_2)$ $\cdots$ $\wedge ValAx(v.id_n, type_n)$ |

**Figure 4.3.** Definition of $ValAx(v, t)$

Execution of an atomic action α can occur only when an entry control point for α is *active*. Among other things, execution causes that active entry control point to become inactive and an exit control point of α to become active. The program state usually encodes which control points are active by representing the information in (implicit) variables, called *program counters*, each of which ranges over some subset of the control points.

The set of control points associated with a statement $S$ is the set of control points associated with the elements of $\mathcal{A}(S)$. A subset of these control points are considered the entry control points for $S$, and a disjoint subset are considered its exit control points. For example, the statement

$$T: \textbf{if } x \leq y \rightarrow m := y \; [] \; x \geq y \rightarrow m := x \; \textbf{fi}$$

has three atomic actions: a guard evaluation action $GEval_{if}(T)$, $m := y$, and $m := x$. The semantics we will ascribe to this statement defines the entry control point for $GEval_{if}(T)$ to be the sole entry control point of $T$ and defines the exit control point for $m := y$ and the exit control point for $m := x$ to be the exit control points for $T$.

In specifying and proving properties of programs, three *control predicates* for each $S$ an atomic action or statement will be useful:

$at(S)$:      an entry control point of $S$ is active.

$after(S)$:   an exit control point of $S$ is active.

$in(S)$:      $at(T)$ holds for some $T \in \mathcal{A}(S)$.

To reason about formulas containing control predicates, we extend Predicate Logic with additional axioms, called *control predicate axioms*. These axioms formalize how the control predicates for a statement or atomic action $S$ relate to the control predicates for constructs that make up $S$ and constructs containing $S$, based on the control flow defined by $S$. The axioms also characterize the entry and exit control points for each $S$ by defining $at(S)$ and $after(S)$. Like the program variable axioms, the control predicate axioms are satisfied by all program states. In fact, the program variable axioms and control predicate axioms completely characterize the set of program states.

In the following, we use operator $\oplus$ (with the same precedence as $\vee$) to denote *n*-way exclusive-or, so that predicate

$$P_1 \oplus P_2 \oplus \; \cdots \; \oplus P_n$$

is *true* when exactly one of $P_1$ through $P_n$ is. For example, $in(S) \oplus after(S)$ asserts that either a control point corresponding to $in(S)$ or one corresponding to $after(S)$ is active, but not both. Note that $P_1 \oplus (P_2 \oplus P_3)$ and $P_1 \oplus P_2 \oplus P_3$ are not equivalent. The first involves two 2-way exclusive-ors and is satisfied if $P_1$, $P_2$, and $P_3$ all hold; the second involves one 3-way exclusive-or and is satisfied only when exactly one of $P_1$, $P_2$, and $P_3$ holds.

We start with some general axioms. The first two are a direct consequence of how $in(S)$ is defined.

(4.7)  *In Axioms*:  (a) $at(S) \Rightarrow in(S)$

(b) For $\mathcal{A}(S)$ containing a single atomic action:  $at(S) = in(S)$


The next axiom asserts that an exit control point for $T$ cannot be active at the same time as an entry control point for $T$ or any of its components.

(4.8)  *Entry/Exit Axiom*:  $\neg(in(T) \wedge after(T))$


Finally, initial states of a program $S$ (say) satisfy $at(S)$, so we conclude axiom (a) below—that $Init_S$ implies $at(S)$. In addition, every state produced during execution of an entire program $S$ satisfies one of the following: (i) $S$ has not yet started, (ii) $S$ has started but not terminated, or (iii) $S$ has terminated. If $S$ has not yet started, then $at(S)$ holds; if $S$ has started but not terminated, then $in(S)$ holds; and if $S$ has terminated, then $after(S)$ holds. This allows us to conclude (b) below.

(4.9)  *Program Control Axioms*:  (a) $Init_S \Rightarrow at(S)$

(b) For $S$ the entire program:  $in(S) \oplus after(S)$


The control predicate axioms for a statement juxtaposition $S_1\ S_2$ (a) define its entry control points, (b) define its exit control points, (c) assert that every exit control point of $S_1$ is an entry control point of $S_2$, (d) define $in(S)$, and (e) assert that control points satisfying $in(S_1)$, $in(S_2)$, and $after(S)$ cannot all be active at the same time.

(4.10)  *Statement Juxtaposition Control Axioms*:  For $S$ the juxtaposition $S_1\ S_2$:

(a) $at(S) = at(S_1)$
(b) $after(S) = after(S_2)$
(c) $after(S_1) = at(S_2)$
(d) $in(S) = (in(S_1) \vee in(S_2))$
(e) $in(S) \vee after(S) \Rightarrow in(S_1) \oplus in(S_2) \oplus after(S)$


The axioms for an **if** statement $S$ (a) define its entry control point, (b) define its exit control points, (c) assert that each exit control point for $GEval_{if}(S)$ is an entry control point for the statement in some guarded command, (d) define $in(S)$, and (e) prevent several control points from being active simultaneously.

(4.11)  **if** *Control Axioms*:  For an **if** statement:

$$S: \textbf{if } B_1 \rightarrow S_1 \ [] \ B_2 \rightarrow S_2 \ [] \ \cdots \ [] \ B_n \rightarrow S_n \ \textbf{fi}$$

(a) $at(S) = at(GEval_{if}(S))$
(b) $after(S) = (after(S_1) \vee after(S_2) \vee \cdots \vee after(S_n))$

(c) $after(GEval_{if}(S)) = (at(S_1) \vee at(S_2) \vee \cdots \vee at(S_n))$
(d) $in(S) = (in(GEval_{if}(S)) \vee in(S_1) \vee in(S_2) \vee \cdots \vee in(S_n))$
(e) $in(S) \vee after(S) \Rightarrow in(GEval_{if}(S)) \oplus in(S_1) \oplus in(S_2) \oplus \cdots \oplus in(S_n)$
    $\oplus after(S_1) \oplus after(S_2) \oplus \cdots \oplus after(S_n)$

The control predicate axioms for a **do** statement $S$ (a) define the entry control points for $GEval_{do}(S)$, (b) assert that at most one of these is active, (c) define the exit control points for $GEval_{do}(S)$, (d) assert that at most one of these is active, (e) define $in(S)$, and (f) prevent several control points from being active simultaneously.

(4.12) **do** *Control Axioms*: For a **do** statement:

$$S: \textbf{do } B_1 \rightarrow S_1 \quad [] \quad B_2 \rightarrow S_2 \quad [] \quad \cdots \quad [] \quad B_n \rightarrow S_n \textbf{ od}$$

(a) $at(GEval_{do}(S)) = (at(S) \vee after(S_1) \vee after(S_2) \vee \cdots \vee after(S_n))$
(b) $at(GEval_{do}(S)) \Rightarrow (at(S) \oplus after(S_1) \oplus after(S_2) \oplus \cdots \oplus after(S_n))$
(c) $after(GEval_{do}(S)) = (after(S) \vee at(S_1) \vee at(S_2) \vee \cdots \vee at(S_n))$
(d) $after(GEval_{do}(S)) \Rightarrow (after(S) \oplus at(S_1) \oplus at(S_2) \oplus \cdots \oplus at(S_n))$
(e) $in(S) = (in(GEval_{do}(S)) \vee in(S_1) \vee \cdots \vee in(S_n))$
(f) $in(S) \vee after(S) \Rightarrow in(GEval_{if}(S)) \oplus in(S_1) \oplus in(S_2) \oplus \cdots \oplus in(S_n)$
    $\oplus after(S)$

To illustrate the use of these control predicate axioms, we prove that $at(S_5) \Rightarrow \neg at(S_6)$ holds in all program states of the program in Figure 4.2.

$\quad at(S_5)$
$=\qquad$ «In Axiom (4.7b)»
$\quad in(S_5)$
$\Rightarrow\qquad$ «**if** Control Axiom (4.11d)»
$\quad in(S_5) \wedge in(S_4)$
$\Rightarrow\qquad$ «**if** Control Axiom (4.11e)»
$\quad \neg in(S_6)$
$=\qquad$ «In Axiom (4.7b)»
$\quad \neg at(S_6)$

## 4.3  Proof Outline Logic

Ultimately, we would like to be able to determine whether a given program satisfies any property that can be specified as a Temporal Logic formula. To start out, we define a logic, called *Proof Outline Logic*, that can be used to solve this problem for a restricted but important class of safety properties. In subsequent chapters, Proof Outline Logic is integrated with Temporal Logic.

## Syntax of Proof Outlines

The formulas of Proof Outline Logic include Predicate Logic formulas and proof outlines. A *proof outline* $PO(S)$ for a program statement or atomic action $S$ is the text of $S$ annotated with an assertion, enclosed in braces ("{" and "}"), before and after $S$ as well as before and after each statement in $S$. Figure 4.4 is an example. A *triple* is a proof outline $\{P\}\ S\ \{Q\}$ in which the only assertions are the one that precedes $S$ and the one that follows $S$.

An *assertion* is a Predicate Logic formula in which

- free variables are program variables and rigid variables and

- all predicates are control predicates or predicates defined by the types of the program variables.

Assertions that depend only on the values of program variables in the current state are called *primitive*. Thus, a primitive assertion may not mention control predicates either explicitly or in clauses of derived terms named in the assertion. For example, in the proof outline of Figure 4.4, $x$ is a program variable, X is a rigid variable, and all assertions except the first and last are primitive.

The assertion that immediately precedes a statement $T$ in a proof outline is called the *precondition* of $T$ and is denoted by $pre(T)$; the assertion that directly follows $T$ is called the *postcondition* of $T$ and is denoted by $post(T)$. For the proof outline in Figure 4.4, this correspondence is summarized in Figure 4.5. Finally, for a proof outline $PO(S)$, we write $pre(PO(S))$ to denote $pre(S)$, $post(PO(S))$ to denote $post(S)$, and we write

(4.13)  $\{P\}\ PO(S)\ \{Q\}$

to specify the proof outline in which $pre(S)$ is $P$, $post(S)$ is $Q$, and all other pre- and postconditions are the same as in $PO(S)$.

---

$$\{x=X \land at(S)\}$$
$$S:\ \textbf{if } x \geq 0 \rightarrow \{x=X \land x \geq 0\}$$
$$S_1:\ \textbf{skip}$$
$$\{x=abs(X)\}$$
$$[]\ x \leq 0 \rightarrow \{x=X \land x \leq 0\}$$
$$S_2:\ x := -x$$
$$\{x=abs(X)\}$$
$$\textbf{fi}$$
$$\{x=abs(X) \land after(S)\}$$

**Figure 4.4.** Computing $abs(x)$

| Assertion | Assertion Text |
|-----------|----------------|
| $pre(S)$ | $x=X \wedge at(S)$ |
| $post(S)$ | $x=abs(X) \wedge after(S)$ |
| $pre(S_1)$ | $x=X \wedge x \geq 0$ |
| $post(S_1)$ | $x=abs(X)$ |
| $pre(S_2)$ | $x=X \wedge x \leq 0$ |
| $post(S_2)$ | $x=abs(X)$ |

**Figure 4.5.** Assertions in a proof outline

## Meaning of Proof Outlines

A proof outline $PO(S)$ associates an assertion $pre(T)$ with control predicate $at(T)$ and an assertion $post(T)$ with control predicate $after(T)$ for every statement $T$ of $S$. The effect is to associate an assertion with the entry and exit control point for each atomic action in $\mathcal{A}(S)$—even though some atomic actions (e.g., guard evaluation actions) are not themselves statements and some statements (e.g., synchronous message-passing statements of §11.2) are not themselves atomic actions.

Assertions are intended to characterize the state as execution proceeds. The proof outline of Figure 4.4, for example, implies that if execution is started at the beginning of $S_1$ with $x=23$ (a state that satisfies $pre(S_1)$), then if $S_1$ terminates, $post(S_1)$ is satisfied by the resulting program state, as is $post(S)$. And if execution is started at the beginning of $S$ with $x=X$, then whatever assertion is next reached—be it $pre(S_1)$ because $X \geq 0$ or $pre(S_2)$ because $X \leq 0$—that assertion will hold when reached, and the next assertion will hold when reached, and so on.

With this in mind, we define a proof outline $PO(S)$ to be valid if it describes a relationship among the program variables and control predicates of $S$ that is invariant and, therefore, is not falsified by execution of $S$. The invariant defined by a proof outline $PO(S)$ is "if a control predicate $cp$ is *true*, then all assertions associated by $PO(S)$ with $cp$ are satisfied"; it is formalized as the *proof outline invariant* for $PO(S)$:

(4.14) $I_{PO(S)}$: $\displaystyle\bigwedge_{T \in Stmts(S)} ((at(T) \Rightarrow pre(T)) \wedge (after(T) \Rightarrow post(T)))$

where $Stmts(S)$ is the set of all statements in program text $S$. For example, the proof outline invariant defined by $PO(S)$ of Figure 4.4 is

$$
\begin{array}{cl}
 & (at(S) \Rightarrow x=X \wedge at(S)) \quad \wedge \quad (after(S) \Rightarrow x=abs(X) \wedge after(S)) \\
\wedge & (at(S_1) \Rightarrow x=X \wedge x \geq 0) \quad \wedge \quad (after(S_1) \Rightarrow x=abs(X)) \\
\wedge & (at(S_2) \Rightarrow x=X \wedge x \leq 0) \quad \wedge \quad (after(S_2) \Rightarrow x=abs(X))
\end{array}
$$

because $Stmts(S)=\{S, S_1, S_2\}$.

Our definition for proof outline validity requires that $I_{PO(S)}$ not be falsified by execution begun in a program state satisfying $I_{PO(S)}$ that could not arise from an initial state. For example,

(4.15)  $\{x=0 \wedge y=0\}$ $S_1$: **skip** $\{x=0\}$ $S_2$: **skip** $\{x=0 \wedge y=0\}$

is *not* valid because execution in a program state satisfying $at(S_2)$, $x=0$, and $y=15$ falsifies the proof outline invariant. The proof outline invariant is falsified because assertion $x=0 \wedge y=0$ does not hold when $after(S_2)$ becomes *true*.

By defining proof outline validity with respect to executions that can start in any program state, we permit reasoning about concurrent programs, because a process can be interrupted and subsequently resumed in a state that it would not have reached uninterrupted and by itself. Provided that the proof outline invariant is satisfied when the process is resumed, subsequent execution by the process will not falsify that invariant.

More than one control predicate can hold in a program state. In (4.15), for example, assertion $x=0 \wedge y=0$ is associated with the control predicates $at(S_1)$ and $at(S_1 S_2)$, both of which hold when the entry control point for $S_1 S_2$ is active. The proof outline in Figure 4.4 illustrates a case where control predicates that hold together are associated with different assertions. If $after(S_1)$ holds, then so does $after(S)$ (due to **if** Control Axiom (4.11b)), but two different assertions ($x=abs(X)$ and $x=abs(X) \wedge after(S)$) are associated by $PO(S)$ with these control predicates.

Our axiomatization of Proof Outline Logic is simplified if the single assertion $pre(PO(S))$ for a valid proof outline $PO(S)$ specifies only states in which $I_{PO(S)}$ is satisfied. Unfortunately, the possibility that multiple assertions can be associated with $at(S)$ causes difficulties. To illustrate, suppose our programming notation contained a **let** statement for declaring local variables whose scope is restricted to a statement $T$:

(4.16)  $S$: **let** *declarations* **in** $T$ **tel**

The control predicate axioms for (4.16) would include $at(S)=at(T)$, since allocation of local variables can be done by a compiler, and therefore no atomic action is executed between the start of $S$ and the start of $T$. Thus, program states that satisfy $at(S)$ also satisfy $at(T)$. In the proof outline of Figure 4.6, however, states satisfying $at(S) \wedge pre(S)$ do not necessarily satisfy $I_{PO(S)}$, because $pre(T)$ is stronger than $pre(S)$.

A proof outline $PO(S)$ is defined to be *self-consistent* if $at(S) \wedge pre(PO(S)) \Rightarrow I_{PO(S)}$ is valid. For example, (4.15) is self-consistent but the proof outline of Figure 4.6 is not. We simply prohibit proof outlines from being valid unless they are self-consistent: a proof outline $PO(S)$ is considered

$\{true\}$
$S:$ **let** $temp$ : Int
   **in** $\{x=3 \wedge y=5\}$
       $T:$ $\begin{bmatrix} temp := y & \{temp=5 \wedge x=3 \wedge y=5\} \\ y := x & \{temp=5 \wedge x=3 \wedge y=3\} \\ x := temp & \{x=5 \wedge y=3\} \end{bmatrix}$
   **tel**
$\{x=5 \wedge y=3\}$

**Figure 4.6.** Swapping $x$ and $y$

---

valid iff $I_{PO(S)}$ (4.14) is an invariant and $PO(S)$ is self-consistent. Formalized in terms of $\mathcal{H}_S^+$-validity[3] of Temporal Logic formulas:

(4.17)  **Valid Proof Outline.**  A proof outline $PO(S)$ is *valid* iff:

   *Self-Consistency:*  $\mathcal{H}_S^+ \vDash (at(S) \wedge pre(PO(S))) \Rightarrow I_{PO(S)})$

   *Invariance:*  $\mathcal{H}_S^+ \vDash (I_{PO(S)} \Rightarrow \Box I_{PO(S)})$                    □

   From this definition of proof outline validity, we infer that rigid variables in proof outlines, like rigid variables in Temporal Logic formulas, relate the values of program variables from one state to the next. This is because there is an implicit universal quantification over the rigid variables in $I_{PO(S)} \Rightarrow \Box I_{PO(S)}$. Thus, that formula is $\mathcal{H}_S^+$-valid iff for any assignment of values to the proof outline's rigid variables, execution of $S$ (i) starts in a state that does not satisfy $I_{PO(S)}$ or (ii) results in a sequence of states that each satisfy $I_{PO(S)}$. Case (i) occurs when the rigid variables are given incorrect values in light of the current values of program variables; case (ii) implies choosing correct values for the rigid variables. For example, the valid proof outline of Figure 4.4 contains a rigid variable X to record the initial value of $x$. Execution in a state where $at(S_2)$ and $x=-23$ hold produces an anchored sequence satisfying $I_{PO(S)} \Rightarrow \Box I_{PO(S)}$, even if $-23$ is not associated with X, because then $I_{PO(S)}$ is *false* (causing $I_{PO(S)} \Rightarrow \Box I_{PO(S)}$ to be satisfied).

   To establish that a proof outline is valid, Self-Consistency and Invariance must be demonstrated. Self-Consistency is not difficult to establish—we prove $at(S) \wedge pre(PO(S)) \Rightarrow I_{PO(S)}$ using our extended Predicate Logic.

   Invariance requires establishing $\mathcal{H}_S^+ \vDash (I_{PO(S)} \Rightarrow \Box I_{PO(S)})$. Since Computational Induction Rule (3.24a) allows us to infer $\mathcal{H}_S^+ \vDash (I_{PO(S)} \Rightarrow \Box I_{PO(S)})$ from $\mathcal{H}_S^+ \vDash (I_{PO(S)} \Rightarrow \bigcirc I_{PO(S)})$, Invariance can be proved by a simplified form of operational reasoning that involves "only" checking the effect of executing each atomic action in every program state. In particular, $\mathcal{H}_S^+ \vDash (I_{PO(S)} \Rightarrow \bigcirc I_{PO(S)})$

---

[3]Recall that $\mathcal{H}_S^+$ is defined by Program-Execution Interpretations (3.81).

follows from showing that if execution of any atomic action $\alpha$ in $\mathcal{A}(S)$ is started in a program state satisfying $I_{PO(S)}$ and $\alpha$ terminates, then the resulting state satisfies $I_{PO(S)}$.

But even the checking required to establish $\mathcal{H}_S^+ \models (I_{PO(S)} \Rightarrow \bigcirc I_{PO(S)})$ is liable to involve lots of tedious work. Therefore, an alternative for demonstrating the validity of a proof outline $PO(S)$ is to employ a logic intended expressly for that purpose. One such logic is given below. The logic eliminates the need for operational reasoning about program execution.

## *Axiomatization*

Proof Outline Logic extends Predicate Logic of §4.2. The axioms and inference rules of ordinary Predicate Logic are extended with program variable axioms and control predicate axioms, as well as axioms and inference rules that allow valid proof outlines and no others to be proved as theorems. We axiomatize proof outlines by giving an axiom or inference rule for **skip**, the assignment statement, statement juxtaposition, **if**, **do**, and the guard evaluation actions, because these are the statements and atomic actions of the programming notation. There are also some statement-independent inference rules. The logic is sound and complete relative to Predicate Logic.

The first axiom of Proof Outline Logic is for **skip**:

(4.18)  **skip** *Axiom*:  For a primitive assertion $P$:  $\{P\}$ **skip** $\{P\}$

The next axiom is for an assignment statement $\overline{x} := \overline{e}$, where $\overline{x}$ is a list $x_1$, $x_2, ..., x_n$ of identifiers (i.e., not elements of records or arrays) and $\overline{e}$ is a list $e_1$, $e_2, ..., e_n$ of expressions[4]:

(4.19)  *Assignment Axiom*:  For a primitive assertion $P$:  $\{P_{\overline{e}}^{\overline{x}}\}\ \overline{x} := \overline{e}\ \{P\}$

A proof outline for the juxtaposition of two statements can be derived from the proof outlines for the statements:

(4.20)  *Statement Juxtaposition Rule*:  $\dfrac{\{P\}\,PO(S_1)\,\{Q\},\quad \{Q\}\,PO(S_2)\,\{R\}}{\{P\}\,PO(S_1)\,\{Q\}\,PO(S_2)\,\{R\}}$

The guard evaluation action for an **if** ensures that the appropriate statement is selected for execution. This is reflected in the following axiom:

---

[4]An axiom for assignment statements whose targets are elements of composite variables is the subject of §4.4.

(4.21) *GEval*$_{if}$*(S) Axiom*:  For an **if** statement

$$S: \text{ if } B_1 \rightarrow S_1 \ [] \ B_2 \rightarrow S_2 \ [] \ \cdots \ [] \ B_n \rightarrow S_n \text{ fi}$$

and a primitive assertion $P$:

$$\{P\} \, GEval_{if}(S) \, \{P \wedge ((at(S_1) \Rightarrow B_1) \wedge \cdots \wedge (at(S_n) \Rightarrow B_n))\}$$

The inference rule for **if** permits a valid proof outline to be inferred from valid proof outlines for its components:

(4.22) **if** *Rule*:  (a)  $\{P\} \, GEval_{if}(S) \, \{R\}$,
  (b)  $R \wedge at(S_1) \Rightarrow P_1, \ \ldots, \ R \wedge at(S_n) \Rightarrow P_n$,
  (c)  $\{P_1\} \, PO(S_1) \, \{Q\}, \ \ldots, \ \{P_n\} \, PO(S_n) \, \{Q\}$

$$\frac{}{\begin{array}{l} \{P\} \\ S: \text{ if } B_1 \rightarrow \{P_1\} \, PO(S_1) \, \{Q\} \\ \phantom{S:} [] \ \cdots \\ \phantom{S:} [] \ B_n \rightarrow \{P_n\} \, PO(S_n) \, \{Q\} \\ \phantom{S:} \text{fi} \\ \{Q\} \end{array}}$$

The guard evaluation action for **do** selects a statement $S_i$ for which the corresponding guard $B_i$ holds; if no guard is *true*, then the exit control point for the **do** becomes active:

(4.23) *GEval*$_{do}$*(S) Axiom*:  For a **do** statement

$$S: \text{ do } B_1 \rightarrow S_1 \ [] \ B_2 \rightarrow S_2 \ [] \ \cdots \ [] \ B_n \rightarrow S_n \text{ od}$$

and a primitive assertion $P$:

$$\{P\} \, GEval_{do}(S) \, \{P \wedge (at(S_1) \Rightarrow B_1) \wedge \cdots \wedge (at(S_n) \Rightarrow B_n) \\ \wedge (after(S) \Rightarrow (\neg B_1 \wedge \cdots \wedge \neg B_n))\}$$

The inference rule for **do** is based on a *loop invariant*, an assertion $I$ that holds before and after every iteration of a loop, and therefore is guaranteed to hold when the **do** terminates—no matter how many iterations occur:

(4.24) **do** *Rule*:  (a)  $\{I\} \, GEval_{do}(S) \, \{R\}$,
  (b)  $R \wedge at(S_1) \Rightarrow P_1, \ \ldots, \ R \wedge at(S_n) \Rightarrow P_n$,
  (c)  $\{P_1\} \, PO(S_1) \, \{I\}, \ \ldots, \ \{P_n\} \, PO(S_n) \, \{I\}$
  (d)  $R \wedge after(S) \Rightarrow I \wedge \neg B_1 \wedge \ldots \wedge \neg B_n$

$$\frac{}{\begin{array}{l} \{I\} \\ S: \text{ do } B_1 \rightarrow \{P_1\} \, PO(S_1) \, \{I\} \\ \phantom{S:} [] \ \cdots \\ \phantom{S:} [] \ B_n \rightarrow \{P_n\} \, PO(S_n) \, \{I\} \\ \phantom{S:} \text{od} \\ \{I \wedge \neg B_1 \wedge \cdots \wedge \neg B_n\} \end{array}}$$

We now turn to the statement-independent inference rules of Proof Outline Logic. Rule of Consequence (4.25) allows the precondition of a proof outline to be strengthened and the postcondition to be weakened, based on deductions possible in Predicate Logic:

(4.25) *Rule of Consequence*: $\dfrac{P' \Rightarrow P, \quad \{P\} \, PO(S) \, \{Q\}, \quad Q \Rightarrow Q'}{\{P'\} \, PO(S) \, \{Q'\}}$

The presence of Predicate Logic formulas in the premise of this rule and the next rule is what forces the completeness of Proof Outline Logic to be relative to Predicate Logic.

Rule of Equivalence (4.26) allows assertions anywhere in a proof outline to be modified. In particular, the rule allows a proof outline $PO'(S)$ for a program $S$ to be inferred from another proof outline $PO(S)$ for that program when $I_{PO(S)}$ and $I_{PO'(S)}$ are equivalent and $PO'(S)$ is self-consistent:

(4.26) *Rule of Equivalence*: $\dfrac{\text{(a) } PO(S), \quad\quad\quad\quad\quad\quad\quad\quad\quad\quad\quad\quad}{PO'(S)}$

(more precisely)

(4.26) *Rule of Equivalence*:  (a) $PO(S)$,
  (b) $I_{PO(S)} = I_{PO'(S)}$,
  (c) $\dfrac{pre(PO'(S)) \wedge at(S) \Rightarrow pre(PO(S))}{PO'(S)}$

Control-Predicate Deletion is a derived rule that allows certain control predicates in assertions to be deleted:

(4.27) *Control-Predicate Deletion*: $\dfrac{\{P \wedge at(S)\} \, PO(S) \, \{Q \vee \neg after(S)\}}{\{P\} \, PO(S) \, \{Q\}}$

This rule is easily derived using Rule of Equivalence (4.26) because:

$$(at(S) \Rightarrow P \wedge at(S)) \;\wedge\; (after(S) \Rightarrow Q \vee \neg after(S))$$
$$= \quad \text{«Predicate Logic»}$$
$$(at(S) \Rightarrow P) \;\wedge\; (after(S) \Rightarrow Q)$$

Control-Point Identity allows control predicates to be added to assertions.

(4.28) *Control-Point Identity*: $\dfrac{\{P\} \, PO(S) \, \{Q\}}{\{P \wedge at(S)\} \, PO(S) \, \{Q \wedge after(S)\}}$

This rule, too, can be derived using Rule of Equivalence (4.26).

The first of the Rigid Variable Rules allows a rigid variable to be renamed or replaced by another constant value; the second allows a conjunct that constrains a rigid variable to be deleted from preconditions where that conjunct is superfluous. Below, we write $PO(S)_{Exp}^X$ to denote a proof outline in which rigid variable X in every assertion is replaced by Exp, an expression involving constants and rigid variables (only).

(4.29) *Rigid Variable Rules*:

(a) $$\dfrac{\{P\}\,PO(S)\,\{Q\}}{\{P_{Exp}^X\}\,PO(S)_{Exp}^X\,\{Q_{Exp}^X\}}$$

(b) For X a rigid variable not occurring free in $P$ or $Q$, $\mathcal{E}$ a term, and $\alpha$ an atomic action:

$$\dfrac{\{P \wedge X=\mathcal{E}\}\ \alpha\ \{Q\}}{\{P\}\ \alpha\ \{Q\}}$$

The Conjunction and Disjunction Rules allow two proof outlines for the same program to be combined. Given proof outlines $PO_A(S)$ and $PO_B(S)$ for a program $S$, let $A_{cp}$ be the assertion that $PO_A(S)$ associates with control predicate $cp$, and let $B_{cp}$ be the assertion that $PO_B(S)$ associates with $cp$. Define $PO_A(S) \otimes PO_B(S)$ to be a proof outline that associates assertion $A_{cp} \wedge B_{cp}$ with each control predicate $cp$. For example, given

$$PO_A(S):\ \{x=5\}\ x:=x+1\ \{x=6\}\ y:=y+1\ \{x=6\}$$

$$PO_B(S):\ \{y=2\}\ x:=x+1\ \{y=2\}\ y:=y+1\ \{y=3\}$$

then $PO_A(S) \otimes PO_B(S)$ is:

$$\{x=5 \wedge y=2\}\ x:=x+1\ \{x=6 \wedge y=2\}\ y:=y+1\ \{x=6 \wedge y=3\}$$

The following Conjunction Rule states that $PO_A(S) \otimes PO_B(S)$ can be inferred from $PO_A(S)$ and $PO_B(S)$:

(4.30) *Conjunction Rule*:  $\dfrac{PO_A(S),\ \ PO_B(S)}{PO_A(S) \otimes PO_B(S)}$

Define $PO_A(S) \oslash PO_B(S)$ to be a proof outline that associates assertion $A_{cp} \vee B_{cp}$ with each control predicate $cp$. The Disjunction Rule allows $PO_A(S) \oslash PO_B(S)$ to be inferred from $PO_A(S)$ and $PO_B(S)$:

(4.31) *Disjunction Rule*:  $\dfrac{PO_A(S),\ \ PO_B(S)}{PO_A(S) \oslash PO_B(S)}$

## Proofs in Proof Outline Logic

A proof in Proof Outline Logic is merely a sequence of proof outlines and Predicate Logic formulas, where each is an axiom or can be derived from previous lines by using inference rules. An example is given below. In it, we show that the proof outline of Figure 4.4 is a theorem. The proof proceeds by working from the inside out, constructing larger proof outlines until the desired formula is obtained.

«**skip** Axiom (4.18)»
   1. $\{x=X \wedge x \geq 0\}$ **skip** $\{x=X \wedge x \geq 0\}$

«Predicate Logic»
   2. $(x=X \wedge x \geq 0) \Rightarrow x=abs(X)$

«Rule of Consequence (4.25) with 1 and 2»
   3. $\{x=X \wedge x \geq 0\}$ **skip** $\{x=abs(X)\}$

«Assignment Axiom (4.19)»
   4. $\{-(-x)=X \wedge -(-x) \leq 0\}\ x := -x\ \{-x=X \wedge -x \leq 0\}$

«Predicate Logic»
   5. $(x=X \wedge x \leq 0) \Rightarrow -(-x)=X \wedge -(-x) \leq 0$
   6. $(-x=X \wedge -x \leq 0) \Rightarrow x=abs(X)$

«Rule of Consequence (4.25) with 5, 4, and 6»
   7. $\{x=X \wedge x \leq 0\}\ x := -x\ \{x=abs(X)\}$

«$GEval_{if}(S)$ Axiom (4.21) where $S$ is

        $S$: if $x \geq 0 \to S_1$ [] $x \leq 0 \to S_2$ fi »
   8. $\{x=X\}\ GEval_{if}(S)\ \{x=X \wedge (at(S_1) \Rightarrow x \geq 0) \wedge (at(S_2) \Rightarrow x \leq 0)\}$

«Predicate Logic»
   9. $(x=X \wedge ((at(S_1) \Rightarrow x \geq 0) \wedge (at(S_2) \Rightarrow x \leq 0)) \wedge at(S_1))$
      $\Rightarrow (x=X \wedge x \geq 0)$
  10. $(x=X \wedge ((at(S_1) \Rightarrow x \geq 0) \wedge (at(S_2) \Rightarrow x \leq 0)) \wedge at(S_2))$
      $\Rightarrow (x=X \wedge x \leq 0)$

«**if** Rule (4.22) with 8, 9, 10, 3, and 7»
  11. $\{x=X\}$
     $S$: **if** $x \geq 0 \to \{x=X \wedge x \geq 0\}$
                  $S_1$: **skip**
                  $\{x=abs(X)\}$
       [] $x \leq 0 \to \{x=X \wedge x \leq 0\}$
                  $S_2$: $x := -x$
                  $\{x=abs(X)\}$
     **fi**
    $\{x=abs(X)\}$

«Control-Point Identity (4.28) with 11»
  12.  $\{x=X \wedge at(S)\}$
      $S:$  **if** $x \geq 0 \rightarrow \{x=X \wedge x \geq 0\}$
            $S_1:$  **skip**
            $\{x=abs(X)\}$
         [] $x \leq 0 \rightarrow \{x=X \wedge x \leq 0\}$
            $S_2:$  $x := -x$
            $\{x=abs(X)\}$
      **fi**
      $\{x=abs(X) \wedge after(S)\}$

## 4.4  Assignment to Composite Variables

Assignment Axiom (4.19) cannot be used for assigning to a component of a composite variable, because (4.19) is formulated in terms of substituting for the target of the assignment statement, and Textual Substitution (2.71) is not defined for replacement of a component of a variable. Moreover, there are difficulties with extending textual substitution to allow substitution for components of a composite variable. For example, is $(i=3 \wedge a[i]=22)_5^{a[3]}$ equal to $i=3 \wedge a[i]=22$ or to $i=3 \wedge 5=22$? To conclude the latter requires inferring that "$a[i]$" is "$a[3]$" in order to do the substitution, which violates the syntactic nature of textual substitution; to conclude the former would result in an assignment axiom that is not sound. We therefore must take a different approach in extending Assignment Axiom (4.19) to handle assigning to composite variables.

### Variables as Functions

To develop an axiom that can handle assignment statements with targets that are components of composite variables, we regard all variables as containing values that are functions. A *function* is a mapping from one set of values, its *domain*, to another set, its *range*. A noncomposite variable contains a function with the single element $\varepsilon$ as its domain and a range that is the same as the type of the variable. The value of the function for argument $\varepsilon$ is just the value of the variable.

An array contains a function whose domain is the set of possible subscript values and whose range is the type of the array. For example,

  **var** $a$ : **array** $[0 .. 10]$ **of** Int

contains a function with domain 0, 1, ..., 10 and range Int. Multidimensional arrays can also be viewed as containing functions. The two-dimensional array

  **var** $a$ : **array** $[1 .. n, \ 1 .. m]$ **of** Real

contains a function that maps a pair of integers $(i, j)$ satisfying $1 \leq i \leq n$ and $1 \leq j \leq m$ into a Real. The array of arrays

(4.32) **var** $a$ : **array** $[1 .. n]$ **of array** $[1 .. m]$ **of** Real

contains a function that maps an integer $i$ satisfying $1 \le i \le n$ into a function that maps an integer $j$ satisfying $1 \le j \le m$ into elements of Real.

Records, too, can be viewed as containing functions. The domain of a record is the set of field names; its range is the union of the types for the fields. For example, the domain of

> **var** *interval* : **record**( *start* : Real;
> *length* : Int;
> *units* : **enum**( *Secs*, *Mins*, *Hrs* ) )

is {*start*, *length*, *units* }, and the range is Int $\cup$ Real $\cup$ {*Secs*, *Mins*, *Hrs* }.

Henceforth, we write a reference to the value of a variable $v$ as a function application $v(\overline{c})$, where $v$ is a function and $\overline{c}$ is a list $c_1 \cdot c_2 \cdot \cdots \cdot c_n$ of zero or more *selectors*. The list of selectors specifies the argument to which the function is applied, according to:

| Variable Type | Reference | Function Application |
|---|---|---|
| noncomposite variable | $v$ | $v(\varepsilon)$ |
| array | $v[i]$ | $v(i)$ |
| record | $v.id$ | $v(id)$ |

Array subscripts and record fields can be mixed, so *student.classes*$[m]$ is written as the function application *student*(*classes*$\cdot m$).

We model an assignment to a component of a composite variable by assigning a new function to the composite variable. Assignment statement $a[c] := e$, for example, is modeled by assigning a function to $a$ that differs only in its value for argument $c$. In order to describe functions constructed in this manner, we employ a notation similar to that given in §2.3 for augmented states. The *function expression* $(v; r \cdot \overline{c} : e)$ denotes a function that is the same as $v$ for all arguments except at $r \cdot \overline{c}$, where its value is $e$.

Two axioms suffice for reasoning about function expressions.

(4.33) *Function Expression Axioms*:

> (a) $(v; \varepsilon : e) = e$
>
> (b) $(v; r \cdot \overline{c} : e)(a) = \begin{cases} (v(a); \overline{c} : e) & \text{for "}a\text{"="}r\text{"} \\ v(a) & \text{for "}a\text{"}\ne\text{"}r\text{"} \end{cases}$

Nested parentheses in function expressions can be omitted without introducing ambiguity by using the rule:

$$(v; \ \overline{c}_1 : e_1; \ \overline{c}_2 : e_2) \ = \ ((v; \ \overline{c}_1 : e_1); \ \overline{c}_2 : e_2)$$

The following examples illustrate the manipulation of function expressions. Assume that $a$ of (4.32) is initialized so that every element $a[i][j]$ equals $i+j$. Thus, $(a; \ 2 \cdot 7 : 15)$ describes an array of arrays where $a[2][7]$ is 15 and every other element $a[i][j]$ equals $i+j$:

$$
\begin{array}{llll}
& (a; \ 2 \cdot 7 : 15)(2)(7) & & (a; \ 2 \cdot 7 : 15)(1)(3) \\
= & \text{«(4.33b)»} & = & \text{«(4.33b)»} \\
& (a(2); \ 7 : 15)(7) & & (a(1))(3) \\
= & \text{«(4.33b)»} & = & \text{«}a[i][j] = i+j \text{ assumed »} \\
& (a(2)(7); \ \varepsilon : 15) & & 4 \\
= & \text{«(4.33a)»} & & \\
& 15 & &
\end{array}
$$

## *Generalized Assignment Axiom*

For any variable $v$, composite or not,

(4.34) $\ v(\overline{c}) := e$

can be viewed as an abbreviation for

(4.35) $\ v := (v; \ \overline{c} : e).$

Moreover, when $\overline{c} \neq \varepsilon$, (4.34) is an assignment statement whose target is an element of a composite variable, while (4.35) is not. We have translated an assignment statement whose target is an element of a composite variable into an equivalent one about which Assignment Axiom (4.19) can be used to reason. Because (4.35) is equivalent to (4.34), we have, for any primitive assertion $P$:

(4.36) $\ \{P^v_{(v; \ \overline{c}:e)}\} \ v(\overline{c}) := e \ \{P\}$

As might be expected, (4.36) simplifies to Assignment Axiom (4.19) when $v(\overline{c})$ denotes a noncomposite variable, because then $\overline{c} = \varepsilon$, so by Function Expression Axiom (4.33a), we conclude $(v; \ \varepsilon : e) = e$.

One final problem must be addressed to obtain an axiom that can handle all multiple assignment statements. In executing

(4.37) $\ x_1 \cdot \overline{c}_1, \ x_2 \cdot \overline{c}_2, \ ..., \ x_n \cdot \overline{c}_n \ := \ e_1, \ e_2, \ ..., \ e_n$

all the expressions in $\overline{c}_i$ and $e_i$ are first evaluated, and only then are updates made to targets $x_1 \cdot \overline{c}_1, x_2 \cdot \overline{c}_2, ..., x_n \cdot \overline{c}_n$ (in that order). Consequently, we cannot simply translate

(4.38) $a[1], a[2] := 22, 33$

into

(4.39) $a, a := (a; \ 1{:}22), (a; \ 2{:}33)$

because (4.38) changes $a[1]$ and $a[2]$, but (4.39) changes only $a[2]$. The correct translation of (4.38) is:

$$a := (a; \ 1{:}22; \ 2{:}33)$$

When translating a multiple assignment statement, we must employ a single function expression that aggregates all the changes to each target variable instead of using a function expression for each target. Consider an assignment statement where multiple references to a given target are grouped:

$$x_1 \cdot \bar{c}_{1,1}, \ ..., \ x_1 \cdot \bar{c}_{1,m}, \quad \cdots \quad x_n \cdot \bar{c}_{n,1}, \ ..., \ x_n \cdot \bar{c}_{n,p}$$
$$:=$$
$$e_{1,1}, \ ..., \ e_{1,m}, \quad \cdots \quad e_{n,1}, \ ..., \ e_{n,p}$$

An equivalent assignment statement in terms of function expressions is:

$$x_1, ..., x_n := (x_1; \bar{c}_{1,1} : e_{1,1}; ...; \bar{c}_{1,m} : e_{1,m}), \ ..., \ (x_n; \bar{c}_{n,1} : e_{n,1}; ...; \bar{c}_{n,p} : e_{n,p})$$

This leads to the following axiom, which is sound for assignment statements whose targets are entire composite variables, noncomposite variables, and elements of composite variables.

(4.40) *Generalized Assignment Axiom*:  For a primitive assertion $P$:

$$\{P^{x_1, \ ..., \ x_n}_{(x_1; \bar{c}_{1,1} : e_{1,1}; ...; \bar{c}_{1,m} : e_{1,m}), \ \cdots \ (x_n; \bar{c}_{n,1} : e_{n,1}; ...; \bar{c}_{n,p} : e_{n,p})} \}$$
$$x_1 \cdot \bar{c}_{1,1}, \ ..., \ x_1 \cdot \bar{c}_{1,m}, \quad \cdots \quad x_n \cdot \bar{c}_{n,1}, \ ..., \ x_n \cdot \bar{c}_{n,p}$$
$$:= \ e_{1,1}, \ ..., \ e_{1,m}, \quad \cdots \quad e_{n,1}, \ ..., \ e_{n,p}$$
$$\{P\}$$

## Examples

The first example illustrates assigning to an element of an array. We calculate a precondition $P$ that makes $\{P\} \ a[3] := 5 \ \{i{=}3 \wedge a[i]{=}22\}$ valid:

> $P$
> $=$      «Generalized Assignment Axiom (4.40)»
> $(i{=}3 \wedge a(i){=}22)^a_{(a; \ 3{:}5)}$
> $=$      «Textual Substitution (2.71)»

$$i=3 \wedge (a; \; 3{:}5)(i)=22$$
$=$ «Function Expression Axiom (4.33b)»
$$i=3 \wedge (a(3); \; \varepsilon{:}5)=22$$
$=$ «Function Expression Axiom (4.33a)»
$$i=3 \wedge 5=22$$
$=$ «Predicate Logic»
*false*

As a second example, we find a precondition $P$ that makes the following valid.

$$\{P\} \; a[i],a[j] := a[j],a[i] \; \{a[i]=X \wedge a[j]=Y\}$$

This proof proceeds along the same lines as the previous one.

$P$
$=$ «Generalized Assignment Axiom (4.40)»
$$(a(i)=X \wedge a(j)=Y)^{a}_{(a; \; i:a(j); \; j:a(i))}$$
$=$ «Textual Substitution (2.71)»
$$(a; \; i{:}a(j); \; j{:}a(i))(i)=X \wedge (a; \; i{:}a(j); \; j{:}a(i))(j)=Y$$
$=$ «Function Expression Axioms (4.33)»
$$(a; \; i{:}a(j); \; j{:}a(i))(i)=X \wedge a(i)=Y$$
$=$ «Predicate Logic and Function Expression Axioms (4.33)»
$$((i \neq j \wedge a(j)=X) \vee (i=j \wedge a(i)=a(j)=X)) \wedge a(i)=Y$$
$=$ «Predicate Logic»
$$a(j)=X \wedge a(i)=Y$$

Thus,

$$\{a[j]=X \wedge a[i]=Y\} \; a[i],a[j] := a[j],a[i] \; \{a[i]=X \wedge a[j]=Y\}$$

is a theorem, and we conclude that $a[i],a[j] := a[j],a[i]$ interchanges elements $a[i]$ and $a[j]$, even if $i=j$.

## 4.5 A Predicate Transformer

Proof Outline Logic provides a way to derive preconditions and postconditions for a given program. As programmers, however, we are more often concerned with synthesis than analysis, so we also require a way to construct a program for a given precondition and postcondition. One solution is to view programs as *predicate transformers*—functions that map predicates to predicates. In particular, knowing how each program fragment $S$ maps primitive postconditions to preconditions provides help in selecting among program fragments that might truthify a given postcondition.

Such a predicate transformer, called *wp*, is the subject of this section. We begin by giving its definition and some general rules for reasoning about

Predicate Logic formulas written in terms of *wp*. Then, we describe the mapping that *wp* defines for the programming notation of §4.1. Finally, we conclude by showing how *wp* can be used in deriving sequential programs.

## Weakest Preconditions

The *weakest precondition* predicate transformer *wp* is defined as follows.

(4.41) **Weakest Precondition.** Given a statement $S$ and a primitive formula $Q$ of Predicate Logic, $wp(S,Q)$ is the weakest primitive formula of Predicate Logic (i.e., specifies the largest set of states) such that execution of $S$ begun in any state satisfying $wp(S,Q)$ is guaranteed to terminate in a state satisfying $Q$.                                                                    □

A number of useful laws about *wp* follow directly from this definition. These laws allow Predicate Logic to be used to simplify and reason about formulas involving *wp*.

First, since no state satisfies *false*, a program cannot terminate in a state satisfying *false*. Thus, there cannot be a state in which execution of $S$ can start that will lead to termination in a state satisfying *false*, and we have:

(4.42) *Excluded Miracle Law*:  $wp(S, false) = false$

Next, note that if $S$ is executed beginning in a state that satisfies both $wp(S,Q)$ and $wp(S,R)$, then according to the definition of *wp*, upon termination the resulting state will satisfy $Q \land R$. In addition (again by definition), a state that satisfies $wp(S, Q \land R)$ also satisfies both $wp(S,Q)$ and $wp(S,R)$. So we have:

(4.43) *Distributivity of Conjunction Law*:
$$(wp(S,Q) \land wp(S,R)) = wp(S, Q \land R)$$

The next two laws can be derived directly from (4.42) and (4.43) using Predicate Logic. (See exercise 4.32.)

(4.44) *Monotonicity Law*:  If $Q \Rightarrow R$ is valid, then $wp(S,Q) \Rightarrow wp(S,R)$ is valid.

(4.45) *Distributivity of Disjunction Law*:  $wp(S,Q) \lor wp(S,R) \Rightarrow wp(S, Q \lor R)$

The converse of (4.45), $wp(S, Q \lor R) \Rightarrow wp(S,Q) \lor wp(S,R)$, is not valid in general. To see this, consider a program that simulates a coin flip:

*flip*: **if** *true* → *outcome* := *heads*
       [] *true* → *outcome* := *tails*
       **fi**

Since *flip* is nondeterministic, we cannot be sure which of the assignment statements will be selected. Thus, there is no start state that guarantees a particular value for *outcome*:

(4.46)  $wp(\textit{flip}, \textit{outcome}=\textit{heads}) = wp(\textit{flip}, \textit{outcome}=\textit{tails}) = \textit{false}$

However, one of the guarded commands will be executed, so *outcome* is *heads* or *tails* when *flip* terminates:

(4.47)  $wp(\textit{flip}, \textit{outcome}=\textit{heads} \vee \textit{outcome}=\textit{tails}) = \textit{true}$

Substitution of (4.46) and (4.47) into the converse of (4.45) yields $\textit{true} \Rightarrow \textit{false}$, so the converse of (4.45) is not valid for *flip*. When $S$ is deterministic, the converse of (4.45) does hold, and the implication can be strengthened to equality.

(4.48)  *Distributivity of Deterministic Disjunction Law*:
$$\text{For deterministic } S, \ wp(S,Q) \vee wp(S,R) = wp(S, Q \vee R)$$

## Calculating Weakest Preconditions

We now turn to rules for determining $wp(S,Q)$ for $S$ an atomic action or a statement of the programming notation described in §4.1. The similarity between these rules and the axioms and inference rules of Proof Outline Logic is not accidental—both Proof Outline Logic and $wp$ formalize execution as a relation between assertions.

The **skip** statement always terminates and has no effect on any program or rigid variable. In order for **skip** to terminate in a state satisfying a primitive formula $Q$ of Predicate Logic, it must be executed in a state satisfying $Q$. This makes **skip** the identity predicate transformer.

(4.49)  For a primitive assertion $Q$:  $wp(\textbf{skip}, Q) = Q$

Execution of a multiple assignment statement $\bar{x} := \bar{e}$ in a program $S$ terminates iff the value computed for each expression $e_i$ is consistent with the declared type of corresponding target $x_i$. Thus, termination requires that $VarAx(S)_{\bar{e}}^{\bar{x}}$ hold before execution is begun. Second, if execution of $\bar{x} := \bar{e}$ does terminate, then the state satisfies $Q$ iff $Q_{\bar{e}}^{\bar{x}}$ holds before execution is begun. Thus, we have[5]

(4.50)  For a primitive assertion $Q$:  $wp(\bar{x} := \bar{e}, Q) = (VarAx(S) \wedge Q)_{\bar{e}}^{\bar{x}}$

---

[5]Generalization for assignment statements whose targets are elements of composite variables is straightforward. Variables are treated as functions (as discussed in §4.4), and $wp(\bar{x} := \bar{e}, Q)$ is defined to require that the selector for each target variable be in the domain of that target.

In order for the statement juxtaposition $S_1 S_2$ to terminate in a state satisfying $Q$, statement $S_2$ must terminate in a state satisfying $Q$. This requires that $S_2$ be started in a state satisfying $wp(S_2,Q)$, which, in turn, requires that $S_1$ terminate in a state satisfying $wp(S_2,Q)$. Execution of $S_1$ in a state satisfying $wp(S_1, wp(S_2,Q))$ ensures the desired result, and we conclude that statement juxtaposition is defined by composition of predicate transformers:

(4.51)  For a primitive assertion $Q$:   $wp(S_1 S_2, Q) = wp(S_1, wp(S_2, Q))$.

Given the **if** statement

(4.52) *IF*: **if** $B_1 \rightarrow S_1$ [] $B_2 \rightarrow S_2$ []  $\cdots$  [] $B_n \rightarrow S_n$ **fi**,

guard evaluation action $GEval_{if}(IF)$ terminates iff at least one guard holds. To ensure, in addition, that execution of $GEval_{if}(IF)$ terminates in a state satisfying $Q$, the initial state must also satisfy $Q$:

(4.53)  For a primitive assertion $Q$:
$$wp(GEval_{if}(IF), Q) = ((B_1 \vee B_2 \vee \cdots \vee B_n) \wedge Q)$$

From this weakest precondition for $GEval_{if}(IF)$, we now define the weakest precondition for an **if** statement. Two restrictions on the initial state ensure that execution of *IF* of (4.52) terminates in a state satisfying a primitive assertion $Q$. First, to ensure termination of the guard evaluation action, the **if** must be started in a state satisfying $wp(GEval_{if}(IF), true)$. Second, if a guarded command $S_i$ can be selected for execution, then $wp(S_i, Q)$ must hold of the initial state. Since $S_i$ is executed only if guard $B_i$ holds, this second requirement is equivalent to

$TRANS(IF)$: $(B_1 \Rightarrow wp(S_1,Q)) \wedge \cdots \wedge (B_n \Rightarrow wp(S_n,Q))$.

By combining these two requirements, we get an expression for the weakest precondition of **if**:

(4.54)  For a primitive assertion $Q$:
$$wp(IF, Q) = (wp(GEval_{if}(IF), true) \wedge TRANS(IF))$$

To define the weakest precondition for a **do** statement

*DO*: **do** $B_1 \rightarrow S_1$ [] $B_2 \rightarrow S_2$ []  $\cdots$  [] $B_n \rightarrow S_n$ **od**

the weakest precondition of a guard evaluation action $GEval_{do}(DO)$ is needed. Execution of $GEval_{do}(DO)$ changes only the active control points, so termination in a state satisfying $Q$ is ensured iff the initial state satisfies $Q$.

(4.55) For a primitive assertion $Q$:  $wp(GEval_{do}(DO), Q) = Q$

To define $wp(DO,Q)$, let predicate $H_j(Q)$ hold for all states in which execution of $DO$ leads to termination after $j$ or fewer iterations in a state satisfying $Q$. Thus, $H_0(Q)$ is the set of states in which no iterations of $DO$ are required to reach a state satisfying a primitive assertion $Q$ and is defined by:

$$H_0(Q) = (wp(GEval_{do}(DO), true) \wedge \neg(B_1 \vee \cdots \vee B_n) \wedge Q)$$

For $0 < j$, predicate $H_j(Q)$ can be defined in terms of $H_{j-1}(Q)$ by observing that $DO$ can be rewritten in terms of $IF$ (4.52):

$$DO: \textbf{do } B_1 \vee \cdots \vee B_n \rightarrow IF \textbf{ od}$$

Thus:

$$H_j(Q) = (H_0(Q) \vee wp(IF, H_{j-1}(Q)))$$

The assertion that $DO$ terminates is equivalent to the assertion that it performs only a finite number of iterations. Thus, we get:

(4.56) For a primitive assertion $Q$:  $wp(DO,Q) = (H_0(Q) \vee H_1(Q) \vee \cdots)$.

As should be clear from (4.56), calculating the weakest precondition for a **do** can be difficult. Fortunately, the following result asserts that performing this calculation is not necessary for proving $P \Rightarrow wp(DO,Q)$.

(4.57) **Precondition for do.** Given a **do** statement

$$DO: \textbf{do } B_1 \rightarrow S_1 \quad [] \quad B_2 \rightarrow S_2 \quad [] \quad \cdots \quad [] \quad B_n \rightarrow S_n \textbf{ od}$$

if a primitive assertion $I$ satisfies

  (i)  for all $i$, $1 \le i \le n$: $I \wedge B_i \Rightarrow wp(S_i, I)$
  (ii)  there   is   an   integer-valued   expression   $\upsilon$   such   that
     $I \wedge (B_1 \vee \cdots \vee B_n) \Rightarrow \upsilon > 0$
  (iii)  for all $i$, $1 \le i \le n$: $I \wedge B_i \wedge V = \upsilon \Rightarrow wp(S_i, V > \upsilon)$
  then $I \Rightarrow wp(DO, I \wedge \neg(B_1 \vee \cdots \vee B_n))$.                          □

In (4.57), *variant function* $\upsilon$ bounds the number of loop iterations still to be performed. This is because condition (iii) asserts that performing an iteration of the loop decreases $\upsilon$, and condition (ii) ensures that when $\upsilon \le 0$, no guard is *true* or $I$ is *false*.

## Program Derivation

We now illustrate how to construct a sequential program $S$ along with a valid proof outline $PO(S)$ satisfying the restriction that $pre(S)$ is $P$ and $post(S)$ is $Q$ for given primitive assertions $P$ and $Q$. The methodology is based on constructing a proof of $P \Rightarrow wp(S,Q)$. We let the shape and structure of $Q$ suggest candidates for $S$ by anticipating the shape that $wp(S,Q)$ will take and reconciling that with the shape of $P$.

(4.58) **Statement Selection Heuristics.** When selecting $S$ to satisfy $P \Rightarrow wp(S,Q)$:

- If $P \Rightarrow Q$ then use **skip** for $S$.

- If $P$ and $Q$ have identical structure, with $Q$ being $P_e^{\bar{v}}$ for some $\bar{v}$ and $\bar{e}$, then investigate using an assignment statement $\bar{v} := \bar{e}$ for $S$.

- If $Q$ is a conjunction of formulas, then investigate using a statement juxtaposition $S_1\, S_2$ for $S$, where $S_1$ truthifies some conjuncts and $S_2$ truthifies others.

- If $Q$ is a disjunction of formulas, then investigate using an **if** for $S$, where each alternative truthifies one of the disjuncts.

- If $Q$ involves bound variables, then investigate using a **do** for $S$.    □

Obviously, facility with Predicate Logic can be helpful in applying these heuristics because it allows $Q$ to be reformulated in ways that bring out hidden structure.

When statement juxtaposition, **if**, or **do** is contemplated for $S$, we proceed in two steps:

(1)    Replace $S$ by a skeleton that is written in terms of some program fragments $S_1$ through $S_n$. Conjecture an intermediate assertion $pre(S_2)$ for a statement juxtaposition $S_1\, S_2$, the guards for an **if**, or the loop invariant for a **do**.

(2)    Identify candidates for program fragments $S_1$ through $S_n$. These choices are each driven by proofs for the obligations $P_i \Rightarrow wp(S_i, Q_i)$ that must be discharged in order to prove $P \Rightarrow wp(S,Q)$.

To choose a **do** requires devising an invariant. This invariant then drives the development of the guarded commands that constitute the **do**. A number of techniques exist for selecting an invariant. They are all based on reformulating a postcondition $Q$ of a **do** in terms of two predicates, $I$ and $\neg B$, in such a way that:

- $I \wedge \neg B \Rightarrow Q$

- it is easy to make $I$ hold initially

Predicate $B$ is the basis for selecting guards $B_1, ..., B_n$ in the **do**. In particular, $B_1 \vee \cdots \vee B_n$ should equal $B$.

Two of the more useful techniques for choosing $I$ are:

(4.59) **Deleting a Conjunct.** Obtain $I$ by deleting a conjunct from $Q$. Choose a conjunct to delete so that it is easy to make $I$ hold initially.  □

(4.60) **Replacing an Expression by a Variable.** Obtain $I$ by replacing a constant, variable, or expression in $Q$ by a fresh variable and adding a conjunct defining values that this new variable may assume.  □

We illustrate these techniques by deriving a program $S$ and a valid proof outline $PO(S)$ such that $pre(S)$ is $P$ and $post(S)$ is $Q$, where:

$P$: $n \geq 0$

$Q$: $0 \leq r^2 \ \wedge \ r^2 \leq n \ \wedge \ n < (r+1)^2$

This yields a program that computes integer approximations to square roots.

As a first attempt, we design a program that enumerates and checks various choices for $r$. We conjecture that a loop can accomplish this. So, we try Deleting a Conjunct (4.59) to obtain a loop invariant $I$ by deleting the third conjunct of $Q$:

$I$: $0 \leq r^2 \ \wedge \ r^2 \leq n$

We choose to delete the third conjunct because it is easy to truthify $I$ by initializing $r$ to 0, since $n \geq 0 \Rightarrow wp(r:=0, I)$. By negating deleted conjunct $n < (r+1)^2$ and using it as the guard, the loop terminates in a state satisfying $I \wedge \neg B$. Thus, we have:

$$\{n \geq 0\}$$
$$r := 0$$
$$\{I: \ 0 \leq r^2 \ \wedge \ r^2 \leq n\}$$
$$\textbf{do } n \geq (r+1)^2 \rightarrow \{I \ \wedge \ n \geq (r+1)^2\} \ \dots \ \{I\} \textbf{ od}$$
$$\{I \ \wedge \ n < (r+1)^2\}$$
$$\{Q\}$$

We complete the loop body so that conditions (i)–(iii) of Precondition for do (4.57) hold. We start by choosing $n - (r+1)^2$ for variant function $\upsilon$ and verify that (ii) holds. This choice of $\upsilon$ is based on the observation that for the loop body to progress towards termination, $r$ must be increased, since $r$ is initially 0 and the guard is *false* when $n < (r+1)^2$. By increasing $r$ in the loop body, $\upsilon$ decreases, as required by (iii). An obvious way to increase $r$ is by executing $r := r+1$. Toward satisfying condition (i), we compute

$$wp(r := r+1, \ I) \ = \ (0 \leq (r+1)^2 \ \wedge \ (r+1)^2 \leq n)$$

and verify that:

$$I \; \wedge \; n{\geq}(r{+}1)^2 \;\; \Rightarrow \;\; 0{\leq}(r{+}1)^2 \; \wedge \; (r{+}1)^2{\leq}n$$

Since this implication is valid, we are done. The final (valid) proof outline is:

$$\{P: \; n{\geq}0\}$$
$$r := 0$$
$$\{I: \; 0{\leq}r^2 \; \wedge \; r^2{\leq}n\}$$
$$\textbf{do} \; n{\geq}(r{+}1)^2 \rightarrow \{I \; \wedge \; n{\geq}(r{+}1)^2\}$$
$$\qquad\qquad r := r{+}1$$
$$\qquad\qquad \{I\}$$
$$\textbf{od}$$
$$\{Q: \; 0{\leq}r^2 \; \wedge \; r^2{\leq}n \; \wedge \; n{<}(r{+}1)^2\}$$

A second program to compute the integer approximation for the square root of $n$ can be obtained using Replacing an Expression by a Variable (4.60). We replace "$r{+}1$" in $Q$ with a fresh variable $s$ and, as required by (4.60), add a conjunct to bound $s$. The result is:

$$I': \; 0{\leq}r^2 \; \wedge \; r^2{\leq}n \; \wedge \; n{<}s^2 \; \wedge \; r{<}s{\leq}n{+}1$$

Again, we use (4.57) in finding a guard. Since $I' \wedge s{=}r{+}1 \Rightarrow Q$, we choose $s{\neq}r{+}1$ as the guard. It is easy to initialize $r$ and $s$ so that $I'$ holds, since:

$$n{\geq}0 \Rightarrow wp(r,s := 0,n{+}1, \; I')$$

Thus, we have:

$$\{P: \; n{\geq}0\}$$
$$r,s := 0,n{+}1$$
$$\{I': \; 0{\leq}r^2 \; \wedge \; r^2{\leq}n \; \wedge \; n{<}s^2 \; \wedge \; r{<}s{\leq}n{+}1\}$$
$$\textbf{do} \; s{\neq}r{+}1 \rightarrow \{I' \; \wedge \; s{\neq}r{+}1\} \; ... \; \{I'\} \, \textbf{od}$$
$$\{I' \; \wedge \; s{=}r{+}1\}$$
$$\{Q: \; 0{\leq}r^2 \; \wedge \; r^2{\leq}n \; \wedge \; n{<}(r{+}1)^2\}$$

Conditions (i)−(iii) of (4.57) drive the design of the loop body. Based on the guard and initialization, we choose $s{-}(r{+}1)$ as the variant function $\upsilon$. Notice that condition (ii) is satisfied:

$$(I' \wedge s{\neq}r{+}1) \;\; \Rightarrow \;\; s{-}(r{+}1){>}0$$

A fast way to decrease $\upsilon$ is by halving the distance between $r$ and $s$, either by increasing $r$ or decreasing $s$. This suggests that the body of the loop be completed as follows.

$\{n\geq 0\}$
$r,s := 0,n+1$
$\{I': \ 0\leq r^2 \ \wedge \ r^2\leq n \ \wedge \ n<s^2 \ \wedge \ r<s\leq n+1\}$
**do** $s\neq r+1 \rightarrow \{I' \ \wedge \ s\neq r+1\}$
        **if** ? $\rightarrow$ ...
               $r := (r+s)$ div 2
        [] ? $\rightarrow$ ...
               $s := (r+s)$ div 2
        **fi** $\{I'\}$
**od**
$\{I' \ \wedge \ s=r+1\}$
$\{Q\}$

The ellipses (...) have been included because additional statements might be necessary to satisfy condition (i) of (4.57). Condition (iii) is now satisfied, provided that statements that replace the ellipses do not increase $\upsilon$.

We now consider the first guarded command in the **if**. It must truthify $I'$, so we compute $wp(r := (r+s)$ div 2, $I')$:

(4.61) $0\leq((r+s)$ div $2)^2 \ \wedge \ ((r+s)$ div $2)^2\leq n \ \wedge \ n<s^2$
        $\wedge \ ((r+s)$ div $2)<s\leq n+1$

Condition (i) of (4.57) does not hold because the second conjunct of (4.61) is not implied by $I'\wedge s\neq r+1$. We remedy this by using the second conjunct as the guard for this guarded command, thereby ensuring that execution of $r := (r+s)$ div 2 does truthify $I'$. A similar argument allows derivation of the second guarded command. This results in the proof outline of Figure 4.7.

The procedure we employed in constructing the two square-root programs of this section is quite powerful and will be used repeatedly. Rather than

---

$\{n\geq 0\}$
$r,s := 0,n+1$
$\{I': \ 0\leq r^2\leq n \ \wedge \ n<s^2 \ \wedge \ r<s<n+1\}$
**do** $s\neq(r+1) \rightarrow \{I' \ \wedge \ s\neq(r+1)\}$
        **if** $((r+s)$ div $2)^2\leq n \rightarrow \{I' \ \wedge \ s\neq(r+1) \ \wedge \ ((r+s)$ div $2)^2\leq n\}$
                    $r := (r+s)$ div 2 $\{I'\}$
        [] $((r+s)$ div $2)^2>n \rightarrow \{I' \ \wedge \ s\neq(r+1) \ \wedge \ ((r+s)$ div $2)^2>n\}$
                    $s := (r+s)$ div 2 $\{I'\}$
        **fi** $\{I'\}$
**od**
$\{I' \ \wedge \ s=(r+1)\}$
$\{Q: \ 0\leq r^2 \ \wedge \ r^2\leq n \ \wedge \ n<(r+1)^2\}$

**Figure 4.7.** Computing a square root

allowing operational considerations to drive program design, we concentrated on discharging obligations associated with constructing a valid proof outline. Our first design decision was the choice of an invariant, and this choice was based on the shapes of formulas in the problem specification. Other design decisions— like whether to decrease the variant function by 1 or, in the second program, by halving—also originated with obligations we extracted from a proof outline. The entire design process was driven by the construction of a proof that the resulting program would satisfy its specification. We did not construct a program and then its proof—the proof led the way. Nor did we let concerns about program execution drive the design, yet the program we ultimately devised did exhibit good performance.

### Historical Notes

Hoare was the first to propose a logic for reasoning about programs [Hoare 69]. His logic is based on a program verification technique described in [Floyd 67]. The technique associates a predicate with each edge in the flowchart for a program in such a way that if execution is started anywhere in the program and the predicate on the corresponding flowchart edge is *true*, then as execution proceeds, the predicate on each subsequent corresponding edge will be *true*. Floyd credits Perlis and Gorn for the idea, mentioning an unpublished paper by Gorn as its earliest appearance. A similar approach was independently developed by Naur [Naur 66]. There, predicates called *general snapshots* are interspersed in the program text.

Other early investigations into formal systems are reported in [Yanov 58], [Igarashi 64], and [de Bakker 68] for proving the equivalence of programs, and in [McCarthy 62] and [Burstall 68] for programs specified as recursive functions. Program verification is almost as old as programming itself, however. Early techniques are given in [Goldstine & von Neumann 47] and [Turing 49]; the Turing paper is reprinted and discussed in [Morris & Jones 84].

Formulas of the logical system in [Hoare 69] were of the form $P \{S\} Q$, although this notation has since been displaced by $\{P\} S \{Q\}$, which is suggestive of assertions being viewed as comments. GHL (Generalized Hoare Logic) of [Lamport 80b] introduced control predicates *at*, *in*, and *after* and extended Hoare's logic to permit reasoning about invariance, expressed by a proof outline. See [Lamport & Schneider 84] for a discussion of the principles on which GHL is based; that paper also makes precise the relationship between GHL and Floyd's verification method, Hoare's logic, and various approaches for reasoning about concurrent programs. Another logic that extends Hoare's logic with control predicates is CPHL [Lamport 88]. Soundness and relative-completeness proofs for Hoare-style logics are given in [Cook 78], [Apt 81], and [Apt & Olderog 91].

Proof Outline Logic is based on GHL. The programming notation axiomatized by Proof Outline Logic has additional control structures but less flexibility about atomicity. Our multiple assignment statement and Assignment Axiom (4.19) are based on [Gries 78]; the **if** and **do** statements are from [Dijkstra 75]; guard evaluation actions were first axiomatized in [Lamport & Schneider 84]; and Generalized Assignment Axiom (4.40) was introduced in [Gries & Levin 80]. The notation used for proof outlines in GHL is more expressive than the notation of Proof Outline Logic, but our notation is closer to conventional annotated programs.

Although many who have written about programming logics use proof outlines, few have formalized them and even fewer have done so correctly. One of the earlier (correct) formalizations appears in [Ashcroft 76]; a natural deduction programming logic of proof outlines is presented in [Constable & O'Donnell 78].

Weakest preconditions were proposed by Dijkstra [Dijkstra 75] and are discussed in detail in [Dijkstra 76a], [Gries 81], and [Cohen 90]. The presentations in [Gries 81] and [Cohen 90] are intended for programmers and contain numerous examples as well as general techniques useful in deriving programs. The two techniques we discussed for choosing a loop invariant, (4.59) and (4.60), are taken from [Gries 81].

## Exercises

**4.1.** For a program $S$ written in the programming notation of §4.1, show how to construct the characteristic predicate for the set $\mathcal{H}_S$ defined in §3.4. Hint: Use structural induction on the syntax of programs.

**4.2.** Construct $VarAx(S)$ if $S$ contains declarations as follows.

   (a)   **var** $x, y$ : Real;   $i, j$ : Int

   (b)   **var** $a$ : **array** $[-3 .. 5]$ **of** Bool

   (c)   **var** $complex$ : **record**( $real$ : Real;
                                   $imaginary$ : Real )

   (d)   **var** $argh$ : **record**( $stuff$ : **array** $[1..5]$ **of record**( $this$ : Nat;
                                                          $that$ : Int );
                        $more$ : Bool )

**4.3.** For the program of Figure 4.2, determine whether each of the following formulas is valid. If the formula is valid, give a proof using Predicate Logic and the control predicate axioms of §4.2.

   (a)   $\neg (at(S_1) \wedge in(S_2))$

   (b)   $at(S_6) \Rightarrow in(S_2)$

   (c)   $after(S_6) \Rightarrow at(S_7)$

   (d)   $at(S_4) \Rightarrow after(GEval_{do}(S_2))$

   (e)   $after(S_7)=after(S_3)$

   (f)   $in(S_5) \Rightarrow in(S_2)$

   (g)   $in(S_5) \Rightarrow \neg in(S_7)$

   (h)   $in(S_5) \Rightarrow \neg at(S_2)$

**4.4.** Given is a statement juxtaposition $S$: $S_1 \, S_2$. Calculate possible values for $at(S)$, $after(S)$, $in(S)$, $at(S_1)$, $after(S_1)$, $at(S_2)$, and $after(S_2)$ by using the control predicate axioms of §4.2 and assuming:

   (a)   $at(S)$ is *true*.

   (b)   $after(S)$ is *true*.

   (c)   $at(S_1)$ is *true*.

   (d)   $after(S_1)$ is *true*.

   (e)   $at(S_2)$ is *true*.

   (f)   $after(S_2)$ is *true*.

**4.5.** Given is an **if** statement:

$$S: \text{if } B_1 \rightarrow S_1 \; [] \; B_2 \rightarrow S_2 \; \text{fi}$$

Calculate possible values for $at(S)$, $after(S)$, $in(S)$, $at(GEval_{if}(S))$, $after(GEval_{if}(S))$, $at(S_1)$, $in(S_1)$, $after(S_1)$, $at(S_2)$, $in(S_2)$, and $after(S_2)$ by using the control predicate axioms of §4.2 and assuming:

(a)   $at(S)$ is *true*.

(b)   $after(S)$ is *true*.

(c)   $at(GEval_{if}(S))$ is *true*.

(d)   $at(S_1)$ is *true*.

(e)   $after(S_1)$ is *true*.

**4.6.** Given is a **do** statement:

$$S: \text{do } B_1 \rightarrow S_1 \; [] \; B_2 \rightarrow S_2 \; \text{od}$$

Calculate possible values for $at(S)$, $after(S)$, $in(S)$, $at(GEval_{do}(S))$, $after(GEval_{do}(S))$, $at(S_1)$, $in(S_1)$, $after(S_1)$, $at(S_2)$, $in(S_2)$, and $after(S_2)$ by using the control predicate axioms of §4.2 and assuming:

(a)   $at(S)$ is *true*.

(b)   $after(S)$ is *true*.

(c)   $at(S_1)$ is *true*.

(e)   $after(S_1)$ is *true*.

**4.7.** For each of the following formulas of Proof Outline Logic, if the given proof outline is valid then provide a proof; otherwise, explain why the given proof outline is not valid.

(a)   $\{y=14\}$ **skip** $\{y=14\}$

(b)   $\{x=0 \wedge y=3\}$ **skip** $\{x=21 \wedge y=3\}$

(c)   $\{y=14 \wedge x>y\}$ **skip** $\{x>12\}$

(d)   $\{\textit{false}\}$ **skip** $\{x=3\}$

(e)   $\{after(S)\}$ $S:$ **skip** $\{x=3\}$

(f)   $\{x=C-1\}$ $x := x+1$ $\{x=C\}$

(g)   $\{\textit{true}\}$ $x := 3$ $\{x=3\}$ $y := 3$ $\{x=3 \wedge y=3\}$

(h)   $\{y=60\}$ $x := 22$ $\{y=60\}$ $x:=23$ $\{y=60\}$

(j)   $\{y=60\}$ $x := 20$ $\{y=3*x\}$

(k)   $\{x=2y\}$ $x,y := 2*x, 2*y$ $\{x=2y\}$

(l)   $\{x=X \wedge y=Y\}$
      **if** $x \leq y \rightarrow \{x \leq y\}$ **skip** $\{x \leq y\}$
      $[] \; y \leq x \rightarrow \{y \leq x\} x,y := y,x$ $\{x \leq y\}$
      **fi** $\{x \leq y\}$

(m)   $\{x=X \wedge y=Y\}$
      **if** $x \leq y \rightarrow \{x \leq y\}$ **skip** $\{X \leq Y\}$
      $[] \; y \leq x \rightarrow \{y \leq x\} x,y := y,x$ $\{X \leq Y\}$
      **fi** $\{X \leq Y\}$

(n)  $\{true\}$ **do** $true \rightarrow \{true\}$ **skip** $\{true\}$ **od** $\{false\}$

(o)  $\{true\}$ **do** $true \rightarrow \{true\}$ **skip** $\{true\}$ **od** $\{x=3\}$

(p)  $\{0 \leq X \wedge 0 \leq Y \wedge x=X \wedge y=Y\}$
     $z := 1$
     $\{I:\ 0 \leq y \wedge z*x^y = X^Y\}$
     **do** $0 < y \wedge even(y) \rightarrow \{I \wedge 0 < y \wedge even(y)\}$
     $\qquad\qquad\qquad\qquad\quad y,x := y \text{ div } 2, x*x$
     $\qquad\qquad\qquad\qquad\quad \{I\}$
     $\quad [\!] \ 0 < y \wedge odd(y) \ \rightarrow \ \{I \wedge 0 < y \wedge odd(y)\}$
     $\qquad\qquad\qquad\qquad\quad y,z := y-1, z*x$
     $\qquad\qquad\qquad\qquad\quad \{I\}$
     **od** $\{z=X^Y\}$

(q)  $\{n \geq 0\}$
     $r := 0 \ \{I:\ 0 \leq r^2 \wedge r^2 \leq n\}$
     **do** $n \geq (r+1)^2 \rightarrow \{I \wedge n \geq (r+1)^2\}$
     $\qquad\qquad\qquad\quad r := r+1 \ \{I\}$
     **od** $\{I \wedge n < (r+1)^2\}$

(r)  $\{n \geq 0\}$
     $r,s := 0, n+1$
     $\{I:\ 0 \leq r^2 \leq n \wedge n < s^2 \wedge r < s < n+1\}$
     **do** $s \neq r+1 \rightarrow \{I \wedge s \neq r+1\}$
     $\qquad\qquad\quad$ **if** $((r+s) \text{ div } 2)^2 \leq n \rightarrow \{I \wedge s \neq r+1 \wedge ((r+s) \text{ div } 2)^2 \leq n\}$
     $\qquad\qquad\qquad\qquad\qquad\qquad\qquad\qquad r := (r+s) \text{ div } 2 \ \{I\}$
     $\qquad\qquad\quad [\!] \ ((r+s) \text{ div } 2)^2 > n \rightarrow \{I \wedge s \neq r+1 \wedge ((r+s) \text{ div } 2)^2 > n\}$
     $\qquad\qquad\qquad\qquad\qquad\qquad\qquad\qquad s := (r+s) \text{ div } 2 \ \{I\}$
     $\qquad\qquad\quad$ **fi** $\{I\}$
     **od** $\{I \wedge s=r+1\}$

(s)  $\{(at(S_1) \vee after(S_3)) \wedge in(S_1) \Rightarrow x=X\}$
     $S_1:$ **skip**
     $\{x=X \wedge after(S_2) \Rightarrow y=Y\}$
     $S_2:$ **skip**
     $\{x=X+1 \vee \neg after(S_3)\}$
     $S_3:$ **skip**
     $\{x=X\}$

(t)  $\{x=5/0\} \ x := x+1 \ \{x=5/0+1\}$

**4.8.** Assume that $\{P\} PO(S) \{Q\}$ is a theorem of Proof Outline Logic. Determine whether each of the following is valid. Justify your answer with a proof or a counterexample.

(a)  $\{at(S)\} PO(S) \{after(S)\}$

(b)  $\{at(S) \Rightarrow P\} PO(S) \{after(S) \Rightarrow Q\}$

(c)  $\{at(S) \vee P\} PO(S) \{after(S) \vee Q\}$

**4.9.** Show how to prove $\{P\} PO(S) \{Q\}$ using Proof Outline Logic, if you can assume that each of the following have been proved.

(a)  $\{at(S) \wedge P\} PO(S) \{after(S) \wedge Q\}$

(b)  $\{at(S) \Rightarrow P\} PO(S) \{after(S) \Rightarrow Q\}$

**4.10.** (a)  Show that if $P$ and $Q$ are primitive and $\{P\}\, x,y := y,x\, \{Q\}$ is a theorem of Proof Outline Logic, then so is

$$\{P\}\ t := x\ \{P'\}\ x := y\ \{Q'\}\ y := t\ \{Q\}$$

for $t$ a fresh variable and suitable assertions $P'$ and $Q'$, by giving $P'$, $Q'$, and a proof of the theorem.

(b)  Is it necessary that $P$ and $Q$ be primitive? If it is, then give an example where your new proof outline is not valid for $P$ or $Q$ that are not primitive.

**4.11.** In some programming notations, the assignment statement $x := y$ div $0$ does not terminate because the value of expression $y$ div $0$ is considered undefined. We might call this statement a *partial assignment statement*, in contrast to the assignment statement of §4.1. Assume that the syntax of expressions is defined by the following grammar.

$expr ::= term \mid expr + term$
$term ::= factor \mid term * factor \mid term$ div $factor$
$factor ::= constant \mid identifier$

(a)  For any *expr* $E$ of this grammar, show how to construct a predicate $def_E$ such that $def_E$ is always defined and is satisfied in exactly those states where $E$ is not "undefined."

(b)  For any *expr* $E$, give a statement in the programming notation of §4.1 that has the same effect as a partial assignment statement $x := E$.

(c)  Give a Proof Outline Logic inference rule for the partial assignment statement $x := E$.

(d)  Demonstrate the soundness of your answer to (c) by replacing $x := E$ by your solution to (b) and showing that the resulting formula can be proved using Proof Outline Logic.

**4.12.** The **if** statement in some programming notations has the form

$S$: **if** $B$ **then** $S_1$ **else** $S_2$ **fi**

where $B$ is a boolean expression and $S_1$ and $S_2$ are statements. Execution of $S$ results in execution of $S_1$ if $B$ is *true* and execution of $S_2$ otherwise.

(a)  Show how to implement this new **if** in terms of the **if** statement of §4.1.

(b)  Give control predicate axioms for this new **if**.

(c)  Give a Proof Outline Logic inference rule for this new **if**.

**4.13.** One might postulate an **if** statement like the one given in §4.1 but having an exit control point that is distinct from the exit control points for each of its guarded commands.

(a)  Give control predicate axioms for this new **if**.

(b)  Give a Proof Outline Logic inference rule for this new **if**.

**4.14.** Two statements $S$ and $S'$ are *pre/post partially equivalent* iff for all primitive assertions $P$ and $Q$: there is a formula $\{P\}\, PO(S)\, \{Q\}$ that is a theorem of Proof Outline Logic iff there is a formula $\{P\}\, PO'(S')\, \{Q\}$ that is also a theorem.

(a)    Prove pre/post partial equivalence of $S$ and $S'$:

$$S: \textbf{do } B_1 \rightarrow S_1 \;[]\; B_2 \rightarrow S_2 \;[]\; \cdots \;[]\; B_n \rightarrow S_n \textbf{ od}$$

$$S': \textbf{do } B_1 \vee B_2 \vee \cdots \vee B_n \rightarrow$$
$$\textbf{if } B_1 \rightarrow S_1 \;[]\; B_2 \rightarrow S_2 [] \cdots [] B_n \rightarrow S_n \textbf{ fi}$$
$$\textbf{od}$$

(b)    The **while** statement

      **while** $B$ **do** *body* **od**

specifies repeated execution of *body* provided that $B$ is *true* at the start of each iteration. The **repeat** statement

      **repeat** *body* **until** $B$

specifies repeated execution of *body* provided that $B$ holds at the the end of the previous execution of *body*. Give control predicate axioms and Proof Outline Logic inference rules for **while** and **repeat**. Then, prove pre/post partial equivalence of $S$ and $S'$:

      $S:$ *body* **while** $\neg B$ **do** *body* **od**

      $S':$ **repeat** *body* **until** $B$

**4.15.** Would replacing the postcondition of $GEval_{if}(S)$ Axiom (4.21) by

$$P \wedge ((at(S_1) \wedge B_1) \vee \cdots \vee (at(S_n) \wedge B_n))$$

change the soundness or completeness of Proof Outline Logic? Explain.

**4.16.** Suppose Rule of Consequence (4.25) were removed from the axiomatization of Proof Outline Logic. Is it possible to modify the other axioms and inference rules so the logic is again complete (relative to Predicate Logic)? If so, what modifications suffice?

**4.17.** Assignment Axiom (4.19) gives a precondition in terms of a syntactic transformation of the postcondition. It is also possible to define an axiom for assignment statements that gives the postcondition in terms of a syntactic transformation of the precondition.

(a)    Give such an assignment axiom.

(b)    Is it easier or harder to construct a proof using this "forward" assignment axiom? Why?

**4.18.** Assignment Axiom (4.19) and **skip** Axiom (4.18) are not sound if $P$ mentions control predicates. Give examples to illustrate this.

**4.19.** Consider the following suggestion for an Assignment Axiom:

$$\{P^{\bar{x}, \, at(S), \, after(S)}_{\bar{e}, \, false, \, true}\} \;\; S: \bar{x} := \bar{e} \;\; \{P\}$$

Would Proof Outline Logic remain sound if this axiom were included? Explain.

**4.20.** The following has been proposed as an alternative to **if** Rule (4.22).

$$\frac{\begin{array}{l}\{P\}\, GEval_{if}(S)\,\{R\},\\ (R \wedge at(S_1)) \Rightarrow (P_1 \wedge B_1), \quad ..., \quad (R \wedge at(S_n)) \Rightarrow (P_n \wedge B_n),\\ \{P_1 \wedge B_1\}\, PO(S_1)\,\{Q_1 \wedge Q\}, \quad ..., \quad \{P_n \wedge B_n\}\, PO(S_n)\,\{Q_n \wedge Q\}\end{array}}{\begin{array}{l}\{P\}\\ \quad S\colon \text{if } B_1 \rightarrow \{P_1 \wedge B_1\}\, PO(S_1)\,\{Q_1\}\\ \qquad [] \;\cdots\\ \qquad [] \; B_n \rightarrow \{P_n \wedge B_n\}\, PO(S_n)\,\{Q_n\}\\ \qquad \textbf{fi}\\ \{Q\}\end{array}}$$

Is this rule sound? If not, explain why.

**4.21.** The following alternative for $I_{PO(S)}$ has been proposed in place of (4.14) for defining validity of a proof outline $PO(S)$:

$$(after(S) \Rightarrow post(S)) \wedge (\bigwedge_{T \,\in\, Stmts(S)} (at(T) \Rightarrow pre(T)))$$

Is this new definition equivalent to the original one? Explain.

**4.22.** The requirement that valid proof outlines be self-consistent is one way to avoid problems that arise when multiple assertions are associated with a single control point. An alternative is simply to require that all assertions associated with a single control point be identical. What, if any, are the difficulties with this alternative?

**4.23.** What Proof Outline Logic axioms or inference rules would become unsound if Valid Proof Outline (4.17) were weakened to require Invariance but not Self-Consistency?

**4.24.** Prove (informally) that for programs written using the notation of §4.1, the following holds:

> For every control point $\lambda$, there is some statement $T$ such that either $at(T)$ or $after(T)$ is *true* iff $\lambda$ is active.

Why should this property be of interest to the designer of a logic like Proof Outline Logic?

**4.25.** Suppose you are given the following theorems of Proof Outline Logic:

$$\{P^1\}\ \textbf{do}\ []_{i=1,m} B_i^1 \rightarrow \{B_i^1 \wedge P^1\}\, S_i^1\, \{P^1\}\ \textbf{od}\ \{P^1 \wedge \bigwedge_{i=1,m} \neg B_i^1\},$$

$$\{P^2\}\ \textbf{do}\ []_{i=1,m} B_i^2 \rightarrow \{B_i^2 \wedge P^2\}\, S_i^2\, \{P^2\}\ \textbf{od}\ \{P^2 \wedge \bigwedge_{i=1,m} \neg B_i^2\},$$

$$\cdots$$

$$\{P^n\}\ \textbf{do}\ []_{i=1,m} B_i^n \rightarrow \{B_i^n \wedge P^n\}\, S_i^n\, \{P^n\}\ \textbf{od}\ \{P^n \wedge \bigwedge_{i=1,m} \neg B_i^n\}$$

What additional theorems must be proved in order for the following also to be a theorem?

$$\{\bigwedge_{i=1,n} P^i\}$$

$$\textbf{do}\ []_{\substack{i=1,n\\j=1,m}} B_j^i \rightarrow \{B_j^i \wedge \bigwedge_{i=1,n} P^i\}\, S_j^i\, \{\bigwedge_{i=1,n} P^i\}\ \textbf{od}$$

$$\{\bigwedge_{i=1,n} P^i \wedge \bigwedge_{\substack{i=1,n\\j=1,m}} \neg B_j^i\}$$

**4.26.** The following test for validity of a proof outline $PO(S)$ has been suggested.

> For every pair of assertions $P$ and $Q$ in $PO(S)$ that are separated by some text $T$ that does not contain assertions, $\{P\}\,T\,\{Q\}$ is a theorem of Proof Outline Logic.

Is this test sound? Is this test complete? Explain.

**4.27.** The following test for validity of a proof outline has been suggested.

**Proof Outline Validity Test.**

(1)   Use the following to simplify each assertion $A$ that contains a control predicate $C$:

(a) If $A$ is $pre(S)$ and $at(S) \Rightarrow C$ then in $A$ replace $C$ by *true*.

(b) If $A$ is $pre(S)$ and $C \Rightarrow \neg at(S)$ then in $A$ replace $C$ by *false*.

(c) If $A$ is $post(S)$ and $after(S) \Rightarrow C$ then in $A$ replace $C$ by *true*.

(d) If $A$ is $post(S)$ and $C \Rightarrow \neg after(S)$ then in $A$ replace $C$ by *false*.

(2)   In the resulting proof outline, identify for each control point $\lambda'$ the immediately preceding control point on every execution path to $\lambda'$. Let this set of control points be $pred(\lambda')$.

(3)   For each control point $\lambda$ in $pred(\lambda')$, identify the code that is executed between when $\lambda$ is active and $\lambda'$ next becomes active. Let this be $exec(\lambda, \lambda')$. Define $A_\lambda$ to be the assertion associated with a control point $\lambda$.

(a) If $exec(\lambda, \lambda')$ does not change any program variable or involve evaluating any guard, then check that $A_\lambda \Rightarrow A_{\lambda'}$ is valid.

(b) If $exec(\lambda, \lambda')$ involves executing some statement $S$, then check that $\{A_\lambda\}\,S\,\{A_{\lambda'}\}$ is a theorem of Proof Outline Logic.

(c) If $exec(\lambda, \lambda')$ is a guard evaluation action and guard $B$ is *true*, then check that $A_\lambda \wedge B \Rightarrow A_{\lambda'}$ is valid.

(d) If $exec(\lambda, \lambda')$ is a guard evaluation action and guards $B_1, B_2, ..., B_n$ are *false*, then check that $(A_\lambda \wedge \neg B_1 \wedge \neg B_2 \wedge \cdots \wedge \neg B_n) \Rightarrow A_{\lambda'}$ is valid.   ☐

(a)   Show that any theorem of Proof Outline Logic satisfies this Proof Outline Validity Test.

(b)   Give a procedure to construct a Proof Outline Logic proof for any proof outline $\{P\}\,PO(S)\,\{Q\}$ that satisfies this test.

**4.28.** Evaluate the following function expressions assuming that $b[1..7]$ is an array of integers initialized so that $(\forall i \in \text{Nat}: 1 \le i \le 7: b[i] = i)$.

(a)   $(b;\ 2{:}3)(2)$

(b)   $(b;\ 1{:}2;\ 2{:}3;\ 3{:}4;\ 1{:}4)(3)$

(c)   $(b;\ 7{:}1;\ 6{:}2;\ 5{:}3;\ 4{:}4;\ 3{:}5)(1)$

(d)   $(b;\ 7{:}1;\ 6{:}2;\ 5{:}3;\ 4{:}4;\ 3{:}5)(6)$

(e)   $(b;\ 7{:}b(7);\ 6{:}b(6);\ 5{:}b(5))(6)$

(f)   $(b;\ b(7){:}6;\ b(1){:}7;\ b(2){:}3;\ b(1){:}5)(7)$

**4.29.** For each of the following formulas, use Generalized Assignment Axiom (4.40) to find a precondition $P$ that makes the formula valid.

(a)  $\{P\}\ a[i]:=24\ \{a[i]=a[j]\}$

(b)  $\{P\}\ a[i],a[j]:=2,3\ \{a[i]=2\}$

(c)  $\{P\}\ a[a[i]]:=i\ \{a[i]=i\}$

(d)  $\{P\}\ i,b[i]:=b[i],i\ \{i=b[i]\}$

(e)  $\{P\}\ i,b[i],b[j]:=b[i],b[j],i\ \{i=b[j]\}$

(f)  $\{P\}\ i,b[i],b[b[i]]:=b[i],b[b[i]],i\ \{i=b[b[i]]\}$

(g)  $\{P\}\ i,b[i],b[b[i]]:=b[i],b[b[i]],i\ \{i\neq b[b[i]]\}$

**4.30.** Simplify each of the following:

(a)  $wp(x:=2*y,\ x=13)$

(b)  $wp(j:=j+1,\ 0<j\wedge(\forall j\in \text{Int}:\ 0\leq i\leq j:\ b[i]=5))$

(c)  $wp(x:=x*y,\ x*y=C)$

(d)  $wp(y,y:=x+1,y+z,\ x=y)$

(e)  $wp(x:=(x-y)*(x+y),\ x+y^2\neq0)$

(f)  $wp(S\ \textbf{if}\ false\ \rightarrow\ \textbf{skip fi},\ Q)$ for any $S$ and $Q$.

(g)  $wp(\textbf{do}\ true\ \rightarrow\ x:=x+1\ \textbf{od},\ Q)$ for any $Q$.

(h)  $wp(i:=0\ \textbf{do}\ i<5\ \rightarrow\ i:=i+1\ \textbf{od},\ i=5)$

(i)  $wp(S,\ i\leq5)$ where

$$S:\ i,stop:=0,false$$
$$\textbf{do}\ \neg stop\wedge i<5\ \rightarrow\ i:=i+1$$
$$[]\ \neg stop\ \rightarrow\ stop:=true$$
$$\textbf{od}$$

**4.31.** With Predicate Logic and $wp$ Laws (4.42)–(4.45) and (4.48), prove or disprove that for any $S$:

(a)  $(wp(S,Q)\wedge wp(S,\neg Q))=false.$

(b)  $(wp(S,Q)\vee wp(S,\neg Q))=true.$

**4.32.** With only Predicate Logic, Excluded Miracle Law (4.42), and Distributivity of Conjunction Law (4.43) prove:

(a)  Monotonicity Law (4.44)

(b)  Distributivity of Disjunction Law (4.45)

**4.33.** Prove that the definitions given for the weakest precondition for **skip**, the assignment statement, statement juxtaposition, **if**, and **do** satisfy Excluded Miracle Law (4.42) and Distributivity of Conjunction Law (4.43).

**4.34.** Show by induction on the structure of $S$ that if $P\Rightarrow wp(S,Q)$, then there exists a theorem of proof outline $PO(S)$ where $pre(S)$ is $P$ and $post(S)$ is $Q$. Your argument should be constructive—it should give a method to construct the proof of $PO(S)$ from a Predicate Logic proof that $P\Rightarrow wp(S,Q)$.

**4.35.** It is possible to use *wp* for defining the semantics of a programming construct.

    (a)    Give an informal, operational description of a construct $S$ that satisfies $wp(S,Q) = false$.

    (b)    Give an informal, operational description of a construct $S$ that satisfies $wp(S,Q) = true$.

    (c)    Which of *wp* Laws (4.42)–(4.45) and (4.48) are satisfied by the constructs defined in (a) and (b)?

**4.36.** With only Predicate Logic and *wp* Laws (4.42)–(4.45) and (4.48), prove Precondition for **do** (4.57).

**4.37.** Show that condition (iii) of Precondition for **do** (4.57) is equivalent to

(iii)′ $I \wedge B_i \Rightarrow wp(v := \upsilon\ S_i, v > \upsilon)$

where $v$ is a fresh variable. Is there any reason to prefer one formulation over the other?

**4.38.** Relate condition (iii) of Precondition for **do** (4.57) to Natural Number $\diamondsuit$ Induction Rule (3.69).

**4.39.** Two statements $S$ and $S'$ are *pre/post totally equivalent* iff for all primitive assertions $P$ and $Q$,

$$(P \Rightarrow wp(S, Q)) = (P \Rightarrow wp(S', Q))$$

is valid.

    (a)    Prove pre/post total equivalence of $S$ and $S'$:

$$S: \mathbf{do}\ B_1 \to S_1\ [\!]\ B_2 \to S_2\ [\!]\ \cdots\ [\!]\ B_n \to S_n\ \mathbf{od}$$

$$S': \mathbf{do}\ B_1 \vee B_2 \vee\ \cdots\ \vee B_n \to$$
$$\mathbf{if}\ B_1 \to S_1\ [\!]\ B_2 \to S_2\ [\!]\ \cdots\ [\!]\ B_n \to S_n\ \mathbf{fi}$$
$$\mathbf{od}$$

    (b)    Prove pre/post total equivalence of $S$ and $S'$:

$$S:\ body\ \mathbf{while}\ \neg B\ \mathbf{do}\ body\ \mathbf{od}$$

$$S':\ \mathbf{repeat}\ body\ \mathbf{until}\ B$$

where the **while** and **repeat** statements are as defined in exercise 4.14.

**4.40.** For each of the following programming problems,

    (i)    restate the problem in terms of restrictions on a proof outline for any program solving the problem,

    (ii)    develop a loop invariant $I$ from the postcondition using Deleting a Conjunct (4.59), and

    (iii)    derive a program and proof outline using the methods of §4.5 and your answers to (i) and (ii).

    (a)    Assume that *val* appears somewhere in integer array $a[1 .. n]$, where $n \geq 1$, and determine the location of its first occurrence.

(b)   Find the largest integer that is both a power of 2 and at most $n$.

(c)   Truthify $0 \leq r^2 \ \wedge \ r^2 \leq n \ \wedge \ n < (r+1)^2$ using an invariant obtained by deleting the second conjunct.

(d)   Given $x$ and $y$, compute $q$ and $r$ satisfying $0 \leq r \ \wedge \ r < y \ \wedge \ q*y + r = x$ without using multiplication or division.

**4.41.** For each of the following programming problems,

   (i)   restate the problem in terms of restrictions on a proof outline for any program solving the problem,

   (ii)  develop a loop invariant $I$ from the postcondition using Replacing an Expression by a Variable (4.60), and

   (iii) derive a program and proof outline using the methods of §4.5 and your answers to (i) and (ii).

(a)   Determine whether array $a[1 .. n]$ contains all zeros.

(b)   Compute the length of the longest plateau in a sorted array $a[1 .. n]$ of integers. A *plateau* is a contiguous sequence of array elements having equal values.

(c)   Find the total number of plateaus in a sorted array $a[1 .. n]$ of integers. (Do not forget plateaus of length 1.)

(d)   Given arrays $f[1 .. n]$ and $g[1 .. m]$ that are both sorted in ascending order, count the number of values that appear in both $f$ and $g$. Assume that neither $f$ nor $g$ contains any duplicate values.

(e)   Given an array $dnf[1 .. n]$ containing 1's, 2's, and 3's, rearrange the elements of $dnf$ so that all the 1's precede the 2's and all the 2's precede the 3's. To interchange elements $dnf[i]$ and $dnf[j]$, your program must use operation $swap(i,j)$. Your program should invoke *swap* at most $n$ times.

**4.42.** For each of the following programming problems,

   (i)   restate the problem in terms of restrictions on a proof outline for any program solving the problem,

   (ii)  develop a loop invariant $I$ from the postcondition, and

   (iii) derive a program and proof outline using the methods of §4.5 and your answers to (i) and (ii).

(a)   Interchange the values of $x$ and $y$, if necessary, so that $x \leq y$.

(b)   Count the number of non-negative values in integer array $b[1 .. n]$.

(c)   Reverse the elements in integer array $a[0 .. n]$, so that $a[0]$ and $a[n]$ are interchanged, $a[1]$ and $a[n-1]$ are interchanged, etc.

(d)   Find the greatest common divisor of positive integers $x$, $y$, and $z$. (The greatest common divisor of three positive integers is the largest integer that divides all three of them.)

(e)   Given three integer-valued functions $f$, $g$, and $h$ with domain and range the positive integers, compute the smallest integer $i$ such that there exist integers $j$ and $k$ satisfying $f(i) = g(j) = h(k)$. Assume that each function is non-decreasing for increasing values of its argument.

(f)    Rearrange the elements in integer array $a[1..n]$ so they are in ascending order. (Correctness requires the final array to be a permutation of the original array.)

(g)    Find the coordinates of some occurrence of a given value *val* in integer array $a[1..n,\ 1..m]$, where each row and each column is sorted. You may assume that *val* occurs at least once.

# Chapter 5

# Concurrency and Interference

We now add statements for concurrency and synchronization to the sequential programming notation of Chapter 4. We also extend Proof Outline Logic, using interference freedom to characterize when a valid proof outline for a concurrent program can be derived from valid proof outlines for its component processes. Synchronization statements are then viewed as mechanisms to prevent interference.

## 5.1 Specifying Concurrency

The **cobegin** statement

(5.1)   $S$: **cobegin** $S_1$ ‖ $S_2$ ‖ $\cdots$ ‖ $S_n$ **coend**

specifies concurrent execution of statements $S_1$, ..., $S_n$, making each a process. Its atomic actions are $\mathcal{A}(S_1) \cup \cdots \cup \mathcal{A}(S_n)$. Execution of $S$ results in interleaving the atomic actions of its processes and terminates when these processes have terminated.

For example,

   **cobegin**   $S$: $x := x+1$   ‖   $T$: $x := x+2$   **coend**

defines processes $S$ and $T$ and contains two atomic actions: $x := x+1$ and $x := x+2$.[1] Two histories are possible for this **cobegin**—one in which execution of $T$ follows execution of $S$ and one in which $S$ follows $T$. Another example of a

---

[1] Recall from §4.1 that assignment statements are implemented as single atomic actions.

**cobegin** is the search program of Figure 5.1, which locates the first instance of a value $V$ in array $a$.


## 5.2  Control Predicate Axioms

The control predicate axioms for a **cobegin** $S$ define $at(S)$, $in(S)$, and $after(S)$ in terms of control predicates for its processes. Axiom (5.2a) below asserts that the entry control point for a **cobegin** is active iff an entry control point for each of its processes is active. Axiom (5.2b) asserts that the exit control point for a **cobegin** is active iff an exit control point for each of its processes is active. Finally, axiom (5.2c) asserts that some control point in the **cobegin** is active whenever a control point in one of its processes is active.

(5.2)   **cobegin** *Control Axioms*:  For a **cobegin** statement:
$$S: \textbf{cobegin } S_1 \ \| \ S_2 \ \| \ \cdots \ \| \ S_n \ \textbf{coend}$$
(a) $at(S) = (at(S_1) \wedge \cdots \wedge at(S_n))$
(b) $after(S) = (after(S_1) \wedge \cdots \wedge after(S_n))$
(c) $in(S) = ((in(S_1) \vee after(S_1)) \wedge \cdots \wedge (in(S_n) \vee after(S_n))$
$\qquad\qquad \wedge \neg(after(S_1) \wedge \cdots \wedge after(S_n)))$


We write $\alpha \| \beta$ to denote that $\alpha$, an atomic action or statement, is executed concurrently with an atomic action or statement $\beta$. Observe that relation $\|$ is symmetric. Whether $\alpha \| \beta$ holds depends only on the syntax of the program

```
var et, ot, x, y : Nat;
    a : array [0 .. n−1] of Int

et, x, ot, y := n, 0, n, 1
cobegin
    do x < min(et,ot) → if a[x]=V → et := x
                        [] a[x]≠V → x := x+2
                        fi
    od
||
    do y < min(et,ot) → if a[y]=V → ot := y
                        [] a[y]≠V → y := y+2
                        fi
    od
coend
k := min(et,ot)
```

**Figure 5.1.** Two-process search program

containing $\alpha$ and $\beta$. For the programming notation we have given thus far, if $\alpha$ is an atomic action in one process of a **cobegin** and $\beta$ is an atomic action in a different process of that **cobegin**, then $\alpha \| \beta$ holds.

When $\alpha \| \beta$ holds, executing $\alpha$ cannot affect the values of $at(\beta)$, $after(\beta)$, or $in(\beta)$. This is formalized by the following.

(5.3)    *Process Independence Axiom*: If $\alpha \| \beta$ holds and $cp(\beta)$ denotes one of the control predicates $at(\beta)$, $in(\beta)$, $after(\beta)$, or their negations, then:

$$\{cp(\beta)\} \ \alpha \ \{cp(\beta)\}$$

## 5.3  Interference Freedom

We desire a Proof Outline Logic inference rule with the following as its conclusion:

(5.4)    $\{P\}$
     $S$: **cobegin**
         $PO(S_1) \ \| \ \cdots \ \| \ PO(S_n)$
       **coend**
     $\{Q\}$

According to Valid Proof Outline (4.17), in order for (5.4) to be valid, it must be self-consistent and $I_{PO(S)}$ must be an invariant. Therefore, we investigate conditions on $P$, $Q$, and $PO(S_1)$ through $PO(S_n)$ to ensure that (5.4) is self-consistent and $I_{PO(S)}$ is an invariant. We then formulate these conditions as Proof Outline Logic formulas, obtaining premises for a sound **cobegin** inference rule.

We first consider conditions for ensuring that $I_{PO(S)}$ for (5.4) is not falsified by execution of $S$. Computational Induction Rule (3.24a) allows $I_{PO(S)} \Rightarrow \Box I_{PO(S)}$ to be deduced from $I_{PO(S)} \Rightarrow \bigcirc I_{PO(S)}$, so it suffices that we identify conditions to ensure that no atomic action $\alpha$ of $S$ falsifies $I_{PO(S)}$. By definition (4.14), $I_{PO(S)}$ for (5.4) is:

$$I_{PO(S_1)} \ \wedge \ \cdots \ \wedge \ I_{PO(S_n)} \ \wedge \ (at(S) \Rightarrow pre(S)) \ \wedge \ (after(S) \Rightarrow post(S))$$

Therefore, executing $\alpha$ cannot falsify $I_{PO(S)}$ iff it cannot falsify $I_{PO(S_1)}$, ..., $I_{PO(S_n)}$, $at(S) \Rightarrow pre(S)$, or $after(S) \Rightarrow post(S)$. We now proceed by cases and show that $\alpha$ cannot falsify:

(i)   $I_{PO(S_i)}$, where $\alpha \in \mathcal{A}(S_i)$

(ii)  $I_{PO(S_j)}$, where $\alpha \notin \mathcal{A}(S_j)$

(iii) $at(S) \Rightarrow pre(S)$

(iv)  $after(S) \Rightarrow post(S)$

For case (i), we must identify a condition to ensure that executing $\alpha$ does not falsify any assertion in proof outline $PO(S_i)$ for the process $S_i$ that contains $\alpha$. An obvious choice is a condition that implies that $PO(S_i)$ is valid, since the invariance requirement of Valid Proof Outline (4.17) for $PO(S_i)$ is exactly what we seek. In general, $\alpha$ can be from any process, so we require:

(5.5)  **Sequential Correctness Condition.** $PO(S_1)$, ..., $PO(S_n)$ are theorems of Proof Outline Logic.                                                     □

For case (ii), we are concerned with finding a condition to ensure that execution of an atomic action $\alpha$ from one process does not falsify the proof outline invariant $I_{PO(S_j)}$ for another. Since $I_{PO(S_j)}$ is just a conjunction (of implications $cp \Rightarrow A_{cp}$), it suffices to identify a condition that ensures that $\alpha$ does not falsify or *interfere with* each of these conjuncts.

Define $pre^*(\alpha)$ to be the predicate that, according to the assertions in the proof outline containing $\alpha$, is satisfied just before $\alpha$ executes:

(5.6)  **Precondition of an Action.** If $\alpha$ is a **skip** or assignment statement with label $S$, or $\alpha$ is guard evaluation action $GEval_{if}(S)$, then:

$$pre^*(\alpha): \ pre(S)$$

If $\alpha$ is guard evaluation action $GEval_{do}(S)$ for a **do**

$$S: \ \mathbf{do} \ B_1 \to S_1 \ [] \ B_2 \to S_2 \ [] \ \cdots \ [] \ B_n \to S_n \ \mathbf{od}$$

then:

$$pre^*(\alpha): \ pre(S) \vee (\bigvee_{1 \le i \le n} post(S_i))$$

                                                                                    □

The condition that $\alpha$ does not falsify an assertion $A$ is then implied by the validity of the *interference freedom triple*:

(5.7)  $NI(\alpha, A)$:  $\{pre^*(\alpha) \wedge A\} \ \alpha \ \{A\}$

In order to prove that $\alpha$ does not falsify conjunct $cp \Rightarrow A_{cp}$ of $I_{PO(S_j)}$, it suffices to prove $NI(\alpha, cp \Rightarrow A_{cp})$. This, in turn, can be demonstrated by proving $NI(\alpha, A_{cp})$, because:

«$NI(\alpha, A_{cp})$»
   1.  $\{pre^*(\alpha) \wedge A_{cp}\} \ \alpha \ \{A_{cp}\}$

«Process Independence Axiom (5.3), since $\alpha \notin \mathcal{A}(S_j)$»
   2.  $\{\neg cp\} \ \alpha \ \{\neg cp\}$

«Rule of Consequence (4.25) with 2, since $pre^*(\alpha) \wedge \neg cp \Rightarrow \neg cp$»
   3.  $\{pre^*(\alpha) \wedge \neg cp\} \ \alpha \ \{\neg cp\}$

«Disjunction Rule (4.31) with 1 and 3»
   4.   $\{pre^*(\alpha) \land (\neg cp \lor A_{cp})\} \; \alpha \; \{\neg cp \lor A_{cp}\}$

«Rule of Equivalence (4.26) with 4, since $(\neg cp \lor A_{cp}) = (cp \Rightarrow A_{cp})$»
   5.   $\{pre^*(\alpha) \land (cp \Rightarrow A_{cp})\} \; \alpha \; \{cp \Rightarrow A_{cp}\}$

Generalizing, we conclude that no atomic action $\alpha$ from one process can interfere with the proof outline invariant for any other process provided that the following condition holds.

(5.8)  **Interference Freedom Condition.** A proof outline

$$\{P\} \; S: \textbf{cobegin} \; PO(S_1) \; \| \; \cdots \; \| PO(S_n) \; \textbf{coend} \; \{Q\}$$

is proved *interference free* by establishing:

> For all atomic actions $\alpha \in \mathcal{A}(S)$:
>> For all $j$, $1 \le j \le n$:
>>> For all assertions $A$ in $PO(S_j)$:
>>>> If $\alpha \| S_j$ then $NI(\alpha, A)$.                     ☐

Case (iii), that $\alpha$ does not falsify $at(S) \Rightarrow pre(S)$, is trivially satisfied because $at(S)$ is made *false* by every atomic action in $S$.

Case (iv) is also trivial except when all but one process $S_i$ have terminated, $I_{PO(S)}$ holds, and $\alpha$ is the last atomic action of $S_i$. Consider that case. For every process $S_j$ that has terminated, the control predicate axioms imply that $after(S_j)$ holds. Because $I_{PO(S)}$ holds, we then conclude that $post(S_j)$ is satisfied. The validity of $PO(S_i)$ from Sequential Correctness Condition (5.5) implies that $post(S_i)$ will be satisfied when $\alpha$ terminates; and Interference Freedom Condition (5.8) implies that no $post(S_j)$ for any other process is falsified by $\alpha$. Thus, $post(PO(S_1)) \land \cdots \land post(PO(S_n))$ or any assertion implied by it will be satisfied when $\alpha$ terminates. So the following suffices.

(5.9)  **Postcondition Condition.**
$$post(PO(S_1)) \land \cdots \land post(PO(S_n)) \Rightarrow post(S) \qquad ☐$$

We next turn to ensuring that proof outline (5.4) is self-consistent, which is the case iff $at(S) \land P \Rightarrow I_{PO(S)}$ is $\mathcal{H}_S^+$-valid. In light of **cobegin** Control Axiom (5.2a) for $at(S)$ in (5.4), it would seem reasonable to expect that whenever $pre(S)$ holds then so should $pre(PO(S_1)) \land \cdots \land pre(PO(S_n))$.

(5.10)  **cobegin Self-Consistency Condition.**
$$pre(S) \Rightarrow pre(PO(S_1)) \land \cdots \land pre(PO(S_n)) \qquad ☐$$

Here is the proof that this condition ensures self-consistency of (5.4).

$pre(S) \Rightarrow pre(PO(S_1)) \wedge \cdots \wedge pre(PO(S_n))$

$=$   «**cobegin** Control Axiom (5.2a)»

$at(S) \wedge pre(S) \Rightarrow$

$\qquad at(S_1) \wedge pre(PO(S_1)) \wedge \cdots \wedge at(S_n) \wedge pre(PO(S_n))$

$\Rightarrow$   «$at(S_i) \wedge pre(PO(S_i)) \Rightarrow I_{PO(S_i)}$ due to self-consistency of

$\qquad PO(S_i)$ from Sequential Correctness Condition (5.5)»

$at(S) \wedge pre(S) \Rightarrow I_{PO(S_1)} \wedge \cdots \wedge I_{PO(S_n)}$

$\Rightarrow$   «$A \wedge B \Rightarrow (A \Rightarrow B)$»

$at(S) \wedge pre(S) \Rightarrow I_{PO(S_1)} \wedge \cdots \wedge I_{PO(S_n)} \wedge (at(S) \Rightarrow pre(S))$

$\Rightarrow$   «**cobegin** Control Axioms (5.2) imply $at(S) \Rightarrow \neg after(S)$»

$at(S) \wedge pre(S) \Rightarrow I_{PO(S_1)} \wedge \cdots \wedge I_{PO(S_n)}$

$\qquad\qquad\qquad\qquad \wedge (at(S) \Rightarrow pre(S)) \wedge (after(S) \Rightarrow post(S))$

$=$   «Definition (4.14) of $I_{PO(S)}$»

$at(S) \wedge pre(S) \Rightarrow I_{PO(S)}$

We have derived four conditions—Sequential Correctness Condition (5.5), Interference Freedom Condition (5.8), Postcondition Condition (5.9), and **cobegin** Self-Consistency Condition (5.10)—to ensure that proof outlines for processes can be combined to form a valid proof outline for the **cobegin** constructed using these processes. A Proof Outline Logic inference rule for **cobegin** results from regarding these four conditions as premises and proof outline (5.4) as the conclusion:

(5.11) **cobegin** *Rule*:

> (a) $PO(S_1), ..., PO(S_n),$
>
> (b) $P \Rightarrow pre(PO(S_1)) \wedge \cdots \wedge pre(PO(S_n)),$
>
> (c) $post(PO(S_1)) \wedge \cdots \wedge post(PO(S_n)) \Rightarrow Q,$
>
> (d) $PO(S_1), ..., PO(S_n)$ are interference free.
>
> ---
> $\{P\}$ **cobegin** $PO(S_1) \parallel \cdots \parallel PO(S_n)$ **coend** $\{Q\}$

## Strengthening and Weakening

To gain experience with **cobegin** Rule (5.11), we develop a proof outline for a trivial concurrent program:

(5.12) **cobegin**   $S: x := x+1$   $\parallel$   $T: x := x+2$   **coend**

First, a theorem is constructed for each process in isolation. This permits premise (a) of **cobegin** Rule (5.11) to be satisfied. Assignment Axiom (4.19) yields:

$\{x=X\}$  $S: x := x+1$  $\{x=X+1\}$

$\{x=X\}$  $T: x := x+2$  $\{x=X+2\}$

We combine these to produce the (not necessarily interference-free or valid) proof outline:

(5.13) $\{P\}$
    **cobegin**
        $\{x=\text{X}\}$   $S: \ x := x+1$   $\{x=\text{X}+1\}$
    $\|$
        $\{x=\text{X}\}$   $T: \ x := x+2$   $\{x=\text{X}+2\}$
    **coend**
    $\{Q\}$

We now check premises (b), (c), and (d) of **cobegin** Rule (5.11). Premise (b) requires that:

$$
\begin{aligned}
& P \ \Rightarrow \ pre(S) \wedge pre(T) \\
= \ & \quad \text{«Substituting for } pre(S) \text{ and } pre(T)\text{»} \\
& P \ \Rightarrow \ x=\text{X} \wedge x=\text{X}
\end{aligned}
$$

We therefore conclude that $P \Rightarrow x=\text{X}$ must be valid and choose $x=\text{X}$ for $P$, noting that we have latitude to strengthen this assertion if necessary.

Premise (c) requires that:

$$
\begin{aligned}
& x=\text{X}+1 \wedge x=\text{X}+2 \ \Rightarrow \ Q \\
= \ & \quad \text{«Predicate Logic»} \\
& false \Rightarrow Q
\end{aligned}
$$

This gives little guidance for choosing $Q$, since $false \Rightarrow Q$ is valid for all $Q$. For the time being, we leave $Q$ unspecified.

To check premise (d), note that $S \| T$ holds. There is one atomic action in $\mathcal{A}(S)$ ($x := x+1$) and two assertions ($pre(S)$ and $post(S)$) in $PO(S)$; and there is one atomic action in $\mathcal{A}(T)$ ($x := x+2$) and two assertions ($pre(T)$ and $post(T)$) in $PO(T)$. Premise (d) therefore requires that $NI(S, pre(T))$, $NI(T, pre(S))$, $NI(S, post(T))$, and $NI(T, post(S))$ be theorems.

We expand $NI(S, pre(T))$ and get:

$$
\begin{aligned}
NI(S, pre(T)): \quad & \{pre^*(S) \wedge pre(T)\} \ S \ \{pre(T)\} \\
& \quad \text{«Precondition of an Action (5.6)»} \\
= \ & \{pre(S) \wedge pre(T)\} \ S \ \{pre(T)\} \\
& \quad \text{«substituting for } pre(S) \text{ and } pre(T)\text{»} \\
= \ & \{x=\text{X} \wedge x=\text{X}\} \ x := x+1 \ \{x=\text{X}\}
\end{aligned}
$$

This triple is not valid, so we conclude that $S$ interferes with $pre(T)$. Similarly, $S$ interferes with $post(T)$ and $T$ interferes with both $pre(S)$ and $post(S)$. We must eliminate this interference.

There are two general approaches for eliminating interference in a proof outline.

(5.14) **Strengthening.** To eliminate interference of atomic action $\alpha$ with an assertion $A$, strengthen $pre^*(\alpha)$ and/or $A$ so that $NI(\alpha, A)$ becomes a theorem.          □

(5.15) **Weakening.** To eliminate interference of atomic action $\alpha$ with an assertion $A$, weaken $A$ so that $NI(\alpha, A)$ becomes a theorem.          □

Strengthening (5.14) can always be used to make $NI(\alpha, A)$ a theorem by selecting for $pre^*(\alpha)$ and $A$ predicates so strong that $pre(NI(\alpha, A))$ is *false*, because any triple with precondition equivalent to *false* is a theorem. However, less extreme strengthenings usually suffice. Weakening (5.15) can always be used to make $NI(\alpha, A)$ a theorem by selecting for $A$ a predicate so weak that $post(NI(\alpha, A))$ is *true*, because any triple with postcondition equivalent to *true* is a theorem. Less extreme weakenings usually suffice.

Constraints on $pre(\alpha)$ and $A$ may limit the use of Strengthening (5.14) and Weakening (5.15). These constraints typically arise in connection with the other premises of **cobegin** Rule (5.11) and the intended use of a proof outline. For example, we reject Strengthening (5.14) as a way to make $NI(S, pre(T))$ a theorem because there is no way to strengthen $pre(S)$ and/or $pre(T)$ and still have these assertions be implied by $P$, as is required by premise (b) of **cobegin** Rule (5.11).[2] Our use of Weakening (5.15) too will be limited. Proof outlines having stronger assertions tend to be more useful, and Weakening (5.15) leads away from such proof outlines.

With Strengthening (5.14) ruled out for $pre(S)$ and $pre(T)$ of (5.13), we try Weakening (5.15) and weaken $pre(T)$ by adding $x=X+1$ as a disjunct. This disjunct is chosen to account for the fact that $pre(T)$ must hold both before and after $S$ is executed. The desire to leave premise (a) satisfied forces weakening of $post(T)$, and we obtain the following proof outline.

```
{P:  x=X}
cobegin
    {x=X}  S:  x := x+1   {x=X+1}
||
    {x=X ∨ x=X+1}  T:  x := x+2   {x=X+2 ∨ x=X+3}
coend
{Q}
```

By expanding $NI(S, pre(T))$ we get:

$$NI(S, pre(T)): \quad \{pre^*(S) \wedge pre(T)\}\ S\ \{pre(T)\}$$

---

[2]Of course, it is possible to strengthen $P$, but there is no basis for doing so.

«Precondition of an Action (5.6)»
$= \{pre(S) \wedge pre(T)\} \ S \ \{pre(T)\}$

«substituting for $pre(S)$ and $pre(T)$»
$= \{x=X \wedge (x=X \vee x=X+1)\} \ x := x+1 \ \ \{x=X \vee x=X+1\}$

«simplifying the precondition»
$= \{x=X\} \ x := x+1 \ \{x=X \vee x=X+1\}$

Now, $NI(S, pre(T))$ is a theorem. Moreover, $P \Rightarrow pre(S) \wedge pre(T)$ remains valid, so premise (b) remains satisfied.

To continue with the interference-freedom obligations for satisfying premise (d), we check whether $NI(T, pre(S))$ is a theorem:

$NI(T, pre(S))$:    $\{pre^*(T) \wedge pre(S)\} \ T \ \{pre(S)\}$

«Precondition of an Action (5.6)»
$= \{pre(T) \wedge pre(S)\} \ T \ \{pre(S)\}$

«substituting for $pre(T)$ and $pre(S)$»
$= \{(x=X \vee x=X+1) \wedge x=X\} \ x := x+2 \ \ \{x=X\}$

«simplifying the precondition»
$= \{x=X\} \ x := x+2 \ \{x=X\}$

It is not. Again, Weakening (5.15) is used to weaken $pre(S)$, and then $post(S)$ is modified so that premise (a) remains satisfied. This results in:

(5.16)   $\{P:\ x=X\}$
     **cobegin**
         $\{x=X \vee x=X+2\} \ S:\ x := x+1 \ \ \{x=X+1 \vee x=X+3\}$
     $\|$
         $\{x=X \vee x=X+1\} \ T:\ x := x+2 \ \ \{x=X+2 \vee x=X+3\}$
     **coend**
     $\{Q\}$

$NI(T, pre(S))$ becomes:

$NI(T, pre(S))$:    $\{pre^*(T) \wedge pre(S)\} \ T \ \{pre(S)\}$

«Precondition of an Action (5.6)»
$= \{pre(T) \wedge pre(S)\} \ T \ \{pre(S)\}$

«substituting for $pre(T)$ and $pre(S)$»
$= \{(x=X \vee x=X+1) \wedge (x=X \vee x=X+2)\}$
$x := x+2$
$\{x=X \vee x=X+2\}$

«simplifying the postcondition»
$= \{x=X\} \ x := x+2 \ \{x=X \vee x=X+2\}$

This is a theorem. Furthermore, this weakening of *pre*(*S*) leaves premise (b) satisfied and leaves *NI*(*S*, *pre*(*T*)) a theorem.

The last two interference-freedom triples are:

$$NI(S, post(T)): \quad \{(x=X \vee x=X+2) \wedge (x=X+2 \vee x=X+3)\}$$
$$x := x+1$$
$$\{x=X+2 \vee x=X+3\}$$

$$NI(T, post(S)): \quad \{(x=X \vee x=X+1) \wedge (x=X+1 \vee x=X+3)\}$$
$$x := x+2$$
$$\{x=X+1 \vee x=X+3\}$$

Both are theorems.

With the postcondition for each process altered, we return to premise (c) of **cobegin** Rule (5.11):

$$post(S) \wedge post(T) \;\Rightarrow\; Q$$
$$= \quad \text{«Substituting for } post(S) \text{ and } post(T)\text{»}$$
$$(x=X+1 \vee x=X+3) \wedge (x=X+2 \vee x=X+3) \;\Rightarrow\; Q$$
$$= \quad \text{«Predicate Logic»}$$
$$x=X+3 \;\Rightarrow\; Q$$

So, we choose $x=X+3$ for $Q$. The resulting Proof Outline Logic theorem is given in Figure 5.2.

The pattern followed in this example is typical. First, to satisfy premise (a) of **cobegin** Rule (5.11), a proof outline for each process is constructed in isolation. Then, premise (b) is used to constrain the precondition of the **cobegin**. Next, to satisfy premise (d), interference-freedom triples are enumerated and checked. If any interference is discovered, then proof outlines for processes are changed and premises (a), (b), and (d) are rechecked. Finally, to satisfy premise (c), the postcondition for the **cobegin** is formed from the conjunction of the postconditions of each proof outline.

As a second example, we construct a proof outline for the two-process search program of Figure 5.1. First, to satisfy premise (a) of **cobegin** Rule

---

$$\{P: \ x=X\}$$
**cobegin**
$$\{x=X \vee x=X+2\} \quad S: \ x := x+1 \quad \{x=X+1 \vee x=X+3\}$$
||
$$\{x=X \vee x=X+1\} \quad T: \ x := x+2 \quad \{x=X+2 \vee x=X+3\}$$
**coend**
$$\{Q: \ x=X+3\}$$

**Figure 5.2.** Simple **cobegin** example

(5.11), a proof outline for each process in isolation is constructed. By combining these, we get the (not necessarily interference-free or valid) proof outline of Figure 5.3, which satisfies premise (a) of **cobegin** Rule (5.11).

Premise (b) is satisfied, because the following is valid:

$$et=n \wedge x=0 \wedge ot=n \wedge y=1 \;\Rightarrow\; I_E \wedge I_O$$

Premise (c) is trivially satisfied, since its antecedent and consequent are identical. Finally, premise (d) requires checking 64 (!) triples—each process has 4 atomic actions and 8 assertions. Fortunately, proving most of these triples is trivial; $E_3$ and $O_3$ are the only atomic actions that might interfere with an assertion in the other process, because they are the only atomic actions that change variables (i.e., $et$ and $ot$) mentioned in assertions of another process.

---

$\{true\}$
$et, x, ot, y := n, 0, n, 1$
$\{et=n \wedge x=0 \wedge ot=n \wedge y=1\}$
**cobegin**
  $\{I_E: (et<n \Rightarrow a[x]=V) \wedge (\forall i \in \text{Int}: 0\leq2*i<x: a[2*i]\neq V) \wedge et\leq n\}$
  $E_1:$ **do** $x<\min(et,ot) \to \{I_E \wedge x<\min(et,ot)\}$
            $E_2:$ **if** $a[x]=V \to \{I_E \wedge x<\min(et,ot) \wedge a[x]=V\}$
                      $E_3:$ $et:=x$  $\{I_E\}$
                  $[]$ $a[x]\neq V \to \{I_E \wedge x<\min(et,ot) \wedge a[x]\neq V\}$
                      $E_4:$ $x:=x+2$  $\{I_E\}$
            **fi** $\{I_E\}$
        **od**  $\{I_E \wedge x\geq\min(et,ot)\}$
$\|$
  $\{I_O: (ot<n \Rightarrow a[y]=V)$
          $\wedge (\forall i \in \text{Int}: 0\leq2*i+1<y: a[2*i+1]\neq V) \wedge ot\leq n\}$
  $O_1:$ **do** $y<\min(et,ot) \to \{I_O \wedge y<\min(et,ot)\}$
            $O_2:$ **if** $a[y]=V \to \{I_O \wedge y<\min(et,ot) \wedge a[y]=V\}$
                      $O_3:$ $ot:=y$  $\{I_O\}$
                  $[]$ $a[y]\neq V \to \{I_O \wedge y<\min(et,ot) \wedge a[y]\neq V\}$
                      $O_4:$ $y:=y+2$  $\{I_O\}$
            **fi** $\{I_O\}$
        **od**  $\{I_O \wedge y\geq\min(et,ot)\}$
**coend**
$\{I_E \wedge x\geq\min(et,ot) \wedge I_O \wedge y\geq\min(et,ot)\}$
$k := \min(et, ot)$
$\{(k<n \Rightarrow a[k]=V) \wedge (\forall i \in \text{Int}: 0\leq i<k: a[i]\neq V)\}$

**Figure 5.3.** Search program proof outline

This observation leads to a general rule for identifying the triples that must actually be checked when trying to establish interference freedom. If an assertion $A$ does not depend on any aspect of the state that is modified by executing $\alpha$, then $\alpha$ cannot interfere with $A$, and $NI(\alpha, A)$ is valid. Thus, if the program variables and control predicates changed by executing $\alpha$ do not appear in $A$, then proving $NI(\alpha, A)$ is an unnecessary formality.

In our programming notation, assignment statements are the only way to change the value of a program variable, and Process Independence Axiom (5.3) allows us to conclude that executing an atomic action in one process cannot change a control predicate corresponding to a control point in another. To formalize this as a rule of Proof Outline Logic, we define

(5.17) **Disjointness Condition.** Atomic action $\alpha$ in one process and assertion $A$ in another are *disjoint* iff

    (a)    no program variable mentioned in $A$ appears as a target of an assignment statement in $\alpha$, and

    (b)    no control predicate in $A$ concerns the process that contains $\alpha$. $\quad\square$

We now have the following Proof Outline Logic rule:

(5.18) *Disjointness NI Rule*: $\dfrac{\alpha \text{ and } A \text{ are disjoint}}{NI(\alpha, A)}$

This rule permits interference freedom to be established simply by identifying and proving only those triples $NI(\alpha, A)$ for which (5.18) cannot be applied.

Back to the proof outline of Figure 5.3, due to Disjointness NI Rule (5.18), only 8 (of the 64) triples need be proved in order to discharge premise (d):

(5.19) $NI(E_3, pre(O_2))$:   $\{pre(E_3) \wedge pre(O_2)\}\, E_3\, \{pre(O_2)\}$

(5.20) $NI(E_3, pre(O_3))$:   $\{pre(E_3) \wedge pre(O_3)\}\, E_3\, \{pre(O_3)\}$

(5.21) $NI(E_3, pre(O_4))$:   $\{pre(E_3) \wedge pre(O_4)\}\, E_3\, \{pre(O_4)\}$

(5.22) $NI(E_3, post(O_1))$:   $\{pre(E_3) \wedge post(O_1)\}\, E_3\, \{post(O_1)\}$

(5.23) $NI(O_3, pre(E_2))$:   $\{pre(O_3) \wedge pre(E_2)\}\, O_3\, \{pre(E_2)\}$

(5.24) $NI(O_3, pre(E_3))$:   $\{pre(O_3) \wedge pre(E_3)\}\, O_3\, \{pre(E_3)\}$

(5.25) $NI(O_3, pre(E_4))$:   $\{pre(O_3) \wedge pre(E_4)\}\, O_3\, \{pre(E_4)\}$

(5.26) $NI(O_3, post(E_1))$:   $\{pre(O_3) \wedge post(E_1)\}\, O_3\, \{post(E_1)\}$

Of these, (5.19)–(5.21) are not valid because executing $et := x$ can interfere with $y < \min(et, ot)$ by changing $et$ so that $et < y$. Similarly, (5.23)–(5.25) are not valid because executing $ot := y$ can interfere with $x < \min(et, ot)$. Triples

(5.22) and (5.26) are theorems—assigning $x$ to $et$ ($y$ to $ot$) when $x < \min(et, ot)$ ($y < \min(et, ot)$) can only reduce the value of $\min(et, ot)$ and therefore cannot falsify $y \geq \min(et, ot)$ ($x \geq \min(et, ot)$).

To eliminate the interference by $E_3$ and $O_3$, we use Weakening (5.15) and replace $x < \min(et, ot)$ in $PO(E_1)$ and $y < \min(et, ot)$ in $PO(O_1)$ by weaker predicates. All that is required in order to satisfy premise (a) for $PO(E_1)$ is that $x < et$ hold, which can be inferred in $pre(E_2)$ from guard $x < \min(et, ot)$ and then propagated to subsequent assertions. All that is required in order to satisfy premise (a) for $PO(O_1)$ is that $y < ot$ hold, which can be obtained in the same manner. The replacement of $x < \min(et, ot)$ by $x < et$ and of $y < \min(et, ot)$ by $y < ot$ results in the proof outline of Figure 5.4. Now (5.19)–(5.26) can be proved. Thus, the proof outline of Figure 5.4 is a theorem of Proof Outline Logic and is, therefore, valid.

---

$\{true\}$
$et, x, ot, y := n, 0, n, 1$
$\{et=n \wedge x=0 \wedge ot=n \wedge y=1\}$
**cobegin**
    $\{I_E\colon (et<n \Rightarrow a[x]=V) \wedge (\forall i \in \text{Int: } 0 \leq 2*i < x\colon a[2*i] \neq V) \wedge et \leq n\}$
    $E_1\colon$ **do** $x < \min(et, ot) \to \{I_E \wedge x < et\}$
        $E_2\colon$ **if** $a[x]=V \to \{I_E \wedge x < et \wedge a[x]=V\}$
            $E_3\colon et := x \quad \{I_E\}$
        $[]\ a[x] \neq V \to \{I_E \wedge x < et \wedge a[x] \neq V\}$
            $E_4\colon x := x+2 \quad \{I_E\}$
      **fi** $\{I_E\}$
    **od** $\{I_E \wedge x \geq \min(et, ot)\}$

$\parallel$

    $\{I_O\colon (ot<n \Rightarrow a[y]=V)$
        $\wedge (\forall i \in \text{Int: } 0 \leq 2*i+1 < y\colon a[2*i+1] \neq V) \wedge ot \leq n\}$
    $O_1\colon$ **do** $y < \min(et, ot) \to \{I_O \wedge y < ot\}$
        $O_2\colon$ **if** $a[y]=V \to \{I_O \wedge y < ot \wedge a[y]=V\}$
            $O_3\colon ot := y \quad \{I_O\}$
        $[]\ a[y] \neq V \to \{I_O \wedge y < ot \wedge a[y] \neq V\}$
            $O_4\colon y := y+2 \quad \{I_O\}$
      **fi** $\{I_O\}$
    **od** $\{I_O \wedge y \geq \min(et, ot)\}$
**coend**
$\{I_E \wedge x \geq \min(et, ot) \wedge I_O \wedge y \geq \min(et, ot)\}$
$k := \min(et, ot)$
$\{(k<n \Rightarrow a[k]=V) \wedge (\forall i \in \text{Int: } 0 \leq i < k\colon a[i] \neq V)\}$

**Figure 5.4.** Search program revised proof outline

## 5.4  Hiding Control Predicates in Derived Terms

A need for control predicates in Proof Outline Logic becomes apparent in constructing a proof outline for the following concurrent program.

(5.27)  $R$:  **cobegin**   $S$: $x := x+1$   ∥   $T$: $x := x+1$   **coend**

Assignment Axiom (4.19) yields proof outlines for each process in isolation.

$\{x=X\}$  $S$: $x := x+1$  $\{x=X+1\}$
$\{x=X\}$  $T$: $x := x+1$  $\{x=X+1\}$

We thus obtain a (not necessarily interference-free or valid) proof outline in which premises (a), (b), and (c) of **cobegin** Rule (5.11) are satisfied.

(5.28)  $\{x=X\}$
    $R$:  **cobegin**
            $\{x=X\}$  $S$: $x := x+1$  $\{x=X+1\}$
        ∥
            $\{x=X\}$  $T$: $x := x+1$  $\{x=X+1\}$
        **coend**
    $\{x=X+1\}$

Premise (d) requires proving four triples:

$NI(S, pre(T))$:   $\{pre(S) \land pre(T)\}$ $S$ $\{pre(T)\}$
$NI(S, post(T))$:   $\{pre(S) \land post(T)\}$ $S$ $\{post(T)\}$
$NI(T, pre(S))$:   $\{pre(T) \land pre(S)\}$ $T$ $\{pre(S)\}$
$NI(T, post(S))$:   $\{pre(T) \land post(S)\}$ $T$ $\{post(S)\}$

The first triple is not valid; executing $x := x+1$ interferes with $x=X$. Since there is no way to strengthen $pre(S)$ and still have it be implied by $pre(R)$, as required by premise (b) of **cobegin** Rule (5.11), we use Weakening (5.15) to modify $pre(S)$, accounting for possible execution of $T$ when $x=X$. We then modify $post(S)$ so that the proof outline for $S$ remains valid. A similar argument suggests that $pre(T)$ and $post(T)$ be weakened, resulting in the following proof outline.

    $\{x=X\}$
    $R$:  **cobegin**
            $\{x=X \lor x=X+1\}$  $S$: $x := x+1$  $\{x=X+1 \lor x=X+2\}$
        ∥
            $\{x=X \lor x=X+1\}$  $T$: $x := x+1$  $\{x=X+1 \lor x=X+2\}$
        **coend**
    $\{x=X+1 \lor x=X+2\}$

Note that $post(R)$ is not as expected, and there is still interference! Weakening assertions again results in another proof outline:

$\{x=X\}$
$R$: **cobegin**
> $\{x=X \lor x=X+1 \lor x=X+2\}$
> $S$: $x := x+1$
> $\{x=X+1 \lor x=X+2 \lor x=X+3\}$
>
> ‖
>
> $\{x=X \lor x=X+1 \lor x=X+2\}$
> $T$: $x := x+1$
> $\{x=X+1 \lor x=X+2 \lor x=X+3\}$
> **coend**
$\{x=X+1 \lor x=X+2 \lor x=X+3\}$

This, too, is unsatisfactory, because $post(R)$ does not imply $x=X+2$ and there is still interference. By now it should be clear that additional weakening along these lines will not produce the desired proof outline.

To understand the problem, return to (5.28), where we were required, but were unable, to prove $NI(S, pre(T))$. The problem is that $pre(T)$ of (5.28) is too strong—the value of $x$ depends on whether $S$ has executed, but $pre(T)$ restricts $x$ to a single value, X. By using control predicates, we can construct assertions in which the values of program variables, like $x$, change as a function of the active control points in another process. This insight allows us to construct another proof outline for (5.27).

First, we construct a proof outline for each process in isolation. The proof outline for the first process is:

(5.29)  $\{at(S) \ \land \ ((at(T) \land x=X) \lor (after(T) \land x=X+1))\}$
$\quad\quad$ $S$: $x := x+1$
$\quad\quad$ $\{after(S) \ \land \ ((at(T) \land x=X+1) \lor (after(T) \land x=X+2))\}$

We give a detailed proof of this theorem to illustrate how control predicates are introduced in a proof outline.

《Assignment Axiom (4.19)》
    1.   $\{x=X\}$   $S$: $x := x+1$   $\{x=X+1\}$
    2.   $\{x=X+1\}$   $S$: $x := x+1$   $\{x=X+2\}$

《Process Independence Axiom (5.3) for $T$ and $S$ in different processes》
    3.   $\{at(T)\}$   $S$: $x := x+1$   $\{at(T)\}$
    4.   $\{after(T)\}$   $S$: $x := x+1$   $\{after(T)\}$

《Conjunction Rule (4.30) using 3 with 1; 4 with 2》
    5.   $\{at(T) \land x=X\}$   $S$: $x := x+1$   $\{at(T) \land x=X+1\}$
    6.   $\{after(T) \land x=X+1\}$   $S$: $x := x+1$   $\{after(T) \land x=X+2\}$

«Disjunction Rule (4.31) with 5 and 6»
  7.   $\{(at(T) \wedge x=X) \vee (after(T) \wedge x=X+1)\}$
       $S:\ x := x+1$
       $\{(at(T) \wedge x=X+1) \vee (after(T) \wedge x=X+2)\}$

«Control-Point Identity (4.28) with 7»
  8.   $\{at(S) \wedge ((at(T) \wedge x=X) \vee (after(T) \wedge x=X+1))\}$
       $S:\ x := x+1$
       $\{after(S) \wedge ((at(T) \wedge x=X+1) \vee (after(T) \wedge x=X+2))\}$

A similar proof establishes:

(5.30)  $\{at(T) \wedge ((at(S) \wedge x=X) \vee (after(S) \wedge x=X+1))\}$
        $T:\ x := x+1$
        $\{after(T) \wedge ((at(S) \wedge x=X+1) \vee (after(S) \wedge x=X+2))\}$

Thus, the following proof outline satisfies premise (a) of **cobegin** Rule (5.11).

(5.31)  $\{at(R) \wedge x=X\}$
        $R:$  **cobegin**
               $\{at(S) \wedge ((at(T) \wedge x=X) \vee (after(T) \wedge x=X+1))\}$
               $S:\ x := x+1$
               $\{after(S) \wedge ((at(T) \wedge x=X+1) \vee (after(T) \wedge x=X+2))\}$
        ||
               $\{at(T) \wedge ((at(S) \wedge x=X) \vee (after(S) \wedge x=X+1))\}$
               $T:\ x := x+1$
               $\{after(T) \wedge ((at(S) \wedge x=X+1) \vee (after(S) \wedge x=X+2))\}$
        **coend**
        $\{after(R) \wedge x=X+2\}$

It is also simple to verify that (5.31) satisfies premises (b), (c), and (d); we omit those steps here.

As the final step in constructing the proof outline, we can delete the control predicates from $pre(R)$ and $post(R)$. Rule of Consequence (4.25) allows $post(R)$ in (5.31) to be weakened to $x=X+2 \vee \neg after(R)$, since

$$(after(R) \wedge x=X+2) \Rightarrow (x=X+2 \vee \neg after(R))$$

is valid. Control-Predicate Deletion (4.27) applied to the result produces the proof outline in Figure 5.5.

In retrospect, it should not be surprising that some theorems of Proof Outline Logic require control predicates in assertions. The set of active control points influences execution by defining which atomic actions can be executed next and therefore defines how the computation can proceed. Control predicates are our way to specify in assertions a set of active control points.

$\{x=X\}$
$R$:  **cobegin**
       $\{at(S) \wedge ((at(T) \wedge x=X) \vee (after(T) \wedge x=X+1))\}$
       $S$:  $x := x+1$
       $\{after(S) \wedge ((at(T) \wedge x=X+1) \vee (after(T) \wedge x=X+2))\}$
  $\|$
       $\{at(T) \wedge ((at(S) \wedge x=X) \vee (after(S) \wedge x=X+1))\}$
       $T$:  $x := x+1$
       $\{after(T) \wedge ((at(S) \wedge x=X+1) \vee (after(S) \wedge x=X+2))\}$
  **coend**
$\{x=X+2\}$

**Figure 5.5.** Incrementing $x$ by 2

---

## Using Derived Terms

The assertions in the proof outline of Figure 5.5 are complex. Each assertion characterizes possible values for $x$ in terms of active control points in another process. The value of $x$ is of interest, but it is given in terms of something that is not of interest—active control points. Assertions should abstract relevant aspects of the state, not obscure them. Apparently, the view of the state provided by program variables and control predicates is not always the most appropriate for understanding a program.

We obtain more suitable abstractions by using derived terms (of §2.3). Below, we define two derived terms: $XS$ equals the amount by which process $S$ has incremented $x$, and $XT$ equals the amount by which process $T$ has incremented $x$.

$$XS: \begin{cases} 0 & \text{if } at(S) \\ 1 & \text{if } after(S) \end{cases} \qquad\qquad XT: \begin{cases} 0 & \text{if } at(T) \\ 1 & \text{if } after(T) \end{cases}$$

We can reformulate the assertions in the proof outline of Figure 5.5 in terms of $XS$ and $XT$ to get the proof outline of Figure 5.6. Note how much simpler the assertions are in that proof outline. Note also how they describe sets of states in a way that is likely to be meaningful to a reader.

In order to use derived terms in assertions, we must have a way to introduce them into Proof Outline Logic theorems. Derived Term Expansion Rule (2.77), which allows a derived term to be replaced according to its definition, provides that way. In particular, we can use Derived Term Expansion Rule (2.77) to relate an assertion that uses the derived term to an assertion that does not. Rule of Consequence (4.25) or Rule of Equivalence (4.26) is then used to effect the replacement. For example, from the definitions of $XS$ and $XT$ we obtain:

$at(S) \wedge ((at(T) \wedge x{=}X) \vee (after(T) \wedge x{=}X{+}1))$
= «Predicate Logic, Textual Substitution (2.71)»
$at(S) \wedge ((at(T) \wedge (x{=}X{+}v)_0^v) \vee (after(T) \wedge (x{=}X{+}v)_1^v))$
= «Derived Term Expansion Rule (2.77), since $at(T) \oplus after(T)$»
$at(S) \wedge (x{=}X{+}v)_{XT}^v$
= «Textual Substitution (2.71)»
$at(S) \wedge x{=}X{+}XT$
= «Predicate Logic»
$(at(S) \wedge 0{=}0 \wedge x{=}X{+}0{+}XT) \vee (after(S) \wedge false)$
= «Textual Substitution (2.71)»
$(at(S) \wedge (v{=}0 \wedge x{=}X{+}v{+}XT)_0^v) \vee$
$(after(S) \wedge (v{=}0 \wedge x{=}X{+}v{+}XT)_1^v)$
= «Derived Term Expansion Rule (2.77), since $at(S) \oplus after(S)$»
$(v{=}0 \wedge x{=}X{+}v{+}XT)_{XS}^v$
= «Textual Substitution (2.71)»
$XS{=}0 \wedge x{=}X{+}XS{+}XT$

Rule of Equivalence (4.26) now allows $pre(S)$ in $PO(R)$ of Figure 5.5 to be replaced by $XS{=}0 \wedge x{=}X{+}XS{+}XT$. Similar reasoning allows the other assertions in Figure 5.5 to be formulated in terms of derived terms $XS$ and $XT$, resulting in $PO(R)$ of Figure 5.6.

## 5.5 Synchronously Altered and Shared Assertions

Demonstrating that a collection of proof outlines is interference-free can be an intimidating prospect. Even when the proof outlines for the individual processes are small, the number of triples that must be proved might be quite large. Fortunately, methods do exist to simplify the task. One such method is based on using Disjointness NI Rule (5.18). In this section, we discuss another.

A term or predicate $p$ is considered *synchronously altered* by a process $S$ iff executing $S$ is required in order to change the value of $p$. For example, a program variable that is read and/or written by process $S$ but only read by other processes is synchronously altered by $S$, as is a control predicate corresponding

---

$\{at(R) \wedge x{=}X\}$
$R:$ **cobegin**
    $\{XS{=}0 \wedge x{=}X{+}XS{+}XT\}$  $S:$ $x := x{+}1$  $\{XS{=}1 \wedge x{=}X{+}XS{+}XT\}$
    $\|$
    $\{XT{=}0 \wedge x{=}X{+}XS{+}XT\}$  $T:$ $x := x{+}1$  $\{XT{=}1 \wedge x{=}X{+}XS{+}XT\}$
    **coend**
$\{after(R) \wedge x{=}X{+}2\}$

**Figure 5.6.**  Using derived terms

to a control point in $S$. Thus, in the proof outline of Figure 5.4, $x$ and $et$ are synchronously altered by process $E_1$, and $y$ and $ot$ by process $O_1$; in Figure 5.6, $XS$ is synchronously altered by $S$, $XT$ is synchronously altered by $T$, but $x$ is synchronously altered by neither process.

An assertion $L$ in the proof outline for a process $S$ is *synchronously altered* if all the terms and predicates occurring in $L$ are synchronously altered by $S$. If $L$ is synchronously altered, then no atomic action in any other process can interfere with $L$. Thus, $NI(\alpha, L)$ is valid whenever $\alpha$ is an atomic action from one process and $L$ is a synchronously altered assertion in another. This provides the basis for the following Proof Outline Logic rule:

(5.32) *Synchronously Altered NI Rule*: For $S_i \| S_j$:

$$\frac{\alpha \in \mathcal{A}(S_i), \quad L \text{ synchronously altered in } PO(S_j)}{NI(\alpha, L)}$$

Synchronously Altered NI Rule (5.32) has applications beyond proof outlines containing only synchronously altered assertions. Consider a proof outline for a concurrent program in which

   (i)   the proof outline for each process in isolation is a theorem,

   (ii)  each assertion $A$ is of the form $L_A \wedge I$ for some fixed $I$, and

   (iii)  $L_A$ is synchronously altered.

As we now show, $NI(\alpha, A)$ is valid for any assertion $A$ from one process and atomic action $\alpha$ from another. Therefore, it is unnecessary to prove interference freedom for a proof outline satisfying conditions (i)–(iii), even though the proof outline contains assertions (e.g., $L_A \wedge I$) that are not synchronously altered.

To demonstrate that $NI(\alpha, A)$ is valid, we proceed as follows. First observe that due to (ii) and (iii) and Precondition of an Action (5.6), $pre^*(\alpha)$ has the form $L_{pre^*(\alpha)} \wedge I$, where $L_{pre^*(\alpha)}$ is synchronously altered by the process containing $\alpha$. Moreover, since, by (ii), $I$ is a conjunct of every assertion in that process, we conclude that the following is valid.

(5.33) $\{L_{pre^*(\alpha)} \wedge I\} \ \alpha \ \{I\}$

Second, for an assertion $A$ in a different process than the one containing $\alpha$, (ii) and (iii) imply that $A$ is of the form $L_A \wedge I$, where $L_A$ is synchronously altered. Thus, Synchronously Altered NI Rule (5.32) allows us to infer $NI(\alpha, L_A)$:

(5.34) $\{L_{pre^*(\alpha)} \wedge I \wedge L_A\} \ \alpha \ \{L_A\}$

Conjunction Rule (4.30) can be used to combine (5.34) with (5.33), producing

$$\{L_{pre^*(\alpha)} \wedge I \wedge L_A\} \ \alpha \ \{L_A \wedge I\}$$

which is $NI(\alpha, A)$. This completes a proof of $NI(\alpha, A)$ from conditions (i)–(iii).

By stipulating that assertions had a certain form, we completely eliminated the need to enumerate and check interference-freedom triples. This can be formalized as a Proof Outline Logic inference rule for **cobegin**. We define $I$ to be a *shared assertion* in $PO(S_1)$, ..., $PO(S_n)$ if it appears as a conjunct of every assertion in each of these proof outlines. By reformulating conditions (i)–(iii) above in terms of a shared assertion, we obtain the following **cobegin** inference rule, which does not require an explicit interference-freedom proof.

(5.35) **cobegin** *with Shared Assertions Rule*:

> (a) $PO(S_1)$, ..., $PO(S_n)$,
> (b) $P \implies pre(PO(S_1)) \wedge \cdots \wedge pre(PO(S_n))$,
> (c) $post(PO(S_1)) \wedge \cdots \wedge post(PO(S_n))) \implies Q$,
> (d) Each assertion $A$ is of the form $L_A \wedge I$, where
> $\quad L_A$ is synchronously altered and $I$ is a shared assertion.

$$\{P\} \text{ cobegin } PO(S_1) \parallel \cdots \parallel PO(S_n) \text{ coend } \{Q\}$$

To illustrate the use of this inference rule, note that proof outlines $PO(S)$ and $PO(T)$ of Figure 5.6 have

$\quad I: \ x=X+XS+XT$

as a shared assertion. This is because every assertion is the conjunction of $I$ and a synchronously altered assertion—in process $S$ the synchronously altered assertions equate the value of $XS$ with 0 or 1; in $T$ they equate $XT$ with 0 or 1. Thus, **cobegin** with Shared Assertions Rule (5.35) applies, and it is not necessary to enumerate and check interference-freedom triples.

It is not difficult to establish that for any program $S$, if $PO(S)$ is valid then there exists another proof outline $PO'(S)$ that has a shared assertion $I$. For $I$, choose proof outline invariant $I_{PO(S)}$, and for an assertion $A$ in $PO(S)$ associated with control predicate $loc(A)$, choose $loc(A)$ for synchronously altered assertion $L_A$.

The use of **cobegin** with Shared Assertions Rule (5.35) is practical only when a shared assertion $I$ of manageable size can be identified. $I$ must be of manageable size because satisfying premise (a) of (5.35) requires that $I$ appear in every assertion. If $I$ is long and unwieldy, then proving these theorems is liable to be just as tedious as the interference-freedom obligation being replaced. Not all proof outlines have short, shared assertions as did the one in Figure 5.6. However, the desire to avoid checking interference freedom explicitly by using **cobegin** with Shared Assertions Rule (5.35) is a powerful incentive for the discovery of such shared assertions—particularly when we construct a program and proof together.

## 5.6 Specifying Synchronization

Interference is sometimes an inevitable consequence of certain execution interleavings. The only way to avoid such interference is by preventing those interleavings. Synchronization mechanisms permit such control.

Two primitive forms of synchronization underlie all synchronization mechanisms. The first, *indivisibility*, combines two or more atomic actions into a single one by eliminating control points. The second, *condition synchronization*, prevents a process from executing when in certain states. These primitive forms differ primarily in whether a process blocks its own execution or blocks execution by others. With indivisibility, a process blocks execution by others; with condition synchronization, a process blocks its own execution.

Define an atomic action to be *enabled* in any state in which it could be executed were its entry point active. Because such states are exactly those that will lead to termination of the atomic action, we conclude that the set of states $enbl(\alpha)$ for which an atomic action $\alpha$ is enabled is defined by the following.

(5.36) $enbl(\alpha)$: $wp(\alpha, true)$

For example, when $\alpha$ is a **skip**:

$$enbl(\mathbf{skip})$$
$$= \quad \text{«definition (5.36) of } enbl(\alpha)\text{»}$$
$$wp(\mathbf{skip}, true)$$
$$= \quad \text{«definition (4.49) of } wp \text{ for } \mathbf{skip}\text{»}$$
$$true$$

As another example, when $\alpha$ is the guard evaluation action for

(5.37) $S$: **if** $B \rightarrow$ **skip fi**

we have:

$$enbl(GEval_{if}(S))$$
$$= \quad \text{«definition (5.36) of } enbl(\alpha)\text{»}$$
$$wp(GEval_{if}(S), true)$$
$$= \quad \text{«definition (4.53) of } wp \text{ for } GEval_{if}(S)\text{»}$$
$$B$$

An atomic action $\alpha$ is defined to be *unconditional* in a program $S$ if and only if $enbl(\alpha)$ holds in all program states; otherwise, $\alpha$ is *conditional* in $S$. Thus, a **skip** is unconditional, and the guard evaluation for an **if** can be conditional.[3] If $\alpha$ is conditional in $S$, then it is possible for execution of $\alpha$ to be

---

[3]If the disjunction of the guards in an **if** is satisfied in all program states, then the guard evaluation action for that **if** is unconditional.

blocked because the state does not satisfy $enbl(\alpha)$. Such an atomic action, then, implements condition synchronization.

In order to allow synchronization mechanisms to be defined, we augment our programming notation with a new type of statement. By surrounding a statement $S$ with angle brackets, we define an *atomic statement*, which is executed as a single atomic action. Thus, $\langle S \rangle$ defines a statement that contains no internal control points and whose execution is blocked unless the state satisfies $wp(S, true)$. Because $S$ might contain internal control points but $\langle S \rangle$ does not, this angle-bracket notation allows indivisibility to be specified; and because $wp(S, true)$ can, in general, differ from $enbl(\alpha)$ for $\alpha$ the first atomic action of $S$, the notation allows condition synchronization to be specified as well.

For example,

(5.38)   $\alpha_1$: $\langle$ **if** $sem > 0 \rightarrow sem := sem - 1$ **fi** $\rangle$

specifies a synchronization mechanism that blocks until decrementing *sem* would leave *sem* non-negative and then—indivisibly—does the decrement. A more pathological atomic statement with the same effect is:

(5.39)   $\alpha_2$: $\langle sem := sem - 1$ **do** $sem < 0 \rightarrow$ **skip od** $\rangle$

Here, both the decrement of *sem* and the **do** are part of a single atomic action, so the decrement is performed only when the resulting state is one from which the **do** is guaranteed to terminate.

The appearance of arbitrary programs inside angle brackets can pose vexing implementation problems, as illustrated by (5.39). However, if atomic statements are used only to describe synchronization mechanisms that already exist, such implementation problems need never be confronted. The question of what synchronization mechanisms are available to the programmer depends on hardware and underlying support software. For the time being, we use angle brackets without restriction. Later, their use will be restricted to statements that model existing synchronization mechanisms.

## Reasoning About Atomic Statements

We now extend Proof Outline Logic for reasoning about programs that contain atomic statements. An atomic statement labeled $S$ contains no internal control points, so we have:

(5.40)   $\langle S \rangle$ *Control Axioms*:  For $S$ an atomic statement $\langle T \rangle$:
       (a) $at(S) = at(T)$
       (b) $in(S) = at(S)$
       (c) $after(S) = after(T)$

This means that a proof outline containing $\langle T \rangle$ associates assertions with $at(\langle T \rangle)$ and $after(\langle T \rangle)$ but not with control points internal to $T$. It also means that $pre^*(\langle T \rangle)$ is simply the precondition of $\langle T \rangle$:

(5.41) **Precondition of an Atomic Statement.** For $\alpha$ an atomic statement $\langle T \rangle$:

$$pre^*(\alpha): \ pre(\langle T \rangle) \qquad\qquad\qquad \square$$

If $P$ and $Q$ are primitive assertions and $\{P\}\,PO(T)\,\{Q\}$ is valid, then $\{P\}\,\langle T \rangle\,\{Q\}$ is also valid. The following Proof Outline Logic inference rule is based on this observation.

(5.42) $\langle S \rangle$ *Rule*: For primitive assertions $P$ and $Q$:

$$\frac{\{P\}\,PO(S)\,\{Q\}}{\{P\}\,\langle S \rangle\,\{Q\}}$$

Second, by definition, an atomic action $\alpha$ cannot be executed to completion in a state satisfying $\neg\, enbl(\alpha)$. Since $\{P\}\,\alpha\,\{Q\}$ is valid if execution of $\alpha$ does not terminate when started in a state satisfying $P$, we have the following (derived) Proof Outline Logic rule.

(5.43) *Blocked Atomic Action Rule*: For any assertion $Q$ and any atomic action or atomic statement $\alpha$:

$$\{\neg\, enbl(\alpha)\}\ \alpha\ \{Q\}$$

Finally, we extend the domain of *wp* so that when $\alpha$ is an atomic statement, $enbl(\alpha)$ can be determined using definition (5.36). This extension is simple because atomic statement $\langle S \rangle$ terminates in a state satisfying a primitive assertion $Q$ exactly when $S$ does.

(5.44) For a primitive assertion $Q$: $wp(\langle S \rangle, Q) \ = \ wp(S, Q)$

It should not be surprising that $S$ and $\langle S \rangle$ have the same weakest precondition. Programs $S$ and $\langle S \rangle$ differ only in their internal control points, and control points are ignored by *wp*.

To illustrate these rules, we analyze (5.38). It is easy to prove the following theorem of Proof Outline Logic when $Q$ is a primitive assertion:

$$\begin{aligned}
&\{Q^{sem}_{sem-1}\}\\
&T: \ \textbf{if } sem > 0 \rightarrow \{Q^{sem}_{sem-1} \wedge sem > 0\}\\
&\qquad\qquad\qquad\quad sem := sem - 1\\
&\qquad\qquad\qquad \{Q \wedge sem \geq 0\}\\
&\ \ \textbf{fi}\\
&\ \{Q \wedge sem \geq 0\}
\end{aligned}$$

Therefore, using $\langle S \rangle$ Rule (5.42), we get:

$$\{Q_{sem-1}^{sem}\} \quad \alpha_1 : \quad \langle T: \ \textbf{if} \ sem > 0 \rightarrow sem := sem - 1 \ \textbf{fi} \rangle \quad \{Q \wedge sem \geq 0\}$$

Furthermore, using definition (5.36) of $enbl(\alpha_1)$, we obtain:

$$
\begin{aligned}
& enbl(\alpha_1) \\
=\ & \text{«definition (5.36) of } enbl(\alpha)\text{»} \\
& wp(\alpha_1, true) \\
=\ & \text{«definition (5.44) of } wp \text{ for } \langle S \rangle \text{»} \\
& wp(T, true) \\
=\ & \text{«definition (4.54) of } wp \text{ for } \textbf{if} \text{ »} \\
& sem > 0
\end{aligned}
$$

From this and Blocked Atomic Action Rule (5.43), we can infer:

$$\{sem \leq 0\} \quad \alpha_1 : \quad \langle \textbf{if} \ sem > 0 \rightarrow sem := sem - 1 \ \textbf{fi} \rangle \quad \{Q \wedge sem \geq 0\}$$

By Disjunction Rule (4.31) we therefore conclude:

$$\{Q_{sem-1}^{sem} \vee sem \leq 0\} \quad \alpha_1 : \quad \langle \textbf{if} \ sem > 0 \rightarrow sem := sem - 1 \ \textbf{fi} \rangle \quad \{Q \wedge sem \geq 0\}$$

Finally, by Rule of Equivalence (4.26) we get:

(5.45)  $\{sem > 0 \Rightarrow Q_{sem-1}^{sem}\}$
$\qquad \alpha_1 : \ \langle \textbf{if} \ sem > 0 \rightarrow sem := sem - 1 \ \textbf{fi} \rangle$
$\qquad \{Q \wedge sem \geq 0\}$

The reader is invited to repeat this exercise for $\alpha_2$ (5.39). Because $wp(\alpha_1, R) = wp(\alpha_2, R)$ holds for any (primitive) predicate $R$, you should be able to prove that $\{sem > 0 \Rightarrow Q_{sem-1}^{sem}\} \, \alpha_2 \, \{Q\}$ is a theorem and that $enbl(\alpha_2)$ is $sem > 0$.

## 5.7  Synchronization and Interference

Both indivisibility and condition synchronization can be used to eliminate interference, as we now show using the proof outline fragment of Figure 5.7. Assume that premises (a), (b), and (c) of **cobegin** Rule (5.11) hold for this proof outline but that $\alpha$ interferes with $A$. Thus, we have that $PO(S_1)$, $PO(S_2)$, $P \Rightarrow pre(S_1) \wedge pre(S_2)$, and $post(S_1) \wedge post(S_2) \Rightarrow Q$ are theorems, but $NI(\alpha, A)$ is not valid.

### Using Indivisibility

An atomic action $\alpha$ cannot interfere with an assertion $A$ if the control points with which $\alpha$ and $A$ are associated cannot be active at the same time.

$\{P\}$
**cobegin**
$\quad S_1: \ \dots \ \{pre(\alpha)\} \ \alpha \ \dots$
$\|$
$\quad S_2: \ \dots \ \{U\} \ \beta \ \{A\} \ \gamma \ \{V\} \ \dots$
**coend**
$\{Q\}$

**Figure 5.7.** Example with interference

---

Thus, eliminating the control point with which $\alpha$ is associated and/or the one with which $A$ is associated eliminates the possibility of $\alpha$ interfering with $A$.

(5.46) **Avoiding Interference by Indivisibility.** If $\alpha$ interferes with $A$, then include $A$ or $\alpha$ in a larger atomic action. $\qquad\square$

There are two ways in which Avoiding Interference by Indivisibility (5.46) might be applied to the proof outline fragment of Figure 5.7. One is to combine $\beta$ and $\gamma$ into a single atomic statement. This results in a new proof outline for $S_2$,

$$S_2: \ \dots \ \{U\} \ \langle\beta \ \gamma\rangle \ \{V\} \ \dots$$

and $NI(\alpha, A)$ need no longer be proved. The other way that Avoiding Interference by Indivisibility (5.46) might be applied is to replace $\alpha$ with a larger atomic statement, say $\alpha'$, that includes $\alpha$ as well as one or more preceding and/or following atomic actions. This results in a new proof outline for $S_1$:

$$S_1: \ \dots \ \alpha': \ \langle\dots \alpha \dots\rangle \ \dots$$

Again, proving interference freedom no longer requires that $NI(\alpha, A)$ be proved, although $NI(\alpha', A)$ must be proved. Presumably, $\alpha'$ has been constructed with this proof obligation in mind.

In addition to providing a way to avoid interference, employing indivisibility reduces the number of interference-freedom triples that must be checked. This reduction is accomplished in two ways. First, the set of atomic actions shrinks, so fewer atomic actions might interfere. Second, the set of control points shrinks, so fewer assertions might be interfered with.

Indivisibility is not without disadvantages, however. The elimination of control points reduces the number of possible execution interleavings, which is rarely a desirable transformation for a concurrent program.

## Using Condition Synchronization

The most direct use of condition synchronization for eliminating interference is to block an atomic action in states where its execution could cause interference.

(5.47) **Avoiding Interference by Blocking.** Interference by an atomic action $\alpha$ with an assertion $A$ can be eliminated by identifying a predicate $B$ such that

$$\{B \wedge pre^*(\alpha) \wedge A\}\, \alpha\, \{A\}$$

is valid and then replacing $\alpha$ by

$$\alpha'\colon\ \langle \mathbf{if}\, B \to \alpha\, \mathbf{fi}\rangle$$

or by any other atomic action $\alpha'$ for which

$$(enbl(\alpha') \Rightarrow B \wedge enbl(\alpha))\ \wedge\ (B \wedge pre(\alpha) \Rightarrow wp(\alpha', post(\alpha)))$$

is valid.                                                                                         □

Thus, we replace $\alpha$ by an atomic action $\alpha'$ that blocks in some additional states (because $enbl(\alpha') \Rightarrow B \wedge enbl(\alpha)$) but otherwise has an equivalent effect.

Viewed assertionally, Avoiding Interference by Blocking (5.47) replaces the obligation to prove $NI(\alpha, A)$ with an obligation $NI(\alpha', A)$ whose proof can be discharged mechanically. This is because by construction, $\alpha$ and $\alpha'$ have the same precondition and equivalent effects (in states where they can be both executed), so we can infer from the validity of $\{B \wedge pre^*(\alpha) \wedge A\}\, \alpha\, \{A\}$ that

(5.48)   $\{B \wedge pre^*(\alpha') \wedge A\}\ \alpha'\ \{A\}$

is also valid. $NI(\alpha', A)$ is now proved as follows.

«(5.48)»
  1.   $\{B \wedge pre^*(\alpha') \wedge A\}\, \alpha'\, \{A\}$

«Blocked Atomic Action Rule (5.43)»
  2.   $\{\neg enbl(\alpha')\}\ \alpha'\ \{A\}$

«Disjunction Rule (4.31) with 1 and 2»
  3.   $\{\neg enbl(\alpha') \vee (B \wedge pre^*(\alpha') \wedge A)\}\ \alpha'\ \{A\}$

  4.   $pre^*(\alpha') \wedge A$
    $\Rightarrow$    «Consequent-Weakening Law (2.30)»
          $\neg enbl(\alpha') \vee (pre^*(\alpha') \wedge A)$
    $=$      «$(A \vee B) = (A \vee (\neg A \wedge B))$»
          $\neg enbl(\alpha') \vee (enbl(\alpha') \wedge pre^*(\alpha') \wedge A)$
    $\Rightarrow$    «$enbl(\alpha') \Rightarrow B$ from Avoiding Interference by
          Blocking (5.47)»
          $\neg enbl(\alpha') \vee (B \wedge pre^*(\alpha') \wedge A)$

«Rule of Consequence (4.25) with 4 and 3»
5. $\{pre^*(\alpha') \wedge A\} \ \alpha' \ \{A\}$

A second use of condition synchronization for eliminating interference arises in connection with Strengthening (5.14) and Weakening (5.15). Both techniques involve changing the assertions in a proof outline. Changes to one assertion, however, usually requires changes to others, so that premises (a), (b), and (c) of **cobegin** Rule (5.11) remain valid. Moreover, making these changes might require modifications to still more assertions. More often than not, these modifications can lead to a point where, for one reason or another, some assertion that must be changed cannot be.

Condition synchronization provides a way to strengthen an assertion without causing changes to propagate throughout a proof outline. Recall that the statement

(5.49)  **if** $B \to$ **skip fi**

blocks until $B$ holds. It can be used to strengthen an assertion by blocking until some desired condition holds.

(5.50)  **Strengthening by Condition Synchronization.** An assertion $pre(T)$ in a proof outline $PO(S)$ can be strengthened to $pre(T) \wedge B$ by proving[4]

$$\{pre(T)\}$$
$$\textbf{if } B \to \{pre(T) \wedge B\} \textbf{ skip } \{pre(T) \wedge B\} \textbf{ fi}$$
$$\{pre(T) \wedge B\}$$
$$T$$
$$\{post(T)\}$$

and replacing

$$\{pre(T)\} \ T \ \{post(T)\}$$

with it in $PO(S)$.                                                        □

Strengthening by Condition Synchronization (5.50) has obvious application when Strengthening (5.14) is used to eliminate interference. According to Strengthening (5.14), one way to eliminate interference of an atomic action $\alpha$ with an assertion $A$ is by strengthening $pre(\alpha)$ with a condition $B$ that makes $NI(\alpha, A)$ valid. When applied to the proof outline of Figure 5.7, this results in a new proof outline for $S_1$.

$S_1$: ... $\{pre(\alpha)\}$
    **if** $B \to \{pre(\alpha) \wedge B\}$ **skip** $\{pre(\alpha) \wedge B\}$ **fi**
    $\{pre(\alpha) \wedge B\}$
    $\alpha$ ...

---

[4]This proof is trivial unless the assertion being strengthened mentions a control predicate.

Note that having made the modification, we must check that no new interference has been introduced. For the proof outline of Figure 5.7, this requires checking that no atomic action in $S_2$ interferes with the new, stronger, assertion $pre(\alpha) \wedge B$.

A second way to use Strengthening (5.14) to avoid $\alpha$ from interfering with $A$ is by strengthening $A$ with a condition $B$ (say) that makes $NI(\alpha, A)$ valid. This, too, is possible using Strengthening by Condition Synchronization (5.50), but doing so can be a bit subtle. In Figure 5.7, for example, simply strengthening $pre(\gamma)$ to $A \wedge B$ prevents $\alpha$ from interfering with $pre(\gamma)$ but does not prevent $\alpha$ from interfering with $post(\beta)$ (i.e., $A$). This problem can be avoided by propagating a stronger assertion from precondition to postcondition through some fragment of a proof outline.

(5.51) **Strengthening by Propagation.** To strengthen an assertion $P$ in a proof outline $PO(S)$:

   (1)   Select other assertions in $PO(S)$ that, if strengthened, would allow $P$ to be strengthened.

   (2)   Use Strengthening by Condition Synchronization (5.50) and strengthen these assertions as necessary to allow $P$ to be strengthened by propagation.                                         □

In the proof outline of Figure 5.7, we might select $pre(\beta)$ (i.e., $U$) and strengthen it. To do so, we select predicates $B'$ and $B$ such that $\{U \wedge B'\} \beta \{A \wedge B\}$ is valid, thereby allowing the desired strengthening of $A$ ($post(\beta)$).

$$
\begin{aligned}
&S_2: \;\dots\; \{U\} \\
&\qquad \textbf{if } B' \rightarrow \{U \wedge B'\} \textbf{ skip } \{U \wedge B'\} \textbf{ fi} \\
&\qquad \{U \wedge B'\} \\
&\qquad \beta \\
&\qquad \{A \wedge B\} \\
&\qquad \gamma \;\dots
\end{aligned}
$$

As before, having made a modification, we must check that new interference has not been introduced. For example, just because $U$ was not interfered with does not imply that $U \wedge B'$ will not be interfered with.

Strengthening by Condition Synchronization (5.50) also has application when Weakening (5.15) is used to eliminate interference. According to Weakening (5.15), interference of an atomic action $\alpha$ with an assertion $A$ can be avoided by weakening $A$ so that $NI(\alpha, A)$ becomes a theorem. A problem can arise after weakening an assertion when the change propagates to other assertions in the proof outline, since the assertions in the resulting proof outline might be interfered with or might be too weak to be useful. Fortunately, the extent of this propagation can be limited with Strengthening by Condition Synchronization (5.50).

For example, when applied to the interference of $\alpha$ with $A$ in Figure 5.7, Weakening (5.15) dictates that we find a disjunct $D$ such that $NI(\alpha, A \vee D)$ is valid and replace $post(\beta)$ (i.e., $A$) by the weaker assertion $A \vee D$. Weakening $post(\beta)$, however, also weakens $pre(\gamma)$ and might falsify

(5.52)  $\{pre(\gamma)\} \, \gamma \, \{post(\gamma)\}$

which is needed for premise (a) of **cobegin** Rule (5.11). Rather than make (5.52) valid by replacing $post(\gamma)$ with a weaker assertion, which further propagates the weakening, we employ condition synchronization to ensure that $V$ holds after $\gamma$ terminates. Assuming that $B$ is chosen such that $\{A \vee D\} \, \gamma \, \{V \vee B\}$ is valid and that no interference is introduced by changing $V$ to $V \vee B$, the revised proof outline for $S_2$ is:

$$
\begin{aligned}
S_2: \; ... \; &\{U\} \\
&\beta \\
&\{A \vee D\} \\
&\gamma \\
&\{V \vee B\} \\
&\textbf{if} \, \neg B \rightarrow \{(V \vee B) \wedge \neg B\} \; \textbf{skip} \; \{(V \vee B) \wedge \neg B\} \, \textbf{fi} \\
&\{V\} \; ...
\end{aligned}
$$

## A Bank Example

To illustrate these techniques, consider a concurrent program to model a bank. The bank manages a collection of $n \geq 1$ accounts

   **var**  *acnt* : **array** $[1..n]$ **of** Int

and employs an auditor to check for embezzlement. Transactions transfer money from one account to another.

A transaction to transfer \$20 from account *mmb* to account *fbs* does not change the total deposits at the bank. We employ a derived term

$$
Tot: \; \Big\{ \; \sum_{i=1}^{t} acnt[i] \quad \text{if } 0 \leq t \leq n
$$

to characterize the total of the balances in accounts $acnt[1..t]$. Assuming that $1 \leq mmb \leq n$, $1 \leq fbs \leq n$, and $fbs \neq mmb$, a proof outline for a program to implement such a transfer of funds is given by:

$$
\begin{aligned}
&\{T = Tot_n^t \wedge acnt[mmb] = M \wedge acnt[fbs] = F \wedge fbs \neq mmb\} \\
&Move: \; acnt[mmb], acnt[fbs] := acnt[mmb] - 20, acnt[fbs] + 20 \\
&\{T = Tot_n^t \wedge acnt[mmb] = M - 20 \wedge acnt[fbs] = F + 20\}
\end{aligned}
$$

While checking the accounts, the auditor sums the bank's deposits.

$\{true\}$
Check: $C_1$: $j, cash := 0, 0$   $\{j=0 \land cash=Tot^t_j\}$
       $C_2$: **do** $j \neq n \rightarrow \{0 \leq j < n \land cash=Tot^t_j\}$
              $C_3$: $cash, j := cash+acnt[j+1], j+1$
              $\{0 \leq j \leq n \land cash=Tot^t_j\}$
       **od**
$\{cash=Tot^t_n\}$

The value in *cash* can then checked to detect embezzlement.

In order to perform an audit while transactions are being processed, *Move* and *Check* might be executed concurrently. This is modeled by regarding each as a process in a **cobegin**, and it requires that the proof outlines for *Move* and *Check* be interference free. Unfortunately, they are not—interference-freedom triples $NI(Move, pre(C_3))$ and $NI(Move, post(C_3))$ are not valid. The problem is that executing *Move* can change $Tot^t_j$ without changing *cash* if $mmb \leq j < fbs$ or $fbs \leq j < mmb$ holds.

There are a variety of ways to eliminate this interference. The simplest is to use indivisibility and eliminate control points internal to $C_2$, as prescribed by Avoiding Interference by Indivisibility (5.46). We construct a single atomic statement that encompasses the **do** in *Check*.

$\{true\}$
Check: $C_1$: $j, cash := 0, 0$   $\{j=0 \land cash=Tot^t_j\}$
       $C_2$: $\langle$**do** $j \neq n \rightarrow cash, j := cash+acnt[j+1], j+1$ **od**$\rangle$
$\{cash=Tot^t_n\}$

The result is a proof outline that satisfies the premises of **cobegin** Rule (5.11). Unfortunately, this change causes almost all of *Check* to be executed without interruption. This can delay execution of *Move*, which might be undesirable.

Another way to eliminate interference of *Move* with $pre(C_3)$ and $post(C_3)$ is to use Strengthening (5.14). $NI(Move, pre(C_3))$ and $NI(Move, post(C_3))$ both become valid if the precondition for the assignment statement in *Move* is strengthened by $(mmb \leq j \land fbs \leq j) \lor (j < mmb \land j < fbs)$. This prevents execution of *Move* when it would falsify $cash=Tot^t_j$. We can use Strengthening by Condition Synchronization (5.50) to achieve the desired strengthening, resulting in a new proof outline for *Move*:

$\{P: \; T=Tot^t_n \land acnt[mmb]=M \land acnt[fbs]=F \land fbs \neq mmb\}$
Move: $M_0$: **if** $(mmb \leq j \land fbs \leq j) \lor (j < mmb \land j < fbs) \rightarrow$
                $\{P \land ((mmb \leq j \land fbs \leq j) \lor (j < mmb \land j < fbs))\}$
                $M_1$: **skip**
                $\{P \land ((mmb \leq j \land fbs \leq j) \lor (j < mmb \land j < fbs))\}$
       **fi** $\{P \land ((mmb \leq j \land fbs \leq j) \lor (j < mmb \land j < fbs))\}$
       $M_2$: $acnt[mmb], acnt[fbs] := acnt[mmb]-20, acnt[fbs]+20$
$\{T=Tot^t_n \land acnt[mmb]=M-20 \land acnt[fbs]=F+20\}$

However, now changes to $j$ by *Check* have the potential to interfere with the assertions in *Move*. Execution of $C_1$, which assigns 0 to $j$, happens not to falsify

(5.53) $(mmb \le j \land fbs \le j) \lor (j < mmb \land j < fbs)$,

because we are assuming that $0 \ne mmb$ and $0 \ne fbs$ hold. Unfortunately, the increment to $j$ in $C_3$ does interfere with (5.53), because adding 1 to $j$ can falsify $j < mmb \land j < fbs$.

There are two ways to eliminate the interference with $j < mmb \land j < fbs$. The first is to employ Avoiding Interference by Indivisibility (5.46) and eliminate the control points associated with assertions containing $j < mmb \land j < fbs$. After doing this and then merging assignment statement $M_2$ into the body of the **if** and finally deleting the superfluous **skip**, $M_1$, the result is the following proof outline for *Move*. Coincidentally, it is exactly what would have been obtained had we initially employed Avoiding Interference by Blocking (5.47) with $M_2$ for $\alpha$.

$$\{P: \ \mathrm{T} = Tot_n^t \land acnt[mmb] = \mathrm{M} \land acnt[fbs] = \mathrm{F} \land fbs \ne mmb\}$$
$$Move: \ \langle \textbf{if} \ (mmb \le j \land fbs \le j) \lor (j < mmb \land j < fbs) \rightarrow$$
$$acnt[mmb], acnt[fbs] := acnt[mmb] - 20, acnt[fbs] + 20 \ \textbf{fi} \rangle$$
$$\{\mathrm{T} = Tot_n^t \land acnt[mmb] = \mathrm{M} - 20 \land acnt[fbs] = \mathrm{F} + 20\}$$

Unfortunately, *Move* is now an unrealistically large atomic statement.

The second way to avoid this new interference is by yet another use of Strengthening (5.14)—this time to remove $j < mmb \land j < fbs$ from the assertions being interfered with. We achieve this strengthening simply by strengthening the guard in the **if**:

$$\{P: \ \mathrm{T} = Tot_n^t \land acnt[mmb] = \mathrm{M} \land acnt[fbs] = \mathrm{F} \land fbs \ne mmb\}$$
$$Move: \ M_0: \ \textbf{if} \ mmb \le j \land fbs \le j \rightarrow \{P \land mmb \le j \land fbs \le j\}$$
$$M_1: \ \textbf{skip}$$
$$\{P \land mmb \le j \land fbs \le j\}$$
$$\textbf{fi}$$
$$\{P \land mmb \le j \land fbs \le j\}$$
$$M_2: \ acnt[mmb], acnt[fbs] := acnt[mmb] - 20, acnt[fbs] + 20$$
$$\{\mathrm{T} = Tot_n^t \land acnt[mmb] = \mathrm{M} - 20 \land acnt[fbs] = \mathrm{F} + 20\}$$

We are not done, though. In deleting $j < mmb \land j < fbs$ from the assertions, assignment statement $C_1$ now does falsify $mmb \le j \land fbs \le j$.

One way to avoid interference by $C_1$ with $pre(M_1)$, $post(M_1)$, and $post(M_0)$ is with Avoiding Interference by Blocking (5.47). For $B$, we choose some predicate that makes $\{B \land pre(C_1) \land A\} C_1 \{A\}$ valid because $B \land A \Rightarrow false$ holds, where $A$ ranges over $pre(M_1)$, $post(M_1)$, and $post(M_0)$. Then, we inhibit execution of $C_1$ whenever $B$ does not hold.

Specifically, we introduce a new program variable *safe* and add assignment statements to *Move* so that $\neg$ *safe* is implied by $pre(M_1)$, $post(M_1)$, and $post(M_0)$. Writing $PO(S) \otimes P$ to denote the proof outline in which every assertion of $PO(S)$ is strengthened by conjunct $P$, we get:

> $\{T = Tot_n^t \wedge acnt[mmb] = M \wedge acnt[fbs] = F \wedge fbs \neq mmb\}$
> *safe* := *false*
> $PO(Move) \otimes \neg safe$
> *safe* := *true*
> $\{T = Tot_n^t \wedge acnt[mmb] = M-20 \wedge acnt[fbs] = F+20\}$

Furthermore, we replace $C_1$ by $\langle \text{if } safe \rightarrow j, cash := 0, 0 \text{ fi} \rangle$. This results in the following proof outline.

> $\{true\}$
> *Check*:  $C_1$: $\langle \text{if } safe \rightarrow j, cash := 0, 0 \text{ fi} \rangle$
> $\qquad\qquad \{j = 0 \wedge cash = Tot_j^t\}$
> $\qquad C_2$: **do** $j \neq n \rightarrow \{0 \leq j < n \wedge cash = Tot_j^t\}$
> $\qquad\qquad\qquad C_3$: $cash, j := cash + acnt[j+1], j+1$
> $\qquad\qquad\qquad \{0 \leq j \leq n \wedge cash = Tot_j^t\}$
> $\qquad\qquad$ **od**
> $\{cash = Tot_n^t\}$

There is no longer any interference, so the design of *Move* and *Check* is finished.

## Historical Notes

The first assertional method for proving properties of concurrent programs was described in [Ashcroft & Manna 71]. It is based on converting a concurrent program into a nondeterministic, sequential one. The method uses flow charts to represent programs; it is not practical because the resulting nondeterministic program can be large and awkward. A second assertional verification method based on transforming the flowchart representation of a concurrent program is described in [Levitt 72]. There, flowcharts for processes that synchronize using semaphores are combined by adding the flow of control implied by process switches at semaphore operations. An extension of Floyd's method [Floyd 67] allows verification conditions to be obtained from such a flowchart. Other methods based on assigning assertions to control points in a flowchart are described in [Lauer 73] and [Newton 74].

Subsequently, Ashcroft developed an approach for extracting verification conditions directly from the flowchart of a concurrent program [Ashcroft 75]. Ashcroft associated an assertion with each control point in the program by defining an assertion for each edge in the flowchart, just as Floyd had proposed for sequential programs. A formula equivalent to our proof outline invariant is defined and shown to be an invariant.

Hoare was the first to address the design of a programming logic for concurrent programs. In [Hoare 72a], he extended the logic of [Hoare 69] with inference rules for parallel composition of processes that synchronize using conditional critical regions. The extended logic could be used to prove partial correctness properties of (only) certain concurrent programs. The logic could not, for example, be used to reason about programs in which processes communicate, because assertions appearing in the proof of one process are not allowed to mention variables local to another. Some of these restrictions are relaxed in [Hoare 75], but that logic is also incomplete, and process interaction is limited to sequences, similar to unbounded message queues.

Interference freedom and the first complete programming logic for partial correctness were developed by Owicki in a Ph.D. thesis [Owicki 75] supervised by Gries [Owicki & Gries 76a]. The work extends Hoare's logic of triples to handle concurrent programs that synchronize and communicate using shared variables. Lamport, working independently, developed an idea ("monotone assertions") similar to interference freedom as part of a more general method for proving both safety and liveness properties of concurrent programs [Lamport 77a]. Unfortunately, the method of [Lamport 77a] is described in terms of the flowchart representation of a concurrent program, and this probably accounted for its failure to attract the attention it deserved.

Lamport's Generalized Hoare Logic (GHL) is a Hoare-style programming logic for reasoning about concurrent programs, motivated by the success of the Owicki-Gries logic [Lamport 80b]. In contrasting the logic of [Owicki & Gries 76a] and GHL, the first significant difference concerns the role of proof outlines. The Owicki-Gries logic is based on triples rather than proof outlines. However, this is deceptive. Had interference freedom been formalized in the logic, the need for treating proof outlines (in addition to tri-. ples) as formulas would probably have become apparent. GHL is based on proof outlines, making formulas a bit more complex but allowing a simple inference rule for **cobegin**.

The second significant difference between the Owicki-Gries logic and GHL is the use of control predicates. Instead of control predicates, the Owicki-Gries logic sometimes requires that additional variables, called auxiliary variables, be added to a program when constructing a proof. (These variables can be thought of as derived terms whose value is computed by the program rather than by a definition.) The debate over the merits of control predicates and auxiliary variables is still active [Lamport 88]. Advocates of auxiliary variables claim that control predicates make proofs operational, ugly, and complex; advocates of control predicates argue that there is no formal basis for establishing that an auxiliary variable correctly captures the intended aspects of the state, so proving something about a program that has auxiliary variables tells nothing about the program of interest, which does not mention auxiliary variables. In Chapter 7, we show how to prove that an auxiliary variable does correctly capture the intended aspects of the state and argue that neither control predicates nor auxiliary variables is sufficient for all purposes.

The final distinction between the Owicki-Gries logic and GHL concerns the class of properties that can be proved. The Owicki-Gries logic was intended for proving only three types of properties: partial correctness, mutual exclusion, and deadlock freedom. The logic could have been extended for proving safety properties, although doing so is subtle. GHL was originally intended for proving safety properties, even for programs where all of the atomic actions have not been specified.

Neither [Owicki & Gries 76a] nor [Lamport 77a] addressed the issue of developing concurrent programs along with their proof outlines. In [Jones 83], interference freedom is used as part of a methodology for developing concurrent programs from partial correctness specifications. To decompose a high-level specification into specifications for lower-level components, rely and guarantee predicates are defined for each component. A *rely* predicate asserts conditions on which the component depends for correct operation, and a *guarantee* predicate asserts conditions the component maintains. In our terminology, invariance of the rely predicate implies that the component will not be interfered with; maintenance of the guarantee predicate by one component is the basis for ensuring invariance of the rely predicate of another.

Another assertional method for reasoning about concurrent programs is discussed in [Soundararajan 84a]. In this method, a compatibility test is used to determine whether proofs of processes can be combined to obtain a proof of the concurrent program comprising those processes. Associated with each process $P$ is a variable that contains the sequence of values stored in each shared variable referenced by $P$. These sequence variables are used only in proofs. Actual assignments to them are not made, but the axioms for assignment statements and other statements that change shared variables encode assignments to the sequence variables. The *compatibility test* determines whether the sequence variables in each of the proofs describe a feasible execution of the entire system by checking that the value of a shared variable read by a process is indeed the last value written. If the sequence variables satisfy this compatibility test, then the individual proofs of the processes can be combined.

Proof Outline Logic is an attempt to combine the best of the Owicki-Gries logic and GHL. Our first attempt at such a combination is reported in [Schneider & Andrews 86]. In the current version of Proof Outline Logic, **cobegin** Rule (5.11) is based on the **cobegin** inference rule in [Owicki & Gries 76a], although the soundness proof for that rule is based on the argument of [Lamport & Schneider 84]. Disjointness Condition (5.17) and corresponding Disjointness NI Rule (5.18) formalize folk theorems. The term "synchronously altered" is borrowed from [Levin & Gries 81], but Synchronously Altered NI Rule (5.32) and the notion of a shared assertion are the Proof Outline Logic formulations of folk theorems for performing interference-freedom proofs; **cobegin** with Shared Assertions Rule (5.35) is based on the method of [Ashcroft 75]. The angle-bracket notation for specifying synchronization was invented by Lamport and formalized in [Lamport 80b]. However, the notation was popularized by Dijkstra, with the earliest published use in [Dijkstra 77a]. The idea that an **if** statement with no *true* guard should delay until some guard becomes *true* originated with [Dijkstra 76b].

The underlying methodology in this chapter—using interference freedom to drive proof construction and to motivate synchronization—has been reported in various example program derivations but has never been formalized. Development of a proof outline based on Strengthening (5.14) and Weakening (5.15) was first described in [Schneider & Andrews 86], as were versions of Avoiding Interference by Indivisibility (5.46) and Strengthening by Condition Synchronization (5.50). Strengthening by Propagation (5.51) is based on work done in collaboration with McCurley [McCurley 88].

The two-process search example of Figure 5.1 was first discussed in [Rosen 74] and popularized in [Owicki & Gries 76a]. The Bank example of §5.7 first appeared in [Lamport 76]. Exercise 5.5 is from [Francez 86].

## Exercises

**5.1.** (a)   Recall from exercise 4.1 that $\mathcal{H}_S$ is the set of histories of program $S$. Give a formal definition of $\mathcal{H}_S$ in terms of $\mathcal{H}_{T_1}, ..., \mathcal{H}_{T_n}$, where $S$ is:

$$S: \textbf{cobegin } T_1 \ \| \ T_2 \ \| \ \cdots \ \| \ T_n \ \textbf{coend}$$

(b)   Give a formal definition of $\mathcal{H}_S$ in terms of $\mathcal{H}_T$, where $S$ is:

$$S: \langle T \rangle$$

(c)   With these definitions and your answer to exercise 4.1, prove that $\mathcal{H}_{S1} = \mathcal{H}_{S2} \cup \mathcal{H}_{S3}$, where:

$S1$: **cobegin** $\langle T_1 \rangle$ ‖ $\langle T_2 \rangle$ **coend**

$S2$: $\langle T_1 \rangle$ $\langle T_2 \rangle$

$S3$: $\langle T_2 \rangle$ $\langle T_1 \rangle$

**5.2.** A statement $S$ *simulates* a statement $T$ iff $\mathcal{H}_S = \mathcal{H}_T$, and therefore every history of $S$ is a history of $T$ and vice versa. Show how 2-process **cobegin** statements

$\qquad$ **cobegin** $S_1$ ‖ $S_2$ **coend**

can be used to simulate an $n$-process **cobegin**:

$\qquad$ **cobegin** $S_1$ ‖ $S_2$ ‖ $\cdots$ ‖ $S_n$ **coend**

**5.3.** Explain the consequences of using each of the following in place of **cobegin** Control Axiom (5.2c).

(a) $\quad in(S) = (in(S_1) \vee in(S_2) \vee \cdots \vee in(S_n))$

(b) $\quad in(S) = ((in(S_1) \oplus after(S_1)) \wedge \cdots \wedge (in(S_n) \oplus after(S_n))$
$\qquad \qquad \wedge \neg(after(S_1) \wedge \cdots \wedge after(S_n)))$

**5.4.** The following program sets $x$ to 0.

$\qquad$ $S$: **cobegin**
$\qquad \qquad$ **do** $x > 0 \rightarrow x := x - 1$ **od**
$\qquad$ ‖
$\qquad \qquad$ **do** $x < 0 \rightarrow x := x + 1$ **od**
$\qquad$ **coend**

Give a Proof Outline Logic theorem $PO(S)$ in which $pre(S)$ is *true* and $post(S)$ is $x = 0$. Be sure to enumerate and discharge all of the interference-freedom theorems needed to prove $PO(S)$.

**5.5.** The following program computes the greatest common divisor of $x1$ and $x2$.

$\qquad$ $S$: $y1, y2 := x1, x2$
$\qquad \qquad$ **cobegin**
$\qquad \qquad \qquad$ **do** $y1 \neq y2 \rightarrow$ **if** $y1 > y2 \rightarrow y1 := y1 - y2$
$\qquad \qquad \qquad \qquad \qquad \quad$ [] $y1 \leq y2 \rightarrow$ **skip**
$\qquad \qquad \qquad \qquad \qquad$ **fi**
$\qquad \qquad \qquad$ **od**
$\qquad \qquad$ ‖
$\qquad \qquad \qquad$ **do** $y1 \neq y2 \rightarrow$ **if** $y2 > y1 \rightarrow y2 := y2 - y1$
$\qquad \qquad \qquad \qquad \qquad \quad$ [] $y2 \leq y1 \rightarrow$ **skip**
$\qquad \qquad \qquad \qquad \qquad$ **fi**
$\qquad \qquad \qquad$ **od**
$\qquad \qquad$ **coend**

Give a Proof Outline Logic theorem $PO(S)$ in which $pre(S)$ is $x1 > 0 \wedge x2 > 0$ and $post(S)$ is $y1 = gcd(x1, x2) \wedge y2 = gcd(x1, x2)$. Be sure to enumerate and discharge all of the interference-freedom theorems needed to prove $PO(S)$.

**5.6.** The following program generalizes to three processes the two-process search given in Figure 5.1.

$t1, x1, t2, x2, t3, x3 := n, 0, n, 1, n, 2$
**cobegin**
    **do** $x1 < \min(t1, t2, t3) \rightarrow$ **if** $a[x1]=V \rightarrow t1 := x1$
                                   [] $a[x1] \neq V \rightarrow x1 := x1+3$
                                   **fi**
    **od**
  ||
    **do** $x2 < \min(t1, t2, t3) \rightarrow$ **if** $a[x2]=V \rightarrow t2 := x2$
                                     [] $a[x2] \neq V \rightarrow x2 := x2+3$
                                   **fi**
  ||
    **do** $x3 < \min(t1, t2, t3) \rightarrow$ **if** $a[x3]=V \rightarrow t3 := x3$
                                     [] $a[x3] \neq V \rightarrow x3 := x3+3$
                                   **fi**
    **od**
**coend**
$k := \min(t1, t2, t3)$

Give a Proof Outline Logic theorem $PO(S)$ in which $pre(S)$ is *true* and $post(S)$ is:

$$(k < n \Rightarrow a[k]=V) \land (\forall i \in \text{Int}:\ 0 \le i < k:\ a[i] \neq V)$$

Be sure to enumerate and discharge all of the interference-freedom theorems needed to prove $PO(S)$.

**5.7.** To prove that both $at(S_1)$ and $at(S_2)$ do not hold at the same time in a given program $S$, it suffices to prove a theorem of a Proof Outline Logic in which $pre(S)$ is *true* and

$$pre(S_1) \Rightarrow \neg at(S_2)$$
$$pre(S_2) \Rightarrow \neg at(S_1)$$

are both valid. For each of the four programs below:

    (i)  Construct such a proof outline using **cobegin** Rule (5.11).

    (ii)  Construct such a proof outline using **cobegin** with Shared Assertions Rule (5.35).

(a)    *free* := *true*
    **cobegin**
        $\underset{i=1,2}{||}$ **do** *true* $\rightarrow \langle$**if** *free* $\rightarrow$ *free* := *false* **fi**$\rangle$
                                $S_i$: **skip**
                                  *free* := *true*
      **od**
    **coend**

(b)    *turn* := 1
    **cobegin**
        **do** *true* $\rightarrow$ **if** *turn*$=1 \rightarrow$ **skip fi**
                      $S_1$: **skip**
                      *turn* := 2
      **od**
  ||

$$\textbf{do } true \rightarrow \textbf{if } turn=2 \rightarrow \textbf{skip fi}$$
$$S_2: \textbf{ skip}$$
$$turn := 1$$
$$\textbf{od}$$
$$\textbf{coend}$$

(c)    $x, y := false, false$
$$\textbf{cobegin}$$
$$x := true$$
$$\textbf{if } \neg y \rightarrow \textbf{skip fi}$$
$$S_1: \textbf{ skip}$$
$$x := false$$
$$\|$$
$$y := true$$
$$\textbf{if } \neg x \rightarrow \textbf{skip fi}$$
$$S_2: \textbf{ skip}$$
$$y := false$$
$$\textbf{coend}$$

(d)    $s := 1$
$$\textbf{cobegin}$$
$$\underset{i=1,2}{\|} \quad \langle \textbf{if } s > 0 \rightarrow s := s-1 \textbf{ fi} \rangle$$
$$S_i: \textbf{ skip}$$
$$s := s+1$$
$$\textbf{coend}$$

**5.8.** Consider a **do** statement:

$$\textbf{do } B_1 \rightarrow S_1 \ [] \ \cdots \ [] \ B_n \rightarrow S_n \textbf{ od}$$

where guards $B_1, ..., B_n$ are not necessarily disjoint.

(a)    Show how to implement this **do** using **cobegin** to achieve nondeterministic selection of a guarded command. Do not use **if** statements containing more than one guarded command.

(b)    Show that your answer to (a) is pre/post partially equivalent to the **do** above. (See exercise 4.14 for the definition of pre/post partially equivalent.)

(c)    Give another implementation of the **do** above, only this time using conditional atomic actions.

(d)    Show that your answer to (c) is pre/post partially equivalent to the **do** above.

**5.9.** The **race** (radically absurd **cobegin** execution) statement

$$\textbf{race } S_1 \ \| \ S_2 \ \| \ \cdots \ \| \ S_n \textbf{ ecar}$$

involves concurrent execution of *contestants* $S_1$ through $S_n$. However, unlike **cobegin**, as soon as some contestant $S_i$ terminates, execution of the other contestants is halted and the **race** terminates.

(a)    Give control predicate axioms for the **race** statement.

(b)    Give a Proof Outline Logic inference rule for **race**.

(c)    Describe an application where the **race** statement is useful.

**5.10.** Execution of the **step** (synchronized transition execution processing) statement

**step**
$$S_1 \mid S_2 \mid ... \mid S_n$$
$$\|$$
$$T_1 \mid T_2 \mid ... \mid T_n$$
$$\|$$
$$...$$
$$\|$$
$$U_1 \mid U_2 \mid ... \mid U_n$$
**pets**

is as follows. First, $S_1, T_1, ..., U_1$ are executed concurrently. Once those statements have terminated, $S_2, T_2, ..., U_2$ are executed. This continues until $S_n, T_n, ..., U_n$ are executed concurrently and terminate.

(a)    Give control predicate axioms for the **step** statement.

(b)    Give a Proof Outline Logic inference rule for **step**.

(c)    Describe a computer architecture where the **step** statement is useful.

**5.11.** How can Interference Freedom Condition (5.8) be simplified for a collection of proof outlines $PO(S_1), ..., PO(S_n)$ in which all assertions are primitive?

**5.12.** Suppose the definition of an interference-freedom triple $NI(\alpha, A)$ were changed to

$$NI(\alpha, A):\quad \{at(\alpha) \wedge loc(A) \wedge A \wedge pre^*(\alpha)\}\ \alpha\ \{loc(A) \Rightarrow A\}$$

where assertion $A$ is associated with control predicate $loc(A)$.

(a)    Will a proof outline that satisfies interference freedom using the definition of $NI(\alpha, A)$ given in §5.3 necessarily satisfy interference freedom using this new definition? If so, give a procedure to transform one proof to the other; if not, give an example that satisfies one definition but not the other.

(b)    Will a proof outline that satisfies interference freedom using this new definition of $NI(\alpha, A)$ necessarily satisfy interference freedom using the definition given in §5.3? If so, give a procedure to translate from one proof to another; if not, give an example that satisfies one definition but not the other.

**5.13.** Suppose the definition of an interference-freedom triple $NI(\alpha, A)$ were changed to:

$$NI(\alpha, A):\quad \{pre(\alpha) \wedge A\}\ \alpha\ \{A\}$$

Explain why $NI(\alpha, A)$ is now sometimes undefined.

**5.14.** Consider the following programming logic, called HLCP. If $I$ is an assertion and $S$ is a program, then

$$[I]\ S\ [I]$$

is an HLCP formula. Assertions can mention program variables, control predicates, and rigid variables. The HLCP formula $[I]\ S\ [I]$ is *valid* iff whenever program $S$ is executed in any state satisfying $(in(S) \vee after(S)) \wedge I$, assertion $I$ will continue to hold of the program's state as each control point is reached.

(a)    Give a Temporal Logic characterization of when $[I]\ S\ [I]$ is valid.

(b)    Give an inference rule whose premises are formulas of Proof Outline Logic and whose conclusion is the HLCP formula $[I]\ S\ [I]$ with the strongest $I$ possible.

(c)     Define the *extended HLCP formula* [P] S [Q] to be *valid* if and only if when-
        ever program S is executed in any state satisfying $in(S) \wedge P$, P continues to
        hold of the state as each control point associated with $in(S)$ is reached, and Q
        holds if a control point associated with $after(S)$ is reached. Show how to for-
        mulate an arbitrary extended HLCP formula [P] S [Q] as an (unextended)
        HLCP formula [I] S [I] such that one is valid iff the other is.

(d)     Given that HLCP formulas $[I]\ S_1\ [I]$, ..., $[I]\ S_n\ [I]$ are each valid, what addi-
        tional premises are needed to infer:

$$[I]\ \textbf{cobegin}\ S_1\ \|\ \cdots\ \|\ S_n\ \textbf{coend}\ [I]\ ?$$

**5.15.** Requirement (b) of Disjointness Condition (5.17) is rather strong. It stipulates that
no control predicate in A concern the same process as the one containing $\alpha$.
Clearly, there are situations in which executing $\alpha$ will not falsify a control predicate
that concerns the process containing $\alpha$. For example, if a process S contains $\alpha$ and

$$(at(\alpha) \vee after(\alpha)) \Rightarrow in(S)$$

is valid, then control predicate $in(S)$ cannot be falsified by executing $\alpha$. Give a
weaker formulation of requirement (b) that allows A to mention control predicates
concerning the process containing $\alpha$.

**5.16.** Disjointness NI Rule (5.18) can be proved sound by giving a procedure to construct
a proof of $NI(\alpha, A)$ whenever requirements (a) and (b) of Disjointness Condition
(5.17) hold. Give this procedure.

**5.17.** A proof outline $PO(S)$ for a program S is *stronger* than another proof outline
$PO'(S)$ if for every assertion A in $PO(S)$ and corresponding assertion $A'$ in $PO'(S)$,
$A \Rightarrow A'$ is valid. What is the strongest Proof Outline Logic theorem that contains
only primitive assertions for the program

$$\textbf{cobegin}\ x := x+1\ \|\ x := x+1\ \textbf{coend}.$$

Explain why your answer is strongest.

**5.18.** One might argue that indivisibility is not a fundamental form of synchronization
because it can be implemented by altering our definition of when an atomic action is
enabled.

(a)     Support this argument by showing that in any given program, $enbl(\alpha)$ can be
        defined for each atomic action $\alpha$ so that a sequence of two particular atomic
        actions $\beta$ and $\gamma$ is always executed indivisibly.

(b)     What problems does defining $enbl(\alpha)$ in this way raise?

**5.19.** (a)     Argue that $\{\neg enbl(\langle S \rangle) \vee wp(S, Q)\}\ \langle S \rangle\ \{Q\}$ is necessarily valid.

(b)     Argue that if $\{P\}\langle S \rangle\ \{Q\}$ is valid then $P \Rightarrow (\neg enbl(\langle S \rangle) \vee wp(S, Q))$ holds,
        so the precondition in the triple of part (a) is as weak as possible.

**5.20.** Is it necessary that the precondition of the funds transfer process *Move* contain the
conjunct $fbs \neq mmb$? Explain.

**5.21.** It is not necessary to delay the auditor, *Check*, or the funds-transfer process, *Move*,
in order to to eliminate the interference in the Bank problem of §5.7. The key is to
employ an additional variable that contains the value of $j$ at the time a transfer is
made by *Move*. Derive this solution.

# Chapter 6

# Safety Properties: Invariance

A safety property asserts that some "bad thing" does not happen during execution. In this chapter, we consider invariance properties, an important class of safety properties. We discuss methods for proving that a program satisfies an invariance property and show how these methods can guide in the development of programs.

## 6.1 Invariance Properties

An *invariance property* is a safety property that can be specified by a Temporal Logic formula

(6.1)   $Init \Rightarrow \Box Etern$

where *Init* and *Etern* are state predicates, i.e., Predicate Logic formulas that do not use past extensions. Property $\{Init \Rightarrow \Box Etern\}$ proscribes current and future states that satisfy *Etern* (the "bad thing") in any anchored sequence whose current state satisfies *Init*. Examples of invariance properties include:

(6.2)   *Mutual Exclusion.* No anchored sequence whose current state satisfies $Init_S$ contains a current or future state with control inside $CS_1$ and $CS_2$:

$$Init_S \Rightarrow \Box \neg (in(CS_1) \wedge in(CS_2))$$

(6.3)   *Partial Correctness.* No anchored sequence whose current state satisfies $at(S) \wedge P$ contains a current or future state in which $S$ has terminated and $Q$ does not hold:

$$at(S) \wedge P \Rightarrow \Box (after(S) \Rightarrow Q)$$

Thus, the "bad thing" for Mutual Exclusion (6.2) is a state satisfying $in(CS_1) \wedge in(CS_2)$ in an execution starting from an initial program state. The "bad thing" for Partial Correctness (6.3) is a state satisfying $after(S) \wedge \neg Q$ in an execution starting from a state satisfying $at(S) \wedge P$.


## 6.2   Verifying Invariance Properties

Given a program $S$, proving $\mathcal{H}_S^+$-validity of $Init \Rightarrow \square Etern$ establishes that $S$ satisfies this invariance property. We observed in §3.4 that ordinary Temporal Logic is sound but not complete for $\mathcal{H}_S^+$-validity. Thus, $Init \Rightarrow \square Etern$ might be $\mathcal{H}_S^+$-valid but not a theorem. We now extend Temporal Logic to obtain $S$-Temporal Logic, a logic that is sound and complete for $\mathcal{H}_S^+$-validity. Since our concern in this chapter is with invariance properties, we restrict attention to identifying Temporal Logic extensions for proving $\mathcal{H}_S^+$-valid formulas of the form $Init \Rightarrow \square Etern$.

To prove $\mathcal{H}_S^+$-validity of $Init \Rightarrow \square Etern$, it suffices to find a Predicate Logic formula $I$ (without past extensions) for which the following are $\mathcal{H}_S^+$-valid:

(6.4)   $Init \Rightarrow I$

(6.5)   $I \Rightarrow \square I$

(6.6)   $I \Rightarrow Etern$

Thus, $I$ is an invariant that is satisfied by program states from which execution cannot lead to the "bad thing" being proscribed by $Init \Rightarrow \square Etern$. Because not all states satisfying $Etern$ are ones from which $Etern$ will continue to hold, $I$ is typically stronger than $Etern$.

The $\mathcal{H}_S^+$-validity of (6.4), (6.5), and (6.6) suffices for proving $\mathcal{H}_S^+$-validity of $Init \Rightarrow \square Etern$, because we can use ordinary Temporal Logic (which is sound for $\mathcal{H}_S^+$-validity) as follows.

$$
\begin{aligned}
&Init \\
\Rightarrow \quad &\text{«(6.4)»} \\
&I \\
\Rightarrow \quad &\text{«(6.5)»} \\
&\square I \\
\Rightarrow \quad &\text{«(6.6)»} \\
&\square Etern
\end{aligned}
$$

We conclude that to make ordinary Temporal Logic complete for invariance properties, we should extend that logic so that (6.4), (6.5), and (6.6) are provable whenever they are $\mathcal{H}_S^+$-valid.

Predicate Logic (as extended in §4.2 with program variable axioms and control predicate axioms for $S$) can be used to prove $\mathcal{H}_S^+$-validity of (6.4) and

(6.6). This is because *Init*, *I*, and *Etern* are formulas of that logic, and the logic is complete.

To show that *I* is an invariant, as required to establish $\mathcal{H}_S^+$-validity of (6.5), involves reasoning about program execution. Proof Outline Logic was designed for this type of reasoning. Recall that according to Valid Proof Outline (4.17), if $PO(S)$ is valid, then $I_{PO(S)} \Rightarrow \Box I_{PO(S)}$ is $\mathcal{H}_S^+$-valid. Since Proof Outline Logic is both sound and complete with respect to proof outline validity, demonstrating that $I \Rightarrow \Box I$ is $\mathcal{H}_S^+$-valid is equivalent to proving a theorem of Proof Outline Logic.

In light of this equivalence, *S*-Temporal Logic is obtained by merging Proof Outline Logic with Temporal Logic. Both logics extend our Predicate Logic for reasoning about program states, so merging them is reasonable. The formulas of *S*-Temporal Logic include those of (ordinary) Temporal Logic and those of Proof Outline Logic, with validity being defined as might be expected: a proof outline is valid iff it satisfies Valid Proof Outline (4.17), and a Temporal Logic formula is valid iff it is $\mathcal{H}_S^+$-valid.

A complete axiomatization for proving invariance properties by using *S*-Temporal Logic requires only that a single inference rule be added to the axiomatizations of Proof Outline Logic and Temporal Logic. This rule allows reasoning done in the Proof Outline Logic fragment of *S*-Temporal Logic to be used in the Temporal Logic fragment. In particular, from a proof outline $PO(S)$ for *S*, the new rule allows us to infer an *S*-Temporal Logic theorem that asserts that $I_{PO(S)}$ is an invariant.

(6.7) *Proof Outline Invariant Rule*: $\qquad \dfrac{PO(S)}{I_{PO(S)} \Rightarrow \Box I_{PO(S)}}$

Soundness of this rule follows directly from Valid Proof Outline (4.17).

The following derived rule of inference summarizes how a proof outline can be used for demonstrating $\mathcal{H}_S^+$-validity of an invariance property.

(6.8) *Safety Consequence Rule*: $\quad \dfrac{\begin{array}{l}\text{(a) } PO(S),\\ \text{(b) } Init \Rightarrow I_{PO(S)},\\ \text{(c) } I_{PO(S)} \Rightarrow Etern\end{array}}{Init \Rightarrow \Box Etern}$

Justification of this rule is based on the argument given above for proving $Init \Rightarrow \Box Etern$ from (6.4), (6.5), and (6.6), only now Proof Outline Invariant Rule (6.7), rather than Temporal Logic, is used to infer that $I \Rightarrow \Box I$ is $\mathcal{H}_S^+$-valid. Safety Consequence Rule (6.8) also follows directly from Proof Outline Invariant Rule (6.7) and $\Box$ Consequence Rule (3.13).

$S$: **cobegin**

       *Prod*: **do** *true* $\rightarrow S_1$: **if** $a-r<N \rightarrow S_2$: $a := a+1$ **fi od**

  ||

       *Cons*: **do** *true* $\rightarrow T_1$: **if** $a-r>0 \rightarrow T_2$: $r := r+1$ **fi od**

  **coend**

**Figure 6.1.** Producer/consumer program

---

## A Producer/Consumer Example

To illustrate the use of Safety Consequence Rule (6.8), we prove that invariance property

(6.9)   $at(S) \wedge a=0 \wedge r=0 \wedge 0\leq N \;\Rightarrow\; \Box(0\leq a-r\leq N)$

is satisfied by program $S$ of Figure 6.1. The exercise is not as contrived as it might seem at first. If $a$ represents the number of items that have been added to a finite-size buffer with capacity $N$, and $r$ represents the number of items that have been removed, then $a := a+1$ in *Prod* models adding an item to the buffer, and $r := r+1$ in *Cons* models removing an item. Invariance property (6.9) asserts that for executions starting from $Init_S$, a state where nothing has been added or removed from the buffer (i.e., $a=0 \wedge r=0$), no process attempts to add an item to a full buffer (i.e., $a-r=N$) or remove an item from an empty buffer (i.e., $a-r=0$). Thus, proving (6.9) establishes that *Prod* and *Cons* correctly synchronize access to a bounded buffer.

A proof outline for $S$ appears as Figure 6.2. To use Safety Consequence Rule (6.8) for proving (6.9), we must show that each premise of the rule is a theorem of $S$-Temporal Logic. Premise (a) is a theorem because the proof outline of Figure 6.2 is a theorem of Proof Outline Logic. Premise (b) is a theorem because the only conjunct in $I_{PO(S)}$ that has an antecedent implied by $at(S) \wedge a=0 \wedge r=0 \wedge 0\leq N$ is $at(S) \Rightarrow at(S) \wedge a=0 \wedge r=0 \wedge 0\leq N$. Here is the proof of premise (c).

$I_{PO(S)}$

$=$      «definition (4.14) of $I_{PO(S)}$»

      $\displaystyle\bigwedge_{T \,\in\, Stmts(S)} ((at(T) \Rightarrow pre(T)) \wedge (after(T) \Rightarrow post(T)))$

$\Rightarrow$     «Each assertion in the proof outline of Figure 6.2 implies
       $0\leq a-r\leq N$, so $pre(T) \Rightarrow Etern$ and $post(T) \Rightarrow Etern$»

      $\displaystyle\bigwedge_{T \,\in\, Stmts(S)} ((at(T) \Rightarrow Etern) \wedge (after(T) \Rightarrow Etern))$

$=$      «Implication Law (2.22a)»

$\{Init_S\colon at(S) \wedge a=0 \wedge r=0 \wedge 0 \le N\}$
$S\colon$ **cobegin**
$\qquad \{0 \le a-r \le N\}$
$\qquad Prod\colon$ **do** $true \to \{0 \le a-r \le N\}$
$\qquad\qquad\qquad\qquad S_1\colon$ **if** $a-r<N \to \{0 \le a-r <N\}$
$\qquad\qquad\qquad\qquad\qquad\qquad S_2\colon a := a+1$
$\qquad\qquad\qquad\qquad\qquad\qquad \{0 \le a-r \le N\}$
$\qquad\qquad\qquad\qquad\quad$ **fi** $\{0 \le a-r \le N\}$
$\qquad\qquad$ **od** $\{false\}$
$\quad \|$
$\qquad \{0 \le a-r \le N\}$
$\qquad Cons\colon$ **do** $true \to \{0 \le a-r \le N\}$
$\qquad\qquad\qquad\qquad T_1\colon$ **if** $a-r>0 \to \{0< a-r \le N\}$
$\qquad\qquad\qquad\qquad\qquad\qquad T_2\colon r := r+1$
$\qquad\qquad\qquad\qquad\qquad\qquad \{0 \le a-r \le N\}$
$\qquad\qquad\qquad\qquad\quad$ **fi** $\{0 \le a-r \le N\}$
$\qquad\qquad$ **od** $\{false\}$
$\quad$ **coend**
$\{false\}$

**Figure 6.2.** Proof outline for producer/consumer

$\qquad \bigwedge\limits_{T \in Stmts(S)} ((\neg at(T) \vee Etern) \wedge (\neg after(T) \vee Etern))$

$=$ «Distributive Law (2.16c)»

$\quad Etern \ \vee \ (\bigwedge\limits_{T \in Stmts(S)} (\neg at(T) \wedge \neg after(T)))$

$\Rightarrow$ «$(\bigwedge\limits_{T \in Stmts(S)} (\neg at(T) \wedge \neg after(T))) \Rightarrow \neg in(S) \wedge \neg after(S)$ due to the control predicate axioms»

$\quad Etern \ \vee \ (\neg in(S) \wedge \neg after(S))$

$=$ «$(\neg in(S) \wedge \neg after(S)) = false$ due to Program Control Axiom (4.9b)»

$\quad Etern \vee false$

$=$ «Or-Simplification Law (2.25c)»

$\quad Etern$

This completes the proof that the program of Figure 6.2 satisfies invariance property (6.9).

## 6.3  Exclusion of Configurations

Safety Consequence Rule (6.8) is based on proving that *Etern* holds for each state that can arise during execution. Another approach for proving $Init \Rightarrow \Box Etern$ is to establish that $\neg Etern$ is *false* in any state that arises during execution. For example, if $P$ holds whenever $at(\alpha)$ does and $Q$ holds whenever $at(\beta)$ does, then $P \wedge Q$ describes the program state when $at(\alpha) \wedge at(\beta)$ holds. The constant *false* is satisfied by no program state, so if $P \wedge Q$ equals *false* then $at(\alpha)$ and $at(\beta)$ cannot both be satisfied. Thus, proving that $P \wedge Q$ is *false* allows us to conclude that execution of $\alpha$ and $\beta$ are mutually exclusive—a state satisfying $at(\alpha) \wedge at(\beta)$ cannot occur.

The general method for proving an invariance property by showing that states satisfying $\neg Etern$ cannot arise during execution is really just a reformulation of premise (c) from Safety Consequence Rule (6.8):

$$I_{PO(S)} \Rightarrow Etern$$
$=\qquad \text{«Implication Law (2.22a)»}$
$$\neg I_{PO(S)} \vee Etern$$
$=\qquad \text{«Commutative Law (2.14b)»}$
$$Etern \vee \neg I_{PO(S)}$$
$=\qquad \text{«Or-Simplification Law (2.25c)»}$
$$Etern \vee \neg I_{PO(S)} \vee false$$
$=\qquad \text{«Implication Law (2.22a)»}$
$$\neg (Etern \vee \neg I_{PO(S)}) \Rightarrow false$$
$=\qquad \text{«De Morgan's Law (2.17b)»}$
$$\neg Etern \wedge I_{PO(S)} \Rightarrow false$$

Thus, we have:

(6.10)  *Exclusion of Configurations Rule*:

$$\begin{array}{l} \text{(a)} \;\; PO(S), \\ \text{(b)} \;\; Init \Rightarrow I_{PO(S)}, \\ \text{(c)} \;\; \neg Etern \wedge I_{PO(S)} \Rightarrow false \\ \hline \qquad\quad Init \Rightarrow \Box Etern \end{array}$$

## *Producer/Consumer Example Revisited*

To illustrate the use Exclusion of Configurations Rule (6.10), we check whether the producer/consumer program of Figure 6.1 is deadlock free. *Deadlock* is a state in which two or more processes remain forever blocked at conditional atomic actions, and invariance property *deadlock freedom* asserts that no execution starting from an initial program state leads to deadlock.[1]

---

[1]Some consider it a deadlock when a single process is forever blocked at a conditional atomic action. We do not, preferring that deadlock occur only in concurrent programs.

(6.11) *Deadlock Freedom*. No anchored sequence whose current state satisfies *Init_S* contains a current or future state in which two or more processes are thereafter blocked at conditional atomic actions.

Since the only conditional atomic actions in the program of Figure 6.1 are the guard evaluation actions of $S_1$ and $T_1$, deadlock freedom for the program is:

(6.12) $at(S) \wedge a=0 \wedge r=0 \wedge 0 \leq N$
$$\Rightarrow \Box \neg (at(S_1) \wedge \neg enbl(GEval_{if}(S_1)) \wedge at(T_1) \wedge \neg enbl(GEval_{if}(T_1)))$$

Based on definition (5.36) of $enbl(\alpha)$, (6.12) is equivalent to:

(6.13) $at(S) \wedge a=0 \wedge r=0 \wedge 0 \leq N$
$$\Rightarrow \Box \neg (at(S_1) \wedge a-r \geq N \wedge at(T_1) \wedge a-r \leq 0)$$

To use Exclusion of Configurations Rule (6.10) with the proof outline of Figure 6.2, it suffices to discharge premise (c), since premises (a) and (b) are identical to things already proved in connection with (6.9). Based on (6.13) and the form of the conclusion of Exclusion of Configurations Rule (6.10), we conclude that *Etern* is:

$$Etern: \quad \neg (at(S_1) \wedge a-r \geq N \wedge at(T_1) \wedge a-r \leq 0)$$

---

$\{Init_S: \ at(S) \wedge a=0 \wedge r=0 \wedge 0<N\}$
$S:$ **cobegin**
           $\{0 \leq a-r \leq N \wedge 0<N\}$
           *Prod*: **do** *true* $\rightarrow$ $\{0 \leq a-r \leq N \wedge 0<N\}$
                             $S_1$: **if** $a-r<N \rightarrow$   $\{0 \leq a-r<N \wedge 0<N\}$
                                           $S_2$: $a := a+1$
                                        $\{0 \leq a-r \leq N \wedge 0<N\}$
                             **fi** $\{0 \leq a-r \leq N \wedge 0<N\}$
           **od** $\{false\}$
    $\|$
           $\{0 \leq a-r \leq N \wedge 0<N\}$
           *Cons*: **do** *true* $\rightarrow$ $\{0 \leq a-r \leq N \wedge 0<N\}$
                              $T_1$: **if** $a-r>0 \rightarrow$   $\{0<a-r \leq N \wedge 0<N\}$
                                           $T_2$: $r := r+1$
                                        $\{0 \leq a-r \leq N \wedge 0<N\}$
                             **fi** $\{0 \leq a-r \leq N \wedge 0<N\}$
           **od** $\{false\}$
**coend**
$\{false\}$

**Figure 6.3.** Revised proof outline for producer/consumer

To satisfy premise (c), we must prove that $\neg Etern \wedge I_{PO(S)}$ implies *false*. Unfortunately, it doesn't; it implies $0 = N = a - r$. Moreover, it is not possible to make premise (c) valid by altering the proof outline of Figure 6.2 to strengthen $I_{PO(S)}$. The program of Figure 6.1 really does deadlock when $N = 0$: *Cons* becomes blocked because the buffer contains no items for *Cons* to consume, and *Prod* becomes blocked because the buffer has no space in which to store items.

One way to eliminate this deadlock is to require that $N > 0$ hold initially. This is accomplished by strengthening $Init_S$ to be $at(S) \wedge a = 0 \wedge r = 0 \wedge N > 0$ and then constructing a new, stronger proof outline. See Figure 6.3. We apply Exclusion of Configurations Rule (6.10) to that proof outline. Premise (a) is satisfied because the proof outline of Figure 6.3 is a theorem of Proof Outline Logic. Premise (b) is still satisfied even though $pre(S)$ has been strengthened, and premise (c) is satisfied because:

$$\begin{aligned}
& \neg Etern \wedge I_{PO(S)} \\
= \quad & \text{«Expanding definitions of } Etern \text{ and } I_{PO(S)} \text{»} \\
& at(S_1) \wedge a - r \geq N \wedge at(T_1) \wedge a - r \leq 0 \wedge 0 < N \wedge 0 \leq a - r \leq N \\
= \quad & \text{«Predicate Logic»} \\
& false
\end{aligned}$$

## 6.4   Direct Use of Proof Outlines

Safety Consequence Rule (6.8) and Exclusion of Configurations Rule (6.10) are sometimes awkward to use because they require constructing and manipulating a long formula, $I_{PO(S)}$. Fortunately, most invariance properties encountered in practice are ones for which explicit construction of $I_{PO(S)}$ is unnecessary. Such properties and (simpler) derived rules of *S*-Temporal Logic are the subject of this section.

### Subsets of Histories

For invariance properties in which $\neg Etern$ is being proscribed only for a subset of histories starting in initial program states, $Init \Rightarrow I_{PO(S)}$ can be discharged without constructing $I_{PO(S)}$. To see how, first observe that such invariance properties are necessarily of the form

(6.14)   $Init_S \wedge P \Rightarrow \Box Etern$

for $P$ a primitive Predicate Logic formula. Examples of such invariance properties are Mutual Exclusion (6.2) and Partial Correctness (6.3).

Next, observe that for a proof outline $PO(S)$, $at(S) \wedge pre(PO(S)) \Rightarrow I_{PO(S)}$ is a theorem due to definition (4.14) of $I_{PO(S)}$. Therefore, in using Safety Consequence Rule (6.8) or Exclusion of Configurations Rule (6.10) to prove $at(S) \wedge P \Rightarrow \Box Etern$, premise (b) is satisfied if $P$ equals $pre(PO(S))$. This results in the following simplified versions of Safety Consequence Rule (6.8) and Exclusion of Configurations Rule (6.10).

**(6.15)** *Precondition Safety Consequence Rule:*

$$\frac{\text{(a) } PO(S),\quad \text{(b) } I_{PO(S)} \Rightarrow Etern}{at(S) \wedge pre(PO(S)) \Rightarrow \Box Etern}$$

**(6.16)** *Precondition Exclusion of Configurations Rule:*

$$\frac{\text{(a) } PO(S),\quad \text{(b) } \neg Etern \wedge I_{PO(S)} \Rightarrow false}{at(S) \wedge pre(PO(S)) \Rightarrow \Box Etern}$$

## Strong Assertions

Another simplification to our rules for proving invariance properties is possible when a proof outline has sufficiently strong assertions. Let $loc(A)$ be the control predicate with which an assertion $A$ is associated in proof outline $PO(S)$. Thus, $I_{PO(S)}$ is equivalent to $\bigwedge_A (loc(A) \Rightarrow A)$, and the following are derived inference rules.

**(6.17)** $I_{PO(S)}$ *Decomposition Rules:*

(a) $$\frac{\text{For each assertion } A \text{ in } PO(S): \quad loc(A) \wedge A \Rightarrow Etern}{I_{PO(S)} \Rightarrow Etern}$$

(b) $$\frac{\text{For each assertion } A \text{ in } PO(S): \quad loc(A) \wedge A \wedge \neg Etern \Rightarrow false}{\neg Etern \wedge I_{PO(S)} \Rightarrow false}$$

These rules make the explicit construction of $I_{PO(S)}$ unnecessary in discharging premises $I_{PO(S)} \Rightarrow Etern$ and $\neg Etern \wedge I_{PO(S)} \Rightarrow false$. With $I_{PO(S)}$ Decomposition Rule (6.17a), $I_{PO(S)} \Rightarrow Etern$ is discharged by checking each assertion individually rather than by combining assertions to form $I_{PO(S)}$. For example, since every assertion in the proof outline of Figure 6.2 implies $0 \leq a - r \leq N$, we infer immediately that $I_{PO}(S) \Rightarrow 0 \leq a - r \leq N$ is a theorem.

## Validity by Location

Finally, for many invariance properties, proving $loc(A) \wedge A \Rightarrow Etern$, as required by $I_{PO(S)}$ Decomposition Rules (6.17), is trivial for all but a few key assertions. Mutual Exclusion (6.2) is an example of such a property. For any assertion $A$ associated with a control point that is not in a critical section, $loc(A) \Rightarrow \neg (in(CS_1) \wedge in(CS_2))$—hence $\quad loc(A) \wedge A \Rightarrow \neg (in(CS_1) \wedge in(CS_2))$— are theorems. Consequently, to prove that a program satisfies Mutual Exclusion (6.2), it is necessary to prove $loc(A) \wedge A \Rightarrow \neg (in(CS_1) \wedge in(CS_2))$ only for control points $loc(A)$ that are inside critical sections.

Partial Correctness (6.3) is another property for which $loc(A) \wedge A \Rightarrow Etern$ need be proved only for a few of the assertions in a proof outline. In Partial Correctness (6.3), $Etern$ is $after(S) \Rightarrow Q$, which holds in all states satisfying $\neg after(S)$. Therefore, $I_{PO}(S) \Rightarrow (after(S) \Rightarrow Q)$ can be proved from $I_{PO(S)}$ Decomposition Rule (6.17a) by showing $after(S) \wedge post(PO(S)) \Rightarrow Q$, and we have:

(6.19) *Partial Correctness Rule*:

$$\frac{PO(S)}{at(S) \wedge pre(PO(S)) \Rightarrow \Box(after(S) \Rightarrow post(PO(S)))}$$

For example, using Partial Correctness Rule (6.19) with the proof outline of Figure 5.4, we conclude:

$$at(S) \Rightarrow \Box(after(S) \Rightarrow ((k < n \Rightarrow a[k] = V)$$
$$\wedge (\forall i \in \text{Int:}\ 0 \le i < k:\ a[i] \ne V)))$$

Thus, if the program of Figure 5.4 is started in an initial state and terminates, then either $k \ge N$ or $a[k]$ is the first occurrence of value $V$ in array $a$.


## 6.5  Developing Programs for Invariance Properties

It is not unusual to be asked to design a program that satisfies some given invariance property. The $S$-Temporal Logic rules of this chapter obviously have application in determining whether this job has been completed. Perhaps not so obvious is that the rules have application in the development of programs. By keeping in mind, during construction of a program, how we intend to prove that it satisfies an invariance property, we can restrict attention to refinements that further our goal. Moreover, constructing proof and program together virtually ensures success in ultimately verifying that the final program satisfies a desired invariance property.

We illustrate this approach to program design by deriving a solution to the mutual exclusion problem, a classical concurrent programming exercise. A *mutual exclusion protocol* ensures that execution of selected statements, called *critical sections*, exclude each other. This is a form of condition synchronization: By making critical sections $CS_1$ and $CS_2$ mutually exclusive, assertions associated with control points in $CS_1$ can be strengthened by the conjunct $\neg in(CS_2)$, and those associated with $CS_2$ can be strengthened by $\neg in(CS_1)$.

Thus, atomic actions in $CS_1$ cannot interfere with assertions in $PO(CS_2)$, and atomic actions in $CS_2$ cannot interfere with assertions in $PO(CS_1)$.

The mutual exclusion problem is usually posed in terms of two processes, each of which executes a critical section and a noncritical section. This setting is illustrated in Figure 6.4. For each process $S_i$, we must design an entry protocol *entry*$_i$ and an exit protocol *exit*$_i$ to ensure that execution of critical sections satisfy Mutual Exclusion (6.2) and the following three properties:

(6.20) *Entry Nonblocking.* Both processes cannot become blocked if both are executing their entry protocols.

(6.21) *NCS Nonblocking.* One process cannot become blocked executing its entry protocol when the other is executing *NCS*.

(6.22) *Exit Nonblocking.* No process can become blocked executing its exit protocol.

These last three properties stipulate that the entry and exit protocols do not block processes without cause. All are invariance properties. Entry Nonblocking (6.20) is a form of Deadlock Freedom (6.11); NCS Nonblocking (6.21) proscribes states in which one process is blocked attempting to enter its critical section while the other executes in its noncritical section; and Exit Nonblocking (6.22) proscribes states in which a process is blocked attempting to exit its critical section.

## Ensuring Mutual Exclusion

It is impossible to formalize nonblocking properties (6.20), (6.21), and (6.22) without first knowing what conditional atomic actions are in the entry and exit protocols. Therefore, we start by constructing entry and exit protocols to ensure Mutual Exclusion (6.2). Once candidate protocols have been developed, we return to the three nonblocking properties.

---

$S$:  **cobegin**
 $S_1$:  **do** *true* $\rightarrow$ *entry*$_1$
   $CS_1$
   *exit*$_1$
   $NCS_1$
  **od**
 ||
 $S_2$:  **do** *true* $\rightarrow$ *entry*$_2$
   $CS_2$
   *exit*$_2$
   $NCS_2$
  **od**
 **coend**

**Figure 6.4.** Mutual exclusion problem

We begin by devising a proof outline for the program of Figure 6.4 with an eye towards verifying Mutual Exclusion (6.2) using the rules of the preceding sections. In this initial proof outline, the entry and exit protocols are **skip** statements since there is no reason to choose otherwise. A failure to prove Mutual Exclusion (6.2) will then identify assertions that must be strengthened for the proof to succeed. The strengthening is implemented by modifying the entry and exit protocols.

Figure 6.5 gives an initial proof outline for the program of Figure 6.4. Because $PO(S)$ of Figure 6.5 is a Proof Outline Logic theorem, premise (a) of Precondition Safety Consequence Rule (6.15) is satisfied. To satisfy premise (b) and conclude that Mutual Exclusion (6.2) holds, we use $I_{PO(S)}$ Decomposition Rule (6.17a). This requires proving

$$(6.23) \quad loc(A) \wedge A \Rightarrow \neg (in(CS_1) \wedge in(CS_2))$$

for each assertion $A$ in the proof outline. Unfortunately, (6.23) is not valid for assertions in $PO(CS_1)$ and $PO(CS_2)$. However, from this failure to prove Mutual Exclusion (6.2), we have learned that assertions in $PO(CS_1)$ must be strengthened so that each implies $\neg in(CS_2)$, and assertions in $PO(CS_2)$ must be strengthened so that each implies $\neg in(CS_1)$.

---

```
{true}
S:  cobegin
        {¬in(CS₁)}
        S₁: do true → {¬in(CS₁)}
                        entry₁: skip
                        {in(CS₁)} PO(CS₁) {¬in(CS₁)}
                        exit₁: skip
                        {¬in(CS₁)} PO(NCS₁) {¬in(CS₁)}
               od {false}
        ‖
        {¬in(CS₂)}
        S₂: do true → {¬in(CS₂)}
                        entry₂: skip
                        {in(CS₂)} PO(CS₂) {¬in(CS₂)}
                        exit₂: skip
                        {¬in(CS₂)} PO(NCS₂) {¬in(CS₂)}
               od {false}
     coend
  {false}
```

**Figure 6.5.** Initial proof outline for mutual exclusion problem

To accomplish this strengthening, we alter the entry protocols. We find predicates $B_1$ and $B_2$ such that

$$I:\ (B_1 \Rightarrow \neg in(CS_2))\ \wedge\ (B_2 \Rightarrow \neg in(CS_1))$$

holds throughout execution. Strengthening by Condition Synchronization (5.50) with guard $B_1$ now can be used to strengthen $pre(PO(CS_1))$ with $B_1$ and anything $I \wedge B_1$ implies—in particular, by $\neg in(CS_2)$. We similarly strengthen $pre(PO(CS_2))$ with $B_2$ and anything that $I \wedge B_2$ implies.

Next, Strengthening by Propagation (5.51) is used to strengthen the other assertions in $PO(CS_1)$ and $PO(CS_2)$ with the same conjuncts. These strengthenings result in the following modifications to the proof outline of Figure 6.5:

$$\cdots$$
$$S_1:\ \ldots\ \{I \wedge \neg in(CS_1)\}$$
$$\qquad\qquad entry_1:\ \textbf{if } B_1 \to \{I \wedge B_1\}\ T_1:\ \textbf{skip }\{I \wedge B_1\}\textbf{ fi}$$
$$\qquad\qquad \{I \wedge B_1\}$$
$$\qquad\qquad PO(CS_1) \otimes (I \wedge B_1)$$
$$\qquad\qquad \cdots$$

$$\|$$
$$S_2:\ \ldots\ \{I \wedge \neg in(CS_2)\}$$
$$\qquad\qquad entry_2:\ \textbf{if } B_2 \to \{I \wedge B_2\}\ T_2:\ \textbf{skip }\{I \wedge B_2\}\textbf{ fi}$$
$$\qquad\qquad \{I \wedge B_2\}$$
$$\qquad\qquad PO(CS_2) \otimes (I \wedge B_2)$$
$$\qquad\qquad \cdots$$
$$\cdots$$

This new proof outline is not interference-free. Execution of $T_2$ falsifies $I \wedge B_1$ (specifically, $\neg in(CS_2)$) in the proof outline of $S_1$. This is because when $T_2$ terminates, $after(T_2)$ holds, and due to the following proof, $in(CS_2)$ holds as well.

$$\qquad\quad after(T_2)$$
$$\Rightarrow\qquad \text{«\textbf{if} Control Axiom (4.11b)»}$$
$$\qquad\quad after(entry_2)$$
$$=\qquad \text{«Statement Juxtaposition Control Axiom (4.10c)»}$$
$$\qquad\quad at(CS_2)$$
$$\Rightarrow\qquad \text{«In Axiom (4.7a)»}$$
$$\qquad\quad in(CS_2)$$

Symmetrically, $T_1$ interferes with $I \wedge B_2$ in the assertions of $PO(S_2)$.

We eliminate interference of $T_2$ with $I \wedge B_1$ by using Strengthening (5.14). We strengthen both $pre(T_2)$ and $I$ so that $pre(T_2) \wedge I \wedge B_1$ equals *false*, making $NI(T_2, I \wedge B_1)$ valid. To accomplish this, strengthen $pre(T_2)$ with the conjunct $at(T_2)$ and modify $I$ so that $I \wedge B_1 \Rightarrow \neg at(T_2)$. Symmetric modifications to eliminate interference of $T_1$ with $I \wedge B_2$ result in the following new definition for $I$,

$I$:  $(B_1 \Rightarrow \neg(in(CS_2) \vee at(T_2)))$  $\wedge$  $(B_2 \Rightarrow \neg(in(CS_1) \vee at(T_1)))$

and the following revised proof outline.

$$
\begin{aligned}
&\cdots\\
S_1: &\ \cdots \ \{I \wedge \neg in(CS_1)\}\\
&\qquad entry_1\colon \ \mathbf{if}\, B_1 \to \{I \wedge at(T_1) \wedge B_1\}\ T_1\colon\ \mathbf{skip}\ \{I \wedge B_1\}\,\mathbf{fi}\\
&\qquad \{I \wedge B_1\}\\
&\qquad PO(CS_1) \otimes (I \wedge B_1)\\
&\qquad \cdots\\
\parallel\\
S_2: &\ \cdots\ \{I \wedge \neg in(CS_2)\}\\
&\qquad entry_2\colon\ \mathbf{if}\, B_2 \to \{I \wedge at(T_2) \wedge B_2\}\ T_2\colon\ \mathbf{skip}\ \{I \wedge B_2\}\,\mathbf{fi}\\
&\qquad \{I \wedge B_2\}\\
&\qquad PO(CS_2)\otimes(I \wedge B_2)\\
&\qquad \cdots\\
&\cdots
\end{aligned}
$$

$NI(T_2, I \wedge B_1)$ and $NI(T_1, I \wedge B_2)$ are valid in this new proof outline, but $GEval_{if}(entry_2)$ may interfere with $I \wedge B_1$ by falsifying $\neg at(T_2)$; similarly, $GEval_{if}(entry_1)$ may interfere with $I \wedge B_2$. One more strengthening of $I$ solves this problem.

$I$:  $(B_1 \Rightarrow \neg(in(CS_2) \vee in(entry_2)))$
$\qquad \wedge\ (B_2 \Rightarrow \neg(in(CS_1) \vee in(entry_1)))$

Finally, we must ensure that execution of the atomic action preceding $entry_2$ does not falsify $I$ in making $at(entry_2)$ hold (and similarly for $entry_1$). We solve this problem by postulating that $pre(entry_1) \Rightarrow \neg B_2$ and $pre(entry_2) \Rightarrow \neg B_1$ are valid. Thus, we have:

$$
\begin{aligned}
&\cdots\\
S_1: &\ \cdots\ \{I \wedge \neg in(CS_1) \wedge \neg B_2\}\\
&\qquad entry_1\colon\ \mathbf{if}\, B_1 \to \{I \wedge at(T_1) \wedge B_1\}\ T_1\colon\ \mathbf{skip}\ \{I \wedge B_1\}\,\mathbf{fi}\\
&\qquad \{I \wedge B_1\}\\
&\qquad PO(CS_1)\otimes(I \wedge B_1)\\
&\qquad \cdots\\
\parallel\\
S_2: &\ \cdots\ \{I \wedge \neg in(CS_2) \wedge \neg B_1\}\\
&\qquad entry_2\colon\ \mathbf{if}\, B_2 \to \{I \wedge at(T_2) \wedge B_2\}\ T_2\colon\ \mathbf{skip}\ \{I \wedge B_2\}\,\mathbf{fi}\\
&\qquad \{I \wedge B_2\}\\
&\qquad PO(CS_2)\otimes(I \wedge B_2)\\
&\qquad \cdots\\
&\cdots
\end{aligned}
$$

Our next task is to define $B_1$ and $B_2$ in terms of program variables, since guards may not mention control predicates. We introduce boolean program variables $in1$ and $in2$ and add assignment statements to the entry and exit protocols so that we can replace $I$ by:

$$I: \quad (\neg in2 \Rightarrow \neg(in(CS_2) \vee in(entry_2)))$$
$$\wedge \ (\neg in1 \Rightarrow \neg(in(CS_1) \vee in(entry_1)))$$

Then, $\neg in2$ can replace $B_1$, and $\neg in1$ can replace $B_2$. We have only to identify assignment statements to ensure that $I$ holds throughout execution and that ensure $pre(entry_1)$ and $pre(entry_2)$ hold when they are reached.

Execution of either $entry_i$ or $CS_i$ causes $\neg(in(CS_i) \vee in(entry_i))$ to become *false*. Therefore, maintaining the truth of $I$ requires that $in1$ be *true* before $entry_1$ is executed and that $in2$ be *true* before $entry_2$ is executed. We accomplish this by adding assignment statement $in1 := true$ before $entry_1$ and $in2 := true$ before $entry_2$. Since these statements are part of the entry protocol, we redefine $entry_i$ to include the assignment statement (labeled $door_i$) and the **if** (labeled $gate_i$). The result is shown in the following proof outline. Notice the revised definition of $I$ to account for the renaming of statements.

$$I: \quad (\neg in2 \Rightarrow \neg(in(CS_2) \vee in(gate_2)))$$
$$\wedge \ (\neg in1 \Rightarrow \neg(in(CS_1) \vee in(gate_1)))$$

...

$S_1$: ...  $\{I \wedge \neg in(CS_1)\}$
$entry_1$: $door_1$: $in1 := true$  $\{I \wedge \neg in(CS_1) \wedge in1\}$
$gate_1$: **if** $\neg in2 \rightarrow \{I \wedge at(T_1) \wedge in1 \wedge \neg in2\}$
$T_1$: **skip** $\{I \wedge in1 \wedge \neg in2\}$ **fi**

$\{I \wedge in1 \wedge \neg in2\}$
$PO(CS_1) \otimes (I \wedge in1 \wedge \neg in2)$

...

$\|$

$S_2$: ...  $\{I \wedge \neg in(CS_2)\}$
$entry_1$: $door_2$: $in2 := true$  $\{I \wedge \neg in(CS_2) \wedge in2\}$
$gate_2$: **if** $\neg in1 \rightarrow \{I \wedge at(T_2) \wedge in2 \wedge \neg in1\}$
$T_2$: **skip** $\{I \wedge in2 \wedge \neg in1\}$ **fi**

$\{I \wedge in2 \wedge \neg in1\}$
$PO(CS_2) \otimes (I \wedge in2 \wedge \neg in1)$

...

...

Unfortunately, these new assignment statements cause interference. Execution of $in1 := true$ falsifies $\neg in1$ in assertions of $S_2$, and $in2 := true$ falsifies $\neg in2$ in assertions of $S_1$. This interference can be removed with Weakening (5.15). Replace $\neg in1$ in assertions of $S_2$ by $\neg in1 \vee after(door_1)$ and replace $\neg in2$ in assertions of $S_1$ by $\neg in2 \vee after(door_2)$. The result is shown in the proof outline of Figure 6.6, which is interference-free. Moreover, because

$$I \wedge (\neg in2 \vee after(door_2)) \ \Rightarrow \ \neg in(CS_2)$$

$$I \wedge (\neg in1 \vee after(door_1)) \;\Rightarrow\; \neg in(CS_1)$$

are valid, (6.23) is valid for each assertion $A$ in the proof outline, so Mutual Exclusion (6.2) is satisfied.

## Nonblocking

Given this entry protocol candidate, we now check whether Entry Nonblocking (6.20) is satisfied.  For our protocol, this property is formalized as

---

```
{true}
S: in1, in2 := ...
    {I: (¬in2 ⇒ ¬(in(CS₂) ∨ in(gate₂)))
       ∧ (¬in1 ⇒ ¬(in(CS₁) ∨ in(gate₁)))}
    cobegin
    {I ∧ ¬in(CS₁)}
S₁: do true → {I ∧ ¬in(CS₁)}
        entry₁: door₁: in1 := true  {I ∧ ¬in(CS₁) ∧ in1}
                gate₁: if ¬in2 → {I ∧ at(T₁) ∧ in1 ∧ (¬in2 ∨ after(door₂))}
                                T₁: skip
                                {I ∧ in1 ∧ (¬in2 ∨ after(door₂))} fi
        {I ∧ in1 ∧ (¬in2 ∨ after(door₂))}
        PO(CS₁)⊗(I ∧ in1 ∧ (¬in2 ∨ after(door₂)))
        {I ∧ ¬in(CS₁)}
        exit₁: skip
        {I ∧ ¬in(CS₁)} PO(NCS₁)⊗(I ∧ ¬in(CS₁))  {I ∧ ¬in(CS₁)}
        od {false}
    ‖
    {I ∧ ¬in(CS₂)}
S₂: do true → {I ∧ ¬in(CS₂)}
        entry₂: door₂: in2 := true  {I ∧ ¬in(CS₂) ∧ in2}
                gate₂: if ¬in1 → {I ∧ at(T₂) ∧ in2 ∧ (¬in1 ∨ after(door₁))}
                                T₂: skip
                                {I ∧ in2 ∧ (¬in1 ∨ after(door₁))} fi
        {I ∧ in2 ∧ (¬in1 ∨ after(door₁))}
        PO(CS₂)⊗(I ∧ in2 ∧ (¬in1 ∨ after(door₁)))
        {I ∧ ¬in(CS₂)}
        exit₂: skip
        {I ∧ ¬in(CS₂)} PO(NCS₂)⊗(I ∧ ¬in(CS₂))  {I ∧ ¬in(CS₂)}
        od {false}
    coend
{false}
```

**Figure 6.6.**  Protocol for Mutual Exclusion (6.2)

(6.24)  $at(S) \Rightarrow \Box \neg (at(gate_1) \wedge \neg enbl(GEval_{if}(gate_1))$
$\wedge\, at(gate_2) \wedge \neg enbl(GEval_{if}(gate_2)))$

because the only conditional atomic actions in the entry protocols are $GEval_{if}(gate_1)$ and $GEval_{if}(gate_2)$.

We select Precondition Exclusion of Configurations Rule (6.16) for proving (6.24). Premise (a) is satisfied by the (valid) proof outline of Figure 6.6. Premise (b) requires that

(6.25)  $at(gate_1) \wedge in2 \wedge at(gate_2) \wedge in1 \wedge I_{PO(S)}$

implies *false*, because $enbl(GEval_{if}(gate_1))$ is $\neg in2$ and $enbl(GEval_{if}(gate_2))$ is $\neg in1$. Unfortunately, (6.25) does not imply *false*; it implies

(6.26)  $at(gate_1) \wedge in2 \wedge at(gate_2) \wedge in1 \wedge I \wedge \neg in(CS_1) \wedge \neg in(CS_2)$.

Either the proof outline of Figure 6.6 is not strong enough to prove (6.24), or this property is not satisfied by our protocol. By working backwards from a state satisfying (6.26), we find that execution of $door_1$ followed by $door_2$ results in a state where $S_1$ is blocked at $gate_1$ and $S_2$ is blocked at $gate_2$. The entry protocol we have developed does not satisfy Entry Nonblocking (6.20).

To eliminate this deadlock, we try weaker guards in $gate_1$ and $gate_2$— weaker guards mean that fewer states will cause blocking. Constraints on these guards can be determined by using an as yet unspecified disjunct $X_i$ to accomplish the weakening for $gate_i$. The proof outline for $S_1$ with such a weaker guard would be:

```
...
{I ∧ ¬in(CS₁)}
entry₁: door₁: in1 := true  {I ∧ ¬in(CS₁) ∧ in1}
        gate₁: if ¬in2 ∨ X₁ →
                    {I ∧ at(T₁) ∧ in1 ∧ (¬in2 ∨ X₁ ∨ after(door₂))}
                    T₁: skip
                    {I ∧ in1 ∧ (¬in2 ∨ X₁ ∨ after(door₂))} fi
{I ∧ in1 ∧ (¬in2 ∨ X₁ ∨ after(door₂))}
PO(CS₁)⊗(I ∧ in1 ∧ (¬in2 ∨ X₁ ∨ after(door₂)))
...
```

Constraints on $X_1$ and $X_2$ that ensure Entry Nonblocking (6.20) is satisfied are now obtained by using the proof outline with weaker guards and repeating the above proof for (6.24). Notice that if $\neg X_1 \wedge \neg X_2 \Rightarrow false$ is valid, then so is

$at(gate_1) \wedge \neg(\neg in2 \vee X_1) \wedge at(gate_2) \wedge \neg(\neg in1 \vee X_2)$
$\wedge\, I \wedge \neg in(CS_1) \wedge in1 \wedge \neg in(CS_2) \wedge in2 \quad \Rightarrow \quad false$

and premise (b) of Precondition Exclusion of Configurations Rule (6.16) is satisfied. Therefore, if $X_1$ and $X_2$ are predicates that cannot simultaneously be *false*, then Entry Nonblocking (6.20) will hold.

An obvious choice is to define a single variable $t$ (say).  By strengthening $I$ to be

$$I:\quad (\neg in2 \Rightarrow \neg(in(CS_2) \vee in(gate_2)))$$
$$\wedge\ (\neg in1 \Rightarrow \neg(in(CS_1) \vee in(gate_1)))$$
$$\wedge\ (t=1 \vee t=2)$$

we can use $t=1$ for $X_1$ and use $t=2$ for $X_2$.  We make the substitution into the proof outlines to get:

$$\cdots$$
$$\{I \wedge \neg in(CS_1)\}$$
$$entry_1\colon\ door_1\colon\ in1 := true\ \ \{I \wedge \neg in(CS_1) \wedge in1\}$$
$$\qquad\quad gate_1\colon\ \textbf{if}\,\neg in2 \vee t=1 \to \{I \wedge at(T_1) \wedge in1$$
$$\wedge (\neg in2 \vee t=1 \vee after(door_2))\}$$
$$T_1\colon\ \textbf{skip}$$
$$\{I \wedge in1 \wedge (\neg in2 \vee t=1 \vee after(door_2))\}\,\textbf{fi}$$
$$\{I \wedge in1 \wedge (\neg in2 \vee t=1 \vee after(door_2))\}$$
$$PO(CS_1) \textcircled{a} (I \wedge in1 \wedge (\neg in2 \vee t=1 \vee after(door_2)))$$
$$\cdots$$
$$\|$$
$$\cdots$$
$$\{I \wedge \neg in(CS_2)\}$$
$$entry_2\colon\ door_2\colon\ in2 := true\ \ \{I \wedge \neg in(CS_2) \wedge in2\}$$
$$\qquad\quad gate_2\colon\ \textbf{if}\,\neg in1 \vee t=2 \to \{I \wedge at(T_2) \wedge in2$$
$$\wedge (\neg in1 \vee t=2 \vee after(door_1))\}$$
$$T_2\colon\ \textbf{skip}$$
$$\{I \wedge in2 \wedge (\neg in1 \vee t=2 \vee after(door_1))\}\,\textbf{fi}$$
$$\{I \wedge in2 \wedge (\neg in1 \vee t=2 \vee after(door_1))\}$$
$$PO(CS_2) \textcircled{a} (I \wedge in2 \wedge (\neg in1 \vee t=2 \vee after(door_1)))$$
$$\cdots$$

This proof outline is not interference-free.  Execution of $GEval_{if}(gate_2)$ falsifies $after(door_2)$ (because $after(door_2)=at(GEval_{if}(gate_2))$) without causing $\neg in2 \vee t=1$ to become *true*.  We solve this problem by inserting a statement, $step_2$, between $door_2$ and $gate_2$.  This statement causes $after(door_2)$ and $at(gate_2)$ to refer to different control points and makes it impossible for $gate_2$ to be executed when $after(door_2)$ holds.  To ensure that $step_2$ itself does not falsify $\neg in2 \vee t=1 \vee after(door_2)$, we implement $step_2$ by the assignment statement $t := 1$.  (The assignment statement $in2 := false$, which also does not interfere with $\neg in2 \vee t=1 \vee after(door_2)$, cannot be used because it falsifies $\neg in2 \Rightarrow \neg(in(CS_2) \vee at(T_2))$ in $I$.)  Similarly, executing $gate_1$ can falsify $after(door_1)$, and this interference is eliminated by adding a statement $step_1$.

The proof outline that results when $step_1$ is added to $S_1$ and $step_2$ is added to $S_2$ is given in Figure 6.7. It is interference-free and is strong enough to establish Mutual Exclusion (6.2) and Entry Nonblocking (6.20).

---

$\{true\}$
$S:\ t, in1, in2 := ...$
 $\quad \{I:\ (\neg in2 \Rightarrow \neg(in(CS_2) \vee in(gate_2))) \wedge (\neg in1 \Rightarrow \neg(in(CS_1) \vee in(gate_1)))$
 $\qquad \wedge\ (t=1 \vee t=2)\}$
 **cobegin**
 $\{I \wedge \neg in(CS_1)\}$
 $S_1:$ **do** $true \to \{I \wedge \neg in(CS_1)\}$
 $\qquad entry_1:\ door_1:\ in1 := true\ \ \{I \wedge \neg in(CS_1) \wedge in1\}$
 $\qquad\qquad step_1:\ t := 2\ \ \{I \wedge \neg in(CS_1) \wedge in1\}$
 $\qquad\qquad gate_1:$ **if** $\neg in2 \vee t=1 \to \{I \wedge at(T_1) \wedge in1$
 $\qquad\qquad\qquad\qquad\qquad\qquad\qquad \wedge (\neg in2 \vee t=1 \vee after(door_2))\}$
 $\qquad\qquad\qquad\quad T_1:$ **skip**
 $\qquad\qquad\qquad\qquad \{I \wedge in1 \wedge (\neg in2 \vee t=1 \vee after(door_2))\}$ **fi**
 $\qquad \{I \wedge in1 \wedge (\neg in2 \vee t=1 \vee after(door_2))\}$
 $\qquad PO(CS_1) \otimes (I \wedge in1 \wedge (\neg in2 \vee t=1 \vee after(door_2)))$
 $\qquad \{I \wedge \neg in(CS_1)\}$
 $\qquad exit_1:$ **skip**
 $\qquad \{I \wedge \neg in(CS_1)\}\ PO(NCS_1) \otimes (I \wedge \neg in(CS_1))\ \{I \wedge \neg in(CS_1)\}$
 $\qquad$ **od** $\{false\}$
 $\|$
 $\{I \wedge \neg in(CS_2)\}$
 $S_2:$ **do** $true \to \{I \wedge \neg in(CS_2)\}$
 $\qquad entry_2:\ door_2:\ in2 := true\ \ \{I \wedge \neg in(CS_2) \wedge in2\}$
 $\qquad\qquad step_2:\ t := 1\ \ \{I \wedge \neg in(CS_2) \wedge in2\}$
 $\qquad\qquad gate_2:$ **if** $\neg in1 \vee t=2 \to \{I \wedge at(T_2) \wedge in2$
 $\qquad\qquad\qquad\qquad\qquad\qquad\qquad \wedge (\neg in1 \vee t=2 \vee after(door_1))\}$
 $\qquad\qquad\qquad\quad T_2:$ **skip**
 $\qquad\qquad\qquad\qquad \{I \wedge in2 \wedge (\neg in1 \vee t=2 \vee after(door_1))\}$ **fi**
 $\qquad \{I \wedge in2 \wedge (\neg in1 \vee t=2 \vee after(door_1))\}$
 $\qquad PO(CS_2) \otimes (I \wedge in2 \wedge (\neg in1 \vee t=2 \vee after(door_1)))$
 $\qquad \{I \wedge \neg in(CS_2)\}$
 $\qquad exit_2:$ **skip**
 $\qquad \{I \wedge \neg in(CS_2)\}\ PO(NCS_2) \otimes (I \wedge \neg in(CS_2))\ \{I \wedge \neg in(CS_2)\}$
 $\qquad$ **od** $\{false\}$
 **coend**
$\{false\}$

**Figure 6.7.** Mutual Exclusion (6.2) and Entry Nonblocking (6.20)

We next check whether NCS Nonblocking (6.21) is satisfied by the entry and exit protocols of Figure 6.7. For our program, this property is formalized by:

$$at(S) \Rightarrow \Box \neg (at(gate_1) \wedge \neg enbl(GEval_{if}(gate_1))$$
$$\wedge (at(GEval_{do}(S_2)) \vee in(NCS_2) \vee after(NCS_2)))$$

$$at(S) \Rightarrow \Box \neg (at(gate_2) \wedge \neg enbl(GEval_{if}(gate_2))$$
$$\wedge (at(GEval_{do}(S_1)) \vee in(NCS_1) \vee after(NCS_1)))$$

We again use Precondition Exclusion of Configurations Rule (6.16). Premise (a) is satisfied by the proof outline of Figure 6.7. Premise (b) would be satisfied by showing that the following are valid.

(6.27)  $at(gate_1) \wedge \neg enbl(GEval_{if}(gate_1))$
$\wedge (at(GEval_{do}(S_2)) \vee in(NCS_2) \vee after(NCS_2)) \wedge I_{PO(S)} \Rightarrow false$

(6.28)  $at(gate_2) \wedge \neg enbl(GEval_{if}(gate_2))$
$\wedge (at(GEval_{do}(S_1)) \vee in(NCS_1) \vee after(NCS_1)) \wedge I_{PO(S)} \Rightarrow false$

Unfortunately, neither is. This should not be surprising, because no program variable is changed when a process exits its critical section. Thus, the program variables provide no way for an entry protocol to determine whether a process *is* executing in its critical section or merely *was* executing in its critical section.

The obvious way to remedy this problem is for the exit protocol to change some program variable(s). Which variable to change is guided by unfulfilled obligations (6.27) and (6.28). In the antecedent of (6.27),

$$(at(GEval_{do}(S_2)) \vee in(NCS_2) \vee after(NCS_2)) \wedge I_{PO(S)}$$

effectively selects assertions associated with control points at, in, and after $NCS_2$. Thus, if each of these assertions implied a predicate $P$ such that $P \wedge \neg enbl(GEval_{if}(gate_1)) \Rightarrow false$, then (6.27) would be satisfied.

Because $\neg enbl(GEval_{if}(gate_1))$ is $in2 \wedge t \neq 1$, two obvious candidates for $P$ are $\neg in2$ and $t=1$. We reject $t=1$ because it would be falsified by executing $step_1$. This leaves $\neg in2$ as our choice for $P$. It is not falsified by executing $S_1$. Thus, to make (6.27) valid, we modify $exit_2$ so that assertions in and after $NCS_2$ can be strengthened by $\neg in2$ and modify the initialization so that the assertion before $entry_2$ can be so strengthened. Assignment statement $in2 := false$ in the exit protocol does the job.

Symmetric reasoning for process $S_2$ leads to the proof outline of Figure 6.8. Variable $t$ can be initialized to either 1 or 2. The proof outline is valid and makes (6.27) and (6.28) valid, which means that our protocol now satisfies NCS Nonblocking (6.21). It is wise to check that Mutual Exclusion (6.2) and Entry Nonblocking (6.20) are still satisfied as well. They are.

$\{true\}$
$S$: $t, in1, in2 := 1, false, false$
　　$\{t=1 \land \neg in1 \land \neg in2 \land$
　　$I$: $(\neg in2 \Rightarrow \neg(in(CS_2) \lor in(gate_2))) \land (\neg in1 \Rightarrow \neg(in(CS_1) \lor in(gate_1)))$
　　　　$\land (t=1 \lor t=2)\}$
　　**cobegin**
　　$\{I \land \neg in(CS_1) \land \neg in1\}$
　　$S_1$: **do** $true \rightarrow \{I \land \neg in(CS_1) \land \neg in1\}$
　　　　　$entry_1$: $door_1$: $in1 := true \quad \{I \land \neg in(CS_1) \land in1\}$
　　　　　　　　$step_1$: $t := 2 \quad \{I \land \neg in(CS_1) \land in1\}$
　　　　　　　　$gate_1$: **if** $\neg in2 \lor t=1 \rightarrow \{I \land at(T_1) \land in1$
　　　　　　　　　　　　　　　　　　　　　　$\land (\neg in2 \lor t=1 \lor after(door_2))\}$
　　　　　　　　　　　　　$T_1$: **skip**
　　　　　　　　　　　　　$\{I \land in1 \land (\neg in2 \lor t=1 \lor after(door_2))\}$ **fi**
　　　　　$\{I \land in1 \land (\neg in2 \lor t=1 \lor after(door_2))\}$
　　　　　$PO(CS_1) \oslash (I \land in1 \land (\neg in2 \lor t=1 \lor after(door_2)))$
　　　　　$\{I \land \neg in(CS_1)\}$
　　　　　$exit_1$: $in1 := false \quad \{I \land \neg in(CS_1) \land \neg in1\}$
　　　　　$PO(NCS_1) \oslash (I \land \neg in(CS_1) \land \neg in1)$
　　　　　$\{I \land \neg in(CS_1) \land \neg in1\}$
　　　　**od** $\{false\}$
　　$\parallel$
　　$\{I \land \neg in(CS_2) \land \neg in2\}$
　　$S_2$: **do** $true \rightarrow \{I \land \neg in(CS_2) \land \neg in2\}$
　　　　　$entry_2$: $door_2$: $in2 := true \quad \{I \land \neg in(CS_2) \land in2\}$
　　　　　　　　$step_2$: $t := 1 \quad \{I \land \neg in(CS_2) \land in2\}$
　　　　　　　　$gate_2$: **if** $\neg in1 \lor t=2 \rightarrow \{I \land at(T_2) \land in2$
　　　　　　　　　　　　　　　　　　　　　　$\land (\neg in1 \lor t=2 \lor after(door_1))\}$
　　　　　　　　　　　　　$T_2$: **skip**
　　　　　　　　　　　　　$\{I \land in2 \land (\neg in1 \lor t=2 \lor after(door_1))\}$ **fi**
　　　　　$\{I \land in2 \land (\neg in1 \lor t=2 \lor after(door_1))\}$
　　　　　$PO(CS_2) \oslash (I \land in2 \land (\neg in1 \lor t=2 \lor after(door_1)))$
　　　　　$\{I \land \neg in(CS_2)\}$
　　　　　$exit_2$: $in2 := false \quad \{I \land \neg in(CS_2) \land \neg in2\}$
　　　　　$PO(NCS_2) \oslash (I \land \neg in(CS_2) \land \neg in2)$
　　　　　$\{I \land \neg in(CS_2) \land \neg in2\}$
　　　　**od** $\{false\}$
　　**coend**
$\{false\}$

**Figure 6.8.** Exit protocol for NCS Nonblocking (6.21)

Finally, we check that Exit Nonblocking (6.22) is satisfied by the program of Figure 6.8.  To do so, we must verify that $S$ satisfies:

(6.29) $at(S) \Rightarrow \Box \neg ((at(exit_1) \wedge \neg enbl(exit_1)) \vee (at(exit_2) \wedge \neg enbl(exit_2)))$

Because each $exit_i$ is implemented by a single unconditional atomic action, from definition (5.36) of $enbl$ we have

$\quad\quad enbl(exit_1) = true$
$\quad\quad enbl(exit_1) = true$

and therefore, by Temporal Logic, (6.29) holds.

This completes the derivation of the solution to the mutual exclusion problem.  Figure 6.8 contains a protocol that satisfies Mutual Exclusion (6.2), Entry Nonblocking (6.20), NCS Nonblocking (6.21), and Exit Nonblocking (6.22).

## Reviewing the Method

The above derivation is based on repeated application of a simple method:

(6.30) **Safety Property Methodology.**  If a program does not satisfy $Init \Rightarrow \Box Etern$:

    (1)    Construct a valid proof outline for the program.

    (2)    Identify assertions that must be strengthened in order to prove $Init \Rightarrow \Box Etern$.

    (3)    Modify the program and proof outline so that the assertions are strengthened.                                                                          □

Of course, step (3) requires creativity—especially since stronger assertions are more likely to be interfered with.  Therefore, strengthening an assertion in some process $S_i$ is typically a two-part process.  First, $S_i$ is modified, ignoring other processes.  This results in a proof outline that is valid in isolation and has the stronger assertions.  Then, that proof outline is considered in the context of the concurrent program, and any interference is eliminated.

For the mutual exclusion problem, we were given a program skeleton (i.e., Figure 6.4) containing some unspecified operations and asked to refine them to make certain invariance properties hold.  The skeleton imposed constraints on the solution, and these simplified our task by restricting possible design choices.  Additional constraints accumulated as the derivation proceeded.  Each invariance property, once satisfied, imposed constraints on subsequent modifications to the entry and exit protocols.  For example, maintaining a valid proof outline from which Mutual Exclusion (6.2) could be proved constrained modifications to the entry protocol so that Entry Nonblocking (6.20) could be proved.

Concurrent programming problems are frequently posed in terms of process skeletons with unspecified operations.  This is because these problems usually arise in connection with some (real) system whose structure is already partially determined. Changes to process skeletons might lead to a trivial solution but might be equivalent to replacing the computer hardware or its operating system—rarely an acceptable solution.

The derivation of a program can be viewed as following a path in a tree. The root of the tree corresponds to the problem statement; each internal node identifies a partial design and simpler problem statement; and each leaf corresponds to a design point from which no further progress is possible. For interesting problems, few of the leaves correspond to solutions and most correspond to dead ends. Therefore, program derivation often requires backtracking. Upon reaching a dead end, we must be prepared to reconsider an earlier design decision and proceed from that point.

In the derivation above, there are a number of decision points that we did not explore but to which we would have returned had a dead end been reached. Perhaps the most important decision was our choice of $I$. We might, for example, have instead introduced a single boolean program variable $lock$, maintained the truth of

$$I: \quad \neg lock \ \Rightarrow \ \neg in(CS_1) \land \neg in(CS_2),$$

and used $\neg lock$ for the guards in both entry protocols. Other choices would also have allowed assertions in the critical sections to be strengthened. Different protocols result from the different choices.

### Historical Notes

Safety properties, as first defined in [Lamport 77a], are equivalent to our invariance properties. The method given in [Lamport 77a] for proving that a program satisfies such a property is based on finding a suitable invariant. This use of invariants, however, did not originate with Lamport. For invariance properties concerning the control state (e.g., mutual exclusion, readers/writers), proofs that use invariants appear in [Dijkstra 71], [Habermann 72], and [Brinch Hansen 72a]. There, program variables are introduced to keep track of various aspects of the control state, and relationships among these variables are shown invariant with respect to the execution of synchronization operations. For invariance properties involving relationships among the control state and program variables, proof methods based on finding an invariant are discussed in [Ashcroft 75] and [Keller 76]. In these methods, $I$ is shown invariant by demonstrating that no program step falsifies $I$. Thus, in terms of $S$-Temporal Logic, these methods are equivalent to TL Invariance Rule (6.31) of exercise 6.4.

Safety Consequence Rule (6.8) is based on a metatheorem of Lamport's Generalized Hoare Logic [Lamport 80b]. Exclusion of Configurations Rule (6.10) is a generalization of a method used in [Owicki & Gries 76a] for proving that a program is free from deadlock and in [Dijkstra 76b] for proving mutual exclusion. $I_{PO(S)}$ Decomposition Rules (6.17) and Partial Correctness Rule (6.19) follow from the methods employed in [Lamport & Schneider 84] to relate assertions and a proof outline invariant.

The literature on the mutual exclusion problem is extensive.  See [Raynal 86] for a summary of protocols and their properties.  The solution developed in §6.5 is based on [Peterson 81].  Because of its simplicity and elegance, this protocol has become a standard in texts in operating systems and concurrent programming.  The protocol is usually presented operationally; the derivation in §6.5 is new.  The first correct solution to the mutual exclusion problem was devised by Dekker and is given in exercise 6.9(h).  The protocol in exercise 6.9(g) is due to Marzullo.

The readers/writers problem of exercise 6.15 is another classical concurrent programming problem.  It was first introduced and solved in [Courtois et al. 71].  Exercise 6.16, to implement barrier synchronization, was inspired by [Jordan 78].  The concurrent $f$, $g$, $h$ problem is Gary Levin's generalization of a sequential programming problem invented by Wim Feijen (and called the "welfare crook" problem in [Gries 81]).

### Exercises

**6.1.** Using Safety Consequence Rule (6.8), prove that the Producer/Consumer program of Figure 6.1 satisfies invariance property (6.13).

**6.2.** Using Safety Consequence Rule (6.8) and the proof outline of Figure 6.7, show that Entry Nonblocking (6.20) holds.

**6.3.** Using Safety Consequence Rule (6.8) and the proof outline of Figure 6.8, show that each of the following holds.

(a)    Mutual Exclusion (6.2)

(b)    Entry Nonblocking (6.20)

(c)    NCS Nonblocking (6.21)

**6.4.** Consider the following $S$-Temporal Logic rule, which has been proposed for establishing that a program satisfies an invariance property.

(6.31) *TL Invariance Rule:*  (a) $Init \Rightarrow I$,
$$\text{(b) } I \Rightarrow \bigcirc I,$$
$$\text{(c) } I \Rightarrow Etern$$
$$\overline{Init \Rightarrow \Box Etern}$$

(a)    Prove the soundness of this rule.

(b)    Show how premise (b) can be discharged by proving a collection of theorems of Proof Outline Logic.

(c)    Characterize the relationship between premise (b) of this rule and premise (a) of Safety Consequence Rule (6.8).

**6.5.** Using Exclusion of Configurations Rule (6.10), prove that the Producer/Consumer program of Figure 6.1 satisfies invariance property (6.9).

**6.6.** Consider the following variation of Precondition Safety Consequence Rule (6.15).

(a) $PO(S)$,
(b) $I_{PO(S)} \Rightarrow Etern$,
(c) $P \Rightarrow pre(PO(S))$
$$\overline{at(S) \wedge P \Rightarrow \Box Etern}$$

Show that any inference possible with this rule is also possible using Precondition Safety Consequence Rule (6.15).

**6.7.** Using Exclusion of Configurations Rule (6.10) and the proof outline of Figure 6.6, show that Mutual Exclusion (6.2) holds.

**6.8.** In the proof outline of Figure 6.6, what if conjunct *in1* were deleted from *post*(*door*$_1$)?

**6.9.** For invariance properties

   (i)   Mutual Exclusion (6.2),

   (ii)  Entry Nonblocking (6.20),

   (iii) NCS Nonblocking (6.21), and

   (iv)  Exit Nonblocking (6.22)

state whether each of the following programs satisfies the property. If it does, give a proof; if it does not, describe a scenario that leads to occurrence of the proscribed "bad thing."

(a)   *free* := *true*
      **cobegin**
          $\underset{i=1,2}{\|}$  **do** *true* → ⟨**if** *free* → *free* := *false* **fi**⟩
                        $S_i$: **skip**
                        *free* := *true*
          **od**
      **coend**

(b)   *turn* := 1
      **cobegin**
          **do** *true* → *entry*$_1$: **if** *turn* = 1 → **skip fi**
                        $CS_1$
                        *exit*$_1$: *turn* := 2
                        $NCS_1$
          **od**
      $\|$
          **do** *true* → *entry*$_2$: **if** *turn* = 2 → **skip fi**
                        $CS_2$
                        *exit*$_2$: *turn* := 1
                        $NCS_2$
          **od**
      **coend**

(c)   *s* := 1
      **cobegin**
          $\underset{i=1,2}{\|}$  ⟨**if** *s* > 0 → *s* := *s* − 1 **fi**⟩
                        $S_i$: **skip**
                        *s* := *s* + 1
      **coend**

(d)   $x, y := false, false$
      **cobegin**
           **do** $true \rightarrow$ $entry_1$: $x := true$ **if** $\neg y \rightarrow$ **skip fi**
                          $CS_1$
                          $exit_1$: $x := false$
                          $NCS_1$
           **od**
      ∥
           **do** $true \rightarrow$ $entry_2$: $y := true$ **if** $\neg x \rightarrow$ **skip fi**
                          $CS_2$
                          $exit_2$: $y := false$
                          $NCS_2$
           **od**
      **coend**


(e)   $s := 1$
      **cobegin**
           $\underset{i=1,2}{∥}$ $\langle$**if** $s > 0 \rightarrow s := s - 1$ **fi**$\rangle$
                          $S_i$: **skip**
                          $s := s + 1$
      **coend**


(f)   $v, w, s := false, false, false$
      **cobegin**
           **do** $true \rightarrow$ $entry_1$: $v, s := s, true$ **do** $v \rightarrow v, s := s, true$ **od**
                          $CS_1$
                          $exit_1$: $s := false$
                          $NCS_1$
           **od**
      ∥
           **do** $true \rightarrow$ $entry_2$: $w, s := s, true$ **do** $w \rightarrow w, s := s, true$ **od**
                          $CS_2$
                          $exit_2$: $s := false$
                          $NCS_2$
           **od**
      **coend**


(g)   $in1, in2 := false, false$
      **cobegin**
           **do** $true \rightarrow$ $entry_1$: **do** $\neg in1 \rightarrow in1 := true$ $v1 := in2$ $in1 := \neg v1$ **od**
                          $CS_1$
                          $exit_1$: $in1 := false$
                          $NCS_1$
           **od**
      ∥
           **do** $true \rightarrow$ $entry_2$: **do** $\neg in2 \rightarrow in2 := true$ $v2 := in1$ $in2 := \neg v2$ **od**
                          $CS_2$
                          $exit_2$: $in2 := false$
                          $NCS_2$
           **od**
      **coend**

(h)    $inl, in2, turn := false, false, 1$
    **cobegin**
        **do** $true \rightarrow entry_1$: $inl := true$
                **do** $in2 \rightarrow$ **if** $turn=2 \rightarrow inl := false$
                                      $\langle$**if** $turn=1 \rightarrow$ **skip fi**$\rangle$
                                      $inl := true$
                        [] $turn \neq 2 \rightarrow$ **skip**
                        **fi**
                **od**
            $CS_1$
            $exit_1$: $turn := 2$
                  $inl := false$
            $NCS_1$
        **od**
    ||
        **do** $true \rightarrow entry_2$: $in2 := true$
                **do** $inl \rightarrow$ **if** $turn=1 \rightarrow in2 := false$
                                          $\langle$**if** $turn=2 \rightarrow$ **skip fi**$\rangle$
                                        $in2 := true$
                    [] $turn \neq 1 \rightarrow$ **skip**
                    **fi**
                **od**
            $CS_2$
            $exit_2$: $turn := 1$
                  $in2 := false$
            $NCS_2$
        **od**
    **coend**

**6.10.** The soundness proof given in §6.3 for Exclusion of Configurations Rule (6.10) that is given in §6.3 is indirect. It shows that the premises of Safety Consequence Rule (6.8) are satisfied whenever the premises of Exclusion of Configurations Rule (6.10) are satisfied. A more direct way to show soundness of Exclusion of Configurations Rule (6.10) is to give a Temporal Logic proof of $Init \Rightarrow \Box Etern$ in which premises (a), (b), and (c) of (6.10) are taken to be axioms. Give such a proof.

**6.11.** Give a soundness proof for $I_{PO(S)}$ Decomposition Rule (6.17a).

**6.12.** A bounded buffer can be implemented by an array $bb[0..N-1]$. Assume that $a$ is the number of elements that have been added to the buffer, $r$ is the number of elements that have been removed from the buffer, and that items are stored in the buffer in the order in which they are inserted. Thus, the contents of the buffer consists of the sequence of items

$$bb[r \bmod N], bb[(r+1) \bmod N], ..., bb[(r+(a-r-1) \bmod N].$$

Modify the program of Figure 6.1, inserting assignment statements involving $bb$ such that the producer inserts values $p[1], p[2], ...$ into the bounded buffer and the sequence of values retrieved by the consumer are stored in $c[1], c[2], ...$ . Your modifications should not involve adding synchronization. Then, prove that your implementation satisfies the invariance property

$$at(S) \wedge a=0 \wedge r=0 \Rightarrow \Box(\forall i \in \text{Int}: \ 0 < i \le r: \ c[i]=p[i]).$$

**6.13.** The *N-exclusion problem* is similar to the mutual exclusion problem except that at most N processes are permitted to be in critical sections at any time. Thus, the mutual exclusion problem is N-exclusion for N=1.

(a)     Give generalized forms of Mutual Exclusion (6.2), Entry Nonblocking (6.20), NCS Nonblocking (6.21), and Exit Nonblocking (6.22) for the N-exclusion problem.

(b)     Derive entry and exit protocols to ensure that these properties are satisfied.

**6.14.** In designing a solution to the mutual exclusion problem, different choices of *I* lead to different protocols. For each of the following choices, derive a protocol and prove that it satisfies Mutual Exclusion (6.2), Entry Nonblocking (6.20), NCS Nonblocking (6.21), and Exit Nonblocking (6.22). Do not use a **do** in the entry or exit protocols for your solution.

(a)     $I: lock \Rightarrow in(CS_1) \vee in(CS_2)$

(b)     $I: (in(CS_1) \Rightarrow v_1 < v_2) \wedge (in(CS_2) \Rightarrow v_2 < v_1) \wedge v_1 \neq v_2$

(c)     $I: (in(CS_1) \Rightarrow v_1 = next) \wedge (in(CS_2) \Rightarrow v_2 = next) \wedge v_1 \neq v_2$

(d)     $I: 0 \leq s \leq 1 \wedge ((s=1)=(\neg in(CS_1) \wedge \neg in(CS_2)))$

**6.15.** Consider a system with *R reader processes* and *W writer processes*. Each reader process is of the form

$$reader_i: \textbf{do } true \rightarrow start\_read$$
$$read_i$$
$$end\_read$$
$$NCS_i$$
$$\textbf{od}$$

and each writer process is of the form

$$writer_i: \textbf{do } true \rightarrow start\_write$$
$$write_i$$
$$end\_write$$
$$NCS_i$$
$$\textbf{od}$$

(a)     Describe invariance properties to ensure that write operations exclude read operations and other write operations, that read operations exclude (only) write operations, but that execution is not otherwise impeded. Formalize these to the extent possible.

(b)     Derive protocols for *start_read, end_read, start_write*, and *end_write* that satisfy the invariance properties of (a). The protocols should not depend on the process identity *i*.

(c)     The requirements in (a) do not prevent reader processes from causing writer processes to be forever blocked at *start_write* operations. This unpleasant behavior can be avoided by preventing new read operations from starting when there is a waiting writer. Formalize this requirement as an invariance property.

(d)     Derive new protocols that satisfy the requirements of (a) and (c). The protocols should not depend on the process identity *i*.

**6.16.** In some numerical algorithms, computation proceeds in phases. Each process executes $phase_0$, $phase_1$, ..., $phase_p$ in sequence, and no process is permitted to start $phase_{i+1}$ until all processes have reached the end of $phase_i$.

(a) Formalize this synchronization problem for $N$ processes in terms of a program skeleton, where execution of two phases is separated by a sequence of instructions labeled *barrier*.

(b) What invariance properties should be satisfied by any implementation of a *barrier* protocol?

(c) Derive an implementation of a *barrier* protocol and prove that it satisfies the requirements enumerated in (b).

**6.17.** Consider a system with $M$ $(1 \leq M)$ processes of type 1 and $F$ $(1 \leq F)$ processes of type 2. Each type $t$ process (where $t$ is 1 or 2) is of the form:

$$S_i: \textbf{do } true \rightarrow start\_t$$
$$CS_i$$
$$end\_t$$
$$N\overline{CS}_i$$
$$\textbf{od}$$

(a) Describe invariance properties that stipulate that type 1 and type 2 processes are not both in their critical sections at the same time, but execution is not otherwise impeded. Formalize these to the extent possible.

(b) Derive protocols for *start_t* and *end_t* that satisfy the invariance properties of (a). The protocols may depend on $t$ but should not depend on the process identity $i$.

(c) The requirements in (a) do not prevent type 1 processes from causing type 2 processes to be blocked forever at *start_2* operations. They also do not prevent type 2 processes from causing type 1 processes to be blocked forever at *start_1* operations. This unpleasant behavior can be avoided by preventing processes of one type from starting new executions of the critical section when processes of the other type are already waiting. Formalize this requirement as an invariance property.

(d) Derive new protocols for *start_t* and *end_t* that satisfy the requirements of (a) and (b). The protocols may depend on $t$ but should not depend on the process identity $i$.

**6.18.** Given are three sequences $f$, $g$, and $h$ such that:

$$f[0] \leq f[1] \leq f[2] \cdots$$
$$g[0] \leq g[1] \leq g[2] \cdots$$
$$h[0] \leq h[1] \leq g[2] \cdots$$

Design a concurrent program consisting of three processes that, if it terminates, sets program variables $i$, $j$, and $k$ to the least integers such that $f[i] = g[j] = h[k]$. In your program, $i$, $j$, and $k$ should be synchronously altered, each by a different process.

**6.19.** Design a 2-process concurrent program that deadlocks when it has computed $x = gcd(X, Y) \wedge y = gcd(X, Y)$, assuming that $x = X \wedge y = Y$ holds initially. Variable $x$ should be synchronously altered by one process and variable $y$ should be synchronously altered by the other. Hint: Use $gcd(x, y) = gcd(X, Y)$ as an invariant.

# Chapter 7

# Safety Properties with Past Terms

For some safety properties, whether a state is considered a "bad thing" depends on the preceding states. We discuss in this chapter how to specify and reason about such safety properties. We show that by extending Predicate Logic, the techniques of Chapter 6 can be used for reasoning about arbitrary safety properties. The chapter also discusses the design of programs satisfying arbitrary safety properties and the role of auxiliary variables in reasoning about programs.

## 7.1 Historical Safety Properties

A safety property, according to Safety Property (2.105), proscribes all anchored sequences that have certain finite prefixes. Thus, every safety property $\mathcal{P}$ has a defining set of finite prefixes; these constitute the "bad thing" for $\mathcal{P}$. For example, the defining set of finite prefixes for invariance property $Init \Rightarrow \Box Etern$ consists of all finite anchored sequences whose current state satisfies state predicate $Init$ and whose final state satisfies state predicate $\neg Etern$.

Not all safety properties are invariance properties. Some sets of finite prefixes cannot be defined using only a current and final state. The property that a program variable $x$ is nondecreasing is an example. The "bad thing" is any finite prefix that contains adjacent states in which the value of $x$ decreases. As another example, finite prefixes where first-come, first-served has been violated can be described only by identifying three states: a state in which the service is requested by some process, a subsequent state in which that process has not yet been served but the service is requested by a second process, and a third (still later) state in which the second process has been served but the first has not.

A *historical safety property* is a safety property whose defining set of finite prefixes cannot be characterized using only current and final states. The property "$x$ is nondecreasing" is a historical safety property, as is first-come, first-served.

## 7.2   Past Extensions to Predicate Logic

Any historical safety property can be specified by Temporal Logic formula *Init* $\Rightarrow \Box Etern$ if a sufficiently expressive Predicate Logic is available. We must be able to write a Predicate Logic formula *Etern* whose value, for an anchored sequence $(\sigma, j)$, depends on past states $\sigma[..j-1]$ as well as current state $\sigma[j]$ *Etern* can then serve as the characteristic predicate for the set of finite prefixes that defines a historical safety property.

New Predicate Logic terms and predicates will enable us to write formulas that depend on past states of an anchored sequence. These new terms and predicates comprise our *past extensions* to Predicate Logic. Their syntax, meaning, and axiomatization is the subject of this section.

### Past Terms and Past Predicates

One form of *past term* consists of a finite sequence of $\Theta$'s (each read "previous") followed by a term. We assign to $\Theta$ the same precedence as is given to the unary operators for Predicate Logic terms. The value of $\sigma[..j][\![\Theta \mathcal{T}]\!]$ is essentially the value of term $\mathcal{T}$ in $\sigma[..j-1]$. See Figure 7.1. For example, the value of $\Theta x$ in $s_0 s_1 s_2$ is the value of $x$ in $s_1$. So, the value of $\Theta x \leq x$ in $s_0 s_1 s_2$ is *true* iff the value of $x$ in $s_1$ is at most the value of $x$ in $s_2$.

Consistent with the view that a Predicate Logic formula is a boolean-valued term, $\Theta$ may be applied to a formula of Predicate Logic, resulting in a *past predicate*. It has the expected meaning based on the definition just given for $\sigma[..j][\![\Theta \mathcal{T}]\!]$:

$$\sigma[..j] \models \Theta P: \quad \begin{cases} \sigma[..j-1] \models P & \text{if } j \geq 1 \\ \text{unspecified (but boolean)} & \text{if } j < 1 \end{cases}$$

Finally, in order to characterize the anchored sequences for which a given past term or past predicate is not unspecified, we introduce the nullary past predicate $def_\Theta$ :

---

| $\mathcal{T}$ | $\sigma[..j][\![\Theta \mathcal{T}]\!]$ |
|---|---|
| constant or rigid variable C | C   if $j \geq 1$ <br> unspecified (but fixed)   if $j < 1$ |
| variable $v$ | $\sigma[j-1][\![v]\!]$   if $j \geq 1$ <br> unspecified (but fixed)   if $j < 1$ |
| term $\mathcal{E}(\mathcal{T}_1, ..., \mathcal{T}_n)$ | $\sigma[..j-1][\![\mathcal{E}(\mathcal{T}_1, ..., \mathcal{T}_n)]\!]$   if $j \geq 1$ <br> unspecified (but fixed)   if $j < 1$ |

**Figure 7.1.** Semantics of past extensions

$\sigma[..j] \models def_{\Theta} : \quad j > 0$

Predicate $def_{\Theta}$ allows formulas to have specified values in any anchored sequence. An example is $def_{\Theta} \Rightarrow \Theta x \leq x$, whose value is specified in all anchored sequences $(\sigma, j)$; in contrast, $\Theta x \leq x$ has an unspecified value if $\sigma$ has only one state, because $\Theta x$ is unspecified in then. Predicate $def_{\Theta}$ also allows us to construct formulas that are satisfied only by anchored sequences $(\sigma, j)$ where $j$ equals 0, because $\neg def_{\Theta}$ is satisfied in exactly those anchored sequences.

Two axioms and an inference rule suffice for most reasoning about formulas that involve past terms and past predicates. They are listed below. The antecedent in the axioms ensures that their past terms have specified values. Past Induction Rule (7.3) allows a theorem $P$ to be proved by induction on the length of a finite sequence of states. The first premise is the base case; it involves proving that $P$ holds for all single-state sequences. The second premise is the induction step.

(7.1)  $\Theta$ *Expression Expansion*:  For $\mathcal{E}(\mathcal{T}_1, ..., \mathcal{T}_n)$ a non-nullary term or formula that is constructed from terms $\mathcal{T}_1, ..., \mathcal{T}_n$:

$$def_{\Theta} \quad \Rightarrow \quad (\Theta\mathcal{E}(\mathcal{T}_1, ..., \mathcal{T}_n) = \mathcal{E}(\Theta\mathcal{T}_1, ..., \Theta\mathcal{T}_n))$$

(7.2)  $\Theta$ *Constant Expansion*:  For a rigid variable or constant C:

$$def_{\Theta} \quad \Rightarrow \quad (\Theta C = C)$$

(7.3)  *Past Induction Rule*:  $\dfrac{\neg def_{\Theta} \Rightarrow P, \quad def_{\Theta} \wedge \Theta P \Rightarrow P}{P}$

## Textual Substitution Revisited

Textual Substitution Laws (2.60) through (2.69) and (3.6) do not address textual substitution into a past term or a past predicate. It is tempting to define $(\Theta\mathcal{T})_e^x$ to be $\Theta(\mathcal{T}_e^x)$. But doing so destroys the soundness of certain of our Predicate Logic laws that use textual substitution. For example, here is an instance of Substitution Equivalence Law (2.76):

(7.4)  $x = y \Rightarrow (\Theta v)_x^y = (\Theta v)_y^y$

If $(\Theta x)_y^x$ were defined to equal $\Theta y$, then (7.4) would simplify to $x = y \Rightarrow \Theta x = \Theta y$, which is not valid.

The problem with (7.4) is the substitution for a variable that is in the scope of a $\Theta$ operator. Antecedent $x = y$ of (7.4) concerns values in the current state, whereas $x$ and $y$ in the consequent are being evaluated in a past state. The values of variables in the current state do not necessarily determine their values in a past state, so we are not substituting "equals for equals" as intended by Substitution Equivalence Law (2.76).

One way to avoid the problem is simply to prohibit textual substitution of a variable that occurs in the scope of a $\Theta$. This prohibition syntactically rules out formulas like (7.4) and eliminates unsoundness that these textual substitutions cause. We adopt this solution. Thus, we do not give axioms concerning textual substitution into a past term or a past predicate, because such substitutions are not permitted.

It would now seem that textual substitution cannot be used to replace a variable or derived term that appears in the scope of a $\Theta$. However, this is not true. Substitution of Equals Rule (2.75) and Substitution Equivalence Law (2.76) can be used for such replacements. For example, we can derive

$$\Theta x = \Theta y \;\Rightarrow\; ((\Theta x + 22 > 15) = (\Theta y + 22 > 15))$$

from the following instance of Substitution Equivalence Law (2.76):

$$(\Theta x = \Theta y) \Rightarrow ((z + 22 > 15)^z_{\Theta x} = (z + 22 > 15)^z_{\Theta y})$$

But a new inference rule is required in order to expand a derived term that appears in the scope of $\Theta$. Consider the following definition of a derived term.

$$YInc: \quad \{\, y + 1 \quad \text{if } true$$

We should be able to prove $def_\Theta \Rightarrow (\Theta y + 1 = \Theta YInc)$. Unfortunately, our rule for replacing a derived term by its definition, Derived Term Expansion Rule (2.77), is not up to this task. With that rule, only occurrences of $YInc$ that do not appear in the scope of a $\Theta$ can be expanded, because of the way textual substitution is used there.

We must generalize Derived Term Expansion Rule (2.77) to allow occurrences of derived terms that are in the scope of a $\Theta$ to be expanded. Let $\Theta^i \mathcal{T}$ denote $\mathcal{T}$ prefixed by $i$ $\Theta$ operators, and let $def^i_\Theta$ denote the predicate $def_\Theta \wedge \Theta def_\Theta \wedge \Theta^2 def_\Theta \wedge \cdots \wedge \Theta^{i-1} def_\Theta$. (When $i$ is 0, $\Theta^i \mathcal{T}$ is defined to be $\mathcal{T}$ and $def^i_\Theta$ is defined to be $true$.)

(7.5)  *Extended Derived Term Expansion Rule:* For $Z$ a derived term

$$Z: \quad \begin{cases} e_1 & \text{if } B_1 \\ \cdots \\ e_n & \text{if } B_n \end{cases}$$

and $P$ a Predicate Logic formula:

$$def_\Theta^i \Rightarrow (\bigwedge_{1\le k\le n} (\Theta^i B_k = \neg(\bigvee_{j\ne k} \Theta^i B_j)))$$

$$def_\Theta^i \Rightarrow (P_{\Theta^i z}^x = ((\Theta^i B_1 \wedge P_{\Theta^i e_1}^x) \vee \cdots \vee (\Theta^i B_n \wedge P_{\Theta^i e_n}^x)))$$

This rule can be understood as a generalization of Derived Term Expansion Rule (2.77). Take the definition for derived term $Z$ and prepend $\Theta^i$ to each $e_j$ and $B_j$. The result will be a definition for $\Theta^i Z$. Use that definition with Derived Term Expansion Rule (2.77) to expand $\Theta^i Z$, adding antecedents in the premise and conclusion to ensure that the past terms do not have unspecified values.

To illustrate the use of Extended Derived Term Expansion Rule (7.5), we prove $def_\Theta \Rightarrow (\Theta y+1=\Theta YInc)$:

«$\Theta$ Constant Expansion (7.2)»
  1.  $def_\Theta \Rightarrow (\Theta true=true)$
  2.  $def_\Theta \Rightarrow (\Theta false=false)$

«Propositional Logic with 1 and 2, since $true=\neg false$»
  3.  $def_\Theta \Rightarrow (\Theta true=\neg \Theta false)$

«Extended Derived Term Expansion Rule (7.5) with 3»
  4.  $def_\Theta \Rightarrow ((\Theta y+1=x)_{\Theta YInc}^x = (\Theta true \wedge (\Theta y+1=x)_{\Theta(y+1)}^x))$

«Textual Substitution (2.71)»
  5.  $def_\Theta \Rightarrow ((\Theta y+1=\Theta YInc) = (\Theta true \wedge (\Theta y+1=\Theta(y+1))))$

«Propositional Logic with 1 and 5, since $A \wedge true=A$»
  6.  $def_\Theta \Rightarrow ((\Theta y+1=\Theta YInc) = (\Theta y+1=\Theta(y+1)))$

«$\Theta$ Expression Expansion (7.1)»
  7.  $def_\Theta \Rightarrow (\Theta(y+1) = (\Theta y+\Theta 1)$

«$\Theta$ Constant Expansion (7.2)»
  8.  $def_\Theta \Rightarrow (\Theta 1=1)$

«Predicate Logic with 6, 7. and 8»
  9.  $def_\Theta \Rightarrow ((\Theta y+1=\Theta YInc) = (\Theta y+1=\Theta y+1))$

«Predicate Logic with 9, since $true = (\Theta y+1=\Theta y+1)$»
  10.  $def_\Theta \Rightarrow ((\Theta y+1=\Theta YInc) = true)$

«Propositional Logic with 10, since $A=(A=true)$»
  11.  $def_\Theta \Rightarrow (\Theta y+1=\Theta YInc)$

## Derived Terms Revisited

Some prefixes of anchored sequences can be characterized only by writing a formula that depends on all past states of the prefix. An example is the set of finite sequences of states in which the value of $x$ is nondecreasing. A formula whose past terms involved $n$ $\Theta$'s can depend on at most $n+1$ of the states in a sequence; however, an arbitrary finite sequence might have more than $n+1$ past states. Thus, extending Predicate Logic with $\Theta$ and $def_\Theta$ does not yield a logic that is sufficiently expressive for our purposes.

A Predicate Logic with the expressiveness we seek results from allowing derived terms to be defined using certain recursive definitions. An example recursive definition of a past term is $Mx$, below. The value of $Mx$ in an anchored sequence $(\sigma, j)$ is the largest value of $x$ in states $\sigma[0], \sigma[1], ..., \sigma[j]$.

$$(7.6) \quad Mx: \begin{cases} x & \text{if } \neg def_\Theta \\ \max(x, \Theta Mx) & \text{if } def_\Theta \end{cases}$$

Note the presence of $\Theta Mx$ in the second clause of the definition of $Mx$; it causes the value of $Mx$ to depend on all states, even though only a fixed number of $\Theta$'s appear in the definition.

$$\sigma[..2][\![Mx]\!]$$
$=$ «definition of $Mx$, since $\sigma[..2] \models def_\Theta$ »
$$\sigma[..2][\![\max(x, \Theta Mx)]\!]$$
$=$ «meaning of $\sigma[..j][\![T]\!]$ and $\sigma[..j][\![v]\!]$»
$$\max(\,\sigma[2][\![x]\!],\ \sigma[..2][\![\Theta Mx]\!]\,)$$
$=$ «meaning of $\sigma[..j][\![\Theta T]\!]$»
$$\max(\,\sigma[2][\![x]\!],\ \sigma[..1][\![Mx]\!]\,)$$
$=$ «definition of $Mx$, since $\sigma[..1] \models def_\Theta$ »
$$\max(\,\sigma[2][\![x]\!],\ \sigma[..1][\![\max(x, \Theta Mx)]\!]\,)$$
$=$ «meaning of $\sigma[..j][\![T]\!]$ and $\sigma[..j][\![v]\!]$»
$$\max(\,\sigma[2][\![x]\!],\ \max(\,\sigma[1][\![x]\!],\ \sigma[..1][\![\Theta Mx]\!]\,))$$
$=$ «meaning of $\sigma[..j][\![\Theta T]\!]$»
$$\max(\,\sigma[2][\![x]\!],\ \max(\,\sigma[1][\![x]\!],\ \sigma[..0][\![Mx]\!]\,))$$
$=$ «definition of $Mx$, since $\sigma[..0] \not\models def_\Theta$ »
$$\max(\,\sigma[2][\![x]\!],\ \max(\,\sigma[1][\![x]\!],\ \sigma[..0][\![x]\!]\,))$$
$=$ «meaning of $\sigma[..j][\![v]\!]$»
$$\max(\,\sigma[2][\![x]\!],\ \max(\,\sigma[1][\![x]\!],\ \sigma[0][\![x]\!]))$$

FDT must be extended for $Mx$ and any derived term that contains a past term or past predicate: FDT is defined in terms of $fdt$, and the definition of $fdt$ in Figure 2.2 covers only terms that are constants, variables, derived terms, function applications, or predicates.

**(7.7)   Extension to $fdt$ Definition.**

| $\mathcal{E}$ | $fdt(\mathcal{E}, ES)$ |
|---|---|
| a past term or past predicate $\Theta^i \mathcal{E}(\mathcal{T}_1, ..., \mathcal{T}_n)$ | $ES$ |

□

Thus, our definition of $Mx$ does not violate condition (i) of Derived Term Restrictions (2.57), which requires:

$$Mx \notin \bigcup_{1 \leq i \leq 2} (\text{FDT}(e_i) \cup \text{FDT}(B_i))$$

Condition (i) of (2.57) was intended to prevent infinite recursion in computing the value of a derived term $Z$. The presence of $\Theta Z$ in the definition of a derived term $Z$ does not cause infinite recursion, however. Extension to *fdt* Definition (7.7) is, therefore, defined so derived terms that appear in the definition of $Z$ but in the scope of a $\Theta$ are not included.

## 7.3  Verifying Historical Safety Properties

Chapter 6 gives a variety of $S$-Temporal Logic rules for proving that a program satisfies an invariance property $Init \Rightarrow \Box Etern$. These rules all are based on constructing a Proof Outline Logic theorem $PO(S)$ to establish that $I_{PO(S)} \Rightarrow \Box I_{PO(S)}$ is $\mathcal{H}_S^+$-valid and then proving $Init \Rightarrow I_{PO(S)}$ and $I_{PO(S)} \Rightarrow Etern$. The same Temporal Logic reasoning works for historical safety properties, but since $Etern$ involves past predicates and terms, so must $I_{PO(S)}$. The rules of Chapter 6 were limited to invariance properties only because proof outlines could not mention past predicates or past terms.

Proof Outline Logic, as axiomatized in Chapters 4 and 5, is not complete when assertions involve past terms and past predicates. Rule of Consequence (4.25) allows past terms and predicates to be introduced into assertions, but only in a limited way. An example of a proof outline that is valid but not provable is $\{x=0\}$ **skip** $\{\Theta x=0\}$. It is not provable because there exists no (nontrivial) formula $Q$ of (ordinary) Predicate Logic for which $Q \Rightarrow \Theta x=0$ is valid, so there can be no theorem $\{x=0\}$ **skip** $\{Q\}$ from which Rule of Consequence (4.25) can be used to infer $\{x=0\}$ **skip** $\{\Theta x=0\}$.

A complete logic for proof outlines is obtained by adding an inference rule for introducing terms involving $\Theta$ into primitive assertions.[1]

(7.8)  $\Theta^i$-*Introduction Rule*: For an atomic action $\alpha$, non-negative integer i, past term $\Theta^{i+1} T$, rigid variable X, and primitive assertions $P$ and $Q$:

$$\frac{\{P\}\ \alpha\ \{Q\}}{\{P^X_{\Theta^i T}\}\ \alpha\ \{Q^X_{\Theta^{i+1} T} \wedge \Theta(P^X_{\Theta^i T}) \wedge def_\Theta\}}$$

---

[1] Recall from §4.3 that a primitive assertion is a state predicate that depends only on the values of program variables in the current state.

$\Theta^i$-Introduction Rule (7.8) is sound because a rigid variable in a proof outline denotes the same value in all states of an anchored sequence. Thus, rigid variable X in the pre- and postconditions of premise $\{P\}\ \alpha\ \{Q\}$ can be uniformly replaced by the value of $\Theta^i\,\mathcal{T}$ in a given anchored sequence. The value of $\Theta^i\,\mathcal{T}$ in anchored sequence $(\sigma, j)$ before $\alpha$ is executed is the same as the value of $\Theta^{i+1}\,\mathcal{T}$ in the anchored sequence $(\sigma, j+1)$ corresponding to termination of $\alpha$. So, if X in precondition $P$ is replaced by $\Theta^i\,\mathcal{T}$, then X in postcondition $Q$ can be replaced by $\Theta^{i+1}\,\mathcal{T}$. The other two conjuncts, $\Theta(P^X_{\Theta^i\mathcal{T}})$ and $def_\Theta$, in the postcondition are satisfied if $\alpha$ terminates, because the anchored sequence before $\alpha$ is executed is the maximal proper prefix of the one produced by executing $\alpha$, and that prefix satisfied precondition $P^X_{\Theta^i\mathcal{T}}$.

To illustrate the use of $\Theta^i$-Introduction Rule (7.8), we prove:

(7.9)   $\{\neg def_\Theta\}\ x := x+1\ \{def_\Theta \Rightarrow \Theta x \le x\}\ x := x+1\ \{def_\Theta \Rightarrow \Theta x \le x\}$

Notice the use of $\Theta^i$-Introduction Rule (7.8) in step 4.

«Assignment Axiom (4.19)»
   1.  $\{x+1=X+1\}\ x := x+1\ \{x=X+1\}$

«Predicate Logic»
   2.  $x=X+1 \Rightarrow X \le x$

«Rule of Consequence (4.25) with 1 and 2»
   3.  $\{x+1=X+1\}\ x := x+1\ \{X \le x\}$

«$\Theta^i$-Introduction (7.8) Rule with 3, using "$x$" for $\mathcal{T}$»
   4.  $\{x+1=x+1\}\ x := x+1\ \{\Theta x \le x \wedge \Theta(x+1=x+1) \wedge def_\Theta\}$

«Predicate Logic»
   5.  $(\Theta x \le x \wedge \Theta(x+1=x+1) \wedge def_\Theta) \Rightarrow (def_\Theta \Rightarrow \Theta x \le x)$

«Rule of Consequence (4.25) with 4 and 5»
   6.  $\{x+1=x+1\}\ x := x+1\ \{def_\Theta \Rightarrow \Theta x \le x\}$

«Predicate Logic»
   7.  $\neg def_\Theta \Rightarrow x+1=x+1$

«Rule of Consequence (4.25) with 6 and 7»
   8.  $\{\neg def_\Theta\}\ x := x+1\ \{def_\Theta \Rightarrow \Theta x \le x\}$

«Predicate Logic»
   9.  $(def_\Theta \Rightarrow \Theta x \le x) \Rightarrow x+1=x+1$

«Rule of Consequence (4.25) with 6 and 9»
   10.  $\{def_\Theta \Rightarrow \Theta x \le x\}\ x := x+1\ \{def_\Theta \Rightarrow \Theta x \le x\}$

«Statement Juxtaposition Rule (4.20) with 8 and 10»
11. $\{\neg def_\Theta\}\ x := x+1\ \{def_\Theta \Rightarrow \Theta x \leq x\}\ x := x+1\ \{def_\Theta \Rightarrow \Theta x \leq x\}$

As a second example, we prove $\{P\}\ \alpha\ \{\Theta P\}$ for any atomic action $\alpha$. If $\alpha$ is an atomic action, then it must be **skip**, an assignment statement, the guard evaluation action for an **if**, or the guard evaluation action for a **do**. The axioms (in Chapter 4) associated with these atomic actions imply that for each such $\alpha$, $\{P\}\ \alpha\ \{true\}$ is a theorem. We can then proceed as follows.

«**skip** Axiom (4.18), Assignment Axiom (4.19), $GEval_{if}(S)$ Axiom (4.21), or $GEval_{do}(S)$ Axiom (4.23), depending on $\alpha$»
1. $\{P\}\ \alpha\ \{true\}$

«$\Theta^i$-Introduction Rule (7.8) with 1, using as X any rigid variable that does not occur free in $P$»
2. $\{P\}\ \alpha\ \{true \wedge \Theta P \wedge def_\Theta\}$

«Predicate Logic»
3. $true \wedge \Theta P \wedge def_\Theta \Rightarrow \Theta P$

«Rule of Consequence (4.25) with 2 and 3»
4. $\{P\}\ \alpha\ \{\Theta P\}$

## Simple Verification Example

We can now use the inference rules of Chapter 6 to prove historical safety properties. As an example, we prove the historical safety property that $x$ is non-decreasing during execution of:

$$S:\ x := x+1\ \ x := x+1$$

That is, we prove that $S$ satisfies:

(7.10) $at(S) \wedge \neg def_\Theta \Rightarrow \Box(def_\Theta \Rightarrow \Theta x \leq x)$

The conclusion of Precondition Safety Consequence Rule (6.15) matches (7.10), the property we wish to verify, if we can derive a theorem $PO(S)$ for which $pre(S)$ is $\neg def_\Theta$. Proof outline (7.9) is such a theorem, so to establish (7.10) we have only to prove $I_{PO(S)} \Rightarrow Etern$, premise (b) of Precondition Safety Consequence Rule (6.15). Here, we use $I_{PO(S)}$ Decomposition Rule (6.17a). This requires showing that $\neg def_\Theta$ and $def_\Theta \Rightarrow \Theta x \leq x$—the assertions in (7.9)—each implies $def_\Theta \Rightarrow \Theta x \leq x$. They do, and that completes the proof.

## 7.4 Developing Programs for Historical Safety Properties

The methodology of §6.5 for deriving programs that satisfy invariance properties also works for deriving programs that satisfy historical safety properties. We start with a program skeleton $S$ and some historical safety property $\mathcal{P}$ of interest. Construction of a proof then leads the construction a program. In particular, we repeatedly employ Safety Property Methodology (6.30) to flesh out $S$ and its proof outline. Each modification is driven by the need to construct a valid proof outline whose assertions are strong enough for proving $\mathcal{P}$.

## Concurrent Reading While Writing

To illustrate Safety Property Methodology (6.30) on a historical safety property, we attack a problem that arises when shared variables are used for communication in a concurrent program. Suppose one process reads these variables by executing a nonatomic operation $READ$; the other writes them by executing a nonatomic operation $WRITE$. Desired is a protocol to synchronize $READ$ and $WRITE$ so that values seen by the reader reflect the state of the shared variables either before a concurrent write has started or after it has completed.

We derive a statement $R$ to control each $READ$ operation and a statement $W$ to control each $WRITE$ operation. The problem description requires that $R$ not terminate with values reflecting an in-progress $WRITE$. This (historical) safety property is specified in Temporal Logic as

(7.11)    $Init_S \Rightarrow \Box(after(R) \Rightarrow \neg BD)$

where derived term $BD$ (an abbreviation for "Bad Data") is satisfied by any anchored sequence such that in the past and current states, the last $READ$ to start overlapped with execution of $WRITE$:

$$BD: \begin{cases} false & \text{if } at(READ) \\ in(WRITE) \vee (def_\Theta \wedge \Theta BD) & \text{if } in(READ) \wedge \neg at(READ) \\ def_\Theta \wedge \Theta BD & \text{if } \neg in(READ) \end{cases}$$

Any valid proof outline having a precondition implied by $Init_S$ and in which $post(R)$ implies $\neg BD$ is sufficient for proving that (7.11) is satisfied, due to $I_{PO(S)}$ Decomposition Rule (6.17a) and Safety Consequence Rule (6.8). Thus, ensuring satisfaction of (7.11) is equivalent to filling out the bodies of $R$ and $W$ in the following proof outline. Note that assertions not pertaining to the proof of (7.11) have been omitted.

(7.12)    $\{Init_S\}$
    $S$: **cobegin** ...
            $R$: ... $READ$ ...
            $\{\neg BD\}$ ...
        $\|$
            ...
            $W$: ... $WRITE$ ...
        **coend**

One way to ensure that $\neg BD$ holds when $R$ terminates is to prevent execution of $READ$ while $WRITE$ is being executed, and vice versa. This, however, can cause execution of $WRITE$ to be delayed—something that is not always acceptable. For example, suppose each digit of a multidigit clock is implemented by a separate shared variable. If the clock is advanced by a process that periodically executes $WRITE$ to store new values in these variables, then the clock's correctness depends not only on what values are written but on when those values are written. Clock accuracy would be compromised if a $WRITE$ were delayed.

$WRITE$ will never be delayed if $W$ contains no conditional atomic actions or loops. We therefore adopt this additional constraint, ruling out exclusion-based readers/writers protocols (like that of exercise 6.15).

In order to proceed, we construct a valid proof outline for $R$ in isolation. The body of $R$ is simply $READ$—there is no justification for including anything else. Moreover, because $\neg BD$ holds when $at(R)$ does, it is easy to construct a proof outline with the desired postcondition. $PO(READ)$ is the proof outline for $READ$ with *true* for every assertion.

(7.13) $\{\neg BD\}$
$\quad\quad R: PO(READ)\textcircled{a}\neg BD$
$\quad\quad \{\neg BD\}$

To include this proof outline in (7.12), however, requires that $W$ not interfere. Unfortunately, it does. Execution of atomic actions in $WRITE$ falsify conjunct $\neg BD$ in all assertions except $pre(READ)$.

To eliminate this interference, we postulate a predicate $p$ such that for every atomic action $\alpha \in \mathcal{A}(WRITE)$, the following holds:

(7.14) $pre(\alpha) \Rightarrow p$

We then use Weakening (5.15) to modify the assertions that formerly were falsified. The result is the following modification of (7.13).

$\quad\quad \{\neg BD\}$
$\quad\quad R: PO(READ)\textcircled{a}(p \vee \neg BD)$
$\quad\quad \{p \vee \neg BD\}$

A problem with this proof outline is that $post(R)$ is now weaker than desired. Moreover, the obvious way to remedy such problems, Strengthening by Condition Synchronization (5.50), does not work. Once $\neg BD$ has been falsified, waiting can never make $\neg BD$ hold again (due to the third clause in the definition of derived term $BD$).

Condition synchronization is not the only way to strengthen an assertion. A loop can be used to strengthen an assertion, because **do** Rule (4.24) has as its postcondition the conjunction of its precondition and another predicate, the loop's guards negated. This suggests that *READ* be made the body of a loop with $p \lor \neg BD$ as loop invariant and $p$ as guard, thereby allowing the postcondition of the loop to be $\neg BD$ because it is implied by $(p \lor \neg BD) \land \neg p$. We thus allow concurrent reading while writing, but prevent data read during a *WRITE* from becoming visible outside of $R$.

$$(7.15) \quad \{I: p \lor \neg BD\}$$
$$R: \textbf{do } p \rightarrow \quad \{I \land \neg BD\}$$
$$PO(READ) \otimes I$$
$$\{I\}$$
$$\textbf{od}$$
$$\{\neg BD\}$$

An easy way to discharge obligation (7.14) is to implement $p$ by a program variable and then bracket *WRITE* with assignment statements to $p$. This is done in the following proof outline fragment, where $PO(WRITE)$ has *true* for each of its assertions.

$$W: \; p := \textit{true}$$
$$PO(WRITE) \otimes p$$
$$p := \textit{false}$$

Unfortunately, when embedded in the **cobegin** of (7.12), final assignment statement $p := \textit{false}$ interferes with $I$ in all assertions of (7.15) except $pre(READ)$. To solve this problem, we again employ Weakening (5.15). We postulate a predicate $q$ that satisfies $pre(p := \textit{false}) \Rightarrow q$ and use $q$ to weaken the assertions in $PO(R)$ that could be falsified by executing $p := \textit{false}$. The revised proof outline for $R$ follows. In it, the weaker loop guard, $p \lor q$, is needed in order to be able to infer $\neg BD$ when the loop terminates, given the weaker loop invariant.

$$\{I: p \lor q \lor \neg BD\}$$
$$R: \textbf{do } p \lor q \rightarrow \quad \{I \land \neg BD\}$$
$$PO(READ) \otimes I$$
$$\{I\}$$
$$\textbf{od}$$
$$\{\neg BD\}$$

The revised protocol for $W$ is:

$$W: \; p := \textit{true}$$
$$PO(WRITE) \otimes p$$
$$q := \textit{true} \; \{q\}$$
$$p := \textit{false}$$

We have succeeded in constructing proof outlines for $R$ and $W$ that are interference free, satisfy the constraints in (7.12), and satisfy the constraints that ensure that *WRITE* is not delayed. However, our protocol has two problems:

(i)  Once $q$ is set to *true* in $W$, the **do** in $R$ loops forever. Useful computation by the process that contains $R$ then becomes impossible.

(ii) A suitable initialization must be devised so that loop invariant $p \lor q \lor \neg BD$ will hold at the start of the **do**.

Although infinite looping of the **do** in $R$ cannot cause (7.11) to be violated, it can be a problem for proving termination and other liveness properties. Nonterminating loops can prevent a "bad thing" from happening, but they might also prevent "good things" from happening. Thus, when liveness properties may be of interest, use of such nonterminating loops is rarely a good practice.

The loop in $R$ will terminate if $\neg(p \lor q)$ holds when $GEval_{do}(R)$ is executed. $W$ truthifies $\neg p$ before exiting, but it cannot also truthify $\neg q$ without causing interference with $I$. Therefore, in order make $\neg(p \lor q)$ hold, we investigate possible places in $R$ to add an assignment statement that will truthify $\neg q$.

The assignment statement must occur in the body of the **do**; otherwise, it will not be executed after the loop has started (and when it would be needed). Also, looking at the assertions in the body of the **do**, we see that the new assignment statement must leave $I$ *true*. Thus, execution of $q := false$ must occur in a state where $p \lor \neg BD$ holds, since $p \lor \neg BD$ implies $I$. By definition, $\neg BD$ holds when $at(READ)$ does, so we can place the assignment statement immediately before *READ*, obtaining the following valid proof outline.

$$\{I: \ p \lor q \lor \neg BD\}$$
$$R: \ \textbf{do } p \lor q \to \ \{I\}$$
$$q := false \ \{I \land \neg BD\}$$
$$PO(READ) \otimes I$$
$$\{I\}$$
$$\textbf{od}$$
$$\{\neg BD\}$$

Now, however, $q := false$ in $R$ interferes with $pre(p := false)$ (which is $q$) in the proof outline for $W$. Recall that we made $q$ a conjunct of $pre(p := false)$ in order to eliminate interference by $p := false$ with $I$ in assertions of the proof outline for $R$. Thus, provided that $pre(p := false)$ remains strong enough for $NI(p := false, I)$ to be valid, we can use Weakening (5.15) to deal with interference by $q := false$. Use of disjunct $\neg BD$ to weaken $pre(p := false)$ does the trick, because executing $q := false$ truthifies $at(READ)$, which implies $\neg BD$, and executing $p := false$ in a state satisfying $\neg BD$ does not falsify $\neg BD$ (hence $I$). Here is the revised proof outline for $W$:

$$W: \ p := true$$
$$PO(WRITE) \otimes p$$
$$q := true \ \{q \lor \neg BD\}$$
$$p := false$$

Finally, we devise an initialization that truthifies loop invariant $p \vee q \vee \neg BD$. Assigning *true* to either $p$ or $q$ will truthify $I$. We choose an assignment statement with target $q$, so that execution of $R$ can terminate without $W$ having to be executed. The final protocol appears as Figure 7.2.

## 7.5  Auxiliary Variables

A valid proof outline $PO(S)$ whose assertions mention a derived term $Z$ sometimes is most easily obtained by first reasoning about a syntactically related program $S'$ and proof outline $PO(S')$ whose assertions do not mention $Z$. This is because a derived term can be simulated by a program variable, called an *auxiliary variable*, that has no effect on program execution.

To implement this simulation, the atomic actions of the original program are augmented with assignments whose targets are the auxiliary variable. These assignments ensure that the value of the auxiliary variable in the augmented program remains equal to the derived term that it simulates. Because an auxiliary variable cannot affect program execution, if $PO(S')$ is a valid proof outline for a program in which auxiliary variable $a$ simulates derived term $Z$, then deleting the assignments to $a$ in $S'$ and substituting $Z$ for $a$ in every assertion of $PO(S')$ will produce a valid proof outline.

---

$\{Init_S\}$
$S$: **cobegin**

    ...

    $R$: $q := true$   $\{I\!: p \vee q \vee \neg BD\}$
        **do** $p \vee q \rightarrow$   $\{I\}$
                $q := false$   $\{I \wedge \neg BD\}$
                $PO(READ)\textcircledR I$
                $\{I\}$
        **od**
        $\{\neg BD\}$
    ...
 $\|$

    ...

    $W$: $p := true$
       $PO(WRITE)\textcircled{\scriptsize $\otimes$} p$
       $q := true$   $\{q \vee \neg BD\}$
       $p := false$

    ...

**coend**

**Figure 7.2.**  Concurrent reading while writing

For example, replacing each atomic action $\alpha$ by $\langle \alpha \ \ mx := \max(mx, x) \rangle$ allows auxiliary variable $mx$ to simulate derived term $Mx$ (7.6). The simulation of $Mx$ by $mx$ allows the proof outline

(7.16) $\{x=Mx\} \ \ x := x+5 \ \ \{x=Mx\} \ \ x := x+10 \ \ \{x=Mx\}$

to be inferred from the following theorem:

(7.17) $\{x=mx\}$
$\quad \alpha_1: \ \langle x := x+5 \ \ mx := \max(mx, x) \rangle$
$\quad \{x=mx\}$
$\quad \alpha_2: \ \langle x := x+10 \ \ mx := \max(mx, x) \rangle$
$\quad \{x=mx\}$

To give a Proof Outline Logic rule for transforming a proof outline that uses an auxiliary variable into one whose assertions use the simulated derived term, we first formalize how auxiliary variables are added to a program.

(7.18) **Adding an Auxiliary Variable.** A variable $a$ is auxiliary in program $S'$ iff:

(i) $a$ appears only in assignments whose target is $a$ and that are part of atomic statements,

(ii) every atomic statement containing an assignment to $a$ remains a syntactically correct atomic statement if that assignment is deleted, and

(iii) for each atomic statement $\alpha'$ containing an assignment to $a$ and each atomic statement $\alpha$ obtained by deleting from $\alpha'$ the assignment to $a$:

$$VarAx(S') \wedge enbl(\alpha) \Rightarrow enbl(\alpha') \qquad \square$$

Accordingly, $d$ is auxiliary in

$\quad$ **if** $b=0 \to c := 1 \ [] \ b \neq 0 \to \langle d := 3 \ \ c := 2 \rangle$ **fi**

but $b$ is not because it appears in a guard, and $c$ is not because $c := 1$ is not part of an atomic statement (and cannot be deleted). As another example, an integer variable $e$ cannot be auxiliary in

$\quad \alpha': \ \langle \textbf{skip} \ e := 0.5 \rangle$

because condition (iii) is violated.

Condition (i) of Adding an Auxiliary Variable (7.18) ensures that the value of an auxiliary variable $a$ is not directly used in computing a value that is assigned to any other variable. This condition also prevents the value of $a$ from influencing the outcome of a guard evaluation action. Condition (ii) ensures that after deleting assignments to an auxiliary variable, a syntactically correct program remains. Finally, condition (iii) ensures that deleting the assignments to an auxiliary variable does not allow an atomic action to be executed when previously it could not be.

We now give the Proof Outline Logic rule for replacing an auxiliary variable $a$ by a derived term $Z$ that it simulates. In the conclusion of the rule, we use $S|_a$ to denote the program obtained by deleting from each atomic statement of $S$ the assignments that mention $a$. And given a proof outline $PO(S)$, we write $PO(S|_a)_Z^a$ to denote the proof outline in which assignments to $a$ have been deleted from the atomic statements of $S$ and every instance of $a$ in the assertions of $PO(S)$ is replaced by $Z$. Premise (b) of the rule is necessary to ensure that $a$ really does simulate $Z$; its role is discussed in the soundness proof given below.

(7.19) *Auxiliary Variable Deletion Rule*:   For $a$ an auxiliary variable in $S$, $Z$ a derived term, and $a$ not occurring free in $Z$:

$$\frac{\text{(a) } PO(S),}{PO(S|_a)_Z^a}\ \text{(b) For every } \alpha \text{ in } \mathcal{A}(S)\colon\ NI(\alpha, a=Z)$$

Note that because $a$ may not occur free in $Z$, when multiple auxiliary variables are eliminated by repeated use of Auxiliary Variable Deletion Rule (7.19), the proof outline that results does not depend on the order in which these variables are eliminated.

Using Auxiliary Variable Deletion Rule (7.19), we can infer (7.16) from (7.17). First, assuming $mx$ has been declared with the same type as $x$, $mx$ in (7.17) satisfies the conditions of Adding an Auxiliary Variable (7.18). Thus, $mx$ can be considered an auxiliary variable in (7.17). Premise (a) of Auxiliary Variable Deletion Rule (7.19) is satisfied because (7.17) is a theorem of Proof Outline Logic. To satisfy premise (b), we must prove:

$$NI(\alpha_1, mx=Mx)\colon\quad \{x=mx \wedge mx=Mx\}\, \alpha_1\, \{mx=Mx\}$$

$$NI(\alpha_2, mx=Mx)\colon\quad \{x=mx \wedge mx=Mx\}\, \alpha_2\, \{mx=Mx\}$$

We give only the proof of $NI(\alpha_1, mx=Mx)$ here; the other proof is similar.

«Assignment Axiom (4.19), Statement Juxtaposition Rule (4.20),
Rule of Consequence (4.25), and $\langle S\rangle$ Rule (5.42)»
1.  $\{x=mx \wedge mx=A\}\ \langle x := x+5\ \ mx := \max(mx, x)\rangle\ \{mx=\max(x, A)\}$

«$\Theta^i$-Introduction Rule (7.8) with 1, using $Mx$ for A»
2.  $\{x=mx \wedge mx=Mx\}$
    $\langle x := x+5\ \ mx := \max(mx, x)\rangle$
    $\{mx=\max(x, \Theta Mx) \wedge \Theta(x=mx \wedge mx=Mx) \wedge \mathit{def}_\Theta\}$

«Predicate Logic»
  3. $mx = \max(x, \Theta Mx) \wedge \Theta(x = mx \wedge mx = Mx) \wedge def_\Theta$
     $\Rightarrow ((mx = \max(x, \Theta Mx) \wedge def_\Theta) \vee (mx = x \wedge \neg def_\Theta))$

«Rule of Consequence (4.25) with 2 and 3»
  4. $\{x = mx \wedge mx = Mx\}$
     $\langle x := x+5 \;\; mx := \max(mx, x)\rangle$
     $\{(mx = \max(x, \Theta Mx) \wedge def_\Theta) \vee (mx = x \wedge \neg def_\Theta)\}$

«Extended Derived Term Expansion Rule (7.5), since
  $def_\Theta = \neg(\neg def_\Theta)$»
  5. $(mx = Mx) = ((def_\Theta \wedge mx = \max(x, \Theta Mx)) \vee (\neg def_\Theta \wedge mx = x))$

«Rule of Equivalence (4.26) with 4 and 5»
  6. $\{x = mx \wedge mx = Mx\} \;\langle x := x+5 \;\; mx := \max(mx, x)\rangle\; \{mx = Mx\}$

## Soundness of Auxiliary Variable Deletion Rule

Auxiliary Variable Deletion Rule (7.19) is fundamentally different from our other inference rules for reasoning about proof outlines. The premises in Auxiliary Variable Deletion Rule (7.19) concern a program that assigns to a variable $a$, but the conclusion concerns a program that does not reference $a$ at all. In each of our other rules, the premises and conclusion refer to program fragments that manipulate the same set of variables.

What is it about the way $S|_a$ is constructed from $S$ that allows construction of a valid proof outline for the latter from a valid proof outline for the former? An answer to this question is found in the soundness proof of Auxiliary Variable Deletion Rule (7.19). We sketch that proof here.

To prove soundness of Auxiliary Variable Deletion Rule (7.19), we show that

(7.20)  $at(S|_a) \wedge pre(PO(S|_a)^a_Z) \Rightarrow I_{PO(S|_a)^a_Z}$

(7.21)  $I_{PO(S|_a)^a_Z} \Rightarrow \Box I_{PO(S|_a)^a_Z}$

are both $\mathcal{H}^+_{S|_a}$-valid whenever premises (a) and (b) of the inference rule are valid.

For a variable $a$ and a sequence $\sigma$ of states, let $\sigma|_a$ be the sequence of states obtained by deleting state component $a$ from the states of $\sigma$. Generalizing to anchored sequences and $\mathcal{H}^+_S$, we define:

$$\mathcal{H}^+_S|_a : \;\; \{(\sigma|_a, i) \mid (\sigma, i) \in \mathcal{H}^+_S\}$$

The conditions of Adding an Auxiliary Variable (7.18) imply that auxiliary variable $a$ cannot affect the way other program variables change during execution (the proof, being tedious, is omitted from this sketch):

(7.22) $\mathcal{H}_S^+|_a = \mathcal{H}_{S|_a}^+$

Thus, in order to prove that (7.20) and (7.21) are $\mathcal{H}_{S|_a}^+$-valid, it suffices to prove that they are $\mathcal{H}_S^+|_a$-valid.

Next, we name the subset of $\mathcal{H}_S^+$ in which $a$ in the current state equals derived term $Z$.

$$\mathcal{H}_S^+(a, Z): \quad \{(\sigma, i) \mid (\sigma, i) \in \mathcal{H}_S^+ \wedge (\sigma, i) \vDash a = Z\}$$

Observe that according to this definition of $\mathcal{H}_S^+(a, Z)$:

(7.23) $\mathcal{H}_S^+(a, Z) \subseteq \mathcal{H}_S^+$

(7.24) $\mathcal{H}_S^+(a, Z) \vDash a = Z$

This means that for any Temporal Logic formula $P$, we can conclude that $P \wedge a = Z$ is $\mathcal{H}_S^+(a, Z)$-valid if $P$ is $\mathcal{H}_S^+$-valid.

Finally, for each anchored sequence $(\sigma, j)$ of $\mathcal{H}_S^+(a, Z)$, there is a set of anchored sequences in $\mathcal{H}_S^+$ that differ from $(\sigma, j)$ only in what values are assigned to variable $a$—one anchored sequence assigns the value of $Z$, and all the other anchored sequences assign different values to $a$. Ignore $a$, and the sets are identical:

(7.25) $\mathcal{H}_S^+|_a = \mathcal{H}_S^+(a, Z)|_a$

With these preliminaries out of the way, we now proceed with the soundness proof. Rather than prove directly that (7.20) and (7.21) are $\mathcal{H}_{S|_a}^+$-valid, we prove the more general result:

(7.26) For $P$ an arbitrary formula of Temporal Logic, if

$$\mathcal{H}_S^+ \vDash (P \wedge (a = Z \Rightarrow \Box(a = Z)))$$

then $\mathcal{H}_{S|_a}^+ \vDash P_Z^a$.

Using (7.26), we then show that (7.20) and (7.21) are $\mathcal{H}_{S|_a}^+$-valid, as follows. Premise (a) of Auxiliary Variable Deletion Rule (7.19) implies $\mathcal{H}_S^+$-validity for

(7.27) $at(S) \wedge pre(PO(S)) \Rightarrow I_{PO(S)}$

(7.28) $I_{PO(S)} \Rightarrow \Box I_{PO(S)}$

due to Valid Proof Outline (4.17). Premise (b) of the rule implies $\mathcal{H}_S^+$-validity for $a = Z \Rightarrow \Box(a = Z)$. Taking the conjunction of (7.27) and (7.28) as $P$ in (7.26), we have:

(i) The premises of Auxiliary Variable Deletion Rule (7.19) imply $\mathcal{H}_S^+ \models (P \wedge (a=Z \Rightarrow \Box(a=Z)))$, as required for (7.26).

(ii) $P_Z^a$ is equivalent to the conjunction of (7.20) and (7.21).

Given (i), (7.26) allows us to conclude that $P_Z^a$ is $\mathcal{H}_{S|_a}^+$-valid. Given (ii), we then conclude that the conjunction of (7.20) and (7.21) is $\mathcal{H}_{S|_a}^+$-valid—exactly what is required to establish soundness of Auxiliary Variable Deletion Rule (7.19).

Proving conclusion $\mathcal{H}_{S|_a}^+ \models P_Z^a$ of (7.26) from its premise $\mathcal{H}_S^+ \models (P \wedge (a=Z \Rightarrow \Box(a=Z)))$ is simply a matter of showing why the latter implies the former.

$$\mathcal{H}_S^+ \models (P \wedge (a=Z \Rightarrow \Box(a=Z)))$$
$\Rightarrow$ «(7.23)»
$$\mathcal{H}_S^+(a, Z) \models (P \wedge (a=Z \Rightarrow \Box(a=Z)))$$
$=$ «(7.24)»
$$\mathcal{H}_S^+(a, Z) \models (a=Z \wedge P \wedge (a=Z \Rightarrow \Box(a=Z)))$$
$\Rightarrow$ «Propositional reasoning»
$$\mathcal{H}_S^+(a, Z) \models (a=Z \wedge P \wedge \Box(a=Z))$$
$=$ «$\Box(x=y) \Rightarrow P_x^v = P_y^v$»
$$\mathcal{H}_S^+(a, Z) \models (a=Z \wedge P \wedge \Box(a=Z) \wedge (\Box(a=Z) \Rightarrow P_a^a = P_Z^a))$$
$\Rightarrow$ «Propositional reasoning»
$$\mathcal{H}_S^+(a, Z) \models (a=Z \wedge P \wedge P_a^a = P_Z^a)$$
$=$ «$P = P_a^a$»
$$\mathcal{H}_S^+(a, Z) \models (a=Z \wedge P_a^a \wedge P_a^a = P_Z^a)$$
$\Rightarrow$ «Propositional reasoning»
$$\mathcal{H}_S^+(a, Z) \models P_Z^a)$$
$\Rightarrow$ «$P_Z^a$ has no free occurrences of $a$»
$$\mathcal{H}_S^+(a, Z)|_a \models P_Z^a)$$
$=$ «(7.25)»
$$\mathcal{H}_S^+|_a \models P_Z^a$$
$=$ «(7.22)»
$$\mathcal{H}_{S|_a}^+ \models P_Z^a$$

## Computational Definitions for Derived Terms

Given a proof outline $PO(S)$, the effort required to discharge premise (b) of Auxiliary Variable Deletion Rule (7.19) is often comparable to proving $PO(S|_a)_Z^a$ directly. Use of an auxiliary variable $a$ becomes attractive when, because we have established by some informal means that $a$ simulates derived term $Z$, premise (b) of Auxiliary Variable Deletion Rule (7.19) need not be proved.

This shortcut is not without risks. The validity of our theorems (i.e., proof outlines) becomes suspect when informal proofs are used for premise (b), since unsound inferences are difficult to identify in proofs that are not completely formal. Fortunately, this reasoning can be made rigorous if necessary: we simply prove the $NI(\alpha, a=Z)$ triples comprising premise (b).

$S$:  $t, in1, in2 := 1, false, false$
  **cobegin**
  $S_1$: **do** $true \rightarrow$ $entry_1$:  $door_1$:  $in1 := true$
                                    $step_1$:  $t := 2$
                                    $gate_1$:  **if** $\neg in2 \lor t=1 \rightarrow T_1$:  **skip fi**
                      $CS_1$
                      $exit_1$:  $in1 := false$
                      $NCS_1$
           **od**
  ||
  $S_2$: **do** $true \rightarrow$ $entry_2$:  $door_2$:  $in2 := true$
                                    $step_2$:  $t := 1$
                                    $gate_2$:  **if** $\neg in1 \lor t=2 \rightarrow T_2$:  **skip fi**
                      $CS_2$
                      $exit_2$:  $in2 := false$
                      $NCS_2$
           **od**
  **coend**

**Figure 7.3.** Mutual exclusion protocol

One way to ensure that $a$ simulates $Z$ is by construction. We define $Z$ to be the current value of $a$. Thus, $Z$ is defined *computationally* by using assignments to an auxiliary variable $a$. To illustrate, we return to the mutual exclusion protocol derived in §6.5 (repeated here as Figure 7.3). The protocol happens to ensure that processes execute their critical sections in first-come, first-served order—a historical safety property for which the "bad thing" is a process executing its critical section when some earlier request has not yet been serviced.

To specify this property in Temporal Logic, we use a derived term $WL$ (an abbreviation for "Wait List") to record the order in which pending critical section execution requests must be satisfied. Let $S_{WL[0]}$ be the process that has made the oldest unsatisfied entry request, let $S_{WL[1]}$ be the next oldest, and so on. Thus, the "bad thing" for first-come, first-served is $at(CS_i) \land WL[0] \neq i$, and we have:

(7.29) *First-Come First-Served Entry*:
$$at(S) \land WL = \varepsilon \;\Rightarrow\; \Box \neg (in(CS_i) \land WL[0] \neq i)$$

(Equivalent formulation $at(S) \land WL = \varepsilon \;\Rightarrow\; \Box (in(CS_i) \Rightarrow WL[0] = i)$ is, to some, a more natural characterization for First-Come First-Served Entry (7.29).)

To define $WL$ computationally, a sequence-valued auxiliary variable $w$ will be used. Two events change the value of $WL$:

  (i)  requesting execution of a critical section and

(ii) satisfying such a request.

In the program of Figure 7.3, $exit_i$ seems a natural implementation for event (ii), since executing $exit_i$ signifies that execution of a critical section has completed. So we replace $exit_i$ with $\langle exit_i \ w := w[1..] \rangle$, causing $w$ to change value in the same way that *WL* does.

For event (i), the first atomic action of $entry_i$ (i.e., $door_i$) seems the natural choice. Closer inspection, however, reveals a flaw in choosing $door_i$ to signify an execution request. Processes executing the protocol of Figure 7.3 cannot distinguish between interleaving $door_1 \ door_2$ and interleaving $door_2 \ door_1$, but making this distinction would be necessary for a process to know whether its request to enter the critical section was first. At the other extreme, equating event (i) with the last atomic action of $entry_i$ (i.e., $T_i$) makes satisfying First-Come First-Served Entry (7.29) trivial—any process reaching $after(gate_i)$ is guaranteed to have its request be the next satisfied. Therefore, we are forced to reject this choice as well. Modification of $GEval_{if}(gate_i)$ would be prohibited by Adding an Auxiliary Variable (7.18). The remaining choice, $step_i$, does not have either of these difficulties. So, we replace $step_i$ with $\langle step_i \ w := w \ i \rangle$, where expression $W \ x$ evaluates to the list that results from appending element $x$ to list $W$. These replacements result in program $S'$ of Figure 7.4.

We can prove that the protocol of Figure 7.3 satisfies First-Come First-Served Entry (7.29) by constructing a proof outline $PO(S)$ for which the following are valid.

---

$S'$: $t, in1, in2 := 1, false, false$
    **cobegin**
    $S_1$: **do** $true \rightarrow entry_1$: $door_1$: $in1 := true$
                            $step_1$: $\langle t := 2 \ w := w \ 1 \rangle$
                            $gate_1$: **if** $\neg in2 \vee t=1 \rightarrow T_1$: **skip fi**
              $CS_1$
              $exit_1$: $\langle in1 := false \ w := w[1..] \rangle$
              $NCS_1$
      **od**
    ‖
    $S_2$: **do** $true \rightarrow entry_2$: $door_2$: $in2 := true$
                           $step_2$: $\langle t := 1 \ w := w \ 2 \rangle$
                           $gate_2$: **if** $\neg in1 \vee t=2 \rightarrow T_2$: **skip fi**
             $CS_2$
             $exit_2$: $\langle in2 := false \ w := w[1..] \rangle$
             $NCS_2$
     **od**
   **coend**

**Figure 7.4.** Augmented mutual exclusion protocol

(7.30)  $at(S) \wedge WL = \varepsilon \Rightarrow pre(PO(S))$

(7.31)  For every atomic action $\alpha$ in $\mathcal{A}(CS_i)$:  $pre(\alpha) \Rightarrow WL[0] = i$

This is because from such a proof outline we can infer the validity of

$$I_{PO(S)} \Rightarrow \neg (in(CS_i) \wedge WL[0] \neq i)$$

by using $I_{PO(S)}$ Decomposition Rule (6.17a). All three premises for Safety Consequence Rule (6.8) are then satisfied.

To construct a proof outline for which (7.30) and (7.31) are valid, we use Auxiliary Variable Deletion Rule (7.19) along with $PO(S')$ in Figure 7.5. That proof outline, which is for $S'$ of Figure 7.4, is written in terms of $I$ defined as follows, where «$a, b, c, ...$» denotes the list $a, b, c, ...$ .

$$
\begin{aligned}
I: \quad & (\neg in1 \Rightarrow \neg (in(CS_1) \vee in(gate_1))) \\
\wedge\ & (\neg in2 \Rightarrow \neg (in(CS_2) \vee in(gate_2))) \\
\wedge\ & (t=1 \vee t=2) \\
\wedge\ & (w=\varepsilon \vee w=\text{«}1\text{»} \vee w=\text{«}1,2\text{»} \vee w=\text{«}2\text{»} \vee w=\text{«}2,1\text{»}) \\
\wedge\ & (1 \in w \Rightarrow in1) \wedge (2 \in w \Rightarrow in2) \\
\wedge\ & (w \neq \varepsilon \Rightarrow w[\,|w|-1] \neq t)
\end{aligned}
$$

Notice also that $at(S') \wedge w = \varepsilon$ implies $pre(PO(S'))$, and $pre(CS_i)$ implies $w[0] = i$. Because $WL$ is defined computationally by $w$, premise (b) of Auxiliary Variable Deletion Rule (7.19) need not be checked when this rule is employed to infer $PO(S)$ from $PO(S')$. Thus, we have completed a proof that the mutual exclusion protocol of Figure 7.3 satisfies First-Come First-Served Entry (7.29).

This example has demonstrated how using an auxiliary variable can provide a simple way to introduce a derived term into proof outline assertions. Computationally specifying a derived term provides a sound basis for believing that an auxiliary variable simulates some derived term of interest, and this belief allows premise (b) of Auxiliary Variable Deletion Rule (7.19) to be ignored. The example also illustrates that computational specifications for derived terms can be easier to construct and understand than equivalent Predicate Logic formulations. Here is a definition for derived term $WL$ used above:

$$
WL: \begin{cases}
\varepsilon & \text{if } \neg def_\Theta \\
\text{«}WL, 1\text{»} & \text{if } def_\Theta \wedge after(step_1) \wedge \Theta \neg after(step_1) \\
\text{«}WL, 2\text{»} & \text{if } def_\Theta \wedge after(step_2) \wedge \Theta \neg after(step_2) \\
WL[1..] & \text{if } def_\Theta \wedge after(exit_1) \wedge \Theta \neg after(exit_1) \\
WL[1..] & \text{if } def_\Theta \wedge after(exit_2) \wedge \Theta \neg after(exit_2) \\
\Theta WL & \text{otherwise}
\end{cases}
$$

It is pretty intimidating. Most programmers are happier dealing with the computational definition, leading to fewer errors when formalizing properties.

$\{w=\varepsilon\}$
$S'$: $t, in1, in2 := 1, false, false$
   $\{\neg in1 \wedge \neg in2 \wedge w=\varepsilon\}$
   **cobegin**
   $S_1$: **do** $true \rightarrow \{I \wedge \neg in1 \wedge (w=\varepsilon \vee w=\text{«2»})\}$
               $entry_1$: $door_1$: $in1 := true$
                      $\{I \wedge in1 \wedge (w=\varepsilon \vee w=\text{«2»})\}$
                 $step_1$: $\langle t := 2\ \ w := w\ 1\rangle$
                      $\{I \wedge in1 \wedge (w[0]=1 \vee w=\text{«2, 1»})\}$
                 $gate_1$: **if** $\neg in2 \vee t=1 \rightarrow \{I \wedge in1 \wedge w[0]=1\}$
                                 $T_1$: **skip**
                                 $\{I \wedge in1 \wedge w[0]=1\}$
                     **fi** $\{I \wedge in1 \wedge w[0]=1\}$
             $PO(CS_1)\otimes(I \wedge in1 \wedge w[0]=1)$
             $exit_1$: $\langle in1 := false\ \ w := w[1..]\rangle$
             $\{I \wedge \neg in1 \wedge (w=\varepsilon \vee w=\text{«2»})\}$
             $PO(NCS_1)\otimes(I \wedge \neg in1 \wedge (w=\varepsilon \vee w=\text{«2»}))$
             $\{I \wedge \neg in1 \wedge (w=\varepsilon \vee w=\text{«2»})\}$

       **od** $\{false\}$
   $\|$

   $S_2$: **do** $true \rightarrow \{I \wedge \neg in2 \wedge (w=\varepsilon \vee w=\text{«1»})\}$
               $entry_2$: $door_2$: $in2 := true$
                      $\{I \wedge in2 \wedge (w=\varepsilon \vee w=\text{«1»})\}$
                 $step_2$: $\langle t := 1\ \ w := {<}w\ 2\rangle$
                      $\{I \wedge in2 \wedge (w[0]=2 \vee w=\text{«1, 2»})\}$
                 $gate_2$: **if** $\neg in1 \vee t=2 \rightarrow \{I \wedge in2 \wedge w[0]=2\}$
                                 $T_2$: **skip**
                                 $\{I \wedge in2 \wedge w[0]=2\}$
                   **fi** $\{I \wedge in2 \wedge w[0]=2\}$
             $PO(CS_2)\otimes(I \wedge in2 \wedge w[0]=2)$
              $exit_2$: $\langle in2 := false\ \ w := w[1..]\rangle$
             $\{I \wedge \neg in2 \wedge (w=\varepsilon \vee w=\text{«1»})\}$
             $PO(NCS_2)\otimes(I \wedge \neg in2 \wedge (w=\varepsilon \vee w=\text{«1»}))$
             $\{I \wedge \neg in2 \wedge (w=\varepsilon \vee w=\text{«1»})\}$

      **od** $\{false\}$
   **coend**

**Figure 7.5.** Proof outline for augmented protocol

Computational specification of derived terms is not without disadvantages. Derived terms that are defined computationally and specifications that mention them are not amenable to formal logical analysis. Moreover, formally deriving consequences from a specification allows us to gain confidence that it correctly captures what we intend. Only by explicitly defining a derived term can logic be used to reason about formulas containing the term.

A second disadvantage of using auxiliary variables to specify derived terms concerns expressiveness. Adding an Auxiliary Variable (7.18) allows only some atomic actions to be augmented with auxiliary variable assignments. This makes it impossible to specify a derived term computationally if the value of the derived term changes as a result of executing atomic actions that may not be so augmented.[2] For example, it would not be possible in the mutual exclusion example above to specify a derived term whose value changed when a guard evaluation action like $GEval_{if}(gate_i)$ is executed.

## 7.6   Some Cautions

It is natural to characterize properties in terms of sequences of interesting events. Our past extensions to Predicate Logic would seem to be ideally suited for formalizing such properties. However, proof outlines involving $\Theta$ are considerably harder to work with than those whose assertions depend only on the current program state. So it is prudent to avoid the past whenever possible. Most safety properties that arise in practice, for example, are actually invariance properties, even though they might seem to involve sequences of events.

When the use of $\Theta$ is unavoidable, care should be taken not to constrain implementations unnecessarily. Like Temporal Logic operator $\bigcirc$, use of $\Theta$ often constrains the number of atomic actions an implementation must execute in performing a state transition. Such constraints rarely are appropriate in a specification, because they limit an implementer's freedom in decomposing state transformations into sets of atomic actions.

Assertions involving $\Theta$ can also be problematic. Those that do not mention $\Theta$ are insensitive to repetition of states. This simplifies proving interference freedom. When $\Theta$ appears in an assertion, every atomic action has the potential to interfere with that assertion. Thus, to simplify interference freedom, terms that are insensitive to repetition of states should be used.

### Historical Notes

Most methods for verifying historical safety properties that use Hoare-style programming logics employ variables to record relevant aspects of a computation's history.

---

[2]This difficulty could be avoided by relaxing our restrictions on which atomic actions can be modified with auxiliary variable assignments.

One approach is to allow such variables to appear in assertions but not in program statements [Soundararajan 84a], [Zwiers & de Roever 89]. A more popular approach is to augment the program with assignment statements to new variables that encode whatever historical information is of interest. The new variables are used in a formal statement of the property as well as in a proof outline to establish that the augmented program satisfies that property. To infer that the original program also satisfies the property of interest, it is asserted that the additional variables can be deleted because they have no effect on program execution. Our method in §7.5 for using auxiliary variables to define derived terms computationally was inspired by this approach. Other methods based on this approach avoid the use of derived terms but involve informal (and unformalizable) proofs that the new variables correctly encode what is desired.

Just when auxiliary variables can be deleted is a subtle question and one that has largely been ignored since they were introduced by Clint for proving partial correctness of coroutines [Clint 73]. First, the presence of an auxiliary variable changes the program state space by adding a component. This means that there will exist properties that are satisfied by a program that has the auxiliary variable but not by the program that results from deleting all references to the variable (e.g., any property that mentions the auxiliary variable). Second, care must be taken to ensure that the existence of assignment statements to auxiliary variables does not change the program state space by adding control points. If it did, then there would exist properties (formulated in terms of control predicates) that might not hold after deleting the auxiliary variable assignment statements. Adding an Auxiliary Variable (7.18) requires that assignments to auxiliary variables be included in atomic statements for exactly this reason. Finally, the exact semantics of assignment affects whether auxiliary variable assignments can be deleted [McCurley 89]. Without condition (iii) of Adding an Auxiliary Variable (7.18), deleting a nonterminating assignment whose target is an auxiliary variable can affect program execution.

Our past extensions to Predicate Logic will be familiar to anyone who has studied temporal logics that have past operators. The utility of such operators for specifying safety properties was first discussed in [Lichtenstein et al. 85]. Our approach differs significantly from most temporal logics that have past operators. We relegate the past to the Predicate Logic fragment, whereas most temporal logics with past operators (e.g., [Prior 67], [Manna & Pnueli 92], [Manna & Pnueli 95]) employ past and future Temporal Logic operators. We could have used either approach.

Lamport was the first to pose and solve the concurrent reading while writing problem [Lamport 77b]. That work was motivated by the desire to develop protocols for multiprocessors that have shared memory. Exercise 7.26 hints at one of Lamport's solutions. The application of such protocols to reading a multidigit clock is discussed in [Lamport 90a]. The protocol in §7.4 is a variation of one developed by Jayanti [Jayanti 90], who was a graduate student at Cornell while this chapter was being written. Our variation is a bit simpler and was discovered while attempting to provide an assertional derivation (and proof) of Jayanti's protocol. Other classical solutions to the concurrent reading while writing problem can be found in Peterson's work [Peterson 83].

Alternative proofs of First-Come First-Served Entry (7.29) for Peterson's mutual exclusion protocol can be found in [Peterson 81], where the protocol was first proposed, and [Manna & Pnueli 83a], where the entire proof is in a temporal logic. The difficulties in deciding what events should signify a process requesting entry into a critical section and what should signify the servicing of a request are actually manifestations of a more fundamental problem. See [Lamport 85a] for a discussion of this.

## Exercises

**7.1.** The following properties all concern a one-lane bridge that is shared by automobile traffic traveling east and west. For each, indicate whether it is an invariance property or a historical safety property.

   (a)   All cars that travel over the bridge are heading east.

   (b)   All cars that travel over the bridge are heading in the same direction.

   (c)   All cars that travel over the bridge at any instant are heading in the same direction.

   (d)   No car waits for more than C cars to pass before it starts across the bridge.

   (e)   At most one car is on the bridge at any instant.

   (f)   At most one car is on the bridge at any instant, and two successive cars travel in opposite directions.

   (g)   At most C cars are permitted on the bridge at any instant.

   (h)   At most C cars are permitted on the bridge during any 24-hour period.

**7.2.** Let $F_{TL}$ be the set of Temporal Logic formulas that can be constructed from (ordinary) Predicate Logic formulas, the Temporal Logic $\square$ operator, and the connectives $\land$ and $\lor$.

   (a)   Can formulas in $F_{TL}$ specify historical safety properties? If so, give an example; otherwise, give an impossibility proof.

   (b)   Suppose $F_{TL}$ were extended to include formulas constructed using the Temporal Logic $\bigcirc$ operator. Can formulas in $F_{TL}$ now specify historical safety properties? If so, give an example; otherwise, give an impossibility proof.

**7.3.** Let *IP* be an arbitrary invariance property and let *HP* be an arbitrary historical safety property. For each of the following, state whether the resulting property is an invariance property, a historical safety property, or not even a safety property. Explain why.

   (a)   *IP*∩*IP*

   (b)   *IP*∪*IP*

   (c)   *IP*∩*HP*

   (d)   *IP*∪*HP*

   (e)   *HP*∩*HP*

   (f)   *HP*∪*HP*

**7.4.** Consider the following derived term definition:

$$Len: \begin{cases} 1 & \text{if } \neg def_\Theta \\ 1 + \Theta Len & \text{if } def_\Theta \end{cases}$$

Decide which of the following are theorems of Predicate Logic. Then, for each, give a proof or describe an anchored sequence that is not a model for the formula.

   (a)   $\Theta(x + \Theta y) = \Theta x + \Theta\Theta y$

   (b)   $x = \Theta(y + z) \land x = \Theta x \implies \Theta(x = y + z)$

(c)    $\Theta x = 5 \vee \Theta x \neq 5$

(d)    $\neg def_\Theta = (Len = 1)$

(e)    $Len > \Theta Len$

(f)    $Len > x \Rightarrow \Theta Len \geq x$

**7.5.** Consider the following derived term definition for $\Diamond$ (read "once"):

$$\Diamond Q: \begin{cases} Q & \text{if } \neg def_\Theta \\ Q \vee \Theta \Diamond Q & \text{if } def_\Theta \end{cases}$$

Decide which of the following are theorems of Predicate Logic. Then, for each, give a proof or describe an anchored sequence that is not a model for the formula.

(a)    $Q \Rightarrow \Diamond Q$

(b)    $(\Diamond Q \wedge \neg def_\Theta) = Q$

(c)    $\Diamond Q \Rightarrow (Q \vee \Theta \Diamond Q)$

(d)    $(def_\Theta \wedge \Theta Q) \Rightarrow \Diamond Q$

**7.6.** Formalize the following as derived terms.

(a)    *Fixed_x* is satisfied by an anchored sequence $(\sigma, j)$ iff the value of $x$ is the same in states $\sigma[..j]$.

(b)    *NonPos* is satisfied by an anchored sequence $(\sigma, j)$ iff the value of $x$ is not positive in states $\sigma[..j]$.

(c)    *Even* is satisfied by an anchored sequence $(\sigma, j)$ iff $j$ is even.

(d)    For any anchored sequence $(\sigma, j)$, term $Done_i$ equals the number of times process $S_i$ completed executing $entry_i$ in $\sigma[..j]$.

(e)    For any anchored sequence $(\sigma, j)$, term $Try_i$ equals the number of times process $S_i$ started executing $entry_i$ in $\sigma[..j]$.

(f)    For any anchored sequence $(\sigma, j)$, term *Waiting* equals the number of processes that have started but not finished executing $entry_i$ in $\sigma[..j]$.

(g)    For any anchored sequence $(\sigma, j)$, term $Sum\_x$ equals the sum of the distinct values that variable $x$ has in $\sigma[..j]$.

**7.7.** Justify soundness for the following:

(a)    $\Theta$ Expression Expansion (7.1)

(b)    $\Theta$ Constant Expansion (7.2)

(c)    Past Induction Rule (7.3)

**7.8.** The following inference rule has been proposed for inclusion in our past extensions to Predicate Logic.

$$\frac{P}{def_\Theta \Rightarrow \Theta P}$$

(a)    Is this rule sound? Justify your answer by giving a soundness proof or a counterexample.

(b)    If sound, is this a derived rule of inference? If so, give a procedure to translate any proof using this rule into a proof that does not use the rule.

**7.9.** Consider the following definition for a derived term $\boxminus P$.

$$\boxminus P: \begin{cases} P & \text{if } \neg def_\Theta \\ P \wedge \Theta \boxminus P & \text{if } def_\Theta \end{cases}$$

Give a proof or describe an anchored sequence that is not a model for each of the following.

(a)   $\boxminus P \Rightarrow P$

(b)   $(P \Rightarrow Q) \Rightarrow (\boxminus P \Rightarrow \boxminus Q)$

(c)   $(P \Rightarrow \Theta P) \Rightarrow (P \Rightarrow \boxminus P)$

**7.10.** Give a proof or describe an anchored sequence that is not a model for each of the following formulas. ($\boxminus P$ is defined above in exercise 7.9 and $\diamondsuit Q$ in exercise 7.5.)

(a)   $Q \Rightarrow \diamondsuit Q$

(b)   $\boxminus P \Rightarrow \diamondsuit P$

(c)   $\boxminus (P \Rightarrow Q) \Rightarrow (\diamondsuit P \Rightarrow \diamondsuit Q)$

(d)   $(\diamondsuit (P \Rightarrow Q)) = (\boxminus P \Rightarrow \diamondsuit Q)$

(e)   $\boxminus P \wedge \diamondsuit Q \Rightarrow \diamondsuit (P \wedge Q)$

**7.11.** Formalize each of the following safety properties as a Temporal Logic formula $Init \Rightarrow \Box Etern$ and explain whether it is an invariance property or a historical safety property.

(a)   The value of $x$ is always divisible by two.

(b)   The value of $x$ is always monotonically decreasing.

(c)   The value of $x$ always differs by no more than 2% from its most recent value.

(d)   The value of $x$ is unchanged from its most recent value.

(e)   Process $S$ executes $exit_S$ only after it has executed $entry_S$.

(f)   Process $S$ executes $CS_S$ after it executes $entry_S$ but before it executes $exit_S$.

(g)   Execution of $S$ takes between 200 and 500 milliseconds. (Assume that program variable $CLOCK$ always contains the correct time.)

(h)   Critical sections $CS_S$ and $CS_T$ strictly alternate.

(i)   While process $S$ is waiting to execute its critical section $CS_S$, process $T$ can enter critical section $CS_T$ at most twice.

(j)   $READ$ operations exclude $WRITE$ operations; $WRITE$ operations exclude $READ$ and $WRITE$ operations; and a stream of $READ$ operations cannot cause a $WRITE$ operation to be delayed indefinitely.

(k)   Among those processes waiting to enter critical sections, the process $S_i$ with the highest priority $\pi(S_i)$ is the next to be granted access.

(l)   The sequence of values retrieved by executing $GET$ operations is a prefix of the sequence of values deposited by executing $PUT$ operations.

**7.12.** In §2.3 we defined predicate $def_T$ for a term $T$ that does not involve past extensions. Is the following extension of that definition sound for integer constant $i > 0$? Why?

$$def_{\Theta^i T}: \quad \Theta^{i-1} def_\Theta \wedge \Theta^i def_T$$

**7.13.** Given any Predicate Logic formulas *Init* and *Etern*, show how to construct another Predicate Logic formula *Etern'* such that properties $\{Init \Rightarrow \Box Etern\}$ and $\{\Box Etern'\}$ are equivalent.

**7.14.** Suppose that *Init* and *Etern* are formulas of Predicate Logic and that both involve past extensions. What class of properties is specified by $Init \Rightarrow \Box Etern$?

**7.15.** Decide which of the following formulas are theorems of Proof Outline Logic. Then, for each, give a proof or describe why it is not valid. (See exercise 7.4 for the definition of derived term *Len* and (7.6) for the definition of *Mx*.)

(a)    $\{x=0\}\ x := 1\ \{\Theta x=0\}$

(b)    $\{true\}$ **skip** $\{x=\Theta x\}$

(c)    $\{\neg def_\Theta\}\ x := x+5\ \{Len=1\}$

(d)    $\{true\}\ \langle$**if** *false* $\rightarrow$ **skip fi**$\rangle\ \{Len=0\}$

(e)    $\{true\}\ \langle$**if** *false* $\rightarrow$ **skip fi**$\rangle\ \{Len=55\}$

(f)    $\{Len=0\}\ x := x+1\ \{Len=1\}\ x := x+1\ \{Len=2\}$

(g)    $\{x=0\}\ x := x+1\ \{x=1\}\ x := x+1\ \{x=Mx\}$

(h)    For *Fixed_x* defined in exercise 7.6(a):

$$\{\neg def_\Theta\}$$
$$\textbf{do } y>0 \rightarrow \{y>0 \wedge Fixed\_x\}$$
$$y := y-1$$
$$\{y\geq 0 \wedge Fixed\_x\}$$
$$\textbf{od } \{y\leq 0 \wedge Fixed\_x\}$$

(i)    For *NonPos* defined in exercise 7.6(b):

$$\{\neg def_\Theta\}$$
$$\textbf{do } x\geq 0 \rightarrow \{x\geq 0\}$$
$$x := x-1$$
$$\{x\geq 0\}$$
$$\textbf{od } \{x<0 \wedge NonPos\}$$

(j)    For $\diamondsuit P$ defined in exercise 7.5:

$$\{x=0 \wedge \neg def_\Theta\}$$
$$\textbf{cobegin}$$
$$\{x=0\}\ x := 1\ \{x=1\}$$
$$\|$$
$$\{x=0 \vee \diamondsuit(x=0)\}$$
$$\textbf{if } x=0 \rightarrow \{x=0 \vee \diamondsuit(x=0)\} \textbf{ skip } \{x=0 \vee \diamondsuit(x=0)\}$$
$$[]\ x\neq 0 \rightarrow \{x=1 \wedge \diamondsuit(x=0)\} \textbf{ skip } \{x=1 \wedge \diamondsuit(x=0)\}$$
$$\textbf{fi } \{\diamondsuit(x=0)\}$$
$$\textbf{coend } \{\diamondsuit(x=0)\}$$

**7.16.** Prove that if $PO(S)$ is a theorem of Proof Outline Logic, then so is

$$\{pre(PO(S))\}\ PO(S)\ \{post(PO(S)) \wedge \boxdot I_{PO(S)}\}$$

where $\boxdot$ is defined in exercise 7.9.

**7.17.** Without using auxiliary variables, show that the mutual exclusion protocol of Figure 7.3 satisfies First-Come First-Served Entry (7.29).

**7.18.** For each of the programs in exercise 6.9:

    (a)    Devise a reasonable definition for derived term *WL* used in First-Come First-Served Entry (7.29).

    (b)    Establish whether the given program satisfies First-Come First-Served Entry (7.29) by either constructing a counterexample or giving a proof outline that can be used to prove that property. Do not use auxiliary variables.

    (c)    Repeat (b), using an auxiliary variable *w* that simulates *WL*.

**7.19.** (a)    Formalize in Temporal Logic the property that derived term *Len* of exercise 7.4 is monotonically nondecreasing during any execution of a program *S*.

    (b)    Prove that *Len* is monotonically nondecreasing during execution of the program in Figure 4.2.

**7.20.** Explain how Proof Outline Logic can be used to reason about the number of atomic actions executed by a program.

**7.21.** Consider the reader/writer problem of exercise 6.15. There, the requirements of parts (a) and (c) do not prevent writer processes from causing reader processes to be forever blocked at *start_read* operations. This unpleasant behavior can be avoided by preventing a new write operation *write$_i$* from starting when there are readers that started waiting before *writer$_i$* executed *start_write*. Formalize this requirement and derive new protocols that, in addition, satisfy the requirements of (a) and (c).

**7.22.** Generalize the concurrent reading while writing protocol in Figure 7.2 to the case where there are N reader processes and a single writer process.

**7.23.** The solution to the concurrent reading while writing problem given in Figure 7.2 involves a shared variable *q*, which is written by both *R* and *W*. It is possible to modify the protocol by adding variables so that each variable is written by only one process. Perform this modification and justify each step in terms of Proof Outline Logic obligations.

**7.24.** Prove that any protocol satisfying *Init* $\Rightarrow \Box \neg (in(WRITE) \wedge in(READ))$ also satisfies (7.11).

**7.25.** Consider a system of N processes, where each executes operations *READ* and *WRITE*. Let derived term *Ar* be the number of processes that are executing *READ* operations and let derived term *Aw* be the number of processes that are executing *WRITE* operations.

    (a)    Give formal definitions for derived terms *Ar* and *Aw*.

    (b)    Prove that any program satisfying

$$Init_S \Rightarrow \Box(Aw=0 \vee (Aw=1 \wedge Ar=0))$$

    also satisfies (7.11).

**7.26.** Another solution to the concurrent reading while writing problem of §7.4 is based on the following observation:

    If the number of writes that have completed before the start of a read is equal to the number of writes that have started by the end of that read, then that read did not overlap any write.

Use this observation to derive an alternative to the program of Figure 7.2. (Hint: implement predicate $p$ in terms of integer counters for the number of writes that have started and the number that have completed.)

**7.27.** In each of the following programs, indicate which of $x$, $y$, and $z$ could be auxiliary given that $a$, $b$, and $c$ are not auxiliary.

(a)  $\langle x,y,z := a,b,b \ \ a := x+y \rangle$

(b)  $\langle x,y := a,b \ \ z := b \ \ a := x+y \rangle$

(c)  $\langle x,y := a,b \ \ z := b \rangle \ a := x+y$

(d)  $\langle x := a \ \ y := b \ \ z := b \ \ a := x+y \rangle$

(e)  **if** $x \geq 0 \rightarrow$ **skip** [] $x \leq 0 \rightarrow \langle x := -x \ \ y := true \rangle$**fi**

(f)  $\langle$**if** $x \geq 0 \rightarrow$ **skip** [] $x \leq 0 \rightarrow y := true$ **fi**$\rangle$

(g)  **if** $x \geq 0 \rightarrow$ **skip** [] $x \leq 0 \rightarrow \langle$**skip** $y := true \rangle$ **fi**

(h)  $y := 0$ **do** $y \leq 5 \rightarrow \langle x := 0 \ \ y := y - 1 \rangle$ **od**

(i)  $y := 0$ **do** $y \leq 5 \rightarrow \langle x := 0 \ \ y := y - 1 \rangle$ **od** $a := x$

**7.28.** Show that Adding an Auxiliary Variable (7.18) implies (7.22).

**7.29.** (a)  Show that the order in which auxiliary variables are deleted by repeated use of Auxiliary Variable Deletion Rule (7.19) is irrelevant.

(b)  When multiple auxiliary variables have been added to a program, is it always possible to delete them in any order by using Auxiliary Variable Deletion Rule (7.19)?

**7.30.** Show that premise (b) of Auxiliary Variable Deletion Rule (7.19) is satisfied for the proof outline of Figure 7.5.

**7.31.** According to Adding an Auxiliary Variable (7.18), assignments to auxiliary variables may not be added to guard evaluation actions.

(a)  If it were possible to associate an auxiliary variable assignment with execution of a guard evaluation action, could all derived terms then be specified computationally?

(b)  If it were possible to associate a different auxiliary variable assignment with each possible outcome of executing a guard evaluation action, could all derived terms then be specified computationally?

**7.32.** In the list of properties and programs that follows:

(i)  Give a Temporal Logic formula that specifies the property, defining any derived terms that you use.

(ii)  Augment the program with auxiliary variables that simulate these derived terms.

(iii)  Construct a proof outline for the augmented program.

(iv)  Using that proof outline, derive a proof outline that can be used to verify the property formalized in (i).

(a)   Property: *x* remains 0 until execution has terminated.

     Program: $x,y := 0,15$
             **do** $y>0 \rightarrow y := y-1$ **od**
             $x := 23$

(b)   Property: The value of *x* never increases after it has decreased.

     Program: $x,y := 50,50$
               **cobegin**
                   **do** $y=50 \rightarrow x := x+1$
                     [] $y=50 \rightarrow$ **skip** **od**
                ||
                   **do** $y=50 \rightarrow y := 49$
                     [] $y=49 \wedge x>0 \rightarrow x := x-1$ **od**
               **coend**

(c)   Property: *x* is never positive after it becomes negative.

     Program: $x,y := 35,76$
               **cobegin**
                   **do** $x>0 \rightarrow x := x+1$
                     [] $x>0 \rightarrow x := x-1$
                     [] $x\leq0 \rightarrow x := x-1$
                   **od**
                ||
                   **do** $x>0 \rightarrow x := x+1$
                     [] $x>0 \rightarrow x := x-1$
                     [] $x\leq0 \rightarrow x := x-1$
                   **od**
               **coend**

(d)   Property: The same critical section is not executed more than 5 times
                 consecutively.

     Program: *free* := *false* *time0*, *time1*, *time2* := $0,0,0$
               **cobegin**
                   **do** *true* $\rightarrow$ ⟨**if** *free* $\wedge$ *time0*$<5 \rightarrow$ *free* := *false* **fi**⟩
                         $CS_0$
                         *time0*, *time1*, *time2* := *time0*$+1,0,0$
                         *free* := *true* **od**
                ||
                   **do** *true* $\rightarrow$ ⟨**if** *free* $\wedge$ *time1* $<5 \rightarrow$ *free* := *false* **fi**⟩
                         $CS_1$
                         *time0*, *time1*, *time2* := $0,$*time1*$+1,0$
                         *free* := *true* **od**
                ||
                   **do** *true* $\rightarrow$ ⟨**if** *free* $\wedge$ *time2* $<5 \rightarrow$ *free* := *false* **fi**⟩
                         $CS_2$
                         *time0*, *time1*, *time2* := $0,0,$*time2*$+1$
                         *free* := *true* **od**
               **coend**

(e)   Property: Processes execute their critical sections in round-robin order.
      Program: $turn := 0$
            **cobegin**
              **do** $true \rightarrow$ **if** $turn = 0 \rightarrow$ **skip fi**
                   $CS_0$
                   $turn := (turn + 1)$ **mod** 3   **od**
          $\parallel$
              **do** $true \rightarrow$ **if** $turn = 1 \rightarrow$ **skip fi**
                   $CS_1$
                   $turn := (turn + 1)$ **mod** 3   **od**
          $\parallel$
              **do** $true \rightarrow$ **if** $turn = 2 \rightarrow$ **skip fi**
                   $CS_2$
                   $turn := (turn + 1)$ **mod** 3   **od**
            **coend**

(f)   Property: $t$ is the number of times any process has executed its critical section.
      Program: $free := false$
            **cobegin**
              $\langle$**if** $free \rightarrow free := false$ **fi**$\rangle$
              $CS_1$
              $free := false$
          $\parallel$
              $\langle$**if** $free \rightarrow free := false$ **fi**$\rangle$
              $CS_2$
              $free := false$
            **coend**

# Chapter 8

# Verifying Arbitrary
# Temporal Logic Properties

Additional axioms and rules are needed for us to go beyond safety properties and be able to reason about properties specified by arbitrary Temporal Logic formulas. These axioms and inference rules of $S$-Temporal Logic are given in this chapter. We also discuss fairness assumptions for **cobegin** implementations, because satisfying a liveness property often requires making assumptions that specific processes will have opportunities to execute. Finally, we describe helpful actions and other techniques for proving eventualities.

## 8.1  $S$-Temporal Logic Revisited

Recall from Chapter 6 that $S$-Temporal Logic is the result of combining Temporal Logic and Proof Outline Logic. Chapters 6 and 7 give rules only for proving safety properties. In this chapter, by adding just a few axioms and inference rules, we obtain a sound and complete logic for verifying any property that can be specified by a Temporal Logic formula. This permits $S$-Temporal Logic to be used for proving all safety properties, liveness properties, and their combinations.[1]

We complete $S$-Temporal Logic by extending it with axioms and inference rules that characterize $\mathcal{H}_S^+$. To see why this works, let $P$ be any Temporal Logic formula that is $\mathcal{H}_S^+$-valid, and let $H_1, H_2, ..., H_n$ be a finite set of Temporal Logic

---

[1]Thus, for proving invariance properties and historical safety properties, $S$-Temporal Logic becomes an alternative to the methods of Chapters 6 and 7. Each method has advantages. The primary advantage of the methods in Chapters 6 and 7 is that reasoning can be done in terms of proof outlines and is, therefore, tightly coupled to the program text. The methods of this chapter, however, do not require a property to be in the form $Init \Rightarrow \Box Etern$.

formulas that are satisfied by elements of $\mathcal{H}_S^+$ and no others. (A finite set of formulas suffices because the number of atomic actions in $S$ is finite and the effects of each atomic action can be characterized by a single Temporal Logic formula.) Thus, by construction, an anchored sequence is in $\mathcal{H}_S^+$ iff it satisfies $H_1 \wedge H_2 \wedge \cdots \wedge H_n$.

We now show that if $H_1, H_2, ..., H_n$ are provable in $S$-Temporal Logic, then so is any $\mathcal{H}_S^+$-valid formula $P$. Since ordinary Temporal Logic is sound for all anchored sequences,

(8.1)   $H_1 \wedge H_2 \wedge \cdots \wedge H_n \implies P$

is valid—it is trivially valid for an anchored sequence that does not satisfy $H_1 \wedge H_2 \wedge \cdots \wedge H_n$, and because $P$ is $\mathcal{H}_S^+$-valid, (8.1) is also satisfied by an anchored sequence that does satisfy $H_1 \wedge H_2 \wedge \cdots \wedge H_n$. Ordinary Temporal Logic is complete, so we conclude that (8.1), being valid, is provable. We therefore can obtain an $S$-Temporal Logic proof of $P$ by extending the proof of (8.1), first with proofs for $H_1$ through $H_n$ and then with TL Modus Ponens (3.8) steps that eliminate each $H_i$ from the antecedent of (8.1).

All that remains is to give axioms and inference rules for deriving $H_1, H_2, ..., H_n$, the Temporal Logic characterization of $\mathcal{H}_S^+$. $\mathcal{H}_S^+$ is defined by Program-Execution Interpretations (3.81). Thus, for any anchored sequence $(\sigma, j)$ an element of $\mathcal{H}_S^+$:

  (i)  if $\sigma$ is finite, then no atomic action is enabled in the final state of $\sigma$, and

  (ii) for $i$ satisfying $0 \le i+j+1 < |\sigma|$, $\sigma[i+j+1]$ is the result of executing some enabled atomic action in $\sigma[i+j]$.

To formalize (i) in Temporal Logic, we use a predicate $exec(S)$ that is satisfied by all states in which an atomic action of $S$ can be executed:

$$exec(S): \quad \bigvee_{\alpha \in \mathcal{A}(S)} (at(\alpha) \wedge enbl(\alpha))$$

Because of the meaning given to $\bigcirc$ by Interpreting Temporal Logic Formula (3.4), if $\sigma$ is finite then for $P$ a Temporal Logic formula, $P = \bigcirc P$ is satisfied in the final position of $\sigma$. Thus, from (i) we get the following axiom of $S$-Temporal Logic.

(8.2)   $\mathcal{H}_S^+$ *Stutter Axiom*:  For $S$ the entire program and $P$ any Temporal Logic formula:

$$\neg exec(S) \implies P = \bigcirc P$$

We formalize (ii), that $\sigma[i+j+1]$ is the result of executing some enabled atomic action in $\sigma[i+j]$, in two parts. The first part asserts that some enabled atomic action must be executed and says how control predicates *at* and *after* change value in successive (and unequal) states of an anchored sequence. Specifically, provided that some atomic action can be executed:

- For one atomic action $\alpha$ in $\mathcal{A}(S)$: $at(\alpha)$ becomes *false* and $after(\alpha)$ becomes *true*.

- For all other atomic actions $\alpha'$ in $\mathcal{A}(S)$ such that $\alpha \parallel \alpha'$: $at(\alpha')$ and $after(\alpha')$ remain unchanged.

This is formalized as the following *S*-Temporal Logic axiom:[2]

(8.3)   $\mathcal{H}_S^+$ *Control Axiom*:   For *S* the entire program:

$$exec(S) \Rightarrow \bigvee_{\alpha \in \mathcal{A}(S)} (at(\alpha) \wedge enbl(\alpha) \wedge \bigcirc after(\alpha) \wedge (\bigwedge_{\substack{\alpha' \in \mathcal{A}(S) \\ \alpha \parallel \alpha'}} frzn(\alpha')))$$

where

$$frzn(\alpha):  at(\alpha) = \bigcirc at(\alpha) \wedge after(\alpha) = \bigcirc after(\alpha)$$

Note that although each of the disjuncts in $\mathcal{H}_S^+$ Control Axiom (8.3) does not explicitly mention all the control predicates that remain unchanged for the process containing $\alpha$, this information is easily derived from what is mentioned there along with the control predicate axioms for the process containing $\alpha$.

The second part of our Temporal Logic characterization of (ii) formalizes how execution of an enabled atomic action $\alpha$ affects the state. We use Proof Outline Logic for this task rather than define an *S*-Temporal Logic axiom for each type of atomic action.

(8.4)   $\mathcal{H}_S^+$ *Triple Rule*:   $\dfrac{\{P\}\,\alpha\,\{Q\}}{at(\alpha) \wedge P \Rightarrow \bigcirc(after(\alpha) \Rightarrow Q)}$

Observe that in contrast to $\mathcal{H}_S^+$ Control Axiom (8.3), this rule does not say anything about whether $\alpha$ or any another atomic action actually is executed.

It is instructive to compare $\mathcal{H}_S^+$ Triple Rule (8.4) with Proof Outline Invariant Rule (6.7). The conclusion of (8.4) is an $\mathcal{H}_S^+$-valid *S*-Temporal Logic formula, even though its premise concerns $\mathcal{H}_\alpha^+$-validity.[3] The conclusion of Proof Outline Invariant Rule (6.7) is also an $\mathcal{H}_S^+$-valid *S*-Temporal Logic formula, but its premise involves $\mathcal{H}_S^+$-validity. Thus, $\mathcal{H}_S^+$ Triple Rule (8.4) allows us to conclude something about a program by reasoning about its parts, whereas Proof Outline Invariant Rule (6.7) does not.

From $\mathcal{H}_S^+$ Control Axiom (8.3) and $\mathcal{H}_S^+$ Triple Rule (8.4), we obtain a derived inference rule of *S*-Temporal Logic that enables conclusions about an entire program to be deduced from conclusions about its individual atomic actions.

---

[2]Recall from §5.2 that $\alpha \parallel \beta$ denotes that $\alpha$ is an atomic action in one process of some **cobegin** and $\beta$ is an atomic action in a different process of that **cobegin**.

[3]According to Valid Proof Outline (4.17), if premise $\{P\}\,\alpha\,\{Q\}$ is a theorem, then $I_{PO(\alpha)} \Rightarrow \Box I_{PO(\alpha)}$ is $\mathcal{H}_\alpha^+$-valid.

(8.5)   *Combining Rule*:   $\dfrac{\text{For all } \alpha \in \mathcal{A}(S):\ at(\alpha) \wedge P \ \Rightarrow\ \bigcirc(after(\alpha) \Rightarrow Q)}{exec(S) \wedge P \ \Rightarrow\ \bigcirc Q}$

To justify this rule, we show how to prove its conclusion if its premises have already been proved.

$exec(S) \wedge P$

$\Rightarrow$     «$\mathcal{H}_S^+$ Control Axiom (8.3)»

$P \ \wedge \displaystyle\bigvee_{\alpha \in \mathcal{A}(S)} (at(\alpha) \wedge enbl(\alpha) \wedge \bigcirc after(\alpha) \wedge ( \bigwedge_{\substack{\alpha' \in \mathcal{A}(S) \\ \alpha \parallel \alpha'}} frzn(\alpha')))$

$\Rightarrow$     «Antecedent-Strengthening Law (2.29)»

$P \ \wedge \displaystyle\bigvee_{\alpha \in \mathcal{A}(S)} (at(\alpha) \wedge \bigcirc after(\alpha))$

$=$     «Choose $\beta$ not occurring free in $P$ or $Q$; Bound Variable Renaming Rule (2.70)»

$P \ \wedge \displaystyle\bigvee_{\beta \in \mathcal{A}(S)} (at(\beta) \wedge \bigcirc after(\beta))$

$=$     «Propositional reasoning, since $\beta$ does not occur free in $P$»

$\displaystyle\bigvee_{\beta \in \mathcal{A}(S)} (P \wedge at(\beta) \wedge \bigcirc after(\beta))$

$\Rightarrow$     «Premise implies $at(\beta) \wedge P \wedge \bigcirc after(\beta) \ \Rightarrow\ \bigcirc Q$»

$\displaystyle\bigvee_{\beta \in \mathcal{A}(S)} \bigcirc Q$

$=$     «Propositional reasoning, since $\beta$ does not occur free in $Q$»

$\bigcirc Q$

One useful consequence of Combining Rule (8.5) is:

(8.6)   *Past $\bigcirc$ Law*:   For Predicate Logic formula $P$: $exec(S) \wedge P \Rightarrow \bigcirc \ominus P$

This law follows because $\{P\} \ \alpha \ \{\ominus P\}$ is a theorem for any atomic action $\alpha$ (as was shown in §7.3). So, using $\mathcal{H}_S^+$ Triple Rule (8.4), we conclude $at(\alpha) \wedge P \Rightarrow \bigcirc(after(\alpha) \Rightarrow Q)$ for all $\alpha$ in $\mathcal{A}(S)$, and the desired result then follows from Combining Rule (8.5). Notice that Past $\bigcirc$ Law (8.6) is a formula only when $P$ is a formula of Predicate Logic and not Temporal Logic. This is so because if $P$ contains a temporal operator, then $\ominus P$ would not be a formula.

## Unbounded *x+y* Example

To illustrate the use of these *S*-Temporal Logic axioms and inference rules, we prove that execution of the program in Figure 8.1 causes $x+y$ to exceed any value. Note that $x$ and $y$ are not given initial values by the program. However, because $x$ and $y$ are declared to be of type integer, we conclude from Program Variable Axioms (4.6) that they each will have some integer value when execution starts.

$S$:  **var** $x, y$ : Int
    **cobegin**
        $L_1$:  **do** *true* $\to$ $T_1$:  $x := x+1$ **od**
    ‖
        $L_2$:  **do** *true* $\to$ $T_2$:  $y := y+1$ **od**
    **coend**

**Figure 8.1.** Computing unbounded $x+y$

---

The property that $x+y$ eventually exceeds any integer N is formalized in Temporal Logic as the eventuality $at(S) \wedge N \in \text{Int} \Rightarrow \Diamond(x+y \geq N)$.  Since $at(S) \wedge N \in \text{Int} \Rightarrow in(S) \wedge N \in \text{Int}$ holds, it suffices to prove:

(8.7)   $in(S) \wedge N \in \text{Int} \Rightarrow \Diamond(x+y \geq N)$

Two rules are given in §3.3 for proving properties of this form: Well-Founded $\Diamond$ Induction Rule (3.68) and Natural Number $\Diamond$ Induction Rule (3.69). The latter seems a better choice for this problem, since $x$ and $y$ are being increased by integers. The conclusion of Natural Number $\Diamond$ Induction Rule (3.69) involves a rigid variable R. We therefore reformulate (8.7) in terms of such a rigid variable; R bounds the amount by which $x+y$ must be increased in order to satisfy $x+y \geq N$.

$\quad in(S) \wedge N \in \text{Int} \Rightarrow \Diamond(x+y \geq N)$
=     «Textual Substitution, since R does not occur free»
$\quad (in(S) \wedge N \in \text{Int} \Rightarrow \Diamond(x+y \geq N))^{R}_{\max(0,\, N-(x+y))}$
=     «TL One-Point Law (3.61a)»
$\quad (\forall R:\ R = \max(0, N-(x+y)):\ in(S) \wedge N \in \text{Int} \Rightarrow \Diamond(x+y \geq N))$
=     «TL Range Law (3.46a)»
$\quad (\forall R:\ R = \max(0, N-(x+y)) \wedge in(S) \wedge N \in \text{Int} \Rightarrow \Diamond(x+y \geq N))$
=     «*VarAx(S)* $\Rightarrow$ ($x \in \text{Int} \wedge y \in \text{Int}$),
$\quad\quad x \in \text{Int} \wedge y \in \text{Int} \wedge N \in \text{Int} \Rightarrow \max(0, N-(x+y)) \in \text{Nat}$»
$\quad (\forall R:\ R \in \text{Nat} \wedge R = \max(0, N-(x+y)) \wedge in(S) \wedge N \in \text{Int}$
$\quad\quad \Rightarrow \Diamond(x+y \geq N))$
=     «TL Range Law (3.46a)»
$\quad (\forall R \in \text{Nat}:\ R = \max(0, N-(x+y)) \wedge in(S) \wedge N \in \text{Int} \Rightarrow \Diamond(x+y \geq N))$

Thus, (8.7) is equivalent to $(\forall R \in \text{Nat}:\ P \Rightarrow \Diamond Q)$, where:

$P$:  $R = \max(0, N-(x+y)) \wedge in(S) \wedge N \in \text{Int}$

$Q$:  $x+y \geq N$

First, premise $P_0^R \Rightarrow \Diamond Q$ of Natural Number $\Diamond$ Induction Rule (3.69) is straightforward to discharge.

$$P_0^R$$
$=$    «Textual Substitution (2.71)»
$$0 = \max(0, N - (x+y)) \wedge in(S) \wedge N \in \text{Int}$$
$\Rightarrow$    «$VarAx(S) \Rightarrow x \in \text{Int} \wedge y \in \text{Int}$,
$\quad\quad x \in \text{Int} \wedge y \in \text{Int} \wedge N \in \text{Int} \wedge 0 = \max(0, N - (x+y)) \Rightarrow x+y \geq N$»
$$(x+y) \geq N$$
$\Rightarrow$    «$\Diamond$ Law (3.16c)»
$$\Diamond(x+y \geq N)$$

The second premise,

(8.8)   $(\forall V \in \text{Nat}: \ P_{V+1}^R \Rightarrow \Diamond(Q \vee P_V^R))$

becomes easy to discharge once we have proved

(8.9)   $x+y=W \wedge in(S) \Rightarrow \Diamond(x+y=W+1 \wedge in(S))$

because (8.8) is equivalent to $(\forall V: \ V \in \text{Nat} \wedge P_{V+1}^R \Rightarrow \Diamond(Q \vee P_V^R))$ and we have the following:

$$V \in \text{Nat} \wedge P_{V+1}^R$$
$=$    «Textual Substitution (2.71)»
$$V \in \text{Nat} \wedge V+1 = \max(0, N - (x+y)) \wedge in(S) \wedge N \in \text{Int}$$
$\Rightarrow$    «$V \in \text{Nat} \wedge V+1 = \max(0, N - (x+y))$
$\quad\quad \Rightarrow V+1 = N - (x+y) \wedge N > (x+y)$»
$$V+1 = N - (x+y) \wedge N > x+y \wedge in(S) \wedge N \in \text{Int}$$
$\Rightarrow$    «(8.9)»
$$\Diamond(V = N - (x+y) \wedge N \geq x+y \wedge in(S)) \wedge N \in \text{Int}$$
$=$    «Frame Law (3.66b)»
$$\Diamond(V = N - (x+y) \wedge N \geq x+y \wedge in(S)) \wedge \Box(N \in \text{Int})$$
$\Rightarrow$    «$\Diamond$ Law (3.16h)»
$$\Diamond(V = N - (x+y) \wedge N \geq x+y \wedge in(S) \wedge N \in \text{Int})$$
$\Rightarrow$    «definition of $\max(a, b)$, since $x \in \text{Int} \wedge y \in \text{Int}$
$\quad\quad$ from $VarAx(S)$»
$$\Diamond(V = \max(0, N - (x+y)) \wedge in(S) \wedge N \in \text{Int})$$
$\Rightarrow$    «definition of $P$»
$$\Diamond P_V^R$$
$\Rightarrow$    «Consequent-Weakening Law (2.30)»
$$\Diamond(Q \vee P_V^R)$$

Thus, all that remains is to prove (8.9).

We start our proof of (8.9) by analyzing how each of the program's atomic actions affects the value of $x+y$. There are four atomic actions: $GEval_{do}(L_1)$,

$T_1$, $GEval_{do}(L_2)$, and $T_2$. For each, we construct a proof outline having as its precondition $x+y=W$ and then use $\mathcal{H}_S^+$ Triple Rule (8.4) to obtain an $S$-Temporal Logic theorem that characterizes the triple:

(8.10)  $at(L_1) \wedge x+y=W \Rightarrow (\bigcirc at(T_1) \Rightarrow \bigcirc(x+y=W))$

(8.11)  $at(T_1) \wedge x+y=W \Rightarrow (\bigcirc after(T_1) \Rightarrow \bigcirc(x+y=W+1))$

(8.12)  $at(L_2) \wedge x+y=W \Rightarrow (\bigcirc at(T_2) \Rightarrow \bigcirc(x+y=W))$

(8.13)  $at(T_2) \wedge x+y=W \Rightarrow (\bigcirc after(T_2) \Rightarrow \bigcirc(x+y=W+1))$

Here, for example, is the proof of (8.13).

      «Proof Outline Logic»
        1.  $\{x+y=W\}$  $T_2$  $\{x+y=W+1\}$

      «$\mathcal{H}_S^+$ Triple Rule (8.4) with 1»
        2.  $at(T_2) \wedge x+y=W \Rightarrow \bigcirc(after(T_2) \Rightarrow x+y=W+1)$

        3.      $at(T_2) \wedge x+y=W \Rightarrow \bigcirc(after(T_2) \Rightarrow x+y=W+1)$
        $\Rightarrow$     «$\bigcirc$ Axiom (3.21b)»
          $at(T_2) \wedge x+y=W \Rightarrow (\bigcirc after(T_2) \Rightarrow \bigcirc(x+y=W+1))$

    We are now ready to prove (8.9). The proof is based on showing that at most two atomic actions can be executed before $T_1$ or $T_2$ must be executed. Don't be discouraged by the length of this proof. Derived rules discussed later in this chapter will allow proofs to be shortened considerably.

        $x+y=W \wedge in(S)$
    $=$      «$in(S)=exec(S)$ for this program»
        $x+y=W \wedge exec(S)$
    $\Rightarrow$    «$\mathcal{H}_S^+$ Control Axiom (8.3); Antecedent-Strengthening Law (2.29)»
        $x+y=W \wedge (\quad (at(L_1) \wedge \bigcirc at(T_1))$
                      $\vee\ (at(T_1) \wedge \bigcirc after(T_1))$
                      $\vee\ (at(L_2) \wedge \bigcirc at(T_2))$
                      $\vee\ (at(T_2) \wedge \bigcirc after(T_2)))$
    $\Rightarrow$    «(8.10), (8.11), (8.12), (8.13)»
        $(\bigcirc at(T_1) \wedge \bigcirc(x+y=W))$
        $\vee\ (\bigcirc after(T_1) \wedge \bigcirc(x+y=W+1))$
        $\vee\ (\bigcirc at(T_2) \wedge \bigcirc(x+y=W))$
        $\vee\ (\bigcirc after(T_2) \wedge \bigcirc(x+y=W+1))$

$=$          «Propositional reasoning»

$((\bigcirc after(T_1) \vee \bigcirc after(T_2)) \wedge \bigcirc (x+y=W+1))$
$\vee ((\bigcirc at(T_1) \vee \bigcirc at(T_2)) \wedge \bigcirc (x+y=W))$

$=$          «$\bigcirc$ Law (3.22a) and (3.22b)»

$\bigcirc ((after(T_1) \vee after(T_2)) \wedge x+y=W+1)$
$\vee \bigcirc ((at(T_1) \vee at(T_2)) \wedge x+y=W)$

$\Rightarrow$          «$\mathcal{H}_S^+$ Control Axiom (8.3), since $at(T_1) \vee at(T_2) \Rightarrow exec(S)$
          Antecedent-Strengthening Law (2.29)»

$\bigcirc ((after(T_1) \vee after(T_2)) \wedge x+y=W+1)$
$\vee \bigcirc (x+y=W \wedge (\quad (at(T_1) \wedge \bigcirc after(T_1))$
$\qquad\qquad\qquad\quad \vee (at(T_2) \wedge \bigcirc after(T_2))$
$\qquad\qquad\qquad\quad \vee (at(T_1) \wedge at(L_2) \wedge \bigcirc at(T_2) \wedge \bigcirc at(T_1))$
$\qquad\qquad\qquad\quad \vee (at(T_2) \wedge at(L_1) \wedge \bigcirc at(T_1) \wedge \bigcirc at(T_2))))$

$=$          «Propositional reasoning»

$\bigcirc ((after(T_1) \vee after(T_2)) \wedge x+y=W+1)$
$\vee \bigcirc (\quad (x+y=W \wedge at(T_1) \wedge \bigcirc after(T_1))$
$\qquad\quad \vee (x+y=W \wedge at(T_2) \wedge \bigcirc after(T_2))$
$\qquad\quad \vee (x+y=W \wedge at(T_1) \wedge at(L_2) \wedge \bigcirc at(T_2) \wedge \bigcirc at(T_1))$
$\qquad\quad \vee (x+y=W \wedge at(T_2) \wedge at(L_1) \wedge \bigcirc at(T_1) \wedge \bigcirc at(T_2)))$

$\Rightarrow$          «(8.10), (8.11), (8.12), (8.13)»

$\bigcirc ((after(T_1) \vee after(T_2)) \wedge x+y=W+1)$
$\vee \bigcirc (\quad (\bigcirc after(T_1) \wedge \bigcirc (x+y=W+1))$
$\qquad\quad \vee (\bigcirc after(T_2) \wedge \bigcirc (x+y=W+1))$
$\qquad\quad \vee (\bigcirc at(T_2) \wedge \bigcirc at(T_1) \wedge \bigcirc (x+y=W))$
$\qquad\quad \vee (\bigcirc at(T_1) \wedge \bigcirc at(T_2) \wedge \bigcirc (x+y=W)))$

$=$          «Propositional reasoning»

$\bigcirc ((after(T_1) \vee after(T_2)) \wedge x+y=W+1)$
$\vee \bigcirc (\quad ((\bigcirc after(T_1) \vee \bigcirc after(T_2)) \wedge \bigcirc (x+y=W+1))$
$\qquad\quad \vee (\bigcirc at(T_2) \wedge \bigcirc at(T_1) \wedge \bigcirc (x+y=W)))$

$=$          «$\bigcirc$ Law (3.22a) and (3.22b)»

$\bigcirc ((after(T_1) \vee after(T_2)) \wedge x+y=W+1)$
$\vee \bigcirc \bigcirc ((after(T_1) \vee after(T_2)) \wedge x+y=W+1)$
$\vee \bigcirc \bigcirc (at(T_2) \wedge at(T_1) \wedge x+y=W)$

$\Rightarrow$          «$\mathcal{H}_S^+$ Control Axiom (8.3), since $at(T_1) \wedge at(T_2) \Rightarrow exec(S)$
          Antecedent-Strengthening Law (2.29)»

$\bigcirc ((after(T_1) \vee after(T_2)) \wedge x+y=W+1)$
$\vee \bigcirc \bigcirc ((after(T_1) \vee after(T_2)) \wedge x+y=W+1)$
$\vee \bigcirc \bigcirc (\quad (at(T_2) \wedge \bigcirc after(T_2) \wedge x+y=W)$
$\qquad\qquad \vee (at(T_1) \wedge \bigcirc after(T_1) \wedge x+y=W))$

$\Rightarrow$ «(8.11), (8.13)»

$\bigcirc((after(T_1) \vee after(T_2)) \wedge x+y=W+1)$
$\vee \bigcirc\bigcirc((after(T_1) \vee after(T_2)) \wedge x+y=W+1)$
$\vee \bigcirc\bigcirc( \quad (\bigcirc after(T_2) \wedge \bigcirc(x+y=W+1))$
$\qquad \vee (\bigcirc after(T_1) \wedge \bigcirc(x+y=W+1)))$

$=$ «$\bigcirc$ Law (3.22a) and (3.22b)»

$\bigcirc((after(T_1) \vee after(T_2)) \wedge x+y=W+1)$
$\vee \quad \bigcirc\bigcirc((after(T_1) \vee after(T_2)) \wedge x+y=W+1)$
$\vee \bigcirc\bigcirc\bigcirc((after(T_2) \vee after(T_1)) \wedge x+y=W+1)$

$\Rightarrow$ «$\bigcirc P \Rightarrow \Diamond P, \ \bigcirc\Diamond P \Rightarrow \Diamond P$»

$\Diamond((after(T_1) \vee after(T_2)) \wedge x+y=W+1)$
$\vee \Diamond((after(T_1) \vee after(T_2)) \wedge x+y=W+1)$
$\vee \Diamond((after(T_2) \vee after(T_1)) \wedge x+y=W+1)$

$\Rightarrow$ «Control predicate axiom, $after(T_1) \vee after(T_2) \Rightarrow in(S)$»

$\Diamond(in(S) \wedge x+y=W+1)$
$\vee \Diamond(in(S) \wedge x+y=W+1)$
$\vee \Diamond(in(S) \wedge x+y=W+1)$

$=$ «Propositional reasoning»

$\Diamond(x+y=W+1 \wedge in(S))$

## 8.2 Unless Properties and Derivatives

The $S$-Temporal Logic axioms and rules of §8.1 can be painful to use, as
we have just seen. They force us to reason about each individual atomic action,
and they represent sets of interleavings by long disjunctions. Moreover, $\bigcirc$ is the
only temporal operator that appears in these axioms and rules. Most properties
of interest to us will be specified using $\square$, $\Diamond$, and $\mathcal{U}$, so further $S$-Temporal
Logic manipulations would be necessary in order to bridge the gap between the
axiomatization of §8.1 and Temporal Logic specifications for properties that
arise in practice.

Derived rules of $S$-Temporal Logic that allow direct proof of properties
involving $\square$, $\Diamond$, and $\mathcal{U}$ are one way to avoid tedious $S$-Temporal Logic manipulations. In this section, we give such rules for directly proving unless properties
of the form $P \Rightarrow P\mathcal{U}Q$ and invariants $I \Rightarrow \square I$. Later, in §8.5, we consider rules
for proving eventuality properties of the form $P \Rightarrow \Diamond Q$.

### Unless Properties

If execution of every atomic action $\alpha$ in $\mathcal{A}(S)$ truthifies $P \vee Q$ when started
in a state satisfying $P \wedge \neg Q$, then any execution of $S$ started in $P$ will satisfy
$P\mathcal{U}Q$. This gives a general method for proving unless properties.

(8.14) $\mathcal{U}$ *Property Rules*:

(a)  $$\frac{\text{For all } \alpha \in \mathcal{A}(S):\quad \{at(\alpha) \wedge P \wedge \neg Q\}\, \alpha\, \{P \vee Q\}}{P \Rightarrow P\,\mathcal{U}\,Q}$$

(b)  $$\frac{\text{For all } \alpha \in \mathcal{A}(S):\quad \{at(\alpha) \wedge P\}\, \alpha\, \{P \vee Q\}}{P \Rightarrow P\,\mathcal{U}\,Q}$$

A formal justification for these derived rules shows how to prove $P \Rightarrow P\,\mathcal{U}\,Q$ from the premise of each. We give the justification here only for $\mathcal{U}$ Property Rule (8.14b) and leave the other for the exercises.

«$\mathcal{H}_S^+$ Stutter Axiom (8.2)»
1.  $\neg exec(S) \wedge P \;\Rightarrow\; \bigcirc P$

«$\mathcal{H}_S^+$ Triple Rule (8.4) and premise of $\mathcal{U}$ Property Rule (8.14b)»
2.  For all $\alpha \in \mathcal{A}(S)$:  $at(\alpha) \wedge P \;\Rightarrow\; \bigcirc(after(\alpha) \Rightarrow P \vee Q)$

«Combining Rule (8.5) with 2»
3.  $exec(S) \wedge P \;\Rightarrow\; \bigcirc(P \vee Q)$

4.  $(\neg exec(S) \wedge P \;\Rightarrow\; \bigcirc P) \wedge (exec(S) \wedge P \;\Rightarrow\; \bigcirc(P \vee Q))$
    $\Rightarrow$   «Consequent-Weakening Law (2.30»
    $(\neg exec(S) \wedge P \;\Rightarrow\; \bigcirc(P \vee Q)) \wedge (exec(S) \wedge P \;\Rightarrow\; \bigcirc(P \vee Q))$
    $\Rightarrow$   «Constructive Dilemma Law (2.33b)); Distributive Law (2.16b)»
    $(\neg exec(S) \vee exec(S)) \wedge P \;\Rightarrow\; \bigcirc(P \vee Q))$
    $=$   «Excluded Middle Law (2.20); And-Simplification Law (2.26b)»
    $P \;\Rightarrow\; \bigcirc(P \vee Q)$

«$\mathcal{U}$ Induction Rule (3.36) with 4»
5.  $P \Rightarrow P\,\mathcal{U}\,Q$

To illustrate the use of $\mathcal{U}$ Property Rule (8.14b), we return to the program of Figure 8.1. That program satisfies the following, which will be useful in §8.4:

(8.15)  $at(GEval_{do}(L_1)) \wedge x=\text{W} \Rightarrow (at(GEval_{do}(L_1)) \wedge x=\text{W})\mathcal{U}(at(T_1) \wedge x=\text{W})$

(8.16)  $at(T_1) \wedge x=\text{W} \Rightarrow (at(T_1) \wedge x=\text{W})\mathcal{U}(in(L_1) \wedge x=\text{W}+1)$

The first is proved from the following theorems using $\mathcal{U}$ Property Rule (8.14b).

$\{at(GEval_{do}(L_1)) \wedge at(GEval_{do}(L_1)) \wedge x=\text{W}\}$
$GEval_{do}(L_1)$
$\{(at(GEval_{do}(L_1)) \wedge x=\text{W}) \vee (at(T_1) \wedge x=\text{W})\}$

$\{at(T_1) \wedge at(GEval_{do}(L_1)) \wedge x=\text{W}\}$
$T_1\colon\ x := x+1$
$\{(at(GEval_{do}(L_1)) \wedge x=\text{W}) \vee (at(T_1) \wedge x=\text{W})\}$

$\{at(GEval_{do}(L_2)) \land at(GEval_{do}(L_1)) \land x{=}\text{W}\}$
$GEval_{do}(L_2)$
$\{(at(GEval_{do}(L_1)) \land x{=}\text{W}) \lor (at(T_1) \land x{=}\text{W})\}$

$\{at(T_2) \land at(GEval_{do}(L_1)) \land x{=}\text{W}\}$
$T_2{:}\ y := y{+}1$
$\{(at(GEval_{do}(L_1)) \land x{=}\text{W}) \lor (at(T_1) \land x{=}\text{W})\}$

A similar proof establishes (8.16).

## *Verifying an Invariant*

An invariant $I$ for a program is a formula for which $I \Rightarrow \Box I$ is $\mathcal{H}_S^+$-valid. According to $\Box$ to $\mathcal{U}$ Law (3.29), $\Box P = P\,\mathcal{U}\,false$, so $I \Rightarrow \Box I$ is equivalent to $I \Rightarrow I\,\mathcal{U}\,false$. Thus, we can prove that a program satisfies $I \Rightarrow \Box I$, for $I$ a Predicate Logic formula,[4] by using $\mathcal{U}$ Property Rule (8.14a) or (8.14b) with $I$ for $P$ and *false* for $Q$.

(8.17)  $\Box$ *Property Rule*:  $\dfrac{\text{For all } \alpha \in \mathcal{A}(S){:}\ \ \{at(\alpha) \land I\}\ \alpha\ \{I\}}{I \Rightarrow \Box I}$

For example, we can prove

$$x{+}y{\geq}\text{N} \Rightarrow \Box(x{+}y{\geq}\text{N})$$

for the program of Figure 8.1 simply by establishing the following theorems of Proof Outline Logic.

$\{at(GEval_{do}(L_1)) \land x{+}y{\geq}\text{N}\}\ GEval_{do}(L_1))\ \{x{+}y{\geq}\text{N}\}$

$\{at(T_1) \land x{+}y{\geq}\text{N}\}\ T_1{:}\ x := x{+}1\ \{x{+}y{\geq}\text{N}\}$

$\{at(GEval_{do}(L_2)) \land x{+}y{\geq}\text{N}\}\ GEval_{do}(L_2)\ \{x{+}y{\geq}\text{N}\}$

$\{at(T_2) \land x{+}y{\geq}\text{N}\}\ T_2{:}\ y := y{+}1\ \{x{+}y{\geq}\text{N}\}$

## 8.3  Fairness Assumptions

More than one atomic action can be enabled at a time during execution of a **cobegin**. Although $\mathcal{H}_S^+$ Control Axiom (8.3) asserts that some atomic action must next be selected for execution, nothing in our $S$-Temporal Logic axiomatization rules out schedulers that discriminate when making the selection. If $P$ is a theorem of $S$-Temporal Logic, then $P$ must be satisfied by $S$ no matter what scheduler is used.

---

[4] $I$ must be a formula of Predicate Logic, or else premise $\{at(\alpha) \land I\}\ \alpha\ \{I\}$, not being a formula of Proof Outline Logic, could not be proved.

For example, having proved $at(S) \wedge N \in \text{Int} \Rightarrow \Diamond(x+y \geq N)$ for program $S$ of Figure 8.1, we can conclude that $x+y$ will exceed any N, even if $x$ is never incremented (because process $L_1$ is discriminated against, hence never executed) or if $y$ is never incremented (because $L_2$ is never executed).[5] Moreover, because we do not preclude schedulers that discriminate against $L_1$ or $L_2$, neither of

(8.18)  $at(S) \wedge N \in \text{Int} \Rightarrow \Diamond(x \geq N)$

(8.19)  $at(S) \wedge N \in \text{Int} \Rightarrow \Diamond(y \geq N)$

is satisfied by $S$ (and neither is an $S$-Temporal Logic theorem).

The **cobegin** implementations one typically encounters in practice do not discriminate when selecting atomic actions. To draw conclusions about only those executions possible with such a **cobegin**, we associate a fairness assumption with it. This fairness assumption, a Temporal Logic formula, characterizes executions (i.e., anchored sequences) that are not possible in light of the scheduler for the **cobegin** at hand.

The weakest possible fairness assumption is *true*. It rules out no executions, permitting even those where some enabled atomic action is never executed. Below, we discuss somewhat stronger fairness assumptions of practical import: unconditional fairness, weak fairness, and strong fairness. Each is defined in terms of restrictions it imposes on execution of a single atomic action. A fairness assumption for an entire program is then constructed by forming a conjunction of these, one conjunct for each atomic action of the program.

## Unconditional Fairness

The natural fairness assumption for unconditional atomic actions, called *unconditional fairness*, stipulates that an atomic action $\alpha$ not be forever blocked. Unconditional fairness for $\alpha$ means that the implementation does not discriminate against executing $\alpha$ once $at(\alpha)$ has become *true*. For the program of Figure 8.1, both (8.18) and (8.19) hold when unconditional fairness is assumed of all atomic actions, because executions consistent with these fairness assumptions cannot forever discriminate against actions in $\mathcal{A}(L_1)$ or in $\mathcal{A}(L_2)$.

It is reasonable to expect unconditional fairness of a **cobegin** implementation. When each process of the **cobegin** is executed by its own processor, known as *multiprocessing*, interleavings that omit atomic actions from some process are simply not possible. When processes share a single processor, called *multiprogramming*, each process is executed for a time-slice and then, in response to an interrupt (usually from a hardware interval-timer), is forced to relinquish the processor. The resulting situation is indistinguishable from one in which each process is executed on its own processor but instructions are executed at varying, nonzero rates.

---

[5]A **cobegin** implementation that discriminates against both $L_1$ and $L_2$ would violate $\mathcal{H}_S^+$ Control Axiom (8.3) and therefore is not of concern.

The fairness assumption $F^u_\alpha$ for unconditional fairness of an unconditional atomic action $\alpha$ rules out executions in which the entry control point of $\alpha$ is active but never executed. Thus, $F^u_\alpha$ rules out anchored sequences in which some suffix satisfies $\Box at(\alpha)$, or equivalently, it rules out anchored sequences that satisfy $\Diamond \Box at(\alpha)$. Therefore, we expect $\neg \Diamond \Box at(\alpha)$ to hold for any execution satisfying $F^u_\alpha$. Since $\neg \Diamond \Box at(\alpha)$ is equivalent to $\Box \Diamond \neg at(\alpha)$, we have:

(8.20) **Unconditional Fairness.** Fairness assumption $F^u_\alpha$ for $\alpha$ an unconditionally fair atomic action is:

$$F^u_\alpha: \quad \Box \Diamond \neg at(\alpha) \qquad\qquad \Box$$

## *Weak and Strong Fairness*

Conditional atomic actions, which cannot be executed in all states, complicate the situation. In the program of Figure 8.2, *Stop*, a conditional atomic action, can have infinitely many opportunities to be executed, yet remain blocked[6] because $c$ happens to be *false* at those times.

To reason about **cobegin** implementations whose schedulers do not discriminate against conditional or unconditional atomic actions, we introduce two other fairness assumptions. *Strong fairness* of $\alpha$ rules out executions where conditional atomic action $\alpha$ remains blocked on a condition that holds infinitely often, and *weak fairness* of $\alpha$ rules out executions where conditional atomic action $\alpha$ remains blocked on a condition that holds continuously from some point on. Strong fairness is sufficient to guarantee termination of the program in Figure 8.2, but weak fairness is not, because $c$ does not hold continuously due to *Loop*. Weak fairness is sufficient to ensure termination of the program in Figure 8.5 (unconditional fairness would not be sufficient, because *Stop* is a conditional atomic action).

Programmers are apt to prefer a **cobegin** that implements strong fairness to one that implements (only) weak fairness, because strong fairness sanctions less

---

$S$:  $T_1$:  $b, c := true, false$
      $T_2$:  **cobegin**
                   *Loop*: **do** $b \rightarrow c := true \;\; c := false$ **od**
              ||
                   *Stop*: $\langle$**if** $c \rightarrow b := false$ **fi**$\rangle$
              **coend**

**Figure 8.2.** Terminates under strong fairness

---

[6]Recall from §4.1 that the guard evaluation action for an **if** blocks until some guard holds.

discrimination. In contrast, a **cobegin** implementer will prefer supporting weak fairness over strong fairness and will prefer supporting neither to supporting either. Weak fairness of an atomic action $\alpha$ is easy to support because an implementation that samples $enbl(\alpha)$ and finds it to be *false* is then not obligated to execute $\alpha$. Thus, it suffices that the routines implementing the **cobegin** periodically receive control and update a set $Rdy$ that contains the atomic actions that satisfy $at(\alpha) \wedge enbl(\alpha)$. Weak fairness follows if the implementation allows no atomic action to remain in $Rdy$ forever—say by always removing the atomic action that has been in the set the longest and executing it.

A **cobegin** implementation that supports strong fairness may be obliged to execute an atomic action $\alpha$ even though repeated samplings of $enbl(\alpha)$ return *false*. This is because strong fairness guarantees that $\alpha$ must be executed if $enbl(\alpha)$ does not continuously remain *false*, a condition that cannot be checked by sampling $enbl(\alpha)$ periodically. Thus, to support strong fairness, the routines implementing a **cobegin** must receive control every time $enbl(\alpha)$ changes, for every atomic action $\alpha$ with $at(\alpha)$ equal to *true*. Such transfers of control are prohibitively expensive when arbitrary conditional atomic actions are allowed.

In many computing systems, the only conditional atomic actions are special synchronization commands, and these are implemented by the same operating system routines that implement **cobegin**. For this restricted set of conditional atomic actions, operating system routines do receive control every time $enbl(\alpha)$ changes; supporting strong fairness is then practical. In one scheme, the implementation maintains a set $Prio$ of atomic actions $\alpha$ that have not been executed since $at(\alpha) \wedge enbl(\alpha)$ was last *true*. The oldest atomic action $\alpha$ satisfying $at(\alpha) \wedge enbl(\alpha)$ and in $Prio$ is next selected for execution.

Strong fairness assumption $F_\alpha^s$ for a conditional atomic action $\alpha$ is formalized as follows. $F_\alpha^s$ rules out anchored sequences that have a suffix in which $\alpha$ remains blocked despite being enabled infinitely often. Thus, $F_\alpha^s$ rules out anchored sequences satisfying $\Diamond(\Box at(\alpha) \wedge \Box\Diamond enbl(\alpha))$ or, equivalently, allows only those anchored sequences satisfying $\neg\Diamond(\Box at(\alpha) \wedge \Box\Diamond enbl(\alpha))$. Since $\neg\Diamond(\Box at(\alpha) \wedge \Box\Diamond enbl(\alpha))$ is equivalent to $\Box(\Diamond\neg at(\alpha) \vee \Diamond\Box\neg enbl(\alpha))$, we have:

(8.21) **Strong Fairness.** Fairness assumption $F_\alpha^s$ for $\alpha$ a strongly fair atomic action is:

$$F_\alpha^s: \quad \Box(\Diamond\neg at(\alpha) \vee \Diamond\Box\neg enbl(\alpha)) \qquad \qquad \Box$$

Weak fairness assumption $F_\alpha^w$ rules out executions that have suffixes in which a conditional atomic action $\alpha$ remains forever blocked despite being active and continuously enabled from some point on. Thus, $F_\alpha^w$ rules out executions that satisfy $\Diamond\Box(at(\alpha) \wedge enbl(\alpha))$. Hence the anchored sequences in $\mathcal{H}_S^+$ that satisfy weak fairness are those that satisfy $\neg\Diamond\Box(at(\alpha) \wedge enbl(\alpha))$, or equivalently, $\Box\Diamond(\neg at(\alpha) \vee \neg enbl(\alpha))$.

(8.22)  **Weak Fairness.**  Fairness assumption $F_\alpha^w$ for $\alpha$ a weakly fair atomic
action is:

$$F_\alpha^w: \quad \Box\Diamond(\neg at(\alpha) \vee \neg enbl(\alpha)) \qquad\qquad \Box$$


The names strong fairness and weak fairness can be rationalized by proving that strong fairness for an atomic action $\alpha$ implies weak fairness for that
action. We prove $F_\alpha^s \Rightarrow F_\alpha^w$ by proving its contrapositive.

$\quad\neg F_\alpha^w$
$=\qquad$ «Weak Fairness (8.22)»
$\quad\neg\Box\Diamond(\neg at(\alpha) \vee \neg enbl(\alpha))$
$=\qquad$ «Temporal Logic»
$\quad\Diamond(\Box at(\alpha) \wedge \Box enbl(\alpha))$
$\Rightarrow\qquad$ «$\Diamond$ Law (3.16c)»
$\quad\Diamond(\Box at(\alpha) \wedge \Box\Diamond enbl(\alpha))$
$=\qquad$ «Temporal Logic»
$\quad\neg\Box(\Diamond\neg at(\alpha) \vee \Diamond\Box\neg enbl(\alpha))$
$=\qquad$ «Strong Fairness (8.21)»
$\quad\neg F_\alpha^s$

Also note that for an unconditional atomic action $\alpha$, strong fairness, weak fairness, and unconditional fairness are equivalent:

$\quad F_\alpha^s$
$=\qquad$ «Strong Fairness (8.21)»
$\quad\Box(\Diamond\neg at(\alpha) \vee \Diamond\Box\neg enbl(\alpha))$
$=\qquad$ «$\alpha$ is unconditional, so $enbl(\alpha)=true$»
$\quad\Box(\Diamond\neg at(\alpha) \vee \Diamond\Box false)$
$=\qquad$ «$\Diamond\Box false = false$»
$\quad\Box(\Diamond\neg at(\alpha) \vee false)$
$=\qquad$ «Or-Simplification Law (2.25c)»
$\quad\Box\Diamond\neg at(\alpha)$
$=\qquad$ «Unconditional Fairness (8.20)»
$\quad F_\alpha^u$
$=\qquad$ «Unconditional Fairness (8.20)»
$\quad\Box\Diamond\neg at(\alpha)$
$=\qquad$ «Or-Simplification Law (2.25c)»
$\quad\Box\Diamond(\neg at(\alpha) \vee false)$
$=\qquad$ «$\alpha$ is unconditional, so $enbl(\alpha)=true$»
$\quad\Box\Diamond(\neg at(\alpha) \vee \neg enbl(\alpha))$
$=\qquad$ «Weak Fairness (8.22)»
$\quad F_\alpha^w$

## Conditions on Fairness Assumptions

Not every Temporal Logic formula makes sense as a fairness assumption. It is not enough that a fairness assumption rule out executions. How they are ruled out is crucial. A fairness assumption may rule out executions only by forcing enabled atomic actions to be executed; it must not rule out executions by prohibiting which atomic action can be next executed. Whether an atomic action can be next executed must remain something that is defined by the program text—even in the presence of a fairness assumption.

To see how restricting executions to those satisfying an arbitrary Temporal Logic formula $F$ might restrict which enabled atomic actions can be next executed, consider the program of Figure 8.3 and let $F$ be $at(S) \Rightarrow \Diamond after(S)$. When $at(T_2)$ holds, an implementation must execute either $Stop$ or $GEval_{do}(Loop)$. First executing $GEval_{do}(Loop)$ causes $F$ to be satisfied, because the **cobegin** will terminate; executing $Stop$ first does not satisfy $F$, because the program will then never terminate. Thus, requiring that $F$ be satisfied implicitly prohibits execution of $Stop$ in any state that satisfies $at(T_2)$. $F$ would not be suitable as a fairness assumption.

Execution of a program ultimately involves a mixture of compilation and interpretation.[7] Unfortunately, neither a compiler nor an interpreter can, in general, determine when execution of an atomic action must be prevented in order to ensure that some arbitrary Temporal Logic formula $F$ will be satisfied. Here is why.

There cannot exist a compiler whose inputs are a program text and $F$ and whose output indicates whether some atomic action can be executed when enabled, because this compiler would have to be able to determine whether an arbitrary loop (e.g., $Loop$ in Figure 8.3) halts—an instance of the well-known (and undecidable) halting problem. Similarly, the impossibility of predicting the future means that an interpreter cannot know whether to block an enabled atomic action. Thus, if we are to have any hope of implementing a fairness assumption $F$, then $F$ had better not prohibit execution of enabled atomic actions.

---

$S$:   $T_1$:  $b := true$
        $T_2$:  **cobegin**
                        $Stop$:  $b := false$
                ‖
                        $Loop$:  **do** $\neg b \to$ **skip od**
                **coend**

**Figure 8.3.**  Terminating program?

---

[7] The program text is translated into atomic actions by a compiler. The operating system scheduler, which selects an atomic action for execution among those that are enabled, the run-time libraries, and computer hardware together constitute an interpreter.

We formalize the requirement that a fairness assumption not prohibit execution of an enabled atomic action as follows. Execution of a program $S$ is characterized by a set $\mathcal{H}_S^+$ of anchored sequences. Execution of $S$ under a fairness assumption $F$ also defines a set of anchored sequences: $\mathcal{H}_S^+ \cap \mathcal{F}$, where $\mathcal{F}$ is the set of models for $F$. If satisfying $F$ prohibits an enabled atomic action from being executed next, then for some $(\sigma, j)$ in $\mathcal{H}_S^+$, there will be a prefix that is not a prefix of any element in $\mathcal{H}_S^+ \cap \mathcal{F}$. This prefix corresponds to the partial execution of $S$ up to and including the atomic action that $F$ prohibits. We can prevent $F$ from imposing such prohibitions by stipulating that for every finite anchored sequence $\beta$, $\beta \propto \mathcal{H}_S^+$ holds iff $\beta \propto (\mathcal{H}_S^+ \cap \mathcal{F})$ does, where $\alpha \propto X$ denotes that $\alpha$ is a finite prefix of some anchored sequence in $X$ and is formally[8] defined by:

(8.23) $\quad \alpha \propto X$: $\quad (\exists (\sigma, j) \in X$: $\alpha \leq (\sigma, j))$

A pair $(\mathcal{P}, \mathcal{Q})$, where both $\mathcal{P}$ and $\mathcal{Q}$ are sets of anchored sequences and $\mathcal{P}$ is a safety property, is defined to be *machine closed* iff

(8.24) $\quad (\forall \beta$: $\beta \propto \mathcal{P} = \beta \propto (\mathcal{P} \cap \mathcal{Q}))$

holds. $\mathcal{H}_S^+$ is a safety property. (The "bad thing" is two adjacent states $\sigma[i..i+1]$ where $\sigma[i] \neq \sigma[i+1]$ but no atomic action in $\mathcal{A}(S)$ transforms $\sigma[i]$ into $\sigma[i+1]$.) Thus, if $(\mathcal{H}_S^+, \mathcal{F})$ is machine closed, then by definition, $F$ does not prohibit any atomic action of $S$ from being the next to be executed. We therefore require that $(\mathcal{H}_S^+, \mathcal{F})$ be machine closed in order for $F$ to be a fairness assumption.

There are two significant consequences of $(\mathcal{H}_S^+, \mathcal{F})$ being machine closed. First, it implies:

(8.25) $\quad \mathcal{H}_S^+ \cap \mathcal{F} \neq \varnothing$,

so a fairness assumption cannot rule out all program executions. The proof of (8.25) is simple, since $\mathcal{H}_S^+$, by construction, is not empty.

$$
\begin{aligned}
&\mathcal{H}_S^+ \neq \varnothing \\
=\quad &\text{«definition of } \beta \propto \mathcal{H}_S^+\text{»} \\
&(\exists \beta: \beta \propto \mathcal{H}_S^+) \\
=\quad &\text{«(8.24) since } (\mathcal{H}_S^+, \mathcal{F}) \text{ is machine closed»} \\
&(\exists \beta: \beta \propto \mathcal{H}_S^+ \cap \mathcal{F}) \\
=\quad &\text{«definition of } \beta \propto \mathcal{H}_S^+ \cap \mathcal{F}\text{»} \\
&\mathcal{H}_S^+ \cap \mathcal{F} \neq \varnothing
\end{aligned}
$$

Second, $(\mathcal{H}_S^+, \mathcal{F})$ being machine closed implies that fairness assumptions cannot alter which safety properties program $S$ satisfies:

---

[8]Recall from §2.4 that $(\sigma, i) \leq (\tau, j)$ means that anchored sequence $(\sigma, i)$ is a prefix of anchored sequence $(\tau, j)$.

(8.26)  For any safety property $\mathcal{P}$:   $(\mathcal{H}_S^+ \cap \mathcal{F} \subseteq \mathcal{P}) = (\mathcal{H}_S^+ \subseteq \mathcal{P})$

Validity of a proof outline, which is essentially an invariance property, is unaffected by the presence of fairness assumptions. Here is the proof of (8.26).

1.    $\mathcal{H}_S^+ \subseteq \mathcal{P}$
$\Rightarrow$    «$\mathcal{H}_S^+ \cap \mathcal{F} \subseteq \mathcal{H}_S^+$»
     $\mathcal{H}_S^+ \cap \mathcal{F} \subseteq \mathcal{P}$

2.    $\mathcal{H}_S^+ \not\subseteq \mathcal{P}$
$=$    «definition of $\not\subseteq$»
     $(\exists \alpha \in \mathcal{H}_S^+ : \ \alpha \notin \mathcal{P})$
$\Rightarrow$    «Safety Property (2.105), since $\mathcal{P}$ is a safety property»
     $(\exists \alpha \in \mathcal{H}_S^+ : \ (\exists \beta : \ \beta \leq \alpha : \ (\forall \gamma \in \Sigma_S^\infty : \ \beta\gamma \notin \mathcal{P})))$
$=$    «definition (8.23) of $\beta \propto \mathcal{P}$»
     $(\exists \beta : \ \beta \propto \mathcal{H}_S^+ : \ (\forall \gamma \in \Sigma_S^\infty : \ \beta\gamma \notin \mathcal{P}))$
$=$    «$(\beta \propto \mathcal{H}_S^+) = (\beta \propto \mathcal{H}_S^+ \cap \mathcal{F})$ since $(\mathcal{H}_S^+, \ \mathcal{F})$ is machine closed»
     $(\exists \beta : \ \beta \propto \mathcal{H}_S^+ \cap \mathcal{F} : \ (\forall \gamma \in \Sigma_S^\infty : \ \beta\gamma \notin \mathcal{P}))$
$=$    «definition (8.23) of $\beta \propto \mathcal{P}$»
     $(\exists \alpha \in \mathcal{H}_S^+ \cap \mathcal{F} : \ (\exists \beta : \ \beta \leq \alpha : \ (\forall \gamma \in \Sigma_S^\infty : \ \beta\gamma \notin \mathcal{P}))$
$\Rightarrow$    «Predicate Logic»
     $(\exists \alpha \in \mathcal{H}_S^+ \cap \mathcal{F} : \ \alpha \notin \mathcal{P})$
$=$    «definition of $\not\subseteq$»
     $\mathcal{H}_S^+ \cap \mathcal{F} \not\subseteq \mathcal{P}$

«Propositional reasoning with 1 and 2»
  3.  $(\mathcal{H}_S^+ \cap \mathcal{F} \subseteq \mathcal{P}) = (\mathcal{H}_S^+ \subseteq \mathcal{P})$

We must also impose a second requirement on a Temporal Logic formula $F$ in order for it to be admissible as a fairness assumption. A fairness assumption should not only provide an abstract and succinct characterization of a scheduler, but should also be useful for reasoning about executions under that scheduler. To this end, we restrict $F$ to be a Temporal Logic formula that is satisfied throughout executions produced by any scheduler it characterizes—not just when execution starts. That is, we require $F$ to be satisfied after each atomic action is selected and executed. If $(\sigma, i)$ is a model for $F$, then so must be every suffix of $(\sigma, i)$.

To summarize the preceding discussion, we require that $F$ satisfy two requirements in order to be a fairness assumption. The first implies that $F$ does not block execution of enabled atomic actions; the second ensures that $F$ is satisfied throughout execution.

(8.27) **Fairness Assumption Requirements.** A Temporal Logic formula $F$ with set of models $\mathcal{F}$ can be a fairness assumption for a program $S$ provided that:

   (i)  $(\mathcal{H}_S^+, \mathcal{F})$ is machine closed.

  (ii)  $\mathcal{F}$ is suffix closed.          □

$F_\alpha^u$, $F_\alpha^s$, and $F_\alpha^w$ satisfy Fairness Assumption Requirements (8.27). But not all Temporal Logic formulas that satisfy Fairness Assumption Requirements (8.27) are equally interesting. The fairness assumptions one encounters in practice are usually conjunctions of unconditional fairness $F_\alpha^u$, strong fairness $F_\alpha^s$, and weak fairness $F_\alpha^w$. These fairness assumptions are popular for three reasons. First, because they are defined in terms of a generic atomic action $\alpha$, they are applicable to all programs. Second, there exist programs that satisfy different liveness properties when execution is constrained to satisfy the fairness assumption. And third—as has already been discussed—they can all be implemented efficiently in the scheduler of an operating system.

## 8.4  Reasoning from Fairness Assumptions

For a program $S$ and a fairness assumption $F$, let $S/F$ denote $S$ restricted to execute in a way that satisfies $F$. Thus,

$$\mathcal{H}_{S/F}^+ = \mathcal{H}_S^+ \cap \mathcal{F}$$

where $\mathcal{F}$ is the set of models for $F$. $S/F$ satisfying a property specified by a Temporal Logic formula $P$ is equivalent to asserting that $\mathcal{H}_{S/F}^+ \subseteq \{P\}$. Therefore, we can establish that $S/F$ satisfies $P$ by using a logic that is sound and complete with respect to $\mathcal{H}_{S/F}^+$-validity—proving $P$ to be a theorem of this logic implies that $P$ is $\mathcal{H}_{S/F}^+$-valid, which implies that every element of $\mathcal{H}_{S/F}^+$ is in $\{P\}$.

$S$-Temporal Logic is sound, but when $\mathcal{H}_{S/F}^+ \neq \mathcal{H}_S^+$ holds, it is not complete with respect to $\mathcal{H}_{S/F}^+$-validity. It is sound because $\mathcal{H}_{S/F}^+$ is a suffix-closed[9] subset of $\mathcal{H}_S^+$. In particular, the axioms of $S$-Temporal Logic are $\mathcal{H}_{S/F}^+$-valid because they are $\mathcal{H}_S^+$-valid and $\mathcal{H}_{S/F}^+ \subseteq \mathcal{H}_S^+$. Soundness of Temporal Generalization Rule (3.11) follows because $\mathcal{H}_{S/F}^+$ is suffix closed; soundness of the other rules follows from $\mathcal{H}_{S/F}^+ \subseteq \mathcal{H}_S^+$ and their soundness for $\mathcal{H}_S^+$-validity.

$S$-Temporal Logic is not complete with respect to $\mathcal{H}_{S/F}^+$-validity when $\mathcal{H}_{S/F}^+ \neq \mathcal{H}_S^+$ holds, because then $F$ is $\mathcal{H}_{S/F}^+$-valid and not $\mathcal{H}_S^+$-valid. $F$ cannot be a theorem of $S$-Temporal Logic because that logic is sound with respect to $\mathcal{H}_S^+$-validity and $F$ is not $\mathcal{H}_S^+$-valid. But $F$ is $\mathcal{H}_{S/F}^+$-valid. Therefore, $F$ is a valid and

---

[9] $\mathcal{H}_{S/F}^+$ is suffix closed because it equals $\mathcal{H}_S^+ \cap \mathcal{F}$ and the intersection of any two suffix-closed sets is itself suffix closed. $\mathcal{H}_S^+$ is suffix closed by construction; $\mathcal{F}$ is suffix closed due to requirement (ii) of Fairness Assumption Requirement (8.27).

unprovable in $S$-Temporal Logic, so $S$-Temporal Logic is incomplete for $\mathcal{H}^+_{S/F}$-validity.

A complete logic for $\mathcal{H}^+_{S/F}$-validity is obtained by adding $F$ as an axiom to $S$-Temporal Logic. We call this logic $S/F$-Temporal Logic. To demonstrate its completeness, we show how to prove in $S/F$-Temporal Logic an arbitrary $\mathcal{H}^+_{S/F}$-valid formula $P$. There are two cases to consider. If $P$ is $\mathcal{H}^+_S$-valid, then $P$ is provable in $S$-Temporal Logic (because $S$-Temporal Logic is complete with respect to $\mathcal{H}^+_S$-validity), and the added axiom $F$ of $S/F$-Temporal Logic does not affect this proof. If, on the other hand, $P$ is not $\mathcal{H}^+_S$-valid, then by construction $F \Rightarrow P$ is $\mathcal{H}^+_S$-valid, and therefore provable in $S$-Temporal Logic. Its proof can be transformed into a proof of $P$ by using axiom $F$ and TL Modus Ponens (3.8).

Of course, having $S/F$-Temporal Logic be sound and complete with respect to $\mathcal{H}^+_{S/F}$-validity is interesting only if $\mathcal{H}^+_{S/F}$ is not empty. A logic with no models (the case where $\mathcal{H}^+_{S/F} = \varnothing$) is trivially sound and complete. We are assured that $\mathcal{H}^+_{S/F}$ is not empty by (i) of Fairness Assumption Requirements (8.27) since according to (8.25), $(\mathcal{H}^+_S, \mathcal{F})$ being machine closed implies that $\mathcal{H}^+_S \cap \mathcal{F} \neq \varnothing$.

## Unbounded x Example

If we assume unconditional fairness for the atomic actions in the program of Figure 8.1, then $x$ will eventually exceed any bound. To illustrate the use of $S/F$-Temporal Logic, we prove this fact. The property that $x$ eventually exceeds any integer N, (8.18), can be proved from

(8.28)  $in(L_1) \wedge N \in \text{Int} \Rightarrow \Diamond(x \geq N)$

because $at(S) \wedge N \in \text{Int} \Rightarrow in(L_1) \wedge N \in \text{Int}$ holds.

It is not difficult to prove that (8.28) is equivalent to

(8.29)  $(\forall R \in \text{Nat}: \; P \Rightarrow \Diamond Q)$

$$\text{where} \qquad P: \; R = \max(0, N-x) \wedge in(L_1) \wedge N \in \text{Int}$$
$$Q: \; x \geq N.$$

Our task, then, is to prove (8.29) a theorem of $S/F^u_S$-Temporal Logic, where fairness assumption $F^u_S$ asserts unconditional fairness for all the atomic actions of $S$:

$$F^u_S: \quad \bigwedge_{\alpha \in \mathcal{A}(S)} F^u_\alpha$$

As in the corresponding proof of §8.1, we employ Natural Number $\Diamond$ Induction Rule (3.69). The premises are discharged in much the same manner as in §8.1. The first premise is:

$$P^R_0$$
$$= \qquad \text{«Textual Substitution (2.71)»}$$

$$0=\max(0, N-x) \wedge in(L_1) \wedge N\in Int$$
$$\Rightarrow \quad \text{«}VarAx(S) \Rightarrow x\in Int; \quad x\in Int \wedge N\in Int \wedge 0=\max(0, N-x) \Rightarrow x\geq N\text{»}$$
$$x\geq N$$
$$\Rightarrow \quad \text{«}\Diamond \text{ Law (3.16c)»}$$
$$\Diamond(x\geq N)$$

The second premise,

(8.30) $(\forall V\in Nat: \; P_{V+1}^R \Rightarrow \Diamond(Q \vee P_V^R))$,

is easy to discharge if we have proved:

(8.31) $x=W \wedge in(L_1) \Rightarrow \Diamond(x=W+1 \wedge in(L_1))$

To prove (8.30), we show that $V\in Nat \wedge P_{V+1}^R \Rightarrow \Diamond(Q \vee P_V^R)$:

$$V\in Nat \wedge P_{V+1}^R$$
$$= \quad \text{«Textual Substitution (2.71)»}$$
$$V\in Nat \wedge V+1=\max(0, N-x) \wedge in(L_1) \wedge N\in Int$$
$$\Rightarrow \quad \text{«}V\in Nat \wedge V+1=\max(0, N-x)$$
$$\Rightarrow V+1=N-x \wedge N>x\text{»}$$
$$V+1=N-x \wedge N>x \wedge in(L_1) \wedge N\in Int$$
$$\Rightarrow \quad \text{«(8.31)»}$$
$$\Diamond(V=N-x \wedge N\geq x \wedge in(L_1)) \wedge N\in Int$$
$$= \quad \text{«Frame Law (3.66b)»}$$
$$\Diamond(V=N-x \wedge N\geq x \wedge in(L_1)) \wedge \Box(N\in Int)$$
$$\Rightarrow \quad \text{«}\Diamond \text{ Law (3.16h)»}$$
$$\Diamond(V=N-x \wedge N\geq x \wedge in(L_1) \wedge N\in Int)$$
$$\Rightarrow \quad \text{«}VarAx(S) \Rightarrow x\in Int,$$
$$\text{definition of } \max(a, b), \text{ since } x\in Int \wedge N\in Int\text{»}$$
$$\Diamond(V=\max(0, N-x) \wedge in(L_1) \wedge N\in Int)$$
$$\Rightarrow \quad \text{«definition of } P\text{»}$$
$$\Diamond P_V^R$$
$$\Rightarrow \quad \text{«Consequent-Weakening Law (2.30)»}$$
$$\Diamond(Q \vee P_V^R)$$

The proof of (8.31), unlike the corresponding proof in §8.1, depends on fairness assumptions. We decompose (8.31) into two obligations, one for each of the atomic actions in process $L_1$:

(8.32) $x=W \wedge at(GEval_{do}(L_1)) \Rightarrow \Diamond(x=W+1 \wedge in(L_1))$

(8.33) $x=W \wedge at(T_1) \Rightarrow \Diamond(x=W+1 \wedge in(L_1))$

Notice that (8.32) and (8.33) together imply (8.31), because from the control predicate axioms we can deduce $in(L_1) = at(GEval_{do}(L_1)) \vee at(T_1)$.

We start with (8.33). The assumption of unconditional fairness for $T_1$ ensures that $T_1$ does not remain enabled forever.

$$x=\text{W} \wedge at(T_1)$$
$\Rightarrow$ «(8.16)»
$$(at(T_1) \wedge x=\text{W})\mathcal{U}(in(L_1) \wedge x=\text{W}+1)$$
$\Rightarrow$ «$\mathcal{U}$ Entailment Law (3.31a)»
$$\Box(at(T_1) \wedge x=\text{W}) \vee \Diamond(in(L_1) \wedge x=\text{W}+1)$$
$=$ «$\Box$ Distributive Law (3.12a)»
$$(\Box at(T_1) \wedge \Box x=\text{W}) \vee \Diamond(in(L_1) \wedge x=\text{W}+1)$$
$=$ «$F_S^u \Rightarrow \neg\Box at(T_1)$»
$$(\neg\Box at(T_1) \wedge \Box at(T_1) \wedge \Box x=\text{W}) \vee \Diamond(in(L_1) \wedge x=\text{W}+1)$$
$\Rightarrow$ «Propositional reasoning»
$$\Diamond(in(L_1) \wedge x=\text{W}+1)$$

To prove (8.32), we first show that the antecedent of (8.33) eventually holds if the antecedent of (8.32) holds.

$$x=\text{W} \wedge at(GEval_{do}(L_1))$$
$\Rightarrow$ «(8.15)»
$$(at(GEval_{do}(L_1)) \wedge x=\text{W})\mathcal{U}(at(T_1) \wedge x=\text{W})$$
$\Rightarrow$ «$\mathcal{U}$ Entailment Law (3.31a)»
$$\Box(at(GEval_{do}(L_1)) \wedge x=\text{W}) \vee \Diamond(at(T_1) \wedge x=\text{W})$$
$=$ «$\Box$ Distributive Law (3.12a)»
$$(\Box at(GEval_{do}(L_1)) \wedge \Box x=\text{W}) \vee \Diamond(at(T_1) \wedge x=\text{W})$$
$=$ «$F_S^u \Rightarrow \neg\Box at(GEval_{do}(L_1))$»
$$(\neg\Box at(GEval_{do}(L_1)) \wedge \Box at(GEval_{do}(L_1)) \wedge \Box x=\text{W})$$
$$\vee \Diamond(at(T_1) \wedge x=\text{W})$$
$\Rightarrow$ «Propositional reasoning»
$$\Diamond(at(T_1) \wedge x=\text{W})$$

Now, (8.32) follows by using $\Diamond$ Catenation Rule (3.20) with (8.33).

The proof that (8.28) holds under unconditional fairness is now complete.

## 8.5  Helpful Actions and Eventualities

In the proofs of (8.32) and (8.33), an unless property $P \Rightarrow P\mathcal{U}Q$ is used to derive an eventuality $P \Rightarrow \Diamond Q$. The general form of these proofs, given in Figure 8.4, and involves discharging two conditions:

(8.34) $P \Rightarrow P\mathcal{U}Q$

(8.35) $P \Rightarrow \Diamond\neg P \vee \Diamond Q$

The first condition specifies a safety property, and the second specifies a liveness property. However, liveness property (8.35), being weaker than our goal $P \Rightarrow \Diamond Q$, should be easier to prove.

$$P$$
$$= \quad \text{«(8.34): } P \Rightarrow P \mathcal{U} Q \text{»}$$
$$P \mathcal{U} Q$$
$$\Rightarrow \quad \text{«}\mathcal{U} \text{ Entailment Law (3.31a)»}$$
$$\Box P \vee \Diamond Q$$
$$\Rightarrow \quad \text{«}\Box \text{ Axiom (3.10a)»}$$
$$(P \wedge \Box P) \vee \Diamond Q$$
$$\Rightarrow \quad \text{«(8.35): } P \Rightarrow \Diamond \neg P \vee \Diamond Q \text{»}$$
$$((\Diamond \neg P \vee \Diamond Q) \wedge \Box P) \vee \Diamond Q$$
$$= \quad \text{«Distributive Law (2.16b)»}$$
$$((\Diamond \neg P \wedge \Box P) \vee (\Diamond Q \wedge \Box P)) \vee \Diamond Q$$
$$= \quad \text{«}\Diamond \text{ Law (3.16b)»}$$
$$((\neg \Box P \wedge \Box P) \vee (\Diamond Q \wedge \Box P)) \vee \Diamond Q$$
$$= \quad \text{«Contradiction Law (2.21); Or-Simplification Law (2.25c)»}$$
$$(\Diamond Q \wedge \Box P) \vee \Diamond Q$$
$$\quad \text{«Or-Simplification Law (2.25d)»}$$
$$\Diamond Q$$

**Figure 8.4.** Proof for $P \Rightarrow \Diamond Q$

---

Different methods for discharging these conditions yield different inference rules for proving $P \Rightarrow \Diamond Q$. Three such rules are given below. All make use of a single idea—helpful actions—in proving (8.35). An atomic action $\alpha$ is a *helpful action* for proving $P \Rightarrow \Diamond Q$ if executing $\alpha$ in a state satisfying $P$ contributes to truthifying $Q$.

As might be expected, we can conclude $P \Rightarrow \Diamond Q$ by proving that if $P$ holds, then some helpful action is eventually executed and afterwards either $P$ holds again or $Q$ holds. To establish this formally, it suffices to postulate the following condition on $P$, where H denotes a set of helpful actions.

$$(8.36) \quad P \Rightarrow (\bigwedge_{\alpha \in H} at(\alpha)) \wedge \Diamond ((\bigvee_{\alpha \in H} after(\alpha)) \vee Q)$$

The first conjunct of (8.36) is the minimum we might expect so that a helpful action can be executed whenever $P$ holds; the second conjunct asserts that if $P$ holds, then either some helpful action is eventually executed or $Q$ is truthified by executing some other action. Note that when $H = \varnothing$, (8.36) implies $P \Rightarrow \Diamond Q$.

Here is the proof of (8.35) from (8.36).

$$P$$
$$\Rightarrow \quad \text{«(8.36)»}$$
$$(\bigwedge_{\alpha \in H} at(\alpha)) \wedge \Diamond ((\bigvee_{\alpha \in H} after(\alpha)) \vee Q)$$
$$\Rightarrow \quad \text{«}after(\alpha) \Rightarrow \neg at(\alpha) \text{, due to control predicate axioms»}$$
$$(\bigwedge_{\alpha \in H} at(\alpha)) \wedge \Diamond ((\bigvee_{\alpha \in H} \neg at(\alpha)) \vee Q)$$

$\Rightarrow$      «Antecedent-Strengthening Law (2.29)»

$\Diamond((\underset{\alpha \in H}{\vee} \neg at(\alpha)) \vee Q)$

$\Rightarrow$      «$(\underset{\alpha \in H}{\vee} \neg at(\alpha)) \Rightarrow \neg P$ by contrapositive of (8.36)»

$\Diamond(\neg P \vee Q)$

$=$      «$\Diamond$ Distributive Law (3.17b)»

$\Diamond \neg P \vee \Diamond Q$

Because (8.34) and (8.35) together imply $P \Rightarrow \Diamond Q$, we conclude that proving (8.34) along with (8.36) also implies $P \Rightarrow \Diamond Q$.

## Well-Founded Eventualities

Well-Founded $\Diamond$ Induction Rule (3.68) is an inference rule for proving an eventuality. Recall that the rule is

$$\frac{(\forall R \in \mathcal{W}: P \Rightarrow \Diamond(Q \vee (\exists V \in \mathcal{W}: V \triangleleft R: P_V^R)))}{(\forall R \in \mathcal{W}: P \Rightarrow \Diamond Q)}$$

for $(\mathcal{W}, \triangleleft)$ a well-founded set, R not occurring free in $Q$, and V not occurring free in $P$ or $Q$. Since the premise of this rule is itself an eventuality, we can make suitable substitutions into (8.34) and (8.36) and use the resulting formulas in place of this premise. The substitutions are given below. Notice that each element R in well-founded set $\mathcal{W}$ can have a different set $H_R$ of helpful actions associated with it.

$P$:  $P$

$Q$:  $Q \vee (\exists V \in \mathcal{W}: V \triangleleft R: P_V^R)$

$H$:  $H_R$

Finally, according to $\mathcal{U}$ Property Rule (8.14b), proving

For all $\alpha \in \mathcal{A}(S)$:  $\{at(\alpha) \wedge P\}$ $\alpha$ $\{P \vee Q \vee (\exists V \in \mathcal{W}: V \triangleleft R: P_V^R)\}$

implies (8.34). We thus obtain the following inference rule.

(8.37) *Eventuality by Unless*: For $(\mathcal{W}, \triangleleft)$ a well-founded set, rigid variable R not occurring free in $Q$, and V not occurring free in $P$ or $Q$:

  (a) For all $\alpha \in \mathcal{A}(S)$:  $\{at(\alpha) \wedge P\}$ $\alpha$ $\{P \vee Q \vee (\exists V \in \mathcal{W}: V \triangleleft R: P_V^R)\}$

  (b) $(\forall R \in \mathcal{W}: P \Rightarrow \underset{\alpha \in H_R}{\wedge} at(\alpha) \wedge$

  $\Diamond((\underset{\alpha \in H_R}{\vee} after(\alpha)) \vee Q \vee (\exists V \in \mathcal{W}: V \triangleleft R: P_V^R)))$

  $$\overline{(\forall R \in \mathcal{W}: P \Rightarrow \Diamond Q)}$$

Premise (a) of the rule implies that for any value R, each atomic action leaves $P$ *true*, truthifies $Q$, or truthifies $P_V^R$ where V<R. Helpful atomic actions (those in $H_R$), however, truthify $Q$ or $P_V^R$ for V<R. This is because according to premise (b), execution of a helpful action $\alpha$ falsifies $P$ by falsifying $at(\alpha)$ for $\alpha \in H_R$.

To see why the premises imply that $Q$ will eventually hold, recall that $\mathcal{W}$ is well founded, so it has no infinite descending chains. We know from premise (b) that whenever $P$ holds, then eventually either some helpful action will be executed or $Q$ will be truthified by some other action. Moreover, from the preceding discussion, execution of a helpful action will truthify $Q$ or $P_V^R$ where V<R. Every decreasing chain of values from R is finite, so only a finite number of helpful actions can truthify $P_V^R$ for progressively smaller values of V. Thus, only a finite number of helpful actions can be executed before $Q$ must hold.

## *Unbounded x+y Example Revisited*

To illustrate the use of Eventuality by Unless (8.37), we return to the program of Figure 8.1 and prove (again) that $x+y$ eventually exceeds any value. We must select $\mathcal{W}$, $P$, and the $H_R$. The premises of (8.37) constrain these so that for any execution, if $Q$ does not hold initially then there is a decreasing (according to <) sequence of values for R such that $P$ holds initially and continues to hold until $Q$ does. Thus, $\mathcal{W}$, $P$, and $H_R$ are interdependent, and our derivation proceeds accordingly.

The amount val by which $x+y$ must still be increased to truthify $x+y \geq N$ is one dimension of $\mathcal{W}$:

$\mathcal{W}$: Nat $\times$ $\cdots$      with $(i, ...)$<$(i', ...)$ if $i < i'$

$P$:   R=(val, ...) $\wedge$ $x+y+$val=N $\wedge$ 0<val $\wedge$ $\cdots$

We now consider possible sets $H_R$ of helpful actions. If $x+y < N$ holds, then increasing $x+y$ decreases the value of R that makes $P$ hold. Therefore, in states satisfying $x+y < N$, any atomic action that increments $x+y$ is helpful: $T_1$ is helpful if $x+y < N \wedge at(T_1)$ holds, and $T_2$ is helpful if $x+y < N \wedge at(T_2)$ holds. Continuing, if $x+y < N$ holds but $at(T_1)$ does not, then an action that truthifies $at(T_1)$ would be helpful because it allows helpful action $T_1$ to be executed. Therefore, we conclude that $GEval_{do}(L_1)$ is a helpful action when $x+y < N \wedge at(GEval_{do}(L_1))$ holds; analogously, $GEval_{do}(L_2)$ is a helpful action when $x+y < N \wedge at(GEval_{do}(L_2))$ is satisfied. This suggests adding the control state of each process as a dimension of $\mathcal{W}$, and we try:

$\mathcal{W}$: Nat $\times$ $C_1$ $\times$ $C_2$

     where: $C_1$: $\{T_1, GEval_{do}(L_1)\}$   with   $T_1$<$GEval_{do}(L_1)$

              $C_2$: $\{T_2, GEval_{do}(L_2)\}$   with   $T_2$<$GEval_{do}(L_2)$

$P$:   R=(val, $\alpha$, $\beta$) $\wedge$ $x+y+$val=N $\wedge$ 0<val $\wedge$ $at(\alpha)$ $\wedge$ $at(\beta)$

$$H_{(val, \alpha, \beta)}: \quad \begin{cases} \{\alpha, \beta\} & \text{if } 0 < val \\ \varnothing & \text{if } 0 \geq val \end{cases}$$

Elements of $\mathcal{W}$ are ordered by the usual lexicographic ordering for Cartesian products (see §3.3).

We now check the premises of Eventuality by Unless (8.37) for the case where $Q$ is:

$Q$:  $x + y \geq N$

It is easy to see that premise (a) holds. The program has four atomic actions: $GEval_{do}(L_1)$, $T_1$, $GEval_{do}(L_2)$, and $T_2$. If $P$ holds for $R = (val, \alpha, \beta)$ and one of assignment statements $T_1$ or $T_2$ is executed, then either $Q$ will hold (because now $x + y = N$) or $P_V^R$ will hold with $V = (val-1, ...)$. In the latter case, $V \triangleleft R$. If one of the guard evaluation actions is executed, then $P_V^R$ will hold, with $V = (val, \alpha', \beta')$, and we conclude $V \triangleleft R$ because either $\alpha' \triangleleft \alpha$ (because $GEval_{do}(L_1)$ was executed) or $\alpha' = \alpha \wedge \beta' \triangleleft \beta$ (because $GEval_{do}(L_2)$ was executed).

Premise (b) follows from $\mathcal{H}_S^+$ Control Axiom (8.3), because every enabled action is helpful. Here is a proof.

$P$

$\Rightarrow$      «definition of $P$ and $H_R$»

$\displaystyle\bigwedge_{\alpha \in H_R} at(\alpha)$

$=$      «for unconditional atomic action $\alpha$, $enbl(\alpha) = true$»

$\displaystyle\bigwedge_{\alpha \in H_R} (at(\alpha) \wedge enbl(\alpha))$

$\Rightarrow$      «$\mathcal{H}_S^+$ Control Axiom (8.3)»

$(\displaystyle\bigwedge_{\alpha \in H_R} (at(\alpha) \wedge enbl(\alpha))) \wedge (\displaystyle\bigvee_{\alpha \in H_R} \bigcirc after(\alpha))$

$\Rightarrow$      «$\bigcirc$ Laws (3.22b)»

$(\displaystyle\bigwedge_{\alpha \in H_R} (at(\alpha) \wedge enbl(\alpha))) \wedge \bigcirc(\displaystyle\bigvee_{\alpha \in H_R} after(\alpha))$

$\Rightarrow$      «$\bigcirc P \Rightarrow \Diamond P$»

$(\displaystyle\bigwedge_{\alpha \in H_R} (at(\alpha) \wedge enbl(\alpha))) \wedge \Diamond(\displaystyle\bigvee_{\alpha \in H_R} after(\alpha))$

$\Rightarrow$      «Antecedent-Strengthening Law (2.29)»

$(\displaystyle\bigwedge_{\alpha \in H_R} at(\alpha)) \wedge \Diamond(\displaystyle\bigvee_{\alpha \in H_R} after(\alpha))$

$\Rightarrow$      «Consequent-Weakening Law (2.30)»

$(\displaystyle\bigwedge_{\alpha \in H_R} at(\alpha))$

$\wedge \Diamond((\displaystyle\bigvee_{\alpha \in H_R} after(\alpha)) \vee Q \vee (\exists V \in \mathcal{W}: V \triangleleft R: P_V^R))$

## Fair Helpful Actions

When helpful actions are fair, we can use fairness assumptions—instead of a direct appeal to $\mathcal{H}_S^+$ Control Axiom (8.3), as just done—to conclude that helpful actions are executed eventually. For weakly-fair helpful actions, proving that $P$ implies $at(\alpha) \wedge enbl(\alpha)$ for every helpful action $\alpha$ ensures that some helpful action will be executed eventually; for strongly-fair helpful actions, proving that $P$ implies $at(\alpha) \wedge \Diamond enbl(\alpha)$ suffices. These insights lead to inference rules for proving eventualities when helpful actions are fair.

Consider a program $S/F$ for which we have proved:

(8.38) $P \Rightarrow P \,\mathcal{U}\, Q$

Moreover, suppose that fairness assumption $F$ implies that all helpful actions are weakly fair:

(8.39) $F \Rightarrow \bigwedge\limits_{\alpha \in H} F_\alpha^w$

If we have also proved

(8.40) $P \Rightarrow (H \neq \varnothing \wedge \bigwedge\limits_{\alpha \in H} (at(\alpha) \wedge enbl(\alpha))) \;\vee\; \Diamond Q,$

then we can prove $P \Rightarrow \Diamond Q$ using the same basic approach as in Figure 8.4. First, observe that according to Implication Law (2.22a), (8.40) is equivalent to:

(8.41) $P \Rightarrow (\neg \Diamond Q \Rightarrow (H \neq \varnothing \wedge \bigwedge\limits_{\alpha \in H} (at(\alpha) \wedge enbl(\alpha))))$

Second, we prove

(8.42) $\Box P \Rightarrow \Diamond Q$

as follows.

$\Box P$
$=$ 〈(8.41)〉
$\Box(\neg \Diamond Q \Rightarrow (H \neq \varnothing \wedge \bigwedge\limits_{\alpha \in H} (at(\alpha) \wedge enbl(\alpha))))$
$\Rightarrow$ 〈$\Box$ Axiom (3.10a)〉
$\Box \neg \Diamond Q \Rightarrow \Box(H \neq \varnothing \wedge \bigwedge\limits_{\alpha \in H} (at(\alpha) \wedge enbl(\alpha)))$
$=$ 〈$\Box$ Distributive Law (3.12a)〉
$\Box \neg \Diamond Q \Rightarrow (\Box(H \neq \varnothing) \wedge \bigwedge\limits_{\alpha \in H} \Box(at(\alpha) \wedge enbl(\alpha)))$
$=$ 〈(8.39), since $F_\alpha^w \Rightarrow \neg\Box(at(\alpha) \wedge enbl(\alpha))$〉
$\Box \neg \Diamond Q \Rightarrow (\Box(H \neq \varnothing) \wedge \mathit{false})$
$=$ 〈Propositional reasoning〉
$\neg \Box \neg \Diamond Q$
$=$ 〈$\Diamond$ Axiom (3.15)〉
$\Diamond \Diamond Q$
$=$ 〈Absorption Law (3.18b)〉
$\Diamond Q$

Finally, we prove $P \Rightarrow \Diamond Q$ using (8.42).

$$
\begin{aligned}
& P \\
\Rightarrow \quad & \text{«(8.38)»} \\
& P \, \mathcal{U} \, Q \\
\Rightarrow \quad & \text{«}\mathcal{U} \text{ Entailment Law (3.31a)»} \\
& \Box P \vee \Diamond Q \\
\Rightarrow \quad & \text{«(8.42)»} \\
& \Diamond Q \vee \Diamond Q \\
= \quad & \text{«Or-Simplification Law (2.25a)»} \\
& \Diamond Q
\end{aligned}
$$

We have shown how to prove the eventuality $P \Rightarrow \Diamond Q$ from (8.38), (8.39), and (8.40). As before, we can use such a proof to discharge the eventuality that is the premise of Well-Founded $\Diamond$ Induction Rule (3.68). We replace the premise with (8.39) and (8.40) after making the substitutions

$P:\ P$

$Q:\ Q \vee (\exists V \in \mathcal{W}:\ V \lhd R:\ P_V^R)$

$H:\ H_R$

and, according to $\mathcal{U}$ Property Rule (8.14b), prove

For all $\alpha \in \mathcal{A}(S)$: $\{at(\alpha) \wedge P\}\ \alpha\ \{P \vee Q \vee (\exists V \in \mathcal{W}:\ V \lhd R:\ P_V^R)\}$

to discharge (8.38). This results in the following rule for proving that $S/F$ satisfies an eventuality $P \Rightarrow \Diamond Q$.

(8.43) *Eventuality by Weakly Fair Helpful Actions*:  For $(\mathcal{W}, \lhd)$ a well-founded set, rigid variable R not occurring free in $Q$, and V not occurring free in $P$ or $Q$:

    (a) For all $\alpha \in \mathcal{A}(S)$: $\{at(\alpha) \wedge P\}\ \alpha\ \{P \vee Q \vee (\exists V \in \mathcal{W}:\ V \lhd R:\ P_V^R)\}$
    (b) $(\forall R \in \mathcal{W}:\ P \Rightarrow (H_R \neq \varnothing \wedge \bigwedge_{\alpha \in H_R} (at(\alpha) \wedge enbl(\alpha)))$
                 $\vee\ \Diamond(Q \vee (\exists V \in \mathcal{W}:\ V \lhd R:\ P_V^R)))$
    (c) $(\forall R \in \mathcal{W}:\ F \Rightarrow \bigwedge_{\alpha \in H_R} F_\alpha^w)$

$$\rule{10cm}{0.4pt}$$

$$(\forall R \in \mathcal{W}:\ P \Rightarrow \Diamond Q)$$

The notable difference between this rule and Eventuality by Unless (8.37) is premise (b). Premise (b) for Eventuality by Weakly Fair Helpful Actions (8.43) can frequently be discharged without using Temporal Logic; this is not the case for rule (8.37). In particular, if $H_R$ is not empty for $R \in \mathcal{W}$, then proving

$$(\forall R \in \mathcal{W}:\ P \Rightarrow \bigwedge_{\alpha \in H_R} (at(\alpha) \wedge enbl(\alpha)))$$

$$S:\ T_1:\ b := \textit{true}$$
$$T_2:\ \textbf{cobegin}$$
$$\textit{Loop}:\ \textbf{do}\ b \to L:\ \textbf{skip od}$$
$$\|$$
$$\textit{Stop}:\ \langle \textbf{if}\ b \to b := \textit{false}\ \textbf{fi} \rangle$$
$$\textbf{coend}$$

**Figure 8.5.** Terminates under weak fairness

suffices to discharge premise (b) of (8.43).

   With reasoning that parallels the derivation of Eventuality by Weakly Fair Helpful Actions (8.43), it is also possible to obtain a rule for proving eventualities when helpful actions are strongly fair. The following (weaker) requirement replaces (8.40).

(8.44)  $P \Rightarrow (H \neq \emptyset \wedge \bigwedge_{\alpha \in H} (at(\alpha) \wedge \Diamond enbl(\alpha))) \vee \Diamond Q$

This gives the following inference rule for proving eventualities in $S/F$.

(8.45)  *Eventuality by Strongly Fair Helpful Actions*:  For $(\mathcal{W}, \prec)$ a well-founded set, rigid variable R not occurring free in $Q$, and V not occurring free in $P$ or $Q$:

    (a)  For all $\alpha \in \mathcal{A}(S)$:  $\{at(\alpha) \wedge P\}\ \alpha\ \{P \vee Q \vee (\exists V \in \mathcal{W}\colon V \prec R\colon P_V^R)\}$

    (b)  $(\forall R \in \mathcal{W}\colon P \Rightarrow (H_R \neq \emptyset \wedge \bigwedge_{\alpha \in H_R} (at(\alpha) \wedge \Diamond enbl(\alpha)))$
$$\vee\ \Diamond(Q \vee (\exists V \in \mathcal{W}\colon V \prec R\colon P_V^R)))$$

    (c)  $(\forall R \in \mathcal{W}\colon F \Rightarrow \bigwedge_{\alpha \in H_R} F_\alpha^S)$

$$\overline{\qquad (\forall R \in \mathcal{W}\colon P \Rightarrow \Diamond Q) \qquad}$$

## Termination Under Weak Fairness

   Termination of the program in Figure 8.5, $at(S) \Rightarrow \Diamond after(S)$, is easy to prove when all its atomic actions are weakly fair. It suffices that we prove

$$at(S) \Rightarrow \Diamond(after(Loop) \wedge after(Stop))$$

because:

        $after(Loop) \wedge after(Stop)$
$=$     «**cobegin** Control Axiom (5.2b)»
        $after(T_2)$
$=$     «Statement Juxtaposition Control Axiom (4.10b)»
        $after(S)$

We start by identifying helpful actions. Assignment statement $T_1$ is helpful when enabled, because executing $T_1$ truthifies $at(T_2)$ and **cobegin** $T_2$ must start in order to terminate. Once $T_2$ begins, execution of *Stop* is helpful, but as long as $b$ is *true*, atomic actions in *Loop* are not. Then, once *Stop* is executed (falsifying $b$), atomic actions in *Loop* become helpful because their execution causes *Loop* to terminate. This suggests the following, where $\mathcal{W}=\{1, 2, 3, 4\}$, and elements of this set are ordered by $<$.

| V | $P^R_V$ | $H_V$ |
|---|---|---|
| 4 | $at(T_1)$ | $\{T_1\}$ |
| 3 | $at(Stop) \wedge b \wedge in(Loop)$ | $\{Stop\}$ |
| 2 | $after(Stop) \wedge \neg b \wedge at(L)$ | $\{L\}$ |
| 1 | $after(Stop) \wedge \neg b \wedge at(GEval_{do}(Loop))$ | $\{GEval_{do}(Loop)\}$ |

Thus, we have:

$P$:  $\quad (R{=}1 \Rightarrow after(Stop) \wedge \neg b \wedge at(GEval_{do}(Loop)))$
$\quad \wedge \quad (R{=}2 \Rightarrow after(Stop) \wedge \neg b \wedge at(L))$
$\quad \wedge \quad (R{=}3 \Rightarrow at(Stop) \wedge b \wedge in(Loop))$
$\quad \wedge \quad (R{=}4 \Rightarrow at(T_1))$

$Q$:  $\quad after(Loop) \wedge after(Stop)$

We now check the premises of Eventuality by Weakly Fair Helpful Actions (8.43).

For premise (a), it suffices to prove the following triples (because all the others have a *false* precondition due to the control predicate axioms).

$\{at(T_1) \wedge P^R_4\}\; T_1\colon b := true\; \{P^R_3\}$
$\{at(Stop) \wedge P^R_3\}\; Stop\colon \langle \textbf{if } b \rightarrow b := false \textbf{ fi}\rangle\; \{P^R_1 \vee P^R_2\}$
$\{at(Loop) \wedge P^R_3\}\; GEval_{do}(Loop)\; \{P^R_3\}$
$\{at(L) \wedge P^R_3\}\; L\colon \textbf{skip}\; \{P^R_3\}$
$\{at(L) \wedge P^R_2\}\; L\colon \textbf{skip}\; \{P^R_1\}$
$\{at(Loop) \wedge P^R_1\}\; GEval_{do}(Loop)\; \{Q\}$

Premise (b) is easy to verify because the following are valid.

$R{=}1 \wedge P \;\Rightarrow\; H_R \neq \varnothing \wedge at(GEval_{do}(Loop)) \wedge enbl(GEval_{do}(Loop))$

$R{=}2 \wedge P \;\Rightarrow\; H_R \neq \varnothing \wedge at(L) \wedge enbl(L)$

$R{=}3 \wedge P \;\Rightarrow\; H_R \neq \varnothing \wedge at(Stop) \wedge enbl(Stop)$

$R{=}4 \wedge P \;\Rightarrow\; H_R \neq \varnothing \wedge at(T_1) \wedge enbl(T_1)$

Finally, premise (c) follows from our choice of $F$:

$$F: \bigwedge_{\alpha \in \mathcal{A}(S)} F_\alpha^w$$

With premises (a) through (c) of Eventuality by Weakly Fair Helpful Actions (8.43) discharged, we conclude:

(8.46) $(\forall R \in \mathcal{W}: P \Rightarrow \Diamond(after(Loop) \wedge after(Stop)))$

We can now prove $(\forall R \in \mathcal{W}: at(S) \Rightarrow \Diamond(after(Loop) \wedge after(Stop)))$:

$$at(S)$$
$= \quad$ «Statement Juxtaposition Control Axiom (4.10a)»
$$at(T_1)$$
$= \quad$ «definition of $P$»
$$P \wedge (R=4)$$
$\Rightarrow \quad$ «Propositional reasoning»
$$P \wedge (R \in \mathcal{W})$$
$\Rightarrow \quad$ «(8.46)»
$$\Diamond(after(Loop) \wedge after(Stop))$$

By TL Quantification Simplification Law (3.54a), we now conclude $at(S) \Rightarrow \Diamond(after(Loop) \wedge after(Stop))$.

## 8.6 Liveness for Mutual Exclusion

In Chapter 6, we proved a number of safety properties for the mutual exclusion protocol of Figure 8.6. What we did not prove, however, is that a process attempting to enter its critical section will eventually do so. We prove this liveness property here.

The property that all requests to enter critical sections are granted is specified by the following Temporal Logic formula.

(8.47) $at(S) \Rightarrow \Box(at(entry_i) \Rightarrow \Diamond at(CS_i))$

It asserts that if execution of $S$ is started at its initialization, then a process $S_i$ that reaches $entry_i$ is guaranteed to reach $CS_i$.

Figure 8.6 leaves unspecified the critical section $CS_i$ and the noncritical section $NCS_i$ of each process $S_i$. Without making some minimal assumptions about these program fragments, little can be guaranteed about properties satisfied by $S$. The first assumption restricts what variables can be changed by $CS_i$ and $NCS_i$. It stipulates that $t$, $in1$, and $in2$ be modified only by the initialization, entry, and exit protocols.

$S$:  $t, in1, in2 := 1, false, false$
   **cobegin**
   $S_1$:  **do** *true* → *entry*$_1$:  *door*$_1$:  $in1 := true$
                           *step*$_1$:  $t := 2$
                           *gate*$_1$:  **if** ¬*in2* ∨ $t=1$ → $T_1$:  **skip fi**
                $CS_1$
                *exit*$_1$:  $in1 := false$
                $NCS_1$
     **od**
   ||
   $S_2$:  **do** *true* → *entry*$_2$:  *door*$_2$:  $in2 := true$
                           *step*$_2$:  $t := 1$
                           *gate*$_2$:  **if** ¬*in1* ∨ $t=2$ → $T_2$:  **skip fi**
                $CS_2$
                *exit*$_2$:  $in2 := false$
                $NCS_2$
     **od**
   **coend**

**Figure 8.6.** Mutual exclusion protocol

(8.48)  For all $\alpha \in (\mathcal{A}(CS_1) \cup \mathcal{A}(NCS_1) \cup \mathcal{A}(CS_2) \cup \mathcal{A}(NCS_2))$:
$$\{t = T \wedge in1 = IN1 \wedge in2 = IN2\}\ \alpha\ \{t = T \wedge in1 = IN1 \wedge in2 = IN2\}$$

Second, for (8.47) to hold, we must assume that no process remains forever in its critical section. That is, we assume:

(8.49)  $in(CS_i) \Rightarrow \Diamond after(CS_i)$

The assumption is necessary because (as proved in §6.5) $S$ satisfies Mutual Exclusion (6.2), so one process forever executing in its critical section would prevent the granting of entry requests made by the other process. With (8.49), we can prove:

(8.50)  $\Box in(CS_i) \Rightarrow false$

Here is the proof.

    $\Box in(CS_i)$
⇒    «$\Box$ Axiom (3.10a)»
    $\Box in(CS_i) \wedge in(CS_i)$
⇒    «(8.49)»
    $\Box in(CS_i) \wedge \Diamond after(CS_i)$

$\Rightarrow$     «$\Diamond$ Law (3.16h)»
$\Diamond(in(CS_i) \wedge after(CS_i))$
$=$     «$in(T) \Rightarrow \neg after(T)$ due to control predicate axiom»
$\Diamond false$
$=$     «$\Diamond$ Axiom (3.15)»
$\neg\Box\neg false$
$\Rightarrow$     «$\Box$ Axiom (3.10a)»
$\neg\neg false$
$=$     «Propositional reasoning »
$false$

Finally, we assume that a process is not starved—it is trivial to satisfy (8.47) if, because a scheduler prevents $S_i$ from executing atomic actions, $S_i$ is unable to truthify $at(entry_i)$. One solution is to postulate that atomic actions are weakly fair.[10]

(8.51) $F: \quad \bigwedge_{\alpha \in \mathcal{A}(S)} F_\alpha^w$

## Proof of Eventual Entry

Let Predicate Logic formula $I$ (to be defined momentarily) characterize the values of $t$, $in1$, and $in2$ in all executions whose first state satisfies $at(S)$:

(8.52) $at(S) \Rightarrow \Box I$

If we also prove that

(8.53) $I \Rightarrow (at(entry_i) \Rightarrow \Diamond at(CS_i))$

is a theorem of $S/F$-Temporal Logic, then (8.47) is easily proved.

«(8.53)»
1. $I \Rightarrow (at(entry_i) \Rightarrow \Diamond at(CS_i))$

«Temporal Generalization Rule (3.11) with 2»
2. $\Box(I \Rightarrow (at(entry_i) \Rightarrow \Diamond at(CS_i)))$

«$\Box$ Axiom (3.10b)»
3. $\Box(I \Rightarrow (at(entry_i) \Rightarrow \Diamond at(CS_i)))$
$\Rightarrow (\Box I \Rightarrow \Box(at(entry_i) \Rightarrow \Diamond at(CS_i)))$

«TL Modus Ponens (3.8) with 2 and 3»
4. $(\Box I \Rightarrow \Box(at(entry_i) \Rightarrow \Diamond at(CS_i)))$

[10]Exercise 8.30 explores other possibilities.

5.     $at(S)$
     $\Rightarrow$      «(8.52)»
     $\Box I$
     $\Rightarrow$      «line 4»
     $\Box(at(entry_i) \Rightarrow \Diamond at(CS_i))$

A choice of $I$ that is too strong would make it impossible to prove (8.52); a choice that is too weak would make it impossible to prove (8.53). Based on what we know about the role that $t$, $in1$, and $in2$ play in the protocol, we try:

$I$:   $at(S) \lor$
     $((t=1 \lor t=2) \land$
     $(in1=(at(step_1) \lor at(gate_1) \lor at(T_1) \lor in(CS_1) \lor at(exit_1)))) \land$
     $(in2=(at(step_2) \lor at(gate_2) \lor at(T_2) \lor in(CS_2) \lor at(exit_2))))$

To prove (8.52), we employ $\Box$ Property Rule (8.17) and prove $\{at(\alpha) \land I\} \; \alpha \; \{I\}$ for every atomic action $\alpha$ in $\mathcal{A}(S)$. This allows us to conclude $I \Rightarrow \Box I$. Since $at(S)$ is a disjunct of $I$, we can use Consequent-Weakening Law (2.30) to prove $at(S) \Rightarrow I$, so $at(S) \Rightarrow \Box I$ follows by Transitivity of Implication (2.39a).

To prove (8.53), we use Eventuality by Weakly Fair Helpful Actions (8.43). This requires defining $\mathcal{W}$, $P$, and $H_R$. We work backwards from goal $at(CS_i)$, identifying what action(s) must be executed for each subgoal to become *true*. For example, executing $T_i$ truthifies $at(CS_i)$, so we regard $T_i$ as a helpful action in states satisfying $at(T_i)$. $GEval_{if}(gate_i)$ truthifies $at(T_i)$, so it is helpful in states where it can be executed. And so on. The reasoning is somewhat operational, but it produces characterizations for a set of stages that precede an entry to $CS_i$.

We associate an element of V in $\mathcal{W}$ with each stage. An ordering ‹ over these elements is defined by the sequence in which the corresponding stages can be occupied as execution progresses. We also associate with each stage a state predicate $J_V^R$ and set of helpful actions $H_V$ for moving from one stage to a lower one (according to ‹). For proving

(8.54)   $(\forall R \in \mathcal{W} : P \Rightarrow \Diamond at(CS_1))$

the definitions of Figure 8.7 seem plausible; the case where $i=2$ is symmetric. Thus, $P$ is defined by

$$P: \quad \bigwedge_{V \in \mathcal{W}} (R=V \Rightarrow J_V^R)$$

where $\mathcal{W} = \{1, 2, 3, ..., 10\}$. Observe that $P_V^R$ is equivalent to $J_V^R$.

We now check premise (a) of Eventuality by Weakly Fair Helpful Actions (8.43). This requires proving

| V | $J_V^R$ | $H_V$ |
|---|---------|-------|
| 10 | $at(door_1) \land I$ | $\{door_1\}$ |
| 9 | $at(step_1) \land in1 \land I$ | $\{step_1\}$ |
| 8 | $at(gate_1) \land in1 \land in2 \land t=2 \land at(gate_2) \land I$ | $\{gate_2\}$ |
| 7 | $at(gate_1) \land in1 \land in2 \land t=2 \land at(T_2) \land I$ | $\{T_2\}$ |
| 6 | $at(gate_1) \land in1 \land in2 \land t=2 \land in(CS_2) \land I$ | $\varnothing$ |
| 5 | $at(gate_1) \land in1 \land in2 \land t=2 \land at(exit_2) \land I$ | $\{exit_2\}$ |
| 4 | $at(gate_1) \land in1 \land \neg in2 \land t=2 \land I$ | $\{gate_1\}$ |
| 3 | $at(gate_1) \land in1 \land in2 \land t=2 \land at(step_2) \land I$ | $\{step_2\}$ |
| 2 | $at(gate_1) \land in1 \land in2 \land t=1 \land at(gate_2) \land I$ | $\{gate_1\}$ |
| 1 | $at(T_1)$ | $\{T_1\}$ |

**Figure 8.7.** Definitions of stages

$$\{at(\alpha) \land P\} \ \alpha \ \{P \lor at(CS_1) \lor (\exists V \in \mathcal{W}: \ V \triangleleft R: \ P_V^R)\}$$

for each atomic action $\alpha$. Figure 8.8 is helpful in this regard. Each box in the figure is labeled with a state predicate $P_V^R$, and there is an edge connecting $P_V^R$ to $P_W^R$ labeled by $\alpha$ iff $at(\alpha) \land P_V^R$ is not *false* and $\{at(\alpha) \land P_W^R\} \ \alpha \ \{P_W^R\}$ is valid. Thus, the arcs describe how execution of atomic actions cause changes from one stage to another. The absence of any edge from $P_W^R$ to $P_V^R$ where $W \triangleleft V$ suffices to discharge premise (a).

To discharge premise (b), it suffices to prove $P_V^R \Rightarrow \bigwedge_{\alpha \in H_V} (at(\alpha) \land enbl(\alpha))$ for each nonempty $H_V$. Only $H_6$ is empty, so we prove the following.

$P_1^R \Rightarrow at(T_1)$

$P_2^R \Rightarrow at(gate_1) \land (\neg in2 \lor t=1)$

$P_3^R \Rightarrow at(step_2)$

$P_4^R \Rightarrow at(gate_1) \land (\neg in2 \lor t=1)$

$P_5^R \Rightarrow at(exit_2)$

$P_7^R \Rightarrow at(T_2)$

$P_8^R \Rightarrow at(gate_2) \land (\neg in1 \lor t=2)$

$P_9^R \Rightarrow at(step_1)$

$P_{10}^R \Rightarrow at(door_1)$

Since $H_6$ is empty, we must prove $P_6^R \Rightarrow \Diamond(Q \lor (\exists V \in \mathcal{W}: \ V \triangleleft 6: \ P_V^R))$. Here is that proof:

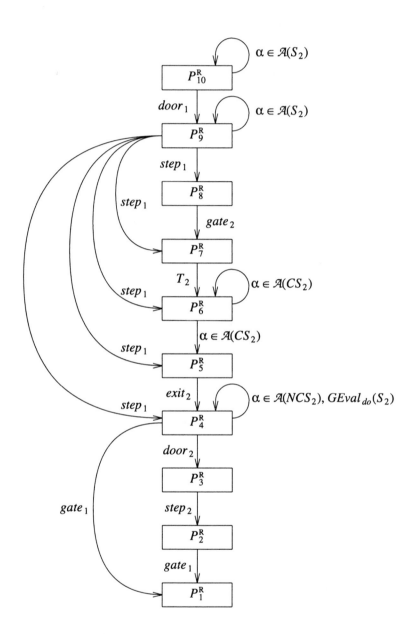

**Figure 8.8.** Proof of premise (a)

$$P_6^R$$
$\Rightarrow$     «$\mathcal{U}$ Property Rule (8.14b) given (8.48)»
$$P_6^R \, \mathcal{U} \, P_5^R$$
$\Rightarrow$     «$\mathcal{U}$ Entailment Law (3.31a) with (8.48)»
$$\Box P_6^R \vee \Diamond P_5^R$$
$\Rightarrow$     «definition of $P_6^R$, $\Box$ Axiom (3.10b), and
        Antecedent-Strengthening Law (2.29)»
$$\Box \, in(CS_2) \vee \Diamond P_5^R$$
$\Rightarrow$     «(8.50)»
$$false \vee \Diamond P_5^R$$
$=$     «Or-Simplification Law (2.25c)»
$$\Diamond P_5^R$$
$=$     « TL One-Point Law (3.61b)»
$$\Diamond(\exists V\colon V=5\colon P_V^R)$$
$\Rightarrow$     «TL Quantification Weakening Law (3.50b)»
$$\Diamond(\exists V\in \mathcal{W}\colon V{<}6\colon P_V^R)$$
$\Rightarrow$     «Consequent-Weakening Law (2.30)»
$$\Diamond(Q \vee (\exists V\in \mathcal{W}\colon V{<}6\colon P_V^R))$$

Premise (c) follows from (8.51).

With premises (a) through (c) of Eventuality by Weakly Fair Helpful Actions (8.43) discharged, we conclude (8.54), $(\forall R\in \mathcal{W}\colon P \Rightarrow \Diamond at(CS_1))$. It is not difficult to prove (8.53) from this, as is required to complete our proof that $S/F$ satisfies (8.47), so all entry requests are granted.

$$(\forall R\in \mathcal{W}\colon P \Rightarrow \Diamond at(CS_1))$$
$\Rightarrow$     «TL Range Narrowing Law (3.48)»
$$(\forall R\colon R{=}10\colon P \Rightarrow \Diamond at(CS_1))$$
$=$     «TL One-Point Law (3.61)»
$$(P \Rightarrow \Diamond at(CS_1))_{10}^R$$
$=$     «Textual Substitution (2.71)»
$$at(door_1) \wedge I \Rightarrow \Diamond at(CS_1)$$
$=$     «Statement Juxtaposition Control Axiom (4.10a)»
$$at(entry_1) \wedge I \Rightarrow \Diamond at(CS_1)$$

## Historical Notes

The axioms and rules of §8.1 that complete $S$-Temporal Logic are inspired by the recipe given in [Manna & Pnueli 83b] for "cooking" a temporal proof system for a pet language. Differences between our axiomatization and the one in [Manna & Pnueli 83b] arise from two sources. First, we include in $\mathcal{H}_S^+$ anchored sequences that correspond to executions starting from arbitrary program states; [Manna & Pnueli 83b] consider only executions starting from program states reachable from an initial state. Second, the treatments of fairness differ.

$\mathcal{U}$ Property Rules (8.14a) and (8.14b) as well as $\Box$ Property Rule (8.17) are similar to rules first proposed in [Lamport 80b]. See [Manna & Pnueli 84] for a large collection of such inference rules to facilitate proving Temporal Logic theorems when reasoning about programs. For example, □ Property Rule (8.17) is known there as INV.

Fairness in concurrent programs can be traced back to properties first postulated in [Dijkstra 65] and [Dijkstra 68b] concerning process execution speeds. The virtues of assuming fairness, however, have not been universally embraced. A debate on the subject can be found in [Dijkstra 88], [Chandy & Misra 88a], and [Schneider & Lamport 88]. An early Temporal Logic formulation of a fairness assumption appears in [Pnueli 79]. Fairness assumptions for atomic actions were first defined and formalized in [Lehman et al. 81] but with somewhat different terminology—*impartial* for what we call unconditional fairness, *just* for what we call weak fairness, and *fair* for what we call strong fairness. Our terminology is taken from [Francez 86], which gives a snapshot of research on fairness through the mid-80s.

The conditions we impose on fairness assumptions are derived from a semantic characterization of fairness in [Apt et al. 87] (see [Apt et al. 88] for an expanded treatment). There, three criteria are postulated for fairness assumptions. The first is called *feasibility*; we call this machine closed, adopting the terminology of [Abadi & Lamport 88], who articulated this condition in connection with a theory of system refinement. The second criterion, *equivalence robustness*, asserts that interchanging two independent actions should not affect whether a fairness assumption is satisfied by an execution. And the final criterion, *liveness enhancement*, asserts that the fairness assumption actually rules out some executions. We do not require that fairness assumptions satisfy these last two criteria; neither is necessary for implementation or reasoning. However, these last two criteria are sensible, and we expect that they would be satisfied by the fairness assumptions one encounters in practice.

A variety of approaches for reasoning about fair executions have been proposed. One, discussed in [Apt & Olderog 83], is to make a connection between fairness and nondeterminism in programs. A program with a fairness assumption is transformed into one having no fairness assumptions but containing a nondeterministic choice statement. We rejected this approach because it would mean developing the logical apparatus to infer properties of one program by proving them for another. Difficulties associated with that are hinted at in §7.5 in connection with auxiliary variable deletion. A second approach for establishing that $P$ is satisfied by execution under a fairness assumption $F$ is simply to prove that $F \Rightarrow P$ is $\mathcal{H}_S^+$-valid [Emerson 83]. This forces us to reason about a somewhat more complicated formula—especially since $F$ is liable to be long. The approach we employ, encoding $F$ as a collection of axioms and proving $P$, seems to have the advantages of the $F \Rightarrow P$ approach but none of the disadvantages.

The use of well-founded sets to prove termination of sequential programs is discussed in [Floyd 67]. Their use for proving properties of concurrent programs was first introduced in [Lehman et al. 81]. There, fairness ensures that some ranking function, whose domain is the program state space and whose range is a well-founded set, decreases eventually (rather than after every atomic action). This is the basis for Eventuality by Weakly Fair Helpful Actions (8.43) and Eventuality by Strongly Fair Helpful Actions (8.45), inference rules we borrowed from [Manna & Pnueli 81c]. The idea of helpful actions (there, called *helpful directions*) was independently reported in [Grumberg et al. 81] for termination of **do** statements with multiple guarded commands. Figure 8.8 is based on the "proof diagrams" of [Manna & Pnueli 84]. A different diagrammatic representation useful for proving eventualities is described in [Owicki & Lamport 82], which extends a scheme first proposed in [Lamport 77a].

Peterson's mutual exclusion protocol has become a benchmark in the verification literature. Other Temporal Logic proofs of eventual entry can be found in [Peterson 81] and [Manna & Pnueli 81c].

## Exercises

**8.1.** For what class of programs is the following alternative to $\mathcal{H}_S^+$ Triple Rule (8.4) sound?

$$\frac{\{P\}\,\alpha\,\{Q\}}{(at(\alpha) \wedge P) \Rightarrow \bigcirc (after(\alpha) \wedge Q)}$$

**8.2.** Given is a sequential program $S$ containing a statement $T$. If $P \Rightarrow wp(T, Q)$ is valid, then what is the strongest $S$-Temporal Logic theorem that can be proved about $P$ and $Q$?

**8.3.** (a) Prove (8.10): $at(L_1) \wedge x + y = W \Rightarrow (\bigcirc at(T_1) \Rightarrow \bigcirc (x + y = W))$

(b) Prove (8.11): $at(T_1) \wedge x + y = W \Rightarrow (\bigcirc after(T_1) \Rightarrow \bigcirc (x + y = W + 1))$

(c) Prove (8.12): $at(L_2) \wedge x + y = W \Rightarrow (\bigcirc at(T_2) \Rightarrow \bigcirc (x + y = W))$

**8.4.** Prove that execution of

> $S$: **var** $x$ : Int
>     **do** $true \rightarrow x := x + 1$ **od**

causes $x$ to exceed any integer value.

**8.5.** Prove that the following program terminates with $x = 0$.

> $S$: **var** $x$ : Int
>     **cobegin**
>         **do** $x > 0 \rightarrow x := x - 1$ **od**
>     $\parallel$
>         **do** $x < 0 \rightarrow x := x + 1$ **od**
>     **coend**

**8.6.** What is the strongest assertion $A$ that can be made about the values of $x$ and $y$ when the following program terminates? To buttress your claim, give an $S$-Temporal Logic proof that $at(S) \Rightarrow \Diamond (after(S) \wedge A)$ is a theorem.

> $S$: **var** $x, y$ : Int
>     **cobegin**
>         **do** $y > 0 \rightarrow y, x := y - 1, x + 1$ **od**
>     $\parallel$
>         **do** $x > 0 \rightarrow x := x - 1$ **od**
>     **coend**

**8.7.** Prove that the following program terminates.

> $x := 0$
> **cobegin**
>     $\langle$**if** $x = 1 \rightarrow$ **skip fi**$\rangle$ $x := 0$
> $\parallel$
>     $\langle$**if** $x = 0 \rightarrow$ **skip fi**$\rangle$ $x := 1$ $\langle$**if** $x = 0 \rightarrow$ **skip fi**$\rangle$
> **coend**

**8.8.** Prove that $at(S) \Rightarrow \square \Diamond at(S_1)$ is an $S$-Temporal Logic theorem for $S$ given below. Make no assumptions about fairness.

```
S: turn := 1
   cobegin
        do true → if turn=1 → skip fi
                  S₁: skip
                  turn := 2
        od
   ‖
        do true → if turn=2 → skip fi
                  S₂: skip
                  turn := 1
        od
   coend
```

**8.9.** For $P$ a state predicate, is

$$after(S) \wedge P \Rightarrow \Box(after(S) \wedge P)$$

a theorem of $S$-Temporal Logic for every program $S$? Justify your answer with a proof or an example for which the formula is not valid.

**8.10.** Give a formal proof of (8.16):

$$at(T_1) \wedge x=W \Rightarrow (at(T_1) \wedge x=W)\mathcal{U}(in(L_1) \wedge x=W+1)$$

**8.11.** Give a formal justification for $\mathcal{U}$ Property Rule (8.14a):

$$\frac{\text{For all } \alpha \in \mathcal{A}(S): \quad \{at(\alpha) \wedge P \wedge \neg Q\} \, \alpha \, \{P \vee Q\}}{P \Rightarrow P \mathcal{U} Q}$$

**8.12.** Prove that $F_\alpha^u$ is equivalent to:

(a)     $\neg\Diamond\Box at(\alpha)$

(b)     $\Box(at(\alpha) \Rightarrow \Diamond after(\alpha))$

**8.13.** Prove that $F_\alpha^s$ is equivalent to:

(a)     $\neg\Diamond(\Box at(\alpha) \wedge \Box\Diamond enbl(\alpha))$

(b)     $\Box\Diamond(\neg at(\alpha) \vee \Box\neg enbl(\alpha))$

(c)     $\Box\Diamond(\neg at(\alpha) \vee \neg\Diamond enbl(\alpha))$

(d)     $\neg\Diamond\Box(at(\alpha) \wedge \Diamond enbl(\alpha))$

(e)     $\Box(\Box\Diamond(at(\alpha) \wedge enbl(\alpha)) \Rightarrow \Diamond after(\alpha))$

**8.14.** Prove that $F_\alpha^w$ is equivalent to:

(a)     $\neg\Diamond\Box(at(\alpha) \wedge enbl(\alpha))$

(b)     $\Box(\Diamond\neg at(\alpha) \vee \Diamond\neg enbl(\alpha))$

(c)     $\Box(\Diamond\Box(at(\alpha) \wedge enbl(\alpha)) \Rightarrow \Diamond after(\alpha))$

**8.15.** The following has been proposed as a fairness assumption.

$$F_\alpha^n: \quad \Box(at(\alpha) \wedge enbl(\alpha) \Rightarrow \bigcirc after(\alpha))$$

(a)     What difficulties, if any, arise if the fairness assumption $F$ for a sequential program $S$ satisfies $F \Rightarrow \bigwedge_{\alpha \in \mathcal{A}(S)} F_\alpha^n$?

(b)     What difficulties, if any, arise if the fairness assumption $F$ for a concurrent program $S$ satisfies $F \Rightarrow \bigwedge_{\alpha \in \mathcal{A}(S)} F_\alpha^n$?

(c)     Give an example of a two-process concurrent program with fairness assumption $F$, $F \Rightarrow \bigwedge_{\alpha \in \mathcal{A}(S)} F_\alpha^n$, that can be implemented with a single processor.

**8.16.** Fairness Assumption Requirements (8.27) gives two conditions that a fairness assumption must satisfy. Sometimes a third condition is also imposed:

$$\text{Exists a program } S: \; \mathcal{H}_S^+ \cap \mathcal{F} \neq \mathcal{H}_S^+$$

(a)     Give an example of a nontrivial fairness assumption that this condition rules out or explain why no such example exists.

(b)     Give an (informal) justification for requiring that a fairness assumption satisfy this third requirement.

**8.17.** Which of the following candidate fairness assumptions satisfy the conditions of Fairness Assumption Requirements (8.27)?

(a)     $at(\alpha) \wedge enbl(\alpha) \Rightarrow \Diamond after(\alpha)$

(b)     $\Box(at(\alpha) \wedge enbl(\alpha) \Rightarrow \Diamond after(\alpha))$

(c)     $\Box(at(\alpha) \wedge enbl(\alpha) \wedge at(\beta) \wedge enbl(\beta) \Rightarrow \bigcirc(after(\alpha) \vee after(\beta)))$

(d)     For $\alpha$ and $\beta$ unconditional atomic actions in different processes:
$$\Box\Diamond at(\alpha) \Rightarrow \Diamond after(\beta)$$

(e)     For $S$ an **if** statement
$$S: \; \textbf{if } B_1 \rightarrow S_1 \; [] \; B_2 \rightarrow S_2 \; [] \; \cdots \; [] \; B_n \rightarrow S_n \; \textbf{fi}$$
$$\Box\Diamond(at(GEval_{if}(S)) \wedge B_i) \Rightarrow \Diamond at(S_i)$$

(f)     For $S$ an **if** statement
$$S: \; \textbf{if } B_1 \rightarrow S_1 \; [] \; B_2 \rightarrow S_2 \; [] \; \cdots \; [] \; B_n \rightarrow S_n \; \textbf{fi}$$
$$\Diamond\Box(at(GEval_{if}(S)) \wedge B_i) \Rightarrow \Diamond at(S_i)$$

**8.18.** For what values of $x1$ and $x2$ does the following program terminate, assuming that all actions are unconditionally fair? Give an $S/F$-Temporal Logic theorem (and proof) to justify your claim.

```
S: y1, y2 := x1, x2
    cobegin
        do y1≠y2 → if y1>y2 → y1 := y1−y2
                   [] y1≤y2 → skip
                   fi
        od
    ||
        do y1≠y2 → if y2>y1 → y2 := y2−y1
                   [] y2≤y1 → skip
                   fi
        od
    coend
```

**8.19.** Determine whether $at(S) \Rightarrow \Box\Diamond at(S_1)$ is an $S$-Temporal Logic theorem for each of the following. Assume that all atomic actions are strongly fair.

(a)    S: *free* := *true*
       **cobegin**
          **do** *true* → ⟨**if** *free* → *free* := *false* **fi**⟩
                 $S_1$: **skip**
                 *free* := *true*
          **od**
        ‖
          **do** *true* → ⟨**if** *free* → *free* := *false* **fi**⟩
                 $S_2$: **skip**
                 *free* := *true*
          **od**
       **coend**

(b)    S: $x, y$ := *false, false*
       **cobegin**
          $x$ := *true*
          **if** ¬$y$ → **skip fi**
          $S_1$: **skip**
          $x$ := *false*
        ‖
          $y$ := *true*
          **if** ¬$x$ → **skip fi**
          $S_2$: **skip**
          $y$ := *false*
       **coend**

(c)    S: $s$ := 1
       **cobegin**
         ⟨**if** $s > 0$ → $s := s - 1$ **fi**⟩
         $S_1$: **skip**
         $s := s + 1$
        ‖
         ⟨**if** $s > 0$ → $s := s - 1$ **fi**⟩
         $S_2$: **skip**
         $s := s + 1$
       **coend**

**8.20.** Without using any of the inference rules presented in §8.5 or beyond, prove that the program of Figure 8.3 terminates when all atomic actions are unconditionally fair.

**8.21.** Without using any of the inference rules presented in §8.5 or beyond, prove that the program of Figure 8.5 terminates when all atomic actions are weakly fair.

**8.22.** Without using any of the inference rules presented in §8.5 or beyond, prove that the program of Figure 8.2 terminates when all atomic actions are strongly fair.

**8.23.** Prove that in the Producer/Consumer program of Figure 6.1, *a* is unbounded, assuming that all atomic actions are strongly fair.

   (i) Construct the proof without using any of the inference rules presented in §8.5 or beyond.

  (ii) Construct the proof without using Eventuality by Weakly Fair Helpful Actions (8.43).

**8.24.** Give an example program and property for which **skip** is a helpful action.

**8.25.** Prove that the program of Figure 8.3 terminates when all atomic actions are unconditionally fair by using:

   (a)   Eventuality by Weakly Fair Helpful Actions (8.43)

   (b)   Eventuality by Strongly Fair Helpful Actions (8.45)

**8.26.** Prove that the program of Figure 8.2 terminates when all atomic actions are strongly
fair by using Eventuality by Strongly Fair Helpful Actions (8.45).

**8.27.** Justify Eventuality by Strongly Fair Helpful Actions (8.45) using the same approach
as was employed to justify Eventuality by Weakly Fair Helpful Actions (8.43).

**8.28.** It is possible to define a single inference rule for concluding

$$(\forall R \in \mathcal{W} \colon P \Rightarrow \Diamond Q)$$

when there are both weakly fair and strongly fair atomic actions. Define $H_R$ to be
the union of two sets: $H_R^s$ and $H_R^w$. Then, have different premises for each of these
sets of actions. Derive such a rule.

**8.29.** Does the protocol of Figure 8.6 satisfy $\Box(at(entry_1) \Rightarrow \Diamond at(CS_1))$? Justify your
answer with a proof or a counterexample.

**8.30.** Prove that the mutual exclusion protocol of Figure 8.6 satisfies

$$at(S) \quad \Rightarrow \quad \Box(at(entry_i) \Rightarrow \Diamond at(CS_i))$$

assuming $at(NCS_i) \Rightarrow \Diamond after(NCS_i)$ instead of assuming that all atomic actions are
weakly fair.

**8.31.** Prove, using Eventuality by Unless (8.37), that the mutual exclusion protocol of
Figure 8.6 satisfies $at(S) \Rightarrow (\Box(at(entry_i) \Rightarrow \Diamond at(CS_i)))$ if all atomic actions are
weakly fair.

**8.32.** Without using any rule introduced in §8.5 or beyond, prove that the mutual exclusion protocol of Figure 8.6 satisfies $at(S) \Rightarrow (\Box(at(entry_i) \Rightarrow \Diamond at(CS_i)))$.

# Chapter 9

# Programming with Fine-Grained Atomic Actions

Real computer hardware does not implement as atomic actions all the assignment statements, guard evaluation actions, and atomic statements of our programming notation. A typical computer can execute only a small, fixed set of unconditional atomic actions; an operating system might add to this a few conditional atomic actions. Thus, there is a gap between the programming model we have been assuming and what is available on an actual computer system.

To bridge the gap, this chapter is about programming using only a realistic set of fine-grained, unconditional atomic actions. (Chapter 10 discusses how to exploit the conditional atomic actions supported by operating systems.) We give methods for inferring safety properties of programs constructed with fine-grained atomic actions by reasoning about programs constructed with coarse-grained ones. We define a subset of our programming notation, all of whose statements are easily compiled into realistic, fine-grained, unconditional atomic actions. Finally, we discuss techniques for programming with this subset. Solutions to classical coordination problems illustrate the techniques.

## 9.1 Pretending Atomicity

It is easier to reason about a concurrent program that has fewer atomic actions, since fewer interleavings are then possible. By combining atomic actions into atomic statements, we reduce the number of atomic actions. But the resulting program may not satisfy the same properties as the original. This happens because control points and intermediate states are eliminated in forming an atomic statement. For example, in what follows, atomic statement $S'$ is obtained by combining the two atomic actions comprising $S$.

$$S:\ y := x+1\ \ x := y$$

$$S': \quad \langle y := x+1 \quad x := y \rangle$$

Even though $S$ and $S'$ each increments $x$ by 1 and sets $y$ to that value, only $S'$ does not falsify $x=y$. This is because execution of $S$ produces an intermediate state that satisfies $x \neq y$, whereas execution of $S'$ does not.

Some properties are unaffected when atomic actions are combined into a single atomic statement. $S$ and $S'$ above both terminate with $x=y$, so this is an example of a property unaffected by combining the two assignment statements. A natural question, then, is what conditions allow us to construct a proof that some program $S'$ built from coarse-grained atomic actions satisfies a given property and then conclude that the same property holds for a program $S$ whose atomic actions have been combined to produce $S'$. In short, we want to know when reasoning about a program with coarse-grained atomic actions tells us something about a program with finer-grained ones.

## Reduction for Invariance Properties

Define $S/T$ to be the program that results when statement $T$ in $S$ is replaced by atomic statement $\langle T \rangle$. Consider a history of $S/T$

$$(9.1) \quad s_0 \xrightarrow{\alpha_1} s_1 \xrightarrow{\alpha_2} s_2 \xrightarrow{\langle T \rangle} s_3 \xrightarrow{\alpha_3} s_4 \cdots$$

where $T$ is the juxtaposition of three atomic actions:

$$T: \quad R \; A \; L$$

History (9.1) satisfies invariance property $Init \Rightarrow \square Etern$ if either $s_0$ does not satisfy $Init$ or all states satisfy $Etern$. For the sake of discussion, assume the latter—that $s_0$ satisfies $Init$ and all states satisfy $Etern$.

Among the histories of $S$ are the $T$-aggregated histories[1]

$$(9.2) \quad s_0 \xrightarrow{\alpha_1} s_1 \xrightarrow{\alpha_2} s_2 \xrightarrow{R} t \xrightarrow{A} t' \xrightarrow{L} s_3 \xrightarrow{\alpha_3} s_4 \cdots$$

which are defined to be histories of $S$ in which no atomic action is interleaved with execution of $T$. Since we have assumed that $Init$ holds in $s_0$ and all the states of (9.1) satisfy $Etern$, we conclude that histories of the form (9.2) satisfy $Init \Rightarrow \square Etern$ if intermediate states $t$ and $t'$ satisfy $Etern$.

To infer that a state $t$ satisfies $Etern$, a proof that execution of $R$ does not falsify $Etern$ suffices:

---

[1]More than one $T$-aggregated history is possible if atomic actions are nondeterministic. If all atomic actions are deterministic, then a single $T$-aggregated history describes the effects of executing sequence $\alpha_1 \, \alpha_2 \, R \, A \, L \, \alpha_3$ of atomic actions.

(9.3)  $\{Etern\}\ R\ \{Etern\}$

To infer that a state $t'$ satisfies *Etern*, a proof that execution of $L$ does not falsify $\neg Etern$ suffices:

(9.4)  $\{\neg Etern\}\ L\ \{\neg Etern\}$

(Validity of (9.4) implies that $L$ was not executed in a state satisfying $\neg Etern$, because, according to (9.2), $L$ terminated in $s_3$, and $s_3$ is known to satisfy *Etern*.) Thus, (9.3) and (9.4) guarantee that a $T$-aggregated history with intermediate states $t$ and $t'$ as in (9.2) satisfies $Init \Rightarrow \Box Etern$ if history (9.1) of $S/T$ does. We have identified conditions that imply that $T$-aggregated histories of $S$ are equivalent to histories of $S/T$, at least with respect to an invariance property $Init \Rightarrow \Box Etern$.

Not all histories of $S$ are $T$-aggregated histories. Atomic actions (from other processes) may be interleaved between $R$ and $A$ and between $A$ and $L$. Here is an example of such a history:

(9.5)  $s_0 \xrightarrow{\alpha_1} s_1 \xrightarrow{R} \hat{s}_2 \xrightarrow{\alpha_2} \hat{t} \xrightarrow{A} \hat{t}' \xrightarrow{\alpha_3} \hat{s}_3 \xrightarrow{L} \hat{s}_4 \cdots$

In order to establish that $S$ satisfies $Init \Rightarrow \Box Etern$, we must show that such histories—as well as the $T$-aggregated histories—satisfy $Init \Rightarrow \Box Etern$. They do satisfy $Init \Rightarrow \Box Etern$ provided that certain commutativity conditions on actions hold. These commutativity conditions allow an arbitrary history of $S$ to be transformed into a $T$-aggregated history, where the $T$-aggregated history satisfies $Init \Rightarrow \Box Etern$ iff the original arbitrary history does.

An atomic action $\rho$ is defined to *right commute* with an atomic action $\alpha$ if the state produced by first executing $\rho$ and then executing $\alpha$ could also result from executing $\alpha$ followed by $\rho$. ("Could" because $\alpha$ and/or $\rho$ may be nondeterministic.) Whether two atomic actions from different processes right commute can be checked using *wp*. This is because if $\rho\alpha$ and $\alpha\rho$ both terminate, then due to Process Independence Axiom (5.3), the same control predicates will be satisfied by the final state of each. States from which $\rho\alpha$ and $\alpha\rho$ both terminate can be described using *wp*, as can the equivalence of the noncontrol aspects of states (since the noncontrol aspects of states are described using primitive state predicates).

(9.6)  **Right Commutativity.** Atomic action $\rho$ right commutes with atomic action $\alpha$ of another process iff for all primitive state predicates $Q$:

$$wp(\rho\alpha, Q) \Rightarrow wp(\alpha\rho, Q) \qquad \Box$$

Similarly, an atomic action $\Lambda$ *left commutes* with an atomic action $\alpha$ if the state produced by first executing $\alpha$ and then executing $\Lambda$ also would be produced by executing $\Lambda$ followed by $\alpha$. Whether two atomic actions from different processes left commute can be checked using *wp*, too.

(9.7)   **Left Commutativity.** Atomic action $\Lambda$ left commutes with atomic action $\alpha$ of another process iff for all primitive state predicates $Q$:

$$wp(\alpha\Lambda, Q) \;\Rightarrow\; wp(\Lambda\alpha, Q) \qquad\qquad \square$$

A history like (9.5) is transformed into a $T$-aggregated history by moving $R$ later and $L$ earlier. Commutativity conditions to permit this are:

(9.8)   $R$ right commutes with every atomic action in every other process.

(9.9)   $L$ left commutes with every atomic action in every other process.

To see why (9.8) and (9.9) suffice, we show how they, in conjunction with (9.3) and (9.4), can be used to prove that history (9.5) satisfies $Init \Rightarrow \square Etern$ if every $T$-aggregated history like (9.2) does.

In order to demonstrate that (9.5) satisfies $Init \Rightarrow \square Etern$, we must show that if $s_0$ satisfies $Init$, then all states satisfy $Etern$. We do this as follows.

- $s_0$ satisfies $Init$ and $Etern$ by our assumptions about history (9.1).

- $s_1$ satisfies $Etern$ by our assumptions about history (9.1).

- $\hat{s}_2$ satisfies $Etern$ due to condition (9.3), given that $s_1$ satisfies $Etern$.

- $\hat{t}$ satisfies $Etern$ because intermediate state $t$ of (9.2) satisfies $Etern$ and condition (9.8) implies that $\hat{t}$ equals some such state $t$. Take $R$ for $\rho$ and $\alpha_2$ for $\alpha$; interchanging $R$ with $\alpha_2$ in history (9.5) produces the prefix of (9.2) that ends with state $t$.

- $\hat{t}'$ satisfies $Etern$ because $\hat{t}'$ equals an intermediate state $t'$ in some $T$-aggregated history (9.2), and $t'$ in every such $T$-aggregated history satisfies $Etern$. State $\hat{t}'$ equals some $t'$ because both are produced by executing atomic action $A$ in state $t$.

- $\hat{s}_3$ satisfies $Etern$ due to (9.4), because we show below that $\hat{s}_4$ satisfies $Etern$.

- $\hat{s}_4$ satisfies $Etern$ because $s_4$ of (9.2) satisfies $Etern$ and condition (9.9) implies that $\hat{s}_4$ and $s_4$ are equal. Take $L$ for $\Lambda$ and $\alpha_3$ for $\alpha$; interchanging $L$ with $\alpha_3$ (as well as interchanging $R$ with $\alpha_2$) produces the prefix of (9.2) that ends with state $s_4$.

This argument can be generalized for histories in which more than one atomic action is executed between $R$ and $A$ and/or between $A$ and $L$. Repeated use of conditions (9.8) and (9.9) allows the $R$ to be moved right and the $L$ to be moved left, producing the desired $T$-aggregated history.

Thus, provided that (9.3), (9.4), (9.8), and (9.9) hold, a history of $S$ satisfies $Init \Rightarrow \square Etern$ iff the corresponding $T$-aggregated history does. We have also seen that $S/T$ satisfies $Init \Rightarrow \square Etern$ if (9.3) and (9.4) hold and all $T$-aggregated histories of $S$ satisfy $Init \Rightarrow \square Etern$. Therefore, whenever (9.3), (9.4), (9.8), and (9.9) hold, we can establish that $S$ satisfies $Init \Rightarrow \square Etern$ by constructing a proof that $S/T$ satisfies $Init \Rightarrow \square Etern$:

(9.10) **Reduction for Invariance Properties.** A program $S$ that contains the statement

$$T: \; R \; A \; L$$

satisfies invariance property $Init \Rightarrow \Box Etern$ if program $S/T$ satisfies $Init \Rightarrow \Box Etern$ and the following hold:

(i)   $\{Etern\} \; R \; \{Etern\}$

(ii)  $\{\neg Etern\} \; L \; \{\neg Etern\}$

(iii) $R$ right commutes with each atomic action in every other process.

(iv)  $L$ left commutes with each atomic action in every other process.   □

When $Etern$ does not concern intermediate states of $T$, a simpler reduction principle applies. The following is the general form taken by such an $Etern$, where $Q$ is some state predicate.

$$Etern: \; Q \vee (\neg at(T) \wedge in(T))$$

Premises (i) and (ii) of Reduction for Invariance Properties (9.10) are always satisfied for this choice of $Etern$. Premise (i) follows by using Rule of Consequence (4.25) with $\{true\} \; R \; \{after(R)\}$, since both $Etern \Rightarrow true$ and $after(R) \Rightarrow \neg at(T) \wedge in(T)$ are valid. Premise (ii) follows by using Rule of Consequence (4.25) with $\{false\} \; L \; \{\neg Etern\}$ and $\neg Etern \wedge at(L) \Rightarrow false$.

(9.11) **Reduction for Invariance Properties Corollary.** A program $S$ that contains statement

$$T: \; R \; A \; L$$

satisfies invariance property

$$Init \Rightarrow \Box (Q \vee (\neg at(T) \wedge in(T)))$$

if program $S/T$ satisfies this property and the following hold:

(i)  $R$ right commutes with each atomic action in every other process.

(ii) $L$ left commutes with each atomic action in every other process.   □

Reduction for Invariance Properties (9.10) and its corollary (9.11) concern whether three atomic actions can be combined into a single atomic statement. It is also possible to combine only two atomic actions into an atomic statement. The trick is to regard one of $R$ or $L$ as being an empty atomic action. The *empty atomic action* changes no component of the state, so it falsifies no state predicate, left commutes with every atomic action, and right commutes with every atomic action.[2] In short, the empty atomic action is one for which premises of Reduction for Invariance Properties (9.10) are discharged trivially.

---

[2]In contrast to the empty atomic action, **skip** does cause a state component—the program counter—to change.

*Applications of Reduction*

Reduction allows us to prove that sequential program

$$S: \quad y := x+1 \quad x := y$$

satisfies partial correctness property

(9.12)  $at(S) \wedge x{=}X \; \Rightarrow \; \Box(after(S) \; \Rightarrow \; x{=}y \wedge x{=}X{+}1)$

by reasoning about $S/S$, the program whose single atomic statement is built from the two atomic actions of $S$:

$$S: \quad \langle y := x+1 \quad x := y \rangle$$

Property (9.12) imposes no restriction on the intermediate states of $S$, since $after(S) \Rightarrow x{=}y \wedge x{=}X{+}1$ is equivalent to:

*Etern*:  $(after(S) \; \Rightarrow \; x{=}y \wedge x{=}X{+}1) \; \vee \; (\neg at(S) \wedge in(S))$

Therefore, we use Reduction for Invariance Properties Corollary (9.11). Its premises (i) and (ii) are vacuously satisfied when there is only one process—take $y := x+1$ to be $R$, $x := y$ to be $A$, and the empty atomic action for $L$.[3] So, a proof that $S/S$ satisfies (9.12) suffices for establishing that $S$ satisfies (9.12). Partial Correctness Rule (6.19) applied to the following proof outline for $S/S$ is then all that is required.

$$\{at(S) \wedge x{=}X\} \; \langle y := x+1 \quad x := y \rangle \; \{x{=}y \wedge x{=}X{+}1\}$$

As a second example, we revisit the producer/consumer program of §6.2. See Figure 9.1. We would like to prove that sequence *out* of the values removed by *Cons* from *buf* is a prefix of sequence *inp* of the values added by *Prod*. This is formalized as the invariance property $Init \Rightarrow \Box Etern$ where:

*Init*:     $at(PC) \; \wedge \; inp{=}INP$

*Etern*:   $out{=}inp[.. \, |out| - 1]$

We use Reduction for Invariance Properties (9.10) twice to reduce the number of atomic actions that must be considered. The first reduction combines $S_2$, $S_3$, and $S_4$ into a single atomic statement and produces $PC/S_2 S_3 S_4$. A second reduction produces $(PC/S_2 S_3 S_4)/T_1 T_2 T_3$ (see Figure 9.2) by combining $T_1$, $T_2$, and $T_3$ into a single atomic statement. The desired invariance property then is proved with Precondition Safety Consequence Rule (6.15) applied

---

[3]It also works to choose the empty atomic action for $R$, $y := x+1$ for $A$, and $x := y$ for $L$.

$PC$: **var** $a, r$ : Int; $v, w$ : Char;
$\qquad$ $buf$: **array** $[0 .. N-1]$ **of** Char;
$\qquad$ $inp, out$ : **seq of** Char

$\quad$ $a, r, out := 0, 0, \varepsilon$
$\quad$ **cobegin**
$\qquad$ $Prod$: **do** $true \rightarrow S_1$: $v, inp := inp[0], inp[1..]$
$\qquad\qquad\qquad\qquad\qquad$ $S_2$: $\langle$**if** $a-r<N \rightarrow$ **skip fi**$\rangle$
$\qquad\qquad\qquad\qquad\qquad$ $S_3$: $buf[a \bmod N] := v$
$\qquad\qquad\qquad\qquad\qquad$ $S_4$: $a := a+1$
$\qquad\qquad\qquad$ **od**
$\quad$ $\|$
$\qquad$ $Cons$: **do** $true \rightarrow T_1$: $\langle$**if** $a-r>0 \rightarrow$ **skip fi**$\rangle$
$\qquad\qquad\qquad\qquad\qquad$ $T_2$: $w := buf[r \bmod N]$
$\qquad\qquad\qquad\qquad\qquad$ $T_3$: $r := r+1$
$\qquad\qquad\qquad\qquad\qquad$ $T_4$: $out := out\ w$
$\qquad\qquad\qquad$ **od**
$\quad$ **coend**

**Figure 9.1.** Producer/consumer program

$PC$: $a, r, out := 0, 0, \varepsilon$
$\quad$ **cobegin**
$\qquad$ $Prod$: **do** $true \rightarrow S_1$: $\quad v, inp := inp[0], inp[1..]$
$\qquad\qquad\qquad\qquad\qquad$ $S_{234}$: $\left\langle$**if** $a-r<N \rightarrow$ **skip fi**$\right.$
$\qquad\qquad\qquad\qquad\qquad\qquad\quad$ $buf[a \bmod N] := v$
$\qquad\qquad\qquad\qquad\qquad\qquad\quad$ $a := a+1 \left.\right\rangle$
$\qquad\qquad\qquad$ **od**
$\quad$ $\|$
$\qquad$ $Cons$: **do** $true \rightarrow T_{123}$: $\left\langle$**if** $a-r>0 \rightarrow$ **skip fi**$\right.$
$\qquad\qquad\qquad\qquad\qquad\qquad\quad$ $w := buf[r \bmod N]$
$\qquad\qquad\qquad\qquad\qquad\qquad\quad$ $r := r+1 \left.\right\rangle$
$\qquad\qquad\qquad\qquad\qquad$ $T_4$: $\quad out := out\ w$
$\qquad\qquad\qquad$ **od**
$\quad$ **coend**

**Figure 9.2.** Reduced producer/consumer program

to a proof outline for $(PC / S_2\,S_3\,S_4)/T_1\,T_2\,T_3$. This twice-reduced program is simpler to analyze; it has about half the number of atomic actions.

Reduction for Invariance Properties (9.10) can be used combine $S_2$, $S_3$, and $S_4$ into an atomic statement if we check that its premises (i) through (iv) hold. Take $S_2$ for $R$, $S_3$ for $A$, and $S_4$ for $L$.

Premise (i) asserts that $S_2$ does not falsify *Etern*. It holds because no variable mentioned in *Etern* is changed by $S_2$. Premise (ii) asserts that $S_4$ does not falsify $\neg$ *Etern*. It holds for the same reason.

Premise (iii) involves showing that $S_2$ right commutes with every atomic action in *Cons*. According to Right Commutativity (9.6), we must show:

(9.13)  $wp(S_2 \, GEval_{do}(Cons), Q) \;\Rightarrow\; wp(GEval_{do}(Cons) \, S_2, Q)$

(9.14)  $wp(S_2 \, T_1, Q) \;\Rightarrow\; wp(T_1 \, S_2, Q)$

(9.15)  $wp(S_2 \, T_2, Q) \;\Rightarrow\; wp(T_2 \, S_2, Q)$

(9.16)  $wp(S_2 \, T_3, Q) \;\Rightarrow\; wp(T_3 \, S_2, Q)$

(9.17)  $wp(S_2 \, T_4, Q) \;\Rightarrow\; wp(T_4 \, S_2, Q)$

We give the details only for (9.16), because it is the only obligation that is nontrivial—it is the only one in which a variable (i.e., $r$) is mentioned by one action and changed by the other.

$$
\begin{aligned}
&\quad wp(S_2 \, T_3, Q) \\
=&\quad \text{«weakest precondition (4.51) for statement juxtaposition } S_2 \, T_3 \text{»}\\
&\quad wp(S_2, wp(T_3, Q)) \\
=&\quad \text{«weakest precondition (4.50) for assignment statement } T_3 \text{»}\\
&\quad wp(S_2, (VarAx(PC) \land Q)^r_{r+1}) \\
=&\quad \text{«weakest precondition (5.44) for atomic statement } S_2 \text{»}\\
&\quad a-r<N \land (VarAx(PC) \land Q)^r_{r+1} \\
\Rightarrow&\quad \text{«number theory»}\\
&\quad a-(r+1)<N \land (VarAx(PC) \land Q)^r_{r+1} \\
=&\quad \text{«Textual Substitution (2.71)»}\\
&\quad (a-r<N \land VarAx(PC) \land Q)^r_{r+1} \\
=&\quad \text{«weakest precondition (4.50) for assignment statement } T_3 \text{»}\\
&\quad wp(T_3, a-r<N \land Q) \\
=&\quad \text{«weakest precondition (5.44) for atomic statement } S_2 \text{»}\\
&\quad wp(T_3, wp(S_2, Q)) \\
=&\quad \text{«weakest precondition (4.51) for statement juxtaposition } T_3 \, S_2 \text{»}\\
&\quad wp(T_3 \, S_2, Q)
\end{aligned}
$$

Finally, premise (iv) requires showing that $S_4$ left commutes with every atomic action in *Cons*. This is done using Left Commutativity (9.7) and proving:

(9.18)  $wp(GEval_{do}(Cons) \, S_4, Q) \;\Rightarrow\; wp(S_4 \, GEval_{do}(Cons), Q)$

(9.19)  $wp(T_1 \, S_4, Q) \;\Rightarrow\; wp(S_4 \, T_1, Q)$

(9.20)  $wp(T_2 \, S_4, Q) \;\Rightarrow\; wp(S_4 \, T_2, Q)$

(9.21) $wp(T_3 S_4, Q) \Rightarrow wp(S_4 T_3, Q)$

(9.22) $wp(T_4 S_4, Q) \Rightarrow wp(S_4 T_4, Q)$

Only (9.19) is nontrivial, and similar reasoning to that used above suffices.

To reduce by $T_1, T_2$, and $T_3$, we take $T_1$ for $R$, $T_2$ for $A$, and $T_3$ for $L$.

Premise (i) of Reduction for Invariance Properties (9.10) stipulates that $T_1$ may not falsify *Etern*; this premise holds because $T_1$ does not alter any variable mentioned in *Etern*. Premise (ii) stipulates that $T_3$ may not falsify $\neg$*Etern*, and it holds for the same reason.

Premise (iii) requires showing that $T_1$ right commutes with every atomic action in $Prod/S_2 S_3 S_4$, and premise (iv) requires showing that $T_3$ left commutes with every atomic action in $Prod/S_2 S_3 S_4$. There are three atomic actions in $Prod/S_2 S_3 S_4$: $GEval_{do}(Prod)$, $S_1$, and $\langle S_2 S_3 S_4 \rangle$. Therefore, premises (iii) and (iv) give rise to the following obligations:

(9.23) $wp(T_1 GEval_{do}(Prod), Q) \Rightarrow wp(GEval_{do}(Prod) T_1, Q)$

(9.24) $wp(T_1 S_1, Q) \Rightarrow wp(S_1 T_1, Q)$

(9.25) $wp(T_1 \langle S_2 S_3 S_4 \rangle, Q) \Rightarrow wp(\langle S_2 S_3 S_4 \rangle T_1, Q)$

(9.26) $wp(GEval_{do}(Prod) T_1, Q) \Rightarrow wp(T_1 GEval_{do}(Prod), Q)$

(9.27) $wp(S_1 T_1, Q) \Rightarrow wp(T_1 S_1, Q)$

(9.28) $wp(\langle S_2 S_3 S_4 \rangle T_1, Q) \Rightarrow wp(T_1 \langle S_2 S_3 S_4 \rangle, Q)$

Checking these is straightforward.

## Reduction for Other Properties

Reduction for Invariance Properties (9.10) and its corollary (9.11) do not easily generalize to handle historical safety properties or liveness properties. The problem with historical safety properties is that they can distinguish *T*-aggregated histories from histories, like (9.5), in which atomic actions are interleaved with *T*. Right and left commutativity concern the final state produced when a sequence of two atomic actions is executed; they say nothing about the intermediate state that arises. Consequently, right and left commutativity do not guarantee that reordering atomic actions produces an equivalent execution with respect to a historical safety property.

Liveness properties are problematic because they, too, can depend on sequences of states. For example, reordering atomic actions may change whether a history is ruled out by Strong Fairness (8.21).

*Reduction for Other Statements*

Reduction for Invariance Properties (9.10) and its corollary (9.11) concern statement juxtapositions. We might want to make other types of statements atomic. For example, we might want to transform

(9.29)  **if** $B$ → **skip fi**

into:

⟨**if** $B$ → **skip fi**⟩

Such a transformation should be reasonable, since semantically (9.29) is a statement juxtaposition—it is a guard evaluation action followed by a **skip**. Reduction for Invariance Properties (9.10) is not applicable, however, because the syntax of statement juxtaposition is not used in (9.29).

Here is another example where the syntax of our programming notation obscures a semantic juxtaposition of atomic actions:

**do** $B_1 → \alpha_1 \alpha_2$  [] $B_2 → \alpha_3 \alpha_4$  **od**

We might want to combine the guard evaluation action, $\alpha_1$, and $\alpha_3$ into a single atomic action. However, it is not even clear how to write the desired program. The following describes a program that would seem to have four (and not three, as intended) atomic actions.

**do** ⟨$B_1 → \alpha_1$⟩$\alpha_2$  [] ⟨$B_2 → \alpha_3$⟩$\alpha_4$  **od**

It is messy, but not difficult, to formulate a version of Reduction for Invariance Properties (9.10) that does not suffer difficulties due to programming language syntax. We would employ a programming notation that allowed any sequence of atomic actions to be regarded as a single atomic action. Then, we would enumerate syntactic constructs that lead to (semantic) juxtapositions of atomic actions. We do not pursue this course here, because the programming notation would be needlessly complex.

## 9.2  Translation-Independent Reasoning

Programs written in high-level languages are not executed directly. Instead, they are translated into a machine language, and the machine language program is executed. Since each machine-language instruction is, by definition, an atomic action, this suggests a way to reason about a high-level language program. Translate it into a machine-language program—either by hand or automatically—and reason about the resulting program.

There are three difficulties with reasoning about the translation rather than the original program. First, machine-language programs are significantly larger than the high-level language programs from which they are derived, so the objects we would reason about become quite large. Second, reasoning about a machine-language program forces us to think at a low level of abstraction. And third, the exercise teaches us nothing about the consequences of employing a different translator or executing the program on a computer with a different machine language.

We would like to reason directly about programs written in high-level languages. Moreover, we would like our conclusions to hold for the machine-language program produced by any reasonable compiler for any reasonable machine language—the conclusions should be *translation-independent*. At least for certain types of properties, these goals are attainable. Reasonable compilers and machine languages share certain characteristics. If these characteristics are the only assumptions we make when reasoning about a high-level language program, then our conclusions will be translation-independent.

One characteristic of a reasonable machine language concerns concurrent accesses to memory.

(9.30) **Memory Atomicity.** Concurrent reads and/or writes to a noncomposite variable are serial. Their order may be arbitrary. □

Memory Atomicity (9.30) stipulates that if one process writes 2 to an integer variable $x$ and another process concurrently writes 4 to $x$, then the final value of $x$ will be 2 or 4—not some combination of these. Also, if one process reads $x$ while another is concurrently writing $x$, then the reader will obtain the value in $x$ just before the write commenced or just after the write completed—not some combination of the old and new values.

Reasonable compilers generate machine-language programs that do not access memory unnecessarily.

(9.31) **Compiler Access Restrictions.** A machine-language program generated for an expression or an assignment statement satisfies:

(i) For each variable $v$ that appears in an expression, the number of machine-language instructions that read $v$ is between 1 and the number of times $v$ is mentioned in that expression.

(ii) For each variable $v$ that appears as a target of an assignment statement, the number of machine-language instructions that write $v$ is between 1 and the number of times $v$ is a target.

(iii) The only other variables read or written are fresh variables that are not already used in the program. □

According to Compiler Access Restrictions (9.31), the machine-language program for $x := y+z$ will read $y$ and $z$ once and write $x$ once. The machine-language program for $x := x+1$ will read $x$ once and write $x$ once. Finally, the machine-language program for $x, y := x+1, x+1$ may read $x$ once or twice (due to (i)), will write $x$ once (due to (ii)), and will write $y$ once (due to (ii)).

## Assignment Statements

If assignment statements are translated into machine-language programs, then execution of an assignment statement might involve several atomic actions. However, for proving some invariance properties, we can pretend (as we have been) that certain assignment statements are executed as if they were single atomic actions. We characterize below when this is possible. When it is, we can determine in a translation-independent way whether an invariance property is satisfied by a program, because translating each assignment statement into its constituent atomic actions is not necessary.

Atomic actions that do not read variables written by other processes and do not write variables read by other processes both left and right commute with atomic actions of other processes. We refer to such atomic actions as *commuting* and all others as *noncommuting*. Provided that an assignment statement translation has at most one noncommuting atomic action, the premises of Reduction for Invariance Properties Corollary (9.11) are satisfied. Also, premises (iii) and (iv) of Reduction for Invariance Properties (9.10) are satisfied.

Compiler Access Restrictions (9.31) gives a way to ensure that the machine-language translation of an assignment statement has at most one non-commuting atomic action. Here are sufficient conditions:

(9.32) **At Most One Assignments.** The machine-language program for an assignment statement $T$ will have at most one noncommuting atomic action if either of the following is satisfied.

    (a)    No expression in $T$ mentions a variable that is written by another process, and at most one target of $T$ is read by another process.

    (b)    At most one expression in $T$ mentions at most once a variable that is written by another process, and no target of $T$ is read or written by another process.          □

Most of the assignment statements in the concurrent programs we have developed satisfy these restrictions. See, for example, the two-process search program of Figure 5.1, the producer/consumer program of Figure 6.1, the mutual-exclusion program of Figure 6.8, and the concurrent-reading-while-writing program of Figure 7.2. Moreover, assignment statements that do not satisfy At Most One Assignments (9.32) can usually be decomposed into sequences of assignment statements (possibly involving additional fresh variables) that do.

Given an assignment statement $T$ that satisfies At Most One Assignments (9.32), we can use Reduction for Invariance Properties Corollary (9.11) to infer that an invariance property $Init \Rightarrow \Box (Q \vee (\neg at(T) \wedge in(T)))$ is satisfied.

In order to conclude that an arbitrary invariance property $Init \Rightarrow \Box Etern$ is satisfied, we must use Reduction for Invariance Properties (9.10). Its premises (iii) and (iv) are implied by At Most One Assignments (9.32), so all that remains is to discharge premises (i) and (ii). These premises are satisfied if the truth of *Etern* is left unchanged by each commuting atomic action in the translation of $T$. From Compiler Access Restrictions (9.31), we deduce that *Etern* is left unchanged by these commuting atomic actions if *Etern* does not mention any variable that is a target in $T$ or any control predicate that changes when $T$ is executed (i.e., $at(T)$, $in(T)$, $after(T)$, and control predicates equal to these).

In summary, we have:

(9.33) **Reduction with At Most One Assignments.** Given is a program $S$ containing an assignment statement $T$ that satisfies At Most One Assignments (9.32).

(a)   For proving an invariance property:

$$Init \;\Rightarrow\; \Box(Q \vee (\neg\, at(T) \wedge in(T)))$$

it suffices to construct a proof outline for $S/T$.

(b)   For proving an invariance property

$$Init \;\Rightarrow\; \Box Etern$$

where *Etern* does not mention any variable that is a target in $T$ or any control predicate that changes when $T$ is executed, it suffices to construct a proof outline for $S/T$.                      □

To better understand the need for At Most One Assignments (9.32) in Reduction with At Most One Assignments (9.33), consider the following concurrent program.

(9.34) **cobegin** $x := x+1$ ∥ $x := 2$ **coend**

This program terminates with $x=2 \vee x=3$ when each assignment statement is executed as a single atomic action. However, a compiler that obeyed Compiler Access Restrictions (9.31) might translate assignment statement $x := x+1$ in (9.34) into a load followed by an add and then a store, where *reg* is some private register:

(9.35) **cobegin**   $reg := x$  $reg := reg+1$  $x := reg$   ∥   $x := 2$   **coend**

Program (9.35)—unlike (9.34)—can terminate in a state in which the final value of $x$ is the initial value incremented by 1. (Execute $x := 2$ between $reg := x$ and $x := reg$.) The problem is that $x := x+1$ does not comply with At Most One Assignments (9.32), and its translation involves two noncommuting atomic actions.

## *Guard Evaluation Actions for* **do**

Guard evaluation actions for **do** statements are also translated into machine-language programs. To understand when such a machine-language program can be treated as a single atomic action, we employ reasoning similar to that used above for assignment statements.

The machine-language program that corresponds to a guard evaluation action will contain noncommuting atomic actions, which read from variables written by other processes, and commuting atomic actions, which do not read from these variables. None of these atomic actions changes any variable that is read by another process, because guard evaluation has no side effects. Thus, provided that *Etern* does not depend on the value of a control predicate that changes when $GEval_{do}(S)$ is executed, $\{Etern\}\,\alpha\,\{Etern\}$ and $\{\neg Etern\}\,\alpha\,\{\neg Etern\}$ are valid for each atomic action $\alpha$ in the translation. This means that premises (i) and (ii) of Reduction for Invariance Properties (9.10) are satisfied. If, in addition, at most one of the atomic actions is noncommuting, then premises (iii) and (iv) also hold.

Part (i) of Compiler Access Restrictions (9.31) gives a way to ensure that at most one atomic action in the translation of the guard evaluation for a **do** is noncommuting. So we have:

(9.36) **Reduction with At Most One do Guards.** For a **do** statement $T$, even if $GEval_{do}(T)$ is not translated into a single atomic action, it suffices to construct a proof outline for $S$ in proving invariance property

$$Init \;\Rightarrow\; \Box Etern$$

provided that (i) *Etern* does not mention any control predicate that changes when $GEval_{do}(T)$ is executed and (ii) the guards of $T$ together mention at most once a variable written by another process.          □

The guards of the **do** statements in just about all[4] of the concurrent programs of previous chapters comply with the restrictions of Reduction with At Most One **do** Guards (9.36).

When guards do not comply, it is usually possible to modify the **do** so that they do: add one or more assignment statements before the **do** and at the end of each guarded statement that is part of the **do**. Execution of the added assignment statements calculate the values of the guards, but in a way that satisfies At Most One Assignments (9.32). For example, if $x$ and $y$ are written by another process, then

**do** $x + y > 0 \rightarrow S$ **od**

might be replaced by

---

[4]The notable exception is the concurrent reading while writing program of Figure 7.2.

$$t := x \quad t := t+y \quad \textbf{do } t>0 \rightarrow S \quad t := x \quad t := t+y \quad \textbf{od}$$

where variable $t$ is neither read nor written by other processes.

Reduction with At Most One **do** Guards (9.36) does not allow the guard evaluation action of the following loop to be considered atomic when $x$ is written by another process.

$$T: \textbf{do} \quad x=0 \rightarrow \textbf{skip} \quad [] \quad x \neq 0 \rightarrow \textbf{skip} \quad \textbf{od}$$

There is a good reason for this. The loop is nonterminating when the guard evaluation action is a single atomic action but may terminate when the guard evaluation is a sequence of atomic actions. Part (i) of Compiler Access Restrictions (9.31) permits a translation of $GEval_{do}(T)$ to read $x$ twice. Should the value read in evaluating $x=0$ be nonzero and the value read in evaluating $x \neq 0$ be zero, then both guards would be found *false* and the loop would terminate. Termination would not occur if $GEval_{do}(T)$ were a single atomic action.

## 9.3  Implementing Condition Synchronization

The guard evaluation action for an **if** statement implements condition synchronization: execution is blocked until some guard holds. Only a few, prespecified, such guard evaluation actions will be available on any real computer system. Therefore, although an **if** statement could have an arbitrary guard $B$, programming with

(9.37)  $S$:  **if** $B \rightarrow T$ **fi**

could be problematic.

We have used statements like (9.37) freely in developing programs. Consequently, we seek a replacement—a statement that is not built from conditional atomic actions but that blocks progress until some boolean expression $B$ holds. The obvious candidate is a **do** with guard $\neg B$.

(9.38)  **Implementing Condition Synchronization.** An **if** statement with an arbitrary guard $B$

$$S: \textbf{if } B \rightarrow T \textbf{ fi}$$

can be replaced by:

$$S: \textbf{do } \neg B \rightarrow \textbf{skip od } T \qquad\qquad \square$$

This leaves the question of termination. With (9.37), execution of $T$ can be prevented if atomic actions from other processes are scheduled whenever $at(S) \wedge B$ holds. A fairness assumption attached to $GEval_{if}(S)$ in (9.37) is needed to ensure that $T$ in (9.37) will be reached.

The (replacement) **do** statement in Implementing Condition Synchronization (9.38) is guaranteed to terminate only if $B$ holds long enough and unconditional fairness is assumed for its atomic actions. That is, the **do** will terminate if we can prove

$$at(S) \wedge \Diamond \Box B \Rightarrow after(S)$$

a theorem of $S'/F$-Temporal Logic, where program $S'$ contains the **do** and $F$ implies unconditional fairness for the **skip** and guard evaluation action $GEval_{do}(S)$. Thus, termination of the replacement is guaranteed when a weakly fair **if**, like (9.37), is replaced according to Implementing Condition Synchronization (9.38).

It is not possible to guarantee that $T$ will be reached when a strongly fair **if** guard evaluation action is replaced with a **do**. The guard evaluation action for such an **if** must, by definition, terminate if $B$ holds infinitely often. But the **do** might not terminate in this situation, because $B$ might be *true* infinitely often but never hold when its guard evaluation action is executed. To solve this problem, we must somehow prevent processes that falsify $B$ from doing so until after the guard evaluation action is executed. This requires changes to the code of these processes—a more global modification than we wish to contemplate here.

### Illustration using Mutual Exclusion Protocol

The mutual exclusion protocol of §6.5 uses an **if** statement to implement condition synchronization. Specifically, for process $S_1$, guard evaluation action $GEval_{if}(gate_1)$ allows $pre(gate_1)$ to be strengthened with the disjunction $\neg in2 \vee t=1 \vee after(door_2)$. This is depicted in the following fragment (taken from Figure 6.8) of the proof outline of process $S_1$.

$$entry_1: door_1: \dots$$
$$\{I \wedge \neg in(CS_1) \wedge in1\}$$
$$gate_1: \textbf{if} \neg in2 \vee t=1 \to \{I \wedge at(T_1) \wedge in1$$
$$\wedge (\neg in2 \vee t=1 \vee after(door_2))\}$$
$$T_1: \dots$$

To replicate this strengthening, we use Implementing Condition Synchronization (9.38) and replace the **if** with a **do** whose guard is the negation of the condition being awaited.

$$entry_1: door_1: \dots$$
$$\{I': I \wedge \neg in(CS_1) \wedge in1\}$$
$$gate_1: \textbf{do} \neg(\neg in2 \vee t=1) \to \{I'\} \textbf{ skip } \{I'\} \textbf{ od}$$
$$\{I \wedge at(T_1) \wedge in1$$
$$\wedge (\neg in2 \vee t=1 \vee after(door_2))\}$$
$$T_1: \dots$$

Unfortunately, this **do** does not satisfy Reduction with At Most One **do** Guards

(9.36), since both *in2* and *t* are written by another process. So, we reformulate the **do** in terms of a local variable $p_1$ and add the necessary assignment statements.

$$entry_1: \ door_1: \ ...$$
$$\{I': \ I \wedge \neg in(CS_1) \wedge in1\}$$
$$p_1 := false$$
$$\{W: \ I' \wedge (p_1 \Rightarrow (\neg in2 \vee t=1 \vee after(door_2)))\}$$
$$gate_1: \ \mathbf{do} \ \neg p_1 \rightarrow \{\neg p_1 \wedge W\}$$
$$p_1 := p_1 \vee \neg in2 \ \{W\}$$
$$p_1 := p_1 \vee (t=1) \ \{W\}$$
$$\mathbf{od} \ \{I \wedge at(T_1) \wedge in1$$
$$\wedge (\neg in2 \vee t=1 \vee after(door_2))\}$$
$$T_1: \ ...$$

The result is a valid proof outline, because it is a theorem of Proof Outline Logic.

After replacing the **if** by the **do**, we might wish to re-prove the liveness property that a process attempting to enter its critical section will eventually do so. This is accomplished by modifying the proof of that property in §8.6. The key observation for extending the proof in §8.6 is that whenever $GEval_{if}(gate_1)$ was a helpful action in the original, the atomic actions in the **do** labeled $gate_1$ are helpful actions. Atomic action $p_1 := false$ is a helpful action whenever it can be executed.

## Awaiting a Disjunction

The transformation used above for the mutual exclusion protocol is actually an instance of a more general technique. We started with an **if** whose guard is a disjunction, where each disjunct mentions at most once a variable that is written by another process:

$$S: \ \{P\} \ \mathbf{if} \ B_1 \vee B_2 \vee \cdots \vee B_n \rightarrow \{Q: \ P \wedge (B_1 \vee B_2 \vee \cdots \vee B_n)\}$$
$$T: \ ...$$

And we replaced this **if** by an instance of the program fragment in Figure 9.3, where the **do** satisfies the condition of Reduction with At Most One **do** Guards (9.36), the assignment statements comply with At Most One Assignments (9.32), and $v$ is a fresh variable.

To establish that the replacement works we must prove three things:

(i) The proof outline of Figure 9.3 is valid in isolation.

(ii) Executing an atomic action from a concurrent process cannot falsify any assertion in Figure 9.3.

(iii) Executing an atomic action in Figure 9.3 cannot falsify any assertion in a concurrent process.

The proof outline of Figure 9.3 is a theorem, so (i) holds. For (ii), it suffices to note that falsifying $W$ is equivalent to falsifying $P$ or $Q$. The interference

$$S: \{P\}$$
$$v := false \quad \{W: P \wedge (v \Rightarrow B_1 \vee B_2 \vee \cdots \vee B_n)\}$$
$$\textbf{do} \neg v \rightarrow \{\neg v \wedge W\}$$
$$v := v \vee B_1 \quad \{W\}$$
$$v := v \vee B_2 \quad \{W\}$$
$$\cdots$$
$$v := v \vee B_n \quad \{W\}$$
$$\textbf{od} \quad \{Q: P \wedge (B_1 \vee B_2 \vee \cdots \vee B_n)\}$$
$$T: \ldots$$

**Figure 9.3.  do** replacement for **if**

---

freedom proof for the original program establishes that neither $P$ nor $Q$ is falsified by executing an atomic action from a concurrent process. Finally, (iii) holds provided that assertions in other processes do not mention $v$ or $at(S)$ (but control predicate $in(S)$ can appear).

The same sort of translation does not work for an **if** where the guard is a conjunction:

$$S: \textbf{if } B_1 \wedge B_2 \wedge \cdots \wedge B_n \rightarrow T: \ldots$$

It is instructive to understand why. Essential to the code in Figure 9.3 is that each $B_i$ is evaluated using a separate atomic action. Since the state may change between execution of these atomic actions, there is no way to determine the existence of a (single) state satisfying $B_1 \wedge B_2 \wedge \cdots \wedge B_n$. The fragment of Figure 9.3 works because a state satisfies $B_1 \vee B_2 \vee \cdots \vee B_n$ whenever any $B_i$ is *true*.

## 9.4  Programming with the Subset

The restrictions in §9.2 and §9.3 can be regarded as defining a subset of our programming notation. This subset contains only certain assignment statements and **do** statements. Furthermore, the subset does not contain **if** statements whose guard evaluation actions require conditional atomic actions.

Invariance properties can be proved in a translation-independent manner for programs written in the subset. Thus, a desire to stay within this subset can drive program development and augment Safety Property Methodology (6.30). In particular, the subset characterizes the statements that do not require further elaboration. We illustrate this below by deriving another solution to the mutual exclusion problem.

## *Mutual Exclusion with Tickets*

Upon entering a crowded bakery in the United States, the usual routine is for a customer to receive a ticket bearing a number. A clerk serves waiting customers, one at a time and in ascending order by ticket number. The numbered tickets are thus used to solve a mutual exclusion problem in which customers are processes and interacting with the clerk constitutes a critical section.

We program this ticket-based scheme as follows. Associated with each process $i$ is a variable $t_i$ that contains the number on the ticket that $i$ has taken; $t_i$ equals $\perp$ whenever $i$ does not have a ticket. Atomic action *GetT* is executed by a process $i$ in order to obtain a ticket. Based on the discussion of the previous paragraph, *GetT* would be expected to satisfy the following proof outline:

$$\{t_i=\perp\} \; GetT(t_i) \; \{t_i\neq\perp\}$$

Process $i$ executes atomic action $WaitMinT(t_i)$ in order to block until $t_i$ is the smallest ticket value held by any process. Thus, *WaitMinT* is assumed to satisfy the following, where $(\downarrow j\colon R\colon e)$ denotes the smallest of $\infty$ and values $e_v^j$ for all $v$ satisfying $R_v^j$. We assume that $\infty$ is not the value of any ticket.

$$\{t_i\neq\perp\} \; WaitMinT(t_i) \; \{t_i\leq(\downarrow j\colon t_j\neq\perp\colon t_j)\}$$

When $WaitMinT(t_i)$ terminates, $t_i$ is the smallest of any ticket currently held by a process. Process $i$ is then allowed to execute its critical section. The proof outline of Figure 9.4 results from this thinking.

To establish that Mutual Exclusion (6.2) is satisfied, we use Exclusion of Configurations Rule (6.10). Premise (a) of this rule requires a valid proof outline for the program containing all the processes. For expository simplicity, we consider the case where there are only two processes. We must therefore determine whether the following proof outline is a theorem of Proof Outline Logic, where the proof outlines for $S_1$ and $S_2$ are instances of Figure 9.4.

---

$$\{t_i=\perp\}$$
$$S_i\colon \quad \textbf{do } true \rightarrow entry_i\colon \; \{t_i=\perp\}$$
$$GetT(t_i) \; \{t_i\neq\perp\}$$
$$WaitMinT(t_i) \; \{t_i\leq(\downarrow j\colon t_j\neq\perp\colon t_j)\}$$
$$PO(CS_i)\otimes(t_i\leq(\downarrow j\colon t_j\neq\perp\colon t_j))$$
$$exit_i\colon \; t_i := \perp \; \{t_i=\perp\}$$
$$PO(NCS_i)\otimes t_i=\perp$$
$$\textbf{od } \{false\}$$

**Figure 9.4.** Proof outline for process $i$ ticket protocol

(9.39)     $\{t_1 = \perp \ \wedge \ t_2 = \perp\}$
   $S:$ **cobegin** $PO(S_1) \ \| \ PO(S_2)$ **coend**
   $\{false\}$

Unfortunately, this proof outline is not a theorem because there is interference. Execution of $GetT(t_1)$ falsifies $t_2 \le (\downarrow j: t_j \ne \perp: t_j)$ if the value assigned to $t_1$ is too small. The interference is avoided if we revise our expectations for $GetT(t_i)$ so that the value assigned to $t_i$ is never too small:

$$\{t_i = \perp\} \ GetT(t_i) \ \{t_i \ne \perp \ \wedge \ t_i \ge (\downarrow j: t_j \ne \perp: t_j)\}$$

The revised proof outline for process $i$ appears as Figure 9.5. Proof outline (9.39) no longer exhibits interference, so premise (a) of Exclusion of Configurations Rule (6.10) is satisfied.

Premise (b) of Exclusion of Configurations Rule (6.10) is easily discharged for $Init$ equal to $at(S)$: we have only to initialize $t_1$ and $t_2$ to $\perp$.

To discharge premise (c) of Exclusion of Configurations Rule (6.10), we must prove that $in(CS_1) \wedge in(CS_2) \wedge I_{PO(S)}$ implies $false$, because $Etern$ for Mutual Exclusion (6.2) with two processes is $\neg (in(CS_1) \wedge in(CS_2))$. In fact, we find that $in(CS_1) \wedge in(CS_2) \wedge I_{PO(S)}$ implies

$$t_1 \le (\downarrow j: t_j \ne \perp: t_j) \ \wedge \ t_2 \le (\downarrow j: t_j \ne \perp: t_j)$$

and this is not $false$ when $t_1 = t_2$ holds. It should not be surprising that Mutual Exclusion (6.2) is violated if the same ticket value is given to both processes.

The obvious solution is to strengthen the postcondition of $GetT(t_i)$ so that unique ticket values are distributed. This leads to a third, stronger, specification for $GetT$

(9.40) $\{t_i = \perp\} \ GetT(t_i) \ \{t_i \ne \perp \ \wedge \ t_i \ge (\downarrow j: t_j \ne \perp: t_j) \ \wedge \ U(i)\}$

where:

$U(i): \ (\forall j: \ j \ne i \wedge t_j \ne \perp: \ t_i \ne t_j)$

---

   $\{t_i = \perp\}$
$S_i:$ **do** $true \rightarrow entry_i:$ $\{t_i = \perp\}$
                 $GetT(t_i) \ \{t_i \ne \perp \ \wedge \ t_i \ge (\downarrow j: t_j \ne \perp: t_j)\}$
                 $WaitMinT(t_i) \ \{t_i \le (\downarrow j: t_j \ne \perp: t_j)\}$
         $PO(CS_i) \otimes (t_i \le (\downarrow j: t_j \ne \perp: t_j))$
         $exit_i: \ t_i := \perp \ \{t_i = \perp\}$
         $NCS_i \otimes t_i = \perp$
     **od** $\{false\}$

**Figure 9.5.** Revised proof outline for process $i$ ticket protocol

We now obtain the stronger proof outline of Figure 9.6 for a process $S_i$. Proof outline (9.39) remains interference-free when it is instantiated using Figure 9.6 for $PO(S_i)$, so premises (a) and (b) are easily discharged. Furthermore, premise (c) is now satisfied because $in(CS_1) \wedge in(CS_2) \wedge I_{PO(S)}$ implies

$$t_1 \leq (\downarrow j: t_j \neq \perp: t_j) \ \wedge \ U(1) \ \wedge \ t_2 \leq (\downarrow j: t_j \neq \perp: t_j) \ \wedge \ U(2)$$

which is equivalent to *false*.

## *Implementing GetT*

An obvious way to implement *GetT* is to use a global counter *tix*:

$$t_i, tix := tix, tix+1$$

This statement does not comply with At Most One Assignments (9.32), so we devise a program fragment with the same effect. This new statement is constructed so that it complies with the restrictions of §9.2 and §9.3.

Use of a loop for *GetT* is suggested by Statement Selection Heuristics (4.58), since conjuncts in the postcondition of (9.40) involve quantification. We use Replacing an Expression by a Variable (4.60) in that postcondition to obtain the following proposal for a loop invariant. The number of processes is N (which we are assuming is 2).

$$0 \leq p_i \leq N \ \wedge \ t_i \neq \perp \ \wedge \ t_i \geq (\downarrow j: 0 < j \leq p_i \wedge t_j \neq \perp: t_j)$$
$$\wedge \ (\forall j: 0 < j \leq p_i \wedge j \neq i \wedge t_j \neq \perp: t_i \neq t_j)$$

Note that when $p_i = N$, this loop invariant implies the postcondition of (9.40).

The first and second conjuncts of the proposed loop invariant are easy to truthify initially. The third conjunct is not. This is because $(\downarrow j: 0 < j \leq p_i \wedge t_j \neq \perp: t_j)$ equals $\infty$ when $t_1, t_2, ..., t_{p_i}$ equal $\perp$, and we cannot use $t_i := \infty$ to initialize $t_i$ since $\infty$ is not a value in the type of $t_i$.

---

$\{t_i = \perp\}$
$S_i$: **do** *true* $\rightarrow$ *entry*$_i$: $\{t_i = \perp\}$
　　　　　　　　*GetT*$(t_i)$ $\{t_i \neq \perp \ \wedge \ t_i \geq (\downarrow j: t_j \neq \perp: t_j)\} \ \wedge \ U(i)\}$
　　　　　　　　*WaitMinT*$(t_i)$ $\{t_i \leq (\downarrow j: t_j \neq \perp: t_j) \ \wedge \ U(i)\}$
　　　　　　$PO(CS_i) \otimes (t_i \leq (\downarrow j: t_j \neq \perp: t_j) \ \wedge \ U(i))$
　　　　　　*exit*$_i$: $t_i := \perp \ \{t_i = \perp\}$
　　　　　　$NCS_i \otimes t_i = \perp$
　　**od** $\{false\}$

**Figure 9.6.** Third proof outline for process $i$ ticket protocol

This problem with the third conjunct does not occur in the postcondition of (9.40) because $(\downarrow j:\ t_j\neq\perp:\ t_j)$ cannot equal $\infty$ since $t_i\neq\perp$ is known to hold. We can exploit this insight to devise a loop invariant whose third conjunct is easy to truthify initially. Note how $t_i$ has been included in the range of the minimization:

$I:\ \ 0\leq p_i\leq N\ \wedge\ t_i\neq\perp\ \wedge\ t_i\geq(t_i\downarrow(\downarrow j:\ 0<j\leq p_i\wedge t_j\neq\perp:\ t_j))$
$\wedge\ (\forall j:\ 0<j\leq p_i\wedge j\neq i\wedge t_j\neq\perp:\ t_i\neq t_j)$

As before, if $p_i=N$ then $I$ implies the postcondition of (9.40).

A coding trick allows us to simplify the manipulation of ticket values. Encode $\perp$ as the integer 0 and assume that other ticket values are positive integers. Then[5] $t_i:=t_i\uparrow(t_{p_i+1}+1)$ assigns a value to $t_i$ that is not $\perp$ and is larger than $t_{p_i+1}$. Assignment statement $t_i:=t_i\uparrow(t_{p_i+1}+1)$ does not comply with At Most One Assignments (9.32), but we can decompose it into a sequence of two assignment statements that do. The resulting protocol for $GetT$ is given in Figure 9.7.

We have developed a routine that can be used in place of $GetT$ and that satisfies (9.40). We next investigate what happens when this routine is substituted for $GetT$ in (9.39). By proving interference freedom, we would establish that our implementation of $GetT$ behaves as required.

Consider the proof outline of Figure 9.6 for process $S_1$ but with $GetT$ replaced according to Figure 9.7. We start by considering assertions in Figure 9.7 for $GetT(t_1)$. The only variable written by $S_2$ mentioned in those assertions is $t_2$, so three atomic actions in $S_2$ must be checked: $exit_2$ and both $p_2,t_2:=0,1$ and $t_2:=t_2\uparrow v_2$.

Execution of $exit_2$ cannot cause the value of $t_i\downarrow(\downarrow j:\ 0<j<p_i\wedge t_j\neq\perp:\ t_j)$ or $t_i\downarrow(\downarrow j:\ 0<j<p_i\wedge t_j\neq\perp:\ t_j)_{p_i+1}^{p_i}$ to increase beyond $t_i$. Thus, it does not cause interference.

---

$\{t_i=\perp\}$
$p_i,t_i:=0,1$
$\{I:\ 0\leq p_i\leq N\ \wedge\ t_i\neq\perp$
$\quad\wedge\ t_i\geq t_i\downarrow(\downarrow j:\ 0<j\leq p_i\wedge t_j\neq\perp:\ t_j)$
$\quad\wedge\ (\forall j:\ 0<j\leq p_i\wedge j\neq i\wedge t_j\neq\perp:\ t_i\neq t_j)\}$
$\mathbf{do}\ p_i\neq N\rightarrow\{p_i\neq N\ \wedge\ I\}$
$\qquad v_i:=t_{p_i+1}+1\ \ \{(I_{p_i+1}^{p_i})_{t_i\uparrow v_i}^{t_i}\}$
$\qquad t_i:=t_i\uparrow v_i\ \ \{I_{p_i+1}^{p_i}\}$
$\qquad p_i:=p_i+1\ \ \{I\}$
$\mathbf{od}\ \{t_i\neq\perp\ \wedge\ t_i\geq(\downarrow j:\ t_j\neq\perp:\ t_j)\ \wedge\ U(i)\}$

**Figure 9.7.** $GetT(t_i)$

---

[5] $v\uparrow w$ denotes the maximum of $v$ and $w$.

We next check whether $p_2, t_2 := 0, 1$ or $t_2 := t_2 \uparrow v_2$ can interfere with assertions of $PO(GetT(t_1))$ in Figure 9.7. The first two conjuncts of $I$, $I^{p_i}_{p_i+1}$, and $(I^{p_i}_{p_i+1})^{t_i}_{t_i \uparrow v_i}$ cannot be falsified by executing either of these assignment statements. We treat each of the last two conjuncts separately.

The third conjunct of $I$, $I^{p_i}_{p_i+1}$, and $(I^{p_i}_{p_i+1})^{t_i}_{t_i \uparrow v_i}$ are unaffected by either assignment statement unless $t_2$ is among the values being minimized. Thus, let us consider the case where $t_2$ is among those values. Decreasing $t_2$ cannot falsify the inequality $t_i \geq t_i \downarrow (\downarrow j: 0 < j \leq p_i \wedge t_j \neq \bot : t_j)$, and increasing $t_2$ cannot cause $t_i \downarrow (\downarrow j: 0 < j \leq p_i \wedge t_j \neq \bot : t_j)$ to exceed $t_i$. Thus, neither $p_2, t_2 := 0, 1$ nor $t_2 := t_2 \uparrow v_2$ can falsify the third conjunct of $I$. A similar argument works for the third conjunct of $I^{p_i}_{p_i+1}$ and $(I^{p_i}_{p_i+1})^{t_i}_{t_i \uparrow v_i}$.

Execution of $t_2 := t_2 \uparrow v_2$ can falsify the final conjunct of $I$, $I^{p_i}_{p_i+1}$, and $(I^{p_i}_{p_i+1})^{t_i}_{t_i \uparrow v_i}$ because the new value of $t_2$ may be the same as $t_1$. This will occur, for example, if the two processes execute $GetT$ in lock step. We eliminate the interference by exploiting process-name uniqueness to break ties. For $t_i$ with value $ti$ and $t_j$ with value $tj$ where $ti \neq \bot$ and $tj \neq \bot$ hold, we redefine $\leq$ and $=$ as follows.

$$t_i = \bot: \quad ti = \bot$$
$$t_i = t_j: \quad (ti = \bot \wedge tj = \bot) \ \vee \ (ti = tj \wedge i = j)$$
$$t_i \leq t_j: \quad ti < tj \ \vee \ (ti = tj \wedge i \leq j)$$

Now it is impossible for $t_1 = t_2$ to hold unless $t_i$ and $t_j$ both equal $\bot$. Moreover, execution of $t_2 := t_2 \uparrow v_2$ cannot falsify the final conjunct of $I$, $I^{p_i}_{p_i+1}$, or $(I^{p_i}_{p_i+1})^{t_i}_{t_i \uparrow v_i}$.

We have shown that no atomic action in $S_2$ can falsify any assertion in the proof outline for $GetT(t_1)$ of Figure 9.7. In order to establish interference freedom, we must also show that no atomic action of $S_2$ falsifies the other assertions in $PO(S_1)$ (Figure 9.6). In particular, we must show that neither $p_2, t_2 := 0, 1$ nor $t_2 := t_2 \uparrow v_2$ falsifies these assertions.

Unfortunately, executing $p_2, t_2 := 0, 1$ does falsify $t_1 \leq (\downarrow j: t_j \neq \bot : t_j)$, because it may cause $(\downarrow j: t_j \neq \bot : t_j)$ to decrease. We avoid the problem by excluding $t_2$ from $(\downarrow j: t_j \neq \bot : t_j)$ until $t_2 > (\downarrow j: t_j \neq \bot : t_j)$ holds. The postcondition of $GetT(t_2)$ in Figure 9.7 suggests that we need only exclude $t_2$ from $(\downarrow j: t_j \neq \bot : t_j)$ until $after(GetT(t_2))$ holds. Figure 9.8 uses these weaker assertions to revise the proof outline of Figure 9.6.

Neither $p_2, t_2 := 0, 1$ nor $t_2 := t_2 \uparrow v_2$ can falsify the assertions of Figure 9.8, because $in(GetT(t_2))$ holds when they are executed. Finally, the atomic action of $GetT(t_2)$ that makes $\neg in(GetT(t_2))$ *true* does not interfere, because it also truthifies $after(GetT(t_2))$, and according to the proof outline of Figure 9.7, $t_2 \geq (\downarrow j: t_j \neq \bot : t_j)$ is also truthified.

The proof outline of Figure 9.8, with its weaker assertions, is sufficient for establishing mutual exclusion of critical sections. Premise (c) of Exclusion of Configurations Rule (6.10) still holds, because $in(CS_i)$ implies $\neg in(GetT(t_i))$.

$\{t_i = \bot\}$
$S_i:$ **do** $true \rightarrow entry_i:$ $\{t_i = \bot\}$
$\qquad\qquad\qquad\quad GetT(t_i)$
$\qquad\qquad\qquad\quad \{t_i \neq \bot \;\wedge\; t_i \geq (\downarrow j: t_j \neq \bot: t_j) \;\wedge\; U(i)\}$
$\qquad\qquad\qquad\quad WaitMinT(t_i)$
$\qquad\qquad\qquad\quad \{t_i \leq (\downarrow j: \neg in(GetT(t_j)) \wedge t_j \neq \bot: t_j) \;\wedge\; U(i)\}$
$\qquad\qquad\quad PO(CS_i) \otimes (t_i \leq (\downarrow j: \neg in(GetT(t_j)) \wedge t_j \neq \bot: t_j) \;\wedge\; U(i))$
$\qquad\qquad\quad exit_i:\; t_i := \bot \; \{t_i = \bot\}$
$\qquad\qquad\quad NCS_i \otimes t_i = \bot$
$\qquad$ **od** $\{false\}$

**Figure 9.8.**  Weaker proof outline for process $i$ ticket protocol

---

## Implementing WaitMinT

The obvious way to implement $WaitMinT(t_i)$ so that it truthifies the postcondition required by Figure 9.8 is by using

**if** $t_i \leq (\downarrow j: \neg in(GetT(t_j)) \wedge t_j \neq \bot: t_j) \rightarrow$ **skip fi**

but this requires a conditional atomic action, which is not likely to be available. Therefore, we use Implementing Condition Synchronization (9.38) and consider:

(9.41)  **do** $\neg (t_i \leq (\downarrow j: \neg in(GetT(t_j)) \wedge t_j \neq \bot: t_j)) \rightarrow$ **skip od**

Unfortunately, this statement mentions control predicates and does not comply with (ii) of Reduction with At Most One **do** Guards (9.36). We therefore try to decompose the guard and obtain a statement that does comply.

Loop (9.41) terminates when $t_i \leq t_j$ for every process $j$ for which $\neg in(GetT(t_j)) \wedge t_j \neq \bot$ holds. It is not difficult to construct a loop that terminates when $t_i \leq t_j \vee t_j = \bot$ holds for a single $t_j$:

(9.42)  **do** $t_i > t_j \neq \bot \rightarrow$ **skip od**

Moreover, the guard for this loop complies[6] with (ii) of Reduction with At Most One **do** Guards (9.36).  And $\neg(t_i > t_j \neq \bot)$, which holds upon termination of (9.42), implies $t_i \leq t_j \vee t_j = \bot \vee \neg in(GetT(t_j))$.

To handle all processes $j$, we investigate a loop with (9.42) in its body. The result is given in Figure 9.9, where $p_i$ is local to process $i$.

---

[6]Note that logically equivalent guard $t_i > t_j \wedge t_j \neq \bot$ does not comply with the restriction of At Most One **do** Guards (9.36) because $t_j$ is mentioned twice.

$\{t_i \neq \perp\}$
$p_i := 0$
$\{I: \ t_i \neq \perp \ \wedge \ 0 \leq p_i \leq N \ \wedge \ t_i \leq (\downarrow j: \ 0 < j \leq p_i \wedge \neg in(GetT(t_j)) \wedge t_j \neq \perp: \ t_j)\}$
$\mathbf{do} \ p_i \neq N \rightarrow \{p_i \neq N \wedge I\}$
$\qquad L: \ \mathbf{do} \ t_i > t_{p_i+1} \neq \perp \rightarrow \{I\} \ \mathbf{skip} \ \{I\} \ \mathbf{od} \ \{I^{p_i}_{p_i+1}\}$
$\qquad p_i := p_i + 1 \ \{I\}$
$\mathbf{od} \ \{t_i \neq \perp \ \wedge \ t_i \leq (\downarrow j: \ \neg in(GetT(t_j)) \wedge t_j \neq \perp: \ t_j)\}$

**Figure 9.9.** *WaitMinT*$(t_i)$

---

We next investigate what happens when this routine is substituted for *WaitMinT* in the proof outline of Figure 9.8 (with *GetT* instantiated according to Figure 9.7). By proving interference freedom, we would establish that the implementation of *WaitMinT* works.

We start by considering assertions in *WaitMinT*$(t_1)$ and show that they are falsified by no atomic action in $S_2$. The only variable changed by $S_2$ that affects these assertions is $t_2$—it affects the third conjunct of $I$,

$$t_i \leq (\downarrow j: \ 0 < j \leq p_i \wedge \neg in(GetT(t_j)) \wedge t_j \neq \perp: \ t_j)$$

and it is changed by executing $exit_2$, $p_2, t_2 := 0, 1$, and $t_2 := t_2 \uparrow (t_{p_2+1} + 1)$. Execution of $exit_2$ can only increase $(\downarrow j: \ 0 < j \leq p_i \wedge t_j \neq \perp: \ t_j)$, which never falsifies $I$. Execution of $p_2, t_2 := 0, 1$ and $t_2 := t_2 \uparrow (t_{p_2+1} + 1)$ occur when $in(GetT(t_2))$ holds, so these statements cannot change the value of:

$$(\downarrow j: \ 0 < j \leq p_i \wedge \neg in(GetT(t_j)) \wedge t_j \neq \perp: \ t_j)$$

Finally, the atomic action of *GetT*$(t_2)$ that makes $\neg in(GetT(t_2))$ *true* does not interfere, because it truthifies *after*$(GetT(t_2))$ and $t_2 \geq (\downarrow j: \ t_j \neq \perp: \ t_j)$.

No statement in Figure 9.9 can falsify an assertion in Figure 9.8, because none of the statements in *WaitMinT* changes anything mentioned in these assertions.

### Nonblocking and Eventual Entry

Solutions to the mutual exclusion problem should satisfy various nonblocking properties as well as a property that states that a process attempting to enter its critical section will eventually do so. We now analyze whether these properties are satisfied by the protocol of Figure 9.8 but with *GetT*$(t_i)$ as defined in Figure 9.7 and *WaitMinT*$(t_i)$ as defined in Figure 9.9.

The protocol contains no conditional atomic actions, so Entry Nonblocking (6.20), NCS Nonblocking (6.21), and Exit Nonblocking (6.22) all trivially hold.

For eventual entry into a critical section (which is formalized in Chapter 8 as (8.47)) to hold, all executions of $L$ in *WaitMinT* must terminate. We sketch the argument for that here, leaving the formal proof for the exercises. Suppose that a process $i$ is executing in *WaitMinT* and $t_k < t_i$ holds for a total of $n$ processes. These $n$ processes will precede $i$ into the critical section, because $t_k > t_i$ holds for any process $k$ that starts executing $GetT(t_k)$ after $i$ starts executing *WaitMinT*($t_i$).

When $n=0$, the guard on $L$ is *false* (by definition of $n$) and $L$ terminates. (This requires an assumption of unconditional fairness.) Consider the case when $n>0$. Thus, there exists a process $k$ such that $t_i > t_k \land t_k \neq \perp$ holds. If process $k$ exits the critical section, then $exit_k$ is executed and the subsequent values for $t_k$ will thereafter satisfy $t_k = \perp \lor t_i < t_k$. Thus, the guard on $L$ for $p_i = k$ will become *false*, and $L$ will terminate (again, assuming unconditional fairness).

It remains only to show that process $k$ will exit the critical section. As in §6.6, we assume that no process executes forever in its critical section. Consequently, if $k$ enters its critical section then it must exit. That $i$ enters its critical section follows by induction, because now there are $n-1$ processes $k$ for which $t_k < t_i$.

## 9.5  Synchronization and Interference Revisited

Avoiding Interference by Indivisibility (5.46) and Avoiding Interference by Blocking (5.47) may require using atomic actions that are not available. Fortunately, there are variations of these techniques that use only atomic actions supported by a typical computer. These variations are the subject of this section.

### *Exclusion Instead of Indivisibility*

Consider a concurrent program in which some unconditional atomic action $\alpha$ in one process interferes with an assertion $pre(S)$ in another:

**cobegin**
      ... $\alpha$ ...
  $\parallel$
      ... $\{pre(S)\}$ $S$ ...
**coend**

We can eliminate this interference by ensuring that $at(\alpha)$ cannot be *true* when $at(S)$ is. Avoiding Interference by Indivisibility (5.46) accomplishes this by substituting a coarse-grained atomic action, thereby eliminating one of the two control points. However, such a substitution is practical only when the needed coarse-grained atomic action is in the machine language. It rarely is.

Instead of eliminating a control point, it suffices for $at(\alpha)$ and $at(S)$ to be in critical sections that are mutually exclusive. So that interference is not simply being exchanged for deadlock, we must guarantee that no process executes forever in these critical sections.

(9.43) **Avoiding Interference by Exclusion.** If $\alpha$ interferes with $pre(S)$, then try making $\alpha$ part of a critical section $CS$ and $pre(S)$ part of another critical section $CS'$ such that

   (i)  $CS$ and $CS'$ are mutually exclusive, and

   (ii)  no process executes forever in $CS$ or $CS'$.       ☐

Mutual exclusion can be implemented using any of a number of protocols. We have already seen mutual exclusion protocols in §6.5 and §9.4, and we will see others in this chapter. Notice that requirement (ii), that critical sections terminate, rules out including in $CS$ or $CS'$ a **do** or **if** whose guard depends on a variable that is changed by another process executing in a mutually exclusive critical section.

Avoiding Interference by Exclusion (9.43) is really just a form of Strengthening (5.14): We strengthen $pre(\alpha)$ and $pre(S)$ to reflect that they are mutually exclusive. In particular, Control-Point Identity (4.28) and the mutual exclusion allow $pre(\alpha)$ to be strengthened to imply $at(\alpha) \wedge \neg at(S)$ and allow $pre(S)$ to be strengthened to imply $at(S) \wedge \neg at(\alpha)$. Such a strengthening makes $pre(NI(\alpha, pre(S)))$ equal to *false*, so $NI(\alpha, pre(S))$ is (trivially) valid.

As an illustration of Avoiding Interference by Exclusion (9.43), consider a concurrent program with an assignment statement that increments $x$ but violates At Most One Assignments (9.32):

(9.44) **cobegin**

       ... $\alpha$: $x := ...$

  ||

       ... $\{P\}$ $x := x+1$ $\{Q\}$ ...

  **coend**

So that At Most One Assignments (9.32) is no longer violated, a sequence of assignments statements might be substituted in place of $x := x+1$.

(9.45) **cobegin**

       ... $\alpha$: $x := ...$

  ||

       ... $\{P\}$ $t := x+1$ $\{P \wedge t=x+1\}$ $S$: $x := t$ $\{Q\}$ ...

  **coend**

Interference freedom of (9.44) unfortunately does not imply interference freedom for (9.45). Atomic action $\alpha$ will falsify $t=x+1$ and will therefore falsify $pre(S)$.

Avoiding Interference by Exclusion (9.43) can be used to prevent $\alpha$ from falsifying $pre(S)$. Assignment statements $t := x+1$ and $x := t$ are placed in a critical section, thereby ensuring that $pre(S)$ appears in a critical section, and atomic action $\alpha$ is placed in a mutually exclusive critical section. Observe that both of these critical sections terminate because neither contains a loop and each comprises only unconditional atomic actions. The result is:

(9.46) **cobegin**

$\qquad$ ... *CS*: *entry* $\alpha$: $x := ... \ exit \ ...$

$\quad$ ||

$\qquad$ ... $\{P\}$
$\qquad$ *entry* $\{P \wedge \neg in(CS)\}$
$\qquad$ *CS'*: $t := x+1 \ \{P \wedge t=x+1 \wedge \neg in(CS)\}$
$\qquad\qquad$ *S*: $x := t \ \{Q \wedge \neg in(CS)\}$
$\qquad$ *exit* $\{Q\}$ ...

$\quad$ **coend**

Now, $NI(\alpha, pre(S))$ has *false* as its precondition, so it is valid. We have used mutual exclusion to eliminate interference.

This example demonstrates one way to program with assignment statements that do not comply with At Most One Assignments (9.32). Such an assignment statement $\bar{x} := \bar{e}$ is presumably being translated into some machine-language program fragment $S_{\bar{x}:=\bar{e}}$ that always terminates and, if executed in isolation, causes $\bar{x}$ to change in the correct way. Include in critical sections $\bar{x} := \bar{e}$ as well as any assignment statement $T_i$ whose targets include variables in $\bar{x}$ or $\bar{e}$. Mutual exclusion of these critical sections implies that execution of $S_{\bar{x}:=\bar{e}}$ is never interleaved with the execution of $T_i$. Thus, $S_{\bar{x}:=\bar{e}}$ is executed as if in isolation.

(9.47) **Atomic Assignments by Exclusion.** Assignment statement

$$S: \ \bar{x} := \bar{e}$$

may be considered a single atomic action if it is included in a critical section and the following are included in mutually exclusive critical sections:

- assertions involving $at(S)$, $in(S)$, and any control predicate $cp$ that satisfies $cp \Rightarrow at(S)$ or $cp \Rightarrow in(S)$,

- expressions that appear in guards or assertions and involve variables of $\bar{x}$, and

- assignment statements that mention variables of $\bar{x}$ and $\bar{e}$.  $\qquad\square$

## Simulating Arbitrary Conditional Atomic Actions

In Avoiding Interference by Blocking (5.47), an atomic action $\alpha$ is replaced by another atomic action $\langle \mathbf{if} \ B \rightarrow \alpha \ \mathbf{fi} \rangle$. Guard $B$ is chosen so that it holds in states in which execution of $\alpha$ does not falsify some predicate of interest; presumably, executing $\alpha$ in other states might. Thus, the two important attributes of $\langle \mathbf{if} \ B \rightarrow \alpha \ \mathbf{fi} \rangle$ are:

(i)  It strengthens the precondition for $\alpha$, because execution of $\langle \mathbf{if} \ B \rightarrow \alpha \ \mathbf{fi} \rangle$ is blocked unless $B$ holds.

(ii) It prevents other atomic actions from falsifying $B$ before $\alpha$ is executed, because of the indivisibility inherent in $\langle \mathbf{if} \ B \rightarrow \alpha \ \mathbf{fi} \rangle$.

Unfortunately, atomic actions like $\langle$if $B \to \alpha$ fi$\rangle$ are usually not part of a machine language. We seek a construction that not only exhibits (i) and (ii) but uses atomic actions likely to be available on a typical machine.

From Implementing Condition Synchronization (9.38), we know that an **if** can be replaced by a **do**, leading us to investigate the replacement of $\{P\}$ $\langle$if $B \to \alpha\rangle$ $\{Q\}$ in

**cobegin**

   ...

$\parallel$

   $S$:   ...   $\{P\}$ $\langle$if $B \to \alpha\rangle$ $\{Q\}$ ...
**coend**

by the following, where $b$ is a fresh variable. We assume that program fragment $S_{b:=B}$ truthifies $b=B$ and that every assignment statement in $S_{b:=B}$ complies with At Most One Assignments (9.32).

(9.48)   $\{P\}$
   $PO(S_{b:=B}) \otimes P$
   $\{P \wedge b=B\}$
   $L$: **do** $\neg b \to \{P\}$   $PO(S_{b:=B}) \otimes P$   $\{P \wedge b=B\}$ **od**
   $\{P \wedge b \wedge b=B\}$
   $\alpha$
   $\{Q\}$

Fragment (9.48) exhibits (i) but not (ii). Although $pre(\alpha)$ implies $B$, execution of a concurrent process might interfere with $pre(\alpha)$ by falsifying $b=B$. In addition, a concurrent process might interfere with the assertions in $PO(S_{b:=B})$ and falsify $b=B$ in that way.

Interference with $b=B$ and the assertions in $PO(S_{b:=B})$ can be eliminated with Avoiding Interference by Exclusion (9.43). Any atomic action $\alpha_i$ that interferes with $b=B$ or the assertions in $PO(S_{b:=B})$ is included in a critical section $CS_i$. However, we cannot simply group $S_{b:=B}$, $L$, and $\alpha$ in a mutually exclusive single critical section $CS$, because this would not satisfy requirement (ii) of Avoiding Interference by Exclusion (9.43), that execution of $CS$ be terminating.[7] We must be a bit more resourceful in forming the critical section. The trick is to include $S_{b:=B}$, $GEval_{do}(L)$, and $\alpha$, but not to include the entire loop. See Figure 9.10.

(9.49)   **Simulating a Conditional Atomic Action.**   Try replacing

   $\quad$ ... $\{P\}$ $\langle$if $B \to \alpha\rangle$ $\{Q\}$ ...

---

[7]This is because an atomic action interfering with $b=B$ would have to be part of another critical section $CS'$. Termination of $CS$ would then depend on a variable changed by another process executing inside a critical section.

with the proof outline in Figure 9.10 provided that each atomic action $\alpha_i$ whose execution can falsify $B$ is included in some critical section $CS_i$ and:

  (i) Execution of a critical section $CS_i$ is mutually exclusive with $CS$.

  (ii) No process executes forever in any of its critical sections.

  (iii) Fresh variable $b$ is used only in $CS$.          □

As with Implementing Condition Synchronization (9.38), we must revisit the question of termination. Termination of the **do** in Figure 9.10 is guaranteed only if $B$ holds long enough for the loop's guard $\neg b$ to become *false*. If the conditional atomic action being simulated is weakly fair, then it must terminate should $B$ hold from some point onward; the **do** of Figure 9.10 will terminate then as well. However, if the conditional atomic action being simulated is strongly fair, then the **do** of Figure 9.10 might not terminate when the conditional atomic action would. Therefore, strongly fair conditional atomic actions should be avoided.

To illustrate Simulating a Conditional Atomic Action (9.49), recall that one of the solutions to the bank problem of §5.7 uses a single conditional atomic action *Move* to perform the funds transfer:

---

...
$\{P\}$
*entry* $\{P \wedge \neg (\bigvee_i in(CS_i))\}$
$PO(S_{b:=B}) \otimes (P \wedge \neg (\bigvee_i in(CS_i)))$
$\{P \wedge b=B \wedge \neg (\bigvee_i in(CS_i))\}$
$CS$: $L$: **do** $\neg b \rightarrow \{P \wedge \neg (\bigvee_i in(CS_i))\}$
            *exit* $\{P\}$
            *entry* $\{P \wedge \neg (\bigvee_i in(CS_i))\}$
            $PO(S_{b:=B}) \otimes (P \wedge \neg (\bigvee_i in(CS_i)))$
            $\{P \wedge b=B \wedge \neg (\bigvee_i in(CS_i))\}$
   **od** $\{P \wedge b=B \wedge b \wedge \neg (\bigvee_i in(CS_i))\}$
  $\alpha$ $\{Q \wedge \neg (\bigvee_i in(CS_i))\}$
  *exit*
$\{Q\}$
...

**Figure 9.10.** Simulating $\langle$**if** $B \rightarrow \alpha$ **fi**$\rangle$

$\{P: \text{ T}=Tot_n^t \wedge acnt[mmb]=\text{M} \wedge acnt[fbs]=\text{F} \wedge fbs \neq mmb\}$
$Move: \ \langle \textbf{if } (mmb \leq j \wedge fbs \leq j) \vee (j < mmb \wedge j < fbs) \rightarrow$
$\qquad\qquad acnt[mmb], acnt[fbs] := acnt[mmb]-20, acnt[fbs]+20 \ \textbf{fi} \rangle$
$\{\text{T}=Tot_n^t \wedge acnt[mmb]=\text{M}-20 \wedge acnt[fbs]=\text{F}+20\}$

Simulating a Conditional Atomic Action (9.49) would be used as follows. To ensure that $mmb \leq j \wedge fbs \leq j$ is not falsified by concurrent execution, we place all updates to $j$ in critical sections. Thus, $C_1$ and $C_3$ in *Check* are placed in critical sections. ($C_1$ initializes $j$ to 0, and $C_3$ increments $j$ by one.) The proof outline for *Move* above is then replaced by the proof outline of Figure 9.11. The revised $C_1$ and $C_3$ do not interfere with $pre(M)$ in Figure 9.11 because their preconditions imply $in(CS_i)$ for some $i$, but $pre(M)$ implies $\neg in(CS_i)$.

## *Use of Signals*

Entry protocols for implementing mutual exclusion tend to be time-consuming. Consequently, repeated execution of *entry* can make the transformation in Simulating a Conditional Atomic Action (9.49) unattractive. The entry protocol was used there to ensure that no process falsifies $B$ when $at(\alpha)$ holds. If some other aspect of the program already prevents this interference, then *entry* (and *exit*) can be deleted. A common instance of this situation is described below.

A *signal b* is a boolean variable that is set to *true* only by one process and set to *false* only by another. We call the process that sets $b$ to *true* the *signaler* and the process that sets $b$ to *false* the *signalee*. A signal $b$ can indicate when it is safe to execute $\alpha$ of $\langle \textbf{if } B \rightarrow \alpha \ \textbf{fi} \rangle$ provided that (i) $b \Rightarrow B$ is an invariant, (ii) execution of only the signaler can affect the truth of $B$, and (iii) $\langle \textbf{if } B \rightarrow \alpha \ \textbf{fi} \rangle$ occurs in the signalee. The following protocol is used.

---

$\{P: \text{ T}=Tot_n^t \wedge acnt[mmb]=\text{M} \wedge acnt[fbs]=\text{F} \wedge fbs \neq mmb\}$
$entry \ \{P \wedge \neg (\underset{i}{\vee} in(CS_i))\}$
$CS: \text{ L}: \textbf{ do } \neg((mmb \leq j \wedge fbs \leq j) \vee (j < mmb \wedge j < fbs)) \rightarrow$
$\qquad\qquad\qquad\qquad\qquad\qquad \{P \wedge \neg (\underset{i}{\vee} in(CS_i))\}$
$\qquad\qquad\qquad\qquad\qquad\qquad exit \ \{P\}$
$\qquad\qquad\qquad\qquad\qquad\qquad entry \ \{P \wedge \neg (\underset{i}{\vee} in(CS_i))\}$
$\qquad \textbf{od } \{P \wedge ((mmb \leq j \wedge fbs \leq j) \vee (j < mmb \wedge j < fbs)) \wedge \neg (\underset{i}{\vee} in(CS_i))\}$
$\qquad M: \ acnt[mmb], acnt[fbs] := acnt[mmb]-20, acnt[fbs]+20$
$\qquad \{\text{T}=Tot_n^t \wedge acnt[mmb]=\text{M}-20 \wedge acnt[fbs]=\text{F}+20 \wedge \neg (\underset{i}{\vee} in(CS_i))\}$
$\quad exit$
$\{\text{T}=Tot_n^t \wedge acnt[mmb]=\text{M}-20 \wedge acnt[fbs]=\text{F}+20\}$

**Figure 9.11.** *Move* replacement

- The signaler sets $b$ to *true* when $B$ holds.
- The signalee waits until $b$ is *true*, executes $\alpha$, then sets $b$ to *false*.
- The signaler is permitted to falsify $B$ only if $\neg b$ holds.

The invariance of $b \Rightarrow B$ ensures that $B$ holds when the signalee finishes waiting for $b$. It remains only to establish that $B$ is not falsified before $\alpha$ is executed by the signalee. By assumption (ii) above, the signaler is the only process that can interfere with $B$. The invariance of $b \Rightarrow B$ requires that $\neg b$ hold before the signaler falsifies $B$. Since only the signalee may assign *false* to $b$, the signalee prevents the signaler from falsifying $B$ when $at(\alpha)$ holds by executing $b := false$ only after $\alpha$ is completed. Formulated in terms of proof outlines, we have:

(9.50) **Signals for Conditional Atomic Actions.** In a valid proof outline, suppose a process $S$ contains

$$... \ \{P\} \ \langle \text{if } B \to \alpha \text{ fi} \rangle \ \{Q\} \ ...$$

and $B$ can be affected only by executing a process $T$. Define

$$Ib: \ (b \Rightarrow B) \wedge (\neg b \Rightarrow \neg at(\alpha))$$

and conjoin $Ib$ to every assertion in the proof outline.

(i) Replace

$$... \ \{P \wedge Ib\} \ \langle \text{if } B \to \alpha \text{ fi} \rangle \ \{Q \wedge Ib\} \ ...$$

in $S$ by:

$$... \ \{I: P \wedge Ib\}$$
$$\text{do } \neg b \to \{I\} \ \text{skip} \ \{I\} \ \text{od}$$
$$\{P \wedge Ib \wedge b \wedge B\}$$
$$\alpha \ \{Q \wedge Ib\}$$
$$b := false \ \{Q \wedge Ib\} \ ...$$

(ii) Replace

$$... \ \{P \wedge Ib\} \ \alpha \ \{Q \wedge Ib\} \ ...$$

as follows for any atomic action $\alpha$ that affects $B$ and is in process $T$:

If $\alpha$ truthifies $B$:

$$... \ \{P \wedge Ib\} \ \alpha \ \{Q \wedge Ib \wedge B\} \ b := true \ \{Q \wedge Ib\} \ ...$$

If $\alpha$ falsifies $B$:

$$... \ \{P \wedge Ib\}$$
$$\text{do } b \to \{P \wedge Ib\} \ \text{skip} \ \{P \wedge Ib\} \ \text{od}$$
$$\{P \wedge Ib \wedge \neg b\}$$
$$\alpha \ \{Q \wedge Ib\} \ ...$$    $\square$

Note that the transformation described in (ii) of Signals for Conditional Atomic Actions (9.50) implicitly assumes that an atomic action that can affect $B$ either truthifies or falsifies $B$. For this to be so, program restructuring—perhaps using conditional statements—may be necessary.

## 9.6  Interlock Instructions

Some machine languages have *interlock instructions*: instructions that, in a single atomic action, both read and write one or more shared variables. Concurrent accesses to variables cannot occur while an interlock instruction is being executed. Thus, interlock instructions strengthen Memory Atomicity (9.30) by ruling out certain interleavings of memory accesses.

Interlock instructions are usually intended to help solve particular concurrent programming problems. They typically do not solve the entire problem but provide help where it is needed most. By solving only a portion of the problem, the cost of the interlock instruction is reduced. However, this does mean that interlock instructions are often quite primitive. Documentation describing the intended uses of a given interlock instruction can be invaluable—the manual that defines a computer's machine language usually contains such information.

### Test and Set

Execution of *test and set*, in a single atomic action, copies the value of a given (shared) variable $v$ into a (presumably local) variable $p$ and then sets $v$ to a constant. An example of such an instruction is:

$TestSet(v, p)$:  $v, p := true, v$

It sets a boolean $v$ to *true* and stores in $p$ the initial value of $v$.

Note that according to Compiler Access Restrictions (9.31), $v, p := true, v$ would compile to a sequence of atomic actions. Moreover, $v, p := true, v$ violates At Most One Assignments (9.32) if $v$ is written by other processes, so Reduction with At Most One Assignments (9.33) does not apply. Thus, it is unrealistic to consider $v, p := true, v$ a single atomic action. *TestSet*, though, is.

*TestSet* facilitates programming mutual exclusion protocols. A process $i$ enters its critical section only if $TestSet(v, p_i)$ is executed and $v$ changes value. Process $i$ can determine that $TestSet(v, p_i)$ caused $v$ to change value by checking whether $p_i$ is *false* after execution. Mutual exclusion is achieved because once $v$ is *true*, subsequent executions of $TestSet(v, p_i)$ leave $v$ *true*. Thus, once $i$ is granted entry to its critical section, entry attempts by other processes are prevented. Upon exiting its critical section, $i$ sets $v$ to *false*, thereby allowing $v$ to change by the next execution of *TestSet*.

The protocol just described for process $i$ is given below; $v$ is assumed to be initially *false*.

(9.51)  $entry_i$:  $p_i := true$
                  **do** $p_i \rightarrow TestSet(v, p_i)$ **od**
        $CS_i$
        $exit_i$:   $v := false$

To prove that Mutual Exclusion (6.2) is satisfied by this protocol, we use Exclusion of Configurations Rule (6.10) to prove $at(S) \Rightarrow \Box \neg (in(CS_1) \wedge in(CS_2))$. The proof outline of Figure 9.12 is a theorem of Proof Outline Logic. Thus, premise (a) is satisfied. Premise (b) with $Init$ instantiated by $at(S)$ is similarly valid. The following calculation discharges premise (c).

$$\neg\neg(in(CS_1) \wedge in(CS_2)) \; \wedge \; I_{PO(S)}$$
$$\Rightarrow \quad \text{«Negation Law (2.19), definition (4.14) of } I_{PO(S)}\text{»}$$
$$in(CS_1) \wedge in(CS_2) \wedge \neg p_1 \wedge \neg p_2 \wedge I$$
$$\Rightarrow \quad \text{«definition of } I \text{ in Figure 9.12»}$$
$$in(CS_1) \wedge in(CS_2) \wedge \neg in(CS_1) \wedge \neg in(CS_2)$$
$$\Rightarrow \quad \text{«Contradiction Law (2.21)»}$$
$$false$$

Unfortunately, (9.51) does not guarantee entry to a critical section. Process $i$ might forever execute the **do** in $entry_i$, even though $v$ is infinitely often *false*. This behavior occurs if execution of $TestSet(v, p_i)$ by $i$ happens only when $v$ equals *true*. The behavior is unlikely to occur when contention for the critical section is low. For example, if execution in the critical section is brief and infrequent, then a process executing its entry protocol will rarely be delayed, and such infinite looping is extremely unlikely. Thus, use of (9.51) should be restricted to low-contention settings.

---

$\{true\}$
$S$:  $v := false$  $\{I$:  $(\neg v \Rightarrow \underset{i}{\wedge} \neg in(CS_i)) \; \wedge \; \underset{i}{\wedge} (in(CS_i) \Rightarrow \neg p_i)$
$\qquad\qquad\qquad\qquad \wedge \; (v \Rightarrow \underset{i}{\wedge} (\neg p_i \wedge \neg at(entry_i)) \Rightarrow \underset{k, k \neq i}{\wedge} \neg in(CS_k)))\}$
$\qquad\quad$ **cobegin**
$\qquad\qquad \parallel \quad \{I\}$
$\qquad\qquad \underset{i}{\quad}$
$\qquad\qquad\quad S_i$: **do** $true \rightarrow \{I\}$
$\qquad\qquad\qquad\qquad\quad entry_i$:  $p_i := true$  $\{I \wedge p_i\}$
$\qquad\qquad\qquad\qquad\qquad\qquad$ **do** $p_i \rightarrow \{I \wedge p_i\}$
$\qquad\qquad\qquad\qquad\qquad\qquad\qquad\quad TestSet(v, p_i)$
$\qquad\qquad\qquad\qquad\qquad\qquad\qquad\quad \{I\}$
$\qquad\qquad\qquad\qquad\qquad\qquad$ **od** $\{I \wedge \neg p_i\}$
$\qquad\qquad\qquad\qquad\qquad PO(CS_i) \otimes (I \wedge \neg p_i)$
$\qquad\qquad\qquad\qquad\qquad exit_i$:   $v := false$  $\{I\}$
$\qquad\qquad\qquad\qquad\qquad PO(NCS_i) \otimes I$
$\qquad\qquad\qquad$ **od**
$\qquad\quad$ **coend**

**Figure 9.12.**  Proof outline for mutual exclusion using *TestSet*

## Compare and Swap

At first glance, the utility of *compare and swap* is difficult to fathom.

$$CompareSwap(t, x, o, n):\ \langle t := (o = x)$$
$$\textbf{if } t \to x := n$$
$$[]\ \neg t \to o := x\ \textbf{fi}\rangle$$

However, this interlock instruction is quite helpful for updating a shared variable using some function of its value. That is, we can use *CompareSwap* to build a protocol that replaces

$$(9.52)\ ...\ \{P\}\ \langle x := f(x)\rangle\ \{Q\}\ ...$$

even when computing $f(x)$ requires multiple atomic actions. Replacing $\langle x := f(x)\rangle$ in our programs is desirable, because it is unrealistic to expect a machine-language instruction to perform such an assignment statement— especially for $f$ an arbitrary function.

The protocol that implements $\langle x := f(x)\rangle$ is quite simple. First, $x$ is stored in a local variable. Next, $f(x)$ is computed. Finally, as a single atomic action, if $x$ has not changed, then a new value is installed; if $x$ has changed, the first two steps are repeated.

$$t_i := false$$
$$\textbf{do } \neg t_i \to old_i := x$$
$$new_i := f(old_i)$$
$$CompareSwap(t_i, x, old_i, new_i)$$
$$\textbf{od}$$

Termination of the **do** is not guaranteed, but it is likely in systems where only a small fraction of the time is spent updating $x$.

A proof outline to replace (9.52) appears in Figure 9.13. To establish interference freedom, we assume that interference freedom has been demonstrated for the proof outline containing (9.52). Thus, no atomic action in another process falsifies $P$ or $Q$. Moreover, from the validity of (9.52) we know that $P \Rightarrow Q^x_{f(x)}$ is valid. Since no atomic action interferes with $P$, we conclude that no atomic action interferes with $P \wedge Q^x_{f(x)}$, with $old_i = x \Rightarrow P \wedge Q^x_{f(old_i)}$, or with $old_i = x \Rightarrow new_i = f(old_i) \wedge P \wedge Q^x_{new_i}$.

## Fetch and Add

Typical of the interlock instruction found in instruction sets for multiprocessors is *fetch and add*:

$$FetchAdd(w, p, e):\ p, w := w, w + e$$

Executing this instruction causes an amount $e$ to be added to a (shared) variable

$\{P\}$
$t_i := false \quad \{I: (t_i \Rightarrow Q) \wedge (\neg t_i \Rightarrow P)\}$
**do** $\neg t_i \rightarrow \{\neg t_i \wedge I\}$
$\qquad old_i := x \quad \{(old_i \neq x \Rightarrow P) \wedge (old_i = x \Rightarrow P \wedge Q^x_{f(old_i)})\}$
$\qquad new_i := f(old_i)$
$\qquad \{(old_i \neq x \Rightarrow P) \wedge (old_i = x \Rightarrow new_i = f(old_i) \wedge P \wedge Q^x_{new_i})\}$
$\qquad CompareSwap(t_i, x, old_i, new_i) \quad \{I\}$
**od** $\{Q\}$

**Figure 9.13.** Proof outline for update using *CompareSwap*

---

$w$ and the initial value of $w$ to be returned in (presumably local) variable $p$.

The popularity of *FetchAdd* on multiprocessors can be attributed to its impact on performance. The designer of a multiprocessor must be careful that shared memory does not become a bottleneck. The problem is that Memory Atomicity (9.30) requires concurrent accesses involving a given memory location to appear serial. So, it would seem that an access by one processor might have to be blocked awaiting the completions of concurrent accesses by others. Such blocking impacts performance.

For *FetchAdd*, however, the blocking can be avoided. Concurrent executions of *FetchAdd* for a given memory location $w$ can be combined before being forwarded to a memory unit storing $w$. Thus, Memory Atomicity (9.30) is maintained without blocking. In particular, execution of $FetchAdd(w, p, e)$ by one processor can be combined by the memory's interface hardware with a $FetchAdd(w, p', e')$ executed concurrently to yield an instruction $FetchAdd(w, temp, e + e')$ that causes $w$ to be updated in the correct way. When the $FetchAdd(w, temp, e + e')$ completes, one of $p, p' := temp, temp + e$ or $p, p' := temp + e', temp$ is executed—neither requires accessing shared memory.

*FetchAdd* generalizes *TestSet*, so it should not be surprising that *FetchAdd* is useful in mutual exclusion protocols. The naive generalization of protocol (9.51), which uses *TestSet*, would be for $w$ to equal 1 initially and a process $i$ to enter its critical section only if it executes $FetchAdd(w, p_i, -1)$ and finds $p_i$ equal to 1 (indicating that $w$ was 1 before the *FetchAdd*). However, unlike *TestSet*, $FetchAdd(w, p_i, -1)$ always changes $w$, so a process that does not find $p_i$ equal to 1 must undo its change to $w$:

(9.54) $entry_i:$ $FetchAdd(w, p_i, -1)$
$\qquad\qquad$ **do** $p_i \leq 0 \rightarrow \alpha: FetchAdd(w, p_i, 1)$
$\qquad\qquad\qquad\quad \beta: FetchAdd(w, p_i, -1)$
$\qquad\qquad$ **od**
$\qquad CS_i$
$\qquad exit_i:$ $\quad FetchAdd(w, p_i, 1)$

Unfortunately, (9.54) allows executions in which no process is permitted to enter a critical section, even when no process is executing in its critical section. In a system with three (or more) processes, it is possible for one process to enter and then exit its critical section and $w \leq 0$ to remain *true* thereafter. The entry protocols of the remaining processes would then never terminate. The problem occurs when processes congregate at control point $\alpha$. While $at(\alpha)$ holds, $w$ is one less than it should be, because that process's unsuccessful *FetchAdd* has not been undone. Since $w$ is at most 1, when a process is at $\alpha$, $w$ cannot be positive—even if the critical section is not in use.

The insidious behavior of (9.54) can be avoided by not executing $FetchAdd(w, p_i, -1)$ when $w \leq 0$ holds:

$$(9.55) \quad entry_i: \ FetchAdd(w, p_i, -1)$$
$$\mathbf{do} \ p_i \leq 0 \rightarrow FetchAdd(w, p_i, 1)$$
$$\mathbf{do} \ w \leq 0 \rightarrow \mathbf{skip} \ \mathbf{od}$$
$$FetchAdd(w, p_i, -1)$$
$$\mathbf{od}$$
$$CS_i$$
$$exit_i: \ FetchAdd(w, p_i, 1)$$

The proof outline from which mutual exclusion can be established for (9.55) is given in Figure 9.14.

## 9.7 Example: Barrier Synchronization

In *barrier synchronization*, a process reaching one of a specified set of control points becomes blocked until all processes have reached control points in that set. An example is $gate_i$ in

$$(9.56) \quad S: \mathbf{cobegin} \ \underset{1 \leq i \leq N}{\parallel} \ S_i: \ U_i \ gate_i \ V_i \quad \mathbf{coend}$$

which is intended to ensure that no process $S_i$ starts executing $V_i$ until every process $S_j$ has completed $U_j$.

Barrier synchronization frequently finds application in computations that iteratively perform scientific calculations. Such a computation is often structured as a concurrent program, where each process loops. Iteration $i$ of the loop of a process produces values that are read by iteration $i+1$ of the other processes, so no process may start its iteration $i+1$ until all processes have completed their iteration $i$.

Barrier synchronization is a safety property. For example, we formalize the synchronization desired of $gate_i$ in (9.56) as the invariance property:

$\{true\}$

$S:\ w := 1\ \{I:\ w \le 1\ \wedge\ \wedge_i\, p_i \le 1\ \wedge\ (w = 1 \Rightarrow \wedge_i \neg\, in(CS_i))$

$\qquad\qquad\qquad \wedge\ \wedge_i\, (in(CS_i) \Rightarrow (p_i = 1))\ \wedge\ \wedge_i\, (in(CS_i) \Rightarrow w \le 0)$

$\qquad\qquad\qquad \wedge\ (w \le 0 \Rightarrow \wedge_i\, (p_i = 1 \Rightarrow \wedge_{k, k \ne i} \neg\, in(CS_k)))\}$

$\qquad$ **cobegin**

$\qquad\qquad \parallel_i \qquad \{I\}$

$\qquad\qquad\qquad S_i:\ \textbf{do}\ true \rightarrow \{I\}$

$\qquad\qquad\qquad\qquad\qquad entry_i:\ FetchAdd(w, p_i, -1)$

$\qquad\qquad\qquad\qquad\qquad\quad \{LI:\ I\ \wedge\ w \le 0\ \wedge\ \wedge_j\, (in(CS_j) \Rightarrow w < 0)\}$

$\qquad\qquad\qquad\qquad\qquad \textbf{do}\ p_i \le 0 \rightarrow \{LI \wedge p_i \le 0\}$

$\qquad\qquad\qquad\qquad\qquad\qquad\qquad FetchAdd(w, p_i, 1)\ \{I\}$

$\qquad\qquad\qquad\qquad\qquad\qquad\qquad \textbf{do}\ w \le 0 \rightarrow \{I\}\ \textbf{skip}\ \{I\}\ \textbf{od}\ \{I\}$

$\qquad\qquad\qquad\qquad\qquad\qquad\qquad FetchAdd(w, p_i, -1)\ \{LI\}$

$\qquad\qquad\qquad\qquad\qquad \textbf{od}\ \{I \wedge p_i > 0\}$

$\qquad\qquad\qquad\qquad\qquad PO(CS_i) \otimes (I \wedge p_i > 0)$

$\qquad\qquad\qquad\qquad\qquad exit_i:\quad FetchAdd(w, p_i, 1)\ \{I\}$

$\qquad\qquad\qquad\qquad\qquad PO(NCS_i) \otimes I$

$\qquad\qquad\qquad \textbf{od}$

$\qquad$ **coend**

**Figure 9.14.** Proof outline for mutual exclusion using *FetchAdd*

---

(9.57) $\quad at(S) \Rightarrow \Box \neg ((\vee_i\, in(U_i))\ \wedge\ (\vee_i\, in(V_i)))$

To illustrate techniques we have seen in this chapter and to show implementations of barrier synchronization, we will develop code for $gate_i$ of (9.56).

As suggested in Safety Property Methodology (6.30), we start by constructing a proof outline for (9.56), with **skip** for the body of $gate_i$. In the proof outlines that follow, $PO(U_i)$ and $PO(V_i)$ are assumed to be valid.

(9.58) $\quad \{at(S)\}$

$\qquad\qquad S:\ \textbf{cobegin}$

$\qquad\qquad\qquad \parallel_{1 \le i \le N}\ S_i:\ \{in(U_i)\}\ PO(U_i) \otimes in(U_i)\ \{after(U_i)\}$

$\qquad\qquad\qquad\qquad\qquad gate_i:\ \textbf{skip}$

$\qquad\qquad\qquad\qquad\qquad \{in(V_i)\}\ PO(V_i) \otimes in(V_i)\ \{after(V_i)\}$

$\qquad\qquad \textbf{coend}$

$\qquad\qquad \{after(S)\}$

Observe that the assertions in (9.58) are not strong enough to conclude that (9.57) holds. Each assertion $A$ must be strengthened so that:

(9.59) If $A$ implies $in(U_i)$, then $A$ also implies $\neg(\vee_j in(V_j))$.

(9.60) If $A$ implies $in(V_i)$, then $A$ also implies $\neg(\vee_j in(U_j))$.

$I_{PO(S)}$ Decomposition Rule (6.17a) and Precondition Safety Consequence Rule (6.15) would then allow us to conclude that (9.57) holds.

## Using a Shared Counter

For a first solution, we employ an integer variable $cnt$ to contain the number of processes $S_i$ that have not yet started executing $gate_i$. We write $(\Sigma i\colon R\colon e)$ to denote the summation of values $e_v^i$ for all $v$ satisfying $R_v^i$.

$$C\colon \quad cnt=(\Sigma i\colon in(U_i) \vee after(U_i)\colon 1)$$

Note that (9.59) and (9.60) hold if

$$(C \wedge cnt \neq 0 \Rightarrow \neg(\vee_i in(V_i))) \quad \wedge \quad (C \wedge cnt=0 \Rightarrow \neg(\vee_i in(U_i)))$$

is made a conjunct of every assertion. Because the second conjunct is valid, each assertion only need be strengthened by:

$$C'\colon \quad cnt=(\Sigma i\colon in(U_i) \vee after(U_i)\colon 1) \quad \wedge \quad (cnt \neq 0 \Rightarrow \neg(\vee_i in(V_i)))$$

We now investigate modifications to proof outline (9.58) so that its assertions satisfy (9.59) and (9.60). Observe that $C'$ is *true* initially if $cnt$ equals N (and N$\neq 0$). A process $S_i$ preserves the first conjunct of $C'$ by decrementing $cnt$ when $S_i$ starts executing $gate_i$, so the **skip** in $gate_i$ is replaced by $cnt := cnt-1$. Finally, we replace the assertions in (9.58) that imply $in(U_i)$ with the stronger $in(U_i) \wedge C' \wedge cnt \neq 0$ and the assertions that imply $in(V_i)$ with the stronger $in(V_i) \wedge C' \wedge cnt=0$. The resulting proof outline is:

(9.61) $\{at(S) \wedge C' \wedge cnt=N\}$
  $S\colon$ **cobegin**
      $\|$   $S_i\colon \{in(U_i) \wedge C' \wedge cnt \neq 0\}$
    $_{1 \leq i \leq N}$      $PO(U_i) @ (in(U_i) \wedge C' \wedge cnt \neq 0)$
         $\{after(U_i) \wedge C' \wedge cnt \neq 0\}$
         $gate_i\colon cnt := cnt-1$
         $\{in(V_i) \wedge C' \wedge cnt=0\}$
         $PO(V_i) @ (in(V_i) \wedge C' \wedge cnt=0)$
         $\{after(V_i) \wedge C' \wedge cnt=0\}$
    **coend**
  $\{after(S) \wedge C' \wedge cnt=0\}$

Proof outline (9.61) is not valid. Conjunct $cnt=0$ in $post(gate_i)$ cannot be justified given the precondition of $gate_i$. To address this problem, we use condition synchronization in $gate_i$ and block execution until $cnt=0$ holds. This gives rise to the valid proof outline in Figure 9.15.

We are not yet done, however. Assignment statement $cnt := cnt-1$ in $gate_i$ does not comply with At Most One Assignments (9.32). We might then employ Atomic Assignments by Exclusion (9.47). Other replacements for $cnt := cnt-1$ would also be possible were interlock instructions available. For example, *CompareSwap* could be used with the protocol of (9.53), taking $old-1$ for $f(old)$. *FetchAdd* could perform the increment directly and efficiently, even if a large number of processes reached $gate_i$ at about the same time.

Next, we turn to the guard evaluation for the **if** statement in $gate_i$. It involves a conditional atomic action. Therefore, we perform the replacement prescribed by Implementing Condition Synchronization (9.38) and complete the development of the code $gate_i$.

$gate_i$:  ...  **do** $cnt \neq 0 \rightarrow$ **skip od**

## Using Boolean Variables

One problem with the barrier synchronization solutions just described is that they require mutual exclusion or interlock instructions. Such machinery is needed in updating $cnt$ because $cnt$ is read and written by all processes. Our subsequent solutions avoid mutual exclusion, since it is expensive to implement, and avoid interlock instructions, since they might not be available. Therefore, our subsequent solutions must avoid variables that are read and written by all processes.

For each process $S_i$, define a boolean variable $g_i$ that records whether $S_i$ has started executing $gate_i$.

---

$\{at(S) \wedge cnt = N \wedge$
$\quad C': (cnt = (\Sigma i: in(U_i) \vee after(U_i): 1))$
$\quad\quad \wedge (cnt \neq 0 \Rightarrow \neg (\underset{i}{\vee} in(V_i)))\}$

$S$: **cobegin**

$\quad\quad \underset{1 \leq i \leq N}{\|} \ S_i: \ \{in(U_i) \wedge C' \wedge cnt \neq 0\}$
$\quad\quad\quad\quad PO(U_i) \otimes (in(U_i) \wedge C' \wedge cnt \neq 0)$
$\quad\quad\quad\quad \{after(U_i) \wedge C' \wedge cnt \neq 0\}$
$\quad\quad\quad\quad gate_i: \ cnt := cnt-1 \ \{C'\}$
$\quad\quad\quad\quad\quad\quad$ **if** $cnt = 0 \rightarrow \{C' \wedge cnt = 0\}$ **skip** $\{C' \wedge cnt = 0\}$ **fi**
$\quad\quad\quad\quad \{in(V_i) \wedge C' \wedge cnt = 0\}$
$\quad\quad\quad\quad PO(V_i) \otimes (in(V_i) \wedge C' \wedge cnt = 0)$
$\quad\quad\quad\quad \{after(V_i) \wedge C' \wedge cnt = 0\}$

$\quad$ **coend**
$\{after(S) \wedge C' \wedge cnt = 0\}$

**Figure 9.15.** Barrier synchronization with $cnt$

$$G: \quad g_i = (in(U_i) \vee after(U_i))$$

As before, note that (9.59) and (9.60) would hold if

$$(G \wedge (\underset{i}{\vee} g_i) \Rightarrow \neg (\underset{i}{\vee} in(V_i))) \quad \wedge \quad (G \wedge \neg (\underset{i}{\vee} g_i) \Rightarrow \neg (\underset{i}{\vee} in(U_i)))$$

is made a conjunct of every assertion. The obvious modification to $G$ is:

$$G': \quad (\underset{i}{\wedge} (g_i = (in(U_i) \vee after(U_i)))) \quad \wedge \quad ((\underset{i}{\vee} g_i) \Rightarrow \neg (\underset{i}{\vee} in(V_i)))$$

because $(\underset{i}{\wedge} (g_i = (in(U_i) \vee after(U_i)))) \wedge \neg (\underset{i}{\vee} g_i)$ implies $\neg (\underset{i}{\vee} in(U_i)))$.

We now change proof outline (9.58) so that its assertions satisfy (9.59) and (9.60). Observe that $G'$ is initially *true* if each $g_i$ is initialized to *true*. A process $S_i$ preserves the first conjunct of $G'$ by setting $g_i$ to *false* when $S_i$ starts executing $gate_i$, so the **skip** in $gate_i$ must be replaced by $g_i := false$. Finally, we replace assertions in (9.58) that imply $in(U_i)$ with $in(U_i) \wedge G' \wedge g_i$ and replace assertions that imply $in(V_i)$ with $in(V_i) \wedge G' \wedge \neg (\underset{i}{\vee} g_i)$. The resulting proof outline is:

(9.62) $\{at(S) \wedge G' \wedge (\underset{i}{\wedge} g_i)\}$

> $S$: **cobegin**
> $\quad \underset{1 \leq i \leq N}{\|} \ S_i: \ \{in(U_i) \wedge G' \wedge g_i\}$
> $\qquad\qquad PO(U_i) \otimes (in(U_i) \wedge G' \wedge g_i)$
> $\qquad\qquad \{after(U_i) \wedge G' \wedge g_i\}$
> $\qquad\qquad gate_i: \ g_i := false$
> $\qquad\qquad \{in(V_i) \wedge G' \wedge \neg (\underset{i}{\vee} g_i)\}$
> $\qquad\qquad PO(V_i) \otimes (in(V_i) \wedge G' \wedge \neg (\underset{i}{\vee} g_i))$
> $\qquad\qquad \{after(V_i) \wedge G' \wedge \neg (\underset{i}{\vee} g_i)\}$
> $\quad$ **coend**
> $\{after(S) \wedge G' \wedge \neg (\underset{i}{\vee} g_i)\}$

The problem with proof outline (9.62) is that $post(gate_i)$ cannot be justified given the precondition of $gate_i$. Again, we solve the problem by adding condition synchronization to $gate_i$; execution of $S_i$ is blocked until $\neg (\underset{i}{\vee} g_i)$ holds. The proof outline of Figure 9.16 results.

The only problem with the protocol in Figure 9.16 concerns the **if**. With Implementing Condition Synchronization (9.38), we get:

$$gate_i: \ g_i := false \ \textbf{do} \ \underset{i}{\vee} g_i \rightarrow \textbf{skip od}$$

A difficulty here is that the guard evaluation action for the **do** reads from more than one shared variable. This problem is solved by changing the **do** so the guard is calculated using a local variable $p_i$ and shared variables are read one at a

$\{at(S) \land (\underset{i}{\land} g_i) \land$

$\quad G': (\underset{i}{\land}(g_i = (in(U_i) \lor after(U_i)))) \land ((\underset{i}{\lor} g_i) \Rightarrow \neg(\underset{i}{\lor} in(V_i)))\}$

$S:$ **cobegin**

$\quad\quad \underset{1 \leq i \leq N}{\|} S_i: \{in(U_i) \land G' \land g_i\}$

$\quad\quad\quad\quad PO(U_i) @ (in(U_i) \land G' \land g_i)$

$\quad\quad\quad\quad \{after(U_i) \land G' \land g_i\}$

$\quad\quad\quad\quad gate_i: g_i := false \ \{G' \land \neg g_i\}$

$\quad\quad\quad\quad\quad\quad \textbf{if} \ \neg(\underset{i}{\lor} g_i) \rightarrow \{G' \land \neg(\underset{i}{\lor} g_i)\} \ \textbf{skip} \ \{G' \land \neg(\underset{i}{\lor} g_i)\} \ \textbf{fi}$

$\quad\quad\quad\quad \{in(V_i) \land G' \land \neg(\underset{i}{\lor} g_i)\}$

$\quad\quad\quad\quad PO(V_i) @ (in(V_i) \land G' \land \neg(\underset{i}{\lor} g_i))$

$\quad\quad\quad\quad \{after(V_i) \land G' \land \neg(\underset{i}{\lor} g_i)\}$

$\quad\quad$ **coend**

$\quad \{after(S) \land G' \land \neg(\underset{i}{\lor} g_i)\}$

**Figure 9.16.**  Barrier synchronization with $g_i$

---

time. The new protocol appears in Figure 9.17. We must check that no atomic action in another process falsifies the assertions in this proof outline. Only atomic actions that change $g_j$ are of concern, and they do not interfere, because they assign *false* to $g_j$, which does not falsify $I_i$.

## Using Signals

Yet another scheme for implementing $gate_i$ is based on signals. We start by augmenting the assertions of (9.58) so that they satisfy conditions (9.59) and (9.60), which are needed to infer that (9.57) holds. The proof outline—far from being valid—is:

(9.63) $\{at(S)\}$

$\quad\quad S:$ **cobegin**

$\quad\quad\quad \underset{1 \leq i \leq N}{\|} S_i: \{in(U_i) \land \neg(\underset{j}{\lor} in(V_j))\}$

$\quad\quad\quad\quad\quad PO(U_i) @ (in(U_i) \land \neg(\underset{j}{\lor} in(V_j)))$

$\quad\quad\quad\quad\quad \{after(U_i) \land \neg(\underset{j}{\lor} in(V_j))\}$

$\quad\quad\quad\quad\quad gate_i:$ **skip**

$\quad\quad\quad\quad\quad \{in(V_i) \land \neg(\underset{j}{\lor} in(U_j))\}$

$\quad\quad\quad\quad\quad PO(V_i) @ (in(V_i) \land \neg(\underset{j}{\lor} in(U_j)))$

$\quad\quad\quad\quad\quad \{after(V_i) \land \neg(\underset{j}{\lor} in(U_j))\}$

$\quad\quad\quad$ **coend**

$\quad\quad \{after(S) \land \neg(\underset{j}{\lor} in(U_j))\}$

Note that $post(gate_i)$ cannot be justified and that concurrent execution can falsify conjuncts $\neg(\underset{j}{\vee} in(V_j))$ and $\neg(\underset{j}{\vee} in(U_j))$ in all of the assertions.

It is tempting to implement $gate_i$ using an **if** that blocks until $\neg(\underset{j}{\vee} in(U_j))$ holds. The result would be a valid proof outline. But because the guard of this **if** involves control predicates from several processes, such a guard would not be amenable to replacement by a signal. Recall that a signal may be set to *true* by only one process.

The solution is to decompose $\neg(\underset{j}{\vee} in(U_j))$ into conditions each of which is truthified by a single process—such conditions could be replaced by signals. From De Morgan's Law (2.17b), we have:

$$\neg(\underset{j}{\vee} in(U_j)) = (\underset{j}{\wedge} \neg in(U_j))$$

This suggests using signals for $\neg in(U_1)$, $\neg in(U_2)$, ..., $\neg in(U_N)$ and, because none of these conditions is falsified once *true*, waiting for them one at a time. The following sequence of N conditional atomic actions blocks until $(\underset{j}{\wedge} \neg in(U_j))$ holds. There is no interference in the proof outline because none of the conditions being awaited is ever falsified.

$$\{P\}$$
$$\langle \textbf{if} \neg in(U_1) \to \textbf{skip fi} \rangle \;\; \{P \wedge (\underset{1 \leq i \leq 1}{\wedge} \neg in(U_i))\}$$
$$\langle \textbf{if} \neg in(U_2) \to \textbf{skip fi} \rangle \;\; \{P \wedge (\underset{1 \leq i \leq 2}{\wedge} \neg in(U_i))\}$$
$$\vdots$$
$$\langle \textbf{if} \neg in(U_N) \to \textbf{skip fi} \rangle \;\; \{P \wedge (\underset{1 \leq i \leq N}{\wedge} \neg in(U_i))\}$$

---

$$\{after(U_i) \wedge G' \wedge g_i\}$$
$$gate_i: \;\; g_i := false \;\; \{G' \wedge \neg g_i\}$$
$$p_i := false \;\; \{I_i: \; G' \wedge (p_i \Rightarrow \underset{k}{\wedge} \neg g_k)\}$$
$$\textbf{do} \neg p_i \to \{I_i \wedge p_i\}$$
$$p_i := true \;\; \{G' \wedge p_i\}$$
$$p_i := p_i \wedge \neg g_1 \;\; \{G' \wedge (p_i \Rightarrow \neg g_1)\}$$
$$p_i := p_i \wedge \neg g_2 \;\; \{G' \wedge (p_i \Rightarrow \neg g_1 \wedge \neg g_2)\}$$
$$...$$
$$p_i := p_i \wedge \neg g_N \;\; \{G' \wedge (p_i \Rightarrow \underset{k}{\wedge} \neg g_k)\}$$
$$\textbf{od}$$
$$\{G' \wedge \underset{k}{\wedge} \neg g_k\}$$

**Figure 9.17.** An implementation of $gate_i$

We can now use Signals for Conditional Atomic Actions (9.50). For each process $S_i$, a signal $b_i$ is introduced such that $b_i \Rightarrow \neg in(U_i)$ holds throughout execution. This means that $b_i$ must be initially *false* and may be assigned *true* any time after $\neg in(U_i)$ becomes *true*—we chose to truthify $b_i = true$ as the first action of $gate_i$. Finally, we replace each of the N conditional atomic actions with a **do** as prescribed by (i) of Signals for Conditional Atomic Actions (9.50). A loop can be used to run through those, resulting in the following protocol for $gate_i$.

$$
\begin{aligned}
&gate_i\colon\ b_i := true \\
&\qquad\quad p_i := 0 \\
&\qquad\quad \textbf{do}\ p_i \neq \mathrm{N} \rightarrow \textbf{do}\ \neg b_{p_i+1} \rightarrow \textbf{skip}\ \textbf{od} \\
&\qquad\qquad\qquad\qquad\quad p_i := p_i + 1 \\
&\qquad\quad \textbf{od}
\end{aligned}
$$

## Historical Notes

A good deal of research has been directed towards finding methods to aggregate atomic actions so that reasoning about concurrent programs can be simplified. Perhaps the earliest work along these lines is reported in [Lipton 75]. There, reduction theorems are given for partial correctness and deadlock freedom properties of programs constructed solely from semaphore operations. That work is extended in [Doeppner 77] to a larger class of safety properties and further extended in [Lamport & Schneider 89] to all invariance properties. A reduction theorem for total correctness is given in [Back 89]. Kleene algebra enables [Cohen 93a] to derive all of these reduction theorems by using algebraic reasoning instead of arguing directly about program execution.

Communication with message-passing provided impetus for other work on aggregating actions. In [Lamport 90b], a reduction theorem is given that allows local operations, send operations, and receive operations in a single process to be grouped; safety as well as some liveness properties are handled. Restrictions on the programmer of a shared memory system are proposed in [Misra 91] so the semantics of message-passing—that a receiver must wait for a sender—can be exploited in reduction for certain liveness properties as well as safety properties. That work is extended to larger classes of liveness properties in [Rao 92] and [Cohen 93b].

A somewhat different approach to reduction is proposed in [Lamport 92]. In that, a collection of fine-grained atomic actions are shown to implement a coarse-grained atomic action by relating the variables of the two program fragments. During execution of the fine-grained operation, the coarse-grained variables first equal the values of the original variables just before the operation is executed, and then all change so that they equal the values of the original variables just after it completes. The approach is general enough to handle all safety and liveness properties.

Reduction for Invariance Properties (9.10) and its corollary (9.11) are taken from [Lamport & Schneider 89]. However, the reduction principles in [Lamport & Schneider 89] are formulated using a semantic characterization of actions and juxtaposition rather than the language-specific definitions used here. Also, slightly weaker commutativity conditions are used in [Lamport & Schneider 89]. Right Commutativity (9.6) and Left Commutativity (9.7) are defined in terms of all states, whereas only program states need be considered for the commutativity conditions in [Lamport & Schneider 89]; see exercise 9.12 for consequences.

At Most One Assignments (9.32) was first discussed in [Owicki & Gries 76a] for partial correctness properties. Some have attributed the insight to John Reynolds, because of an acknowledgment in [Owicki & Gries 76a]. This attribution is incorrect; discussions with Gries, Owicki, and Reynolds corroborate Reynolds's noninvolvement in this aspect of the work. Memory Atomicity (9.30) is a long-standing assumption about the operation of a memory; one early mention appears in [Dijkstra 68b]. Compiler Access Restrictions (9.31) and translation-independent reasoning are not explicitly mentioned in the literature. Use of a **do** to block progress until some predicate holds is an old programming technique, sometimes called "spinning" or "busy waiting."

The ticket-based mutual exclusion protocol of §9.4 is based on [Lamport 79], which gives a variant of the bakery algorithm first described in [Lamport 74]. We make stronger assumptions about the value returned by a read that is concurrent with a write than those made in [Lamport 74] and [Lamport 79]. The protocol in [Lamport 74] assumes that if a read overlaps a write, then an arbitrary value is returned; the protocol in [Lamport 79] requires a read that overlaps a write to return a value between zero and the value being written (but methods to implement this are discussed in the paper as well).

That critical sections are a way to avoid interference was known to Gries and Owicki, although they never wrote about it. The code for Simulating a Conditional Atomic Action (9.49) is based on the implementation of conditional critical regions given in [Brinch Hansen 72b] and can be found in [Andrews 91]. Signals for Conditional Atomic Actions (9.50) was inspired by the Flag Synchronization Principles of [Andrews 91].

Test and set appears in the instruction set of the IBM System 360, first announced in April 1964 and actually operational at a customer site in June 1965. In defining the instruction set of the IBM System 370, compare and swap was added. Our implementation of mutual exclusion using test and set is taken from [IBM 70], and our routine to implement $\langle x := f(x) \rangle$ using compare and swap is taken from [IBM 73]. According to [Gottlieb et al. 83], a predecessor of fetch and add was first proposed in [Draughon et al. 67]. Also see [Gottlieb et al. 83] for solutions to most standard synchronization problems in terms of an instruction very similar to fetch and add. The NYU Ultracomputer, its successor the IBM RP3, Columbia University's CHoPP, and the Cray T3D all include fetch and add in their instruction sets [Almasi & Gottlieb 94]. A surprising universality result concerning compare and swap is proved in [Herlihy 91]. Herlihy proves that neither test and set nor fetch and add can be used to construct wait-free and lock-free implementations of objects; compare and swap can.

Henry Jordan is usually credited with first defining barrier synchronization and discussing hardware to support its implementation [Jordan 78]. The implementations we give in §9.7 are impractical because they ignore memory contention. See [Mellor-Crummey & Scott 91] for a good discussion of real implementations.

## Exercises

**9.1.** Which, if any, of the following properties are satisfied when the angle brackets are removed from

$$S: \langle x := x+1 \quad y := y+1 \rangle$$

and $S$ is assumed to label the entire juxtaposition? For properties that are satisfied, give a proof; otherwise, describe an execution that violates the property.

(a)    $\Box(x=y)$

(b)   $at(S) \wedge x=y \Rightarrow \Box(x=y)$

(c)   $at(S) \wedge x=y \Rightarrow \Box(\neg in(S) \Rightarrow x=y)$

(d)   $at(S) \wedge x=y \Rightarrow \Box(in(S) \Rightarrow x \geq y)$

(e)   $at(S) \wedge x=y \Rightarrow \Box(in(S) \Rightarrow x \leq y)$

(f)   $in(S) \wedge x=y \Rightarrow \Box(in(S) \Rightarrow x \geq y)$

(g)   $in(S) \wedge x=y \Rightarrow \Box(after(S) \Rightarrow x \leq y)$

**9.2.** Consider a concurrent program $S$ containing atomic statement $T$:

$T$: $\langle$**if** $sem > 0 \rightarrow$ **skip fi** $sem := sem - 1\rangle$

Suppose $S$ satisfies $at(S) \wedge sem > 0 \Rightarrow \Box(sem \geq 0)$.

(a)   Give an example of $S$ where $at(S) \wedge sem > 0 \Rightarrow \Box(sem \geq 0)$ would be violated if the angle brackets were removed.

(b)   Give an example of $S$ where $at(S) \wedge sem > 0 \Rightarrow \Box(sem \geq 0)$ would not be violated if the angle brackets were removed.

**9.3.** Determine whether atomic action $\rho$ right commutes with atomic action $\alpha$. Justify your answer using Right Commutativity (9.6).

(a)   $\rho$: $x, y := y, x$   and   $\alpha$: $x, y := y, x$.

(b)   $\rho$: $x := x+1$   and   $\alpha$: $y := y+2$.

(c)   $\rho$: $x := x+2$   and   $\alpha$: $x := x+2$.

(d)   $\rho$: $x := x+2$   and   $\alpha$: $x := x*2$.

(e)   $\rho$: $x, y := 2*x, 2*y$   and   $\alpha$: $x := y$.

(f)   $\rho$: $\langle$**if** $x > 0 \rightarrow$ **skip fi**$\rangle$   and   $\alpha$: $x := x+1$.

(g)   $\rho$: $x := x+1$   and   $\alpha$: $\langle$**if** $x > 0 \rightarrow$ **skip fi**$\rangle$.

(h)   $\rho$: $\langle$**if** $x > 0 \rightarrow$ **skip fi**$\rangle$   and   $\alpha$: $x := x-1$.

**9.4.** Determine whether atomic action $\Lambda$ left commutes with atomic action $\alpha$. Justify your answer using Left Commutativity (9.7).

(a)   $\Lambda$: $x, y := y, x$   and   $\alpha$: $x, y := y, x$.

(b)   $\Lambda$: $x := x+1$   and   $\alpha$: $y := y+2$.

(c)   $\Lambda$: $x := x+2$   and   $\alpha$: $x := x+2$.

(d)   $\Lambda$: $x := x+2$   and   $\alpha$: $x := x*2$.

(e)   $\Lambda$: $x, y := 2*x, 2*y$   and   $\alpha$: $x := y$.

(f)   $\Lambda$: $\langle$**if** $x > 0 \rightarrow$ **skip fi**$\rangle$   and   $\alpha$: $x := x+1$.

(g)   $\Lambda$: $x := x+1$   and   $\alpha$: $\langle$**if** $x > 0 \rightarrow$ **skip fi**$\rangle$.

(h)   $\Lambda$: $\langle$**if** $x > 0 \rightarrow$ **skip fi**$\rangle$   and   $\alpha$: $x := x-1$.

**9.5.** (a)   Right Commutativity (9.6) concerns actions $\alpha$ and $\rho$ from different processes. Suppose they are from the same process. Under what circumstances will first executing $\rho$ and then executing $\alpha$ produce the same state as executing $\alpha$ and then $\rho$?

(b)    Why can't *wp* be used to characterize when two atomic actions from the same process right commute?

**9.6.** It is not difficult to prove that $x \geq 0 \Rightarrow \Box x \geq 0$ is satisfied by the following program.

   *S*: **cobegin** $\langle t := x+1 \ \ x := t \rangle$  ‖  $\langle t := x+1 \ \ x := t \rangle$  **coend**

Is it also satisfied by the program obtained by deleting the angle brackets? Use reduction to justify your answer.

**9.7.** It is not difficult to prove that $at(S) \wedge x = X \Rightarrow \Box(after(S) \Rightarrow X+2)$ is satisfied by the following program.

   *S*: **cobegin** $\langle t := x+1 \ \ x := t \rangle$  ‖  $\langle t := x+1 \ \ x := t \rangle$  **coend**

Is it also satisfied by the program obtained by deleting the angle brackets? Use reduction to justify your answer.

**9.8.** It is not difficult to prove that

$$at(S) \Rightarrow \Box(after(S) \Rightarrow ((m = x \vee m = y) \wedge (m \leq x \wedge m \leq y)))$$

is satisfied by the following program.

   *S*: $\langle \textbf{if } x \leq y \rightarrow m := x \ \ [] \ \ y \leq x \rightarrow m := y \ \textbf{fi} \rangle$

Is it also satisfied by the program obtained by deleting the angle brackets? Use reduction to justify your answer.

**9.9.** Give detailed proofs for (9.13)–(9.15) and (9.17).

**9.10.** Give detailed proofs for (9.18)–(9.22).

**9.11.** Give detailed proofs for (9.23)–(9.28).

**9.12.** Consider the following variation on the producer/consumer program of Figure 9.1. In it, unbounded integer variables *a* and *r* have been replaced by bounded variables *am* and *rm* according to $am = a \bmod 2N$ and $rm = r \bmod 2N$.

```
S: cobegin
      Prod: do true → S₁: v, inp := inp[0], inp[1..]
                       S₂: ⟨if a−r mod 2N < N →   skip fi⟩
                       S₃: buf[a mod N] := v
                       S₄: a := a+1 mod 2N
            od
   ‖
      Cons: do true → T₁: ⟨if a−r > 0 mod 2N →   skip fi⟩
                       T₂: w := buf[r mod N]
                       T₃: r := r+1 mod 2N
                       T₄: out := out w
            od
   coend
```

Is it possible to perform the same reductions on this program as done for the producer/consumer program of Figure 9.1? Explain why or why not.

**9.13.** Suppose Memory Atomicity (9.30) were weakened.

   **Weak Memory Atomicity.** Concurrent reads to a noncomposite variable are serial. Concurrent writes to a noncomposite variable are serial but their order may be arbitrary. A concurrent read and write to a noncomposite variable may return an arbitrary value.                        □

Given is a program $S$ designed for execution on a computer that satisfies Weak Memory Atomicity.

(a)    If $S$ is correct when executed on a computer that satisfies Weak Memory Atomicity, will $S$ also be correct when executed on a computer that satisfies Memory Atomicity (9.30)? Justify your answer.

(b)    Explain how to transform $S$ so that when it is executed on a computer satisfying Memory Atomicity (9.30) it will exhibit all behaviors it could produce on a computer satisfying Weak Memory Atomicity.

**9.14.** Variables $x$ and $y$ are written by one process, and the following assignment statements are found in a different concurrent process. Indicate which, if any, comply with At Most One Assignments (9.32). For those that do not, give a sequence of assignment statements that changes the variables in the same way and do comply.

(a)    $x := t+1$

(b)    $x := t+x$

(c)    $x, t := t, 1$

(d)    $x, x := 1, 1$

(e)    $x, x := 1, x$

(f)    $x, y := x+1, y+1$

(g)    $x := x+x$

**9.15.** The following clause is proposed as a third alternative in At Most One Assignments (9.32).

(c)    At most one target is read by another process and at most one expression contains only once a variable that is read or written by another process.

Explain why or why not this extension should be permitted.

**9.16.** Variables $x$ and $y$ are written by one process, and the following **do** statements are found in a different concurrent process. Indicate which, if any, comply with the conditions of Reduction with At Most One **do** Guards (9.36). For those that do not, modify the **do** by adding assignment statements so the result complies with At Most One Assignments (9.32) and Reduction with At Most One **do** Guards (9.36).

(a)    **do** $x=0 \rightarrow$ **skip od**

(b)    **do** $x=y \rightarrow$ **skip od**

(c)    **do** $x=0 \rightarrow$ **skip** [] $y=0 \rightarrow$ **skip od**

(d)    **do** $x=y+1 \rightarrow$ **skip** [] $x=y+2 \rightarrow$ **skip od**

(e)    **do** $x=0 \rightarrow$ **skip** [] $t=1 \rightarrow$ **skip od**

**9.17.** The **do** in the program of Figure 7.2 does not comply with the conditions of Reduction with At Most One **do** Guards (9.36). Propose a replacement that does comply. Prove that the resulting program still satisfies (7.11).

**9.18.** If the guards in an **if** mention more than one variable that is written by other processes, then Compiler Access Restrictions (9.31) imply that guard evaluation cannot be performed as a single atomic action. Unlike with **do**, it is not possible to rewrite the guards so they use local variables and add assignment statements before an **if**. Explain why.

**9.19.** Show how to use Implementing Condition Synchronization (9.38) to transform each of the following **if** statements into a **do**. If necessary, modify the **do** so it complies with Reduction with At Most One **do** Guards (9.36). Assume that $x$ and $y$ are written by a concurrent process.

   (a)     **if** $x=y \to T$ **fi**

   (b)     **if** $x=1 \lor y=2 \to T$ **fi**

   (c)     **if** $\neg(x \le 23 \le y) \to T$ **fi**

   (d)     **if** $\neg(x \le y \land x < 23) \to T$ **fi**

   (e)     **if** $x=3 \to T$ **fi**

**9.20.** Prove that

$$S: \mathbf{do} \neg B \to \mathbf{skip\ od}\ \ T$$

reaches $T$ whenever the weakly fair **if**

$$S: \mathbf{if}\ B \to \mathbf{skip\ fi}\ \ T$$

would reach $T$.

**9.21.** Flesh out the proof hinted at in §9.3 that a process attempting to enter its critical section will eventually do so when the entry protocol of §9.3 is employed.

**9.22.** A proposed replacement for

$$S: \{P\}\ \mathbf{if}\ B_1 \land B_2 \land \cdots \land B_n \to \{Q\}\ T: \ldots$$

is the following.

$$
\begin{aligned}
&S: \{P\} \\
&\quad v := false\ \ \{W\!:\ P \land (v \Rightarrow B_1 \land B_2 \land \cdots \land B_n)\} \\
&\quad \mathbf{do}\ \neg v \to \{\neg v \land W\} \\
&\qquad\qquad v := v \land B_1\ \ \{W\} \\
&\qquad\qquad v := v \land B_2\ \ \{W\} \\
&\qquad\qquad \ldots \\
&\qquad\qquad v := v \land B_n\ \ \{W\} \\
&\quad \mathbf{od}\ \{Q\} \\
&T: \ldots
\end{aligned}
$$

   (a)    Is the replacement fragment a theorem of Proof Outline Logic? If so, give the proof; if not, explain why not.

   (b)    What problems with the proposed replacement limit its utility?

**9.23.** Assume that *GetT* and *WaitMinT* in the ticket protocol of Figure 9.6 are implemented as follows:

$$GetT(t_i):\ t_i, tix := tix, tix+1$$

$$WaitMinT(t_i):\ \mathbf{if}\ t_i \le (\downarrow j\!:\ t_j \ne \bot\!:\ t_j) \to \mathbf{skip\ fi}$$

Prove for (9.39):

     (a)    Mutual exclusion of $CS_1$ and $CS_2$.

     (b)    Neither $S_1$ nor $S_2$ forever blocks attempting to enter its critical section.

**9.24.** Formalize the argument discussed at the end of §9.4 by giving a Temporal Logic proof that a process attempting to enter its critical section will eventually do so.

**9.25.** Does the final ticket protocol of §9.4—Figures 9.7, 9.8, and 9.9—guarantee that processes enter critical sections in first-come, first-served order?

     (a)    Formalize first-come, first-served order for the protocol and argue that your formalization is reasonable.

     (b)    Determine whether the property is satisfied. If it is, give a proof; if it is not, give an execution that violates the property.

**9.26.** Suppose assignment statement $v_i := t_{p_i+1} + 1$ in the **do** of $GetT(t_i)$ is replaced by:

$$v_i := t_{p_i+1} + 1 \quad v_i := v_i + t_i$$

Would the resulting protocol still ensure the following? Give a proof or counterexample for each.

     (a)    Mutual exclusion of $CS_1$ and $CS_2$.

     (b)    Neither $S_1$ nor $S_2$ forever blocks attempting to enter its critical section.

**9.27.** Suppose assignment statement $v_i := t_{p_i+1} + 1$ in the **do** of $GetT(t_i)$ is replaced by:

$$v_i := t_{p_i+1} \quad v_i := v_i + t_i$$

Would the resulting protocol still ensure the following? Give a proof or counterexample for each.

     (a)    Mutual exclusion of $CS_1$ and $CS_2$.

     (b)    Neither $S_1$ nor $S_2$ forever blocks attempting to enter its critical section.

**9.28.** Suppose only Weak Memory Atomicity (see exercise 9.13) holds when the final ticket protocol of §9.4—Figures 9.7, 9.8, and 9.9—is executed. Does the protocol still satisfy the following properties? Give a proof or counterexample for each.

     (a)    Mutual exclusion of $CS_1$ and $CS_2$.

     (b)    Neither $S_1$ nor $S_2$ forever blocks attempting to enter its critical section.

**9.29.** The following program violates At Most One Assignments (9.32).

     **cobegin**   $S$: $x := x+1$  ||  $T$: $x := x+2$  **coend**

Elaborate $S$ and $T$ so that all assignment statements in the program do satisfy At Most One Assignments (9.32). Use Avoiding Interference by Exclusion (9.43) where necessary, so that the final value of $x$ is 3. Construct a proof that $x=3$ holds if your program terminates.

**9.30.** The following program computes the greatest common divisor of $x1$ and $x2$ but involves statements that do not support translation-independent reasoning.

$S: \; y1, y2 := x1, x2$
> **cobegin**
> > **do** $y1 \neq y2 \rightarrow$ **if** $y1 > y2 \rightarrow y1 := y1 - y2$
> > > $[] \; y1 \leq y2 \rightarrow$ **skip**
> > > **fi**
> >
> > **od**
>
> $\parallel$
>
> > **do** $y1 \neq y2 \rightarrow$ **if** $y2 > y1 \rightarrow y2 := y2 - y1$
> > > $[] \; y2 \leq y1 \rightarrow$ **skip**
> > > **fi**
> >
> > **od**
> **coend**

(a)    Indicate which guards and assignment statements cause problems.

(b)    Further elaborate the program, applying Avoiding Interference by Exclusion (9.43) if necessary, so the resulting program does support translation-independent reasoning. Construct a theorem of Proof Outline Logic to establish that the resulting program computes the greatest common divisor of $x1$ and $x2$.

**9.31.** The following programs each employ one or more atomic actions that is typically not part of a machine language.

>    (i)   Indicate which atomic actions are problematic and why.

>    (ii)  Replace the problematic atomic actions. Use Avoiding Interference by Exclusion (9.43) and Simulating a Conditional Atomic Action (9.49) as necessary.

(a)    $turn := 1$
> **cobegin**
> > **do** $true \rightarrow$ **if** $turn = 1 \rightarrow$ **skip fi**
> > > $S_1:$ **skip**
> > > $turn := 2$
> >
> > **od**
>
> $\parallel$
>
> > **do** $true \rightarrow$ **if** $turn = 2 \rightarrow$ **skip fi**
> > > $S_2:$ **skip**
> > > $turn := 1$
> >
> > **od**
> **coend**

(b)    $free := true$
> **cobegin**
> > $\underset{i=1,2}{\parallel}$ **do** $true \rightarrow \langle$ **if** $free \rightarrow free := false$ **fi** $\rangle$
> > > $S_i:$ **skip**
> > > $free := true$
> >
> > **od**
> **coend**

**9.32.** What, if any, difficulties would be caused if $S_{b:=B}$ were replaced by $b := B$ in Figure 9.10? Explain.

**9.33.** Suppose a process $S$ is of the form:

$$S: \ \ldots \{B\} \ T: \ \langle \textbf{if } B \rightarrow \textbf{skip fi} \rangle \ \ldots$$

If $T$ is replaced according to Signals for Conditional Atomic Actions (9.50), then $S$ may not execute $b := true$ after truthifying $B$, because $S$ is the signalee. Why shouldn't the signalee be permitted to execute $b := true$ once $B$ holds?

**9.34.** Using each of the following interlock instructions, give *entry* and *exit* protocols for mutual exclusion of critical sections.

   (a)     $TSL(v, p)$:   $v, p := false, v$

   (b)     $Swap(v, w)$:   $v, w := w, v$

   (c)     $CompareSwap(t, x, o, n)$:   $\langle t := (o = x)$
$$\textbf{if } t \rightarrow x := n$$
$$[] \ \neg t \rightarrow o := x$$
$$\textbf{fi} \rangle$$

   (d)     $FetchOr(w, p, e)$:   $p, w := w, w \vee e$

   (e)     $Decr(v, s)$:   $v, s := v-1, (v-1=0)$

**9.35.** Prove that (9.54) ensures mutual exclusion of critical sections.

**9.36.** Consider a four-phase concurrent program, where $gate1_i$, $gate2_i$, and $gate3_i$ implement barrier synchronization.

$$S: \textbf{cobegin} \quad \mathop{\|}_{1 \leq i \leq N} \ S_i: \ U_i \ \ gate1_i$$
$$V_i \ \ gate2_i$$
$$W_i \ \ gate3_i$$
$$X_i$$

      **coend**

   (a)     Formalize the safety property that stipulates that $gate1_i$, $gate2_i$, and $gate3_i$ work as intended.

   (b)     One implementation of $gate1_i$, $gate2_i$, and $gate3_i$ uses three integer counters like *cnt* of §9.7. Derive a solution that is in this spirit but uses fewer than three counters.

   (c)     Another implementation of $gate1_i$, $gate2_i$, and $gate3_i$ uses three sets of boolean variables like the $g_i$ of §9.7. Derive a solution that is in this spirit but does not use as many sets of boolean variables.

   (d)     A third implementation of $gate1_i$, $gate2_i$, and $gate3_i$ uses three sets of signals like the $b_i$ of §9.7. Derive a solution that is in this spirit but does not use as many sets of signals.

**9.37.** Usually, barrier synchronization controls the start of a loop iteration, as in the following.

$$S: \textbf{cobegin} \quad \mathop{\|}_{1 \leq i \leq N} \ S_i: \ \textbf{do } true \rightarrow U_i \ \ gate_i \ \textbf{od coend}$$

   (a)     Formalize the safety property that stipulates that $gate_i$ works as intended.

   (b)     Derive an implementation of $gate_i$ using counters.

(c)     Derive an implementation of *gate*$_i$ using boolean variables.

(d)     Derive an implementation of *gate*$_i$ using signals.

**9.38.** The barrier synchronization implementations in §9.7 can lead to memory contention, because all processes repeatedly read and write the same set of variables. One
way to avoid this problem is by using an additional process, which serves as a coordinator. The coordinator determines when each process $S_i$ has reached *gate*$_i$; execution of *gate*$_i$ terminates only when the coordinator takes some action.

(a)     Derive this solution.

(b)     Assume that the number N of processes is a power of 2. Instead of a separate
coordinator process, each $S_i$ can serve as the coordinator for $S_{2i}$ and $S_{2i+1}$.
Derive this solution.

# Chapter 10

# Semaphores, Locks, and Conditional Critical Regions

Looping by a process to wait for a condition consumes processor cycles without helping the awaited condition to become *true*. Other processes must be executed if we want the condition truthified. Since it is the operating system that multiplexes a processor among processes, wasted processor cycles are avoided if the operating system implements primitives to await and signal conditions. These primitives implement conditional atomic actions because they can block, but their execution also changes which processes the operating systems considers eligible for execution.

This chapter discusses primitives implemented by operating systems for awaiting and signaling conditions. We start with semaphores and locks. They are easy to implement but can be difficult to use. We then present the split binary semaphore method for implementing mutual exclusion and condition synchronization. Finally, we describe a higher-level mechanism, called conditional critical regions.

## 10.1  Semaphores

A *semaphore* is a non-negative integer variable. Semaphores are declared to have type Sem, so for a semaphore $s$ we have:

$ValAx(s, \text{Sem})$:  $s \in \text{Nat}$

The $\mathbf{P}(s)$ statement blocks until semaphore $s$ can be decremented by 1 without falsifying $ValAx(s, \text{Sem})$ and then decrements $s$. Thus, $\mathbf{P}(s)$ is modeled by the following atomic statement:

(10.1)    $P(s)$:    $\langle$**if** $s > 0 \rightarrow s := s - 1$ **fi**$\rangle$

$V(s)$ is modeled by an atomic statement that increments $s$ by 1:

(10.2)    $V(s)$:    $s := s + 1$

Execution of $V(s)$, therefore, can unblock a process that is attempting $P(s)$.

A variety of fairness assumptions have been associated with $P$ and $V$ statements. Usually, the fairness assumption is attached to the semaphore and applies to all statements naming that semaphore. A *strongly fair* semaphore is one whose $P$ and $V$ statements satisfy Strong Fairness (8.21): a $P$ is not delayed forever on a strongly fair semaphore $s$ if infinitely many $V(s)$ statements are executed. Analogously, a *weakly fair* semaphore is one whose $P$ and $V$ statements satisfy Weak Fairness (8.22): a $P$ is not delayed forever on a weakly fair semaphore if the semaphore remains positive.

Semaphores are a surprisingly versatile synchronization tool. They can implement mutual exclusion, as shown in Figure 10.1 where the $CS_i$ are mutually exclusive by virtue of semaphore $mx$. Semaphores can also implement condition synchronization. Figure 10.2, for example, is a version of the producer/consumer program of Figure 9.1 but with $P$ and $V$ statements as the only conditional atomic actions.

To use Proof Outline Logic and Temporal Logic for reasoning about programs with semaphores, we axiomatize $P$ and $V$. A Proof Outline Logic axiom for $P$ is derived at the end of §5.6. Assignment Axiom (4.19) is used to derive the following axiom for $V$ from (10.2).

(10.3)    $P$ *Axiom*: For a primitive assertion $P$:    $\{s > 0 \Rightarrow P_{s-1}^{s}\}$ $P(s)$ $\{P\}$

(10.4)    $V$ *Axiom*: For a primitive assertion $P$:    $\{P_{s+1}^{s}\}$ $V(s)$ $\{P\}$

These axioms allow the proof outline of Figure 10.3 to be derived. A key step in the derivation concerns the triple for $entry_i$, so we give the details for it.

---

**var** $mx$ : Sem
$mx := 1$
**cobegin**
$\parallel$ $S_i$: **do** $true \rightarrow entry_i$: $P(mx)$
  $\phantom{\parallel}_i$ $\phantom{S_i: \textbf{do} true \rightarrow}$ $CS_i$
  $\phantom{\parallel S_i: \textbf{do} true \rightarrow}$ $exit_i$: $V(mx)$
  $\phantom{\parallel S_i: \textbf{do} true \rightarrow}$ $NCS_i$
    **od**
**coend**

**Figure 10.1.** Mutual exclusion with semaphores

$PC$: **var** $a, r$ : Nat;   $v, w$ : Char;
      $buf$: **array** $[0..N-1]$ **of** Char;
      $inp, out$ : **seq of** Char;
      $slots, portions$ : Sem

$a, r, out := 0, 0, \varepsilon$
$slots, portions := N, 0$
**cobegin**
    $Prod$: **do** $true \rightarrow v, inp := inp[0], inp[1..]$
                          $\mathbf{P}(slots)$
                          $buf[a \bmod N] := v$
                          $a := a+1$
                          $\mathbf{V}(portions)$
         **od**
$\parallel$
    $Cons$: **do** $true \rightarrow \mathbf{P}(portions)$
                          $w := buf[r \bmod N]$
                          $r := r+1$
                          $\mathbf{V}(slots)$
                          $out := out\ w$
        **od**
**coend**

**Figure 10.2.** Producer/consumer with semaphores

---

«Process Independence Axiom (5.3) for each other process $S_j$,
Conjunction Rule (4.30), and Rule of Consequence (4.25)»
  1. $\{V=(\Sigma j:\ j\neq i:\ in(CS_j) \vee after(CS_j):\ 1)\}$
    $entry_i$
    $\{V=(\Sigma j:\ j\neq i:\ in(CS_j) \vee after(CS_j):\ 1)\}$

«Control-Point Identity (4.28), control predicate axioms, and Rule of
Consequence (4.25) »
  2. $\{\neg(in(CS_i) \vee after(CS_i))\}\ entry_i\ \{in(CS_i)\}$

«Conjunction Rule (4.30) with 1 and 2; Rule of Consequence (4.25)»
  3. $\{V=(\Sigma j:\ in(CS_j) \vee after(CS_j):\ 1)\}$
    $entry_i$
    $\{V+1=(\Sigma j:\ in(CS_j) \vee after(CS_j):\ 1)\}$

«**P** Axiom (10.3)»
  4. $\{mx>0 \Rightarrow (mx-1=1-(V+1))\}\ entry_i\ \{mx=1-(V+1)\}$

«Predicate Logic»
  5. $(mx-1=1-(V+1)) \implies (mx>0 \Rightarrow (mx-1=1-(V+1)))$

«Rule of Consequence (4.25) with 4 and 5»
   6. $\{mx-1=1-(V+1)\}$ $entry_i$ $\{mx=1-(V+1)\}$

«Conjunction Rule (4.30) with 3 and 6»
   7. $\{mx-1=1-(V+1)$ $\wedge$ $V=(\Sigma\,j\!:\ in(CS_j)\vee after(CS_j)\!:\ 1)\}$
      $entry_i$
      $\{mx=1-(V+1)$ $\wedge$ $V+1=(\Sigma\,j\!:\ in(CS_j)\vee after(CS_j)\!:\ 1)\}$

«Predicate Logic»
   8. $mx=1-(\Sigma\,j\!:\ in(CS_j)\vee after(CS_j)\!:\ 1)$
      $\wedge$ $V=(\Sigma\,j\!:\ in(CS_j)\vee after(CS_j)\!:\ 1)$
      $\Rightarrow mx-1=1-(V+1)$ $\wedge$ $V=(\Sigma\,j\!:\ in(CS_j)\vee after(CS_j)\!:\ 1)$

   9. $mx=1-(V+1)$ $\wedge$ $V+1=(\Sigma\,j\!:\ in(CS_j)\vee after(CS_j)\!:\ 1)$
      $\Rightarrow mx=1-(\Sigma\,j\!:\ in(CS_j)\vee after(CS_j)\!:\ 1)$

«Rule of Consequence (4.25) with 8, 7, and 9»
  10. $\{mx=1-(\Sigma\,j\!:\ in(CS_j)\vee after(CS_j)\!:\ 1)$
      $\wedge$ $V=(\Sigma\,j\!:\ in(CS_j)\vee after(CS_j)\!:\ 1)\}$
      $entry_i$
      $\{mx=1-(\Sigma\,j\!:\ in(CS_j)\vee after(CS_j)\!:\ 1)\}$

«Rigid Variable Rule (4.29b)»
  11. $\{mx=1-(\Sigma\,j\!:\ in(CS_j)\vee after(CS_j)\!:\ 1)\}$
      $entry_i$
      $\{mx=1-(\Sigma\,j\!:\ in(CS_j)\vee after(CS_j)\!:\ 1)\}$

Note that the assertions in the proof outline of Figure 10.3 together with $ValAx(mx,\ Sem)$ are strong enough to establish that the program of Figure 10.1 satisfies Mutual Exclusion (6.2).

---

```
var mx : Sem
mx := 1
{I:  mx=1-(Σ j: in(CS_j) ∨ after(CS_j): 1)}
cobegin
|| S_i: {I}
i      do true → {I}
                entry_i: P(mx) {I}
                PO(CS_i)⊗I
                {I}
                exit_i: V(mx) {I}
                PO(NCS_i)⊗I
                {I}
          od {I}
      coend {I}
```

**Figure 10.3.** Proof outline for mutual exclusion with semaphores

## Implementing Semaphores

Since an operational semantics—(10.1) and (10.2)—for **P** and **V** statements has been given in terms of our programming notation, we can use a technique from Chapter 9 to construct program fragments that implement **P** and **V**. Each semaphore is represented by an integer variable, and we make use of existing *entry* and *exit* protocols for mutual exclusion.

Simulating a Conditional Atomic Action (9.49) gives a way to implement **P**(*s*):

(10.5)   **P**(*s*):   *entry* **do** $s \leq 0 \rightarrow$ *exit entry* **od** $s := s - 1$ *exit*

Because executing **V**(*s*) can affect condition $s \leq 0$, Simulating a Conditional Atomic Action (9.49) requires that the code for **V**(*s*) be mutually exclusive with checking $s \leq 0$ and executing $s := s - 1$ in (10.5). This means that **V**(*s*) must be implemented by:

(10.6)   **V**(*s*):   *entry* $s := s + 1$ *exit*

Implementations (10.5) and (10.6) are not without problems. First, the *entry* and *exit* protocols are likely to be time-consuming, and when $s \leq 0$ they are executed repeatedly by (10.5). Second, looping in (10.5) until $s > 0$ holds wastes processor cycles.

Finally, there is an issue of fairness. A problem can occur when $s \leq 0$ holds and several processes execute **P**(*s*). Even though **V**(*s*) might be executed infinitely often, a given process $S$ still might never complete its **P**(*s*). This undesirable behavior occurs if other processes executing **P**(*s*) succeed but then rejoin the blocked processes by again executing a **P**(*s*). Process $S$ never completes its **P**(*s*) although $s > 0$ holds infinitely often, so Strong Fairness (8.21) does not hold of the **P**(*s*) implementation. Weak Fairness (8.22), which does hold for **P**(*s*) implementation (10.5), is not strong enough to guarantee that any given process will complete its **P**(*s*) (because the condition blocking $S$ never holds continuously).

The problems with (10.5) are avoided if we integrate support for semaphores into the operating system routines that allocate processors to processes. With this approach, information is stored by the operating system about each process and each semaphore. Stored for a process is whether that process is executable or blocked. Only processes that are marked as being executable may be allocated processors. Stored for a semaphore $s$ is its value $s.val$ and a queue $s.blocked$ of processes that are blocked, waiting to complete **P**(*s*) statements.

**P** and **V** statements are then implemented by operating system routines. These routines, along with all code concerned with allocating processors to processes, are made mutually exclusive by disabling interrupts while they are executed. The routine for **P**(*s*) decrements $s.val$ if $s.val > 0$ holds; otherwise, the process executing the $\mathbf{P}(s)$ is marked as being blocked and is appended to *s.blocked*. The routine for $\mathbf{V}(s)$ increments *s.val* if *s.blocked* is empty; otherwise, the first process on *s.blocked* is removed from the list and marked as being executable.

Because *s.blocked* is a queue, a $\mathbf{V}(s)$ causes the oldest blocked process to become executable. Thus, Strong Fairness (8.21) holds for this implementation. Also, the looping of (10.5) is avoided, because a process awaiting $s > 0$ is never allocated a processor.

## 10.2   Change of Variable to use Semaphores

An arbitrary conditional atomic action $\langle \textbf{if } B \rightarrow T \textbf{ fi} \rangle$ can sometimes be replaced by a $\mathbf{P}$. This is done by changing how the variables mentioned in $B$ and $T$ are represented. Their values are encoded in a semaphore.

(10.7)   **Change of Variables for Semaphores.** A conditional atomic action $\alpha$ that truthifies $post(\alpha)$ is replaced by $\mathbf{P}(sem)$ as follows.

    (1)   Define a predicate $A_{sem}$ such that execution of $\mathbf{P}(sem)$ truthifies $post(\alpha)$ if started in any state where $sem > 0 \wedge A_{sem}$ holds.

    (2)   Replace $\alpha$ with $\mathbf{P}(sem)$. Postulate a precondition for $\mathbf{P}(sem)$ that implies $A_{sem}$.

    (3)   Ensure that $A_{sem}$ holds when $\mathbf{P}(sem)$ is reached. This may require augmenting assertions of the proof outline and/or adding $\mathbf{V}(sem)$ statements before or after statements that change variables mentioned in $A_{sem}$.    □

Two examples serve to illustrate the use of the method.

### Producer/Consumer Derivation

Recall the producer/consumer program of Figure 9.1. The body of the consumer,

$$T_1: \quad \langle \textbf{if } a - r > 0 \rightarrow \textbf{ skip fi} \rangle$$
$$T_2: \quad w := buf[r \bmod N]$$
$$T_3: \quad r := r + 1$$
$$T_4: \quad out := out\ w$$

contains a single conditional atomic action, $T_1$. $T_1$ awaits $a - r > 0$. Moreover, this condition is an inequality, like the condition in operational model (10.1) for $\mathbf{P}$. Steps (1) and (2) of Change of Variables for Semaphores (10.7) suggest that we define a semaphore *portions* to encode the value of $a - r$, and that we define a predicate $A_{portions}$ to ensure that $a - r > 0$ holds after executing $\mathbf{P}(portions)$ if $portions > 0 \wedge A_{portions}$ holds before. Then, according to step (2), we replace $T_1$

by **P**(*portions*).  The following proof outline results.

$\{A_{portions}: \ portions = a - r\}$
$T_1: \ \textbf{P}(portions) \ \ \{portions \geq 0 \wedge portions + 1 = a - r \wedge a - r > 0\}$
$T_2: \ w := buf[r \bmod N] \ \ \{portions + 1 = a - r\}$
$T_3: \ r := r + 1 \ \ \{portions = a - r\}$
$T_4: \ out := out \ w \ \ \{portions = a - r\}$

The producer, by executing $a := a + 1$, falsifies conjuncts $portions = a - r$ and $portions + 1 = a - r$ in this proof outline for the consumer.  The conjuncts would be reestablished if the producer incremented $portions$ by 1 along with the execution of $a := a + 1$.  So, according to step (3) of Change of Variables for Semaphores (10.7), we augment $S_4$ in the producer with **V**(*portions*) and obtain the following protocol.

$S_1: \ v, inp := inp[0], inp[1..]$
$S_2: \ \langle \textbf{if } a - r < N \rightarrow \textbf{ skip fi} \rangle$
$S_3: \ buf[a \bmod N] := v$
$S_4: \ \langle a := a + 1 \ \textbf{V}(portions) \rangle$

We next tackle conditional atomic action $S_2$ in the consumer.  Ordinary algebra allows its condition $a - r < N$ to be put in the same form as the inequality in the condition for a **P**:

$$(a - r < N) \ = \ (0 < N - (a - r))$$

A semaphore *slots* that encodes $N - (a - r)$ thus allows use of a **P** to await the condition in $S_2$.  Steps (1) and (2) of Change of Variables for Semaphores (10.7) yield the following:

(10.8)  $\{A_{slots}: \ slots = N - (a - r)\}$
$S_1: \ v, inp := inp[0], inp[1..] \ \ \{slots = N - (a - r)\}$
$S_2: \ \textbf{P}(slots) \ \ \{slots \geq 0 \wedge slots + 1 = N - (a - r) \wedge a - r < N\}$
$S_3: \ buf[a \bmod N] := v \ \ \{slots + 1 = N - (a - r)\}$
$S_4: \ \langle a := a + 1 \ \textbf{V}(portions) \rangle \ \ \{slots = N - (a - r)\}$

Execution of $T_3$ ($r := r + 1$) by the consumer falsifies conjuncts $slots = N - (a - r)$ and $slots + 1 = N - (a - r)$ in this proof outline, but, as before, including **V**(*slots*) in $T_3$ eliminates the problem.

(10.9)  $\{A_{portions}: \ portions = a - r\}$
$T_1: \ \textbf{P}(portions) \ \ \{portions \geq 0 \wedge portions + 1 = a - r \wedge a - r > 0\}$
$T_2: \ w := buf[r \bmod N] \ \ \{portions + 1 = a - r\}$
$T_3: \ \langle r := r + 1 \ \textbf{V}(slots) \rangle \ \ \{portions = a - r\}$
$T_4: \ out := out \ w \ \ \{portions = a - r\}$

Finally, atomic statements $S_4$ and $T_3$ are decomposed. Instead of using *portions* and *slots* in the proof outline of Figure 10.4, we use derived terms that account for the state between the increment and **V**:

$$Portions: \begin{cases} portions & \text{if } \neg after(S) \\ portions+1 & \text{if } after(S) \end{cases} \qquad Slots: \begin{cases} slots & \text{if } \neg after(T) \\ slots+1 & \text{if } after(T) \end{cases}$$

We have derived a program that is identical to the one in Figure 10.2! Furthermore, the assertions of the proof outline (along with *ValAx(Slots*, Sem) and *ValAx(Portions*, Sem)) are strong enough to establish that $0 \le a-r \le N$ always holds, so we have proved that no process adds an item when the buffer is full (i.e., $a-r=N$) or removes an item when the buffer is empty (i.e., $a-r=0$).

---

*PC*: **var** $a, r$ : Nat;   $v, w$ : Char;
          *buf*: **array** $[0..N-1]$ **of** Char;
          *inp*, *out* : **seq of** Char;
          *slots*, *portions* : Sem

$a, r, out := 0, 0, \varepsilon$  $\{a=0 \land r=0\}$
*slots*, *portions* $:= N, 0$  $\{Slots=N-(a-r) \;\land\; Portions=a-r\}$
**cobegin**
     *Prod*: **do** *true* $\to$ $\{Slots=N-(a-r)\}$
                         $v, inp := inp[0], inp[1..]$  $\{Slots=N-(a-r)\}$
                         **P**(*slots*)
                         $\{Slots \ge 0 \land Slots+1=N-(a-r) \land a-r<N\}$
                         $buf[a \bmod N] := v$  $\{Slots+1=N-(a-r)\}$
                         $S: a := a+1$  $\{Slots=N-(a-r)\}$
                         **V**(*portions*)  $\{Slots=N-(a-r)\}$
               **od** $\{Slots=N-(a-r)\}$

     ||

     *Cons*: **do** *true* $\to$ $\{Portions=a-r\}$
                         **P**(*portions*)
                         $\{Portions \ge 0 \land Portions+1=a-r \land a-r>0\}$
                         $w := buf[r \bmod N]$  $\{Portions+1=a-r\}$
                         $T: r := r+1$  $\{Portions=a-r\}$
                         **V**(*slots*)  $\{Portions=a-r\}$
                         $out := out \; w$  $\{Portions=a-r\}$
               **od** $\{Portions=a-r\}$
**coend** $\{Slots=N-(a-r) \;\land\; Portions=a-r\}$

**Figure 10.4.** Producer/consumer proof outline

## N-Exclusion Derivation

As a second illustration of Change of Variables for Semaphores (10.7), consider the problem of ensuring that at most N processes execute in critical sections at the same time. (When N equals 1, this is the mutual exclusion problem.) Assume that processes have the form:

$S$: **cobegin**
 $\parallel\limits_{i}$ $S_i$: **do** $true \rightarrow entry_i$
 $\qquad\qquad CS_i$
 $\qquad\qquad exit_i$
 $\qquad\qquad NCS_i$
 $\qquad$ **od**
 **coend**

It suffices to derive protocols for $entry_i$ and $exit_i$ so that

$(10.10)$ $\quad at(S) \;\Rightarrow\; \Box(\text{N}\geq(\Sigma\,j\colon\; in(CS_j) \vee after(CS_j)\colon\; 1))$

is satisfied, because $(\Sigma\,j\colon\; in(CS_j) \vee after(CS_j)\colon\; 1) \geq (\Sigma\,j\colon\; in(CS_j)\colon\; 1)$ is valid.

Safety Property Methodology (6.30) leads us to a protocol (below) where $entry_i$ is a conditional atomic action. The presence of control predicates in the guard of $entry_i$ is not a problem here, since we expect to replace this conditional atomic action with a **P**. Note that $\text{N}\geq(\Sigma\,j\colon\; in(CS_j) \vee after(CS_j)\colon\; 1)$ is implied by each assertion below, so according to $I_{PO(S)}$ Decomposition Rule (6.17a) and Precondition Safety Consequence Rule (6.15), we conclude that (10.10) is satisfied.

$\{I\colon\; \text{N}\geq(\Sigma\,j\colon\; in(CS_j) \vee after(CS_j)\colon\; 1)\}$
...
$\{I\}$
$entry_i\colon\; \langle\textbf{if } \text{N}>(\Sigma\,j\colon\; in(CS_j) \vee after(CS_j)\colon\; 1) \rightarrow \textbf{skip fi}\rangle\;\{I\}$
$PO(CS_i)\otimes I$
$exit_i\colon\; \textbf{skip}\;\{I\}$
...

The guard in $entry_i$ can be put in the same form as the guard in a **P**:

$\qquad \text{N}>(\Sigma\,j\colon\; in(CS_j) \vee after(CS_j)\colon\; 1)$
$=\qquad \text{«Algebra»}$
$\qquad 0<\text{N}-(\Sigma\,j\colon\; in(CS_j) \vee after(CS_j)\colon\; 1)$

Therefore, we try introducing a semaphore $mx$ whose value always satisfies $mx=\text{N}-(\Sigma\,j\colon\; in(CS_j) \vee after(CS_j)\colon\; 1)$. For this equation to hold initially, $mx$ must be initialized to N. Steps (1) and (2) of Change of Variables for Semaphores (10.7) then yield the following.

$$mx := \mathrm{N}$$
$$\{I:\ mx = \mathrm{N} - (\Sigma j:\ in(CS_j) \vee after(CS_j):\ 1)\}$$
...

$$\{A_{mx}:\ I\}$$
$$entry_i:\ \mathbf{P}(mx)\ \{mx+1 = \mathrm{N} - (\Sigma j:\ in(CS_j) \vee after(CS_j):\ 1)\}$$
$$PO(CS_i) \otimes I$$
$$exit_i:\ \mathbf{skip}$$
$$\{mx-1 = \mathrm{N} - (\Sigma j:\ in(CS_j) \vee after(CS_j):\ 1)\}$$
...

The only problem with what we have derived is that $post(exit_i)$ does not imply $I$, because $post(exit_i)$ mentions $mx-1$ wherever $I$ mentions $mx$. This problem would be solved by incrementing $mx$, and we therefore replace the **skip** in $exit_i$ by $\mathbf{V}(mx)$. The result of these changes is a protocol like that of Figure 10.3, but with 1 replaced by N.

## 10.3  Binary Semaphores and Locks

A *binary semaphore* is a semaphore, declared to have type Bin_Sem, whose value is at most 1.[1] Thus, for a binary semaphore $b$:

$$ValAx(b, \text{Bin\_Sem}):\ \ b=0 \vee b=1$$

The $\mathbf{P_b}(b)$ statement blocks until $b=1$ and then sets $b$ to 0, the result of decrementing $b$ by 1; $\mathbf{V_b}(b)$ blocks until $b=0$ and then sets $b$ to 1, the result of incrementing $b$ by 1.

(10.11) $\mathbf{P_b}(b):\ \ \langle \mathbf{if}\ b=1 \rightarrow b := 0\ \mathbf{fi} \rangle$

(10.12) $\mathbf{V_b}(b):\ \ \langle \mathbf{if}\ b=0 \rightarrow b := 1\ \mathbf{fi} \rangle$

As with general semaphores, Proof Outline Logic axioms for $\mathbf{P_b}$ and $\mathbf{V_b}$ follow from operational semantics (10.11) and (10.12) for these statements:

(10.13) $\mathbf{P_b}$ *Axiom*: For a primitive assertion $P$:  $\{b=1 \Rightarrow P_0^b\}\ \mathbf{P_b}(b)\ \{P\}$

(10.14) $\mathbf{V_b}$ *Axiom*: For a primitive assertion $P$:  $\{b=0 \Rightarrow P_1^b\}\ \mathbf{V_b}(b)\ \{P\}$

General semaphores often can be replaced by binary ones. An analysis of the mutual exclusion protocol in Figure 10.1, for example, reveals that $mx$

[1]The term *general semaphore* is sometimes used for a semaphore whose value is not bounded from above.

always satisfies $mx=0 \vee mx=1$.[2] Therefore, if $mx$ is replaced by a binary sema-
phore $b$, $\mathbf{P}(mx)$ is replaced by $\mathbf{P_b}(b)$, and $\mathbf{V}(mx)$ is replaced by $\mathbf{V_b}(b)$, then the
resulting protocol remains a solution to the mutual exclusion problem. Note that
$\mathbf{V_b}(b)$ never blocks when this replacement is made. Thus, $\mathbf{V_b}(b)$ here could be
implemented by the assignment statement $b := 1$, an optimization so prevalent
that $b := 1$ is often taken to be the operational semantics of $\mathbf{V_b}$ instead of (10.12).

Not all general semaphores can be replaced by binary semaphores, though.
Semaphores *slots* and *portions* in the producer/consumer solution of Figure 10.2
store values greater than 1, so they cannot be replaced by binary semaphores.

## Locks

Two classes of statements—*acquire* and *release*—are usually provided for
a *lock*. The exact semantics of these statements depends on the nature of the
lock, but an acquire may block, a release never blocks, and both statements
preserve an axiom associated with the type of lock. A general semaphore $s$ could
be considered a lock. The axiom is $ValAx(s, \text{Sem})$, $\mathbf{P}(s)$ is an acquire, and $\mathbf{V}(s)$
is a release.

Locks supported by operating systems usually embody more functionality
than semaphores. An example is the *exclusive lock*, an alternative to semaphores
for implementing mutual exclusion. Associated with each exclusive lock is an
*owner*. The owner is either $\varnothing$ or the name of a process. Execution by a process
$S$ of $\mathbf{acq}(x)$ for an exclusive lock $x$ blocks until either the lock has no owner or $S$
is the owner; $S$ is then made the owner. Execution of $\mathbf{rel}(x)$ by a process $S$ never
blocks and makes $\varnothing$ the owner of $x$ if $S$ was the owner.

To formalize this description of an exclusive lock $x$, we give an axiom
$ValAx(x, \text{Excl\_lock})$ and operational semantics for $\mathbf{acq}(x)$ and $\mathbf{rel}(x)$. Let $SYS$
denote the set of processes.

$ValAx(x, \text{Excl\_lock})$:  $x=\varnothing \vee x \in SYS$

For statements appearing in a process $S$:

> $\mathbf{acq}(x)$:  $\langle \mathbf{if}\, x=S \vee x=\varnothing \rightarrow x := S\ \mathbf{fi} \rangle$
>
> $\mathbf{rel}(x)$:  $\langle \mathbf{if}\, x=S \rightarrow x := \varnothing\ [\!]\ x \neq S \rightarrow \mathbf{skip}\ \mathbf{fi} \rangle$

From this operational semantics, we derive the following Proof Outline Logic
axioms for $\mathbf{acq}(x)$ and $\mathbf{rel}(x)$ appearing in a process $S$:

(10.15)  $\mathbf{acq}(x)$ *Axiom*:  For a primitive assertion $P$:

$$\{x=S \vee x=\varnothing \Rightarrow P_S^x\}\ \mathbf{acq}(x)\ \{P\}$$

---

[2]We infer that $mx$ is bounded above by 1 from $I$ in the proof outline of Figure 10.3; we infer
that $mx$ is an integer and is bounded below by 0 from $ValAx(mx, \text{Sem})$.

(10.16) **rel**($x$) *Axiom*:  For a primitive assertion $P$:

$$\{(x \neq S \wedge P) \vee (x = S \wedge P_\varnothing^x)\}\ \mathbf{acq}(x)\ \{P\}$$

When an exclusive lock $x$ is used to implement mutual exclusion, **acq**($x$) is executed at the start of each critical section and **rel**($x$) at the end. Observe that a process does not become blocked if it executes a second **acq**($x$) without first executing **rel**($x$). This is useful if processes executing in critical sections might be restarted—say, because of a failure. A restarted process can re-enter a critical section, and other processes are prevented from executing in critical sections in the interim. Such functionality is difficult to implement using semaphores.

Another form of lock commonly supported by operating systems is the *read/write lock*. Read and write operations on a file are expected to appear serial, even though each operation might involve several accesses to the file, and accesses from concurrent operations could be interleaved. A file-read operation (we assume) does not cause the state of the file to change, so concurrently performing read operations is indistinguishable from serially performing them. A write, on the other hand, may change the state of the file. The desired appearance of serial behavior is thus guaranteed only if write operations do not overlap reads or other writes. Read/write locks facilitate this type of synchronization.

A read/write lock provides statements for blocking the start of a read or write to ensure that no write operation on a given file is concurrent with a read or a write on that file. Each read operation is preceded by an **acq**$_\mathbf{R}$($F$) statement and terminated with a **rel**$_\mathbf{R}$($F$) statement, where $F$ is a read/write lock associated with the file; each write is preceded by an **acq**$_\mathbf{W}$($F$) statement and terminated with a **rel**$_\mathbf{W}$($F$) statement. Axiom *ValAx*($F$, Read_Write) is formulated in terms of the number $r_F$ of in-progress read operations and the number $w_F$ of in-progress write operations.

$$ValAx(F, \text{Read\_Write}):\ \ (w_F = 0 \vee (r_F = 0 \wedge w_F = 1))$$
$$\wedge\ ValAx(r_F, \text{Nat})\ \wedge\ \ ValAx(w_F, \text{Nat})$$

$\mathbf{acq_R}(F)$:  $\langle \mathbf{if}\ w_F = 0 \rightarrow r_F := r_F + 1\ \mathbf{fi}\rangle$

$\mathbf{rel_R}(F)$:  $\langle r_F := r_F - 1\rangle$

$\mathbf{acq_W}(F)$:  $\langle \mathbf{if}\ w_F = 0 \wedge r_F = 0 \rightarrow w_F := w_F + 1\ \mathbf{fi}\rangle$

$\mathbf{rel_W}(F)$:  $\langle w_F := w_F - 1\rangle$

From this operational semantics, we derive the following Proof Outline Logic axioms:

(10.17) **acq**$_\mathbf{R}$($F$) *Axiom*:  For a primitive assertion $P$:

$$\{w_F = 0 \Rightarrow P_{r_F+1}^{r_F}\}\ \mathbf{acq_R}(F)\ \{P\}$$

(10.18)  **rel$_R$**$(F)$ *Axiom*:  For a primitive assertion $P$:   $\{P^{r_F}_{r_F-1}\}$ **rel$_R$**$(F)$ $\{P\}$

(10.19)  **acq$_W$**$(F)$ *Axiom*:  For a primitive assertion $P$:
$$\{w_F=0 \wedge r_F=0 \;\Rightarrow\; P^{w_F}_{w_F+1}\} \; \textbf{acq}_W(F) \; \{P\}$$

(10.20)  **rel$_W$**$(F)$ *Axiom*:  For a primitive assertion $P$:   $\{P^{w_F}_{w_F-1}\}$ **rel$_W$**$(F)$ $\{P\}$

## 10.4  Split Binary Semaphore Method

A set $\mathcal{B}$ of binary semaphores $b_1, b_2, ..., b_N$ constitutes a *split binary sema-phore* if at any time at most one of $b_1$ through $b_N$ equals 1. Thus, for split binary semaphore $\mathcal{B}$, we can assert the following:

(10.21)  *ValAx*$(\mathcal{B},$ Split_bin$)$:   $(\forall b \in \mathcal{B}\!: \; b=0 \vee b=1) \quad \wedge \quad 0 \le (\underset{b\in\mathcal{B}}{\Sigma} \; b) \le 1$

A split binary semaphore can ensure mutually exclusive execution of criti-cal sections. Each critical section is assumed to be a sequential program frag-ment whose execution starts with a **P$_b$** and ends with a **V$_b$**, both of which name elements of the split binary semaphore. The same binary semaphore need not be named in both the **P$_b$** and the **V$_b$**. In fact, by naming different semaphores in the **P$_b$** and **V$_b$**, condition synchronization becomes possible—when a critical section terminates, only some of the critical sections that are protected by the split binary semaphore become executable. In particular, if a **V$_b$**$(b)$ is executed when a criti-cal section ends, then only critical sections that start with a **P$_b$**$(b)$ may be exe-cuted next.

We now codify the discipline for executing **P$_b$** and **V$_b$** statements that name elements of split binary semaphores. There are three parts. The first ensures mutual exclusion of critical sections, the second implements condition synchronization, and the third concerns freedom from certain kinds of deadlock.

An atomic action $\alpha$ of $\mathcal{A}(S)$ is defined to be in a critical section of split binary semaphore $\mathcal{B}$ iff in every execution of $S$:

- each execution of $\alpha$ is preceded by a **P$_b$** that names an element of $\mathcal{B}$, and no intervening **P$_b$** or **V$_b$** names an element of $\mathcal{B}$; and

- either $\alpha$ is a **V$_b$** that names an element of $\mathcal{B}$, or each execution of $\alpha$ is fol-lowed by a **V$_b$** that names an element of $\mathcal{B}$, and there is no intervening **P$_b$** or **V$_b$** that names an element of $\mathcal{B}$.

Mutual exclusion for the critical sections of $\mathcal{B}$ then follows from *ValAx*$(\mathcal{B},$ Split_bin$)$. In fact, the following invariant is maintained, where $CS_\mathcal{B}$ is the set of atomic actions in critical sections of $\mathcal{B}$.

(10.22) $X_\mathcal{B}$: $(0 = \sum_{b \in \mathcal{B}} b) = (\exists \alpha \in CS_\mathcal{B}: at(\alpha))$

$$\wedge \ (\forall \alpha \in CS_\mathcal{B}: at(\alpha) \Rightarrow (\forall \alpha' \in CS_\mathcal{B}: \alpha \neq \alpha': \neg at(\alpha')))$$

Observe that $X_\mathcal{B} \wedge at(\alpha) \wedge at(\alpha')$ is *false* if $\alpha$ and $\alpha'$ are distinct and both are in $CS_\mathcal{B}$. This means that $NI(\alpha, pre(\alpha'))$ is valid, and we conclude that no atomic action $\alpha$ in a critical section can interfere with $pre(\alpha')$ for $\alpha'$ also an atomic action in a critical section:

(10.23) **Split Binary Semaphores [Mutual Exclusion].** If execution of $\mathbf{P_b}$ and $\mathbf{V_b}$ statements that name elements of $\mathcal{B}$ alternate, then no atomic action in a critical section of $\mathcal{B}$ interferes with the precondition of any other atomic action in a critical section of $\mathcal{B}$. ☐

Condition synchronization is supported by restricting when a semaphore may be named in the $\mathbf{V_b}$ statements that end critical sections. For $C_i$ a primitive predicate, the restrictions preserve the truth of $b_i = 1 \Rightarrow C_i$ and therefore ensure that $C_i$ will hold whenever execution of $\mathbf{P_b}(b_i)$ completes.

(10.24) **Split Binary Semaphores [Condition Synchronization].** For $b_i$ an element of a split binary semaphore $\mathcal{B}$ and $C_i$ a primitive assertion, if

(i)  $C_i$ is implied by the precondition of every $\mathbf{V_b}(b_i)$, and

(ii)  atomic actions that can falsify $C_i$ are in critical sections of $\mathcal{B}$,

then $C_i$ will hold whenever an execution of $\mathbf{P_b}(b_i)$ terminates. ☐

Since $C_i$ is primitive, condition (i) implies that executing $\mathbf{V_b}(b_i)$ preserves the truth of $b_i = 1 \Rightarrow C_i$. Condition (ii) ensures that no other atomic action falsifies $b_i = 1 \Rightarrow C_i$ because $b_i = 0$ holds whenever such an atomic action might execute.

Split Binary Semaphores [Condition Synchronization] (10.24) can lead to deadlock. $ValAx(\mathcal{B}, Split\_bin)$ (10.21) implies that at most one element of a split binary semaphore $\mathcal{B}$ may be 1. Suppose $b_i$ is that element. If no process's next $\mathbf{P_b}$ names $b_i$, then every process will become blocked executing its next $\mathbf{P_b}$, and the system will deadlock.

This deadlock is avoided if a $\mathbf{V_b}$ statement naming $b_i$ is executed only when some process will name $b_i$ in its next $\mathbf{P_b}$. We therefore introduce a non-negative integer program variable $n_i$ whose value, when no process is executing in a critical section, gives the number of processes whose next $\mathbf{P_b}$ will name $b_i$. Deadlock is avoided if

(10.25) $DF_\mathcal{B}$: $(0 = \sum_{b \in \mathcal{B}} b) \vee (\forall b_i \in \mathcal{B}: n_i = 0 \Rightarrow b_i = 0)$

holds throughout execution. This is because $\mathbf{V_b}(b_i)$ falsifies the first disjunct but only falsifies $n_i = 0 \Rightarrow b_i = 0$ if $n_i = 0$ holds. Thus, $DF_\mathcal{B}$ remains *true* when $\mathbf{V_b}(b_i)$

is executed if $n_i \neq 0$ holds. Therefore, to maintain the truth of $DF_{\mathcal{B}}$, a $\mathbf{V_b}(b_i)$ is executed only when some process will name $b_i$ in its next $\mathbf{P_b}$.

Here, then, is a template for the statement to end a critical section:

$$(10.26)\ \ V_{\mathcal{B}}\colon\ \mathbf{if}\ \ \underset{b_i \in \mathcal{B}}{[]}\ \ C_i \wedge n_i > 0 \rightarrow \mathbf{V_b}(b_i)\ \ \mathbf{fi}$$

However, this **if** statement may cause another form of deadlock. If none of its guards holds, then its execution will block. One solution is to require that some guard of (10.26) hold whenever the statement is reached. That is, we require

$$pre(L_j)\ \ \Rightarrow\ \ \underset{b_i \in \mathcal{B}}{\vee}\ (C_i \wedge n_i > 0)$$

to be valid for every instance $L_j$ of (10.26).

A third form of deadlock is possible unless some element $b_i$ of $\mathcal{B}$ is initially 1 and some process executes $\mathbf{P_b}(b_i)$ as its first $\mathbf{P_b}$. Otherwise, each process reaching a critical section of $\mathcal{B}$ will block at the $\mathbf{P_b}$ that begins the critical section. Some care must be exercised in selecting the element $b_i$ that is initialized to 1 because we also require that both $b_i = 1 \Rightarrow C_i$ and $DF_{\mathcal{B}}$ hold.

Thus far, we have placed no restrictions on when $n_i$ is changed except to require that $n$ be accurate when some element of $\mathcal{B}$ is nonzero or a $\mathbf{V_b}$ is about to be executed. Assignments to $n_i$, however, must not falsify $n_i > 0$ in $pre(\mathbf{V_b}(b_i))$ of (10.26). Such interference does not occur when the assignment increases $n_i$ or is part of a critical section of $\mathcal{B}$. This, then, constitutes one restriction on how $n_i$ may be changed. Second, assignment statements that mention $n_i$ on both their left- and right-hand sides do not comply with At Most One Assignments (9.32). When such statements are included in critical sections, they need not be further decomposed—Atomic Assignments by Exclusion (9.47) applies. This is the basis for a second restriction on how $n_i$ may be changed. (Assignment statements to $n_i$ that do comply with At Most One Assignments (9.32) may appear anywhere provided that they do not interfere with $n_i > 0$.)

We summarize our strategy to avoid deadlock and manipulate the $n_i$:

(10.27)  **Split Binary Semaphores [Deadlock Avoidance].** For each element $b_i$ of a split binary semaphore $\mathcal{B}$, introduce a counter $n_i$ such that:

> (i)   Whenever no process is executing in a critical section of $\mathcal{B}$ or $in(V_{\mathcal{B}})$ holds, $n_i$ is the number of processes whose next $\mathbf{P_b}$ will name $b_i$.

> (ii)  Assignment statements to $n_i$ that do not comply with At Most One Assignments (9.32) are in critical sections of $\mathcal{B}$.

> (iii) Assignment statements to $n_i$ do not falsify $in(CS) \vee n_i > 0$, where $CS$ is any critical section for $\mathcal{B}$.

(iv)  Every critical section ends by executing:

$$V_{\mathcal{B}}: \quad \textbf{if} \quad []_{b_i \in \mathcal{B}} \ C_i \wedge n_i > 0 \rightarrow \textbf{V}_{\textbf{b}}(b_i) \quad \textbf{fi}$$

(v)  For each instance $L_j$ of $V_{\mathcal{B}}$, $pre(L_j)$ implies $\bigvee_{b_i \in \mathcal{B}} (C_i \wedge n_i > 0)$.

$\square$

Note that $V_{\mathcal{B}}$ may be nondeterministic, since more than one $C_i$ may hold at a given time and it is possible that $n_i > 0$ holds for each. There may be good reasons for one of the *true* guards to be selected over the others. We can implement priority simply by strengthening the guards. Provided that condition (v) of Split Binary Semaphores [Deadlock Avoidance] (10.27) remains satisfied, the strengthening will not introduce deadlock. The strengthening constitutes a form of scheduling.

Support for fairness is one place where strengthening the guards of $V_{\mathcal{B}}$ is particularly useful. This is because without making a fairness assumption about $GEval_{if}(V_{\mathcal{B}})$, some critical section may be treated unfairly. Consider a process attempting to enter a critical section with associated condition $C_i$. Entry might be guaranteed if $C_i$ holds at the start of every critical section execution from some point onwards, a form of weak fairness. Or, entry might be guaranteed if $C_i$ holds infinitely often at the start of critical section executions, a form of strong fairness.

One way to support these fairness assumptions is to record at the start of each critical section the binary semaphores and values of associated conditions on which processes are blocked. This information is used to strengthen the guards of $V_{\mathcal{B}}$ so that only one guard is *true* at a time. In implementing weak fairness, only the guard corresponding to the *true* condition $C_i$ that has held at the start of every critical section execution and on which a process is blocked the longest would be *true*. For strong fairness, only the guard corresponding to the *true* condition $C_i$ on which a process is waiting the longest would be *true*. Observe that strengthening guards of $V_{\mathcal{B}}$, however, is not sufficient to implement either fairness assumption. $\textbf{P}_{\textbf{b}}$ and $\textbf{V}_{\textbf{b}}$ must also be strongly fair—otherwise, if several processes are blocked on $b_i$, then $\textbf{V}_{\textbf{b}}$ statements might never unblock the process that has been waiting the longest.

## Readers/Writers with Split Binary Semaphores

Consider a database that is shared by a collection of processes. Assume that every program fragment $R_i$ to read the database is bracketed by $\textbf{acq}_{\textbf{R}}$ and $\textbf{rel}_{\textbf{R}}$,

... $\textbf{acq}_{\textbf{R}} \ R_i \ \textbf{rel}_{\textbf{R}}$ ...

and that every program fragment $W_j$ to write the database is bracketed by $\textbf{acq}_{\textbf{W}}$ and $\textbf{rel}_{\textbf{W}}$,

$$\ldots\ \mathbf{acq_W}\ \ W_j\ \ \mathbf{rel_W}\ \ldots$$

Desired are protocols for $\mathbf{acq_R}$, $\mathbf{rel_R}$, $\mathbf{acq_W}$, and $\mathbf{rel_W}$ to prevent writing that is concurrent with either reading or writing. Moreover, assume that read/write locks are not available, so we must ourselves implement their functionality. Thus, for the concurrent program $S$ we desire the following invariance property to hold:

(10.28)  $at(S) \Rightarrow \Box(nw=0 \lor (nw=1 \land nr=0))$

> where:

$$nr: \ \big\{ (\Sigma i\colon in(R_i)\colon\ 1) \quad \text{if } true$$
$$nw: \ \big\{ (\Sigma j\colon in(W_j)\colon\ 1) \quad \text{if } true$$

We start by adding assignments to $\mathbf{acq_R}$, $\mathbf{rel_R}$, $\mathbf{acq_W}$, and $\mathbf{rel_W}$ to introduce program variables $ar$ and $aw$ that satisfy:

(10.29)  $I$:       $ar \geq nr\ \land\ aw \geq nw$

Observe that $I \land (aw=0 \lor (aw=1 \land ar=0))$ implies $nw=0 \lor (nw=1 \land nr=0)$. Thus, a program that satisfies

(10.30)  $at(S) \Rightarrow \Box(aw=0 \lor (aw=1 \land ar=0))$

also satisfies (10.28). After adding assignments to $ar$ and $aw$ to maintain $I$, we get:

| | |
|---|---|
| ... | ... |
| $\{I\}$ | $\{I\}$ |
| $\mathbf{acq_R}$: $ar := ar+1$ $\{I\}$ | $\mathbf{acq_W}$: $aw := aw+1$ $\{I\}$ |
| $PO(R_i) \otimes I$ | $PO(W_j) \otimes I$ |
| $\{I \land ar > nr\}$ | $\{I \land aw > nw\}$ |
| $\mathbf{rel_R}$: $ar := ar-1$ | $\mathbf{rel_W}$: $aw := aw-1$ |
| $\{I\}$ | $\{I\}$ |
| ... | ... |

The assignments to $ar$ and $aw$ do not comply with At Most One Assignments (9.32). But if we include these assignments in critical sections, Atomic Assignments by Exclusion (9.47) applies and there is no need to decompose the statements further. We use Split Binary Semaphores [Mutual Exclusion] (10.23) to implement the critical sections. The set of binary semaphores that comprise the split binary semaphore is unknown at this point, so semaphore names are not given in the $\mathbf{P_b}$ and $\mathbf{V_b}$ statements.

$\ldots \; \{I\}$                                             $\ldots \; \{I\}$

$\mathbf{acq_R}\colon \; \mathbf{P_b}(?) \; \{I\}$                           $\mathbf{acq_W}\colon \; \mathbf{P_b}(?) \; \{I\}$

       $ar := ar+1 \; \{I \wedge ar > nr\}$               $aw := aw+1 \; \{I \wedge aw > nw\}$

       $vr_i\colon \; \mathbf{V_b}(?) \; \{I\}$                         $vw_j\colon \; \mathbf{V_b}(?) \; \{I\}$

$PO(R_i) \otimes I$                                 $PO(W_j) \otimes I$

$\{I \wedge ar > nr\}$                             $\{I \wedge aw > nw\}$

$\mathbf{rel_R}\colon \; pr_i\colon \; \mathbf{P_b}(?) \; \{I \wedge ar > nr\}$      $\mathbf{rel_W}\colon \; pw_j\colon \; \mathbf{P_b}(?) \; \{I \wedge aw > nw\}$

       $ar := ar-1 \; \{I\}$                         $aw := aw-1 \; \{I\}$

       $\mathbf{V_b}(?)$                                $\mathbf{V_b}(?)$

$\{I\} \; \ldots$                                     $\{I\} \; \ldots$

We next check whether there is interference in these proof outlines. $I$ appears both before and after each atomic action, so it is not falsified. Other conjuncts concerning $ar$, $nr$, $aw$, and $nw$ are not falsified if $I$ is strengthened to:

$I\colon \quad ar \geq nr \; \wedge \; aw \geq nw$
$\quad \wedge \quad ar = (\Sigma\, i\colon \; in(vr_i) \vee in(R_i) \vee in(pr_i) \vee after(pr_i)\colon \; 1)$
$\quad \wedge \quad aw = (\Sigma\, j\colon \; in(vw_j) \vee in(W_j) \vee in(pw_j) \vee after(pw_j)\colon \; 1)$

Unfortunately, the assertions in our proof outlines are not strong enough to infer that (10.30) is satisfied. This becomes apparent if we try to prove (10.30) with Safety Consequence Rule (6.8), using $I_{PO(S)}$ Decomposition Rule (6.17a) to discharge premise (c). For each assertion $A$,

$$loc(A) \wedge A \;\; \Rightarrow \;\; (aw = 0 \vee (aw = 1 \wedge ar = 0))$$

must be valid, and it isn't. We must strengthen the assertions.

An obvious strengthening is to conjoin $aw = 0 \vee (aw = 1 \wedge ar = 0)$ to each assertion. But this change destroys the validity of the proof outlines above. Neither $pre(ar := ar+1)$ nor $pre(aw := aw+1)$ would be strong enough to justify $aw = 0 \vee (aw = 1 \wedge ar = 0)$ in the postconditions for these statements.

Execution of $ar := ar+1$ truthifies $aw = 0 \vee (aw = 1 \wedge ar = 0)$ only if started in a state satisfying $wp(ar := ar+1, \; aw = 0 \vee (aw = 1 \wedge ar = 0))$:

$\quad\quad wp(ar := ar+1, \; aw = 0 \vee (aw = 1 \wedge ar = 0))$
$=\quad$ «weakest precondition (4.50) for $ar := ar+1$»
$\quad\quad aw = 0 \vee (aw = 1 \wedge ar+1 = 0)$
$=\quad$ «$I$ implies $ar \geq 0$, so $ar+1 = 0$ is *false*»
$\quad\quad aw = 0$

Thus, we must strengthen $pre(ar := ar+1)$ so that it implies $aw = 0$.

We similarly calculate the states in which $aw := aw+1$ should be executed.

$\quad\quad wp(aw := aw+1, \; aw = 0 \vee (aw = 1 \wedge ar = 0))$
$=\quad$ «weakest precondition (4.50) for $aw := aw+1$»
$\quad\quad aw+1 = 0 \vee (aw+1 = 1 \wedge ar = 0)$

$$= \qquad \text{«}I \text{ implies } aw \geq 0, \text{ so } aw+1=0 \text{ is } false\text{»}$$
$$aw+1=1 \wedge ar=0$$
$$= \qquad \text{«algebra»}$$
$$aw=0 \wedge ar=0$$

We conclude that $pre(aw := aw+1)$ must be strengthened to imply $aw=0 \wedge ar=0$.

The strengthening of $pre(ar := ar+1)$ and $pre(aw := aw+1)$ can be accomplished with Split Binary Semaphores [Condition Synchronization] (10.24), because $ar := ar+1$ and $aw := aw+1$ each immediately follows a $\mathbf{P_b}$ that starts a critical section. We therefore define a binary semaphore for each of the two conditions that must be awaited and a binary semaphore for the condition *true* associated with executing $\mathbf{rel_R}$ and $\mathbf{rel_W}$. Here, then, is the proposed breakdown for the split binary semaphore:

| Name | Condition |
|------|-----------|
| $m$  | *true* |
| $br$ | $aw=0$ |
| $bw$ | $aw=0 \wedge ar=0$ |

We now insert semaphore names into the $\mathbf{P_b}$ statements and strengthen $I$ to include the conjuncts $b_i=1 \Rightarrow C_i$ for the desired condition synchronization. The following proof outlines result.

$I$:  $\quad ar \geq nr \ \wedge \ aw \geq nw$
$\quad\quad \wedge \ \ ar=(\Sigma i: \ in(vr_i) \vee in(R_i) \vee in(pr_i) \vee after(pr_i): \ 1)$
$\quad\quad \wedge \ \ aw=(\Sigma j: \ in(vw_j) \vee in(W_j) \vee in(pw_j) \vee after(pw_j): \ 1)$
$\quad\quad \wedge \ \ aw=0 \vee (aw=1 \wedge ar=0)$
$\quad\quad \wedge \ \ br=1 \Rightarrow aw=0$
$\quad\quad \wedge \ \ bw=1 \Rightarrow aw=0 \wedge ar=0$

```
...  {I}                              ...  {I}
acqR: Pb(br) {I ∧ aw=0}              acqW: Pb(bw) {I ∧ aw=0 ∧ ar=0}
      ar := ar+1 {I ∧ ar>nr}               aw := aw+1 {I ∧ aw>nw}
      vri: Vb(?) {I}                        vwj: Vb(?) {I}
PO(Ri)⊛I                             PO(Wj)⊛I
{I ∧ ar>nr}                          {I ∧ aw>nw}
relR: pri: Pb(m) {I ∧ ar>nr}         relW: pwj: Pb(m) {I ∧ aw>nw}
      ar := ar−1 {I}                        aw := aw−1 {I}
      Vb(?)                                 Vb(?)
{I} ...                              {I} ...
```

Condition (i) of Split Binary Semaphores [Condition Synchronization] (10.24) cannot be checked now because semaphores are not (yet) named in $\mathbf{V_b}$ statements. Condition (ii) holds because all assignments to $ar$ and $aw$ occur in critical sections of the split binary semaphore.

All that remains is to fill in the $V_b$ statements with semaphores. Here, we employ Split Binary Semaphores [Deadlock Avoidance] (10.27). Conditions (i) through (iii) are discharged by adding assignments to variables $n_m$, $n_{br}$, and $n_{bw}$; condition (iv) is discharged by defining:

$$V_{rw}: \quad \textbf{if } n_m > 0 \rightarrow V_b(m)$$
$$[] \ n_{br} > 0 \wedge aw = 0 \rightarrow V_b(br)$$
$$[] \ n_{bw} > 0 \wedge aw = 0 \wedge ar = 0 \rightarrow V_b(bw)$$
$$\textbf{fi}$$

Finally, condition (v) is discharged by proving that the precondition for each of these **if** statements implies:

$$n_m > 0 \ \vee \ (n_{br} > 0 \wedge aw = 0) \ \vee \ (n_{bw} > 0 \wedge aw = 0 \wedge ar = 0)$$

Assignments to $n_m$, $n_{br}$, and $n_{bw}$ are straightforward to formulate for **acq$_R$** and **acq$_W$**. To execute in **acq$_R$**, a $P_b(br)$ must have been completed and the next $P_b$ (in **rel$_R$**) must name $m$. So, assignment statement $n_m, n_{br} := n_m + 1, n_{br} - 1$ is indicated. Similarly, executing in **acq$_W$** involves completing a $P_b(m)$ and then (in **rel$_W$**) executing $P_b(m)$: assignment statement $n_m, n_{bw} := n_m + 1, n_{bw} - 1$ describes this. Thus, we get:

```
...  {I}
acqR: Pb(br)  {I ∧ aw=0}
         ar, nm, nbr := ar+1, nm+1, nbr−1  {I ∧ ar > nr}
         vri: Vrw  {I}
PO(Ri)⊗I
{I ∧ ar > nr}
relR: pri: Pb(m)  {I ∧ ar > nr}
         ar := ar−1  {I}
         Vrw
{I}  ...
```

```
...  {I}
acqW: Pb(bw)  {I ∧ aw=0 ∧ ar=0}
         aw, nm, nbw := aw+1, nm+1, nbw−1  {I ∧ aw > nw}
         vwj: Vrw  {I}
PO(Wj)⊗I
{I ∧ aw > nw}
relW: pwj: Pb(m)  {I ∧ aw > nw}
         aw := aw−1  {I}
         Vrw
{I}  ...
```

It is not clear what assignments to $n_m$, $n_{br}$, and $n_{bw}$ are appropriate in **rel$_R$** and **rel$_W$**. We do know that $n_m$ should be decremented, since a $P_b(m)$ must complete in order to execute in $\text{rel}_R$ and $\text{rel}_W$. However, if the process will next read from the database, then $n_{br}$ should be incremented because $br$ is named in the first $\mathbf{P_b}$ of $\text{acq}_R$. Moreover, if the process will next write to the database, then $n_{bw}$ should be incremented. We are faced with a dilemma.

We dodge the problem by modifying $\text{acq}_R$ and $\text{acq}_W$ and inserting $\mathbf{P_b}(m)$ at the very start of each. Now, $\text{acq}_R$ and $\text{acq}_W$ both start with a $\mathbf{P_b}$ on the same semaphore. With this change, the values of $n_m$, $n_{br}$, and $n_{bw}$ need not be altered by $\text{rel}_R$ and $\text{rel}_W$. Changes must be made to $\text{acq}_R$ and $\text{acq}_W$, though. In $\text{acq}_R$, there is now a $\mathbf{P_b}(m)$ followed by a $\mathbf{P_b}(br)$, so between them, $n_m$ should be decremented and $n_{br}$ should be incremented; in $\text{acq}_W$, there is now a $\mathbf{P_b}(m)$ followed by a $\mathbf{P_b}(bw)$, so between them, $n_m$ should be decremented and $n_{bw}$ should be incremented. Finally, a $V_{rw}$ must be inserted immediately after the updates to $n_m$, $n_{br}$, and $n_{bw}$, so that the alternation of $\mathbf{P_b}$ and $\mathbf{V_b}$ statements needed by Split Binary Semaphores [Mutual Exclusion] (10.23) is preserved.

$$
\begin{aligned}
&\ldots\ \{I\}\\
&\textbf{acq}_R\colon\ \mathbf{P_b}(m)\ \{I\}\ n_m, n_{br} := n_m-1, n_{br}+1\ \{I\}\ V_{rw}\ \{I\}\\
&\qquad\quad\ \mathbf{P_b}(br)\ \{I \wedge aw=0\}\\
&\qquad\quad\ ar, n_m, n_{br} := ar+1, n_m+1, n_{br}-1\ \{I \wedge ar > nr\}\\
&\qquad\quad\ vr_i\colon\ V_{rw}\ \{I\}\\
&PO(R_i)@I\\
&\{I \wedge ar > nr\}\\
&\textbf{rel}_R\colon\ pr_i\colon\ \mathbf{P_b}(m)\ \{I \wedge ar > nr\}\\
&\qquad\quad\ ar := ar-1\ \{I\}\\
&\qquad\quad\ V_{rw}\\
&\{I\}\ \ldots
\end{aligned}
$$

$$
\begin{aligned}
&\ldots\ \{I\}\\
&\textbf{acq}_W\colon\ \mathbf{P_b}(m)\ \{I\}\ n_m, n_{bw} := n_m-1, n_{bw}+1\ \{I\}\ V_{rw}\ \{I\}\\
&\qquad\quad\ \mathbf{P_b}(bw)\ \{I \wedge aw=0 \wedge ar=0\}\\
&\qquad\quad\ aw, n_m, n_{bw} := aw+1, n_m+1, n_{bw}-1\ \{I \wedge aw > nw\}\\
&\qquad\quad\ vw_j\colon\ V_{rw}\ \{I\}\\
&PO(W_j)@I\\
&\{I \wedge aw > nw\}\\
&\textbf{rel}_W\colon\ pw_j\colon\ \mathbf{P_b}(m)\ \{I \wedge aw > nw\}\\
&\qquad\quad\ aw := aw-1\ \{I\}\\
&\qquad\quad\ V_{rw}\\
&\{I\}\ \ldots
\end{aligned}
$$

Lastly, we check condition (v) of Split Binary Semaphores [Deadlock Avoidance] (10.27). We must prove that the precondition of each $V_{rw}$ implies one of its guards. For this purpose, we must strengthen $I$ with three more conjuncts. Let conjunct $I_n$ imply that $n_m$, $n_{br}$, and $n_{bw}$ each has the value stipulated in condition (i) of Split Binary Semaphores [Deadlock Avoidance] (10.27). N is assumed to denote the total number of processes.

$I:$     $ar \geq nr \;\wedge\; aw \geq nw$
  $\wedge\;\; ar = (\Sigma i\colon\; in(vr_i) \vee in(R_i) \vee in(pr_i) \vee after(pr_i)\colon\; 1)$
  $\wedge\;\; aw = (\Sigma j\colon\; in(vw_j) \vee in(W_j) \vee in(pw_j) \vee after(pw_j)\colon\; 1)$
  $\wedge\;\; aw = 0 \vee (aw = 1 \wedge ar = 0)$
  $\wedge\;\; br = 1 \Rightarrow aw = 0$
  $\wedge\;\; bw = 1 \Rightarrow aw = 0 \wedge ar = 0$
  $\wedge\;\; I_n$
  $\wedge\;\; n_m + n_{br} + n_{bw} = \mathrm{N}$
  $\wedge\;\; ar + n_{br} + aw + n_{bw} \leq n_m + n_{br} + n_{bw}$

All three of the new conjuncts of $I$ are left *true* by every assignment statement. By subtracting $n_{br} + n_{bw}$ from both sides of the final conjunct, we deduce that $I$ implies $ar + aw \leq n_m$. The proof that a guard of $V_{rw}$ holds whenever $V_{rw}$ is reached is now straightforward, since $I$ is in the precondition of each $V_{rw}$.

$\qquad\quad I$
$\Rightarrow \qquad$ «Conjunct $I_n$ implies $n_m \geq 0$»
$\quad n_m > 0 \;\vee\; (n_m = 0 \wedge I)$
$= \qquad$ «$I$ implies $ar + aw \leq n_m$, $ar \geq 0$, and $aw \geq 0$, so $I \wedge n_m = 0$
$\qquad\qquad$ implies $ar = 0 \;\wedge\; aw = 0$»
$\quad n_m > 0 \;\vee\; (n_m = 0 \wedge ar = 0 \wedge aw = 0 \wedge I)$
$= \qquad$ «Conjunct $I_n$ implies $n_{br} \geq 0$»
$\quad n_m > 0$
$\quad\vee\; (n_{br} > 0 \wedge n_m = 0 \wedge ar = 0 \wedge aw = 0 \wedge I)$
$\quad\vee\; (n_{br} = 0 \wedge n_m = 0 \wedge ar = 0 \wedge aw = 0 \wedge I)$
$\Rightarrow \qquad$ «Predicate Logic»
$\quad n_m > 0$
$\quad\vee\; (n_{br} > 0 \wedge aw = 0)$
$\quad\vee\; (n_{br} = 0 \wedge n_m = 0 \wedge ar = 0 \wedge aw = 0 \wedge I)$
$\Rightarrow \qquad$ «$I$ implies $n_m + n_{br} + n_{bw} = \mathrm{N}$, so $I \wedge n_{br} = 0 \wedge n_m = 0$
$\qquad\qquad$ implies $n_{bw} = \mathrm{N} > 0$»
$\quad n_m > 0 \;\vee\; (n_{br} > 0 \wedge aw = 0) \;\vee\; (n_{bw} > 0 \wedge ar = 0 \wedge aw = 0)$

This completes the derivation of the solution. The protocols—with assertions removed—are given in Figure 10.5.

With the protocols of Figure 10.5, a sequence of reads can prevent execution of a write. This happens because reads are never blocked when $ar > 0$ holds but writes are. We can eliminate such *writer-starvation* by blocking the start of a new read whenever there is a blocked write attempt. Recall that reads are started by executing $V_b(br)$ in $V_{rw}$ and that $n_{bw}$ is the number of blocked writes. Thus, writer-starvation is avoided by strengthening the second guard of $V_{rw}$ so that $V_b(br)$ is executed only if $n_{bw} = 0$:

(10.31) $V_{rwp}$:  **if** $n_m > 0 \rightarrow V_b(m)$
$\qquad\qquad$ [] $n_{bw} = 0 \wedge n_{br} > 0 \wedge aw = 0 \rightarrow V_b(br)$
$\qquad\qquad$ [] $n_{bw} > 0 \wedge aw = 0 \wedge ar = 0 \rightarrow V_b(bw)$
$\qquad\qquad$ **fi**

$$\dots$$

$$\textbf{acq}_\textbf{R}\colon\ \textbf{P}_\textbf{b}(m)\quad n_m, n_{br} := n_m-1, n_{br}+1\quad V_{rw}$$
$$\qquad\qquad \textbf{P}_\textbf{b}(br)\quad ar, n_m, n_{br} := ar+1, n_m+1, n_{br}-1\quad V_{rw}$$
$$R_i$$
$$\textbf{rel}_\textbf{R}\colon\ \textbf{P}_\textbf{b}(m)\quad ar := ar-1\quad V_{rw}$$
$$\dots$$

$$\dots$$

$$\textbf{acq}_\textbf{W}\colon\ \textbf{P}_\textbf{b}(m)\quad n_m, n_{bw} := n_m-1, n_{bw}+1\quad V_{rw}$$
$$\qquad\qquad \textbf{P}_\textbf{b}(bw)\quad aw, n_m, n_{bw} := aw+1, n_m+1, n_{bw}-1\quad V_{rw}$$
$$W_j$$
$$\textbf{rel}_\textbf{W}\colon\ \textbf{P}_\textbf{b}(m)\quad aw := aw-1\quad V_{rw}$$
$$\dots$$

where:

$$V_{rw}\colon\ \textbf{if } n_m>0 \to \textbf{V}_\textbf{b}(m)$$
$$\qquad [] \ n_{br}>0 \land aw=0 \to \textbf{V}_\textbf{b}(br)$$
$$\qquad [] \ n_{bw}>0 \land aw=0 \land ar=0 \to \textbf{V}_\textbf{b}(bw)$$
$$\qquad \textbf{fi}$$

**Figure 10.5.** Protocols for reading and writing

---

After performing this strengthening, we must check that we have not introduced deadlock. So, we recheck condition (v) of Split Binary Semaphores [Deadlock Avoidance] (10.27).

$$I$$
$$\Rightarrow\quad \text{«Conjunct } I_n \text{ implies } n_m \geq 0\text{»}$$
$$\quad n_m>0 \ \lor\ (n_m=0 \land I)$$
$$=\quad \text{«Conjunct } I_n \text{ implies } n_{bw} \geq 0\text{»}$$
$$\quad n_m>0 \ \lor\ (n_m=0 \land n_{bw}=0 \land I) \ \lor\ (n_m=0 \land n_{bw}>0 \land I)$$
$$=\quad \text{«}I \text{ implies } ar+aw \leq n_m, ar \geq 0, \text{ and } aw \geq 0, \text{ so } I \land n_m=0$$
$$\qquad \text{implies } ar=0 \ \land\ aw=0\text{»}$$
$$\quad n_m>0$$
$$\quad \lor\ (n_m=0 \land n_{bw}=0 \land ar=0 \land aw=0 \land I)$$
$$\quad \lor\ (n_m=0 \land n_{bw}>0 \land ar=0 \land aw=0 \land I)$$
$$\Rightarrow\quad \text{«Predicate Logic»}$$
$$\quad n_m>0 \ \lor\ (n_{bw}=0 \land ar=0 \land aw=0) \ \lor\ (n_{bw}>0 \land ar=0 \land aw=0)$$

There is no deadlock, so $V_{rwp}$ can replace $V_{rw}$ in the protocols of Figure 10.5. The resulting protocol is known as the *writers priority* solution. Of course, it now becomes possible for a series of writes to block all reads. Exercises 10.25 through 10.28 explore alternatives that address this problem.

360        Chapter 10    Semaphores, Locks, and Conditional Critical Regions

## 10.5  Conditional Critical Regions

The split binary semaphore method is essentially a protocol to synchronize a set of critical sections so that

- their execution is mutually exclusive, and

- each critical section may be executed only in a state satisfying some associated condition.

Unfortunately, the critical sections and associated conditions in the resulting programs are virtually impossible to identify. For example, in Figure 10.5 a myriad of details—involving counters, $P_b$ statements, and $V_b$ statements—must be understood to find the critical sections and the condition associated with each.

To address this problem, one might devise a notation for explicitly defining a critical section and its associated condition. The *conditional critical region* statement

(10.32)  $S_i$:   **region** $r$ **when** $B_i \rightarrow CS_i$ **end**

is just such a notation. $S_i$, also called a **region** $r$ statement, specifies that *body* $CS_i$ be blocked until *condition* $B_i$ holds and that execution of $CS_i$ is mutually exclusive with the bodies of all other **region** $r$ statements. We call $r$ the *region identifier*.

A fairness assumption prevents discrimination against one or another blocked process. We might stipulate that the body of a **region** $r$ statement be executed if from some point onwards, the condition holds whenever no other process is executing in a **region** $r$ statement—a form of weak fairness. Alternatively, we might stipulate that the body be executed if infinitely often the condition holds whenever no other process is executing in a **region** $r$ statement—a form of strong fairness.

As an illustration of conditional critical regions, in Figure 10.6 we reformulate the reading/writing protocols of Figure 10.5. It is now easy to recognize critical sections and their associated conditions. Note also how the conditional critical regions resemble the conditional atomic actions in §10.3 that give operational semantics for acquire and release statements on read/write locks. The conditional critical regions, however, have a very different semantics from the conditional atomic actions—conditional atomic actions are executed indivisibly, while **region** statements are not.

Conditional critical regions provide a single construct for specifying both condition synchronization and mutual exclusion. As such, **region** statements are useful in controlling interference. A **region** statement with a condition $B$ blocks the first atomic action $\alpha$ of its body until $B$ holds. Operationally, blocking $\alpha$ prevents execution in states where an assertion could be falsified. Assertionally, blocking $\alpha$ means that $pre(\alpha)$ can be strengthened with $B$. It should be easier to prove $NI(\alpha, A)$ when, by virtue of the condition synchronization, $pre(NI(\alpha, A))$ has been so strengthened.

```
...
acq_R: region rw when aw=0 → ar := ar+1 end
R_i
rel_R: region rw when true → ar := ar−1 end
...


...
acq_W: region rw when aw=0 ∧ ar=0 → aw := aw+1 end
W_j
rel_R: region rw when true → aw := aw−1 end
...
```

**Figure 10.6.** Conditional critical regions for reading and writing

Use of mutual exclusion to control interference is the subject of Avoiding Interference by Exclusion (9.43) and Atomic Assignments by Exclusion (9.47). The bodies of all **region** statements with the same region identifier are mutually exclusive. Operationally, this mutual exclusion precludes executing an atomic action from the body of a **region** $r$ statement when an assertion in the body of another **region** $r$ statement should hold. Assertionally, the mutual exclusion allows the preconditions of atomic actions in the body of each **region** $r$ statement to be strengthened with a conjunct that states that no control point in the body of another **region** $r$ statement is active.

### Axiomatization of **region** Statements

Execution of a **region** $r$ statement $S_i$ involves a guard evaluation action $GEval_{ccr}(S_i)$, which blocks until the condition holds and the body of no other **region** $r$ statement is being executed. Control predicate axioms for a **region** $r$ statement $S_i$ (a) define its entry control point to be the start of the guard evaluation action, (b) define its exit control point to coincide with the end of its body, (c) define $in(S_i)$, (d) assert that the body is executed after the guard evaluation action is completed, and (e) stipulate that the bodies of all **region** $r$ statements are mutually exclusive.

(10.33) *Conditional Critical Region Control Axioms*: For a **region** $r$ statement:

$$S_i: \text{region } r \text{ when } B_i \to CS_i \text{ end}$$

(a) $at(S_i) = at(GEval_{ccr}(S_i))$
(b) $after(S_i) = after(CS_i)$
(c) $in(S_i) = in(GEval_{ccr}(S_i)) \vee in(CS_i)$
(d) $at(CS_i) = after(GEval_{ccr}(S_i))$

(e) Define $CCR_r$ to be a set such that $j \in CCR_r$ iff $CS_j$ is the body of some **region** $r$ statement:

$$in(CS_i) \Rightarrow \bigwedge_{\substack{j \in CCR_r \\ j \neq i}} \neg in(CS_j)$$

The postcondition of the Proof Outline Logic axiom for $GEval_{ccr}(S_i)$ is its precondition strengthened by the condition being awaited:

(10.34) $GEval_{ccr}(S_i)$ *Axiom*:  For a **region** statement

$$S_i: \textbf{region } r \textbf{ when } B_i \rightarrow CS_i \textbf{ end}$$

and a primitive assertion $P$:

$$\{P\}\ GEval_{ccr}(S_i)\ \{P \wedge B_i\}$$

The Proof Outline Logic inference rule for a conditional critical region uses proof outlines for the guard evaluation action and for the body.

(10.35) **region** *Rule*:

$$\frac{\begin{array}{l} \text{(a)}\ \{P\}\ GEval_{ccr}(S_i)\ \{R\} \\ \text{(b)}\ (R \wedge at(CS_i)) \Rightarrow P' \\ \text{(c)}\ \{P'\}\ PO(CS_i)\ \{Q\} \end{array}}{\{P\}\ S_i: \textbf{region } r \textbf{ when } B_i \rightarrow \{P'\}\ PO(CS_i)\ \{Q\}\textbf{ end}\ \{Q\}}$$

In using **region** Rule (10.35), typically $R$ and $P'$ will both be $P \wedge B_i$. Also, assertions are often structured as the conjunction of a shared assertion and a synchronously altered assertion, as discussed in §5.5.

An example of a proof outline involving conditional critical regions appears in Figure 10.7. It shows that the reading/writing protocols of Figure 10.6 satisfy (10.29) and (10.30), so they do indeed prevent writing that is concurrent with either reading or writing.

## Implementing Conditional Critical Regions

Based on the operational semantics described above for **region** statement (10.32), the same effect is achieved by the following program fragment

(10.36) $GEval_{ccr}(S_i)$: $\langle \textbf{if}\, \neg\, in_r \wedge B_i \rightarrow in_r := true\ \textbf{fi}\rangle$
$\quad\quad\quad\quad CS_i$
$\quad\quad\quad\quad in_r := false$

where boolean variable $in_r$ is associated with region identifier $r$ and is initially *false*. The problem of implementing conditional critical regions thus boils down to implementing the conditional atomic action labeled $GEval_{ccr}(S_i)$ in (10.36).

...
$\{I\}$
$\textbf{acq}_R$: **region** $rw$ **when** $aw = 0 \rightarrow \{I \wedge aw = 0\}$
$$ar := ar + 1 \ \{I\} \ \textbf{end}$$
$PO(R_i) \otimes I$
$\{I \wedge ar > nr\}$
$\textbf{rel}_R$: **region** $rw$ **when** $true \rightarrow \{I \wedge ar > nr\}$
$$ar := ar - 1 \ \{I\} \ \textbf{end}$$
$\{I\}$
...


...
$\{I\}$
$\textbf{acq}_W$: **region** $rw$ **when** $aw = 0 \wedge ar = 0 \rightarrow \{I \wedge aw = 0 \wedge ar = 0\}$
$$aw := aw + 1 \ \{I\} \ \textbf{end}$$
$PO(W_j) \otimes I$
$\{I \wedge aw > nw\}$
$\textbf{rel}_W$: **region** $rw$ **when** $true \rightarrow \{I \wedge aw > nw\}$
$$aw := aw - 1 \ \{I\} \ \textbf{end}$$
$\{I\}$
...

where:

$I$:     $ar \geq nr \ \wedge \ aw \geq nw$
$\wedge \ \ ar = (\Sigma i: \ in(R_i) \vee at(\textbf{rel}_R) \vee after(GEval_{ccr}(\textbf{rel}_R)): \ 1)$
$\wedge \ \ aw = (\Sigma j: \ in(W_j) \vee at(\textbf{rel}_W) \vee after(GEval_{ccr}(\textbf{rel}_W)): \ 1)$
$\wedge \ \ aw = 0 \vee (aw = 1 \wedge ar = 0)$

**Figure 10.7.**  Proof outline for reading and writing protocols

---

One approach to implementing $GEval_{ccr}(S_i)$ uses Simulating a Conditional Atomic Action (9.49). $GEval_{ccr}(S_i)$ is replaced by

(10.37)  *entry* $S_{b := \neg in_r \wedge B_i}$
     $T:$ **do** $\neg b \rightarrow exit$ *entry* $S_{b := \neg in_r \wedge B_i}$ **od**
     $in_r := true$
     *exit*

where:

- $b$ is a fresh variable for each $GEval_{ccr}(S_i)$ being implemented.
- program fragment $S_{b := \neg in_r \wedge B_i}$ assigns $\neg in_r \wedge B_i$ to $b$.

- Any atomic action $\alpha'$ that might falsify $\neg in_r \wedge B_i$ is bracketed by *entry* and *exit* so that $\alpha'$ cannot be executed if $at(in_r := true)$, $in(S_{b := \neg in_r \wedge B_i})$, or $at(GEval_{do}(T))$ holds.[3]

It is not possible for a program, like a compiler for example, to determine which atomic actions satisfy the above characterization of $\alpha'$. This is because making such a determination would require the compiler to prove Predicate Logic theorems. A conservative solution is to bracket with *entry* and *exit* all atomic actions that change variables mentioned in $B_i$. Unfortunately, the result is costly, because executions of *entry* and *exit* will be frequent.

An alternative solution is to restrict which variables may appear in the conditions of **region** statements.

(10.38) **Conditional Critical Regions [Condition Restriction].** Variables
named in the condition of a **region** $r$ statement may be changed only in
the body of **region** $r$ statements.                                          □

Recall that bodies of **region** $r$ statements are mutually exclusive. Given Conditional Critical Regions [Condition Restriction] (10.38), this mutual exclusion suffices to ensure that a condition is not falsified after it has been tested but before the body is executed.

Let $entry_r$ and $exit_r$ denote mutual exclusion entry and exit protocols in which all variables have been subscripted with $r$. The effect of this subscripting is that program fragments bracketed by $entry_r$ and $exit_r$ are mutually exclusive with respect to each other but not with respect to program fragments bracketed by $entry_{r'}$ and $exit_{r'}$ when $r$ and $r'$ are different variables. By using the mutual exclusion of $entry_r$ and $exit_r$ instead of implementing mutual exclusion of bodies using $in_r$, we obtain the following alternative to (10.37) for implementing (10.36).

(10.39)  $entry_r \ S_{b := B_i}$
       **do** $\neg b \rightarrow exit_r \ entry_r \ S_{b := B_i}$ **od**
       $CS_i$
       $exit_r$

The proof outline of Figure 10.8, adapted from Figure 9.10, shows for (10.39) that $B_i$ holds before $CS_i$ is executed and that $\neg in(CS_j)$ for $j \in CCR_r$ holds throughout body $CS_i$. (Recall that $j \in CCR_r$ iff $CS_j$ is the body of some **region** $r$ statement.) Thus, (10.39) satisfies the safety properties we expect of a **region** statement implementation.

Another implementation of **region** statement (10.32) is obtained with the split binary semaphore method. Region identifier $r$ is associated with a split

---

[3]Note that $in_r := false$, which appears at the end of (10.36), is not such an $\alpha'$ because $in_r := false$ does not falsify $\neg in_r \wedge B_i$.

$$\{P\}$$
$$entry_r \; \{P \wedge \neg (\bigvee_{j \in CCR_r,\, j \neq i} in(CS_i))\}$$
$$PO(S_{b\,:=\,B_i}) \otimes (P \wedge \neg (\bigvee_{j \in CCR_r,\, j \neq i} in(CS_i)))$$
$$\{P \wedge b = B_i \wedge \neg (\bigvee_{j \in CCR_r,\, j \neq i} in(CS_i)))\}$$
$$\mathbf{do}\; \neg b \rightarrow \{P \wedge \neg (\bigvee_{j \in CCR_r,\, j \neq i} in(CS_i))\}$$
$$exit_r \; \{P\}$$
$$entry_r \; \{P \wedge \neg (\bigvee_{j \in CCR_r,\, j \neq i} in(CS_i))\}$$
$$PO(S_{b\,:=\,B_i}) \otimes (P \wedge \neg (\bigvee_{j \in CCR_r,\, j \neq i} in(CS_i)))$$
$$\{P \wedge b = B_i \wedge \neg (\bigvee_{j \in CCR_r,\, j \neq i} in(CS_i)))\}$$
$$\mathbf{od}\; \{P \wedge B_i \wedge \neg (\bigvee_{j \in CCR_r,\, j \neq i} in(CS_i))\}$$
$$PO(CS_i) \otimes \neg (\bigvee_{j \in CCR_r,\, j \neq i} in(CS_i))$$
$$\{\neg (\bigvee_{j \in CCR_r,\, j \neq i} in(CS_i))\}$$
$$exit_r$$
$$...$$

**Figure 10.8.** Conditional critical region implementation

---

binary semaphore $\{mr, br_1, ..., br_N\}$, where $N$ is the number of **region** $r$ statements. The **region** $r$ statement $S_i$ is translated into the code of Figure 10.9. The translation works as intended provided that we satisfy the conditions of Split Binary Semaphores [Mutual Exclusion] (10.23), Split Binary Semaphores [Condition Synchronization] (10.24), and Split Binary Semaphores [Deadlock Avoidance] (10.27). We now check these.

Split Binary Semaphores [Mutual Exclusion] (10.23) requires that execution of $\mathbf{P_b}$ and $\mathbf{V_b}$ statements alternate. Observe that the translation of Figure 10.9 satisfies this condition when $CS_i$ contains no $\mathbf{P_b}$ and $\mathbf{V_b}$ statements naming elements of the split binary semaphore associated with region identifier $r$. If such $\mathbf{P_b}$ and $\mathbf{V_b}$ statements result only from translation of **region** $r$ statements, the condition of Split Binary Semaphores [Mutual Exclusion] (10.23) is easily satisfied provided that:

(10.40) **Conditional Critical Regions [Nesting].** A **region** $r$ statement may not be directly or indirectly nested within another **region** $r$ statement.  □

In addition, Conditional Critical Regions [Nesting] (10.40) prevents certain deadlocks. A **region** $r$ statement that is nested in a **region** $r$ statement—by

$$S_i:\ \alpha_1:\ \mathbf{P_b}(mr)$$
$$\alpha_2:\ nr_m, nr_i := nr_m - 1, nr_i + 1$$
$$\alpha_3:\ \mathbf{if}\ nr_m > 0 \rightarrow \mathbf{V_b}(mr)$$
$$[]\!\!\!\!\!\!\!\underset{1 \le j \le N}{}\ nr_j > 0 \wedge B_j \rightarrow \mathbf{V_b}(br_j)\ \mathbf{fi}$$
$$\alpha_4:\ \mathbf{P_b}(br_i)$$
$$\alpha_5:\ nr_m, nr_i := nr_m + 1, nr_i - 1$$
$$CS_i$$
$$\alpha_6:\ \mathbf{if}\ nr_m > 0 \rightarrow \mathbf{V_b}(mr)$$
$$[]\!\!\!\!\!\!\!\underset{1 \le j \le N}{}\ nr_j > 0 \wedge B_j \rightarrow \mathbf{V_b}(br_j)\ \mathbf{fi}$$

**Figure 10.9.** Translation of a **region** statement $S_i$

---

its very placement—cannot be executed without violating the mutual exclusion of bodies associated with region identifier $r$. So, the nesting would cause deadlock. Presumably, in nesting **region** $r$ statements, it was condition synchronization that was sought. For example, one might hope that the following (prohibited) construction causes execution of $S_2$ to be blocked until $B'$ holds.

(10.41)  **region** $r$ **when** $B \rightarrow S_1$
            **region** $r$ **when** $B' \rightarrow S_2$ **end**
            $S_3$
            **end**

A simple modification produces the desired effect and complies with Conditional Critical Regions [Nesting] (10.40): the inner **region** $r$ statement is changed to use a different region identifier.

For the translation of Figure 10.9, Split Binary Semaphores [Condition Synchronization] (10.24) requires that atomic actions that falsify any of the $B_j$ be included in the critical sections associated with the split binary semaphore for $r$. This is implied by Conditional Critical Regions [Condition Restriction] (10.38).

Conditions (i) though (iii) of Split Binary Semaphores [Deadlock Avoidance] (10.27) are satisfied by both assignment statements in the translation of Figure 10.9. Condition (iv) is satisfied by the presence of $\alpha_3$ and $\alpha_6$. Condition (v) is satisfied by **if** statement $\alpha_6$ of Figure 10.9 because guard $nr_m > 0$ necessarily holds given the increment of $nr_m$ that precedes $\alpha_6$. But condition (v) is not necessarily satisfied by **if** statement $\alpha_3$.

Blocking of $\alpha_3$ is due entirely to the conditions in **region** $r$ statements and is not due to the details of the translation. That is, $\alpha_3$ blocks only if it is possible for the original program to deadlock because each process is attempting to execute some **region** $r$ statement $S_i$ with a *false* condition $B_i$. To see why, we argue as follows. If $nr_m > 0$ holds, then $\alpha_3$ does not block. Therefore, assume that

$nr_m = 0$ holds. This means that the next $\mathbf{P_b}$ attempted by each process will name one of $br_1$ through $br_N$. From Figure 10.9, we conclude that each process is attempting to execute some **region** $r$ statement $S_i$ and that the associated condition for $S_i$ is *false*. So, the original program would deadlock.

A final implementation alternative for conditional critical regions employs direct support from the operating system. Here, a process attempting to execute a **region** $r$ statement with condition $B_i$ invokes an operating system routine. This routine allows the process to progress only if no process is executing the body of a **region** $r$ statement and if $B_i$ holds; otherwise, an element is placed on a queue associated with region identifier $r$, and the processor is allocated to another process. A process also invokes an operating system routine whenever it completes the body of a **region** $r$ statement. This routine checks the queue for region identifier $r$ to see whether any of the blocked processes could now be allocated a processor. When several processes are eligible, one is selected based on the fairness properties that must be satisfied.

In this operating-system-based implementation, a condition $B_i$ on which some process is blocked is checked only when the body of a **region** statement completes. $B_i$ may become *true* at some other time, but this will go unnoticed. There are two ways to combat this problem. The first is to define a third operating system routine, which is invoked whenever a process makes a change that might affect a condition awaited by some process. Presumably, a compiler would generate code that invoked this routine at suitable points. The approach has the same drawback as implementation (10.37), which required bracketing all atomic actions that change variables mentioned in $B_i$. The second approach is again to require that Conditional Critical Regions [Condition Restriction] (10.38) hold. Now, condition $B_i$ may be changed only by executing the body of a **region** $r$ statement, so conditions need to be checked only in the operating system routine invoked when a body terminates.

### Historical Notes

Semaphores were first proposed by Dijkstra in [Dijkstra 68b]. That paper actually was written in 1965 as a technical note (EWD 123) in Edsger W. Dijkstra's EWD series. Both binary and general semaphores are introduced in [Dijkstra 68b], and they are used to solve the mutual exclusion problem and the bounded buffer problem. Unlike other synchronization statements in vogue at the time, like **wait**($e$) and **cause**($e$), the effects of a **V** are remembered if a matching **P** has not yet been performed. This symmetry of **P** and **V** allowed Dijkstra to argue that semaphores should be easier to program with. A subsequent paper [Dijkstra 71] further discusses and illustrates the use of semaphores. This paper also introduced an alternative to semaphores that, when fleshed out, became known as a "monitor" (see below).

Dijkstra, a Dutchman, chose Dutch words when naming statements to manipulate semaphores. **P** is the first letter of the Dutch word "passeren," which means "to pass"; **V** is the first letter of "vrijgeven," the Dutch word meaning "to release." In some presentations, **P** is called "wait" or "down," and **V** is called "signal" or "up."

An operating system built in the late 1960s by Dijkstra and his research group supported and used semaphores for process synchronization. The kernel of the system even translated interrupts to look like **V**'s on system-defined semaphores. The operating system was named the "THE" system after the Dutch Technical University, Technische Hogeschool Eindhoven (T.H.E.), which housed the effort. The THE system ran on an Electrologica EL XS computer with 32K 27-bit words of main memory. A paper describing the system was presented at the first ACM Symposium on Operating Systems Principles in October 1967 and was ultimately published as [Dijkstra 68a]. The paper remains a classic, not because it discussed semaphores but because it was the first to propose hierarchical level structures for building systems. Each level implements a virtual machine that is more attractive to program than the one implemented by the level below it.

As semaphores were studied and used, deficiencies were noted and improvements proposed. Patil [Patil 71] introduces a problem—the cigarette smoker's problem—and argues that solving this problem requires either conditional statements or a more powerful **P**. The required **P** would atomically decrement a set of semaphores once all are positive. Patil's result is refuted by [Parnas 75], which gives a solution to the cigarette smoker's problem using ordinary **P** and **V** statements without conditional statements. The lesson of [Parnas 75], however, is that whether conditional statements are needed does not constitute an interesting question.

In [Belpaire & Wilmotte 74], a more primitive set of synchronization constructs is proposed. **P** and **V** can be constructed by composing these constructs, as can synchronization primitives well suited for other concurrent programming problems. The constructs in [Belpaire & Wilmotte 74] are the basis for the synchronization mechanisms used in a redesign of the operational flight software for the U.S. Navy's A-7E aircraft [Faulk & Parnas 88]. Another interesting set of synchronization constructs are the eventcounts and sequencers of [Reed & Kanodia 79]. These are easily implemented on multiprocessors because unlike semaphores, they are not defined in terms of mutually exclusive access to variables. Finally, various fairness assumptions and their implications for implementing mutual exclusion with semaphores is the subject of [Stark 82]. Exercise 10.2 is based on this work.

A method of proving deadlock freedom and mutual exclusion for programs that employ semaphores is discussed in [Habermann 72], where solutions to a mutual exclusion problem and a bounded buffer problem are analyzed. Habermann's method is shown to be incomplete in [Clarke 80], which also gives a characterization of the class of programs for which Habermann's method does work. Another axiomatization of semaphore statements is given in [Martin 81]. This axiomatization involves relating the number of suspended **P** statements, completed **P** statements, and completed **V** statements. Martin's framework also allows semaphores, asynchronous message-passing, and synchronous message-passing to be compared. Hoare-style axioms for **P** and **V** are given in [Owicki 75] and [Owicki & Gries 76a]. The same approach is employed there as the one used in §10.1 to justify **P** Axiom (10.3) and **V** Axiom (10.4).

Change of Variables for Semaphores (10.7) is based on a method first published in [Andrews 89]. Our method is more general, though. The method in [Andrews 89] requires transforming existing program statements so that they have the same form as **P** and **V**, whereas Change of Variables for Semaphores (10.7) is based on encoding variables using a semaphore and replacing conditional atomic actions by **P** statements.

Operational semantics (10.12) of $V_b$ differs from that given in [Dijkstra 68b]. We regard $V_b$ as a conditional atomic action, whereas [Dijkstra 68b] defines $V_b$ as an unconditional atomic action that always sets the semaphore to 1. Our semantics (which is also reported in [Andrews 89]) follows from a desire to characterize the value of a binary semaphore in terms of its initial value, the number of completed $P_b$ statements, and the number of completed $V_b$ statements. Such a characterization would not be possible using the unconditional atomic actions of [Dijkstra 68b].

The use of locks for synchronization is prevalent in database systems. A thorough discussion can be found in [Gray & Reuter 93]. See [McCurley 88] for the derivation of Hoare-style axioms for lock statements.

The split binary semaphore method was first mentioned in [Hoare 74]. It was popularized by [Dijkstra 79], which derives protocols for the readers/writers problem like the protocols we develop in §10.4. The readers/writers problem itself was introduced in [Courtois et al. 71]. Another tutorial on split binary semaphores appears in [Martin & Snepscheut 89]. In [Dijkstra 80], a split binary semaphore is used to implement a general semaphore. (See exercise 10.21.) Split binary semaphores are also used in [Martin & Burch 85] and [Udding 86] to implement fair mutual exclusion protocols.

Unstructured use of semaphore statements can lead to programming errors. An oversight might cause access to a shared variable to remain unprotected by a critical section or might cause the **P** and **V** bracketing a critical section to name the wrong semaphore(s). These problems led researchers to devise programming notations that convey synchronization requirements in a more structured manner. The hope was that a suitable syntax would allow the compiler to flag potential errors.

The first proposals along these lines are made in [Hoare 72a], where conditional critical regions are offered as an alternative to semaphores. Each shared variable is associated with a region identifier $r$, so a compiler could check that all references to shared variables are mutually exclusive by checking that the references appear in the bodies of suitable **region** statements. This restriction was not imposed in our formulation of conditional critical regions, but its presence would eliminate the need to check certain forms of interference. (See exercise 10.37.)

Condition synchronization is explicit in a **region** statement. The benefits of this are discussed in [Brinch Hansen 72a] in connection with the reader/writer solutions of [Courtois et al. 71], but a rejoinder to some of Brinch Hansen's comments appears in [Courtois et al. 72]. In [Brinch Hansen 72b], Brinch Hansen extends Hoare's conditional critical regions with constructs that allow a process executing anywhere in the body of a **region** statement to relinquish mutual exclusion and block. One extension is a statement that allows a process to block until a boolean expression becomes *true*—Hoare's conditional critical regions correspond to the special case where this statement starts the body. A second extension, intended for scheduling, provides an **await**($e$) statement to block and add a process to event queue $e$, and a **cause**($e$) statement to remove and unblock a process on event queue $e$. Note that with the advent of event queues, we have come full circle and returned to using synchronization constructs that are not symmetric.

Proof rules for establishing the partial correctness of programs with conditional critical regions are given in [Hoare 72a]. Those rules are not complete, and this led to the rules in [Owicki 75] and [Owicki & Gries 76b] for proving partial correctness, mutual exclusion, and deadlock freedom. The rules in [Owicki 75] and [Owicki & Gries 76b], however, are not complete for other invariance properties; we believe the rules in §10.5 are complete for all safety properties.

A number of researchers have studied the implementation of conditional critical regions, because the problem is intellectually challenging and of practical import. A method for determining which conditions need not be rechecked when a process finishes a conditional critical region is the subject of [Schmid 76]. Prudence dictates that unnecessary condition evaluations be avoided, since a processor-context switch might be required in order to evaluate a condition on which another process is blocked, and context switches are expensive.

However, most work in implementing conditional critical regions concerns designing protocols for providing the mutual exclusion and condition synchronization inherent in

**region** statements. One of the first such efforts is due to Martin Rem and is reported in [Dijkstra 77b]. It uses a split binary semaphore with three components. An assertional correctness proof of Rem's protocol appears in [Gries 77]. Two protocols, each involving a split binary semaphore with two components, are given in [Kessels & Martin 79]. All of these protocols require processes to loop, repeatedly evaluating *false* boolean conditions for **region** statements they attempt to enter. The protocol in Figure 10.9 also employs split binary semaphores but does not involve looping. However, our protocol does require each process to have access to the variables mentioned in the conditions of **region** statements of other processes.

The monitor was the final step in the development of programming notations that control concurrent access to shared data. A *monitor* consists of some variables and some procedures to manipulate those variables. A monitor's variables can be read and written only from within the monitor's procedures. Execution of the monitor's procedures is mutually exclusive. Thus, a monitor can be viewed as a syntax that groups in one place the bodies of all **region** *r* statements for each region identifier *r*, along with any shared variables that are associated with that region identifier. Monitors, which were studied in the mid 1970s, combined the prevailing insights about abstract data type definitions with conditional critical regions.

We do not treat monitors in this text because their primary innovation over conditional critical regions is in modularity and visibility of variables. Monitors were quite popular in the 1970s, and many programming notations supported them. But the construct was found too restrictive, and its popularity faded. The very restrictions that allowed compilers to analyze programs written in terms of monitors had proved to be a straitjacket in building systems. Discussions of monitors do appear in [Andrews 91] and [Andrews & Schneider 83]; a survey of proof rules appears in [Buhr et al. 95].

## Exercises

**10.1.** (a)   Are strong fairness and weak fairness the same for **V** statements? Prove that they are or give a program that illustrates the difference.

(b)   Are strong fairness and weak fairness the same for $V_b$ statements? Prove that they are or give a program that illustrates the difference.

**10.2.** Each of the following has been proposed as a fairness assumption for semaphores.

(i)   Whenever **P** statements are blocked, executing a **V** unblocks the oldest blocked **P**.

(ii)   Whenever **P** statements are blocked, executing a **V** unblocks some blocked **P**.

(a)   Give a program that exhibits different behavior for (i) and (ii).

(b)   Explain whether (i) should or should not be considered a fairness assumption and why.

(c)   Explain whether (ii) should or should not be considered a fairness assumption and why.

**10.3.** (a)   Justify the following alternative to **P** Axiom (10.3) by showing that it is a derived rule of inference of Proof Outline Logic.

For primitive assertions $P$ and $Q$:

$$\frac{P \wedge s > 0 \ \Rightarrow\ Q^s_{s-1}}{\{P\}\ \mathbf{P}(s)\ \{Q\}}$$

(b)    Is this inference rule sound if $P$ and $Q$ are not primitive assertions?

**10.4.** The following triples would have to be proved in deriving the proof outline of Figure 10.4. Give a proof for each.

(a)    $\{Slots = N - (a - r)\}$
       $\mathbf{P}(slots)$
       $\{Slots \geq 0 \wedge Slots + 1 = N - (a - r) \wedge a - r < N\}$

(b)    $\{Slots = N - (a - r)\}$ $\mathbf{V}(portions)$ $\{Slots = N - (a - r)\}$

(c)    $\{Portions = a - r\}$
       $\mathbf{P}(portions)$
       $\{Portions \geq 0 \wedge Portions + 1 = a - r \wedge a - r > 0\}$

(d)    $\{Portions = a - r\}$ $\mathbf{V}(slots)$ $\{Portions = a - r\}$

**10.5.** For the following program, prove that at most N processes may execute a critical section at any time.

```
var mx : Sem
mx := N
cobegin
‖  S_i:  do true → entry_i:  P(mx)
 i                 CS_i
                   exit_i:  V(mx)
                   NCS_i
       od
coend
```

**10.6.** For the following program, prove that at most 1 process may execute a critical section at any time.

```
var bx : Bin_Sem
bx := 1
cobegin
‖  S_i:  do true → entry_i:  P_b(bx)
 i                 CS_i
                   exit_i:  V_b(bx)
                   NCS_i
       od
coend
```

**10.7.** What sequence of semaphore statements can be used to replace $Sa$, $Sb$, $Ta$, and $Tb$ in the following program so that $at(S) \wedge 0 \leq V \Rightarrow \Box(loc \leq V)$ is satisfied?

```
S:  loc := V
    cobegin
        do true → Sa  loc := loc − 1  Sb  od
    ‖
        do true → Ta  loc := loc + 1  Tb  od
    coend
```

**10.8.** Give a proof for the following theorem of Proof Outline Logic.

$$\textbf{var } mx : \text{Sem}$$
$$mx := 1$$
$$\{I: \; (mx=1 \Rightarrow (\forall j: \; \neg(in(CS_j) \vee after(CS_j)))) \; \wedge$$
$$(mx=0 \Rightarrow (\exists j: \; (in(CS_j) \vee after(CS_j))$$
$$\wedge (\forall k: \; k \neq j: \; \neg(in(CS_k) \vee after(CS_k)))))\}$$

$$\textbf{cobegin}$$
$$\| \; S_i: \; \{I\}$$
$$\quad \textbf{do } true \rightarrow \{I\}$$
$$\qquad\qquad entry_i: \; \textbf{P}(mx) \; \{I \wedge mx=0 \wedge in(CS_i)\}$$
$$\qquad\qquad PO(CS_i) \otimes (I \wedge mx=0 \wedge in(CS_i))$$
$$\qquad\qquad \{I \wedge mx=0 \wedge after(CS_i)\}$$
$$\qquad\qquad exit_i: \; \textbf{V}(mx) \; \{I\}$$
$$\qquad\qquad PO(NCS_i) \otimes I$$
$$\qquad\qquad \{I\}$$
$$\quad \textbf{od}$$
$$\textbf{coend}$$

**10.9.** Prove that the following program satisfies $at(S) \Rightarrow \Box(at(A) \vee at(B) \Rightarrow a=b)$.

$$S: \; \textbf{var } a, b : \text{Nat};$$
$$\qquad r, s, t, u : \text{Sem}$$

$$a, b, r, s, t, u := 0, 0, 0, 0, 0, 0$$
$$\textbf{cobegin}$$
$$\quad \textbf{do } true \rightarrow \textbf{V}(r) \; \textbf{P}(s)$$
$$\qquad\qquad\qquad A: \; \textbf{V}(t) \; \textbf{P}(u)$$
$$\qquad\qquad\qquad a := a+1$$
$$\quad \textbf{od}$$
$$\|$$
$$\quad \textbf{do } true \rightarrow \textbf{V}(s) \; \textbf{P}(r)$$
$$\qquad\qquad\qquad B: \; \textbf{V}(u) \; \textbf{P}(t)$$
$$\qquad\qquad\qquad b := b+1$$
$$\quad \textbf{od}$$
$$\textbf{coend}$$

**10.10.** (a)    Assume that each element of some set of atomic actions has a unique label $L_i$, where $1 \leq i \leq n$. Define a derived term #$L$ equal to the number of times that atomic actions from this set have been executed.

    (b)    For a semaphore $s$, suppose:

         •    Each **P** statement has a unique label $P_i$, where $1 \leq i \leq n_P$.

         •    Each **V** statement has a unique label $V_i$, where $1 \leq i \leq n_V$.

         Give the formula that relates $s$, #$P$, and #$V$.

    (c)    Let #$P$ and #$V$ be as defined in (a) and (b). Reformulate $ValAx(s, \text{Sem})$, (10.1), and (10.2) so that they no longer mention $s$, assuming that the initial value of $s$ is A. #$P$ and #$V$ may appear in guards in the reformulations of operational semantics (10.1) and (10.2).

    (d)    Based on the reformulations of (c), derive axioms for **P**($s$) and **V**($s$).

**10.11.** The operating system routines for **P** and **V** discussed at the end of §10.1 are assumed to be mutually exclusive. Is this mutual exclusion requirement necessary? What would happen were it relaxed?

**10.12.** Derive a solution to the readers/writers problem using the change-of-variable method discussed in §10.2. Your solution should prevent writing by a process that is concurrent with either reading or writing by another.

**10.13.** Why couldn't a binary semaphore be considered a lock, with $P_b$ regarded as an acquire statement and $V_b$ regarded as a release statement?

**10.14.** Derive the following axioms for statements involving binary semaphores by showing that the triples are theorems of Proof Outline Logic for operational semantics (10.11) and (10.12).

  (a)    $\mathbf{P_b}$ Axiom (10.13)
  (b)    $\mathbf{V_b}$ Axiom (10.14)

**10.15.** An alternative operational semantics for $\mathbf{P_b}$ and $\mathbf{V_b}$ is:

$$\mathbf{P_b}(b): \quad \langle \mathbf{if}\ b>0 \rightarrow b := b-1\ \mathbf{fi} \rangle$$
$$\mathbf{V_b}(b): \quad \langle \mathbf{if}\ b<1 \rightarrow b := b+1\ \mathbf{fi} \rangle$$

Derive axioms for $\mathbf{P_b}$ and $\mathbf{V_b}$ for this alternative operational semantics.

**10.16.** Derive the following axioms for statements that appear in a process $S$ by showing that they are theorems of Proof Outline Logic.

  (a)    $\mathbf{acq}(x)$ Axiom (10.15)
  (b)    $\mathbf{rel}(x)$ Axiom (10.16)

**10.17.** Derive the following axioms by showing that they are theorems of Proof Outline Logic.

  (a)    $\mathbf{acq_R}(F)$ Axiom (10.17)
  (b)    $\mathbf{rel_R}(F)$ Axiom (10.18)
  (c)    $\mathbf{acq_W}(F)$ Axiom (10.19)
  (d)    $\mathbf{rel_W}(F)$ Axiom (10.20)

**10.18.** Use derived terms and past operators to give an alternative operational semantics and axioms for $\mathbf{P_b}(b)$ and $\mathbf{V_b}(b)$ statements. Your alternatives may not mention $b$ but may assume that the initial value of $b$ is A and may involve derived terms and past operators in guards. Hint: Follow the procedure outlined in exercise 10.10.

**10.19.** Use derived terms and past operators to give an alternative operational semantics and axioms for $\mathbf{acq}(x)$ and $\mathbf{rel}(x)$ statements for exclusive locks. Your alternatives may not mention $x$ but may assume that the initial value of $x$ is $\emptyset$ and may involve derived terms and past operators in guards. Hint: Follow the procedure outlined in exercise 10.10.

**10.20.** Derive $entry_i$ and $exit_i$ for the following program so that at most N processes can execute in their critical sections at the same time. Use the split binary semaphore method.

**cobegin**
$\|$ $S_i$: **do** *true* $\rightarrow$ *entry$_i$*
$\quad\quad\quad\quad CS_i$
$\quad\quad\quad\quad exit_i$
$\quad\quad\quad\quad NCS_i$
$\quad$ **od**
**coend**

**10.21.** Show how to implement a general semaphore $s$ using the split binary semaphore method. To do this, define a split binary semaphore and any additional variables that are required. Then exhibit program fragments that can be substituted for:

(a)  an initialization $s := V$

(b)  a $\mathbf{P}(s)$ statement

(c)  a $\mathbf{V}(s)$ statement

**10.22.** Consider a system with $M$ $(1 \le M)$ processes of type 1 and $F$ $(1 \le F)$ processes of type 2. Each type $t$ process (where $t$ is 1 or 2) is of the following form, where $CS_t$ is called a type $t$ critical section.

$\quad\quad S_i$: **do** *true* $\rightarrow$ *start_t*
$\quad\quad\quad\quad\quad CS_t$
$\quad\quad\quad\quad\quad end\_t$
$\quad\quad\quad\quad\quad NCS_i$
$\quad\quad$ **od**

Use the split binary semaphore method to derive protocols for *start_1*, *end_1*, *start_2*, and *end_2* that will prevent type 1 and type 2 critical sections from being interleaved but will allow any number of type 1 critical sections or any number of type 2 critical sections to be interleaved.

**10.23.** Use the split binary semaphore method to derive a protocol for *gate$_i$* in

$\quad\quad S$: **cobegin** $\quad \| \atop {1 \le i \le N}$ $S_i$: $U_i$ *gate$_i$* $V_i$ **coend**

to ensure that no process $S_i$ starts executing $V_i$ until every process $S_j$ has completed $U_j$.

**10.24.** Formalize assertion $I_n$, which is used in §10.4 for the readers/writers protocols derivation.

**10.25.** What strengthening of the guards in $V_{rw}$ of Figure 10.5 causes blocked readers to have priority over blocked writers?

**10.26.** The following alternative to (10.31) has been proposed. It is supposed to prevent a sequence of reads from blocking execution of any write and a sequence of writes from blocking execution of any read.

**if** $n_m > 0 \rightarrow \mathbf{V_b}(m)$
$[]$ $n_{bw} = 0 \wedge n_{br} > 0 \wedge aw = 0 \rightarrow \mathbf{V_b}(br)$
$[]$ $n_{br} = 0 \wedge n_{bw} > 0 \wedge aw = 0 \wedge ar = 0 \rightarrow \mathbf{V_b}(bw)$
**fi**

What problems would replacing $V_{rw}$ by this **if** statement cause?

**10.27.** Suppose (10.31) is augmented with a fourth guarded command:

> **if** $n_m > 0 \rightarrow \mathbf{V_b}(m)$
> [] $n_{bw} = 0 \wedge n_{br} > 0 \wedge aw = 0 \rightarrow \mathbf{V_b}(br)$
> [] $n_{bw} > 0 \wedge aw = 0 \wedge ar = 0 \rightarrow \mathbf{V_b}(bw)$
> [] $n_{br} > 0 \wedge n_{bw} > 0 \wedge \;\wedge aw = 0 \wedge ar = 0 \rightarrow \mathbf{V_b}(bw)$
> **fi**

What problems, if any, does it cause? What problems, if any, does it solve?

**10.28.** Give modifications to the protocols of Figure 10.5 to ensure that at least one write is permitted every *seqR* reads and at least one read is permitted every *seqW* writes.

**10.29.** Some of the guards in the occurrences of $V_{rw}$ in Figure 10.5 are always *false*. For each occurrence of $V_{rw}$ in Figure 10.5, identify which guards are always *false* and, for each, explain why.

**10.30.** The following would have to be proved in deriving the proof outline of Figure 10.7. Give a proof for each.

(a)   $\{I\}$
      **acq$_R$: region** *rw* **when** $aw = 0 \rightarrow \{I \wedge aw = 0\}$
$$ar := ar + 1 \quad \{I\} \text{ end } \{I\}$$

(b)   $\{I \wedge ar > nr\}$
      **rel$_R$: region** *rw* **when** *true* $\rightarrow \{I \wedge ar > nr\}$
$$ar := ar - 1 \quad \{I\} \text{ end}$$
      $\{I\}$

(c)   $\{I\}$
      **acq$_W$: region** *rw* **when** $aw = 0 \wedge ar = 0 \rightarrow \{I \wedge aw = 0 \wedge ar = 0\}$
$$aw := aw + 1 \quad \{I\} \text{ end}$$
      $\{I\}$

(d)   $\{I \wedge aw > nw\}$
      **rel$_W$: region** *rw* **when** *true* $\rightarrow \{I \wedge aw > nw\}$
$$aw := aw - 1 \quad \{I\} \text{ end}$$
      $\{I\}$

**10.31.** Show how to use conditional critical regions in place of semaphores. To do this, give **region** statements that can be substituted for:

(a)   an initialization $s := V$

(b)   a $P(s)$ statement

(c)   a $V(s)$ statement

**10.32.** Show how to use conditional critical regions in place of binary semaphores. To do this, give **region** statements that can be substituted for:

(a)   an initialization $b := V$

(b)   a $\mathbf{P_b}(b)$ statement

(c)   a $\mathbf{V_b}(b)$ statement

**10.33.** Consider a system with $M$ $(1 \leq M)$ processes of type 1 and $F$ $(1 \leq F)$ processes of type 2. Each type $t$ process (where $t$ is 1 or 2) is of the following form, where $CS_t$

is called a type $t$ critical section.

$$S_i: \textbf{do } true \to start\_t$$
$$CS_t$$
$$end\_t$$
$$\overline{NCS}_i$$
$$\textbf{od}$$

Derive **region** statements for $start\_1$, $end\_1$, $start\_2$, and $end\_2$ that will prevent type 1 and type 2 critical sections from being interleaved but will allow any number of type 1 critical sections or any number of type 2 critical sections to be interleaved.

**10.34.** Use conditional critical regions to give a version of the producer/consumer program of Figure 9.1.

**10.35.** Discuss the consequences—for soundness, for completeness, and for ease of use—when the axiomatization of conditional critical regions is changed as follows.

(i)  Conditional Critical Region Control Axiom (10.33e) is deleted.

(ii)  The postcondition of $GEval_{ccr}(S_i)$ Axiom (10.34) is strengthened to:

$$P \wedge B_i \wedge ( \underset{\substack{j \in CCR_r \\ j \neq i}}{\wedge} \neg in(CS_j))$$

**10.36.** Explain why adding $at(CS_i)$ to the postcondition of $GEval_{ccr}(S_i)$ Axiom (10.34) would make it easy to prove $NI(GEval_{ccr}(L), A)$ valid for any assertion $A$ in the body of a **region** $r$ statement.

**10.37.** The interference-freedom obligations are simplified for programs that use conditional critical regions when the following restriction is imposed.

> Each variable that is read or written by two or more processes is associated with some region identifier $r$ and may only be read or written from within **region** $r$ statements.

(a)  How are the interference-freedom obligations simplified for primitive assertions?

(b)  How are the interference-freedom obligations simplified for arbitrary assertions?

**10.38.** Suggest fairness assumptions for $GEval_{ccr}(S_i)$.

**10.39.** One alternative to (10.41) is a sequence of three **region** statements.

$$\textbf{region } r \textbf{ when } B \to S_1 \textbf{ end}$$
$$\textbf{region } r \textbf{ when } B' \to S_2 \textbf{ end}$$
$$\textbf{region } r \textbf{ when } true \to S_3 \textbf{ end}$$

What added conditions must be discharged in order for this alternative to work?

# Chapter 11

# Message Passing and
# Distributed Programming

Absence of shared memory is the defining characteristic of a *distributed system*. Processes in such a system coordinate by reading and writing shared objects called communications channels. Thus, concurrent programs for distributed systems, or *distributed programs*, are fundamentally no different from other concurrent programs: all use shared objects of one sort or another for synchronization and communication.

However, the shared objects (communications channels) in a distributed system can be read and written only in restricted ways. These restrictions make designing distributed programs more difficult than designing shared-memory concurrent programs. Overcoming this difficulty is a subject of this chapter.

Two common forms of message passing are described: asynchronous message-passing, which is frequently supported by an operating system, and synchronous message-passing, which more often appears in concurrent programming notations. Other message-passing primitives are likely to be derivatives of these. We then turn to techniques for deriving programs that use message-passing. We illustrate the techniques by applying them to two classical distributed programming problems.

## 11.1 Asynchronous Message-Passing

With *asynchronous message-passing*, a send statement

(11.1)    **send** *expr* **on** *C*

is an unconditional atomic action. To execute (11.1), *expr* is evaluated and a message with that value is *sent* on channel *C*.

A receive statement

(11.2)   **receive** *m* **from** *C*

blocks until some message is eligible for receipt on channel *C*; an eligible message is then *received* by assigning it to *m*. The *eligible* messages on a channel are those that have been sent on the channel but not yet received.

Various guarantees are typically made about whether messages sent must become eligible and the order in which eligible messages may be received. These guarantees are usually associated with the channel.

- With a *reliable channel*, every message sent eventually becomes eligible for receipt.

- With an *unreliable channel*, some messages may never become eligible for receipt—the lost messages might be victims of hardware failures, noise bursts, or buffer overruns.

- With a *virtual circuit*, messages are received in the order sent.

- With a *datagram service*, no order is imposed on the receipt of messages.

## Axiomatization of Asynchronous Message-Passing

To axiomatize send statement (11.1) and receive statement (11.2), we translate them into atomic actions about which we already know how to reason. We concentrate here on reliable virtual circuits, since they are so popular.[1] A channel *C* that implements a reliable virtual circuit is modeled by an implicit shared variable *C* that contains the sequence of eligible messages in the order they have been sent. Initially, shared variable *C* equals $\varepsilon$.

(11.3)   *Virtual Circuit Initialization Axiom*:   For a program *S* with a reliable virtual circuit *C*:
$$Init_S \;\Rightarrow\; C = \varepsilon$$

Send statement (11.1) has the same effect as assignment statement[2]

(11.4)   $C := C \; expr$

and receive statement (11.2) is equivalent to atomic statement

(11.5)   $\langle \textbf{if } C \neq \varepsilon \rightarrow m, C := C[0], C[1..] \textbf{ fi} \rangle$ .

---

[1]See exercise 11.6 for an axiomatization of unreliable virtual circuits and exercise 11.7 for an axiomatization of an unreliable datagram service.

[2]Recall, expression *C expr* evaluates to the result of appending the value of *expr* to *C*.

Fairness assumptions for send and receive statements are inherited from their translations. Consequently, only fairness assumptions that are suitable for the translation may be associated with a send or receive statement. Unconditional Fairness (8.20), for example, is suitable for (11.4), so we are allowed to associate this fairness assumption with a send statement. Since either Strong Fairness (8.21) or Weak Fairness (8.22) could apply to (11.5), either of these could be associated with a receive statement.

Proof Outline Logic axioms for (11.1) and (11.2) are obtained by deriving theorems about their translations (11.4) and (11.5). The send statement axiom is an instance of Assignment Axiom (4.19); the receive statement axiom follows from $\langle S \rangle$ Rule (5.42), **if** Rule (4.22), $GEval_{if}(S)$ Axiom (4.21), and Assignment Axiom (4.19).

(11.6) *Reliable Virtual Circuit Send Axiom*: For a primitive assertion $P$:

$$\{P^C_{C\,expr}\} \ \textbf{send } expr \textbf{ on } C \ \ \{P\}$$

(11.7) *Reliable Virtual Circuit Receive Axiom*: For a primitive assertion $P$:

$$\{C \neq \varepsilon \Rightarrow P^{m,\,C}_{C[0],\,C[1..]}\} \ \ \textbf{receive } m \textbf{ from } C \ \ \{P\}$$

To illustrate the use of these axioms, consider the simple client/server system *CliServ* of Figure 11.1. Client *Client* truthifies $val = x * x$ by sending $x$ to server *Server*, which does the actual multiplication and sends back the product.

A first proof outline for *CliServ* uses the two axioms above in order to obtain valid proof outlines for *Client* and *Server* in isolation. Notice that *pre*(*CliServ*) asserts that $G$ and $H$ both equal $\varepsilon$, as per Virtual Circuit Initialization Axiom (11.3).

---

*CliServ*: **cobegin**
      *Client*: **send** $x$ **on** $G$
                **receive** $val$ **from** $H$
    ||
      *Server*: **receive** $v$ **from** $G$
              **send** $v * v$ **on** $H$
   **coend**

**Figure 11.1.** Client/server system

$\{G=\varepsilon \wedge H=\varepsilon\}$
*CliServ*: **cobegin**
$\qquad \{G=\varepsilon \wedge H=\varepsilon\}$
$\qquad$ *Client*: $C_1$: **send** $x$ **on** $G$ $\{H \neq \varepsilon \Rightarrow H[0]=x*x\}$
$\qquad \qquad \quad$ $C_2$: **receive** *val* **from** $H$
$\qquad \{val=x*x\}$
$\quad \parallel$
$\qquad \{G \neq \varepsilon \Rightarrow G[0]=x\}$
$\qquad$ *Server*: $S_1$: **receive** $v$ **from** $G$ $\{v=x\}$
$\qquad \qquad \quad$ $S_2$: **send** $v*v$ **on** $H$
$\qquad \{true\}$
$\qquad$ **coend**
$\{val=x*x\}$

Unfortunately, this proof outline for *CliServ* is not interference free. Send statement $S_2$ in *Server* falsifies conjunct $H=\varepsilon$ of $pre(C_1)$ in *Client*. But $S_2$ cannot be executed when $at(C_1)$ holds, so we use Strengthening (5.14) and add conjunct $\neg at(C_1)$ to $pre(S_2)$. Based on Reliable Virtual Circuit Receive Axiom (11.7), validity of $PO(Server)$ now requires that the consequent of $pre(S_1)$ be strengthened. Once this is done, the proof outline of Figure 11.2 results; it is interference free.

This example illustrates the two ways that information can be conveyed by a message. Messages transfer not only values from one process to another but also transfer predicates. The message sent (by $C_1$) from *Client* to *Server* transfers a value (the value of $x$ when $C_1$ was executed) as well as two predicates: (i) that $x$ equals the value in the message and (ii) control predicate $\neg at(C_1)$. In fact, values in a message generally have no meaning unless a predicate is transferred as well. The transferred predicate says how the message's

---

$\{G=\varepsilon \wedge H=\varepsilon\}$
*CliServ*: **cobegin**
$\qquad \{G=\varepsilon \wedge H=\varepsilon\}$
$\qquad$ *Client*: $C_1$: **send** $x$ **on** $G$ $\{H \neq \varepsilon \Rightarrow H[0]=x*x\}$
$\qquad \qquad \quad$ $C_2$: **receive** *val* **from** $H$
$\qquad \{val=x*x\}$
$\quad \parallel$
$\qquad \{G \neq \varepsilon \Rightarrow G[0]=x \wedge \neg at(C_1))\}$
$\qquad$ *Server*: $S_1$: **receive** $v$ **from** $G$ $\{v=x \wedge \neg at(C1)\}$
$\qquad \qquad \quad$ $S_2$: **send** $v*v$ **on** $H$
$\qquad \{true\}$
$\qquad$ **coend**
$\{val=x*x\}$

**Figure 11.2.** Client/server proof outline

value relates to the values of the sender's variables. Predicates are frequently transferred by messages. For example, a message whose value never varies—such as an acknowledgement message—almost certainly is being used to transfer a predicate.

A second thing to learn from Figure 11.2 concerns pre- and postconditions of receive statements. It might seem as if the postcondition of a receive should be obtained from the preconditions of the sends that name the same channel. That, however, is not how we constructed the pre- and postconditions for the receive statements in Figure 11.2. Instead, we conjectured a postcondition for the receive and then calculated a suitable precondition (by using Reliable Virtual Circuit Receive Axiom (11.7)). Interference-freedom proofs for send statements demonstrate that messages eligible for receipt justify the conjectured receive postconditions.

## Restrictions on Channels

It is not practical to implement a channel that is named by receive statements in more than one process. This is because executing a receive on such a channel could entail communicating with every process that might also receive from that channel. The communication would be necessary whether the implementation delivers a copy of each sent message to all potential receivers or to one:

- If a copy of each sent message is delivered to all potential receivers, then the receive statement's implementation requires communication so that other sites can know to delete their copies of a message that has been received.

- If a copy of a sent message is delivered to only one potential receiver, then the receive statement's implementation might have to communicate in order to locate a message eligible for receipt.

Communication with every process is unnecessary if all receive statements that name a given channel appear in the same process:

(11.8)   **Channel Destination Restriction.** For each channel $C$, only one process may contain receive statements that name $C$; any process may contain send statements that name $C$.                                                    □

For programs that satisfy Channel Destination Restriction (11.8), it is reasonable to postulate a predicate $msg(C)$ that can be a guard in **if** and **do** statements and that holds iff a message on channel $C$ is eligible for receipt. *Server* of Figure 11.3, which generalizes *Server* of Figure 11.2, uses such guards. Guards $msg(G_1)$ and $msg(G_2)$ of the **if** statement prevent *Server* in Figure 11.3 from being blocked awaiting a message on one channel when there is a message available on the other. There is simply no convenient way to program this functionality without such guards.

$$Server: \textbf{do} \ true \rightarrow \textbf{if} \ msg(G_1) \rightarrow \textbf{receive} \ v \ \textbf{from} \ G_1$$
$$\textbf{send} \ v*v \ \textbf{on} \ H$$
$$[] \ msg(G_2) \rightarrow \textbf{receive} \ v \ \textbf{from} \ G_2$$
$$\textbf{send} \ v+v \ \textbf{on} \ H$$
$$\textbf{fi}$$
$$\textbf{od}$$

**Figure 11.3.** Enhanced server

---

Channel Destination Restriction (11.8) ensures that $msg(C)$ cannot be falsified in assertions of the process containing receive statements that name $C$. This is because when send and receive statements are defined by translations (11.4) and (11.5), the meaning of $msg(C)$ is given by the translation:

$$msg(C): \ C \neq \varepsilon$$

Execution of send translation (11.4) truthifies but never falsifies $msg(C)$. Execution of receive translation (11.5) can falsify $msg(C)$, but Channel Destination Restriction (11.8) requires all receive statements that can falsify $msg(C)$ to be in a single process. And those receives, by definition, cannot interfere with the assertions in that process.

(11.9)  **Interference Freedom of $msg(C)$.** If channel $C$ satisfies Channel Destination Restriction (11.8), then no execution can falsify predicate $msg(C)$ in assertions of the process that contains receive statements for $C$.   □

## 11.2  Synchronous Message-Passing

With *synchronous message-passing*, a send statement

(11.10)  $S: \ C!expr$

which names a channel $C$, blocks until a matching receive statement

(11.11)  $R: \ C?m$

is ready for execution, where a send and a receive statement *match* iff they are in different processes and name the same channel. The *channel action* for send $S$ and receive $R$

$$\zeta_{S,R}: \ m := expr$$

is then executed.

Notice that unlike the translations given in §11.1 for asynchronous message-passing statements, each synchronous-send and synchronous-receive statement is not simply being replaced by another atomic action. Additional atomic actions—the channel actions—are involved in the translation.

We extend the syntax of the **cobegin** statement to account for these additional atomic actions. A **cobegin**$^+$ statement

$S$: **cobegin**$^+$

$\qquad S_1 \;\|\; S_2 \;\|\; \cdots \;\|\; S_n$

**coend**

is executed like an ordinary **cobegin** statement, but $\mathcal{A}(S)$ includes channel actions. Specifically, $\mathcal{A}(S)$ is defined to contain all channel actions for synchronous-send and receive statements appearing in $S_1$ through $S_n$ in addition to the atomic actions in $\mathcal{A}(S_1)$, $\mathcal{A}(S_2)$, ..., $\mathcal{A}(S_n)$.

With synchronous message-passing, a send statement blocks until the message it is sending is received. This semantics has a surprising consequence: it enables the transfer of information from receiver to sender. The proof outline of Figure 11.4 illustrates such an information transfer. The postconditions of send statements $S_1$ and $S_2$ hold when reached because a synchronous-send statement and its matching receive are executed simultaneously. Were asynchronous message-passing used instead, assertions $post(S_1)$ and $post(S_2)$ would have to be weaker (to account for messages that had been sent but not yet received).

We end with a comment about fairness assumptions for synchronous message-passing. Fairness assumptions are most sensible to programmers if formulated in terms of the programming notation rather than in terms of modeling artifacts, like channel actions. A fairness assumption for synchronous message-passing should be formalized in terms of send and receive statements. For

---

$\{x=14\}$
$T$: **cobegin**$^+$
$\qquad \{x=14\}$
$\qquad S$: $S_1$: $C\,!23$  $\{x=23\}$
$\qquad\qquad S_2$: $C\,!39$  $\{x=39\}$
$\|$
$\qquad \{true\}$
$\qquad R$: $R_1$: $C\,?x$  $\{true\}$
$\qquad\qquad R_2$: $C\,?x$  $\{true\}$
$\quad$ **coend**
$\{x=39\}$

**Figure 11.4.** Predicate transfer to sender

example, a fairness assumption that prevents discrimination against a receive $R$ with matching sends $S_1, S_2, ..., S_n$ is:

$$\Box\Diamond((\underset{1\leq i\leq n}{\lor} at(S_i)) \land at(R)) \;\Rightarrow\; \Box\Diamond after(R)$$

Notice that there is no mention of channel action $\zeta_{S,R}$, even though execution of $\zeta_{S,R}$ is what is really at issue.

## Reasoning About Synchronous Message-Passing Statements

We start by axiomatizing channel actions and then generalize the derivation of **cobegin** Rule (5.11) to obtain a rule for **cobegin**$^+$ statements.

A channel action $\zeta_{S,R}$ is executed only when both $S$ and $R$ are ready to execute. Thus, execution of $\zeta_{S,R}$ is concurrent with (a) all processes except the ones containing $S$ and $R$, and (b) channel actions for send and receive statements appearing in any process that does not contain $S$ or $R$.

(11.12) **Channel Action Independence.**

    (a)    For $\alpha$ a statement or atomic action of a different process from the one containing send statement $S$ or receive statement $R$: $\zeta_{S,R} \,\|\, \alpha$

    (b)    For $\alpha$ a channel action $\zeta_{S',R'}$ where the processes containing $S'$ and $R'$ are different from the processes containing $S$ and $R$: $\zeta_{S,R} \,\|\, \alpha$         $\Box$

Control predicate axioms for a channel action $\zeta_{S,R}$ stipulate that (a) $\zeta_{S,R}$ can be executed when $S$ and $R$ have been reached and (b) the control states of the processes containing $S$ and $R$ advance to states satisfying $after(S) \land after(R)$ when $\zeta_{S,R}$ terminates.

(11.13) *Channel Action Control Axioms*:   For send statement $S$ and matching receive statement $R$:

        (a)  $at(\zeta_{S,R}) = at(S) \land at(R)$

        (b)  $after(\zeta_{S,R}) = after(S) \land after(R)$

Assignment Axiom (4.19) forms the basis for the Proof Outline Logic axiom for a channel action:

(11.14) *Channel Action Axiom*:   For a channel action

$$\zeta_{S,R}\!: \; m := expr$$

and a primitive assertion $P$:

$$\{P^m_{expr}\} \; \zeta_{S,R} \; \{P\}$$

Processes of a **cobegin**$^+$ statement may mention synchronous-send and synchronous-receive statements. Proof Outline Logic theorems for such processes will be needed. To construct these proof outlines, we use axioms for synchronous-send and synchronous-receive statements. A synchronous-send or receive statement blocks when executed in isolation, since in isolation, no matching synchronous message-passing statement is being executed concurrently. In isolation, then, the postcondition of a synchronous-send or receive statement is never reached. A postcondition that is never reached can assert anything, and we have:

(11.15) *Synchronous Send Axiom*: $\{W\}$ *C!expr* $\{X\}$

(11.16) *Synchronous Receive Axiom*: $\{Y\}$ *C?m* $\{Z\}$

Similar reasoning led to the unconstrained pre- and postconditions in Blocked Atomic Action Rule (5.43).

The control predicate axioms for a **cobegin**$^+$ statement are the same as those for an ordinary **cobegin** statement: **cobegin** Control Axioms (5.2).

We next investigate conditions to ensure that proof outline

(11.17) $\{P\}$
$\quad$ $T$: **cobegin**$^+$
$\quad\quad\quad$ $PO(S_1)$ $\|$ $\cdots$ $\|$ $PO(S_n)$
$\quad\quad$ **coend**
$\quad$ $\{Q\}$

is valid. These conditions will become premises for a sound Proof Outline Logic inference rule that has (11.17) as its conclusion. The same approach is used in §5.3 for developing **cobegin** Rule (5.11).

According to Valid Proof Outline (4.17), validity of (11.17) requires that it be self-consistent and that $I_{PO(T)}$ be an invariant. Proof Outline (11.17) is self-consistent iff $at(T) \wedge P \Rightarrow I_{PO(T)}$ is $\mathcal{H}_T^+$-valid. Since **cobegin** Control Axiom (5.2a) for $at(T)$ is also sound for a **cobegin**$^+$ statement, self-consistency of (11.17) is equivalent to:

$$at(S_1) \wedge \cdots \wedge at(S_n) \wedge P \Rightarrow I_{PO(T)}$$

Therefore, **cobegin** Self-Consistency Condition (5.10)

$$pre(T) \Rightarrow pre(PO(S_1)) \wedge \cdots \wedge pre(PO(S_n))$$

ensures self-consistency of (11.17).

We next turn to conditions for ensuring that $I_{PO(T)}$ is an invariant. Consider an atomic action $\alpha$ in $\mathcal{A}(T)$, for $T$ defined in (11.17). According to definition (4.14), $I_{PO(T)}$ is:

(11.18) $I_{PO(S_1)} \land \cdots \land I_{PO(S_n)} \land (at(T) \Rightarrow pre(T)) \land (after(T) \Rightarrow post(T))$

Thus, it suffices to find conditions that ensure that $\alpha$ does not falsify each of the conjuncts of (11.18). That obligation can be partitioned into the following cases, based on the conjunct of (11.18) and the source of atomic action $\alpha$.

  (i)   $I_{PO(S_i)}$ and $\alpha \in \mathcal{A}(S_i)$

  (ii)  $I_{PO(S_i)}$, $\alpha \in \mathcal{A}(S_j)$, and $S_i$ is distinct from $S_j$

  (iii) $I_{PO(S_i)}$, $\alpha$ is a channel action $\zeta_{S,R}$, and $\zeta_{S,R} \parallel S_i$ does not hold.

  (iv) $I_{PO(S_i)}$, $\alpha$ is a channel action $\zeta_{S,R}$, and $\zeta_{S,R} \parallel S_i$ holds.

  (v)  $at(T) \Rightarrow pre(T)$

  (vi) $after(T) \Rightarrow post(T)$

For case (i), any condition that implies that $PO(S_i)$ is valid suffices, since the invariance requirement of Valid Proof Outline (4.17) for $PO(S_i)$ is exactly what we seek. In particular, Sequential Correctness Condition (5.5), that $PO(S_1)$, ..., $PO(S_n)$ are theorems, is sufficient.

Case (ii) concerns finding a condition to ensure that execution of an atomic action $\alpha$ from one process does not falsify the proof outline invariant $I_{PO(S_j)}$ for another. That, however, is implied by what Interference Freedom Condition (5.8) establishes, because $\mathcal{A}(S_j) \subseteq \mathcal{A}(T)$ holds.

For case (iii), consider a channel action $\zeta_{S,R}$. Execution of $\zeta_{S,R}$ necessarily starts in a state satisfying $at(S) \land at(R)$ and terminates in a state satisfying $after(S) \land after(R)$. Thus, if $I_{PO(T)}$ holds and $\zeta_{S,R}$ is executed, then $\zeta_{S,R}$ must have executed in a state satisfying $pre(S) \land pre(R)$. We would ensure that $I_{PO(S_i)}$ is not falsified by $\zeta_{S,R}$ if we could guarantee that $post(S) \land post(R)$ holds when $\zeta_{S,R}$ terminates or, equivalently, that the following Proof Outline Logic formula is a theorem:

$$CAC(\zeta_{S,R}): \quad \{pre(S) \land pre(R)\} \; \zeta_{S,R} \; \{post(S) \land post(R)\}$$

Thus, what follows guarantees that both $post(S)$ and $post(R)$ hold when $\zeta_{S,R}$ terminates, for any channel action $\zeta_{S,R}$.

(11.19) **Channel Action Condition.** For all channel actions $\zeta_{S,R}$: $CAC(\zeta_{S,R})$. $\square$

Notice that $CAC(\zeta_{S,R})$ is trivially valid when its precondition is equivalent to *false*. This would be the case if $at(S)$ cannot hold at the same time that $at(R)$ does. It should not be surprising that $CAC(\zeta_{S,R})$ is trivially valid if $S$ and $R$ never are executed together.

Case (iv) requires proving that execution of $\zeta_{S,R}$ does not falsify any assertion $A$ in proof outline $PO(S_i)$, where neither $S$ nor $R$ is a statement of $S_i$. This can be formalized using interference freedom triples $NI(\zeta_{S,R}, A)$ provided that we have defined $pre^*(\zeta_{S,R})$, since definition (5.7) of $NI(\alpha, A)$ is written in terms of $pre^*(\alpha)$. Recall that predicate $pre^*(\alpha)$ is satisfied just before $\alpha$ is executed. So, we have:

(11.20) **Precondition of Channel Action.** For $\zeta_{S,R}$ a channel action:

$$pre^*(\zeta_{S,R})\text{:}\quad pre(S) \wedge pre(R) \qquad\qquad \square$$

Because $\zeta_{S,R} \in \mathcal{A}(T)$ holds, Interference Freedom Condition (5.8) handles case (iv) too.

Case (v), that $\alpha$ does not falsify conjunct $at(T) \Rightarrow pre(T)$, is trivially satisfied for any $\alpha$ in $\mathcal{A}(T)$, because $at(T)$ is falsified by every atomic action in $\mathcal{A}(T)$.

Finally, case (vi) is also trivial except when execution of $\alpha$ truthifies $after(S_1) \wedge \cdots \wedge after(S_n)$. From cases (i) through (iv), we conclude that $post(S_i) \wedge \cdots \wedge post(S_n)$ holds when $\alpha$ terminates. Thus, if Postcondition Condition (5.9)

$$post(PO(S_1)) \wedge \cdots \wedge post(PO(S_n)) \;\Rightarrow\; post(T)$$

is discharged, $post(S)$ will hold as required.

We have argued that five conditions—Sequential Correctness Condition (5.5), Interference Freedom Condition (5.8), Channel Action Condition (11.19), and Postcondition Condition (5.9)—ensure that $I_{PO(T)}$ is an invariant. In addition, **cobegin** Self-Consistency Condition (5.10) ensures that (11.17) is self-consistent. By combining these, we ensure that (11.17) is valid and therefore get a Proof Outline Logic rule for **cobegin$^+$**:

(11.21) **cobegin$^+$ Rule:**

$$\frac{\begin{array}{l}\text{(a) } PO(S_1),\ ...,\ PO(S_n), \\ \text{(b) } CAC(\zeta_{S,R}) \text{ for all channel actions } \zeta_{S,R}, \\ \text{(c) } PO(S_1),\ ...,\ PO(S_n) \text{ are interference free,} \\ \text{(d) } P \Rightarrow pre(PO(S_1)) \wedge \cdots \wedge pre(PO(S_n)), \\ \text{(e) } post(PO(S_1)) \wedge \cdots \wedge post(PO(S_n)) \Rightarrow Q.\end{array}}{\{P\}\ \textbf{cobegin}^+\ PO(S_1)\ \|\ \cdots\ \|\ PO(S_n)\ \textbf{coend}\ \{Q\}}$$

## Examples

As a simple illustration for **cobegin$^+$** Rule (11.21), we derive proof outline $PO(T)$ of Figure 11.4. For premise (a), we prove $PO(S)$ and $PO(R)$ in isolation. $PO(S)$ results from using Statement Juxtaposition Rule (4.20) to combine two uses of Synchronous Send Axiom (11.15); $PO(R)$ results from using Statement Juxtaposition Rule (4.20) to combine two uses of Synchronous Receive Axiom (11.16).

Premise (b) requires proving four triples:

$$CAC(\zeta_{S_1,R_1}): \quad \{x=14 \wedge true\} \ \zeta_{S_1,R_1} \ \{x=23 \wedge true\}$$
$$CAC(\zeta_{S_1,R_2}): \quad \{x=14 \wedge true\} \ \zeta_{S_1,R_2} \ \{x=23 \wedge true\}$$
$$CAC(\zeta_{S_2,R_1}): \quad \{x=23 \wedge true\} \ \zeta_{S_2,R_1} \ \{x=39 \wedge true\}$$
$$CAC(\zeta_{S_2,R_2}): \quad \{x=23 \wedge true\} \ \zeta_{S_2,R_2} \ \{x=39 \wedge true\}$$

All are theorems. Here, for example, is the proof of $CAC(\zeta_{S_1,R_1})$; the others are proved similarly.

«Channel Action Axiom (11.14)»
1.  $\{23=23 \wedge true\} \ \zeta_{S_1,R_1} \ \{x=23 \wedge true\}$

«Predicate Logic»
2.  $(x=14 \wedge true) \Rightarrow (23=23 \wedge true)$

«Rule of Consequence (4.25) with 1 and 2»
3.  $\{x=14 \wedge true\} \ \zeta_{S_1,R_1} \ \{x=23 \wedge true\}$

Premise (c), that $PO(S)$ and $PO(R)$ are interference free, holds vacuously. $\mathcal{A}(T)$ contains only channel actions. Because each such channel action $\zeta_{X,Y}$ involves a send statement from process $S$ and a receive statement from process $R$, neither $\zeta_{X,Y} \| S$ nor $\zeta_{X,Y} \| R$ holds, so there are no interference-freedom triples to prove.

Premises (d) and (e) follow trivially. So, the proof outline of Figure 11.4 follows from **cobegin$^+$** Rule (11.21).

A more substantial example is given in Figure 11.5. This program swaps elements between nonempty sets $Bx$ and $Bn$ until no element in $Bn$ is larger than any element in $Bx$. Proof outlines $PO(N)$ and $PO(X)$ are straightforward to prove in isolation, so this discharges premise (a) of **cobegin$^+$** Rule (11.21).

To discharge premise (b), eight triples must be checked: $CAC(\zeta_{S1_N,R1_X})$, $CAC(\zeta_{S1_N,R2_X})$, $CAC(\zeta_{S2_N,R1_X})$, $CAC(\zeta_{S2_N,R2_X})$, $CAC(\zeta_{S1_X,R1_N})$, $CAC(\zeta_{S1_X,R2_N})$, $CAC(\zeta_{S2_X,R1_N})$, and $CAC(\zeta_{S2_X,R2_N})$. Expanding these, we get the following; all are easily proved using Channel Action Axiom (11.14).

(11.22) $\{I \ \wedge \ mx=\max(Bn) \ \wedge \ I \ \wedge \ mn=\min(Bx)\}$
$\zeta_{S1_N,R1_X}: vx := mx$
$\{I \ \wedge \ vx=mx=\max(Bn) \ \wedge \ I \ \wedge \ mn=\min(Bn) \ \wedge \ vx \geq \max(Bn)\}$

(11.23) $\{I \ \wedge \ mx=\max(Bn)$
$\wedge \ I \ \wedge \ B=Bn \cup Bx \cup \{vn,vx\} \ \wedge \ vx \in Bx \ \wedge \ mn=\min(Bx)\}$
$\zeta_{S1_N,R2_X}: vx := mx$
$\{I \ \wedge \ vx=mx=\max(Bn)$
$\wedge \ I \ \wedge \ B=Bn \cup Bx \cup \{vn,vx\} \ \wedge \ mn=\min(Bx) \ \wedge \ vx \geq \max(Bn)\}$

$\{I: \; B=Bn \cup Bx \;\; \wedge \;\; Bn \neq \varnothing \;\; \wedge Bx \neq \varnothing \}$
**cobegin**
   $N: \; \{I\}$
       $mx := \max(Bn) \quad \{I \;\; \wedge \;\; mx = \max(Bn)\}$
       $S1_N: \; Cx!mx \quad \{I \;\; \wedge \;\; vx = mx = \max(Bn)\}$
       $R1_N: \; Cn?vn$
       $\{LI_N: \; I \;\; \wedge \;\; B=Bn \cup Bx \cup \{vn, vx\} \;\; \wedge \;\; vx = mx = \max(Bn)$
               $\wedge \;\; vn \leq \min(Bx)\}$
       **do** $vn < \max(Bn) \rightarrow \{LI_N \;\; \wedge \;\; vn < \max(Bn)\}$
                       $\alpha_N: \; Bn := (Bn - \{mx\}) \cup \{vn\}$
                       $\{I \;\; \wedge \;\; B=Bn \cup Bx \cup \{vn, vx\} \;\; \wedge \;\; vn \in Bn\}$
                       $mx := \max(Bn)$
                       $\{I \;\; \wedge \;\; B=Bn \cup Bx \cup \{vn, vx\} \;\; \wedge \;\; vn \in Bn$
                        $\wedge \;\; mx = \max(Bn)\}$
                       $S2_N: \; Cx!mx$
                       $\{I \;\; \wedge \;\; B=Bn \cup Bx \cup \{vn, vx\} \;\; \wedge \;\; vn \in Bn$
                        $\wedge \;\; vx = mx = \max(Bn)\}$
                       $R2_N: \; Cn?vn \quad \{LI_N\}$
       **od** $\{vn \geq \max(Bn) \;\; \wedge \;\; LI_N\}$
$\|$
   $X: \; \{I\}$
       $mn := \min(Bx) \quad \{I \;\; \wedge \;\; mn = \min(Bx)\}$
       $R1_X: \; Cx?vx$
       $\{I \;\; \wedge \;\; mn = \min(Bn) \;\; \wedge \;\; vx \geq \max(Bn)\}$
       $S1_X: \; Cn!mn$
       $\{LI_X: \; I \;\; \wedge \;\; B=Bn \cup Bx \cup \{vn, vx\} \;\; \wedge \;\; vn = mn = \min(Bx)$
                $\wedge \;\; vx \geq \max(Bn)\}$
       **do** $vx > \min(Bx) \rightarrow \{LI_X \;\; \wedge \;\; vx > \min(Bx)\}$
                       $\alpha_X: \; Bx := (Bx - \{mn\}) \cup \{vx\}$
                       $\{I \;\; \wedge \;\; B=Bn \cup Bx \cup \{vn, vx\} \;\; \wedge \;\; vx \in Bx\}$
                       $mn := \min(Bx)$
                       $\{I \;\; \wedge \;\; B=Bn \cup Bx \cup \{vn, vx\} \;\; \wedge \;\; vx \in Bx$
                        $\wedge \;\; mn = \min(Bx)\}$
                       $R2_X: \; Cx?vx$
                       $\{I \;\; \wedge \;\; B=Bn \cup Bx \cup \{vn, vx\} \;\; \wedge \;\; mn = \min(Bx)$
                        $\wedge \;\; vx \geq \max(Bn)\}$
                       $S2_X: \; Cn!mn \quad \{LI_X\}$
       **od** $\{vx \leq \min(Bx) \;\; \wedge \;\; LI_X\}$
**coend** $\{\max(Bn) \leq \min(Bx) \;\; \wedge \;\; B=Bn \cup Bx\}$

**Figure 11.5.** Sort the sets

(11.24) $\{I \;\wedge\; B=Bn \cup Bx \cup \{vn, vx\} \;\wedge\; vn \in Bn \;\wedge\; mx=\max(Bn)$
$\qquad \wedge\; I \;\wedge\; mn=\min(Bx)\}$
$\zeta_{S2_N,R1_X}: \; vx := mx$
$\{I \;\wedge\; B=Bn \cup Bx \cup \{vn, vx\} \;\wedge\; vn \in Bn \;\wedge\; vx=mx=\max(Bn)$
$\qquad \wedge\; I \;\wedge\; mn=\min(Bn) \;\wedge\; vx \geq \max(Bn)\}$

(11.25) $\{I \;\wedge\; B=Bn \cup Bx \cup \{vn, vx\} \;\wedge\; vn \in Bn \;\wedge\; mx=\max(Bn)$
$\qquad \wedge\; I \;\wedge\; B=Bn \cup Bx \cup \{vn. vx\} \;\wedge\; vx \in Bx \;\wedge\; mn=\min(Bx)\}$
$\zeta_{S2_N,R2_X}: \; vx := mx$
$\{I \;\wedge\; B=Bn \cup Bx \cup \{vn, vx\} \;\wedge\; vn \in Bn \;\wedge\; vx=mx=\max(Bn)$
$\qquad \wedge\; I \;\wedge\; B=Bn \cup Bx \cup \{vn, vx\} \;\wedge\; mn=\min(Bx) \;\wedge\; vx \geq \max(Bn)\}$

(11.26) $\{I \;\wedge\; mn=\min(Bn) \;\wedge\; vx \geq \max(Bn) \;\wedge\; I \;\wedge\; vx=mx=\max(Bn)\}$
$\zeta_{S1_X,R1_N}: \; vn := mn$
$\{LI_X \;\wedge\; LI_N\}$

(11.27) $\{I \;\wedge\; mn=\min(Bn) \;\wedge\; vx \geq \max(Bn)$
$\qquad \wedge\; I \;\wedge\; B=Bn \cup Bx \cup \{vn, vx\} \;\wedge\; vn \in Bn \;\wedge\; vx=mx=\max(Bn)\}$
$\zeta_{S1_X,R2_N}: \; vn := mn$
$\{LI_X \;\wedge\; LI_N\}$

(11.28) $\{I \;\wedge\; B=Bn \cup Bx \cup \{vn, vx\} \;\wedge\; mn=\min(Bx) \;\wedge\; vx \geq \max(Bn)$
$\qquad \wedge\; I \;\wedge\; vx=mx=\max(Bn)\}$
$\zeta_{S2_X,R1_N}: \; vn := mn$
$\{LI_X \;\wedge\; LI_N\}$

(11.29) $\{I \;\wedge\; B=Bn \cup Bx \cup \{vn, vx\} \;\wedge\; mn=\min(Bx) \;\wedge\; vx \geq \max(Bn)$
$\qquad \wedge\; I \;\wedge\; B=Bn \cup Bx \cup \{vn, vx\} \;\wedge\; vn \in Bn \;\wedge\; vx=mx=\max(Bn)\}$
$\zeta_{S2_X,R2_N}: \; vn := mn$
$\{LI_X \;\wedge\; LI_N\}$

Note that (11.23), (11.24), (11.27), and (11.28) concern channel actions that are never actually executed by this program. Nevertheless, these triples must be proved as part of premise (b). We happily embrace this (somewhat tedious) task, because it saves us from the significantly harder job of understanding enough about program execution to identify matching sends and receives that actually are executed together.

Next, we discharge premise (c), Interference Freedom Condition (5.8). No interference triples need to be checked for the channel actions, because each channel action involves send and receive statements from process $N$ and process $X$, and every assertion is part of the proof outline for one of these processes. Of the remaining atomic actions, only assignment statements $\alpha_N$ and $\alpha_X$ are of concern; Disjointness NI Rule (5.18) applies to all others. We must prove that $\alpha_X$ does not falsify $vn \leq \min(Bx)$ and that $\alpha_N$ does not falsify $vx \geq \max(Bn)$. That $\alpha_X$ does not falsify $vn \leq \min(Bx)$ follows because $LI_X$ in $pre(\alpha_X)$ implies $mn=\min(Bx)$, so removing $mn$ from $Bx$ can cause $\min(Bx)$ only to increase.

Moreover, $pre(\alpha_X)$ implies $vx > \min(Bx)$, so adding $vx$ to $Bx - \{mn\}$ cannot cause $\min(Bx)$ to decrease. Interference freedom for $\alpha_N$ is similar.

Premises (d) and (e) are straightforward theorems of Predicate Logic. And that discharges the obligations for using **cobegin**$^+$ Rule (11.21) to infer the proof outline in Figure 11.5.

## Guarded Channel Actions

Concurrent programming notations that support synchronous message-passing often allow receive statements to appear along with the boolean expressions in guards of **if** and **do** statements. We call such guards *receive guards*. A guarded command with a receive guard is executed only if the boolean expression evaluates to *true* and the receive statement in the guard would not block. The server of Figure 11.6, for example, uses receive guards to implement semaphore **P** and **V** statements. A client executes $P!yyy$ (where $yyy$ may be anything) in order to perform $\mathbf{P}(sem)$ and executes $V!yyy$ in order to perform $\mathbf{V}(sem)$.

In what follows, it will be convenient to label guards. Evaluation of receive guard $R$ in a guarded command

(11.30)  $R$:  $B$; $C?m \rightarrow ...$

produces one of three possible outcomes. The guard *fails* if boolean expression $B$ evaluates to *false*; the guard *blocks* if $B$ evaluates to *true* but executing $C?m$ would block because a matching send is not being attempted by another process; and the guard *succeeds* if $B$ evaluates to *true* and $C?m$ would not block. (A guard without a receive statement fails if the boolean expression evaluates to *false* and succeeds if the boolean expression evaluates to *true*.)

With receive guards, an **if** blocks until evaluating one or more of its guards succeeds. Then, a guard that succeeds is selected nondeterministically, the receive statement (if any) is executed, and control is transferred to the statement being guarded. A **do** with receive guards terminates when all of its guards fail. Otherwise, the **do** blocks until evaluating one of the guards succeeds, nondeterministically selects a guard that succeeds, executes the receive statement (if any) in the guard, and transfers control to the statement being guarded.

We reason about **if** and **do** statements that have receive guards much as for **if** and **do** statements without receive guards, but using generalized axioms for the guard evaluation actions. The axiom for the guard evaluation action $GEval_{if}(T)$ of an **if** statement $T$ with receive guards is:

---

> **do** $sem > 0$; $P?xxx \rightarrow sem := sem - 1$
> [] $V?xxx \qquad\quad \rightarrow sem := sem + 1$
> **od**

**Figure 11.6.** Semaphore from synchronous message-passing

(11.31) *GEval $_{if}$(T) Axiom*:  For an **if** statement

$$
\begin{aligned}
T: \ &\textbf{if} \ \ B_1; C_1?m_1 \to T_1 \\
&[] \qquad \cdots \\
&[] \quad B_n; C_2?m_n \to T_n \\
&[] \quad B_1' \to T_1' \\
&[] \qquad \cdots \\
&[] \quad B_n' \to T_n' \\
&\textbf{fi}
\end{aligned}
$$

and a primitive assertion *P*:

$$
\begin{aligned}
\{P\} \ GEval_{if}(T) \ \{P \land (at(T_1) \Rightarrow Q_1) \land \ \cdots \ \land (at(S_n) \Rightarrow Q_n) \\
\land (at(T_1') \Rightarrow B_1') \land \ \cdots \ \land (at(T_n') \Rightarrow B_n')\}
\end{aligned}
$$

The postcondition given by *GEval $_{if}$(T)* Axiom (11.31) allows anything (i.e., $Q_1$, ..., $Q_n$) to be asserted following a receive guard. This is sound because receive guards necessarily fail or block when *GEval $_{if}$(T)* is executed in isolation, so the assertion following a receive guard could not be reached. Note that when there are no receive guards, *GEval $_{if}$(T)* Axiom (11.31) simplifies to *GEval $_{if}$(S)* Axiom (4.21).

The axiom for the guard evaluation action *GEval $_{do}$(T)* of a **do** statement *T* with receive guards is:

(11.32) *GEval $_{do}$(T) Axiom*:  For a **do** statement

$$
\begin{aligned}
T: \ &\textbf{do} \ \ B_1; C_1?m_1 \to T_1 \\
&[] \qquad \cdots \\
&[] \quad B_n; C_2?m_n \to T_n \\
&[] \quad B_1' \to T_1' \\
&[] \qquad \cdots \\
&[] \quad B_n' \to T_n' \\
&\textbf{od}
\end{aligned}
$$

and a primitive assertion *P*:

$$
\begin{aligned}
\{P\} \ GEval_{do}(T) \ \{P \land (at(T_1) \Rightarrow Q_1) \land \ \cdots \ \land (at(T_n) \Rightarrow Q_n) \\
\land (at(T_1') \Rightarrow B_1') \land \ \cdots \ \land (at(T_n') \Rightarrow B_n') \\
\land (after(T) \Rightarrow (\neg B_1 \land \ \cdots \ \land \neg B_n \\
\land \neg B_1' \land \ \cdots \ \land \neg B_n'))\}
\end{aligned}
$$

Here, too, anything can be asserted following a receive guard. When there are no receive guards, *GEval $_{do}$(T)* Axiom (11.32) is equivalent to *GEval $_{do}$(S)* Axiom (4.23).

A form of channel action is used to model the transfer of values to a receive guard from a matching send statement. To model execution of a receive guard *R* (11.30) and matching send statement *S* (11.10), we use the *conditional channel action*[3]:

$$\xi_{S,R}: \quad \langle \textbf{if } B \rightarrow m := expr \textbf{ fi} \rangle$$

The Proof Outline Logic axiom for $\xi_{S,R}$ is obtained by regarding $\xi_{S,R}$ as a program statement and using the axioms and inference rules of Proof Outline Logic.

(11.33) *Conditional Channel Action Axiom*: For a conditional channel action

$$\xi_{S,R}: \quad \langle \textbf{if } B \rightarrow m := expr \textbf{ fi} \rangle$$

and a primitive assertion $P$:

$$\{B \Rightarrow P^m_{expr}\} \; \xi_{S,R} \; \{P\}$$

Like an (ordinary) channel action, a conditional channel action $\xi_{S,R}$ is concurrent with (a) all processes except the ones containing $S$ and $R$ and (b) all channel actions and conditional channel actions for send and receive statements in different processes from $S$ and $R$.

(11.34) **Conditional Channel Action Independence.**

    (a)    For $\alpha$ a statement or atomic action in a different process from the one containing send statement $S$ or receive guard $R$: $\xi_{S,R} \| \alpha$

    (b)    For $\alpha$ a channel action $\zeta_{S',R'}$ or conditional channel action $\xi_{S',R'}$ in a process distinct from those containing send statement $S$ and receive statement $R$: $\xi_{S,R} \| \alpha$       □

Control predicate axioms for a conditional channel action $\xi_{S,R}$ stipulate that (a) $\xi_{S,R}$ is executed when $S$ and the guard evaluation action containing $R$ have been reached and (b) the control states of the processes containing $S$ and $R$ advance when $\xi_{S,R}$ terminates.

(11.35) *Receive-Guard Channel Action Control Axioms*: For a synchronous-send statement $S$ and matching receive guard:

$$R: B\;; C?m \rightarrow U: \; \ldots$$

If $R$ is in an **if** statement labeled $L$:

    (a)    $at(\xi_{S,R}) = at(S) \wedge at(GEval_{if}(L))$

    (b)    $after(\xi_{S,R}) = after(S) \wedge at(U)$

If $R$ is in a **do** statement labeled $L$:

    (a)    $at(\xi_{S,R}) = at(S) \wedge at(GEval_{do}(L))$

    (b)    $after(\xi_{S,R}) = after(S) \wedge at(U)$

---

[3]Conditional channel actions are slightly more complicated than ordinary channel actions, and the notation $\xi_{S,R}$ for a conditional atomic action was selected because it looks slightly more complicated than the notation $\zeta_{S,R}$ for an ordinary channel action.

Analogous to Channel Action Condition (11.19), the following obligations ensure that when the receive in a receive guard can be executed, it truthifies the postcondition being asserted.

(11.36) **Conditional Channel Action Condition.** For each conditional channel action $\xi_{S,R}$ derived from the guarded command

$$R:\ B;\ C?m \to U:\ ...$$

(a)   For receive guard $R$ appearing in an **if** statement labeled $L$, prove:

$$CAC(\xi_{S,R}):\ \{pre(S) \wedge pre(GEval_{if}(L))\}$$
$$\xi_{S,R}$$
$$\{post(S) \wedge pre(U)\}$$

(b)   For receive guard $R$ appearing in a **do** statement labeled $L$, prove:

$$CAC(\xi_{S,R}):\ \{pre(S) \wedge pre^*(GEval_{do}(L))\}$$
$$\xi_{S,R}$$
$$\{post(S) \wedge pre(U)\}\qquad\square$$

Finally, Interference Freedom Condition (5.8) may require proving $NI(\alpha, A)$ when $\alpha$ is a conditional channel action. This means that $pre^*(\alpha)$ must be defined:

(11.37) **Precondition of Conditional Channel Action.** For a conditional channel action $\xi_{S,R}$ :

(a)   For $\xi_{S,R}$ derived from a receive guard in an **if** statement labeled $L$:

$$pre^*(\xi_{S,R}):\ pre(S) \wedge pre(GEval_{if}(L))$$

(b)   For $\xi_{S,R}$ derived from a receive guard in a **do** statement labeled $L$:

$$pre^*(\xi_{S,R}):\ pre(S) \wedge pre^*(GEval_{do}(L))\qquad\square$$

## Examples

As an illustration, a proof outline for a program having receive guards is given in Figure 11.7. The program incorporates the semaphore server of Figure 11.6, and as a result, the $CS_i$ are mutually exclusive (assuming the $CS_i$ and $NCS_i$ do not assign to *sem* or communicate with *SemSrvr*). Derived term *Adj* mentioned in $I$ is defined by:

$$Adj:\ \begin{cases} -1 & \text{if } at(Sinc) \\ +1 & \text{if } at(Sdec) \\ 0 & \text{if } \neg at(Sinc) \wedge \neg at(Sdec) \end{cases}$$

Premise (a) of **cobegin$^+$** Rule (11.21) requires constructing proof outlines for *SemSrvr* and $S_i$ in isolation. Both $PO(SemSrvr)$ and $PO(S_i)$ are straightforward to prove.

$\{true\}$
$sem := 1$   $\{I:\ sem + Adj \geq 0$
$\qquad\qquad\qquad \land\ \ sem + Adj = 1 - (\Sigma j:\ in(CS_j) \lor after(CS_j):\ 1)\}$
$T:$ **cobegin**$^+$
$\quad$ $SemSrvr$: $\{I\}$
$\qquad\qquad$ **do** $R_P$: $sem > 0;\ P?xxx\ \to\ \{I\}\ Sinc:\ sem := sem - 1\ \{I\}$
$\qquad\qquad$ $[]\ R_V$: $V?xxx\qquad\qquad \to\ \{I\}\ Sdec:\ sem := sem + 1\ \{I\}$
$\qquad\qquad$ **od** $\{I\}$

$\quad \|\ S_i$: $\{I\}$
$\quad\ _i\qquad$ **do** $true \to \{I\}$
$\qquad\qquad\qquad\quad entry_i$: $P!97\ \{I\}$
$\qquad\qquad\qquad\quad PO(CS_i)\otimes I$
$\qquad\qquad\qquad\quad \{I\}$
$\qquad\qquad\qquad\quad exit_i$: $V!22\ \{I\}$
$\qquad\qquad\qquad\quad PO(NCS_i)\otimes I$
$\qquad\qquad\qquad\quad \{I\}$
$\qquad\quad$ **od** $\{I\}$
$\quad$ **coend** $\{true\}$

**Figure 11.7.** Mutual exclusion with synchronous message-passing

---

In order to discharge premise (b), we must prove:

$$CAC(\xi_{entry_i,R_P}):\ \ \{I \land I\}\ \xi_{entry_i,R_P}\ \{I \land I\}$$

$$CAC(\xi_{exit_i,R_V}):\ \ \{I \land I\}\ \xi_{exit_i,R_V}\ \{I \land I\}$$

Each is straightforward, given Conditional Channel Action Axiom (11.33).

We discharge premise (c)—Interference Freedom Condition (5.8)—by checking atomic actions in $\mathcal{A}(T)$. For conditional channel actions, $\xi_{entry_i,R_P}$ and $\xi_{exit_i,R_V}$, Conditional Channel Action Axiom (11.33) is used in proving $NI(\alpha, I)$. For the other atomic actions, $I$ appears as both a pre- and postcondition, so $NI(\alpha, I)$ holds, and we conclude that these atomic actions do not falsify any assertion.

Finally, premises (d) and (e) are trivial.

## Implementation of Synchronous Message-Passing

The difficult part in implementing synchronous message-passing is determining whether some matching pair of send and receive statements is ready to be executed. We use the program of Figure 11.8 to illustrate why. One difficulty arises from the independence of channel names and process names. To find a statement that is ready to be executed and matches a given send or receive, every process might have to be checked, since the channel name gives no indication of what processes might contain a matching statement. Receive guards lead to a second difficulty. A process executing a guard evaluation action with receive guards could be ready to execute any from a set of receives. But once a receive has been selected and executed, that process is no longer ready to execute any of the other receives.

One simple implementation of synchronous message-passing uses asynchronous message-passing along with an additional process, *matchmaker*, that serves as a clearinghouse. In order to execute a synchronous message-passing statement $T$, asynchronous message-passing is used to send a request message to *matchmaker* and await its reply. The reply contains a channel name and the name of a process that is ready to execute a synchronous message-passing statement that matches $T$.

The request message sent to *matchmaker* contains the name of the sender and describes the synchronous message-passing statement(s) that the sender is ready to execute, be it (i) a send, (ii) a receive, or (iii) a set of receives (arising from guard evaluation for an **if** or **do**). Two request messages $m$ and $m'$ are said to *intersect* if they come from different processes and a send described in one message matches a receive described in the other.

To process request messages, *matchmaker* maintains a subset *pending* of the request messages it has received, such that:

> *MInv*: Set *pending* contains the request messages for which no reply has been sent, and no two elements of *pending* intersect.

Initially, *pending* is empty. When *matchmaker* receives a request message $m$, *MInv* is truthified either by (i) adding $m$ to *pending* or by (ii) removing from *pending* a message $m'$ that intersects $m$ and then sending replies for $m$ and $m'$.

Details for *matchmaker* are sketched in Figure 11.9. Channel $MM$ is used to send request messages to *matchmaker*. A channel named $P_i$ is associated with each process $P_i$ that sends requests to *matchmaker* and is used by *matchmaker* to send replies to the process $src(msg)$ that originally sent request message $msg$. A

---

$$\textbf{cobegin}^+$$
$$T_1: \textbf{if } C1?v \rightarrow C2?w$$
$$[] \ C2?v \rightarrow C1?w$$
$$\textbf{fi}$$

$$\|$$
$$T_2: C1!23$$
$$\|$$
$$T_3: C2!45$$
$$\textbf{coend}$$

**Figure 11.8.** Troublesome to implement

$pending := \varnothing$  $\{MInv\}$
**do** $true \rightarrow$ $\{MInv\}$
           **receive** $m$ **from** $MM$
           **if** $\neg\,(\exists m' \in pending\colon\ m'$ intersects $m) \rightarrow$
                                  $pending := pending \cup \{m\}$  $\{MInv\}$
           [] $(\exists m' \in pending\colon\ m'$ intersects $m) \rightarrow$
                                Choose $m'\colon\ m' \in pending \wedge m'$ intersects $m$
                                $pending := pending - \{m'\}$
                                **send** $m$ **on** $src(m')$
                                **send** $m'$ **on** $src(m)$
                                $\{MInv\}$
      **fi** $\{MInv\}$
**od**

**Figure 11.9.** Sketch for *matchmaker*

---

reply comprising an intersecting request message contains all the information needed to allow a synchronous message-passing exchange. So, *matchmaker* returns such a request message as its reply.

A decentralized implementation of synchronous message-passing is easily constructed from this centralized one. The role of *matchmaker* is distributed among a collection of processes: $RSrvr_i$ (for "Remote Server"), $LSrvr_i$ (for "Local Server"), and $TSrvr_i$ (for "Token Server") for each process $P_i$. Whereas a process $P_i$ in the original system would communicate with *matchmaker*, in the decentralized implementation, $P_i$ communicates with $LSrvr_i$.

In the decentralized implementation, *pending* is represented by a union of disjoint subsets $pending_k$; each initially equals $\varnothing$:

$$pending\colon\ \Big\{ \bigcup_{1 \leq k \leq N} pending_k$$

Under this representation, an element can be added to *pending* simply by adding it to one of the subsets $pending_i$. Element $m$ is then removed from *pending* by removing $m$ from the single $pending_i$ that contains $m$. One scheme is to partition the channels into $N$ subsets and associate one of these subsets with each $pending_i$.

Process $RSrvr_i$ is used to remove request messages from $pending_i$. See Figure 11.10. Just as with *matchmaker*, a request message is removed from *pending* only when it intersects some other request message being processed. $RSrvr_i$ receives messages on channel $Chk_i$. If some element $m'$ of $pending_i$ intersects the message received, then $RSrvr_i$ returns $m'$ on channel $Resp_{src(m)}$ and deletes $m'$ from $pending_i$ (thereby deleting $m'$ from *pending*); otherwise, $RSrvr_i$ returns $\phi$ on channel $Resp_{src(m)}$.

$\{RI_i:\ MInv\,\}$
**do** $true \rightarrow \{RI_i\}$
        **receive** $m_i$ **from** $Chk_i$
        **if** $\neg\,(\exists m' \in pending_i\colon\ m'$ intersects $m_i) \rightarrow$
                        **send** $\phi$ **on** $Resp_{src(m_i)}$
        $[]\ (\exists m' \in pending_i\colon\ m'$ intersects $m_i) \rightarrow$
                        Choose $m'\colon\ m' \in pending_i \,\wedge$
                                      $m'$ intersects $m_i$
                        $pending_i := pending_i - \{m'\}$
                        **send** $m'$ **on** $Resp_{src(m_i)}$
        **fi**
    **od**

**Figure 11.10.** Outline for $RSrvr_i$

---

Process $LSrvr_i$ takes the place of *matchmaker* for process $P_i$. See Figure 11.11. $P_i$ sends request messages on channel $LSrvr_i$ (rather than $MM$) and awaits responses on channel $P_i$. In *matchmaker*, one request message is handled at a time. This holds for our decentralized implementation as well. To prevent $LSrvr_1, \ldots, LSrvr_N$ from simultaneously processing requests, mutual exclusion entry and exit protocols are used. At most one of $LSrvr_1, \ldots, LSrvr_N$ can process a request at a time. $LSrvr_i$ adds a message to $pending_i$ only if it cannot find an intersecting message in $pending_1, \ldots, pending_N$.

All that remains is to implement $entry_i$ and $exit_i$. We cannot use the mutual exclusion protocols of earlier chapters, because they employ variables that are read or written by multiple processes. Absence of shared variables is the essence of a distributed system. So, we employ a protocol based on a *token*, using asynchronous message-passing to transfer the token from one process to another.

A single instance of the token is created, and only the token holder is permitted to execute its critical section. A token holder relinquishes the token by sending it to another process, which, upon receiving the token, becomes the token holder. Thus, a token-based mutual exclusion protocol implements four rules:

    T1:    A process attempting to execute *entry* waits to become the token holder.

    T2:    A process executing *exit* relinquishes the token to some other process.

    T3:    Any process that is sent the token eventually becomes the token holder.

    T4:    A token holder eventually relinquishes the token.

$\{SI_i\colon\ MInv\,\}$
**do** $true \to \{SI_i\}$

> **receive** $m_i$ **from** $LSrvr_i$
> $entry_i$
> $found_i := false\quad j_i := 0$
> $\{SI_i'\colon\ SI_i$
> $\qquad \wedge\ 0 \le j_i \le N$
> $\qquad \wedge\ \neg found_i \Rightarrow m$ intersects no message in
> $\qquad\qquad (\underset{1\le k\le j_i}{\cup}\ pending_k)\ \}$
> **do** $j_i < N \wedge \neg found_i \to \{SI_i'\}$
>> **send** $m_i$ **on** $Chk_{j_i+1}$
>> **receive** $rply_i$ **from** $Resp_i$
>> **if** $rply_i = \phi \to j_i := j_i+1\quad\{SI_i'\}$
>> $[\,]\ rply_i \ne \phi \to found_i := true$
>>> **send** $m_i$ **on** $P_{src(rply_i)}$
>>> **send** $rply_i$ **on** $P_i$
>>> $\{SI_i'\}$
>>
>> **fi** $\{SI_i'\}$
>
> **od**
> **if** $\neg found_i \to pending_i := pending_i \cup \{m_i\}\quad\{SI_i\}$
> $[\,]\ found_i \to$ **skip** $\{SI_i\}$
> **fi** $\{SI_i\}$
> $exit_i$

**od**

**Figure 11.11.** Outline for $LSrvr_i$

---

Rules T2 and T3 imply that a process may receive the token even though it is not waiting to become the token holder. This suggests using a process $TSrvr_i$ on behalf of each process $LSrvr_i$. Boolean variables $atmpt_i$ and $ok_i$ permit communication between $TSrvr_i$ and $LSrvr_i$: $atmpt_i$ is *true* if process $LSrvr_i$ awaits the token; $ok_i$ is *true* if process $LSrvr_i$ is the token holder. Thus, we replace the entry and exit protocols with:

$entry_i$: $atmpt_i := true\quad$ **if** $ok_i \to$ **skip fi**

$exit_i$: $ok_i, atmpt_i := false, false$

Code for $TSrvr_i$ is given in Figure 11.12.

Performance is best if the second guarded command in Figure 11.12 is never selected, since then superfluous message-delivery delays are avoided—the token is sent only to processes executing entry protocols. This optimization is accomplished when $nxt(i)$ is a function that exploits information about the

$ok_i := false$
**do** $true \rightarrow$ **receive** $tok_i$ **from** $TokChnl_i$
      **if** $atmpt_i \rightarrow ok_i := true$
              **if** $\neg atmpt_i \rightarrow$ **skip fi**
              **send** $tok_i$ **on** $TokChnl_{nxt(i)}$
      [] $\neg atmpt_i \rightarrow$ **send** $tok_i$ **on** $TokChnl_{nxt(i)}$
      **fi**
**od**

**Figure 11.12.** Outline for $TSrvr_i$

---

identities of processes $i$ attempting to execute $entry_i$. Such information could be communicated by adding a **send** to $entry_i$.

## 11.3  Derivation of Distributed Programs

Distributed programs are concurrent programs that satisfy an additional restriction, which embodies the defining characteristic of a distributed system—the absence of shared memory:

(11.38) **Distributed Program Restriction.** For each program variable $v$, at most one process reads and/or writes $v$.      □

To derive a distributed program, we employ a two-step process. In the first step, an ordinary concurrent program is developed, ignoring (for the most part) Distributed Program Restriction (11.38). In a second step, the concurrent program is modified to comply with Distributed Program Restriction (11.38). The modifications—discussed below—involve replacing shared-variable accesses with local-variable accesses and adding message-passing statements to keep the local variables consistent with the shared variables they replace.

Consider a statement $T$ that mentions a variable $x$. Suppose $x$ is also mentioned in another process, and to comply with Distributed Program Restriction (11.38), we have decided that $x$ should be read and written only by that other process. How do we modify $T$?

Two general techniques are applicable, depending on how $x$ is being accessed:

(11.39) **Eliminating Shared-Variable Reads.** If evaluation of a variable or a predicate $x$ by statement $T$ must be eliminated, then:

(1) Use some form of message passing to transfer the current value of $x$ to a local variable in the process containing $T$.

(2) Ensure termination of any receive statements used in step (1) by having send statements in the process that can evaluate $x$. □

(11.40) **Eliminating Shared-Variable Writes.** If writing variable $x$ by statement $T$ must be eliminated, then:

(1) Replace updates to $x$ in $T$ by updates to a new local variable $lx$ (say).

(2) Use some form of message passing to transfer the updated value of $lx$ to the process that can update $x$.

(3) Insert receive statements into the process that can update $x$ to alter the value of $x$ so that it remains consistent with updates made to the new local variables. □

The use of these techniques is best demonstrated with an example. One follows.

## Use of a Spanning Tree

The problem we tackle arises in network management. Suppose a computer network consists of a set $Net$ of sites $0, 1, ..., N$. Each site $i$ has a value $v_i$ and can exchange messages only with the sites in $nbr_i$, its set of neighbors. Given is an associative and commutative operator $\psi$. Desired is a distributed program with one process per site. The process at site 0 should assign to $s_0$ and truthify:

$$(11.41) \quad s_0 = \underset{0 \le k \le N}{\psi} v_k$$

For example, if $\psi$ is set union (i.e., "$\cup$") and $v_i$ is the singleton set containing a unique name of each site $i$, then computing $s_0$ is equivalent to site 0 determining the names of all sites in the network. Alternatively, if $\psi$ is max (i.e., "$\uparrow$") and $v_i$ is the unique name of each site $i$, then computing $s_0$ yields a single site name (the maximum)—the name of a site that could serve a distinguished role.

Our solution to the problem exploits a *spanning tree*, a directed graph whose nodes are $Net$ and whose edges comprise unique paths from site 0 to every other site. Edges of the spanning tree correspond to a subset of the extant network communications channels. Let $tnbr_i$ be the set of sites to which there are spanning tree edges from a site $i$. Define $pred_i$ such that $pred_0$ is 0 and, for $i \ne 0$, $pred_i$ is the unique site $j$ such that $i \in tnbr_j$:

$$pred_i: \begin{cases} j & \text{iff } i \in tnbr_j \\ 0 & \text{otherwise} \end{cases}$$

Thus, $tnbr_i \subseteq nbr_i$, $j \in tnbr_i$ iff $(i, j)$ is an edge of the spanning tree, and $i \in tnbr_{pred_i}$ iff $i \neq 0$. Define $p^*(ss)$ to be the set of nodes reachable along zero or more spanning tree edges from sites in set $ss$.

Figure 11.13 contains a concurrent program that truthifies (11.41). (Exercise 11.28 deals with the derivation of this program; exercise 11.29 discusses a protocol for initialization.) To understand how the program works, look at loop invariant $I$ and process $T_i$. We infer from the first conjunct in $I$ that each site $i$ stores in $s_i$ the result of applying $\psi$ to $v_i$ and all $v_j$ for sites $j$ in $p^*(d_i)$. The sites in $tnbr_i$ are initially in $nd_i$ (for "not done"), and they are moved, one by one, into $d_i$ (for "done")—the second and third conjuncts concern this. The loop terminates when $nd_i$ is empty. From the third conjunct of $I$, having $nd_i$ empty means that all sites in $tnbr_i$ are in $d_i$. Since by the definition of a spanning tree, every site is reachable using spanning tree edges from site 0, we conclude that every site must be in $p^*(\{0\})$. Thus, when the loop at process $T_0$ terminates, $p^*(\{0\})=Net$ holds, and according to the first conjunct of $I$, $s_0$ contains the desired value.

We now transform the concurrent program of Figure 11.13 into a distributed one. Each variable must be associated with a single process and must obey Distributed Program Restriction (11.38). For the program of Figure 11.13, only two accesses need to be modified if subscripts on variable names are taken to designate the process with which each variable is associated:

(1)   $nd_j=\varnothing$ in the guard of the **if** in $T_i$ involves reading a variable $nd_j$ associated with another process $T_j$;

---

$\{(\forall k \in Net:\ s_k=v_k\ \wedge\ nd_k=tnbr_k\ \wedge\ d_k=\varnothing)\}$
**cobegin**

  $\underset{i}{\|}$  $\{I: (\forall k \in Net:\ s_k=v_k\psi(\underset{j \in p^*(d_k)}{\psi}\ v_j)\ \wedge\ nd_k \cap d_k=\varnothing\ \wedge\ nd_k \cup d_k=tnbr_k)\}$

   $T_i$: **do** $nd_i \neq \varnothing \to \{nd_i \neq \varnothing\ \wedge\ I\}$
         **if** $\underset{j \in tnbr_i}{[]}\ j \in nd_i\ \wedge\ nd_j=\varnothing \to$
                       $\{j \in nd_i\ \wedge\ nd_j=\varnothing\ \wedge\ nd_i \neq \varnothing\ \wedge\ I\}$
                       $nd_i, d_i, s_i := nd_i-\{j\}, d_i \cup \{j\}, s_i\psi s_j$
                       $\{I\}$
          **fi** $\{I\}$
        **od** $\{nd_i=\varnothing\ \wedge\ d_i=tnbr_i\ \wedge\ s_i=\underset{j \in p^*(\{i\})}{\psi}\ v_j)\}$

**coend**
$\{(\forall k \in Net:\ d_k=tnbr_k\ \wedge\ s_k=\underset{j \in p^*(\{i\})}{\psi}\ v_j)\}$

**Figure 11.13.** Calculating with a spanning tree

(2)    $s_i \psi s_j$ in the assignment statement of the **if** in $T_i$ involves reading a variable $s_j$ associated with another process $T_j$.

So, we explore transformations to eliminate the two problematical accesses to shared variables.

To address (2), we apply Eliminating Shared-Variable Reads (11.39). We introduce a local variable $sj_i$ and receive $s_j$ into it. Asynchronous message-passing is used, with $C_j^i$ denoting a channel from site $j$ to site $i$. (The notation $C_j^i$ is intended to be suggestive of site $j$ appearing below site $i$ in the spanning tree. The only channels that will actually be used by the program are $C_0^0$ and $C_j^i$ for $j \in tnbr_i$.) Receive statement $R_i$ is inserted just before the assignment statement that accessed $s_j$, and $I$ is strengthened with $L_i$ to characterize the states of channels incident on $T_i$. See Figure 11.14.

The proof outline of Figure 11.14 remains interference free. For each process $T_k$ distinct from $T_i$, two statements have the potential to falsify $L_i$: (i) receive statement $R_k$ and (ii) the assignment statement in the loop at $T_k$.

- Execution of $R_k$ cannot falsify conjunct $C_i^{pred_i} = \varepsilon$; it can only truthify it. Execution of $R_k$ cannot falsify conjunct $(\forall j \in tnbr_i: C_j^i \neq \varepsilon \Rightarrow C_j^i[0] = s_j)$, because $R_k$ names channel $C_j^k$ and we are assuming $k \neq i$ since processes $T_i$ and $T_k$ are distinct.

- Execution of the assignment statement in the loop at $T_k$ can falsify $(\forall j \in tnbr_i: C_j^i \neq \varepsilon \Rightarrow C_j^i[0] = s_j)$ if $k \in tnbr_i$ holds. But the first conjunct of

---

$\{(\forall k \in Net: s_k = v_k \ \wedge \ nd_k = tnbr_k \ \wedge \ d_k = \emptyset \ \wedge \ (\forall j \in Net: C_j^k = \varepsilon))\}$
**cobegin**

$\quad \| \atop i \ \{I: (\forall k \in Net: s_k = v_k \psi( \underset{j \in p^*(d_k)}{\psi} v_j) \ \wedge \ nd_k \cap d_k = \emptyset \ \wedge \ nd_k \cup d_k = tnbr_k)$

$\qquad \wedge \ L_i: C_i^{pred_i} = \varepsilon \ \wedge \ (\forall j \in tnbr_i: C_j^i \neq \varepsilon \Rightarrow C_j^i[0] = s_j)\}$

$\qquad T_i: \textbf{do } nd_i \neq \emptyset \rightarrow \{nd_i \neq \emptyset \ \wedge \ I\}$

$\qquad\qquad\qquad \textbf{if } \underset{j \in tnbr_i}{\square} \ j \in nd_i \ \wedge \ nd_j = \emptyset \rightarrow$

$\qquad\qquad\qquad\qquad\qquad \{j \in nd_i \ \wedge \ nd_j = \emptyset \ \wedge \ nd_i \neq \emptyset \ \wedge \ I\}$

$\qquad\qquad\qquad\qquad\qquad R_i: \textbf{receive } sj_i \textbf{ from } C_j^i$

$\qquad\qquad\qquad\qquad\qquad \{j \in nd_i \ \wedge \ nd_j = \emptyset \ \wedge \ nd_i \neq \emptyset \ \wedge \ I \ \wedge \ sj_i = s_j\}$

$\qquad\qquad\qquad\qquad\qquad nd_i, d_i, s_i := nd_i - \{j\}, d_i \cup \{j\}, s_i \psi sj_i$

$\qquad\qquad\qquad\qquad\qquad \{I\}$

$\qquad\qquad\qquad \textbf{fi } \{I\}$

$\qquad\qquad \textbf{od } \{nd_i = \emptyset \ \wedge \ d_i = tnbr_i \ \wedge \ s_i = \underset{j \in p^{\uparrow}(\{i\})}{\psi} v_j)\}$

**coend**
$\{(\forall k \in Net: d_k = tnbr_k \ \wedge \ s_k = \underset{j \in p^{\uparrow}(\{i\})}{\psi} v_k)\}$

**Figure 11.14.** Reference to $s_j$ eliminated

$L_k$ in the precondition of this assignment statement implies that $C_k^{pred_k}=\varepsilon$ holds, so $C_k^i \neq \varepsilon \Rightarrow C_k^i[0]=s_k$ is not falsified because its antecedent remains *false*.

We must add a send statement on channel $C_j^i$, or else receive statement $R_i$ will never terminate. The send statement must not falsify

$$C_j^{pred_j} \neq \varepsilon \Rightarrow C_j^{pred_j}[0]=s_j$$

in $L_i$. The value of $s_j$ is not changed after $nd_j=\varnothing$ holds, which suggests sending $s_j$ after the loop in $T_j$ terminates. So a send of value $s_i$ is inserted just after the loop of $T_i$.

Also, we must transform the program of Figure 11.14 to eliminate the access to $nd_j$ in the guard evaluation action of the **if**. Again we use Eliminating Shared-Variable Reads (11.39), this time employing the state of a channel to allow a process $i$ to determine whether $nd_j=\varnothing$ holds. The precondition of the send in process $T_i$ implies $nd_i=\varnothing$. Moreover, once $nd_i=\varnothing$ holds, it remains true. Thus, we have as an invariant $msg(C_k^{pred_k}) \Rightarrow nd_k=\varnothing$ for all sites $k$, and we can replace guard $nd_j=\varnothing$ with $msg(C_j^{pred_j})$. The resulting program appears in Figure 11.15.

---

$\{(\forall k \in Net: s_k=v_k \wedge nd_k=tnbr_k \wedge d_k=\varnothing \wedge (\forall j \in Net: C_j^k=\varepsilon))\}$
**cobegin**
   $\|\ \{I: (\forall k \in Net: s_k=v_k \Psi(\underset{j \in p^*(d_k)}{\Psi} v_j) \wedge nd_k \cap d_k=\varnothing \wedge nd_k \cup d_k=tnbr_k$
             $\wedge\ msg(C_k^{pred_k}) \Rightarrow nd_k=\varnothing)$
         $\wedge\ L_i: C_i^{pred_i}=\varepsilon \wedge (\forall j \in tnbr_i: C_j^i \neq \varepsilon \Rightarrow C_j^i[0]=s_j)\}$

     $T_i:$ **do** $nd_i \neq \varnothing \rightarrow \{nd_i \neq \varnothing \wedge I\}$
            **if** $\underset{j \in tnbr_i}{[]}\ j \in nd_i \wedge msg(C_j^{pred_j}) \rightarrow$
                        $\{j \in nd_i \wedge nd_j=\varnothing \wedge nd_i \neq \varnothing \wedge I\}$
                        $R_i:$ **receive** $sj_i$ **from** $C_j^i$
                        $\{j \in nd_i \wedge nd_j=\varnothing \wedge nd_i \neq \varnothing \wedge I \wedge sj_i=s_j\}$
                        $nd_i, d_i, s_i := nd_i-\{j\}, d_i \cup \{j\}, s_i \Psi sj_i$
                        $\{I\}$
            **fi** $\{I\}$
         **od** $\{nd_i=\varnothing \wedge d_i=tnbr_i \wedge s_i=\underset{j \in p^*(\{i\})}{\Psi} v_j)\}$
         **send** $s_i$ **on** $C_i^{pred_i}$ $\{nd_i=\varnothing \wedge d_i=tnbr_i \wedge s_i=\underset{j \in p^*(\{i\})}{\Psi} v_j)\}$
**coend**
$\{(\forall k \in Net: d_k=tnbr_k \wedge s_k=\underset{j \in p^*(\{i\})}{\Psi} v_k)\}$

**Figure 11.15.** Distributed program

## 11.4  Shared-Variable Representations

Eliminating Shared-Variable Reads (11.39) and Eliminating Shared-Variable Writes (11.40) treat variables as objects whose implementation is opaque and preordained. Another approach for complying with Distributed Program Restriction (11.38) is to alter how information is represented in variables.

(11.42) **Change of Representation.** If more than one process accesses a variable $x$, then:

> (1)  A new representation for $x$ is designed in terms of components that are each accessed by only a single process.

> (2)  The original program is transformed by replacing accesses to $x$ by accesses to the components of the new representation.     □

For example, a set-valued variable $x$ that is accessed by multiple processes might be represented as the union of subsets, where each subset $x_i$ is accessed only by process $i$:

(11.43)  $x: \quad \bigcup_i x_i$

Under representation (11.43), a process $i$ would add an element to $x$ by adding the element to $x_i$. So, we are representing a variable $x$ that is accessed by multiple processes in terms of a collection of variables $x_i$ that each are accessed by a single process. The decentralized synchronous message-passing implementation in §11.2 was obtained by changing the representation of *pending* in this way.

Changing how information is represented may change a program's performance. Representation (11.43) allows elements to be added to $x$ cheaply—as an update to one of the $x_i$. But in order to evaluate $e \in x$ under representation (11.43), $\bigvee_i (e \in x_i)$ must be calculated, and this calculation may require every process $i$ to evaluate $e \in x_i$. Thus, evaluating $e \in x$ under representation (11.43) may involve communication with each process $i$ that contains one of the $x_i$. Evaluation of $e \in x$ has become rather expensive.

The suitability of a given representations depends both on the costs of various operations and on how frequently these operations will be performed. When $e \in x$ is expected to be evaluated frequently, an alternative to (11.43) is to create a copy $x_i$ of $x$ for each process $i$. This representation is sometimes known as *full replication*, and each $x_i$ is called a *replica*. Evaluation of $e \in x$ is now cheap, since a process $i$ need only evaluate $e \in x_i$. But under full replication, adding an element to $x$ is expensive, because the element must be added to each replica. Another candidate representation for $x$ uses a single variable, stored by a *manager process*. Now evaluating $e \in x$ and adding an element to $x$ both require a message exchange with the manager process.

We now illustrate Change of Representation (11.42) in the design of a distributed program.

## Distributed-Termination Detection

When a distributed system is employed to execute a discrete-event simulation, a distinct process is used for each activity being simulated. An activity is initiated by sending a message to the appropriate process. The entire distributed simulation terminates once all messages have been delivered and all processes modeling activities have terminated.

By abstracting from simulations and activities, we obtain the following problem description for the protocol to detect termination of a distributed simulation:

(11.44) **Distributed-Termination Detection.** A distributed system consists of processes 1, ..., N−1. Each process $i$ is either idle, in which case predicate $idle(i)$ holds, or active, in which case $\neg idle(i)$ holds. An *active* process may send *basic* messages, but an *idle* process may not. Whether idle or active, processes may send *control* messages as part of executing the termination-detection protocol. An active process may become idle spontaneously, but an idle process becomes active only when it receives a basic message. Design a protocol that determines whether all basic messages have been received and $idle(i)$ holds for all processes $i$.     □

Desired is a protocol $S$ that satisfies a safety property $DS$ and a liveness property $DL$. Safety property (11.45) stipulates that when $S$ terminates, a (fresh) program variable $q$ indicates whether all processes are idle.

(11.45) $DS$: $Init_S \;\Rightarrow\; \Box(after(S) \land q \;\Rightarrow\; Q)$

where $Q$ is defined by:

$Q$:  $(\forall i:\; 1 \le i < \text{N}:\; idle(i))$

Stronger safety property $Init_S \Rightarrow \Box(after(S) \land Q \Rightarrow q)$, might seem preferable. To satisfy it, however, would require setting $q$ to *true* even if all processes become idle after the protocol has terminated. That would be impossible.

Liveness property (11.46) stipulates that if all processes are idle throughout execution of the protocol, then the protocol terminates with $q$ set to *true*. It rules out satisfying $DS$ simply by assigning *false* to $q$.

(11.46) $DL$: $Init_S \;\Rightarrow\; (((in(S) \land Q)\mathcal{U}\,after(S)) \Rightarrow \Diamond(after(S) \land q)$

A stronger liveness property might have a weaker antecedent than $(in(S) \land Q)\mathcal{U}\,after(S)$ to describe the condition under which the protocol must terminate with $q$ set to *true*. However, care must be taken in formulating this weaker antecedent. Otherwise, the new liveness property might inadvertently require the protocol to set $q$ based on information that is not available, such as information about changes to $idle(i)$ after the protocol terminates.

If we ignore Distributed Program Restriction (11.38), an obvious way to satisfy $DS$ and $DL$ is by using an assignment statement:

(11.47) $\{true\}$ $S$: $q := (\forall i: 1 \le i < N: idle(i))$ $\{q \Rightarrow (\forall i: 1 \le i < N: idle(i))\}$

Each assertion in (11.47) implies $after(S) \wedge q \Rightarrow Q$, so according to $I_{PO(S)}$ Decomposition Rule (6.17a) and Precondition Safety Consequence Rule (6.15), $S$ satisfies $DS$. That $S$ satisfies $DL$ is easily established using Temporal Logic.

A problem with (11.47) is the unrealistically coarse atomic action. We might expect that in a distributed system, only process $i$ may evaluate $idle(i)$. This leads us to replace $S$ with a **do** whose body references the $idle(i)$ predicates one at a time.

$$\{true\}$$
$$S: q, t := true, 1$$
$$\{I: 1 \le t \le N \wedge (q \Rightarrow (\forall i: 1 \le i < t: idle(i)))\}$$
$$\textbf{do } t \neq N \rightarrow \{t \neq N \wedge I\} \ q, t := q \wedge idle(t), t+1 \ \{I\} \textbf{ od}$$
$$\{q \Rightarrow (\forall i: 1 \le i < N: idle(i))\}$$

Two events in the distributed system being monitored have the potential to interfere with this proof outline:

(i)  receipt of a basic message

(ii)  a process becoming idle

We now consider each.

Receipt of a basic message by a process $p$ falsifies $idle(p)$. Thus, when $q \wedge p < t$ holds, receipt of a basic message by a process $p$ falsifies $I$. Weakening (5.15) can eliminate this interference. We reject the obvious weakening

$$1 \le t \le N \wedge (q \Rightarrow ( \quad (\forall i: 1 \le i < t: idle(i))$$
$$\vee \ (\exists i: 1 \le i < t: \neg idle(i))))$$

because it makes $I$ too weak to be useful. We seek a weakening that causes $q$ to satisfy $q \Rightarrow (\forall i: 1 \le i < N: idle(i))$ when the **do** terminates, even though $q \Rightarrow (\forall i: 1 \le i < t: idle(i))$ has been falsified.

Suppose synchronous message-passing is being used for communication.[4] Thus, a receive statement can be executed only if the matching send statement is executed simultaneously. From conjunct $q \Rightarrow (\forall i: 1 \le i < t: idle(i))$ of $I$, we conclude that if $q \wedge I$ is falsified then some process $j$, where $t \le j < N$ holds, must have simultaneously executed a send statement. (Idle processes may not execute send statements, and we infer from $I$ that $idle(i)$ holds for all processes $i$ such that $1 \le i < t$. Thus, $t \le j$ must hold.) This leads to a weaker $I$.

---

[4]Exercise 11.33 considers the variation where asynchronous message-passing is employed.

$$I: \quad 1 \le t \le N \quad \wedge \quad (q \Rightarrow ( \quad (\forall i: \ 1 \le i < t: \ idle(i))$$
$$\vee \ (\exists i: \ t \le i < N: \ \neg idle(i))))$$

It is not falsified by processes receiving basic messages.

Note that assignment statement $q, t := q \wedge idle(t), t+1$ does not falsify the new disjunct $(\exists i: \ t \le i < N: \ \neg idle(i))$ of $I$. If $idle(t)$ holds, then incrementing $t$ leaves the truth of the new disjunct unchanged; if, on the other hand, $\neg idle(t)$ holds, then the assignment statement sets $q$ to *false*, which makes the second conjunct of $I$ trivially *true*.

We now address potential interference caused by event (ii) above, a process becoming idle. When a process $i$ becomes idle, $idle(i)$ changes from *false* to *true*. If $i \ge t$ holds, then this transition may falsify $(\exists i: \ t \le i < N: \ \neg idle(i))$, which, in turn, could falsify $I$.

A further use of Weakening (5.15) allows us to eliminate this interference. For each process $p$, a new variable $wa_p$ ("was active") is introduced. Assume that processes being monitored obey the following.

*Idle Rule*:  Variable $wa_p$ is set to *true* whenever $idle(p)$ is set to *true*.

Thus, $wa_p$ records whether $idle(p)$ has held at some time in the past. $I$ is now weakened with a third disjunct, so that $I$ is no longer falsified when $idle(i)$ changes from *false* to *true*.

$$I: \quad 1 \le t \le N \quad \wedge \quad (q \Rightarrow ( \quad (\forall i: \ 1 \le i < t: \ idle(i))$$
$$\vee \ (\exists i: \ t \le i < N: \ \neg idle(i))$$
$$\vee \ (\exists i: \ t \le i < N: \ wa_i)))$$

The assignment to $q$ is changed (see below) so that incrementing $t$ does not falsify this weaker $I$. In particular, if $\neg wa_t$ holds, then disjunct $(\exists i: \ t \le i < N: \ wa_i)$, hence $I$, cannot be falsified by incrementing $t$; if $wa_t$ holds, then the new assignment statement sets $q$ to *false*, so the second conjunct of $I$ holds trivially.

$$\{true\}$$
$$S: \ q, t := true, 1$$
$$\{I: \ 1 \le t \le N \quad \wedge \quad (q \Rightarrow ( \quad (\forall i: \ 1 \le i < t: \ idle(i))$$
$$\vee \ (\exists i: \ t \le i < N: \ \neg idle(i))$$
$$\vee \ (\exists i: \ t \le i < N: \ wa_i)))\}$$
$$\textbf{do } t \ne N \rightarrow \{t \ne N \wedge I\}$$
$$q, t := q \wedge idle(t) \wedge \neg wa_t, t+1 \quad \{I\} \textbf{ od}$$
$$\{q \Rightarrow (\forall i: \ 1 \le i < N: \ idle(i))\}$$

This program terminates but does not satisfy liveness property *DL* (11.46). Unless all the $wa_p$ are initially *false*, $S$ cannot set $q$ to *true*, and *DL* cannot be satisfied. Some obvious alternatives for addressing this problem are:

(i)   assume $Init_S \Rightarrow (\forall i: \ 1 \le i < N: \ \neg wa_i)$ holds

(ii)  design a special protocol to perform the initialization

(iii)  augment $S$

Approach (iii) is the one pursued here.

In an actual application, we would expect $S$ to be executed repeatedly until it terminates with $q$ equal *true*. This means that each repetition of $S$ can perform initialization for the next repetition. Note that $S$ needs to truthify

$$WA:\ (\forall i:\ 1\le i<N:\ \neg wa_i)$$

only if all processes are idle, because only then is satisfying $DL$ nontrivial. So, we augment $S$ to ensure that if all processes remain idle during execution of $S$, then $WA$ will hold when $S$ terminates.

Since $I$ must be preserved while $S$ is executed, we calculate a condition that implies $wp(wa_p := false, I)$. It is straightforward to show:

$$(I \wedge \neg q) \vee (t=1) \vee (I \wedge q \wedge p<t) \ \Rightarrow\ wp(wa_p := false, I)$$

Thus, assignment statement $wa_{t-1} := false$ can be inserted as the last statement of the loop body (see below), since $I \wedge 1\le t-1 < t$ holds there. The proof that when all processes remain idle the augmented protocol truthifies $WA$ is simple and therefore omitted.

```
{true}
S: q, t := true, 1
   {I: 1≤t≤N ∧ (q ⇒ (   (∀i: 1≤i<t: idle(i))
                      ∨ (∃i: t≤i<N: ¬idle(i))
                      ∨ (∃i: t≤i<N: wa_i)))}
   do t≠N → {t≠N ∧ I}
            q, t := q ∧ idle(t) ∧ ¬wa_t, t+1  {I}
            wa_{t-1} := false  {I}
   od
{q ⇒ (∀i: 1≤i<N: idle(i))}
```

With the assignment statement inserted, we obtain a protocol where each complete execution of the protocol does the initialization necessary for repeating the protocol. The protocol doesn't satisfy $DL$ but instead satisfies

$$Init_S \Rightarrow$$
$$(((in(S) \wedge Q)\,\mathcal{U}\,after(S)) \Rightarrow \Diamond(after(S) \wedge WA)$$
$$\wedge\ ((WA \wedge (in(S) \wedge Q)\,\mathcal{U}\,after(S)) \Rightarrow \Diamond(after(S) \wedge q)))$$

which suffices in applications where $S$ will be executed repeatedly.

We now turn attention to transforming $S$ into a distributed program. First, the loop is replaced by a **cobegin**. Each of the $N-1$ iterations of the **do** is executed by a separate process. In the **cobegin**, guard $t=p$ at the start of a process $S_p$ ensures that the loop iteration implemented by $S_p$ occurs at the right time.

$\{true\}$
$S:\ q, t := true, 1$
$\quad \{I:\ 1 \le t \le N \ \wedge \ (q \Rightarrow (\quad (\forall i:\ 1 \le i < t:\ idle(i))$
$\qquad\qquad\qquad\qquad\qquad \vee\ (\exists i:\ t \le i < N:\ \neg idle(i))$
$\qquad\qquad\qquad\qquad\qquad \vee\ (\exists i:\ t \le i < N:\ wa_i)))\}$
**cobegin**
$\quad \underset{1 \le p < N}{\|}\quad \{I\ \wedge\ t \le p\}$
$\qquad\qquad S_p:\ \textbf{if}\ t = p \rightarrow \{I\ \wedge\ t = p\}$
$\qquad\qquad\qquad\qquad q, t := q \wedge idle(p) \wedge \neg wa_p, p+1$
$\qquad\qquad\qquad\qquad \{I\ \wedge\ t \ge p+1\}$
$\qquad\qquad\qquad\qquad wa_p := false\quad \{I\ \wedge\ t \ge p+1\}$
$\qquad\qquad \textbf{fi}\ \{I\ \wedge\ t \ge p+1\}$
**coend** $\{I\ \wedge\ t \ge N\}$
$\{q \Rightarrow (\forall i:\ 1 \le i < N:\ idle(i))\}$

Accesses to $q$ in this program do not comply with Distributed Program Restriction (11.38). One solution is to use Change of Representation (11.42), encoding $q$ by new variables $q_1, q_2, ..., q_N$. The value of $t$, which ranges from 1 to N, defines which of these variables currently represents $q$:

$$q:\ \left\{ q_t\ \text{if}\ 1 \le t \le N \right.$$

We now recode accesses to $q$ according to the new representation.

- The assignment to $q$ labeled $S$ also truthifies $t = 1$, so $q$ is replaced by $q_1$ there.

- The assignment to $q$ in a process $S_p$ also truthifies $t = p+1$, so target $q$ is replaced by $q_{p+1}$. The $q$ in the expression there is replaced by $q_p$ because $t = p$ holds when this $q$ is evaluated.

- Since $t = N$ holds in $post(S)$, the $q$ there is replaced by $q_N$.

$\{true\}$
$S:\ q_1, t := true, 1$
$\quad \{I:\ 1 \le t \le N \ \wedge \ (q \Rightarrow (\quad (\forall i:\ 1 \le i < t:\ idle(i))$
$\qquad\qquad\qquad\qquad\qquad \vee\ (\exists i:\ t \le i < N:\ \neg idle(i))$
$\qquad\qquad\qquad\qquad\qquad \vee\ (\exists i:\ t \le i < N:\ wa_i)))\}$
**cobegin**
$\quad \underset{1 \le p < N}{\|}\quad \{I\ \wedge\ t \le p\}$
$\qquad\qquad S_p:\ \textbf{if}\ t = p \rightarrow \{I\ \wedge\ t = p\}$
$\qquad\qquad\qquad\qquad q_{p+1}, t := q_p \wedge idle(p) \wedge \neg wa_p, p+1$
$\qquad\qquad\qquad\qquad \{I\ \wedge\ t \ge p+1\}$
$\qquad\qquad\qquad\qquad wa_p := false\quad \{I\ \wedge\ t \ge p+1\}$
$\qquad\qquad \textbf{fi}\ \{I\ \wedge\ t \ge p+1\}$
**coend** $\{I\ \wedge\ t \ge N\}$
$\{q_N \Rightarrow (\forall i:\ 1 \le i < N:\ idle(i))\}$

Accesses to $t$ do not comply with Distributed Program Restriction (11.38), either. Variable $t$ is being used to block execution of a process $S_p$ until processes $S_1$ through $S_{p-1}$ have terminated. This is accomplished by awaiting $t=p$ at the start of $S_p$. Therefore, we investigate use of a receive statement in place of $GEval_{if}(S_p)$. Specifically, Eliminating Shared-Variable Reads (11.39) is employed to transfer predicate $t=p$ from $S_{p-1}$ (the process that truthifies $t=p$) to $S_p$ (the process awaiting $t=p$).

$$\{I \ \wedge \ t \leq p\}$$
$$S_p: \ Rcv_p: \ C_p^{p-1}?... \quad \{I \ \wedge \ t=p\}$$
$$q_{p+1}, t := q_p \wedge idle(p) \wedge \neg wa_p, p+1 \quad \{I \ \wedge \ t=p+1\}$$
$$Snd_p: \ C_{p+1}^p!... \quad \{I \ \wedge \ t \geq p+1\}$$
$$wa_p := false \ \{I \ \wedge \ t \geq p+1\}$$

We are postulating a channel $C_p^{p-1}$ from each process $p-1$ to process $p$.

Note that the assignment to variable $t$ in $S_p$ is no longer needed, since $t$ is no longer read by any process. Therefore, we delete this assignment statement, and—because $t$ is still used in the proof outline—we introduce a derived term $t$ to simulate the value of the deleted variable.

$$t: \begin{cases} 1 & \text{if } \neg(\exists i: \ 1 \leq i \leq N: \ (at(Snd_i) \vee after(Snd_i) \vee after(S_i))) \\ (\uparrow i: \ 1 \leq i \leq N \wedge (at(Snd_i) \vee after(Snd_i) \vee after(S_i)): \ i+1) & \text{otherwise} \end{cases}$$

Here, then, is the simplified program for process $S_p$.

$$\{I \ \wedge \ t \leq p\}$$
$$S_p: \ Rcv_p: \ C_p^{p-1}?... \quad \{I \ \wedge \ t=p\}$$
$$q_{p+1} := q_p \wedge idle(p) \wedge \neg wa_p \quad \{I \ \wedge \ t=p+1\}$$
$$Snd_p: \ C_{p+1}^p!... \quad \{I \ \wedge \ t \geq p+1\}$$
$$wa_p := false \ \{I \ \wedge \ t \geq p+1\}$$

The final step in the derivation is to change accesses to the $q_i$'s and the $wa_i$'s in order to comply with Distributed Program Restriction (11.38). We associate $q_p$ and $wa_p$ with process $S_p$. Thus, the only problem with the code just derived for $S_p$ is the assignment statement that updates $q_{p+1}$. That problem is handled with Eliminating Shared-Variable Writes (11.40): $q_{p+1}$ is computed, stored in $qn_p$ at process $p$, and then sent to process $S_{p+1}$.

$$\{I \ \wedge \ t \leq p\}$$
$$S_p: \ Rcv_p: \ C_p^{p-1}?q_p \quad \{I \ \wedge \ t=p\}$$
$$qn_p := q_p \wedge idle(p) \wedge \neg wa_p$$
$$\{I \ \wedge \ t=p+1 \ \wedge \ qn_p=(q_p \wedge idle(p) \wedge \neg wa_p)\}$$
$$Snd_p: \ C_{p+1}^p!qn_p \quad \{I \ \wedge \ t \geq p+1\}$$
$$wa_p := false \ \{I \ \wedge \ t \geq p+1\}$$

Finally, we replace initial assignment statement $q_1, t := true, 1$ in $S$ by a new process:

> $\{true\}$
> $Snd_0$:  $C_1^0 \,!true$
> $\{I \ \wedge \ t \geq 1\}$

And we add a process to receive the value sent by $S_{N-1}$.

> $\{true\}$
> $Rcv_N$:  $C_N^{N-1} ?q_N$
> $\{q_N \Rightarrow (\forall i: \ 1 \leq i < N: \ idle(i))\}$

By assembling all the processes into a single **cobegin$^+$** we obtain the program of Figure 11.16.

By introducing synchronous message-passing statements, we incur the obligation to discharge premise (b) of **cobegin$^+$** Rule (11.21). This involves proving $CAC(\zeta_{X,Y})$ for each of the channel actions of every channel $C_j^i$. Specifically, we prove $CAC(\zeta_{Snd_0, Rcv_1})$, $CAC(\zeta_{Snd_p, Rcv_{p+1}})$ for $1 \leq p < N$, and $CAC(\zeta_{Snd_{N-1}, Rcv_N})$:

$$\{true \ \wedge \ I \ \wedge \ t \leq 1)\} \ \ \zeta_{Snd_0, Rcv_1} \ \ \{I \ \wedge \ t \geq 1 \ \wedge \ I \ \wedge \ t=1\}$$

---

> $\{true\}$
> $S$:  **cobegin$^+$**
>
> > $\{true\}$  $Snd_0$:  $C_1^0 \,!true$  $\{I \ \wedge \ t \geq 1\}$
> >
> > $\|$ $\{true\}$  $Rcv_N$:  $C_N^{N-1} ?q_N$  $\{q_N \Rightarrow (\forall i: \ 1 \leq i < N: \ idle(i))\}$
> >
> > $\underset{1 \leq p < N}{\|}$ $\quad \{I \ \wedge \ t \leq p\}$
> > $\qquad S_p$:  $Rcv_p$:  $C_p^{p-1} ?q_p$  $\{I \ \wedge \ t=p\}$
> > $\qquad\qquad qn_p := q_p \wedge idle(p) \wedge \neg wa_p$
> > $\qquad\qquad \{I \ \wedge \ t=p+1 \ \wedge \ qn_p = (q_p \wedge idle(p) \wedge \neg wa_p)\}$
> > $\qquad\qquad Snd_p$:  $C_{p+1}^p \,!qn_p$  $\{I \ \wedge \ t \geq p+1\}$
> > $\qquad\qquad wa_p := false$  $\{I \ \wedge \ t \geq p+1\}$
> >
> > **coend** $\{I \ \wedge \ t \geq N\}$
> > $\{t=N \ \wedge \ q_N \Rightarrow (\forall i: \ 1 \leq i < N: \ idle(i))\}$

**Figure 11.16.** Distributed-termination detection

$$\{I \;\wedge\; t=p+1 \;\wedge\; qn_p=(q_p \wedge idle(p) \wedge \neg wa_p) \;\wedge\; I \;\wedge\; t\leq p+1\}$$
$$\zeta \, Snd_p,Rcv_{p+1}$$
$$\{I \;\wedge\; t\geq p+1 \;\wedge\; I \;\wedge\; t=p+1\}$$

$$\{I \;\wedge\; t=N \;\wedge\; qn_{N-1}=(q_{N-1} \wedge idle(N-1) \wedge \neg wa_{N-1}) \;\wedge\; true\}$$
$$\zeta \, Snd_{N-1},Rcv_N$$
$$\{I \;\wedge\; t\geq N \;\wedge\; q_N \Rightarrow (\forall i:\ 1\leq i<N:\ idle(i))\}$$

All can be proved using Channel Action Axiom (11.14).

## Historical Notes

An operating system designed in 1967 for the Danish RC 4000 computer (manufactured by Regnecentralen) was the first to support message passing [Brinch Hansen 70]. Message passing was selected over the T.H.E. system's semaphores [Dijkstra 68a] because message passing was believed to be more robust when "some processes may turn out to be black sheep and break the rules of the game" [Brinch Hansen 70]. In the RC 4000 operating system, all communication and synchronization is achieved by processes sending and receiving 8-word message buffers. Because the pool of message buffers is finite, a send blocks if no message buffer is available. Thus, the RC 4000 software does not implement asynchronous message-passing as defined in §11.1, although by allocating a sufficiently large pool of message buffers, the illusion of asynchronous message-passing can be created. A predicate like our $msg(C)$ is provided.

ISPL (Incremental Systems Programming Language) [Balzer 71] was among the first programming notations to support message passing. It is a PL/1-like language with *data semaphores*, which are general semaphores whose operations not only synchronize their callers but also convey data. The *P-data* statement, for example, is like a receive; the *V-data* statement resembles a send. The designers of ISPL were concerned with unifying communications mechanisms for file I/O, terminal I/O, communication between user programs, and programs obtaining services from an operating system kernel. Their solution was called a *port*; it transformed communications targeted to any of these destinations into operations on data semaphores.

Another early programming notation that supported message passing, Gypsy [Ambler et al. 77], augments Pascal. Gypsy's send and receive statements have similar semantics to the sends and receives of the RC 4000 operating system. The Gypsy project's focus was to provide tools for implementing formally verified communications software, and Hoare-style proof rules were developed along with the programming notation [Good et al. 79]. For reasoning, Gypsy's send and receive statements were viewed as assignment statements to sequence-valued variables. Each of these variables contains the history of sends and receives on a channel. By representing channels using their histories and imposing restrictions on what could be mentioned in assertions, proofs of Gypsy programs did not involve interference-freedom obligations. However, the restrictions made it impossible to specify or prove certain safety properties.

Hoare-style axiomatizations for asynchronous message-passing statements are also given in [Schlichting & Schneider 84]. Both unreliable datagrams and reliable virtual circuits are treated. As with Gypsy, the axioms for send and receive statements are formulated in terms of histories, but now assertions are not restricted. The resulting logic is more expressive and more powerful than the logic in [Good et al. 79], but proofs do have interference-freedom obligations. Because receive statements are not directly translated into conditional atomic actions, the axiomatizations in [Schlichting & Schneider 84] involve satisfaction obligations analogous to those of [Levin & Gries 81] (see below).

The idea that predicates as well as values are transferred by messages first appeared in [Schlichting & Schneider 84]; extensions are explored in [Bernstein 87].

Synchronous message-passing originated with the Communicating Sequential Processes (CSP) notation proposed in [Hoare 78]. That proposal is the basis for a number of concurrent programming notations [Bal et al. 89]. Perhaps the best known is Occam [Inmos 84], which runs on the Inmos Transputer, a microprocessor designed to serve as a processing element in parallel supercomputers.

Aspects of the original CSP proposal were controversial. The absence of buffering (i.e., the choice of synchronous message-passing) is criticized in [Kieburtz & Silberschatz 79], as are consequences of the proposed channel-naming scheme. (In [Hoare 78], channels are unidirectional and link pairs of processes. A process executing a send or receive simply names the other endpoint in order to specify the channel.) An argument is made in [Bernstein 80] for allowing send statements in the guards of **if** and **do** statements. The problem with such "send guards" is the cost and complexity of their implementation. Nevertheless, implementations are given in [Bagrodia 89], [Bernstein 80], [Schneider 82], [Schwarz 78], [Silberschatz 79], and [Snepscheut 81]. (The implementation in [Buckley & Silberschatz 83] is known to be flawed.)

Hoare's original CSP proposal was not accompanied by proof rules. Three Hoare-style proof systems then followed. Each involved some new type of obligation for reconciling the pre- and postconditions of matching send and receive statements.

In the logic of [Apt et al. 80] for CSP, each process is proved in isolation, and then a cooperation proof is performed to check whether these proofs can be combined. The axioms in [Apt et al. 80] for send and receive statements allow anything to be asserted as their postconditions; the *cooperation proof* establishes that assumptions made in the postcondition of a send or receive statement will, in fact, be true whenever execution of that statement terminates. The cooperation proof involves constructing an invariant to characterize pairs of matching send and receive statements that actually exchange messages during some program execution (so-called *semantic matching*). The invariant is formulated using program as well as auxiliary variables, but auxiliary variables may not be shared. Because no variables are shared, there is no interference-freedom obligation.

The logic of [Levin & Gries 81] for CSP also allows anything to be asserted as the postconditions of send and receive statements. A satisfaction proof is then performed to show that these assertions are sound. The *satisfaction proof* comprises an obligation for each matching pair of send and receive statements—whether or not this pair of statements actually transfers a message; there is no need explicitly to construct an invariant or to calculate semantic matching, as with cooperation proofs. Shared auxiliary variables are necessary for completeness of the logic, so interference-freedom obligations must be discharged.

With the logic of [Soundararajan 84b], send and receive statements are modeled as assignments to sequence-valued variables (as in Gypsy), called *traces*, that record the history of communications. A program proof involves first constructing a proof outline for each process in isolation. Then, these proof outlines are combined according to an inference rule that requires the communication histories of processes to be compatible. The *compatibility test* ensures that a value received by one process is indeed plausible in light of sends by the other.

In [Lamport & Schneider 84], these new types of obligations are all shown to follow from a single principle: modeling send-receive statement pairs by atomic actions (i.e., channel actions) rather than modeling each send and receive statement by a separate atomic action. The axiomatization of §11.2 is based on the approach in [Lamport & Schneider 84].

If process behavior is entirely specified by predicates on traces, then the specification for the parallel composition of a process network is simply the conjunction of the specifications for the component process. The first such *network proof system* was proposed in [Misra & Chandy 81]; a number of others followed—see [Widom et al. 92] for one such logic and citations to others.

The sort program of Figure 11.5 was first described in [Dijkstra 77c], where W.H.J. Feijen is credited with originally formulating the problem. The centralized implementation of synchronous message-passing is from [Andrews 91], as is the idea to transform this centralized implementation into a decentralized one; our particular decentralized implementation, however, is new.

Message-passing statements are sometimes packaged to form higher-level constructs. For example, a *remote procedure call* statement is equivalent to a send statement followed by a receive statement, and a *remote procedure* statement is effectively a receive statement followed by a procedure body and then a send statement. The remote procedure call statement is attractive because its semantics are so similar to a sequential programming construct with which most programmers are familiar. Moreover, remote procedure calls are especially well suited for programming client/server systems—the client makes a remote procedure call and the server executes a remote procedure to render the service.

Remote procedures were first proposed in connection with the Arpanet [Postel & White 74]. Inclusion of remote procedures in various programming notations used by operating system researchers led to interest in their use, semantics, and implementation [Birrell & Nelson 84], [Spector 82].

Another notable higher-level message-passing construct is the rendezvous or accept statement. This construct was popularized by the Ada programming notation [Dod 81], which was mandated for certain projects by the United States government. (One is reminded of the satiric reformulation of the Golden Rule: "He who owns the gold makes the rules.")

This chapter does not discuss remote procedures, rendezvous, or other higher-level packagings simply because their axiomatizations require no techniques beyond what was discussed. Proof Outline Logic inference rules can be constructed for these statements using the same approach as used in §11.1 and §11.2. See exercise 11.14. We also have not discussed multicasts or more complicated message-delivery orderings for the same reason. For example, an axiomatization for causally ordered delivery can be found in [Stoller & Schneider 95].

Another aspect of message-passing ignored in this text concerns ways to specify destinations that are eligible to receive a message. All the message-passing statements we give have used channels for this. The literature, however, describes a variety of other schemes. One is given in exercises 11.5 and 11.12; see [Andrews & Schneider 83] and [Bal et al. 89] for surveys of the possibilities.

A compelling case is made in [Lamport 82] that derivation and reasoning about distributed programs is fundamentally the same as derivation and reasoning about concurrent programs having shared memory. To illustrate the point, Lamport derives a distributed algorithm for maintaining routing tables in a network where links can fail. A similar view is advanced in [Chandy & Misra 86], where it is illustrated by deriving a family of distributed quiescence-detection algorithms. Other examples—encompassing a broad collection of problems—in [Chandy & Misra 88b] further demonstrate the virtues of viewing a distributed program as a restricted form of a shared-memory concurrent one rather than as a new animal. The spanning tree algorithm, which we chose to illustrate the point (in §11.3), is an Echo Algorithm [Chang 82].

The idea that one might represent the information contained by some data structure in a variety of ways was first discussed in [Hoare 72b] as a basis for refining program designs. An elegant formalization is given in [Lamport 83b], where the notion of a *refinement mapping* is introduced for this purpose.

The distributed-termination detection problem was introduced in [Francez 80]. It was motivated by the desire to detect deadlock in CSP programs but has since been shown to arise in a variety of other situations as well. The literature devoted to the problem is quite large, so we do not survey it here. The solution we give in §11.4 is from [Dijkstra et al. 83], and a more recent paper that unifies a number of protocols is [Tel & Mattern 93]. An excellent survey on distributed simulation, by the way, is [Misra 86].

Exercise 11.3 is based on a problem given in [Misra & Chandy 81]; Exercise 11.7 is from [Schlichting & Schneider 84], and exercise 11.36 is from [McCurley & Schneider 86].

## Exercises

**11.1.** Enumerate and discharge the proof obligations for establishing that *PO(CliServ)* of Figure 11.2 is interference free.

**11.2.** Give a Proof Outline Logic theorem characterizing the values of the variables as execution proceeds in each of the following programs. Include implicit variables that model channels. Enumerate and discharge the proof obligations for establishing interference freedom of your proof outline.

(a)     **cobegin**
      $x := 1$    **send** $x$ **on** $C$
    ‖
      **receive** $y$ **from** $C$
    **coend**

(b)     **cobegin**
      $x := 1$    **send** *"xIsOne"* **on** $C$    $x := 0$
    ‖
      **receive** *sgnl* **from** $C$
    **coend**

(c)     **cobegin**
      $x := 1$
      **send** *"xIsOne"* **on** $C$
      **receive** *cont* **from** $D$
      $x := 2$
    ‖
      **receive** *sgnl* **from** $C$
      $y := x$
      **send** *"moveOn"* **on** $D$
    **coend**

(d)     **cobegin**
      $x := 1$    **send** *"xIsOne"* **on** $C$    $x := 2$
    ‖
      **receive** *sgnl* **from** $C$    $y := x$    **send** *"moveOn"* **on** $D$
    **coend**

(e)    **cobegin**
            $i := 0$
            **do** $i \neq N \rightarrow$ **send** $b\,[i]$ **on** $C$    $i := 1+1$  **od**
       ‖
            $j := 0$
            **do** $j \neq N \rightarrow$ **receive** $c\,[j]$ **from** $C$    $j := j+1$  **od**
       **coend**

(f)    **cobegin**
            $i := 0$
            **do** $i \neq N \rightarrow$ **send** $b\,[i]$ **on** $C$
                              **receive** $ack$ **from** $D$
                              $i := 1+1$
            **od**
       ‖
            $j := 0$
            **do** $j \neq N \rightarrow$ **receive** $c\,[j]$ **from** $C$
                              **send** "$xxx$" **on** $D$
                              $j := j+1$
            **od**
       **coend**

**11.3.** Construct a theorem of Proof Outline Logic that can be used to establish that the following process merges the $\infty$-terminated nondecreasing sequences of values it receives on channels *inp1* and *inp2* and outputs the result on channel *out*. Assume that $\infty$ is larger than any other value.

> *merge*:  **receive** $v$ **on** *inp1*
>         **receive** $w$ **on** *inp2*
>         **do** $v < w \rightarrow$ **send** $v$ **on** *out*
>                            **receive** $v$ **on** *inp1*
>         [] $v > w \rightarrow$ **send** $w$ **on** *out*
>                            **receive** $w$ **on** *inp2*
>         [] $v = w \neq \infty \rightarrow$ **send** $v$ **on** *out*
>                            **receive** $v$ **on** *inp1*
>         **od**

**11.4.** Show that each of the following is a Proof Outline Logic theorem.

(a)    Reliable Virtual Circuit Send Axiom (11.6), where a send statement is equivalent to (11.4).

(b)    Reliable Virtual Circuit Receive Axiom (11.7), where a receive statement is equivalent to (11.5).

**11.5.** Some operating systems support a form of asynchronous message-passing in which send and receive statements do not name channels. The send statement

> **send** *expr* **on** $T$

causes *expr* to be evaluated and a message with that value to be sent to process $T$. The receive statement

> **receive** $m$

executed by a process $T$ blocks until some message that has been sent to $T$ becomes eligible.

(a)    What data structure would be appropriate for the implicit shared variable(s) used to model such message-passing statements? To what should it be initialized.

(b)    Give an assignment statement that implements the semantics of this alternative send statement.

(c)    Propose an axiom for the alternative send statement. Justify your proposal by showing that it is a theorem of Proof Outline Logic, assuming the operational semantics for **send** you gave in (b).

(d)    Give an atomic statement that implements the semantics of this alternative receive statement.

(e)    Propose an axiom for the receive statement. Justify your proposal by showing that it is a theorem of Proof Outline Logic, assuming the operational semantics for **receive** you gave in (d).

(f)    Give a translation from the alternative send and receive statements to the asynchronous message-passing statements defined in §11.1.

**11.6.** Suppose channel *UVC* is an unreliable virtual circuit.

(a)    What data structure would be appropriate for the implicit shared variable(s) used to model *UVC*? To what should it be initialized?

(b)    Give an assignment statement that implements the semantics of a send statement on *UVC*.

(c)    Propose an axiom for the send statement. Justify your proposal by showing that it is a theorem of Proof Outline Logic, assuming the operational semantics for **send** you gave in (b).

(d)    Give an atomic statement that implements the semantics of a receive statement on *UVC*.

(e)    Propose an axiom for the receive statement. Justify your proposal by showing that it is a theorem of Proof Outline Logic, assuming the operational semantics for **receive** you gave in (d).

(f)    Give a theorem of Proof Outline Logic to characterize the values of $x$ and $y$ as execution of the following program proceeds.

$$x, y := 3, 4$$
**cobegin**
    **send** 1 **on** *UVC*
    **send** 2 **on** *UVC*
||
    **receive** $x$ **from** *UVC*
    **receive** $y$ **from** *UVC*
**coend**

(g)    Give program fragments that serve as replacements for the send and receive statements of §11.1. These fragments should use unreliable virtual circuits. Show that your fragments work by proving that one is pre/post partially equivalent to Reliable Virtual Circuit Send Axiom (11.6) and the other is pre/post partially equivalent to Reliable Virtual Circuit Receive Axiom (11.7). (Pre/post partial equivalence is defined in exercise 4.14.)

**11.7.** Suppose channel *UDS* supports an unreliable datagram service.

(a)    What data structure would be appropriate for the implicit shared variable(s) used to model *UDS*? To what should it be initialized?

(b)    Give an assignment statement that implements the semantics of a send statement on *UDS*.

(c)    Propose an axiom for the send statement. Justify your proposal by showing that it is a theorem of Proof Outline Logic, assuming the operational semantics **send** you gave in (b).

(d)    Give an atomic statement that implements the semantics of a receive statement on *UDS*.

(e)    Propose an axiom for the receive statement. Justify your proposal by showing that it is a theorem of Proof Outline Logic, given the operational semantics for receive you gave in (d).

(f)    Give a theorem of Proof Outline Logic to characterize the values of $x$ and $y$ as execution of the following sequential program proceeds.

> **send** 1 **on** *UDS*
> **send** 2 **on** *UDS*
> **receive** $x$ **from** *UDS*
> **receive** $y$ **from** *UDS*

(g)    Give program fragments that serve as replacements for the send and receive statements of §11.1. These fragments should use unreliable datagrams. Show that your fragments work by proving that one is pre/post partially equivalent to Reliable Virtual Circuit Send Axiom (11.6) and the other is pre/post partially equivalent to Reliable Virtual Circuit Receive Axiom (11.7). (Pre/post partial equivalence is defined in exercise 4.14.)

**11.8.** Consider the following program, where *Server* is defined in Figure 11.3 and both $G_1$ and $G_2$ are reliable virtual circuits.

> **cobegin**
>    *Server*
> ‖
>    $S_1$: **send** 2 **on** $G_1$
>       **send** 2 **on** $G_2$
>       **receive** $x$ **from** $H$
>       **receive** $y$ **from** $H$
> **coend**

(a)    Construct a valid proof outline whose assertions characterize the values of $x$ and $y$ as execution proceeds.

(b)    Enumerate the obligations that must be discharged in order to establish that your proof outline is interference free.

**11.9.** The proof outline of Figure 11.4 remains valid if $post(R_1)$ is strengthened to $x=23$ and $post(R_2)$ is strengthened to $x=39$. Demonstrate this by showing the strengthened proof outline to be a theorem.

**11.10.** Suppose the synchronous-send statements in the program of Figure 11.4 were replaced by asynchronous sends, and the synchronous-receive statements were replaced by asynchronous receives, where channel $C$ is a reliable virtual circuit. Would the proof outline of the figure still be valid? If not, devise one that characterizes the value of $x$ as execution proceeds and show that this new proof outline is a theorem.

**11.11.** Give a Proof Outline Logic theorem to characterize the values of the variables in each of the following programs. Enumerate and discharge any obligations for proving your theorems.

  (a)  **cobegin**$^+$
      $C!1$  ||  $C?y$
    **coend**

  (b)  **cobegin**$^+$
      $x := 1$  $C!x$  ||  $C?y$
    **coend**

  (c)  **cobegin**$^+$
      $x := 1$  $C!xxx$  $D?ok$  $x := 2$
    ||
      $C?yyy$  $y := x$  $D!cont$
    **coend**

  (d)  **cobegin**$^+$
      $x := 1$  $C!xxx$  $x := 2$
    ||
      $C?yyy$  $y := x$
    **coend**

  (e)  **cobegin**$^+$
      $i := 0$  **do** $i \neq N \to C!b[i]$  $i := i+1$ **od**
    ||
      $j := 0$  **do** $j \neq N \to C?a[j]$  $j := j+1$ **od**
    **coend**

**11.12.** Some concurrent programming notations support a form of synchronous message-passing where send and receive statements do not name channels. The send statement $S!expr$ in process $T$ blocks until a receive statement $T?m$ in process $S$ is ready to execute. The two statements are then executed together by performing the assignment statement $m := expr$. Devise a channel action to model this form of synchronous message-passing.

**11.13.** Asynchronous **send** and **receive** statements on a virtual circuit can be replaced by synchronous send and receive statements if an additional process is added to the program. The additional process buffers messages that are eligible for receipt.

  (a)  Give the code for **send, receive,** and the additional process in this translation.

  (b)  Give a procedure to translate a theorem of Proof Outline Logic proved using Reliable Virtual Circuit Send Axiom (11.6), Reliable Virtual Circuit Receive Axiom (11.7), and Interference Freedom Condition (5.8) into a corresponding theorem about the translation.

**11.14.** The Ada programming notation supports a variant of synchronous message-passing called *rendezvous*. A process containing a statement

**call** $C(in\_arg \# out\_arg)$

is blocked until some other process executes the statement

$C$: **accept**$(in\_parm \# out\_parm)$
    $S$
**end**

and vice versa. Execution of these statements together is equivalent to:

$in\_parm := in\_arg \ \ S \ \ out\_arg := out\_parm$

(a)    Show how to translate **call** and **accept** statements into synchronous message-passing statements.

(b)    Based on this translation, give axioms and inference rules for Proof Outline Logic reasoning about programs with **call** and **accept** statements.

**11.15.** Because messages sent with synchronous message-passing statements are not buffered, program execution may be affected if synchronous message-passing statements are simply replaced by asynchronous message-passing statements. What additional property must a program satisfy to ensure that replacing synchronous message-passing statements with asynchronous ones does not lead to any unpleasant surprises?

**11.16.** The following proof outline is a minor modification of the one in Figure 11.4.

    $\{true\}$
    $T$: **cobegin**$^+$
        $\{true\}$
        $S$: $S_1$: $C!23$ $\{x=23\}$
            $S_2$: $C!39$ $\{x=39\}$
    $\|$
        $\{true\}$
        $R$: $R_1$: $C?x$ $\{true\}$
            $R_2$: $C?x$ $\{true\}$
    **coend**
    $\{x=39\}$

Check Channel Action Condition (11.19) for this modified proof outline. If a triple cannot be proved, explain why the problem does not arise for the corresponding triple for Figure 11.4.

**11.17.** (a)    Suppose

$|Bn \cup Bx| \ = \ |Bn| + |Bx|$

holds before execution of the program in Figure 11.5. Will it necessarily hold when the program terminates? If not, what additional assumption(s) about $Bn$ and $Bx$ ensure that $|Bn \cup Bx| \ = \ |Bn| + |Bx|$ holds when the program terminates?

(b)    Justify your answer to (a) with a valid proof outline. Enumerate the requirements for discharging Channel Action Condition (11.19) and for proving interference freedom.

**11.18.** (a)    Suppose

$|Bn| = B_1 \ \wedge \ |Bx| = B_2$

holds before execution of the program in Figure 11.5. Will this necessarily hold when the program terminates? If not, what additional assumption(s) about $Bn$ and $Bx$ ensure that $|Bn|=B_1 \;\wedge\; |Bx|=B_2$ holds when the program terminates?

(b)    Substantiate your answer to (a) with a valid proof outline. Enumerate the requirements for discharging Channel Action Condition (11.19) and for proving interference freedom.

**11.19.** An alternative semantics for a **do** with receive guards is the following:

> A **do** with receive guards terminates when each of its guards either fails or blocks.

(a)    Which semantics—the one in §11.2 or the above alternative—would be preferred by a compiler-writer implementing the run-time system for a programming notation having **do** with receive guards?

(b)    For the alternative semantics, what (if any) changes are necessary to $GEval_{do}(T)$ Axiom (11.32)?

**11.20.** Show that Conditional Channel Action Axiom (11.33) is a Proof Outline Logic theorem.

**11.21.** Prove that critical sections $CS_i$ are mutually exclusive in the following program.

> **cobegin$^+$**
>
>      $MutexSrvr$: **do** $\underset{i}{[]}$   $Ent_i?xxx \rightarrow Ext_i?xxx$   **od**
>
> $\underset{i}{\|}$    $S_i$: **do** $true \rightarrow entry_i$:   $Ent_i!i$
>                                   $CS_i$
>                              $exit_i$:   $Ext_i!i$
>                                   $NCS_i$
>             **od**
>
> **coend**

**11.22.** (a)    Prove that critical sections $CS_i$ are mutually exclusive in the following program.

> **cobegin$^+$**
>
>      $MutexSrvr$: **do** $\underset{i}{[]}$   $true \rightarrow Ent_i?xxx \; Ext_i?xxx$   **od**
>
> $\underset{i}{\|}$    $S_i$: **do** $true \rightarrow entry_i$:   $Ent_i!i$
>                                   $CS_i$
>                              $exit_i$:   $Ext_i!i$
>                                   $NCS_i$
>             **od**
>
> **coend**

(b)    What property expected of a mutual exclusion protocol is not satisfied by the protocol?

**11.23.** Prove that critical sections $CS_i$ are mutually exclusive in the following program. The code for $TSrvr_i$ appears in Figure 11.12.

$$ok_1, ..., ok_N := false, ..., false$$
**cobegin**

|| $TSrvr_i$
  i

|| $S_i$: **do** $true \rightarrow entry_i$: $atmpt_i := true$  **if** $ok_i \rightarrow$ **skip fi**
  i                        $CS_i$
                           $exit_i$: $ok_i, atmpt_i := false, false$
                           $NCS_i$
              **od**
**coend**

**11.24.** An alternative to the decentralized implementation of *matchmaker* in §11.2 is based on replicating *pending* rather than partitioning it. In the alternative, associated with each process $P_i$ is a set *pending$_i$*, which is a replica of *pending* used by *matchmaker*. Equality of replicas is maintained by ensuring that the same sequence of changes is applied to each. Sketch how to achieve this consistency among replicas for a decentralized implementation of *matchmaker*. Your implementation should not involve sequence numbers of any sort on request messages. (Hint: Employ mutual exclusion.)

**11.25.** Modify the sketch of $TSrvr_i$ in Figure 11.12 and its associated *entry* protocol in order to prevent the second guarded command of $TSrvr_i$ from being selected.

**11.26.** Use asynchronous message-passing statements with Eliminating Shared-Variable Reads (11.39) and Eliminating Shared-Variable Writes (11.40) to transform each of the following programs so that it complies with Distributed Program Restriction (11.38). The transformed program should terminate with the same values for $x$ and $y$ as the original. Variable $x$ should be associated with process $S_x$, and variable $y$ should be associated with process $S_y$.

(a)    $x, y := 2, 5$
       **cobegin**
           $S_x$: $x := 1$  $x := y$  $y := 2$  $y := x$
       ||
           $S_y$: **skip**
       **coend**

(b)    $x, y := 2, 5$
       **cobegin**
           $S_x$: $x := 1$  $x := y$
       ||
           $S_y$: $y := 2$  $y := x$
       **coend**

(c)    $x, y := 2, 5$
       **cobegin**
           $S_x$: $y := x+1$  **if** $y \neq x+1 \rightarrow$ **skip fi**
       ||
           $S_y$: $\langle$**if** $y = x+1 \rightarrow y := y+1$**fi**$\rangle$
       **coend**

**11.27.** Suppose that a value $v_i$ is stored at site $i$ in a computer network comprising sites $Net = \{0, 1, ..., N\}$. Let $nbr_i$ be the set of sites that may directly communicate with site $i$. Desired is a program to truthify:

$$total = \sum_{k \in Net} v_k$$

A program has been proposed and construction of a proof outline started:

> *Init*
> **cobegin**
> $\underset{i \in Net}{||}$ $\qquad \{I_i: d_i \subseteq Net \ \wedge \ ttl_i = \sum_{k \in d_i} v_k\}$
> $\qquad S_i: \textbf{ do } \underset{j, i \neq j}{[]} d_i \cap d_j = \varnothing \to \{I_i \ \wedge \ d_i \cap d_j = \varnothing\}$
> $\qquad\qquad\qquad\qquad\qquad ttl_i, d_i := ttl_i + ttl_j, d_i \cup d_j$
> $\qquad\qquad\qquad\qquad\qquad \{I_i\}$
> $\qquad\quad$ **od**
> **coend**

(a)   Propose an assignment statement for *Init*.

(b)   The program does not comply with Distributed Program Restriction (11.38). Show how to transform it into a program that does. Use asynchronous message-passing. Associate with each process $i$ the variables subscripted with $i$.

(c)   Prove that your program works or explain why it does not.

**11.28.** Derive the program given in Figure 11.13 to truthify:

$$s_0 = \underset{k \in Net}{\forall} v_k$$

(a)   Show that $PO(T_i)$ is a theorem of Proof Outline Logic (in isolation).

(b)   Enumerate and discharge any obligations needed for showing interference freedom.

**11.29.** By virtue of its precondition, the proof outline in Figure 11.15 assumes that initialization has been done to truthify:

$$(\forall k \in Net: s_k = v_k \ \wedge \ nd_k = tnbr_k \ \wedge \ d_k = \varnothing)$$

Extend the derivation given in §11.3 and eliminate that initialization assumption. Do this by designing an initial assignment statement for each process $T_i$.

**11.30.** Transform the program of Figure 11.13 into one that complies with Distributed Program Restriction (11.38) but uses synchronous message-passing statements (instead of the asynchronous message-passing statements used to obtain the distributed program of Figure 11.15).

**11.31.** Derive a distributed program consisting of a process at each site in a computer network comprising a set $Net = \{1, 2, ..., N\}$ of sites, where $nbr_i$ is the set of sites with which $i$ can directly communicate. Your program should construct a spanning tree by truthifying:

$$tnbr_i \subseteq nbr_i \ \wedge \ (Net, \underset{k \in Net}{\cup} (\{k\} \times tnbr_k)) \text{ is a spanning tree}$$

**11.32.** The text suggests that liveness property $DL$ (11.46) for the distributed-termination detection protocol could be weakened.

(a)   Give a (nontrivial) weakening of $DL$ that is satisfied by the distributed-termination detection program of Figure 11.16, assuming that $Init_S \Rightarrow (\forall i:\ 1 \le i < N:\ \neg wa_i)$ holds.

(b)   Prove that the distributed-termination detection program of Figure 11.16 satisfies the weaker liveness property you proposed in (a).

**11.33.** The distributed-termination detection program of Figure 11.16 assumes that synchronous message-passing is used for basic and control messages.

(a)   Derive a protocol for the case where asynchronous message-passing is used for control messages but synchronous message-passing continues to be used for basic messages.

(b)   Derive a protocol for the case where asynchronous message-passing is used for control messages and basic messages.

**11.34.** Suppose value $v_i$ is stored at each site $i$ in a computer network comprising sites $Net = \{0, 1, ..., N-1\}$. The network topology is a ring. Consequently, a site $i$ may communicate only with site $(i+1)$ mod N. Channel $C_i$ is the reliable virtual circuit that links sites $i$ and $(i+1)$ mod N. Given is an associative and commutative operator $\psi$ with identity 0. Desired is a distributed program comprising one process per site. The process at site 0 should truthify:

$$Q:\ s_0 = \underset{0 \le k < N}{\psi}\ v_k$$

(a)   Derive a program that uses asynchronous message-passing statements and truthifies $Q$.

(b)   Derive a program that uses synchronous message-passing statements and truthifies $Q$.

**11.35.** Suppose that a value $v_i$ is stored at each site $i$ in a computer network comprising sites $Net = \{0, 1, ..., N-1\}$. The network topology is a star with site 0 at the center. For a site $i$, where $i \ne 0$, channel $IN_i$ links $i$ to site 0, and channel $OUT_i$ links site 0 to site $i$. Channels are reliable virtual circuits. Given is an associative and commutative operator $\psi$ with identity 0. Desired is a distributed program comprising one process per site. The process at site 0 should truthify:

$$Q:\ s_0 = \underset{0 \le k < N}{\psi}\ v_k$$

(a)   Derive a program that uses asynchronous message-passing statements and truthifies $Q$.

(b)   Derive a program that uses synchronous message-passing statements and truthifies $Q$.

**11.36.** Suppose that a value $v_i$ is stored at each site $i$ in a computer network comprising sites $Net = \{0, 1, ..., N-1\}$. Sites communicate with each other by radio broadcasts. Each site is assigned a distinct frequency on which it sends messages, and all sites constantly monitor all frequencies in order to receive messages. The result is a form of asynchronous message-passing. However, because different frequencies exhibit different propagation characteristics, only a subset of the sites may receive each broadcast. These subsets do not change, and it is known that there always exists a communication path between every pair of sites.

To broadcast a message, a site executes:

**send** *m*

Execution of this statement by a site $j$ causes a message to be sent to each site $i$ such that $j \in pred_i$. To receive a message, a site executes:

**receive** *m*

This receives the oldest previously sent but not yet received message.

Desired is a distributed program such that each site $i$ computes $nbr_i$, the set of sites that receive broadcasts from $i$.

(a)    What data structure would be appropriate for the implicit shared variable(s) used to model this message passing.  To what should it be initialized?

(b)    Give a statement that implements the semantics of the send statement, propose a Proof Outline Logic axiom, and justify your proposal by showing that it is a theorem of Proof Outline Logic.

(c)    Give a statement that implements the semantics of the receive statement, propose a Proof Outline Logic axiom, and justify your proposal by showing that it is a theorem of Proof Outline Logic.

(d)    Derive a program to solve the problem.  (Hint:  If each process initially broadcasts its identity, then a process $i$ can compute $pred_i$.)

# Chapter 12

# Putting It Together

Around 1885, French painters Georges Seurat (1859–1891) and Paul Signac (1863–1935) developed a style of painting variously known as pointillism, divisionism, or neo-impressionism. Instead of brush strokes, small dots of pure color are placed on the canvas. The dots fuse at normal viewing distance and create the illusion of regions having color and texture. Seurat's *A Sunday on La Grande Jatte – 1884* is among the best-known examples of pointillist painting; it is reproduced on the cover of this text.

Even to computer scientists unfamiliar with Seurat, Signac, or pointillism, the idea of dots fusing into regions should be a familiar one. It is the approach used to render images on computer displays (individual pixels are illuminated) and on computer printers (dots of ink are placed on the page). It is also the approach used for publishing pictures in newspapers and magazines.

Chapters 2 through 11 have discussed "dots." With your nose to the canvas, it is hard to recognize shapes. So, in this chapter, we take a step back and look at the bigger picture, discussing elements common to logical and algebraic methods for reasoning about concurrent programs. We also talk about their applicability and practicality. The mental tools described in this book, like all tools, are better suited for some tasks than others. Therefore, we close with a discussion of intellectual leverage that formal methods might provide today and in the future.

## 12.1  On Languages

In developing a method for analyzing whether a program satisfies a property, we must choose how to represent programs and properties. This choice has consequences:

- If programs are represented using a notation that can be executed efficiently, then what is verified can be executed.

- If properties are represented using a notation that is reasonably expressive, then requirements of interest can be formalized as properties.

The ideal representation, then, would be an expressive notation that could be executed efficiently. Such a notation, unfortunately, does not seem to exist. Logics, because of their expressive power, are not executable. And imperative programming notations lack the kind of expressiveness we seek, because their descriptions of "what" must be accompanied by explanations of "how."

Two avenues of compromise are open to us. We might employ a single, albeit nonideal, language to represent programs and properties. Or we might employ two distinct languages and provide a means to relate programs (formulas of one) to properties (formulas of the other). Both avenues lead to viable methods for reasoning about programs. A survey of those methods here would take us too far afield, but a brief discussion of the avenues is instructive.

## Single-Language Approach

In one variant of the single-language approach, programs are represented as properties. An encoding, and not the program text itself, is then subjected to analysis. Provided that a high-level view of execution is taken, short formulas encode programs. The method is attractive for reasoning about algorithms— algorithms, because a high-level view of execution is sensible for that domain. More detailed encodings of execution could, in theory, enable reasoning about programs. In practice, the approach then becomes unwieldy because long formulas are needed.

A second variant of the single-language approach encodes properties as programs. The programming notations for such methods are accompanied by meaning-preserving algebraic laws for transforming one program into another. A program that satisfies a specification is derived systematically by using the algebraic laws to transform the specification into a form that executes efficiently. For example, among the laws might be

$$\text{``}\textbf{skip} \;\; x := expr\text{''} \;\;\; = \;\;\; \text{``}x := expr \;\; \textbf{skip}\text{''}$$

to assert that **skip** commutes with assignment statements.

This second variant of the single-language approach tends to bias specifications towards "how" and away from "what." Also, for reasons not entirely understood, obtaining a rich set of algebraic laws for a concurrent programming notation depends on the presence of synchronous message-passing and the absence of shared memory. (A shared variable is modeled as a process that responds to read and write requests sent to it in messages.) The absence of shared memory and the imposition of synchronous message-passing makes it difficult to reason directly about programs that use other mechanisms for synchronization and communication; it also makes certain properties moot (e.g., mutual exclusion) that nevertheless are important in some settings.

## *Two-Language Approach and Beyond*

An alternative to the single-language approach employs both a programming notation that is efficiently executed and a property notation that is sufficiently expressive. It is known as the two-language approach. The developer of a two-language approach faces the problem of devising the apparatus needed to show that a program satisfies a property. A logic is generally used, embedding the relation between program texts and the properties they satisfy into the logic's relation between syntax and semantics. Algebraic laws to manipulate a property and obtain a program are precluded, given the use of two distinct languages.

One example of the two-language approach would be to employ a Temporal Logic, like the one in Chapters 3 and 8, along with an imperative programming notation. For relating programs and properties, we would use the axioms and inference rules of $S$-Temporal Logic, but with $\mathcal{H}_S^+$ Triple Rule (8.4) replaced by an axiom for each atomic action of the programming notation.

The method of this book adds proof outlines to a two-language approach involving Temporal Logic and an imperative programming notation. The result is not exactly a three-language approach, because the programming notation is embedded in the language of proof outlines. Nevertheless, another language and another logic (Proof Outline Logic) do mean more complexity. What is gained?

Proof outlines link points in the program text to assertions about the program's state. The text of a proof outline thereby provides a static representation of something dynamic: the program state. Moreover, this linking is done in a natural way. Contrast a proof outline with its proof outline invariant. Both encode the exact same information about states, but the information is far less accessible when packaged as the proof outline invariant. Whether developing or analyzing a program, we benefit from seeing how each statement contributes to the property of interest. The assertions of a proof outline provide that information (at least with respect to safety properties). So, what is gained by adding proof outlines to the picture is better support for programming methodology.

## 12.2  Principles for Verifying Safety and Liveness Properties

Step back from our logics, with their innumerable axioms and inference rules, and you find two simple principles—one for verifying safety properties and another for verifying liveness properties. Moreover, because every property is the conjunction of safety and liveness properties (see §2.4), these two principles suffice for proving that a program satisfies any property. Principles so fundamental are worth discussing.

### *Safety Properties*

All safety properties can be proved using invariance arguments. An *invariance argument* for proving that some bad thing $B$ cannot happen during execution involves finding a Predicate Logic formula $I$ such that:

(12.1)   $I$ is initially *true*.

(12.2)   $I$ is not falsified by any atomic action of the program.

(12.3)   If $I$ holds, then $B$ does not.

Typically, $I$ is stronger than $B$, because $B$ not having happened does not imply that $B$ cannot happen in the future. The stronger $I$ rules out states from which $B$ could be *true* in the future (as well as ruling out states in which $B$ currently is *true*).

Notice how an invariance argument is bound up in Safety Consequence Rule (6.8) for verifying invariance properties. There, the role of $I$ is played by the proof outline invariant. Valid Proof Outline (4.17) implies that the proof outline invariant is not falsified by any atomic action of the program, so condition (12.2) is met. Conditions (12.1) and (12.3) of the invariance argument are premises of Safety Consequence Rule (6.8), so they too must be discharged in any proof that employs Safety Consequence Rule (6.8).

This only shows the role of invariance arguments for verifying invariance properties—one particular form of safety property. Arbitrary safety properties are the subject of Chapter 7. But that chapter contains no new $S$-Temporal Logic rules; it is devoted to extensions to Predicate Logic and Proof Outline Logic so that arbitrary safety properties can be recast in the form handled by the rules of Chapter 6. Thus, invariance arguments also underly our method for verifying arbitrary safety properties.

In this light, the axioms and inference rule of Proof Outline Logic can be seen as supporting invariance arguments by providing an apparatus for constructing proof outline invariants. For each atomic action, statement, and program fragment, the Proof Outline Logic axioms and inference rules restrict assertions. The proof outline invariant that results cannot be falsified by any atomic action. With Proof Outline Logic, $I$ in our invariance argument need not be divined; instead, it can be constructed systematically from the program text.

## Liveness Properties

All liveness properties can be proved using well-foundedness arguments. A *well-foundedness argument* for proving that some good thing $G$ happens during execution involves finding a well-founded ordering ‹ on program states such that:

(12.4)   $G$ holds in any state that is ‹-minimal.

(12.5)   Atomic actions started in a state $s$ not satisfying $G$ terminate in a state $t$ where $t$‹$s$ holds.

(12.6)   Some atomic actions are guaranteed to be executed eventually.

The justification that well-foundedness arguments suffice for verifying any liveness property is somewhat technical; we give only an outline here.

Recall that every property defines a set of histories. The sets of interest to us can be recognized by a type of automaton, called a *Buchi automaton*, that accepts infinite-length inputs. Like an ordinary finite-state automaton, a Buchi automaton has a finite number of states, and a subset of these are designated as *accept* states. A history is accepted by a Buchi automaton iff it causes the automaton to enter accept states infinitely often.

The Buchi automaton for a liveness property will have as its accept states a proper subset of the automaton's states. Inputs are rejected that have a suffix in which no accept state is entered. That some inputs are rejected should not be surprising, since any nontrivial liveness property rules out some histories. The mechanism by which the inputs are rejected, though, is critical for understanding the relationship between liveness properties and well-foundedness arguments.

Define a set $Q$ of automaton states to be *strongly connected* iff there is a sequence of transitions from any element of $Q$ to any other but without involving automaton states outside of $Q$. Define a *reject knot* $\kappa$ to be a maximal strongly connected subset of the automaton states that contains no accept states. A Buchi automaton for a liveness property necessarily contains at least one reject knot— because that is the only way it can reject inputs—and rejects any input having a suffix that only enters states in a reject knot.

We prove that a program satisfies a property by showing that no history of the program is rejected by the Buchi automaton for the property. For liveness properties, this can be done with a well-foundedness argument, as follows: Equate $G$ with entering an accept state and conclude from conditions (12.4) through (12.6) that it is impossible for the Buchi automaton to remain forever in a reject knot. That, then, is the connection between well-foundedness arguments and verifying liveness properties.

Given this connection, we should not be surprised to find that our rules for verifying liveness properties are all based on well-foundedness arguments. The two Temporal Logic rules for proving eventualities—Well-Founded $\Diamond$ Induction Rule (3.68) and Natural Number $\Diamond$ Induction Rule (3.69)—employ well-founded sets; the variant function $\upsilon$ used in Precondition for do (4.57) to bound the number of loop iterations is an encoding of a well-foundedness argument; and all the $S$-Temporal Logic inference rules of §8.5 for exploiting fairness assumptions in proving eventualities involve well-founded sets.

## 12.3  Proofs Only Increase Confidence

The methods in this text are intended to increase confidence that a program will behave as intended. At their heart are proofs in a formal logic. However, the term "proof" here can be misleading, for it connotes a certainty that would be misplaced. We do not prove that a program, if executed by a computer, will work correctly. We prove something about two approximations—one for program execution and another for working correctly. Any certainty brought by a proof applies only to these approximations.

First, the meaning we ascribe to programs is just an approximation of what happens when it is copper and silicon actually doing the execution. A compiler and a computer—both rather complex and potentially flawed artifacts—sit between the objects of our analysis and the phenomenon we seek to analyze. Even were the compiler and hardware flawless, what they actually implement is likely to differ from the model of execution axiomatized by our logics. For example, a real computer will have a finite number of finite-sized memory words; Proof Outline Logic and $S$-Temporal Logic ignore this aspect of reality. According to these logics, programs run with no constraints on memory or data representation. And memory limits are not the only way in which our execution model idealizes reality.

We could extend our logics to characterize a more realistic execution model. But doing so adds complexity to the logics and proofs. So instead, someone concerned, for example, about overflow for a variable $v$ is invited to prove an invariance property bounding the values assigned to $v$. As you might imagine, such proofs are tedious. Fortunately, discrepancies between reality and our idealization can be ignored if our goal is (merely) increased confidence. A proof with respect to an idealized model of execution increases confidence in a program, because errors revealed while constructing the proof would also have been errors in the realistic execution model.

A second form of approximation we are making concerns acceptable program behavior. We prove that a program satisfies the property specified by one or another Temporal Logic formula, but that is not the same as proving that the program exhibits acceptable behavior. A Temporal Logic formula might not specify the property we intend, and we might not have identified all the properties that comprise acceptable behavior. To increase our confidence in a Temporal Logic specification, we check that it implies what we expect by defining sanity conditions and proving that they are implied by the specification. However, no formal analysis technique can prove that a formal text is consistent with an informal understanding.

Finally, there is always the risk of errors in proofs. In principle, proofs can be checked mechanically, and today there are computer programs to do this checking (although we are unaware of any for the particular logics described in this text). Such proof-checking environments should become more prevalent as they grow more powerful and easier to use. Not too long ago, arithmetic calculators could be found only in accounting offices, whereas now they are abundant. We predict a similar future for "logic calculators."

In the absence of automated support, people check proofs by reading and studying them. The more readers, the more likely it is that an error in the proof will be detected. A difficulty then arises for the sort of proofs of concern to us—proofs that programs satisfy properties. Fewer people have the incentive to read these proofs, so the proof-checking social process is attenuated.

However, unlike proofs found in mathematics and computer science journals, proofs of programs typically have few (if any) deep or subtle steps. Steps in our proofs tend to be simple, and therefore the proofs can be completely rigorous. It is tedious, but plausible, for a reader to check such a proof completely. So, the very reason our proofs are unattractive to read might also facilitate checking them. The social process that serves published proofs in journals so well just might be useful for program proofs.

## 12.4  A Tool and Applications

The programs treated in this book are tiny in comparison with today's software systems, and constructing proofs for even our tiny programs was nontrivial. It seems safe to conclude that proofs for large programs are not feasible today and to predict that this will remain so for the foreseeable future. What role, then, can there be for a methodology like ours?

Our methods do work well for small programs, providing a systematic way to derive a program that satisfies a specification. Moreover, a byproduct of that derivation is a formal proof that the program satisfies the specification. The derivation is handy for explaining why one or another detail of the program is needed, since each variable and statement can be traced to some step and proof obligation. The proof is a useful maintenance tool, because it enables us to answer questions about disruption that might be caused by modifying the program. Thus, our methods provide a way to understand programs without thinking in terms of execution.

The question about the role of our methodology, then, is really a question about the role of small programs. Can methods for constructing small programs help in constructing large programs? They can. For one thing, any large program is constructed from smaller components. And for writing those smaller components, the methods help. We need not even be completely formal. We can state invariants in English and then use those invariants to guide changing the shared state by a routine we are writing. In fact, we did exactly this at the end of §11.2 in developing a synchronous message-passing implementation. Similarly, a well-founded ranking can guide our choice of statements, so that some liveness property of interest will be satisfied.

Moreover, subtle pieces of systems usually have short formal specifications and are implemented by algorithms having short high-level descriptions. Synchronization routines, network routing and management algorithms, fault-tolerance algorithms—the trickiest parts of a software system—usually can be described in a page or so of high-level code written in terms of suitable abstractions. One might speculate about why this is the case. For us, that it is the case is all that matters, because it means that those parts of a system most in need of our analysis machinery are suitable subjects. Of course, there is the risk of performing the analysis and then making an error when instantiating the abstractions. One must certainly be careful that the properties assumed by the abstractions are implemented by their realizations.

Today, there is a pressing need for software that we can trust. Errors in programs have already caused deaths. Moreover, the problem is getting worse, because software is being used more and more in mission-critical and life-critical applications. The methods in this text provide one way to increase our confidence in programs. At first, they may seem strange and difficult, for we reason about something that is dynamic—program execution—by using something that is static—logical formulas. Practice, however, does make the methods familiar and less difficult. And programmers who are comfortable with the methods become more effective at writing software that can be trusted.

> *Bit by bit,*
> *Putting it together ...*
> *Piece by piece—*
> *Only way to make a work of art.*
> *Every moment makes a contribution,*
> *Every little detail plays a part.*
> *Having just the vision's no solution.*
> *Everything depends on execution:*
> *Putting it together—*
> *That's what counts.*
>
> —From "Putting It Together" in Act II of
> Stephen Sondheim's Broadway musical
> *Sunday in the Park with George*

## Historical Notes

The partitioning of verification methods into single-language and two-language approaches was suggested in [de Roever 86]. A partisan of the two-language approach, de Roever was commenting on a lecture given by Milner, who is the developer of a well-known single-language approach. Examples of the single-language approach include process algebras, such as CCS (Calculus of Communicating Systems) [Milner 80] and CSP (Communicating Sequential Processes) [Hoare 85], as well as logics like TLA (Temporal Logic of Actions) [Lamport 94]. Process algebras generally take programming languages as their starting points; in contrast, TLA is based on a specification notation (a linear-time temporal logic).

Our discussion of the role of invariance and of well-foundedness arguments in proving safety and liveness properties is based on [Alpern & Schneider 87], which gives the first proofs for relating invariance arguments with safety properties and for relating well-foundedness arguments with liveness properties. See [Eilenberg 74] for an introduction to Buchi automata.

As the field has matured, there have been several lengthy and—at times—heated debates about the benefits and practicality of program verification. We do not survey those debates here, for we could not do justice to either side in a limited space. However, two debates are directly related to material discussed in this chapter. One centers on the contention in [DeMillo et al. 79] that proof checking is a social process and proofs of programs are not interesting enough to attract the necessary critical mass of readers. A second debate, sparked by [Fetzer 88], questioned the utility of programming logics because they axiomatize ideal execution models rather than realistic ones. Both [DeMillo et al. 79] and [Fetzer 88] are worth reading by a student of programming logics.

# References

[Abadi & Lamport 88]   Abadi, M., and L. Lamport. The existence of refinement mappings. *Proc. Third Annual Symposium on Logic in Computer Science* (Edinburgh, Scotland, July 1988), IEEE Computer Society, 165-177.

[Almasi & Gottlieb 94]   Almasi, G.S., and A. Gottlieb. *Highly Parallel Computing*. Second edition. The Benjamin Cummings Publishing Company, Redwood City, California, 1994.

[Alpern et al. 86]   Alpern, B., A.J. Demers, and F.B. Schneider. Safety without stuttering. *Information Processing Letters 23*, 4 (Nov. 1986), 177-180.

[Alpern & Schneider 85]   Alpern, B., and F.B. Schneider. Defining liveness. *Information Processing Letters 21*, 4 (Oct. 1985), 181-185.

[Alpern & Schneider 87]   Alpern, B., and F.B. Schneider. Recognizing safety and liveness. *Distributed Computing 2*, 3 (Dec. 1987), 117-126.

[Ambler et al. 77]   Ambler, A.L., D.I. Good, J.C. Browne, W.F. Burger, R.M. Cohen, C.G. Hoch, and R.E. Wells. GYPSY: A language for specification and implementation of verifiable programs. *Proc. of an ACM Conference on Language Design for Reliable Software*, SIGPLAN Notices 12, 3 (March 1977), 1-10.

[Andrews 89]   Andrews, G.R. A method for solving synchronization problems. *Science of Computer Programming 13*, 4 (Dec. 1989), 1-21.

[Andrews 91]   Andrews, G.R. *Concurrent Programming: Principles and Practice*. The Benjamin Cummings Publishing Company, Redwood City, California, 1991.

[Andrews & Schneider 83]   Andrews, G., and F.B. Schneider. Concepts and notations for concurrent programming. *ACM Computing Surveys 15*, 1 (March 1983), 3-43.

[Apt 81]   Apt, K.R. Ten years of Hoare's Logic: A survey—Part I. *ACM TOPLAS 3*, 4 (Oct. 1981), 431-483.

[Apt et al. 80]   Apt, K.R., N. Francez, and W.P. de Roever. A Proof System for Communicating Sequential Processes. *ACM TOPLAS 2*, 3 (July 1980), 359-385.

[Apt et al. 87]   Apt, K.R., N. Francez, and S. Katz. Appraising fairness in languages for distributed computing. *Proc. Fourteenth Annual ACM Symposium on Principles of Programming Languages* (Munich, West Germany, Jan. 1987), ACM, 189-198.

[Apt et al. 88]   Apt, K.R., N. Francez, and S. Katz. Appraising fairness in languages for distributed computing. *Distributed Computing 2*, 4 (Aug. 1988), 226-241.

[Apt & Olderog 83]   Apt, K.R., and E.R. Olderog. Proof rules and transformation dealing with fairness. *Science of Computer Programming 3*, 1 (April 1983), 65-100.

[Apt & Olderog 91]   Apt, K.R., and E.R. Olderog. *Verification of Sequential and Concurrent Programs*. Springer-Verlag, New York, 1991.

[Ashcroft 75]   Ashcroft, E. Proving assertions about parallel programs. *Journal of Computer and System Sciences 10*, 1 (Feb. 1975), 110-135.

[Ashcroft 76]   Ashcroft, E. Program verification tableaus. Technical Report CS-76-01. University of Waterloo, Waterloo, Ontario, Canada, Jan. 1976.

[Ashcroft & Manna 71]   Ashcroft, E., and Z. Manna. Formalization of properties of parallel programs. *Machine Intelligence 6* (1971), Edinburgh University Press, 17-41.

[Back 89]   Back, R.J.R. A method for refining atomicity in parallel algorithms. *Proc. PARLE '89 Parallel Architectures and Languages Europe*, E. Odijk, M. Rem, and J.-C. Syre (eds.), Lecture Notes in Computer Science Volume 366, Springer-Verlag, Berlin, 1989, 199-216.

[Bagrodia 89]   Bagrodia, R. Synchronization of asynchronous processes in CSP. *ACM TOPLAS 11*, 4 (Oct. 1989), 585-597.

[Bal et al. 89]   Bal, H.E., J.G. Steiner, and A.S. Tanenbaum. Programming languages for distributed computing systems. *ACM Computing Surveys 21*, 3 (Sept. 1989), 261-322.

[de Bakker 68]   de Bakker, J.W. Axiomatics of simple assignment statements. M.R.94, Mathematisch Centrum, Amsterdam, 1968.

[de Bakker et al. 86]   de Bakker, J.W., W.P. de Roever, and G. Rozenberg (eds.). *Current Trends in Concurrency*. Lecture Notes in Computer Science Volume 224, Springer-Verlag, New York, 1986.

[Balzer 71]   Balzer, R.M. PORTS—A method for dynamic interprogram communication and job control. *Proc. of the 1971 Spring Joint Computer Conference 38*, AFIPS Press, 1971, 485-489.

[Barringer 85]  Barringer, H. *A Survey of Verification Techniques for Parallel Programs*. Lecture Notes in Computer Science Volume 191, Springer-Verlag, New York, 1985.

[Bell & Machover 77]  Bell, J., and M. Machover. *A Course in Mathematical Logic*. North Holland, New York, 1977.

[Belpaire & Wilmotte 74]  Belpaire, G., and J.P. Wilmotte. A semantic approach to the theory of parallel processes. *Proc. of International Computing Symposium 1973* (Davos, Switzerland, 1973), North Holland, New York, 1974, 159-164.

[Ben-Ari 82]  Ben-Ari, M. *Principles of Concurrent Programming*. Prentice Hall International, Englewood Cliffs, N.J., 1982.

[Ben-Ari et al. 81]  Ben-Ari, M., Z. Manna, and A. Pnueli. The temporal logic of branching time. *Conference Record of Eighth Annual ACM Symposium on Principles of Programming Languages* (Williamsburg, Virginia, Jan. 1981), ACM, 164-176.

[Bernstein 80]  Bernstein, A.J. Output guards and nondeterminism in "Communicating Sequential Processes." *ACM TOPLAS 2*, 2 (April 1980), 234-238.

[Bernstein 87]  Bernstein, A.J. Predicate transfer and timeout in message passing systems. *Information Processing Letters 24*, 1 (Jan. 1987), 43-52.

[Bernstein & Lewis 93]  Bernstein, A.J., and P.M. Lewis. *Concurrency in Programming and Database Systems*. Jones and Bartlett, Boston, Mass., 1993.

[Birrell & Nelson 84]  Birrell, A.D., and B.J. Nelson. Implementing remote procedure calls. *ACM TOCS 2*, 1 (Feb. 1984), 39-59.

[Brinch Hansen 70]  Brinch Hansen, P. The nucleus of a multiprogramming system. *CACM 13*, 4 (Aug. 1970), 238-241, 250.

[Brinch Hansen 72a]  Brinch Hansen, P. A comparison of two synchronizing concepts. *Acta Informatica 1*, 3 (1972), 190-199.

[Brinch Hansen 72b]  Brinch Hansen, P. Structured multiprogramming. *CACM 15*, 7 (July 1972), 574-578.

[Brinch Hansen 77]  Brinch Hansen, P. *The Architecture of Concurrent Programs*. Prentice Hall, Englewood Cliffs, N.J., 1977.

[Buckley & Silberschatz 83]  Buckley, G., and A. Silberschatz. An effective implementation of the generalized input-output construct of CSP. *ACM TOPLAS 5*, 2 (April 1983), 223-235.

[Buhr et al. 95]  Buhr, P., M. Fortier, and M.H. Coffin. Monitor classification. *ACM Computing Surveys 27*, 1 (March 1995), 63-109.

[Burstall 68]  Burstall, R.M. Proving properties of programs by structural induction. Experimental Programming Reports, No. 17. DMIP, Edinburgh, 1968.

[Burstall 74]   Burstall, R.M.  Program proving as hand simulation with a little induction. *Information Processing 74*, North Holland, New York, 1974, 308-312.

[Chandy & Misra 86]   Chandy, K.M., and J. Misra.  An example of stepwise refinement of distributed programs: Quiescence detection. *ACM TOPLAS 8*, 3 (July 1986), 326-343.

[Chandy & Misra 88a]   Chandy, K.M., and J. Misra. Another view of "Fairness." *Software Engineering Notes 13*, 3 (July 1988), 21.

[Chandy & Misra 88b]   Chandy, K.M., and J. Misra. *Parallel Program Design: A Foundation*. Addison-Wesley, Reading, Mass., 1988.

[Chang 82]   Chang, E.J.H. Echo algorithms: Depth parallel operations on general graphs. *IEEE Trans. on Software Engineering SE-8*, 4 (July 1982), 391-401.

[Church 56]   Church, A. *Introduction to Mathematical Logic*. Princeton University Press, Princeton, New Jersey, 1956.

[Clarke 80]   Clarke, E.M. Synthesis of resource invariants for concurrent programs. *ACM TOPLAS 2*, 3 (July 1980), 338-358.

[Clint 73]   Clint, M. Program proving: Coroutines. *Acta Informatica 2*,1 (1973), 50-63.

[Cohen 90]   Cohen, Ed. *Programming in the 1990s*. Springer-Verlag, New York, 1990.

[Cohen 93a]   Cohen, Ernie. A programmers guide to reduction. Technical Report, Bellcore.

[Cohen 93b]   Cohen, Ernie. *Modular Progress Proofs of Asynchronous Programs*. Ph.D. thesis, University of Texas at Austin, 1993.

[Constable & O'Donnell 78]   Constable, R.L., and M.J. O'Donnell. *A Programming Logic*. Winthrop Publishers, Cambridge, Mass., 1978.

[Cook 78]   Cook, S.A. Soundness and completeness of an axiom system for program verification. *SIAM Journal on Computing 7*, 1 (1978), 70-90.

[Courtois et al. 71]   Courtois, P.J., F. Heymans, and D.L. Parnas. Concurrent control with readers and writers. *CACM 14*, 10 (Oct 1971), 667-668.

[Courtois et al. 72]   Courtois, P.J., F. Heymans, and D.L. Parnas. Comments on "A Comparison of Two Synchronizing Concepts by P.B. Hansen." *Acta Informatica 1*, 4 (1972), 375-376.

[de Roever 86]   de Roever, W.P. Questions to Robin Milner—A responder's commentary. *Information Processing 86*, H.J. Kugler (ed.), Elsevier Science Publishers B.V., North-Holland, 1986, 515-518.

[DeLong 70]   DeLong, H. *A Profile of Mathematical Logic*. Addison-Wesley, Reading, Mass. 1970.

[DeMillo et al. 79]   DeMillo, R., R.J. Lipton, and A. Perlis. Social processes and proofs of theorems and programs. *CACM 22*, 5 (May 1979), 271-280.

[Dijkstra 65]   Dijkstra, E.W.   Solution of a problem in concurrent programming control. *CACM 8*, 9 (Sept. 1965), 569.

[Dijkstra 68a]   Dijkstra, E.W.   The structure of T.H.E. multiprogramming system. *CACM 11*, 5 (May 1968), 341-346.

[Dijkstra 68b]   Dijkstra, E.W.   Cooperating sequential processes. In *Programming Languages*, F. Genuys (ed.), Academic Press, New York, 1968.

[Dijkstra 71]   Dijkstra, E.W.   Hierarchical ordering of sequential processes. *Acta Informatica 1* (1971), 115-138.

[Dijkstra 75]   Dijkstra, E.W.   Guarded commands, nondeterminacy and formal derivation of programs. *CACM 18*, 8 (Aug. 1975), 453-457.

[Dijkstra 76a]   Dijkstra, E.W.   *A Discipline of Programming*. Prentice Hall, N.J., 1976.

[Dijkstra 76b]   Dijkstra, E.W.   A personal summary of the Gries-Owicki theory. EWD554 (March 1976), in *Selected Writings on Computing: A Personal Perspective*, E.W. Dijkstra, Springer-Verlag, New York, 1982.

[Dijkstra 77a]   E.W. Dijkstra.   On making solutions more and more fine-grained. EWD622 (May 1977), in *Selected Writings on Computing: A Personal Perspective*, E.W. Dijkstra, Springer-Verlag, New York, 1982.

[Dijkstra 77b]   Dijkstra, E.W.   On two beautiful solutions designed by Martin Rem. EWD629, in *Selected Writings on Computing: A Personal Perspective*, E.W. Dijkstra, Springer-Verlag, New York, 1982.

[Dijkstra 77c]   Dijkstra, E.W.   A correctness proof for communicating processes—A small exercise. EWD607, in *Selected Writings on Computing: A Personal Perspective*, E.W. Dijkstra, Springer-Verlag, New York, 1982.

[Dijkstra 79]   Dijkstra, E.W.   A tutorial on the split binary semaphore. EWD703, in *Theoretical Foundations of Programming Methodology*, M. Broy and G. Schmidt (eds.), Reidel, 1982.

[Dijkstra 80]   Dijkstra, E.W.   The superfluity of the general semaphore. EWD734, April 1980.

[Dijkstra 85]   Dijkstra, E.W.   Mainly on our use of the predicate calculus. EWD905, Feb. 1985.

[Dijkstra 88]   Dijkstra, E.W.   Position paper on "Fairness." *Software Engineering Notes 13*, 2 (April 1988), 18-20.

[Dijkstra & Feijen 84]   Dijkstra, E.W., and W.H.J. Feijen.   *Een methode van programmeren*, Academic Service, Amsterdam, 1984.

[Dijkstra et al. 83]   Dijkstra, E.W., W.H.J. Feijen, and A.J.M. van Gasteren. Derivation of a termination detection algorithm for distributed computations. *Information Processing Letters 16*, 5 (June 1983), 217-219.

[Dod 81]   Department of Defense.   *Programming Language Ada: Reference Manual*. Lecture Notes in Computer Science Volume 106, Springer-Verlag, New York, 1981.

[Doeppner 77]   Doeppner, T.W.  Parallel program correctness through refinement. *Proc. Fourth Annual ACM Symposium on Principles of Programming Languages* (Los Angeles, CA, Jan. 1977), ACM, 155-159.

[Draughon et al. 67]   Draughon, E., R. Grishman, J. Schwartz, and A. Stein. Programming considerations for parallel computers. Report IMM 362, Courant Institute of Mathematical Sciences. New York University, New York, Nov. 1967.

[Eilenberg 74]   Eilenberg, S. *Automata, Languages, and Machines.* Volume A, Academic Press, New York, 1974.

[Emerson 83]   Emerson, E.A.  Alternative semantics for temporal logics. *Theoretical Computer Science 26* (1983), 121-130.

[Emerson & Clarke 81]   Emerson, E.A., and E.M. Clarke.  Characterizing correctness properties of parallel programs as fixpoints. *Proc. Seventh Colloquium on Automata, Languages, and Programming* (Noordwijkerhout, the Netherlands, July 1980), J.W. de Bakker and J. van Leeuwen (eds.), Lecture Notes in Computer Science Volume 85, Springer-Verlag, Heidelberg, 1980, 169-181.

[Emerson & Halpern 83]   Emerson, E.A., and J.Y. Halpern.  "Sometimes" and "not never" revisited: On branching versus linear time. *Conference Record of the Tenth Annual ACM Symposium on Principles of Programming Languages* (Austin, Texas, Jan 1983), ACM, 127-140.

[Enderton 72]   Enderton, H.B.  *A Mathematical Introduction to Logic.* Academic Press, New York, 1972.

[Faulk & Parnas 88]   Faulk, S.R., and D.L. Parnas.  On synchronization in hard-real-time systems. *CACM 31*, 3 (March 1988), 274-287.

[Fetzer 88]   Fetzer, J.H. Program verification: The very idea. *CACM 31*, 9 (Sept. 1988), 1048-1063.

[Fillman & Friedman 84]   Fillman, R.E., and D.P. Friedman.  *Coordinated Computing Tools and Techniques for Distributed Software.* McGraw Hill, New York, 1983.

[Floyd 67]   Floyd, R.W. Assigning meanings to programs. *Proc. Symposia in Applied Mathematics 19*, 1967, 19-31.

[Francez 80]   Francez, N. Distributed termination. *ACM TOPLAS 2*, 1 (Jan. 1980), 42-55.

[Francez 86]   Francez, N. *Fairness.* Springer-Verlag, New York, 1986.

[Francez & Pnueli 76]   Francez, N., and A. Pnueli. A proof method for cyclic programs. *Acta Informatica 9*, 2 (1978), 133-157.

[Gabbay et al. 80]   Gabbay, D., A. Pnueli, S. Shelah, and J. Stavi. The temporal analysis of fairness. *Conference Record of Seventh Annual ACM Symposium on Principles of Programming Languages* (Las Vegas, Nevada, Jan. 1980), ACM, 163-173.

[Gabbay et al. 94]   Gabbay, D., I. Hodkinson, and M. Reynolds. *Temporal Logic: Mathematical Foundations and Computational Aspects*, Vol. 1., Oxford University Press, Oxford, 1994.

[Goldblatt 87]   Goldblatt, R. *Logics of Time and Computation*. CSLI Lecture Notes Number 7, Center for the Study of Language and Information, Leland Stanford Junior University, Stanford, CA, 1987.

[Goldstine & von Neumann 47]   Goldstine, H.H., and J. von Neumann. Planning and coding of problems for an electronic computing instrument. Report for U.S. Ord. Dept. In *Collected Works of J. von Neumann*, Vol. 5, A. Taub (ed.), Pergamon, New York, 1965, 80-151.

[Good et al. 79]   Good, D.I., R.M. Cohen, and J. Keeton-Williams. Principles of proving concurrent programs in GYPSY. *Conference Record of Sixth ACM Symposium on Principles of Programming Languages* (San Antonio, Texas, Jan. 1979), ACM, 42-52.

[Gottlieb et al. 83]   Gottlieb, A., B.D. Lubachevsky, and L. Rudolph. Basic techniques for the efficient coordination of very large numbers of cooperating sequential processors. *ACM TOPLAS 5*, 2 (April 1983), 164-189.

[Gray & Reuter 93]   Gray, J.N., and A. Reuter. *Transaction Processing: Concepts and Techniques*. Morgan Kaufman Publishers, San Mateo, California, 1993.

[Gries 77]   Gries, D. A proof of correctness of Rem's semaphore implementation of the **with-when** statement. Technical Report TR 77-314, Cornell University, Ithaca, New York, 1977.

[Gries 78]   Gries, D. The multiple assignment statement. *IEEE Trans. on Software Engineering SE-4*, 2 (March 1978), 87-93.

[Gries 81]   Gries, D. *The Science of Programming*. Springer-Verlag, New York, 1981.

[Gries & Levin 80]   Gries, D., and G.M. Levin. Assignment and procedure call proof rules. *ACM TOPLAS 2*, 4 (Oct. 1980), 564-579.

[Gries & Schneider 93]   Gries, D., and F.B. Schneider. *A Logical Approach to Discrete Math*. Springer-Verlag, New York. 1993.

[Grumberg et al. 81]   Grumberg, O., N. Francez, J.A. Makowsky, and W.P. de Roever. A proof rule for fair termination of guarded commands. *Algorithmic Languages*, J.W. de Bakker and J.C. Van Vliet (eds.), North Holland, Amsterdam, 1981, 399-416

[Habermann 72]   Habermann, A.N. Synchronization of communicating processes. *CACM 15*, 3 (March 1972), 171-176.

[Hailpern 82]   Hailpern, B.T. *Verifying Concurrent Processes Using Temporal Logic*. Lecture Notes in Computer Science Volume 129, Springer-Verlag, Heidelberg, 1982.

[Hehner 84]   Hehner, E.C.R. *The Logic of Programming*. Prentice Hall International, Englewood Cliffs, New Jersey, 1984.

[Herlihy 91]   Herlihy, M.P. Wait-free synchronization. *ACM TOPLAS 13*, 1 (Jan. 1991), 123-149.

[Hoare 69]   Hoare, C.A.R. An axiomatic basis for computer programming. *CACM 12*, 10 (Oct. 1969), 576-580.

[Hoare 72a]   Hoare, C.A.R. Towards a theory of parallel programming. In *Operating Systems Techniques*, C.A.R. Hoare and R. Perrot (eds.), Academic Press, New York, 1972.

[Hoare 72b]   Hoare, C.A.R. Proof of correctness of data representations. *Acta Informatica 1*, 4 (1972), 271-281.

[Hoare 74]   Hoare, C.A.R. Monitors: An operating system structuring concept. *CACM 12*, 10 (Oct. 1974), 548-557.

[Hoare 75]   Hoare, C.A.R. Parallel programming: An axiomatic approach. *Computer Languages 1*, 1975, Pergamon Press, 151-160.

[Hoare 78]   Hoare, C.A.R. Communicating sequential processes. *CACM 21*, 8 (Aug. 1978), 666-677.

[Hoare 85]   Hoare, C.A.R. *Communicating Sequential Processes*. Prentice Hall International, Englewood Cliffs, N.J., 1985.

[Hofstadter 79]   Hofstadter, D.R. *Gödel, Escher, Bach: An Eternal Golden Braid*. Basic Books, New York, 1979.

[Holt et al. 78]   Holt, R.C., G.S. Graham, E.D. Lazowska, and M.A. Scott. *Structured Concurrent Programming with Operating Systems Applications*. Addison-Wesley, Reading, Mass., 1978.

[Holt 83]   Holt, R.C. *Concurrent Euclid, The UNIX System, and Tunis*. Addison-Wesley, Reading, Mass., 1983.

[Hughes & Cresswell 68]   Hughes, G.E., and M.J. Cresswell. *An Introduction to Modal Logic*. Methuen, London, 1968.

[IBM 70]   IBM Corporation. *IBM System/360 Principles of Operation*. Ninth edition, IBM Systems Reference Library, File No. S360-01, Order No. GA22-6821-8, Nov. 1970.

[IBM 73]   IBM Corporation. *IBM System/370 Principles of Operation*. Fourth edition, GA22-7000-3, Jan. 1973.

[Igarashi 64]   Igarashi, S. *An Axiomatic Approach to Equivalence Problems of Algorithms with Applications*. Ph.D. thesis, University of Tokyo, 1964.

[Inmos 84]   INMOS Ltd. *Occam Programming Manual*. Prentice Hall International, Englewood Cliffs, N.J., 1984.

[Jayanti 90]   Jayanti, P., A. Sethi, and E. Lloyd. Minimal shared information for concurrent reading and writing. Technical report 90-13, Department of Computer and Information Sciences, University of Delaware, Newark, DE, 1990.

[Jones 83]   Jones, C.B. Tentative steps towards a development method for interfering programs. *ACM TOPLAS 5*, 4 (Oct. 1983), 576-619.

[Jordan 78]   Jordan, H. A special purpose architecture for finite element analysis. *Proc. 1978 International Conference on Parallel Processing* (Detroit, Michigan, Aug. 1978), IEEE Computer Society, 263-266.

[Keller 76]   Keller, R.M. Formal verification of parallel programs. *CACM 19*, 7 (July 1976), 371-384.

[Kessels & Martin 79]   Kessels, J.L.W., and A.J. Martin. Two implementations of the conditional critical region using a split binary semaphore. *Information Processing Letters 8*, 2 (Feb. 1979), 67-71.

[Kieburtz & Silberschatz 79]   Kieburtz, R.B., and A. Silberschatz. Comments on "Communicating Sequential Processes." *ACM TOPLAS 1*, 2 (Oct. 1979), 218-225.

[Kindler 94]   Kindler, E. Safety and liveness properties: A survey. *Bulletin of the European Association for Theoretical Computer Science 53* (June 1994), 268-272.

[Kroger 84]   Kroger, F. A generalized nexttime operator in temporal logic. *Journal of Computer Systems and Science 29*, 261-280.

[Kroger 87]   Kroger, F. *Temporal Logic of Programs*. EATCS Monographs on Theoretical Computer Science, Springer-Verlag, Berlin, 1987.

[Lamport 74]   Lamport, L. A new solution of Dijkstra's concurrent programming problem. *CACM 17*, 8 (Aug. 1974), 453-455.

[Lamport 76]   Lamport, L. Towards a theory of correctness for multi-user data base systems. Technical Report CA-7610-0712, Massachusetts Computer Associates, Wakefield, Mass., Oct. 1976.

[Lamport 77a]   Lamport, L. Proving the correctness of multiprocess programs. *IEEE Trans. on Software Engineering SE-3*, 2 (March 1977), 125-143.

[Lamport 77b]   Lamport, L. Concurrent reading while writing. *CACM 20*, 11 (Nov. 1977), 806-811.

[Lamport 79]   Lamport, L. A new approach to proving the correctness of multiprocess programs. *ACM TOPLAS 1*, 1 (July 1979), 84-97.

[Lamport 80a]   Lamport, L. "Sometime" is sometimes "not never." *Conference Record of Seventh Annual ACM Symposium on Principles of Programming Languages* (Las Vegas, Nevada, Jan. 1980), ACM, 174-185.

[Lamport 80b]   Lamport, L. The "Hoare Logic" of concurrent programs. *Acta Informatica 14* (1980), 21-37.

[Lamport 82]   Lamport, L. An assertional correctness proof of a distributed algorithm. *Science of Computer Programming 2*, 3 (Dec. 1982), 175-206.

[Lamport 83a]   Lamport, L. What good is temporal logic? *Information Processing 83*, R.E.A. Mason (ed.), Elsevier Science Publishers B.V., North-Holland, 1983, 657-668.

[Lamport 83b]   Lamport, L.  Specifying concurrent program modules. *ACM TOPLAS 5*, 2 (April 1983), 190-222.

[Lamport 85a]   Lamport, L.  What it means for a concurrent program to satisfy a specification: Why no one has specified priority. *Conference Record of Twelfth Annual ACM Symposium on Principles of Programming Languages* (New Orleans, Louisiana, Jan. 1985), ACM, 78-83.

[Lamport 85b]   Lamport, L.  Basic concepts. In *Distributed Systems—Methods and Tools for Specification*, M. Paul and H.J. Siegert (eds.), Lecture Notes in Computer Science Volume 190, Springer-Verlag, Berlin, 1985.

[Lamport 88]   Lamport, L.  Control predicates are better than dummy variables for reasoning about program control. *ACM TOPLAS 10*, 2 (April 1988), 267-281.

[Lamport 90a]   Lamport, L.  Concurrent reading and writing clocks. *ACM TOCS 8*, 4 (Nov. 1990), 305-310.

[Lamport 90b]   Lamport, L.  A theorem on atomicity in distributed algorithms. *Distributed Computing 4*, 2 (June 1990), 59-68.

[Lamport 92]   Lamport, L.  The reduction theorem. TLA note dated 12 April 1992. Available on the World Wide Web via http://www.research.digital.com/SRC/tla/.

[Lamport 94]   Lamport, L.  The Temporal Logic of Actions. *ACM TOPLAS 16*, 3 (May 1994), 872-923.

[Lamport & Schneider 84]   Lamport, L., and F.B. Schneider. The "Hoare Logic" of CSP and all that. *ACM TOPLAS 6*, 2 (April 1984), 281-296.

[Lamport & Schneider 89]   Lamport, L., and F.B. Schneider. Pretending atomicity. Technical Report 44, Digital Systems Research Center, May 1989.

[Lauer 73]   Lauer, H.C.  *Correctness in Operating Systems*. Ph.D. thesis, Computer Science Department, Carnegie-Mellon University, Pittsburgh, Pa. 1973.

[Lehman et al. 81]   Lehman, D., A. Pnueli, and J. Stavi. Impartiality, justice and fairness: The ethics of concurrent termination. *Proc. Eighth Colloquium on Automata, Languages and Programming*, Lecture Notes in Computer Science Volume 115, Springer-Verlag, Heidelberg, 1981, 264-277.

[Levin & Gries 81]   Levin, G.M., and D. Gries. A proof technique for communicating sequential processes. *Acta Informatica 15* (1981), 281-302.

[Levitt 72]   Levitt, K.N. The application of program-proving techniques to the verification of synchronization processes. *Proc. AFIPS Fall Joint Computer Conference*, AFIPS Press, 1972, 33-47.

[Lichtenstein et al. 85]   Lichtenstein, O., A. Pnueli, and L. Zuck. The glory of the past. *Proc. Workshop on Logics of Programs* (Brooklyn, New York, June 1985), R. Parikh (ed.), Lecture Notes in Computer Science Volume 193. Springer-Verlag, Berlin, 196-218.

[Lipton 75]  Lipton, R.J.  Reduction:  A method of proving properties of parallel programs. *CACM 18* ,12 (Dec. 1975), 717-721.

[Manna & Pnueli 81a]  Manna, Z., and A. Pnueli.  Verification of concurrent programs: The temporal framework.  In *The correctness problem in Computer Science*, R.S. Boyer and J.S. Moore (eds.), Academic Press, New York, 1981, 215-273.

[Manna & Pnueli 81b]  Manna, Z., and A. Pnueli.  Verification of concurrent programs: Temporal proof principles. *Proc. Workshop on Logics of Programs* (Yorktown Heights, New York, May 1981), D. Kozen (ed.), Lecture Notes in Computer Science Volume 131, Springer-Verlag, Berlin, 200-281.

[Manna & Pnueli 81c]  Manna, Z., and A. Pnueli.  Verification of concurrent programs: A temporal proof system. *Foundations of Computer Science IV, Distributed Systems Part 2*, J.W. de Bakker and J. van Leeuwen (eds.), Mathematical Centre Tracts 159, Amsterdam 1983, 163-255.

[Manna & Pnueli 83a]  Manna, Z., and A. Pnueli.  Proving precedence properties: The temporal way. *Proc. Tenth Colloquium on Automata, Languages, and Programming* (Barcelona, Spain, July 1983), J. Diaz (ed.), Lecture Notes in Computer Science Volume 154, Springer-Verlag, Heidelberg, 491-512.

[Manna & Pnueli 83b]  Manna, Z., and A. Pnueli.  How to cook a temporal proof system for your pet language. *Conference Record of the Tenth Annual ACM Symposium on Principles of Programming Languages* (Austin, Texas, Jan 1983), ACM, 141-154.

[Manna & Pnueli 84]  Manna, Z., and A. Pnueli.  Adequate proof principles for invariance and liveness properties of concurrent programs. *Science of Computer Programming 4*, 3 (Dec. 1984), 257-289.

[Manna & Pnueli 89]  Manna, Z., and A. Pnueli.  The anchored version of the temporal framework.  In *Linear Time, Branching Time and Partial Order in Logics and Models for Concurrency*, J.W. de Bakker, W.P. de Roever, and G. Rozenberg (eds.), Lecture Notes in Computer Science Volume 354, Springer-Verlag, New York, 1989, 201-284.

[Manna & Pnueli 90]  Manna, Z., and A. Pnueli.  A hierarchy of temporal properties. *Proc. Ninth Symposium on Principles of Distributed Computing* (Quebec City, Quebec, Canada, Aug. 1990), ACM, 377-408.

[Manna & Pnueli 92]  Manna, Z., and A. Pnueli. *Temporal Logic of Reactive Systems: Specification*. Springer-Verlag, New York, 1992.

[Manna & Pnueli 95]  Manna, Z., and A. Pnueli. *Temporal Logic of Reactive Systems: Safety*. Springer-Verlag, New York, 1995.

[Martin 81]  Martin, A.J.  An axiomatic definition of synchronization primitives. *Acta Informatica 16*, 2 (1981), 219-235.

[Martin & Burch 85]  Martin, A.J., and J. Burch.  Fair mutual exclusion with unfair P and V operations. *Information Processing Letters 21*, 2 (Aug. 1985), 97-100.

[Martin & Snepscheut 89]   Martin, A.J., and J.L.A. van de Snepscheut. Design of synchronization algorithms. *Constructive Methods in Computing Science*, M. Broy, (ed.), NATO ASI Series F: Computer and Systems Sciences, Vol. 55, Springer-Verlag, Heidelberg, 1989, 447-478.

[McCarthy 62]   McCarthy, J. Towards a mathematical science of computation. *Proc. IFIP Congress 1962*, North Holland, Amsterdam, 1962, 21-28.

[McCarthy & Hayes 69]   McCarthy, J., and P.J. Hayes. Some philosophical problems from the standpoint of artificial intelligence. *Machine Intelligence 4* (1969), Edinburgh University Press, 463-502.

[McCurley 88]   McCurley, E.R. *An Assertional Characterization of Serializability and Locking.* Ph.D. thesis, Computer Science Department, Cornell University, Ithaca, New York, 1988.

[McCurley 89]   McCurley, E.R. Auxiliary variables in partial correctness programming logics. *Information Processing Letters 33*, 3 (Nov. 1989), 131-134.

[McCurley & Schneider 86]   McCurley, R., and F.B. Schneider. Derivation of a distributed algorithm for finding paths in directed networks. *Science of Computer Programming 6*, 1 (Jan. 1986), 1-9.

[Mellor-Crummey & Scott 91]   Mellor-Crummey, J.M., and M.L. Scott. Algorithms for scalable synchronization on shared-memory multiprocessors. *ACM TOCS 9*, 1 (Feb. 1991), 21-65.

[Milner 80]   Milner, R. *A Calculus of Communicating Systems.* Lecture Notes in Computer Science Volume 92, Springer-Verlag, Berlin, 1980.

[Misra 86]   Misra, J. Distributed-discrete event simulation. *ACM Computing Surveys 18*, 1 (March 1986), 39-65.

[Misra 91]   Misra, J. Loosely-coupled processes. *Proc. PARLE '91 Parallel Architectures and Languages Europe*, E.H.L. Aarts, J. van Leeuwen, and M. Rem (eds.), Lecture Notes in Computer Science Volume 506, Springer-Verlag, Berlin, 1991, 1-26.

[Misra & Chandy 81]   Misra, J., and K.M. Chandy. Proofs of networks of processes. *IEEE Trans. on Software Engineering SE-7*, 4 (July 1981), 417-426.

[Morris & Jones 84]   Morris, F.L., and C.B. Jones. An early program proof by Alan Turing. *Annals of the History of Computing 6*, 2 (April 1984), 139-143.

[Naur 66]   Naur, P. Proof of algorithms by general snapshots. *BIT 6*, 4, 310-316.

[Newton 74]   Newton, G. Proving properties of interacting processes. Technical Report 74-9, University of Washington, Seattle, Washington, 1974.

[Owicki 75]   Owicki, S.S. *Axiomatic Proof Techniques for Parallel Programs.* Ph.D. thesis, Computer Science Department, Cornell University, Ithaca, New York, 1975.

[Owicki & Gries 76a]   Owicki, S.S., and D. Gries. An axiomatic proof technique for parallel programs I. *Acta Informatica 6*, 4 (1976), 319-340.

[Owicki & Gries 76b]   Owicki, S.S., and D. Gries. Verifying properties of parallel programs: An axiomatic approach. *CACM 19*, 5 (May 1976), 279-285.

[Owicki & Lamport 82]   Owicki, S.S., and L. Lamport. Proving liveness properties of concurrent programs. *ACM TOPLAS 4*, 3 (July 1982), 455-495.

[Parnas 75]   Parnas, D.L. On a solution to the cigarette smoker's problem (without conditional statements). *CACM 18*, 3 (March 1975), 181-183.

[Patil 71]   Patil, S.S. Limitations and capabilities of Dijkstra's semaphore primitives for coordination among processes. MIT Project MAC Memo 57, Feb. 1971.

[Peterson 81]   Peterson, G.L. Myths about the mutual exclusion problem. *Information Processing Letters 12*, 3 (June 1981), 115-116.

[Peterson 83]   Peterson, G.L. Concurrent reading while writing. *ACM TOPLAS 5*, 1 (Jan. 1983), 46-55.

[Pnueli 77]   Pnueli, A. The temporal logic of programs. *Proc. Eighteenth Annual Symposium on Foundations of Computer Science* (Providence, R.I., Nov. 1977), ACM, 46-57.

[Pnueli 79]   Pnueli, A. The temporal semantics of concurrent programs. *Proc. Symposium on Semantics of Concurrent Computation* (Evian, France, July 1979), G. Kahn (ed.), Lecture Notes in Computer Science Volume 70, Springer-Verlag, Heidelberg, 1979, 1-20.

[Postel & White 74]   Postel, J.B. and J.E. White. Procedure call protocol documents version 2. Request for comments 674, Network Working Group, SRI Augmentation Research Center, December 1974.

[Prior 57]   Prior, A.N. *Time and Modality*. Oxford University Press, Oxford, 1957.

[Prior 67]   Prior, A.N. *Past, Present and Future*. Oxford University Press, Oxford, 1967.

[Quine 61]   Quine, W.V.O. *Methods of Logic*. Holt, Reinhart and Winston, New York, 1961.

[Rao 92]   Rao, J.R. *Building on the UNITY Experience: Compositionality, Fairness, and Probability in Parallelism*. Ph.D. thesis, University of Texas at Austin, 1992.

[Raynal 86]   Raynal, M. *Algorithms for Mutual Exclusion*. The MIT Press, Cambridge, Mass., 1986.

[Reed & Kanodia 79]   Reed, D., and R. Kanodia. Synchronization with eventcounts and sequencers. *CACM 22*, 2 (Feb. 1979), 115-123.

[Rescher & Urquhart 71]   Rescher, N., and A. Urquhart. *Temporal Logic*. Springer-Verlag, New York, 1971.

[Rosen 74]  Rosen, B.K.  Correctness of parallel programs: The Church-Rosser approach. IBM Research Report RC5107, T.J. Watson Research Center, Yorktown Heights N.Y., 1974.

[Schlichting & Schneider 84]  Schlichting, R.D., and F.B. Schneider. Using message passing for distributed programming: Proof rules and disciplines. *ACM TOPLAS 6*, 3 (July 1984), 402-431.

[Schmid 76]  Schmid, H.A. On the efficient implementation of conditional critical regions and the construction of monitors. *Acta Informatica 6*, 3 (1976), 227-249.

[Schneider 82]  Schneider, F.B. Synchronization in distributed programs. *ACM TOPLAS 4*, 2 (April 1982), 125-148.

[Schneider 87]  Schneider, F.B. Decomposing properties into safety and liveness using predicate logic. Technical Report 87-874. Dept. of Computer Science, Cornell University, Oct. 1987.

[Schneider & Andrews 86]  Schneider, F.B., and G.R. Andrews. Concepts for concurrent programming. In *Current Trends in Concurrency*, J.W. de Bakker, W.P. de Roever, and G. Rozenberg (eds.), Lecture Notes in Computer Science Volume 224, Springer-Verlag, New York, 1986, 669-716.

[Schneider & Lamport 88]  Schneider, F.B., and L. Lamport. Another position paper on "Fairness." *Software Engineering Notes 13*, 3 (July 1988), 18-20.

[Schwarz 78]  Schwarz, J.S. Distributed synchronization of communicating sequential processes. Technical report, Department of Artificial Intelligence. University of Edinburgh, July 1978.

[Schwartz & Melliar-Smith 81]  Schwartz, R.L., and P.M. Melliar-Smith. Temporal logic specification of distributed systems. *Proc. of the Second International Conference on Distributed Computing Systems* (Paris, France, April 1981), IEEE Computer Society, 446-454.

[Silberschatz 79]  Silberschatz, A. Communication and synchronization in distributed systems. *IEEE Trans. on Software Engineering SE-5*, 6 (Nov. 1979), 542-546.

[Sistla 85]  Sistla, A.P. On characterization of safety and liveness properties in temporal logic. *Proc. Fourth Symposium on Principles of Distributed Computing* (Minaki, Canada, Aug. 1985), ACM, 39-48.

[Sistla 86]  Sistla, A.P. On characterization of safety and liveness properties in temporal logic. Technical Report, GTE Laboratories Inc., Waltham, Mass. March 1986, revised July 1986.

[Smullyan 68]  Smullyan, R.M. *First-Order Logic*. Springer-Verlag, New York, 1968.

[Snepscheut 81]  van de Snepscheut, J.L.A. Synchronous communication between asynchronous components. *Information Processing Letters 13*, 3 (Dec. 1981), 127-130.

[Soundararajan 84a]  Soundararajan, N. A proof technique for parallel programs. *Theoretical Computer Science 31* (1983), 13-29.

[Soundararajan 84b]  Soundararajan, N. Axiomatic semantics of communicating sequential processes. *ACM TOPLAS 6*, 4 (Oct. 1984), 647-662.

[Spector 82]  Spector, A.Z. Performing remote operations efficiently on a local computer network. *CACM 25*, 4 (April 1982), 246-260.

[Stark 82]  Stark, E.W. Semaphore primitives and starvation-free mutual exclusion. *JACM 29*, 4 (Oct. 1982), 1049-1072.

[Stoller & Schneider 95]  Stoller, S.D., and F.B. Schneider. Verifying programs that use causally-ordered message-passing. *Science of Computer Programming 24*, 2 (April 1995), 105-128.

[Tel & Mattern 93]  Tel, G., and F. Mattern. The derivation of distributed termination detection algorithms from garbage collection schemes. *ACM TOPLAS 15*, 1 (Jan. 1993), 1-35.

[Turing 49]  Turing, A.M. Checking a large routine. *Report of a Conference on High Speed Automatic Calculating Machines*, University Mathematics Laboratory, Cambridge, 67-69.

[Udding 86]  Udding, J.T. Absence of individual starvation using weak semaphores. *Information Processing Letters 23*, 3 (Oct. 1986), 159-162.

[Widom et al. 92]  Widom, J.W., D. Gries, and F.B. Schneider. Trace-based network proof systems: Expressiveness and completeness. *ACM TOPLAS 14*, 3 (July 1992), 396-416.

[Yanov 58]  Yanov, Y.I. Logical operator schemes. *Kybernetika 1* (1958).

[Zwiers & de Roever 89]  Zwiers, J., and W.P. de Roever. Predicates are predicate transformers: A unified compositional theory of concurrency. *Proc. Eighth Symposium on Principles of Distributed Computing* (Edmonton, Alberta, Canada, Aug. 1989), ACM, 265-280.

# Index

# Y
Yanov, Y.I., 122, 449

# Z
Zuck, L., 82, 444
Zwiers, J., 229, 449